THE PAPERS OF

James Madison

PRESIDENTIAL SERIES

VOLUME 3

3 NOVEMBER 1810–4 NOVEMBER 1811

EDITED BY

J. C. A. STAGG

JEANNE KERR CROSS   SUSAN HOLBROOK PERDUE

UNIVERSITY PRESS OF VIRGINIA

CHARLOTTESVILLE AND LONDON

This volume of *The Papers of James Madison* has been edited with financial aid from the National Endowment for the Humanities, an independent federal agency, the National Historical Publications and Records Commission, and the University of Virginia. Financial support has also been provided by the John Stewart Bryan Memorial Foundation, the Florence Gould Foundation, and the Kanter Family Foundation. The publication of this volume has been supported by a grant from the National Historical Publications and Records Commission.

First published 1996

∞ The paper used in this publication meets the minimum requirements of the American National Standard for Information Sciences—Permanence of Paper for Printed Library Materials, ANSI z39.48-1984.

Library of Congress Cataloging-in-Publication Data
(Revised for vol. 3)

Madison, James, 1751–1836.
    The papers of James Madison.

    Includes bibliographical references and index.
    Contents: v. 1. 1 March–30 September 1809 — v. 2. 1 Oct. 1809–2 Nov. 1810 / edited by J. C. A. Stagg, Jeanne Kerr Cross, Susan Holbrook Perdue — v. 3. 3 Nov. 1810– 4 Nov. 1811 / edited by J. C. A. Stagg, Jeanne Kerr Cross, Susan Holbrook Perdue.
    1. United States Politics and government 1809–1817 Sources.   2. United States Foreign relations 1809–1817 Sources.   3. United States History War of 1812 Sources. 4. Madison, James, 1751–1836 Archives.   I. Rutland, Robert Allen, 1922   .   II. Title.
    E302.M19   1984   973.5′1′092   83-6953
    ISBN 0-8139-0991-0 (v. 1 : alk. paper)
    ISBN 0-8139-1345-4 (v. 2 : alk. paper)
    ISBN 0-8139-1632-1 (v. 3 : alk. paper)

Printed in the United States of America

To

DAVID A. SHANNON

1920–1991

Contents

CONTENTS

CONTENTS

1811

CONTENTS

CONTENTS

CONTENTS

CONTENTS

CONTENTS

CONTENTS

Preface

The documents in this volume deal with events in James Madison's first administration between 3 November 1810 and 4 November 1811. As was the case with the preceding volume in this series, this twelve-month period was dominated by foreign policy problems. On 2 November 1810 Madison had issued a proclamation announcing that in three months' time the United States, under the terms of Macon's Bill No. 2, would impose non-intercourse against Great Britain unless that nation had revoked its orders in council in the interval. This action, in turn, was based on the assumption that France, as the duc de Cadore implied to American minister John Armstrong on 5 August 1810, had by 1 November already repealed its own anti–neutral trade restrictions embodied in the Berlin and Milan decrees.

Madison's 2 November proclamation was one of the most controversial decisions he ever took as president, in part because of the circumstances that had led up to it, but even more so because of the consequences that were to flow from it. Many observers were skeptical that Napoleon either had repealed his decrees by 1 November 1810 or would do so at any time thereafter, and the policy of French officials in continuing to detain or seize American vessels under "municipal regulations," if not under the Berlin and Milan decrees, seemed to justify their doubts. Indeed, accounts reaching Washington from Europe throughout the winter of 1810–11 raised so many questions about the status of the French decrees and the sincerity of Napoleon's conduct that at the end of January 1811 the chairman of the House committee on foreign relations, John Wayles Eppes, suggested to Madison that legislation to give effect to his November proclamation be delayed until the arrival of more favorable news.

The president was certainly puzzled by the obvious contradictions and ambiguities in French policy. Throughout 1811 he and his cabinet colleagues scrutinized every scrap of information from Europe as part of a never-ending quest to fathom Napoleon's true intentions toward the United States. Madison's private correspondence on the subject barely conceals his personal irritation that the French emperor, by failing to encourage American trade in ways that highlighted the full extent of British violations of neutral rights, was not merely harming American interests but also undermining his own measures of commercial warfare against his enemy. Publicly, however, Madison always maintained that the French decrees had, in fact, been removed and that Great Britain was therefore obliged to reciprocate by lifting the orders in council or suffer the consequences for not doing so. Accordingly, as the third session of the Eleventh

Congress drew to a close, Madison finally signed into law on 2 March 1811 the bill giving legislative effect to the policy he had proclaimed in November 1810.

Unfortunately, Great Britain failed to respond as Madison would have liked. The ministry of Spencer Perceval believed there was no evidence that the Berlin and Milan decrees had been repealed, and they rebuffed the requests made by the American minister, William Pinkney, for the removal of both the orders in council and the more extensive blockade of northern Europe that had been proclaimed in May 1806. These rejections exhausted Pinkney's patience, and the minister, after six years of service in London, decided to return home in February 1811. As the minister was preparing for his departure, however, George III collapsed into a state of permanent insanity, and arrangements were begun to install the Prince of Wales at the head of a regency council. Pinkney doubted that this change would produce any benefit for the United States, but when Madison first received the news in March 1811, he anticipated that the Prince Regent might form a new ministry by replacing his father's Tory ministers with his own Whig friends. Since the latter group included some who in the past had expressed more liberal attitudes toward the United States than had Spencer Perceval and his colleagues, the president allowed himself to hope that a new ministry might agree at least to modify the more rigorous aspects of Great Britain's treatment of neutrals.

Madison's optimism was short-lived. Although the Prince Regent announced he would send a minister to Washington to fill the vacancy left by Madison's dismissal of Francis James Jackson in November 1809, he did not replace the cabinet he had inherited from his father. As evidence of the regent's inactivity in this matter became clear, Madison, in turn, began to doubt there could be any negotiated settlement of the grievances between the two nations. Indications of the president's suspicions began to appear in *National Intelligencer* editorials as early as mid-April 1811, and his worst fears were more than amply confirmed by mid-July, particularly after the new British minister, Augustus John Foster, arrived in Washington and completed the first round of his negotiations with the secretary of state. Certainly Foster was authorized to settle one long-standing American grievance, the *Chesapeake* affair of 1807, but he offered no concessions at all on the other major points in dispute—the orders in council and the blockade of May 1806. Yet Foster was not merely powerless to negotiate the removal of Great Britain's trade restrictions. He had also been instructed to maintain that his government would lift its offending orders and blockades only after Napoleon had restored neutral commerce to the condition in which it stood before November 1806 or when French officials allowed American shippers to carry British produce and manufactures into Continental ports as neutral property. As a practical matter, this last demand was virtually impossible for the United States to fulfill, and Madison never even considered making any effort to attempt it. Nor was the president prepared to allow the Perceval ministry to impose restrictive and self-interested definitions of American neutrality on his administration for however long it might take Great Britain to loosen Napoleon's control over the ports of Continental Europe. As the full extent of the British position became apparent to him, Madison responded on 24 July 1811 by issuing a summons for the Twelfth Congress to assemble for an early session in the first week of November 1811.

As was the case with his proclamation of 2 November 1810, this decision was a most significant one, and the president's motives in making it require careful consideration. As some of the documents in this volume suggest, by the middle of 1811 Madison was well aware that the diplomacy of commercial restriction, espoused by him and his predecessor as an alternative to war with Great Britain, was both unpopular and seemingly ineffective. The Perceval ministry, regardless of the depressed conditions in Great Britain in 1811, simply did not respond to economic coercion; and many British merchants were able to evade Madison's nonintercourse policy by smuggling cargoes into the United States through ports and rivers in both Spanish East Florida and Great Britain's own Canadian colonies. That the British ministry seemed prepared to encourage such activities while also continuing to harass American trade at every possible opportunity could be inferred from its willingness to increase the size of the Royal Navy squadron operating off the American coast; and when Commodore John Rodgers in the *President* severely damaged one of these British vessels, the *Lille Belt*, in an accidental encounter off the Virginia capes in April 1811, the episode provoked a sustained outburst of anti-British sentiment in the American press.

Furthermore, both the president's Federalist opponents and a growing number of his Republican supporters were becoming impatient with the prolonged stalemate in Anglo-American relations, and they were increasingly critical of Madison's apparent willingness to tolerate it. Mercantile communities throughout New England sent the president memorials protesting the harmful effect of commercial restrictions on the local economy, and they demanded he abandon his efforts to use trade as a diplomatic weapon. In most instances, Madison was unmoved by these criticisms, although he did respond sometimes with arguments to the effect that neither national honor nor national interest would be served if Great Britain were allowed to control American commerce at will. The town meeting of New Bedford, Massachusetts, however, decided in June 1811 to counter such presidential statements with a more carefully crafted petition, the contents of which deliberately turned Madison's own words against him in order to show that his policies had failed to attain any of the goals he had proclaimed to justify their imposition. The New Bedford petitioners also declared that the effects of the administration's measures were totally destructive of the purposes for which the Union had been formed, and they even hinted to the president that if trade restrictions were ever justified, they should be enforced as an attribute not of "the power of regulating commerce, but of prosecuting War." The petitioners probably advanced this suggestion in the belief that Madison would never risk war under any circumstances at all, and it is perhaps regrettable that no documentary evidence has survived to indicate the president's reaction on this occasion.

From the opposite side of the political spectrum, too, Madison had always had his critics, especially among the more stridently Anglophobic newspaper editors in the Atlantic coastal cities, and they were now demanding a stronger response to British violations of American neutrality. By the summer of 1811 Madison was thus subjected to sharply conflicting domestic pressures to change his policies as he confronted a Great Britain that was as unyielding as ever; and he was fully aware of the dilemma this situation presented to him—namely, whether to abandon his lifelong goal of encouraging and protecting American commerce against the rivalry of Great Britain or to advance it by means more belligerent than any president had hitherto been willing to attempt. After he had issued his call on 24 July to convene the Twelfth Congress in the first week of November, the president undoubtedly contemplated these matters further at Montpelier during his annual retreat in August and September 1811. There was still time for both him and Spencer Perceval to reconsider their respective positions before November, but Madison, for his part, found no easy solutions to his difficulties during these weeks. Nor was the news from Great Britain any better after the administration had reassembled in Washington in the first week of October. As he prepared to meet the new session of Congress, the president evidently concluded that it would be impossible for him either to persevere with the status quo or to return to the more stringent forms of commercial restriction that had been pursued by the Jefferson administration before 1809. He therefore rejected these options and began instead to draft a message requesting Congress to prepare for war with Great Britain. At the conclusion of this volume he was ready to present it to the legislators as they gathered in Washington on 5 November 1811.

While difficulties with France and Great Britain occupied much of Madison's attention throughout 1811, they were by no means the only foreign policy issues requiring his attention. Relations with Denmark also reached a crisis point as that nation detained and confiscated American vessels in record numbers in the belief that neutral flags, sometimes sailing under the protection of Royal Navy convoys, were being misused as a cover for British commerce. Since Napoleon entertained similar suspicions about the abuse of neutral flags in the Baltic, the fate of American property in Danish ports could not be very easily divorced from the larger problem of the extent to which Great Britain was, in fact, exploiting neutral commerce in eastern Europe in order to undermine the French emperor's Continental System. Nevertheless, Madison wished to extricate the United States from this aspect of the Anglo-French conflict, and in November 1810 he appointed George W. Erving as special minister to Copenhagen in an effort to do so. Presumably the president believed that Erving would defend American interests in the Baltic region more effectively than one of his more tedious correspondents, George Joy, had been able to do, but the special minister did not depart the United States until March 1811 and he did not reach his destination until June. Thereafter the results of his efforts were few, and Erving made little progress toward accomplishing his goals before the outbreak of the War of 1812.

Closer to home, the disintegration of the Spanish-American empire continued throughout 1810 and 1811. Here Madison's first concern was to give effect to his proclamation of 27 October 1810 extending American jurisdiction over portions of the province of West Florida. In the weeks following their declaration of independence from Spain on 26 September 1810, the members of the West Florida convention moved rapidly to provide a constitution for their future government, and by 22 November they had completed the business of electing a legislature and a governor. Orleans territorial governor William C. C. Claiborne therefore found himself confronting a functioning administration when he arrived on the Gulf Coast to implement the president's proclamation. On 10 December Claiborne, with some difficulty, persuaded Fulwar Skipwith, the first and only chief executive of West Florida, to acquiesce in Madison's refusal to recognize his government, but it was less clear whether Claiborne and the handful of other United States officials in the region could prevent some of the more ardent supporters of Floridian independence from launching filibustering expeditions against Mobile, the remaining Spanish enclave within the province. Any fears Madison might have had on this score, however, proved to be largely unfounded, and one of his more frequent correspondents in this volume, Mississippi territorial magistrate Harry Toulmin, kept him fully informed of the movements of potential filibusterers as well as his own efforts to hamper them.

As Claiborne completed the details of extending American authority over West Florida, the president turned his attention to coping with the possible diplomatic consequences of his annexation of Spanish territory. To forestall the possibility that either France or Great Britain might attempt to claim or to occupy the remainder of the Floridas in order to discourage further American encroachments, Madison sought and obtained congressional authority in January 1811 to occupy Spanish East Florida. That authority was to be exercised in the event of either the local authorities agreeing to transfer the province to the United States or a foreign power attempting to occupy it. On that basis, the president then renewed the mission he had assigned to George Mathews of Georgia in the summer of 1810 and instructed him, together with John McKee of Natchez, to negotiate with the local Spanish officials for the transfer of both East Florida and Mobile, in West Florida, to the United States (see *PJM-PS*, 2:310, 312–13). Neither Mathews nor McKee, however, was able to carry out his mission as directed, and beginning in the fall of 1811 the former attempted to acquire East Florida for the United States by fomenting a rebellion against the Spanish authorities. He did so in the belief that both his instructions and his conversations with Madison in January 1811 were sufficient authority for his actions.

The administration, after learning that Mathews had seized Amelia Island in March 1812 as a first move to bring East Florida under American authority, was to deny this argument vigorously; but it has always been a matter of dispute whether Mathews's actions in the fifteen months after his departure from Washington in January 1811 were fundamentally in conflict with Madison's intentions or whether they actually came close to fulfilling them. This dispute cannot be conclusively resolved on the basis of the documentary record on which this edition is based, but it is possible to demonstrate that by January 1811 Madison was aware that Mathews had already made contact with Spanish citizens in East Florida who had expressed an interest in seeing the establishment of American authority in the region provided they received some assistance and encouragement from the United States. And there is, moreover, no evidence to indicate that in the months after January 1811 Madison ever explicitly discouraged his agent from pursuing contacts with these disaffected Spanish subjects in East Florida before Mathews embarked on the seizure of Amelia Island in March 1812.

In the dramatic events occurring in the more distant Spanish-American colonies in 1810–11, the United States was more of an observer than it was a participant. In fact, the revolt commenced in Mexico in September 1810 under the leadership of Manuel Hidalgo y Costilla had been crushed by April 1811 without so much as the barest of references to it appearing in the president's correspondence as published in this volume. It should not be inferred from this silence, however, that Madison had no interest in affairs in Mexico. It is clear that he followed developments there as best he could, largely through the accounts published in the newspapers and in the reports sent to the State Department by Americans closer to the scene, such as William Shaler in Havana and Governor Claiborne on the Gulf Coast. Among the reports sent by Shaler, who continued to operate under the instructions Madison had given him in 1810, was the news that Hidalgo had attempted, albeit without success, to send a minister or an agent to the United States. By May 1811, when the failure of what proved to be merely the first phase of the Mexican revolution against Spain was apparent, Madison remarked in a conversation with the French minister that it was the refusal of the Mexican *criollos* to support Hidalgo's cause that had been instrumental in his defeat. The president further observed that this state of affairs would leave the *peninsulares* in Mexico more dependent on the *criollos* than had been the case previously and thus less able to prevent any future revolt against their rule. It is perhaps unlikely, therefore, that Madison was greatly surprised when an agent who represented the remnants of Hidalgo's supporters in the Tamaulipas province of Mexico eventually succeeded in contacting the State Department in October 1811 seeking American assistance for his cause (Shaler to Monroe, 25 Apr. 1811 [DNA: RG 59, CD, Havana]; Sérurier to Cadore, 5 May 1811 [AAE: Political Correspondence, U.S., vol. 65]; Francisco Mariano Sora and José Bernardo Gutiérrez de Lara to Monroe, 27 Sept. 1811 [DNA: RG 59, CD, Mexico City]).

On the South American mainland, Venezuela, as had been the case in 1810, made the most rapid progress toward independence from Spain. In December 1810 the Caracas junta organized elections for a national congress that met in March 1811. Its members, inspired by the *Sociedad Patriótica* under the leadership of Simón Bolivar and Francisco de Miranda, declared Venezuela an independent republic on 5 July 1811. Preliminary to the declaration, the national congress renewed the initiative that the Caracas junta had made to the United States in June 1810 by dispatching Telésforo d'Orea and José Rafael Revenga on another diplomatic mission to Washington, this time to seek not merely arms and assistance but also recognition, an alliance, and open commercial treaties which the Venezuelans assumed would be of mutual benefit to both nations.

Madison's response was cautious. Although he met with the Venezuelan delegates on 18 May 1811 and showed considerable interest in recent developments in their homeland, particularly in the extent of British commercial influence there, he was reluctant to extend recognition to a regime that at the time of the meeting still acknowledged the rights of Ferdinand VII. To have acted under such circumstances, the secretary of state explained to Orea, would have violated the considerations that governed the president's policy of not recognizing any of the provisional authorities in either the Iberian Peninsula or the Spanish-American colonies pending the outcome of the war between Spain and France. The most that Madison was prepared to do for the Venezuelans was to encourage them to declare their independence and to consent to their request that Robert Lowry, the commercial agent he had sent to La Guaira in the summer of 1810, be given a regular commission as consul (Telésforo d'Orea to Monroe, 17 May 1811 [DNA: RG 59, NFL, Colombia]; Orea to Miguel José Sanz, 21 May 1811, Cristobal L. Mendoza, ed., "Las primeras relaciones diplomaticas de Venezuela con los Estados Unidos: Correspondencia de Orea," *Boletin de la Academia Nacional de la Historia*, 27 [1944]: 349–52).

The president's desire to avoid the consequences of a premature recognition of a new regime also governed his reaction to the overtures made to him by leaders of other insurrectionary movements in South America. Over the summer of 1811 Madison received letters sent to him earlier in the year by recently established juntas in the viceroyalties of the Río de la Plata and New Granada. Their contents reported the progress made in breaking away from Madrid and requested in return some degree of American recognition and support as well as the establishment of trade relations. The Buenos Aires junta even sent delegates to negotiate for this purpose to Washington, where they arrived in October 1811. As had been the case with Orea and Revenga in May, Madison did little more than appoint an additional consul to the port of Buenos Aires while also extending the jurisdiction of Joel Roberts Poinsett, whom he had dispatched to the Río de la Plata in 1810, to the provinces of Chile and Peru. Yet even as he took these limited steps, Madison evidently realized that the issue of recognizing new authorities in Spanish America could not be postponed indefinitely and that he would almost certainly have to face it again in the future. Accordingly, in October 1811 he decided to raise the subject in his next message to Congress, despite the misgivings of his colleague Gallatin and at the risk of incurring diplomatic displeasure from Great Britain and Spain as he did so. But, again, his approach to the problem was cautious; and at this stage he merely chose to sound out the opinion of the legislators so that the United States would not be "unprepared for whatever order of things that may ultimately be established" (Annual Message to Congress, 5 November 1811, Madison, *Writings* [Hunt ed.], 8: 162–63).

On the domestic front, the main event of 1811 was the reconstruction of the president's cabinet after the dismissal of Secretary of State Robert Smith in late March and his replacement by James Monroe of Virginia. The tensions between Gallatin and Smith in the cabinet were long-standing, and sometime after May 1810 it would seem that differences between Madison and his secretary of state also hardened into mutual dislike. These conflicts were then transferred to an open quarrel over the issues of whether Napoleon had repealed the Berlin and Milan decrees and whether the administration should enforce nonintercourse against Great Britain. Not only did Smith disagree with Madison's decisions on both matters, but he made the fact of his disagreement public knowledge throughout Washington. As the lengthy memorandum he prepared on the subject sometime in April 1811 reveals, Madison resented Smith's disloyalty, while Gallatin, who was by now deeply enraged at the role of Robert Smith's brother, Samuel, and other disaffected Republicans in the United States Senate in defeating administration policy measures ranging from Macon's Bill No. 1 to the recharter of the Bank of the United States, finally told the president that he would resign rather than endure the situation any longer.

Madison was thus confronted with a painful choice. The loss of Gallatin's skills in the Treasury Department would be a severe blow to the administration, but the removal of Robert Smith was not likely to come without a political price either, the more so as many of Madison's friends and correspondents in the spring of 1811 were hinting that Smith and his network of relatives, supporters, and sympathetic newspaper editors throughout the mid-Atlantic states were already plotting to oppose the president's reelection in 1812. This last matter was to receive some discussion in the press over the summer of 1811, but how far Madison was worried about it is difficult to say. Probably more decisive in his calculations in dismissing Robert Smith, at least in the short run, were his concern about the imminent departure of Gallatin and an unwillingness to jeopardize unnecessarily any forthcoming negotiations with the new British minister that the Prince Regent had just appointed to Washington. From the president's perspective, it would probably have seemed pointless to embark on yet another attempt to settle Anglo-American disagreements while Robert Smith remained in the cabinet. The secretary, after all, had not acquitted himself with distinction in his dealings with the last two British ministers in Washington, and, given his rebellious conduct in openly questioning the very bases of the president's policies, he promised to be an even less effective advocate of Madison's case against Great Britain than he had been in the past.

In this context, the removal of Smith and his replacement by Monroe seemed to offer Madison the best prospect for solving his diplomatic difficulties while at the same time restoring a greater degree of unity and purpose to both his cabinet and the heterogeneous, faction-ridden coalition of his Republican supporters. Although estranged from Madison ever since the Jefferson administration had rejected the treaty he and William Pinkney had negotiated with Great Britain in 1806, Monroe was not without experience in negotiating the thickets of Anglo-American maritime disputes, and the acquaintances he had made of some of the more liberal Whigs in London might now prove to be useful if, as Madison hoped, the Prince Regent gave them places in a new ministry. And on the purely personal level, Monroe's appointment to the cabinet would also restore the amicable relations between the two Virginians that had existed before 1806.

For his part, Monroe, who had been elected governor of Virginia in January 1811, was more than eager to return to the national political scene. He responded quickly and positively to Madison's overtures, and after a brief and unsuccessful effort to commit the president in advance to some of his positions on Anglo-American relations, he accepted the appointment to the State Department. The new secretary entered on his duties on 5 April 1811, hoping that he would be able to negotiate an acceptable agreement with the British minister over the summer. Here Monroe was to be disappointed, mainly because Lord Wellesley's instructions to Foster precluded the possibility of any sort of compromise settlement, but also in part because he found that his own powers of diplomatic persuasion throughout July 1811 were in many ways restricted by the conduct of his predecessor in office. In the last week of June, in an effort to vindicate himself against the stigma of having been dismissed by Madison, Robert Smith openly attacked both the president and his policies in an *Address* to the people of the United States.

The contents of this pamphlet did not make for pleasant reading. Smith accused Madison of many failings, including the charge that he had connived at improper financial transactions, but the main burden of his argument was that the president's diplomacy was weak and indecisive to the point that he willingly endured both insults from Great Britain and deception from France at the same time. And to the extent that Smith's *Address* called into question yet again whether Napoleon had repealed the Berlin and Milan decrees and even whether Madison himself believed that the decrees had been removed, it also undercut Monroe's efforts to establish the fact of French repeal as the basis for the president's case that the orders in council should be lifted. Both the British minister in Washington and his superiors in London were able to point to the claims made in Robert Smith's *Address* in support of their refusal to admit that the United States had a valid case for a more generous treatment of its neutral rights.

Madison was greatly irritated by the appearance of Smith's pamphlet, but, as he told Jefferson, he could hardly enter a public debate himself in order to counter the harmful impressions its publication had created. That task was left to the president's friend and minister-designate to France, Joel Barlow, who, in conjunction with William Lee and a State Department clerk, John B. Colvin, did indeed refute the former secretary's allegations in the newspapers. The result was an acrimonious public controversy lasting several weeks, during which the competing claims about how well Robert Smith had been able to perform his State Department duties could have only further embarrassed the president. The final outcome may have been more favorable to Madison than it was to Smith, but the disclosures made throughout July and August 1811 could also be regarded as evidence that the president had tolerated for too long conflicts among his colleagues that had done nothing to advance the effectiveness of his policies.

One other major matter that engaged Madison's attention throughout 1811 was the growing hostility between American settlers and the Indian inhabitants of the northwestern and southern frontiers. In the former region, the settlers, including some of Madison's correspondents in this volume, became greatly alarmed at the activities of the Shawnee Prophet, Lalawethika, and his brother, Tecumseh. From a township located at the junction of the Tippecanoe and Wabash Rivers in the Indiana Territory, the Prophet had inspired a religious movement to regenerate the culture of the Shawnee and other northwestern native peoples, while Tecumseh urged these same groups to resist the implementation of the land cessions that had been made to the United States in the 1809 Treaty of Fort Wayne. As a result of several incidents of conflict, or near-conflict, settlers throughout the Northwest demanded military protection from the United States government. Their requests were generally backed by the territorial governors throughout the region, and especially by Indiana governor William Henry Harrison, who had long been convinced that Tecumseh was scheming to create a federation of Indian peoples in alliance with the British in Upper Canada. It is unlikely that Madison shared all of Harrison's fears on this last score, but the president nevertheless became sufficiently concerned about the situation to authorize the governor in June 1811 to assemble a military force to disperse the Prophet and his followers, should events make it necessary to do so. Madison stressed to Harrison, however, his hope that extreme measures would not be required; and even as the governor hastened to assemble his troops in order to begin his march to Tippecanoe, the president clung to the belief that it would be possible to avoid a serious conflict with the Indians.

In these dealings with the Northwestern Indians, Madison was largely governed by the wish not to make matters any worse than they already were, but he does not seem to have been quite so cautious in his conduct toward the Indians on the southern frontier. The native peoples of western Georgia and the Mississippi Territory, most notably those residing in the upper townships of the Muskogee (or Creek) confederation, were experiencing problems similar to those of their northwestern counterparts in responding to American demands for land, trade, and access through their territories. This last issue, in particular, was a most difficult one as it required the cutting of a major road from Tennessee through the heart of the Creek country to the Mobile region, but Madison made it very clear to his old friend Benjamin Hawkins, the Creek Indian agent, that he should press the Indians to make the necessary concessions. By September 1811, Hawkins had succeeded in doing so, but neither he nor Madison appears to have anticipated the full cost of their victory. Even more so than was to be the case in the Northwest, substantial numbers of the Creek people became increasingly angry about their dealings with the United States. Their grievances, however, were ignored, and this would ultimately lead them, too, into involvement in the war with Great Britain for which Madison was about to prepare.

Acknowledgments

In the preparation of this volume the editors wish to acknowledge the assistance of Timothy D. W. Connelly and Donald L. Singer of the National Historical Publications and Records Commission for their willingness to locate and copy a wide range of obscure and remote documents from the collections of the National Archives. We would also like to thank our graduate assistants Taylor Fain, Peter Kastor, and James Lewis for all their efforts with the transcription and annotation. A special word of thanks is due to David Cox and Cecilia Brown for their help with translations, and also to Ann Miller for sharing with us her extensive knowledge of the history of the Virginia Piedmont. John Catanzariti of the Papers of Thomas Jefferson, John Van Horne of the Library Company of Philadelphia, and Richard A. Kerr of Harrisburg, Pennsylvania, readily fulfilled tasks for us that we could not otherwise have easily accomplished. And as always, we remain indebted to the staffs of the University of Virginia Library and the Papers of George Washington.

Editorial Method

The guidelines used in editing *The Papers of James Madison* were explained in volumes 1 and 8 of the first series (1:xxxiii–xxxix and 8:xxiii) and also in the first volume of the secretary of state series (1:xxv–xxvii). These guidelines have been followed in the presidential series. Considerable effort has been made to render the printed texts as literal, faithful copies of the original manuscripts, but some exceptions must be noted. Missing or illegible characters and words in a damaged or torn manuscript are restored by conjecture within angle brackets. Words consistently spelled incorrectly, as well as variant or antiquated spellings, are left as written; however, misspelled words that may appear to be printer's errors are corrected through additions in brackets or followed by the device [*sic*]. The brackets used by Madison and other correspondents have been rendered as parentheses. Slips of the pen have been silently corrected, but substantial errors or discrepancies have been noted. Most addresses and postmarks, as well as most notations or dockets made by various clerks, editors, and collectors through the years, have not been recognized in the provenance unless germane to an understanding of the document. Routine endorsements Madison made on documents late in his lifetime have not been noted. When the enclosures mentioned are newspapers or other ephemeral publications that would have been immediately separated from the document, the absence of such items has not been noted in the provenance.

As has already been noted in previous volumes in this series, the amount of material surviving from Madison's two presidential administrations has required the editors to adopt a policy of increased selectivity. The primary criterion in the editors' decision to print, abstract, or omit a document is a judgment on the extent to which it illuminates James Madison's thoughts or his personal or official life. The degree of involvement he had with the document, either as recipient or sender, is of paramount concern. Other considerations, though not decisive in themselves, have been whether the document was of a routine nature (such as a letter of transmittal, application, or recommendation) or was of intrinsic interest in adding a new dimension to our understanding of the man or, in the case of a lengthy document, whether it had been previously published in an easily accessible source such as *American State Papers* or *The Territorial Papers of the United States*. A large number of bureaucratic documents bearing his signature were generated as a result of the broad responsibilities of Madison's office; those that produce little useful information and do not warrant abstracting are silently omitted (such as letters of appointment and ship's papers). Occasionally, omitted documents are referred to in the notes.

In preparing abstracts the editors have tried to summarize the contents of manuscripts, avoiding unnecessary detail while providing readers with a guide to the most important issues raised and the writer's approach. Editorial additions to these abstracts (except for purposes of identification) appear in brackets or in footnotes. Place-name spellings in abstracts have been modernized and variant spellings of personal names standardized.

Depository Symbols

In the provenance section following each document the first entry indicates the source of the text. If the document was in private hands when copied for this edition, the owner and date of possession are indicated. If the document was in a private or public depository in the United States, the symbol listed in the Library of Congress's *Symbols of American Libraries* (14th ed.; Washington, 1992) is used. When the symbol DLC stands alone, it indicates the Madison Papers in the Library of Congress. Documents in the National Archives, Washington, are designated DNA with the record group and in most cases a second symbol corresponding to the official classification. In the case of foreign depositories, explanations of the symbols are below. The location symbols for depositories used in this volume are:

AAE   Archives du Ministère des Affaires Etrangères, Paris
AHN   Archivo Histórico Nacional, Madrid
CSmH   Henry E. Huntington Library, San Marino, California
CtY   Yale University, New Haven
DeGE   Eleutherian Mills Historical Library, Greenville, Delaware
DLC   Library of Congress, Washington, D.C.
DNA   National Archives, Washington, D.C.
    CD   Consular Despatches
    DD   Diplomatic Despatches
    DL   Domestic Letters
    IC   Instructions to Consuls
    IM   Instructions to Ministers
    LAR   Letters of Application and Recommendation
    LOAG   Letters from and Opinions of Attorneys General
    LRIA   Letters Received by the Secretary of War Relating to Indian Affairs
    LRRS   Letters Received by the Secretary of War, Registered Series
    LRUS   Letters Received by the Secretary of War, Unregistered Series

	LSIA	Letters Sent by the Secretary of War Relating to Indian Affairs
	LSMA	Letters Sent by the Secretary of War Relating to Military Affairs
	LSP	Letters Sent to the President
	ML	Miscellaneous Letters
	NFL	Notes from Foreign Legations
	PPR	Presidential Pardons and Remissions
	TP	Territorial Papers
GBL		British Museum, London
GBLUc		University College, London
ICHi		Chicago Historical Society, Illinois
ICU		University of Chicago, Illinois
InU		Indiana University, Bloomington
KB		Kungliga Biblioteket, Stockholm
KyHi		Kentucky Historical Society, Frankfort
MdBS		Saint Mary's Seminary and University, Baltimore
MdHi		Maryland Historical Society, Baltimore
MH		Harvard University, Cambridge, Massachusetts
MHi		Massachusetts Historical Society, Boston
MoSHi		Missouri Historical Society, St. Louis
NHi		New-York Historical Society, New York City
NIC		Cornell University, Ithaca, New York
NjHi		New Jersey Historical Society, Newark
NjP		Princeton University, Princeton, New Jersey
NN		New York Public Library, New York City
NNMus		Museum of the City of New York
OHi		Ohio State Historical Society, Columbus
PHC		Haverford College, Haverford, Pennsylvania
PHi		Historical Society of Pennsylvania, Philadelphia
PRO		Public Record Office, London
PU		University of Pennsylvania, Philadelphia
RHi		Rhode Island Historical Society, Providence
RPB-JH		Brown University, John Hay Library, Providence
ViU		University of Virginia, Charlottesville
ViW		College of William and Mary, Williamsburg, Virginia

Abbreviations

FC   File copy. Any version of a letter or other document retained by the sender for his own files and differing little if at all from the completed version. A draft, on the other hand, is a preliminary sketch, often incomplete and varying frequently in expression from the finished version. Unless otherwise noted, both are in the sender's hand. A letterbook copy is a retained duplicate, often bound in a chronological file, and usually in a clerk's hand.

JM   James Madison.

Ms   Manuscript. A catchall term describing numerous reports and other papers written by JM, as well as items sent to him which were not letters.

RC   Recipient's copy. The copy of a letter intended to be read by the addressee. If the handwriting is not that of the sender, this fact is noted in the provenance.

Tr   Transcript. A copy of a manuscript, or a copy of a copy, customarily handwritten and ordinarily not by its author or by the person to whom the original was addressed.

Abstracts and Missing Letters. In most cases a document is presented only in abstract form because of its trivial nature, its great length, or a combination of both. Abstracted letters are noted by the symbol §.

The symbol ¶ indicates a "letter not found" entry, with the name of the writer or intended recipient, the date, and such other information as can be surmised from the surviving evidence. If nothing other than the date of the missing item is known, however, it is mentioned only in the notes to a related document.

Short Titles for Books and Other
Frequently Cited Materials

In addition to these short titles, bibliographical entries are abbreviated if a work has been cited in a previous volume of the series.

Annals of Congress.   *Debates and Proceedings in the Congress of the United States* . . . (42 vols.; Washington, 1834–56).

ASP.   *American State Papers: Documents, Legislative and Executive, of the Congress of the United States* . . . (38 vols.; Washington, 1832–61).

Brant, *Madison.*   Irving Brant, *James Madison* (6 vols.; Indianapolis and New York, 1941–61).

Callahan, *List of Officers of the Navy.*   Edward W. Callahan, *List of Officers of the Navy of the United States and of the Marine Corps from 1775 to 1900* (New York, 1900).

Carter, *Territorial Papers.*   Clarence Carter et al., eds., *The Territorial Papers of the United States* (28 vols.; Washington, 1934–75).

DAR Patriot Index. National Society of the Daughters of the American Revolution, *DAR Patriot Index* (Washington, 1966).

Esarey, *Letters of Harrison.* Indiana Historical Commission, *Governors Messages and Letters,* vols. 7 and 9, *Messages and Letters of William Henry Harrison,* ed. Logan Esarey (2 vols.; Indianapolis, 1922).

Evans. Charles Evans, ed., *American Bibliography . . . 1639 . . . 1820* (12 vols.; Chicago, 1903–34).

Ford, *Writings of Jefferson.* Paul Leicester Ford, ed., *The Writings of Thomas Jefferson* (10 vols.; New York, 1892–99).

Ford, *Writings of J. Q. Adams.* Worthington Chauncey Ford, ed., *The Writings of John Quincy Adams* (7 vols.; New York, 1913–17).

Heitman, *Historical Register.* Francis B. Heitman, *Historical Register and Dictionary of the United States Army, from Its Organization, September 29, 1789, to March 2, 1903* (2 vols.; Washington, 1903).

Madison, *Letters* (Cong. ed.). [William C. Rives and Philip R. Fendall, eds.], *Letters and Other Writings of James Madison* (published by order of Congress; 4 vols.; Philadelphia, 1865).

Madison, *Writings* (Hunt ed.). Gaillard Hunt, ed., *The Writings of James Madison* (9 vols.; New York, 1900–1910).

Malone, *Jefferson and His Time.* Dumas Malone, *Jefferson and His Time* (6 vols.; Boston, 1948–81).

Mayo, *Instructions to British Ministers.* Bernard Mayo, ed., *Instructions to the British Ministers to the United States, 1791–1812,* Annual Report of the American Historical Association for the Year 1936, vol. 3 (Washington, 1941).

Miller, *Treaties.* Hunter Miller, ed., *Treaties and Other International Acts of the United States of America* (8 vols.; Washington, 1930–48).

PJM. William T. Hutchinson et al., eds., *The Papers of James Madison* (1st ser., vols. 1–10, Chicago, 1962–77, vols. 11–17, Charlottesville, Va., 1977–91).

PJM-PS. Robert A. Rutland et al., eds., *The Papers of James Madison: Presidential Series* (3 vols. to date; Charlottesville, Va., 1984—).

PJM-SS. Robert J. Brugger et al., eds., *The Papers of James Madison: Secretary of State Series* (3 vols. to date; Charlottesville, Va., 1986—).

Rowland, *Claiborne Letter Books.* Dunbar Rowland, ed., *Official Letter Books of W. C. C. Claiborne, 1801–1816* (6 vols.; Jackson, Miss., 1917).

Senate Exec. Proceedings. *Journal of the Executive Proceedings of the Senate of the United States of America* (3 vols.; Washington, 1828).

Shaw and Shoemaker. R. R. Shaw and R. H. Shoemaker, comps., *American Bibliography: A Preliminary Checklist for 1801–1819* (22 vols. to date; New York, 1958—).

Swem and Williams, *Register.* Earl G. Swem and John W. Williams, eds., *A Register of the General Assembly of Virginia, 1776–1918, and of the Constitutional Conventions* (Richmond, 1918).

Syrett and Cooke, *Papers of Hamilton.*   Harold C. Syrett and Jacob E. Cooke, eds., *The Papers of Alexander Hamilton* (26 vols.; New York, 1961–79).

U.S. Statutes at Large.   *The Public Statutes at Large of the United States of America . . .* (17 vols.; Boston, 1848–73).

Van Horne, *Papers of Latrobe.*   John C. Van Horne and Lee W. Form-walt, eds., *The Correspondence and Miscellaneous Papers of Benjamin Henry Latrobe* (3 vols.; New Haven, 1984–88).

VMHB.   *Virginia Magazine of History and Biography.*

WMQ.   *William and Mary Quarterly.*

Madison Chronology

1810

3 December– 2 March 1811	Third session of Eleventh Congress.
5 December	JM delivers annual message to Congress.

1811

3 January	JM requests from Congress discretionary authority to occupy Spanish East Florida.
16 February	Receives Louis Sérurier as minister from France.
2 March	Signs bill enforcing nonintercourse against Great Britain under provisions of Macon's Bill No. 2.
ca. 14 March	Authorizes Richard Brent to inquire if James Monroe would accept appointment to State Department.
19 March	Requests resignation of Robert Smith as secretary of state; offers him position of minister to Russia.
20 March	Offers James Monroe position of secretary of state.
2 July	Receives Augustus John Foster as minister from Great Britain.
24 July	Issues proclamation to convene first session of Twelfth Congress on 4 Nov. 1811.
25 July	JM and Dolley Madison leave Washington for Montpelier.
ca. 29 July	Arrive at Montpelier.
ca. 27–29 August	Thomas Jefferson and James Monroe visit JM at Montpelier.
14–17 September	JM and Dolley Madison visit Jefferson at Monticello.
30 September	Leave Montpelier for Washington.
3 October	Arrive at Washington.
ca. 1 November	JM prepares annual message to Congress.

Significant Federal Officers

1811

President Madison's Cabinet

Secretary of State	Robert Smith / James Monroe
Secretary of War	William Eustis
Secretary of the Treasury	Albert Gallatin
Secretary of the Navy	Paul Hamilton
Attorney General	Caesar A. Rodney

Supreme Court

Chief Justice	John Marshall
Associate Justices	Samuel Chase
	William Johnson
	Henry Brockholst Livingston
	Joseph Story
	Thomas Todd
	Bushrod Washington

Other Ranking Positions

Vice President	George Clinton
Speaker of the House of Representatives	Joseph B. Varnum
U.S. Minister to Great Britain	William Pinkney
U.S. Minister to France	John Armstrong / Joel Barlow
Postmaster General	Gideon Granger
Chief Clerk, State Department	John Graham

THE PAPERS OF

James Madison

From Oliveira & Sons

Sɪʀ!   Nᴏʀғᴏʟᴋ 3rd. November. 1810

We have duly received, your favour of 29th ultimo;[1] covering a dft. on the U. S. Branch Bank for $192.25.

This is to enclose a bill of lading, of the two QrCasks Brazil wine; and another containing thirty three gals, balance of the hhd of same kind, already fined.

We shall be happy to serve you at any time, with Madeira wines, *warranted genuine and of the best qualities;* which, will become cheaper, if imported, directly for your own use. With the greatest deference And respect we remain Sir! Your Obt Servts.

Oʟɪᴠᴇɪʀᴀ & Sᴏɴs.

2 QrCasks Old Brazil	$95	$190.—
33 gals	Do at the rate of $95 for 26 gals	120.—
3 Cases	$ 1.25	3.75
Drayage		25
		$314.

Oʟ & Sᴏɴs

RC (DLC). Docketed by JM. Enclosure not found. Filed with the RC are a receipt (1 p.), dated 2 Nov. 1810 and signed by J. Williamson, for three quarter-casks of Madeira wine from Oliveira & Sons to be delivered to the collector at Alexandria; and an undated account (1 p.) totaling $331.50 for another shipment of wine for JM.

1. Letter not found (calendared in *PJM-PS*, 2:602).

§ To Napoleon. *3 November 1810, Washington.* "I have lately received the letter of your Imperial and Royal Majesty bearing date the 3 of April last,[1] announcing the Marriage of your Majesty with the Arch Dutchess Maria Louisa of Austria." Offers "our Cordial congratulation."

Tr (AAE: Political Correspondence, U.S., 63:260). 1 p.

1. *PJM-PS*, 2:294.

§ From a Meeting of Citizens of the Indiana Territory. *4 November 1810.* Praises JM for the "firmness and patriotic Zeal" of his conduct toward the European belligerents while also complaining of the activities of Great Britain and its sympathizers in corrupting "our aboriginal neighbours." Expresses confidence in the administration of territorial governor William Henry Harrison "on the late momentous occasion of Indian affairs."[1] Assumes that JM is familiar with Harrison's virtues but declares that the governor merits "the entire confidence" of the people of Indiana and that he is "entitled to the Patronage of the *President* of the United States—and . . . worthy of employ in any station."

RC (DNA: RG 59, TP, Indiana, vol. 1). 4 pp. Signed by William Fleming and Willis Stucker on behalf of a "numerous assemblage of a people occupying a respectable section of the Indiana Territory." Printed under the date of 11 Nov. 1810 in Esarey, *Letters of Harrison*, 1:485–87.

1. This was probably a reference to Harrison's confrontation with the Shawnee leader Tecumseh at a council held in August at Vincennes (see John Smith to JM, 7 Sept. 1810, and enclosure, *PJM-PS*, 2:532–33). After the council, Harrison had sought War Department authority to march a detachment of regular troops and territorial militia to the upper line of the 1809 Fort Wayne purchase in order to "have erected a strong picketed work" that would be "beyond the reach of an assault from the Indians." JM refused to sanction the operation for "various" reasons, among them being "the lateness of the season and the existing state of things in West Florida which may require the whole of our disposable force on the Western waters" (Harrison to William Eustis, 5 and 10 Oct. 1810, Eustis to Harrison, 26 Oct. 1810, Esarey, *Letters of Harrison*, 1:474–75, 475–76, 482).

§ Presidential Proclamation. *5 November 1810, Washington.* JM issues a "full and entire pardon" to all deserters from the U.S. Army and Navy who have taken shelter in West Florida and who, desirous of returning to duty, "shall within Six months from the date hereof surrender themselves to the Commanding officer of any military post . . . or to any Commanding officer in the Naval service."

Letterbook copy (DNA: RG 59, PPR). 1 p.

To Benjamin Rush

DEAR SIR   WASHINGTON Novr. 6. 1810

I thank you for the "Report" on the African Trade, accompanying your favor of the 29th.[1] We have been for some time aware of the evasions of the Act of Congs. on this subject; by means of foreign flags &c procured by our Citizens. But it is very difficult to bring the offenders to justice here; and the foreign Govts. with which the task lies, have not employed their authority for the purpose. If any mode by which our laws could be made effectual, could be devised, there is no reason to distrust the disposition of Congs. to adopt it. The disposition of the Executive will appear in the inclosed paper,[2] of which it is not wished that any public use should be made. It is an answer to Mr. Pinkney, who had been applied to by Mr. Stephen who was Counsel for the Captors, in the very case decided as in the printed Sheet which came with the pamphlet. Be assured Dr. Sir of my great esteem and most friendly wishes.

JAMES MADISON

RC (DLC: Rush Papers).

1. *PJM-PS*, 2:601–2 and n. 1.

2. JM evidently enclosed a copy of Robert Smith to William Pinkney, 16 June 1810 (DNA: RG 59, IM), instructing the American minister on how far he might encourage British efforts to suppress the slave trade (see Rush to JM, 29 Oct. 1810, *PJM-PS*, 2:602 n. 2).

From Harry Toulmin

[6 November 1810]

. . . of some troops for this place: but I know not on what foundation. If only two or three hundred men came; I think it highly probable that several from our settlement would join them: but I have no great apprehension that any body of men will go from this place *alone*, to attack Mobile. Lawyer Kennedy a Major of the militia seems indeed very solicitous to impress the idea, that as the Convention has now become the ruling power in Florida, it will be lawful to leave the territory and serve under their banners against Mobile: but to remove this idea, and to satisfy the people of this district of the impolicy & unlawfulness of joining in any such expedition, I have written a sort of circular letter to the leading men in the different settlements, of which I inclose a copy.[1]

I also take leave to inclose a copy of a letter to my friend Genl. Thomas:[2] for as I know that what little exertions I make, tho' well intended, will be sadly misrepresented, I deem it a matter of prudence to make you acquainted with the whole.

I have just apprized Govr. Holmes of my apprehensions. I wish after all, that they may prove ill founded: but lest Mobile should shortly fall into other hands, I am aware of the importance of your being prepared for the event. I am dear sir very respectfully your faithful & obedt Sert

H. TOULMIN.

RC (DNA: RG 59, TP, Mississippi, vol. 2); enclosures (ibid., vol. 1). RC incomplete; first page or pages missing. Cover (addressed to JM) docketed by John Graham, "Private / Judge Toulmin to Sec. of State—6th Novr 1811." Date here assigned on the basis of the contents of the fragment and the assumption that Graham inadvertently wrote "1811" instead of "1810" when he received the letter, probably sometime early in 1811. For enclosures, see nn. 1 and 2.

1. Toulmin forwarded a copy of a letter addressed "To Captain———/ Washington County," dated 4 Nov. 1810 at Fort Stoddert (2 pp.; printed in Carter, *Territorial Papers, Mississippi*, 6:130–31). In it he referred to an enclosed copy of a letter to him from JM indicating the president's disapproval of filibustering activities against Spanish Florida (see JM to Toulmin, 5 Sept. 1810, *PJM-PS*, 2:525). The judge emphasized that U.S. law prohibited engaging in military activity against a foreign power and warned that "any imprudent acts of ours" would jeopardize American efforts to obtain the Spanish province peacefully and risk involving the nation in a war. "The constituted authorities of the nation are certainly the best

judges, and they are the only legal judges, when and in what manner we should extend the limits of the American territory."

2. Toulmin's 5 Nov. 1810 letter to Philemon Thomas (2 pp.), written from Fort Stoddert, congratulated Thomas on his success in liberating his district from "the spanish yoke" and commended the West Florida convention for its "moderate" conduct. The thrust of the letter, however, was to warn West Floridians not to act in ways that conflicted with JM's policies. Should future West Floridian actions compromise U.S. neutrality, Toulmin feared, "it may eventually be the means of altering entirely the relations of the United States with foreign nations, and of putting it out of their power to render . . . support and protection to the independence and liberty of the Floridas." Advising Thomas not to countenance the schemes of those "most desperate, unprincipled and abandoned men" who would "in contempt of the national authority, engage in enterprizes against a neighbouring province," Toulmin instead advised that the West Florida authorities continue to seek the protection of the U.S., since the "good understanding which is now commencing with the emperor of the French, opens a prospect, I think, of an entire change being effected, through the whole of the Floridas, without affording just occasion of umbrage to any European power."

From John R. Bedford

SIR   NASHVILLE Nov. 8th. 1810

A belief, that every information relative to the crisis in West Florida, coming in a garb that will entitle it to some credence, may not be altogether unacceptable to the executive, induces me to repeat the intrusion of the copies of two more letters on your attention.[1] I do this the more readily, upon the possible supposition, that you may not receive, from a more authentic source, more satisfactory intelligence of the dispositions & real wishes of the Convention & people of West Florida—a country & people who will become perhaps, a subject of very interesting & important deliberation with the executive.

Mr. Barrow has been induced to give me these details of the state of his country and the people, I apprehend, by considerations of the strongest personal regard and to gratify an high degree of interest, that he correctly supposed to actuate me, by reason of much local & personal acquaintance, acquired during a very leisure tour through that country & the adjoining Territories two years ago—but, as he alledges, to obtain the benefits of my opinions & advice, which, I know he values greatly above their intrinsic worth.

To foster his friendly confidence, and to invite a continuance of his full & frank communications upon the political occurrences of his country, I replied from time to time, with perfect freedom & sincerity of thought— expressing views of the political situation of his country, and the measures, it would therefore be incumbent to adopt & persue with steady energy— enforcing the doctrine, that the integrity of their interests was essentially linked with that of the U. States—suggesting & elucidating the impolicy of an alliance with the other Spanish American provinces—warning him with strong emphasis, against the fatal security of an unsuspecting confidence in the fidelity of their Gove[r]nor & many others, whose greater immediate benefits would prompt opposition to any measures of a revolutionary tendency, and which would necessarily be secret & insidious—and therefore urging, as the best measure of self prese[r]vation, to assume the rights of self government upon popular principles. In all which, it gives me some satisfaction, to find my views were not so incorrect as to mislead; nor my predictions not far short of being amply verified, except in the measure of absolute revolution, which is yet in the progress of experiment.

Under every circumstance & my knowledge of Mr. Barrow, I cannot withold entire confidence in the honesty & correctness of all his communications. In the two inclosed copies, you will remark a difference in their tenor, but an emphatic concordance in the views intimated in the first, with the actual events of the 22d. Septr., stated in the second.

I have not thought it worth while to communicate any thing upon this Subject derived through this channel, to any one, but Gove[r]nor Blount, save, yourself: and to him, because in several conversations last summer, he manifested so lively an interest in every thing relating to our South Western Frontier; and especially, as far as it might be involved in the fate of West Florida.

If herein, I have been unseasonably intrusive, please, do me the justice to counterballance the inconvenience thereof, by the misapplied good will, that led to my unprofitable communications. I am with perfect good wishes & entire Respect your Obt. Sevt.

J. R. Bedford

RC and enclosures (DLC). Enclosures both marked "(Copy)"; in Bedford's hand (see n. 1).

1. As he had done on 4 July and 26 Aug. 1810 (see *PJM-PS*, 2:399–400, 508–10), Bedford forwarded copies of letters he had received from William Barrow. The first (3 pp.), written at Bayou Sara on 11 Sept. 1810, described the opening meeting of the West Florida convention at St. Johns Plains in late July in order to answer criticisms that Bedford apparently had made of the delegates' decision to pledge allegiance to Ferdinand VII. "At our first meeting," Barrow wrote, "we were in a measure strangers to one another" when "it was proposed by some to take an oath of allegiance to Ferdinand 7th. Upon this, you will judge, how we, that thought otherwise must feel, finding men to believe that was essential to be done. But when we came to argue upon that subject, only one appeared in favor of it. Then we thought it proper not to say much upon any subject." Barrow also defended the convention's decisions to lay taxes and to make laws for West Florida, assuring Bedford that the delegates were "firm Americans; and only act now as they do, to preserve peace & harmony, untill times justify other measures." After the convention reassembled in November, Barrow continued, its members hoped "to know the determination of the U. States towards us," not doubting that "the great mass of the people are in favor of our becoming in union with the U. S."

Barrow's second letter (3 pp.) was written from West Florida on 10 Oct. 1810 and reported the attack by convention forces on the Spanish fort at Baton Rouge on 22–23 Sept. and the West Floridian declaration of independence on 26 Sept. Barrow hoped that the U.S. would "receive us and add us to one of the adjoining Territories, that we may become a part of that nation. The present Convention is entirely in favor of that measure." He also warned that if the U.S. did not act promptly, "another *Boddy* may not be so much in favor of it as the present is. . . . For now I assure you is the moment—the word liberty is an enchanting sound here. We are in great spirits now—but malitia men will soon become weary; and I fear ours may." Barrow worried about future divisions in the West Florida convention, especially since men such as Shepherd Brown were able to rally "a party" to defend the rights of Ferdinand VII. In this context Barrow justified the seizure of the fort at Baton Rouge as a measure necessary to save lives, and he marveled that so much had already been achieved with so little bloodshed.

From Robert Patton

DEAR SIR, PHILADA. 8th Novr. 1810.

Your favour of 29th Octr.[1] was handed to me, a few days since, by Thomas Mc.Graw. I am really sorry to hear that you have been so unfortunate as to lose one of the first pair of Greys, & fear that it will be difficult to replace him. I have been through all our stables, but, I have not been so fortunate as to find a pair, or even a single horse, fit to match the others.

On examining the horse mentioned to you by the Secretary at War, I find he is much too white for your others, & the owner asks me three hundred dollars for him, which, I think too much by 100. I will continue to look out, & if I procure either one, or a pair, I will send them forward. Should you, Sir, in the mean time, procure one, you will be pleased to write me least, I should purchase also. Please to present my best respect to your amiable Lady & believe me With the greatest respect Your Obedient Servt

ROBT. PATTON

RC (DLC).

1. Letter not found (calendared in *PJM-PS*, 2:603).

From an Unidentified Correspondent

SIR NEW YORK 8h. November 1810

A meeting of the merchants of this city is now called[1] to solicit advice, respecting the effect of your late Proclamation.[2]

Permit a stranger, but a friend to your administration to offer a few reasons, the effect of his experience, why your advice should be explicit.

When the late law establishing a non-intercourse was about to go into effect, all those who respected the edicts of their country and esteemed the administration then in power withheld their orders, and relinquished the advantages of their trade; at the same time, to the writers knowledge, english agents, and persons politically adverse to the existing administration, either placing reliance on the mildness or weakness of our government, gave directions to their factors, to ship as long as american vessels could be found to bring out their shipments. Their importations were immense, which, by an ill judged lenity, after they had arrived in complete defiance of the law, were released to them; and thus aliens & disrespectful citizens, were permitted to make immense sums, while he who respected the laws had spent an unprofitable season, or perhaps had sustained a loss.

This, sir, was too mortifying, and by weakning the reliance of even the friends of the administration, was calculated to make future laws disrespected by all.

You will therefore, Sir, see the propriety of making such explanations, as will place all on an equal footing, will assure all persons that the government will *itself* hereafter *respect* its *own laws*, and will consequently leave the transgressor without excuse. From a sincere

FRIEND OF THE PRESENT ADMINISTRATION

RC (NN).

1. No report of any such meeting has been found.
2. Presidential Proclamation, 2 Nov. 1810 (*PJM-PS*, 2:612–13).

§ From Benjamin Chambers. *8 November 1810, Lawrenceburg.* "I have been absent for 7 Mo past in which time my family have been embarrassed for the want of the money due me from the U. States. . . . The roads I made are travelled by great numbers of persons and allowed to be well done—and I flattered myself that Mr Ewings amendments & alterations . . . would not be deducted from my Acct.[1] . . . Mr Jennings our representative told me that Mr Ewing would sighn a petition in my favour praying a further Allowance for my services. Astonishing as this may appear it is a fact that I have been Kept out of the Small Sum due me for more than two years." Hopes JM will order the account to be paid.

RC (DNA: RG 49, ML). 2 pp. Docketed by Gallatin with a note to treasury auditor Richard Harrison requesting information on the state of the account that included the roads Chambers had contracted to open in the Indiana Territory. Beneath Gallatin's note, Harrison responded on 20 Dec. 1810 that the sum of $4,199.52 advanced to John Badollet had been transferred to the debit of Nathaniel Ewing and the account settled and closed on 28 June. Another note by Gallatin the following day requested Daniel Sheldon to show him the report on the account to see "whether Chambers stands charged or credited &c." Printed in Carter, *Territorial Papers, Indiana*, 8:55–56.

1. Benjamin Chambers, a surveyor, had been engaged by John Badollet, register of the Vincennes Land Office, to open roads "from Vincennes to the Indian Boundary line established by the treaty of Greenville in the direction to the North Bend, and from Clarksville to

intersect the above road on the East Side of the eastern fork of White river and from vincennes to the mississippi oposite the town of St Louis." Chambers had written to JM in 1809 to protest that part of his payment had been wrongly withheld and that land office receiver Nathaniel Ewing had employed men to complete the roads at his expense. JM referred Chambers's complaints to Gallatin, who on 21 Dec. 1810 explained to Chambers the principles on which his department had settled the account with Badollet and Ewing "which embraces your own." In the event that Chambers still believed that money was owed to him, Gallatin wrote, "you should transmit to the Comptroller your account stated on your own principles: and . . . the account will be definitively settled accordingly" (Chambers to Gallatin, 10 Nov. 1808, Chambers to JM, 29 June 1809, Gallatin to Chambers, 7 Aug. 1809, Carter, *Territorial Papers, Indiana*, 7:614–16, 658–59, 665; Gallatin to Chambers, 21 Dec. 1810, ibid., 8:67–68).

From Tench Coxe

Sir   November 10. 1810.

The great intrinsic importance of Banking institutions, both associated and incorporated, will be considered, I trust, by you as a sufficient apology for this respectful solicitation of a small portion of your valuable time.

The system of commerce and credit, and the laws of property in the United Kingdom of Great Britain & Ireland have been considered, as on the whole, the most perfect in Europe. Yet it is certain, that excluding entirely the evidences of their public debt of 4100 millions of Dollars, the administrations of their banks, public & private, have suffered themselves to inundate their whole commercial & financial field with an embarrassing flood of circulating paper and with an unascertained quantity of bank credits given in the form of discounted pr⟨ivate⟩ obligations, notes, or bills, and loans to the British & foreign Governments.

The incorporated Banks of G. Britain & Ireland have also practiced another grant of credit in the acquisition of a portion of their national and other public debts to an amount fully equal to their whole clear estate and equivalent to the sum total of the coin usually supposed to be possessed in Great Britain & Ireland.

In many cases also of individual embarrassment, arising often out [of] the gambling operations of the Stock exchange, the insolvent estates of such persons, and of many others have obtained extensive credits [*illegible*] of evidences of further portions of the public debt.

It appears necessary that we should consider in time the solemn admonition of these great & undeniable facts, and that we should not know *in time* & *yet in vain*, that the United Kingdoms of Great Britain & Ireland besides their immense discount credits, have apparently in circulation five hundred & sixty Millions of paper dollars of associate and incorporated companies, the legal tender of which, in all payments, they have reported by a special legislative committee, that they cannot for years discontinue, or abridge.

As a very strong inducement to new measures of caution & prudence, it ought not to be reserved, that there are no proofs of an unwise or criminal maladministration of banking institutions in the British Kingdoms more ⟨cle⟩ar and notorious than some, which have occurred in two or three of our own states. It is in the ground of the foreign & domestic cases most re[s]pectfully suggested, Sir, that the nature, the operations, and the consequences of Banking institutions, abroad and at home, appear to require a timely, sober, honest and profound consideration in order to prevent the ills, which legislative, directorial, and individual errors may occasion them to produce to this fine country, which by the favor of Heaven, is yet orderly, sound & happy.

The history of corporations of business & property, in many countries abundantly proves their errors, their misconduct & their necessities, & the injuries they have sometimes brought upon other parts of the community and upon the state itself.

The use of the deposits of public treasures is in effect a temporary loan enabling the Banks to discount & is worth some compensation, in reason & practical Business.

The Monopoly of *paper bills of credit redeemable on demand* is also worth some compensation, both in reason and in practice.

As our public debts shall be discharged, the community and individuals will have occasion for banks to employ their private and their public monies.

It is necessary to render perfectly visible the solid benefits resulting to Banking institutions from the transfer to them of the Monopoly of issuing paper bills of credit bearing no interest. This Monopoly, as enjoyed and exercised in Pennsylvania for example, was very considerable and was often happily applied to public uses, and to private objects.

If a grant of £15.000 ⅌ Annum, for example, for 25 years ⟨was⟩ made by the legislature of that province to the crown for the defence of the cisatlantic colonies, it could be raised without a tax on persons or property, by the legislative issue of £⟨4⟩00000 in paper bills of credit, guarrantied by the Province. These bills were loaned on solid personal & Landed security to the builders of mills, and other private improvers, & produced at the lawful interest of six ⅌ Cent the whole grant to the crown of £15000 & £9000 ⅌ annum as a sinking fund. In the same manner an emission was made to build the fortifications on the Delaware & the Light House. Other operations of the same nature were thus conveniently & profitably performed. A few thousand Bank Stockholders enjoy at present all these advantages of the issue of paper Bills in the United States; & they have been induced, like those of Great Britain & Ireland, to issue too much paper taken alltogether, & seperately also, in some serious instances, in order to encrease the profits of this gainful, unlimited & dangerous portion of their business.

It is certain that the governors and managers of public & private banks

9

have in some instances in all countries been inconsiderate & imprudent; deceitful and fraudulent; shameless & unfaithful, to the injury of the stockholders & creditors of the banks, the commercial credit of the Country, and the best interests of their States. The Question of the responsibility of the directors of these institutions is respectfully conceived to require the most serious consideration. It is perfectly reasonable, for so far as the legislative grant of a Corporate Being, Agency & benefit extends they may be considered as compensated public trustees and functionaries, who ought to be under A responsibility essential[ly] official.

After the liberty [of] these preliminary and explanatory observations, I propose respectfully to submit a few examples of the kin⟨d of⟩ cautionary provisions, which recent circumstances abroad & at home appear to require, in order to avoid those evils which have subjected banks to embarrassment, discredit & odium, individuals to danger, fraud & ruin, & the state to dishonor, confusion and alarm, disordering its finances in time of need, & threatening it with fearful agitations. I have the honor to be, Sir, your most respectful Servt.

Draft (PHi: Coxe Papers). Damaged by tears at folds. Docketed by Coxe, "To the Chief Magis. on Banks."

§ From James Burrill, Jr., and Gold S. Silliman. *10 November 1810, Newport, Rhode Island.* "In compliance with the request of a number of the gentlemen of the Bar of this State, we have the honor to transmit to you the enclosed resolutions."

RC and enclosure (DNA: RG 59, LAR, 1809–17, filed under "Robbins"). RC 1 p. Enclosure (2 pp.) is a set of resolutions recommending Asher Robbins for the Supreme Court seat vacated by the death of William Cushing, signed by Burrill as chairman of the meeting of Rhode Island attorneys and by Silliman as secretary, 10 Nov. 1810. RC and enclosure forwarded in Silliman to Robert Smith, 12 Nov. 1810 (ibid.).

§ From the Merchants and Underwriters of Philadelphia. *10 November 1810, Philadelphia.* During "the last and present year," vessels belonging to or insured by the memorialists have been seized by cruisers commissioned by Denmark and "condemned under the most frivolous pretences." The principal grounds for condemnation are "that the documents found on board the captured vessels were forged, and not genuine, particularly, that the certificates obtained from The French consular offices were false, or that such vessels had been visited by, or sailed under convoy of British armed ships." The memorialists can establish that the vessels are exclusively American property, that their documentation is "genuine and duly authenticated," and that "in most instances where American vessels were found in company with British armed ships, they had either fallen in with them by accident, or were obliged by fear to accompany them." In addition, because Americans have been excluded from ports in Holstein and Prussia, there are large numbers of vessels at Gothenburg, and "from recent occurrences in Europe your Memorialists are led to serious apprehensions for the safety of the American vessels and cargoes . . . in the Ports of Sweden." They request that the U.S. government intervene by appointing a special agent to protest the injuries done in Denmark and Norway and to secure American property in Sweden.[1]

RC (DNA: RG 76, Denmark, Convention of 1830, Letters Regarding Claims). 3 pp. Signed by Thomas FitzSimons and forty-nine others. Enclosed in a covering letter addressed to Robert Smith, 10 Nov. 1810, signed by FitzSimons and three others (ibid.).

1. JM was to receive similar petitions from other merchant groups in cities along the Atlantic coast (see the petition from the merchants and underwriters of Baltimore, 20 Nov. 1810; also the undated petition from the merchants of Boston, published in the Boston *Columbian Centinel*, 26 Dec. 1810). For JM's nomination of George W. Erving as special agent to Denmark on 12 Dec. 1810, see Richard Law to JM, 28 July 1810 (*PJM-PS*, 2:447 n. 1).

From C. T. Chapman

COLLECTOR'S OFFICE ALEXANDRIA

SIR   12 November 1810

I have taken the liberty to enclose to you certificates for Three quarter Casks of Wine for the President of the United States sent to my care by Mesrs. Oliveira & Sons of Norfolk[1]—and now on board the Sloop Eliza Ann Captain Evans bound to this City; who I have directed to deliver the same to you. His charges you will please pay and as soon as I pay the freight and charges from Norfolk and at this place will furnish you with a Bill thereof. Most respectfully, I am sir Your Obt Servant

C T CHAPMAN/Dy Coll

RC (DLC). Docketed by JM.

1. See Oliveira & Sons to JM, 3 Nov. 1810, and n.

From Andrew Ellicott

DEAR SIR.   LANCASTER Novbr. 14th. 1810.

While you were Secretary of State, I frequently troubled you with forwarding my communications to the National Institute of France,[1] and being some time indebted to the Institute several letters, and communications, I wish to know if they can be forwarded as formerly thro' the department of State, to our minister, or publick functionary at Paris?

I feel some ambition to continue this correspondence, arising I presume from being the only native born american astronomer, now corresponding with the Institute, on the subject of astronomy: however, I should not have found leisure for some time to come, to have made out my present communication, had I not been impelled by the tyranny of Mr. Snyder's administration, to abandon tra[n]sacting business, as an agent, in the different publick offices of this Commonwealth.

I resided some time under the despotism of Spain,[2] which I found infinitely milder, and more dignified, than Snyderite democracy in this State, which appears to be so far at open war with the arts, sciences, and literature, that not one single person who had the slightest pretension to either has been left in office. The following anecdote, attested by the Journals of our State legislature, will amply establish the fact of this war against science. Some time last winter, a false report got abroad, that I had been one evening looking at the stars thro' a telescope belonging to the Commonwealth; this report was immediately followed by a resolution of the house of representatives, to prevent my making use of that instrument![3] The resolution was lost in the Senate.

There must certainly be something very grateful in the persecution of a poor republican philosopher, who otherwise would scarcely know he was in the world, and who is either immersed in his study among his books, or engaged in cultivating a garden, and pruning his young trees with his own hands, and who has been fifteen months at one time in the service of his country, without ever once laying down on a bed, or sleeping in a house; and six years under the administration of Mr. [M]cKean, that he was never absent one day from the office over which he presided.

Political intolerance among republicans, who claim the freedom of opinion as a birth-right, and religious intolerance among christians, whose religion is founded on brotherly love, and charity, has always appeared to me a paradox, and sometimes almost induced me to believe, that there are but few real republicans, and christians in the world. Whenever I think of intolerance, the following picture of it by Voltaire never fails presenting itself to my view. "Quoi! monstre qui seras brûlé à tout jamais dans l'autre monde, & que je ferai-brûler dans celui-ci dès que je le pourrai, tu as l'insolence de lire *de Thou & Bayle* qui sont mis à l'index à Rome? Quand je te prêchais de la part de *Dieu* que *Samson* avait tué mille Philistins avec une mâchoire d'ane, ta tête plus dure que l'arsenal dont *Samson* avait tiré ses armes m'a faite connaître par un léger movement de gauche à droite que tu n'en croyais rien. Et quand je disais que le diable Asmodée, qui tordit le coû par jalousie aux sept maris de *Saraï* chez les Mèdes etait enchainé dans la haute Egypte, j'a[i] vu une petite contraction de tes lèvrès nommée en latin *cachinnus*, me signifier que dans le fond de l'ame l'histoire d'*Asmodée* t'etait en dérision."[4] The election of Simon Snyder, which I confess I did not oppose, tho' from my knowledge of the man, my conscience frequently warned me that as a patriot I ought, has led me almost to suspect, that the same writer is correct when he says, "les hommes sont très-rarement dignes de se gouverner aux-mêmes."[5] The french nation certainly agree with Voltaire.

You see, that I write to you with all the familiarity of an old friend, and I assure you that my friendship is not in the least diminished by time. I am sir, with great respect and esteem, your sincere friend.

ANDW. ELLICOTT.

RC (DLC).

1. See, for example, Ellicott to JM, 20 Feb. 1802 (*PJM-SS*, 2:480).

2. Ellicott alluded to the years from 1796 to 1800 when he was engaged in establishing the boundary line between the U.S. and the American possessions of Spain following the ratification of Pinckney's treaty (see *PJM-SS*, 1:202–4).

3. The resolution Ellicott complained of was introduced and passed on 17 Feb. 1810 (*Journal of the Twentieth House of Representatives of the Commonwealth of Pennsylvania* [Lancaster, 1809 (1810); Shaw and Shoemaker 21024], pp. 553, 563).

4. "What! monster who will burn forever in the next world and whom I would burn in this world if I could, you have the insolence to read *de Thou and Bayle* who are placed on the index in Rome? When I preach to you on behalf of *God* that *Samson* had killed one thousand Philistines with the jawbone of an ass, your head, harder than the arsenal from which *Samson* drew his weapons, indicated to me by a slight movement from left to right, that you believe none of it. And when I say that the devil Asmodeus, who from jealousy wrung the necks of the seven husbands of *Sarah* while she was with the Medes, was imprisoned in Upper Egypt, I observed a slight curling of your lip, known in Latin as *cachinnus* [to mock with laughter], telling me that at the bottom of your soul you regarded the story of Asmodeus as ridiculous" (editors' translation). The editors have been unable to identify these sentences positively as a direct quotation from Voltaire. The anecdotes and the sentiments, however, can be found in almost any edition of Voltaire's *Dictionnaire philosophique* (see the entries under Asmodée, Samson, and Tolérance), and it is possible that Ellicott blended them into continuous sentences which he then rendered in French in a style resembling that of the French philosophe (*Dictionnaire philosophique*, vols. 17–20 of *Œuvres complètes de Voltaire* [52 vols.; Paris, 1877–85], 17:434–36, 20:396–99, 517–26).

5. "Mankind is rarely worthy of self-government." Possibly this was Ellicott's recollection of Voltaire's question in the second section of his essay on government in the *Dictionnaire philosophique*: "What, then, is the destiny of mankind? Scarcely any great nation is self-governing" (editors' translation) (ibid., 20:287).

From James Maury

LIVERPOOL 14 NOVr 1810

DEAR SIR,

Annexed is the copy of what I had the honor to write to you on the 11th Ulto,[1] since which the Adeline arrived safe in this river; but, before getting into Dock, recieved injury & considerably damaged her cargo, in which damage your consignment participated, & 1786 ℔ were cut off, for which I claim on the Underwriters.[2]

The immense influx of our produce since the expiration of the Non-intercourse law, in front of so unpromising a prospect for exportation to the continent, added to a long continuation of failures (which still continue): & these to an extent far beyond example; have all contributed to the depression of this market, the state of which is such at this juncture, that even such Tobaccoes as yours cannot be estimated at more than 3d a 3½d ⅌ ℔. I have made no sale nor do I think of it at present. At all events I wish first to hear from you.

It is well that I was so ⟨guarded?⟩ in the information about General Armstrong; for, not many days after, I understood it was incorrect. With perfect respect I have the honour to be your most obedient Servant

JAMES MAURY

RC (DLC). Docketed by JM.

1. *PJM-PS*, 2:575.

2. Maury's account of sales of JM's tobacco shipped on the *Adeline*, dated 8 Mar. 1814 (DLC), includes a credit for the amount of £14 6s. 8d. received from the underwriters for damage.

From Peter Stephen DuPonceau

SIR   PHILADELPHIA 15th. Novr. 1810

I had the honor of mentioning to you when you was last in this City in 1805. that I had made, for my private use, a Translation of the first Book of Bynkershoek's Quæstiones Juris Publici.[1] I have Since been induced to publish it, & I beg leave to present you with the first Copy of it that has issued from the press. It is an homage due to the Statesman who has best understood & appreciated the merits of my Author, & who has given to the World the most correct Character of his Writings. Permit me to offer it to you also as a feeble testimony of my respect & veneration for your Character, & of my attachment to your person. I have the honor to be With the greatest consideration & respect Sir Your most obedient and very humble servant

PETER S. DU PONCEAU[2]

RC (DLC).

1. DuPonceau published the first book of Cornelius van Bynkershoek's *Quaestionum juris Publici . . .* (1737 ed.), with notes, as *A Treatise on the Law of War . . . Being the First Book of His "Questiones juris publici"* (Philadelphia, 1810; Shaw and Shoemaker 19697). In the introduction to his translation (p. xix), DuPonceau commended JM for his "correct and judicious praise" of Bynkershoek in his 1806 pamphlet, *An Examination of the British Doctrine, Which Subjects to Capture a Neutral Trade, Not Open in Time of Peace.*

2. Peter Stephen DuPonceau (1760–1844), born and educated in France, came to the U.S. in 1777 as a secretary to Baron von Steuben. He also served Robert R. Livingston in the same capacity during the latter's tenure as secretary for foreign affairs in the 1780s. In 1785 he commenced the practice of law in Philadelphia where he subsequently became known for his translations of works on constitutional and international law as well as for his contributions to history and philology.

From Lafayette

My dear Sir   PARIS 15h November 1810

I am Sure You Have Had the Goodness to Answer My Long triplicate the Last of Which Went By the John Adams.[1] Several Subsequent Letters Have Been Sent By me. The last ones I Had from You are dated May the 18h and 19h.[2]

It is a Comfort to me to think that You and our friend Mr. Jefferson Have Received Notes Which do in a Measure Account for My pecuniary Situation and alleviate the Blame that one inattentive to peculiar Circumstances might in a much Greater degree Lay Upon me.[3]

I Had prepared Communications and Calculations fit to Explain and Advocate the Means I Am Necessitated to take for my Relief. They shall go By another Opportunity. I am allowed only time to Say a few Words, and Beg You Will Communicate these Lines to our Excellent friend Jefferson.

My debts to Mm Baring, parish, parker, preble and Ridgeway form an Enormous Mass which increasing interests to all, except Mr. parish who was paid Annually, Have Swelled to a most Alarming degree. The Mortgages preclude the possibility Even to think of a Loan Any Where.

If You are pleased to Recur to Your Letter of the 18h May Stating the Value of my pointe Coupee Lands, and Whatever Augmentation May take place Within the time When those Gentlemen Must Be paid, from Which the Yearly interest Ought Be deducted, You Will find it a Very Great Advantage for me to Clear those debts now With part of My Lands at the Rate of Near 15 dollars, 75 francs an acre. Mr. david parish Has kindly Advised and promoted the Arrangement. Every friend in Europe thought it Was the only mode of Salvation for me. I think So too Yet Such Was My Reluctance to part With Any part of the Land, Such My fear to incur Your disapprobation and that of Mr. Jefferson, that What Every Body thinks ought to Be a matter of choice, I Y⟨ie⟩ld to as a Matter of Necessity.

The dispositions of All ⟨of⟩ those Gentlemen in Europe are favorable. I write to Mr. Ridgeway And Hope He Will not Be disatisfied With me. My Brother Grammont[4] is also Willing to take Lands.

I am affraid to See that this Operation must Cost me 8000 Acres. Let me Again Entreat You to Compare the price With Your Valuation on the 18h

May as M. duplantier gave it. You Will aknowledge there is, in the indispensable Bargain, full Scope for Every Hope that May Be formed Within a few years. Large Capitalists Might Calculate otherwise. But I am to Escape Ruin not to Seek profit. Honesty Commands me to Clear the Way, as much as I Can, for my Creditors.

There Remain two thousand of those acres, a fine property for me, and the Lands Near the City, a Security for future Wealth, at Least a Security for the payment of my other debts—for You See that the Creditors thereby paid are those Who Never Would Have Contributed to My Ruin, But By their Being in the Way of My finding More Monney.

I Have not Had to Spend more Capitals, I live frugally, my farming Has Not Been Unfortunate, the Little Expenses in addition to Revenue Are inconsiderable, Yet Such is the increase of interests Rolling Upon Each other, Of Ruinous Loans to pay former ones, &c &c. that I Who, at the time the Grant Was Made, Would With Hundred thousand dollars Have Paid all Remaining charges of Revolutions, proscription, Captivity, and Reestablishement in france, Must Now, to Be Saved from threatening Engagements, find, over and above the 8000 Acres, a Very Large Sum.

It Has Hitherto Be[en] My Hope I Could Upon the Remaining Mortgage obtain a Loan of forty or fifty thousand dollars. That Hope is at an End. M. david parish, the only Ressource that Was Left declares, and this Very day more positively than Ever,[5] Has Experienced the impossibility to find Monney Upon those Lands. He knows all the Monneyd people of England, Holland, Germany, and france. Alarmed as He is for My Situation, Sensible of the delays attending an American Relief, He thinks that there alone, Either By a Loan, or By Sale of Lots Near the town I Can find preservation from impending Ruin.

To Avoid it through the Means Which Congress Have Been pleased to grant, and through Your friendly Exertions, My dear Sir, Would add a most lively Gratification to the other feelings Which Cannot fail to attend a Man Emerging from Such A Danger—to Avoid Which I Have done Every thing that My principles and Character Could allow.

I don't Write to M. duplantier putting it all in Your Hands, and Wishing the Good Effect of Your Attempt May Not Be too late. But too Much Has Been Said in former letters to Need illustration.

I know mr. Russel Has writen By this Vessel, and shall only add that With the Most Grateful Regard I am forever Your Affectionate friend

LAFAYETTE

I Have obtained time to write two letters Which With that to Mr. Ridgeway I take the Liberty to inclose ⟨to Mr.⟩ Russel for the Government packet: that for mr. duplantier Being Submitted to you with the Request to Have the goodness to write to Him and forward it if it Has Your Approbation.

RC (PHi); FC (NIC: Dean Collection). RC postmarked New York, 11 [Feb.?]. Docketed by JM. FC, in an unidentified hand, does not include postscript.

1. Lafayette to JM, 24 Mar. 1810 (*PJM-PS*, 2:283–84).

2. *PJM-PS*, 2:343, 346.

3. For a discussion of Lafayette's financial problems, see Madison and Lafayette's Louisiana Lands, 26 Oct. 1809 (*PJM-PS*, 2:35–38).

4. Alexandre-Marie-François, marquis de Sales-Théodule Grammont (1765–1841), was Lafayette's brother-in-law (*Biographie universelle* [1843–65 ed.], 17:322).

5. In the FC, "he" has been added here interlinearly.

§ From a Committee of Citizens of Muscle Shoals. *Ca. 15 November 1810.* Petitions JM on the article of the treaty between the U.S. and the Cherokee Nation[1] reserving "a certain Tract of Land, including the western Banks of the Muscle Shoals, on the Tennessee River, in favour of John D. Chism,[2] and sundry Indian, and White Families, at that Time, then and there residing," which stipulated that the U.S. would extinguish the Chickasaw claims to the tract, if any, in favor of those mentioned.[3] "A great Number of good Citizens, who have large Families," have given "almost their all for a small Tract of Land within the said Reserve, and only taken quit-claim Titles"; they will be left with the "disagreeable alternative, of returning to the miserable State of Tenants, so oppressive . . . and hostile to the Rights, and Liberties of Mankind." Petitioners further state that they have organized courts, laws, and a militia. They urge JM not to regard them as intruders or cut them off "as an insignificant Fraction of the Community" but to protect them and ignore "false and incorrect Representations" coming from "malicious Persons" residing among the Chickasaw.

RC (DNA: RG 75, LRIA). 2 pp. Signed by David Hudspeth, chairman, Stephen Duncan, clerk, and eight members of the committee. Undated. Enclosed in Return J. Meigs to William Eustis, 28 Nov. 1810 (ibid.). Docketed by Meigs, "Muscle Shoal's / a Memorial to the President of the U. S. left at my Office 17th. November 1810, for the Post office." Docketed by a War Department clerk as received 17 Dec. 1810.

1. In a treaty signed at Washington on 7 Jan. 1806 by Secretary of War Henry Dearborn and seventeen chiefs and headmen of the Cherokee Nation, the latter had ceded to the U.S. a substantial part of their southwestern hunting grounds, including an area in dispute between the Cherokee and the Chickasaw (see *ASP, Indian Affairs*, 1:704; Charles H. Fairbanks and John H. Goff, *Cherokee and Creek Indians: Ethnographic Report on Royce Area 79* [New York, 1974], pp. 425–37).

2. John D. Chisholm, a Loyalist who had married into the Cherokee Nation, had been actively involved in William Blount's conspiracy in 1796. He exercised considerable influence in Indian affairs by virtue of his alliances with such Lower Town Cherokee leaders as Doublehead, and he was one of a group of large Tennessee landowners whose properties were set aside as reservations in the land cessions between the Cherokee Nation and the U.S. Following the division of the Cherokee Nation in 1808 over the issue of land sales, he moved in the summer of 1809 to Arkansas where he remained prominent as a leader of the western branch of the Cherokee (McLoughlin, *Cherokee Renascence*, pp. 42, 60, 95, 99, 102–5, 120–22, 145, 152, 217, 220).

3. JM received a very similar petition, undated and bearing 108 signatures, including those of some of the members of the Muscle Shoals committee (4 pp.; docketed as received Decem-

ber 1810), from the settlers on the tract known as Doublehead's Reserve (see Eli Townsend and others to JM, ca. 15 Nov. 1810 [DNA: RG 107, LRRS, D-56:5]).

§ From Edward Lloyd.[1] *15 November 1810, Annapolis.* "At the request of the Republican members of the House of Delegates of this State, I have taken the liberty of enclosing to you the within Recommendation."

RC and enclosure (DNA: RG 59, LAR, 1809–17, filed under "Bland"). RC 1 p. Enclosure (2 pp.) is a 13 Nov. 1810 letter signed by thirty-nine General Assembly delegates recommending Theodorick Bland for U.S. attorney in the event of the resignation of the incumbent, John Stephen.

1. Edward Lloyd (1779–1834) had served as a Republican representative in the Ninth and Tenth Congresses (1806–9). From 1809 to 1811 he was governor of Maryland.

§ From George Joy. *16 November 1810, Copenhagen.* Informs JM he has credible information that some of his letters have been put ashore at Gothenburg, including a letter for JM enclosed in one addressed to Warder & Sons of Philadelphia. Cannot account for the captain's conduct, nor can he discern the fate of the letters. The *Eclipse* of Philadelphia sailed with a similar set of papers, "but I enclose such Copies as I had, or could get ready." Mentions a report from two sources of an armistice between the Turks and the Russians. Was unable to confirm the report in his talks with the Russian minister, but if it is true, "it cannot fail to be important." In a postscript notes that he is enclosing a partial copy of a letter to William Pinkney, "to be continued and followed by such other Communications, as my own Avocations may allow me to transcribe from my stenographic Copies."

RC and enclosures (DLC). RC 3 pp. At the bottom of the RC, Joy listed the enclosures: a partial copy of Joy to William Pinkney, 27 Oct. 1809 (10 pp.), and copies of Joy to Hans R. Saabye, 22 Aug. 1810 (8 pp.) and 1 Sept. 1810 (2 pp.); Saabye to Joy, 11 Sept. 1810 (2 pp.); Joy to Robert Smith, 24 Sept. 1810 (2 pp.); and Joy to JM, 7 and 8 Oct. and 16 Sept. 1810 (see *PJM-PS*, 2:545, 574).

From John G. Jackson

Dr. Sir.   Clarksburg Novr. 17th. 1810

We have just closed the warmest contested Election here I ever witnessed. McKinley whom you know was the Republican candidate Wilson who ran twice against me the federal one the votes were on the 4th. day at night in this County (Harrison) McKinley 404 } 155 majority. The Polls
                                      Wilson   249
were kept open in Monongalia where both Candidates attended four days also: & on the evening of the second day Wilson led 160 votes. I have heard from Wood where McKinley got a Majority of 40 so that from the best calculation he will succeed by a Majority of 80 or 100 in the district of six

Counties.¹ This will be a triumph indeed as it was believed by the opposition & given up by our friends hitherto that I alone could succeed in the district. I personated McKinley here & by unprecedented exertions prevented W from obtaining a Majority over him. It was affirmed that McKinley was engaged in the Western insurrection & excepted by proclamation of Genl. Washington (then President) from a general pardon,² I have pledged myself that the assertion is false, & pray you my dear Sir to request Mr. Grayham to furnish me with copies of the Proclamations issued in that case & a certificate that none others were issued with the seal of State affixed that I may redeem my pledge to the People. I encountered also the most audacious charge I ever heard, made in the address of the person who represented Mr. W to the People. It was, that Congress at midnight made an appropriation of two millions for no specified object—had drawn out the money from the treasury—& divided it as was presumed among the members as there was no account rendered. You see my dear Sir that you have the solace of the Citizen who thanked fortune that he had not alone suffered by the conflagration of the Town. For we too here have to bear a share of lies the most infamous & unfounded. Mrs. M will explain to you the accompanying packet. With sincerest regard Your Mo. Obt Servt

J G JACKSON

RC (DLC).

1. William McKinley was elected to replace Jackson in the first Virginia congressional district following the latter's resignation after his inability to recover fully from the wounds he had received in his duel with Joseph Pearson (see *PJM-PS*, 2:125 and n. 2). In the April 1811 election for the Twelfth Congress, however, McKinley lost the seat to his Federalist opponent, Thomas Wilson (see Jackson to JM, 19 Apr. 1811).

2. The delegates from Ohio County, Virginia, had been excluded from the amnesty arranged on 21–23 Aug. 1794 by the U.S. commissioners and a committee of delegates representing the various counties involved in the Whiskey Rebellion. McKinley had been a member of the Ohio County delegation, and he was, therefore, among those who were exempted from the "full, free, and entire pardon" for the Whiskey rebels issued by Virginia governor Henry Lee in the name of the president on 29 Nov. 1794 (see Syrett and Cooke, *Papers of Hamilton*, 17:131 n. 3, 378, 380 n. 14).

From Christopher Ellery

SIR   PROVIDENCE, R. I. Nov. 20. 1810.

The inclosed statement of facts was intended for general circulation, but, for the moment, is confined to individuals.¹ I transmit it to the President of the United States because I wish him to be informed that the Governor of this State is, at best, a despot and that the Senator U. S. lately elected is his creature—his miserable tool. J. B. Howel was chosen by *one* majority.² It was in his power, having one vote himself, to say to the republican party in the convention, "choose me, or the federalist, Burrill, shall be the senator": the same power had the Governor, Fenner; he also having a vote: all which being perfectly understood by the other members of the assembly, *they submitted*. Every of your moments is precious—therefore am I concise, but my manner, if disrespectful, does not correspond with my heart, which, assuredly, is full of respect & attachment for you, Sir, whose most obedient servant I have the honor to be, ever—

CHRIST. ELLERY

RC (DLC). Enclosure not found, but see n. 1.

1. The enclosure was very likely another copy of a printed broadside that Ellery forwarded to Albert Gallatin at the same time he wrote to JM (see Ellery to Gallatin, 20 Nov. 1810, *Papers of Gallatin* [microfilm ed.], reel 21). This was an account of the nomination and election of a successor to Elisha Mathewson in the U.S. Senate at a convention of the Republican members of the Rhode Island General Assembly held on 30 Oct. 1810. The Republicans, confident of their majority, entrusted the selection of their candidate to the members from Providence, who, after deciding that Mathewson could not be reelected, chose Henry Smith. The governor, James Fenner, objected, after which Smith declined the nomination. The Republicans next selected Jonathan Russell, to whom Fenner also objected on the grounds that he was out of the country. The governor indicated his own preference for David Howell but failing that declared he would accept the nomination of Howell's son, Jeremiah. Many Republicans, however, were unhappy with the situation, and Jeremiah Howell defeated the Federalist candidate, James Burrill, Jr., by only one vote—his own. The account concluded by denouncing Fenner for his personal proscription of Republican candidates chosen by a majority vote in the party convention, a practice that he had also followed during earlier legislative sessions.

2. Jeremiah Brown Howell (1771–1822) served one term in the U.S. Senate from 1811 to 1817. Throughout the first session of the Twelfth Congress he generally supported the preparedness policies sought by JM and his administration, and in the May 1812 congressional caucus he voted for JM's renomination for a second term. He was, however, to vote against the declaration of war against Great Britain in June 1812 (see Leland R. Johnson, "The Suspense Was Hell: The Senate Vote for War in 1812," *Indiana Magazine of History*, 65 [1969]: 251).

§ From the Merchants and Underwriters of Baltimore. *20 November 1810, Baltimore*. Complains of heavy losses suffered by the memorialists from arbitrary and illegal seizures of American vessels in the ports of northern Europe. The "unworthy pretext" for these seizures is the certificates of French consuls in the U.S., issued "in Conformity to Orders from their Government" but denounced in France by the official gazette of the emperor as "false and Forgeries." The aggressions complained of have occurred principally in Denmark and Norway, and "the more Weighty Interference of Government" is necessary to obtain redress. The memorialists are also concerned about the safety of a large number of American vessels at Gothenburg. They suggest the appointment of a special agent to "warn our unsuspecting Mariners of the capricious Changes of Tyranny," to "remonstrate against lawless Depredations, and unjust Detentions," and to help secure American property in Swedish ports; "and as auxiliary to the Success of his Operations, A plan may

be devised, and executed, for detecting, and exposing Frauds, on our Flag, and discriminating between the real and fictitious Americans—the fair, and the false
Traders."

RC (DNA: RG 76, Denmark, Convention of 1830, Letters Regarding Claims). 4 pp.
Signed by Robert Gilmor, president of the Marine Insurance Company, and thirty-five others.

§ From William Thomas and Others. *20 November 1810, Annapolis.* Recommends
either Elias Glenn or Thomas Beale Dorsey for district attorney of Maryland after
the resignation of John Stephen.[1]

RC (DNA: RG 59, LAR, 1809–17, filed under "Glenn"). 2 pp. Signed by Thomas and five
other members of the Maryland Senate. JM also received a letter recommending Glenn from
Philip Reed, U.S. senator from Maryland, written the same day (ibid.; 2 pp.).

   1. On 10 Dec. 1810, JM nominated Dorsey to be U.S. attorney for Maryland. When Dorsey resigned the post after little more than a year, JM nominated Glenn as his replacement
(*Senate Exec. Proceedings,* 2:156, 254).

§ From Edwin Lewis.[1] *21 November 1810, "Franklin near St. Stephens."* Complains
of "injuries and oppressions" from local federal officials, "subjects on which I ad-
ressed you while you were Secretary of State[2] which is the reason I address you now
as President." Is disappointed that there has been no inquiry into the conduct of
Captain Swain[3] or into the decisions of the land commissioners. Requests that Governor Holmes be instructed to make inquiries into his complaints and also into the
conduct of the assistant agent of the Choctaw trading house, who pulled down a
kitchen and made off with lumber belonging to Fort St. Stephens. Requests that
further inquiries be made about Judge Toulmin, Capt. Edmund Pendleton Gaines,
George Gaines, Thomas Malone, and others, stating that "I have been oppressed
by officers of Govt. for no cause except a firm resolution to maintain the laws of the
land." Expresses indignation about "foreigners who are promoted to offices in my
Country, [which] is not the inheritance my father expected to transmit to his un-
born childred [*sic*]." Refers JM to Thomas Blount and Willis Alston, members of
Congress, the former of whom "lives in the Country I was raised in." Mentions in
a postscript that he sent George Poindexter a transcript "shewing how Capt. Swain
a Country man of Judge Toulmins was dismissed and never called to answer has he
power to Dispence with the laws of the land."

RC (DNA: RG 107, LRRS, L-126:5). 3 pp. Docketed by a War Department clerk as received 21 Dec. 1810.

   1. Edwin Lewis was a settler in the Mississippi Territory, where as early as 1803 he had
participated in the agitation for a more liberal federal land policy to encourage immigration.
He evidently quarreled with U.S. officials over conflicting land titles, especially in cases where
a judicial decision was required to resolve overlapping British and American claims. His en-
thusiasms led him to support filibustering expeditions from Mississippi against the Spanish
authorities in Mobile, an issue that only increased his hatred for Judge Harry Toulmin, whose
conduct he was still protesting as late as 1816 (Carter, *Territorial Papers, Mississippi,* 5:279–82,
438–40, 693, 6:184, 220, 265–67, 698–99; Cox, *The West Florida Controversy,* pp. 478, 639–
40; Lewis to JM, 10 Dec. 1810).

2. No earlier letters from Lewis to JM have been found.

3. Possibly Thomas Swaine, a captain in the Fourth U.S. Infantry, who had died in 1808 (Heitman, *Historical Register*, 1:938).

To Andrew Ellicott

DEAR SIR   WASHINGTON, NOVR. 22. 1810

I have read[1] your letter of the 14th., and shall consider any aid, in facilitating your intercourse with the National Institute at Paris, as too much due to the object of it, not to be readily afforded. Your letters forwarded either to me or to the Dept. of State will be always attended to, in making up the communications to our Minister at this place. With my friendly wishes accept assurances of my respect, & esteem.

JAMES MADISON

Printed copy (*University of California Chronicle*, 27 [1925]: 342).

1. The transcriber probably misread JM's "recd" as "read."

§ From Harry Toulmin. *22 November 1810, Fort Stoddert.* Writes again to inform JM of "the situation of this country in the present critical state of affairs" as he fears that certain American citizens will do "some rash act . . . highly injurious to the cause of peace and good order." The population of the district is divided into three settlements. In the settlement near and above St. Stephens there is "little or no stir," but in the settlement at the forks of the Tombigbee and Alabama Rivers, "which is composed entirely or very generally of emigrants from Georgia, it is said that there is a strong disposition to join in the newly projected attack on Mobile." Settlers are invited by "men in public office either openly or secretly" to go "below the line" where it is argued "they are out of the reach of American laws." The idea is circulated that "they will become entitled to the plunder they may seize & to a permanent donation of 640 acres of land."

"As to the Tensaw settlement," on the east side of the Alabama River, "it was expected that they would be nearly unanimous. I went through it last week. The Captain of the Militia there told me that he had assembled the people . . . [and] caused to be read to them a letter which I addressed to him inclosing a copy of one from the President:[1] but that a stranger who calls himself Dr M'Carty and Major Bufford, (formerly of S. Carolina) a justice of the orphans court, had warmly recommended the expedition. . . . Major Buford, afterwards saw me, expressed his doubts & promised to pursue a contrary course," but "the policy, sometimes practiced here" is to prepare "for all events, by taking both sides of a disputed question." Relays reports that some of the local militia officers have resigned and "have been indemnified by new commissions under the Commonwealth of Florida filled up in this district: though if this be a fact I feel confident that their agent in this country has exceeded his powers." Remains concerned about this man, who considers himself injured by Toulmin's actions and has threatened that "he would have satisfaction." Regards this declaration as important only "inasmuch as it indicates his sanguine expectations of success." Has doubts, however, "whether they will be able to raise more than barely enough to begin the work of mischief. . . . One single hundred, I suspect will be the utmost that they will be able to induce to go below the line. They cannot take the fort [at Mobile], but they may occasion the destruction of the town and a considerable loss of property to the inhabitants. Mobile is entirely exposed to the guns of the fort, & must become a heap of ruins, should the assailants seek shelter among the houses."

Was informed on 21 Nov. by Kennedy that a party of sixty or seventy was then proceeding to attack a temporary fort at the mouth of the Pascagoula. Was not aware that the settlement below the line contained so many men and does not know where they have come from.

"It has been gathered . . . that the partizans in this quarter have already made provision for supplies of food and ammunition, and it is publicly said, that those who mean to join in the expedition are to assemble on Sunday next at a bluff below the line on the eastern bank of the east channel of the Mobile." Will thereafter be able to form a more accurate estimate of "the real strength of the combination." Doubts whether he will have grounds for "judicial interference," but if there should be sufficient evidence for a prosecution, he will "comply with the obligations of the law, without waiting to calculate the probable result."

Was at Mobile a few days ago and found the people "alarmed and cautious." Those who dared speak said that American possession of the country would be "universally acceptable." The commandant treated him with kindness but "entered into no political discussion," as he is too completely subordinate to the governor-general to have an opinion of his own.

Expressed to Innerarity his belief that the best way to avert "the impending storm" would be to ask the U.S. government to take possession of the country,[2] as this would be sufficient reason for the convention at Baton Rouge to suspend "hostile approaches" and would "paralize any intrigues which might be going on with any European power." Innerarity responded that "to hint such a thing at Mobile would be construed into treason in Mobile: but if Govr. Folch was there, he was a man of sense, and would calmly weigh a suggestion without criminating the author." Hopes his expressing this unauthorized idea was not improper.

Encloses a copy of a letter from Pensacola to Colonel Sparks;[3] believes that a copy was also sent to Governor Holmes, but it will take at least a month for an answer to arrive. Sparks's response was that he would take all legitimate steps to preserve good relations between the U.S. and Spain, and he has indeed done all he could to prevent arms and ammunition from falling into the hands of the conspirators. Also encloses a letter describing "the state of parties" at Baton Rouge.[4] The writer was a colonel in the Kentucky militia. "I have in reply expressed strongly to him my impressions as to the dangerous consequences of the measures now pursuing in this district."

RC and enclosures (DLC). RC 7 pp. Docketed by JM, with his note: "inclosing letters from Folch & Ballinger." Printed in Carter, *Territorial Papers, Mississippi*, 6:135–39. For enclosures, see nn. 3 and 4.

1. See Toulmin to JM, 6 Nov. 1810, and n. 1.

2. Toulmin had made this suggestion to James Innerarity in a letter he wrote on 15 Nov. 1810. Innerarity's response, however, must have taken place during a meeting between the two in Mobile a few days later, before the arrival of Governor Folch in the town on 21 Nov. (see *American Historical Review*, 2 [1896–97]: 701–2, 703).

3. Toulmin enclosed a copy of Vicente Folch's letter to Richard Sparks, 13 Nov. 1810 (1 p.), requesting him to use all possible means to "dissipate the hostile projects that Reuben Kemper is preparing within the limits of the U. S. against his catholic Majesty's possessions."

4. The enclosure is a 3 Nov. 1810 letter Toulmin had received from John Ballinger (3 pp.), reporting on the proceedings of the West Florida convention in the summer and fall, including the attack on the fort at Baton Rouge on 22–23 Sept. Ballinger described the convention members as "moderate" men rather than "Republicans," who were driven to extreme measures by threats of "Death & proscription" from the "violent Aristocrats and the old American Tories." Although order had been restored in the province, Ballinger was uncertain about the future. "Our Councils," he wrote, "are much Divided. A part are for prosecuting the War [against Spain] With Vigor, Another part are for waiting for the interference of the United States." He hinted that Toulmin should inform the U.S. government of the situation, since he believed "the Great Mass of the People wants nothing more than to become American Citizens." They would, he added, prefer death to continuing dependence on Spain but would otherwise accept any protection offered them, including that of France. "Many true Americans who are well acquainted with the Cautious Policy of the United States has [*sic*] no Confidence in their interference." The letter concludes with a prayer that the U.S. "may Save this Country from the fangs of Joseph Napolean."

From Paul Hamilton

DEAR SIR   CAPITOL HILL Novr. 24th. 1810

I beg leave to send you the letters accompanying this, received from Genl. Smith of Baltimore by yesterday's mail, which I would in person have presented you with, but for an indisposition which confines me to the house. It is necessary for me only to remark that, the agency[1] to which the General refers is a subject entirely new to me, having had neither conversation nor correspondence with him respecting it. I am Sir with great respect &c yrs.

PAUL HAMILTON

RC (DLC). Enclosures not found, but see n. 1.

1. On 22 Nov. 1810 Samuel Smith had written to Hamilton enclosing correspondence to suggest that the agent to be sent to Denmark be dispatched with "Vessels of force" to protect American vessels in the Baltic. As Smith reminded the secretary, he had raised this issue during the last session of the Senate with his proposal "to vest the President with the power to Employ all our Navy in the protection of our Commerce." Smith also wanted naval vessels sent to the Mediterranean and to Haiti, and he requested Hamilton to hint to JM "the necessity of his having the authority to Employ the Navy for the national protection." Specifically, the senator wanted JM to include these subjects in his annual message to Congress (DNA: RG 45, Misc. Letters Received).

From George Jackson

SIR, ZANESVILLE 24 Novr. 1810

I beg the liberty to state to you that my friends or a few of them in this place have recomended myself & a Mr. Samuel Herrick of this place, to you[1] as fit persons, Mr. Herrick to fill the office of District atty. for the State of Ohio in the roome of Mr. Creton,[2] who I am told has resigned for the sake of a seat in the Legislature, where I have the Honor to be also, I should not truble you at this time if it was not Impresed strong on my mind, that the Late Administration as well as yourself are oftin imposed upon by improper recomendations, by which means Fedrelist or quids very frekquently Get apoined to office, and dicided Republicans neglected, who has eequal Clame both in talent and Charactor, to the office bestoed upon men who has and dose acted in oppisition to the late and present administration of our hapy Goverment, myself are recomended to you for Marshal of this state, as soon as that office is vacant, it is at present fu'ld by Genl. Lewis Cass who is by many of our freinds thought to be at Least a very doubtfull Character as respects Politicks and who I am told has got the Fedral Judges to recomend him to you for district atty. and to cap his sucess Messers. Tiffen and Worthington, now Sir, I am bold to Say that Mr Cass the Present Marshal is a very Suspicias Character with myself he has to my knowledge apointed some very voilent Fedral Characters as his Assistants and I know of none who acts under him to be republicans, when he by the late Law of Congress has assistants in every County Genl. Cass has in my opinion, acted very unworanted with me, he was the first that mentioned to me he should resign the office of Marshal, and advised me to aske for it and observed having a personal acquantance with the President, I most succeed, at the same time that this was in contemplation, he Cass was a making aplecation to Gover Huntington for a Mr. Granger at least a very Doubtfull Character and a person of no visible property. I beg pardon for this digr[e]ssion, and hope that yourself and famaly are in Good health; I am very respectfully your Most obent Very Humble Sert

GEO: JACKSON

NB I hope you will excuse this scrall as I am lame in my right arme and cannot will right.

RC (DLC). Cover marked "Private" by Jackson.

1. See John G. Jackson to JM, 29 Sept. 1810 (*PJM-PS*, 2:563–64 and n. 1).

2. William Creighton, Jr., had been appointed U.S. attorney for Ohio in December 1804 (*Senate Exec. Proceedings*, 1:476, 477).

From William Pinkney

LONDON. 24h. Novr. 1810.

I send by this opportunity a Letter to the Secretary of State, entreating your permission to return to America.[1] I have not thought it necessary to mention in that Letter my Motives for this apparently abrupt Request; but you will I am sure be at no Loss to conjecture them.

I ask your Leave *at this Time* to close my Mission here because I find it impossible to remain. I took the Liberty to suggest to you, in my Letter by Mr. Ellis, that I was not unwilling, though I had no Desire, to continue a little longer;[2] but, upon a recent Inspection of my private Affairs, it appears, that my pecuniary means are more completely exhausted than I had supposed, and that to be honest I must hasten Home.

The Compensation (as it is oddly called) allotted by the Government to the Maintenance of its Representatives abroad, is a Pittance, which no Economy however rigid or even Mean can render adequate. It never was adequate I should think; but it is *now* (especially in London) far short of that fair Indemnity for unavoidable Expences, which every Government, no Matter what its Form, owes to its Servants.

I have in Fact been a constant and progressive Loser, and at Length am incapable of supplying the Deficiencies of the public Allowance. Those Deficiencies have been hitherto supplied by the Sacrifice of my own Capital in America, or by my Credit, already pushed I perceive as far as the Remnant of that Capital will justify, and I fear somewhat farther. I cannot, as an honourable Man, with my Eyes open to my Situation, push it farther, and of Course I must retire. I do not mean to exaggerate the Amount of my Capital thus dissipated in a thankless Office. It was not very large—it *could not* be so. I have spent too much of my Life (how faithfully none will have the Injustice to question) in the public Service, to admit of *that*. But such as it was, it had its Value as a Stake, in Case of Accidents, for those about me, and, being now gone, cannot hereafter eke out a scanty Salary. It is superfluous to say that I have no other Resource.

This is the Consideration which has urged me to write for my Recall *at this Moment*.

There are others, however, which ought perhaps to have produced the same Effect at even an earlier period, and *would* have produced it if I had followed my own Inclinations rather than a Sense of Duty to you and to the people. Some of these Considerations respect myself individually, and need not be named; for they are as nothing in Comparison with those which look to my Family. Its Claims to my Exertions for its Benefit in my profession have been too long neglected. Age is stealing fast upon me, and I shall soon have lost the Power of retrieving the Time which has been wasted in Endeavours (fruitless it should seem) to deserve well of my Country. Every Day will as it passes make it more difficult to resume the Habits which I have twice improvidently abandoned. At present, I feel no Want of cheerful Resolution to seek them again as old Friends which I ought never to have quitted, and no Want of Confidence that they will not disown me. How long that Resolution, if not acted upon, may last, or that Confidence may stand up in the Decline of Life, I cannot know and will not try.

I trust it is not necessary for me to say how much your kindness, and that of your Predecessor, has contributed to subdue the Anxieties of my Situation, and to make me forget that I ought to leave a Post, at once so perilous and so costly, to richer and to abler Hands. Those who know me will believe that my Heart is deeply sensible of that Kindness, and that my Memory will preserve a faithful Record of it while it can preserve a Trace of any thing.

I am in Danger of making this a long Letter. I will only add to it, therefore, that I shall prepare myself (in the Expectation of receiving your permission) to return to the U. S. as soon as the Season will allow me to do so with Convenience to my Family, and that, if my Duty should, in any View of it, require a more prompt Departure, I shall not hesitate to act as it requires. Believe me to be, with sincere Respect & affectionate Attachment, Dear Sir, your faithful and Obedient Servant

WM. PINKNEY.

RC (DLC: Rives Collection, Madison Papers). Docketed by JM.

1. Pinkney to Robert Smith, 24 Nov. 1810 (DNA: RG 59, DD, Great Britain).
2. See Pinkney to JM, 13 Aug. 1810 (*PJM-PS*, 2:482).

¶ From Alfred Madison. Letter not found. *24 November 1810*. Described as a two-page letter in the lists probably made by Peter Force (DLC, series 7, container 2).

From David Howell

(Confidential)

SIR,   PROVIDENCE Nov: 26. 1810.

After prevailing on the late Judge Cushing to retain his office for several years, under the failure of his powers, lest a Republican Should succeed him, the Federalists have had the address to unite with that Fraction of the Republican party in this State, which is inimical to Governor Fenner & his

Friends, in recommending Asher Robbins, Esquire, of Newport, in this State, to succeed him.[1]

I am of opinion that the slender condition of Mr Robbins's health would illy comport with the arduous duties of that office; & that other & Stronger objections might be found in his political character, as a Monarchist, &c. & in his moral ch⟨a⟩racter as a Speculator &c. and that, in his conduct & exhibitions as a Lawyer, have not been found Specimens of that candour, & of those legal Talents, which are required in a judge.

I hope I shall be excused in adding a Suggestion that the present District Judge in this State,[2] (having been previously District Attorney for several years,) has laboriously & with credit discharged the duties of his present office, (to which he was named by the late President) & endeavoured to avoid the active Scenes of party, & is, in my opinion, on every ground of pretensions, more worthy of this promotion than Mr Robbins.

I have expected that the Hon: J Q. Adams,[3] or some other Gentleman in whose character & good attachments confidence could be placed, would be called to succeed Mr Cushing.

It is expected that Governor Fenner will write you on this Subject,[4] & that time will be allowed for advice from all quarters. As one mean of increasing your confidence in our most excellent ⟨Go⟩vernor I have enclosed the republican re⟨so⟩lutions passed in this Town Feby. 6. 1809.[5] Our Ticket for General Officers last April, which prevailed, is also enclosed—And I shall only add, as proof that Governor Fenners Friends have the ascendancy, that my only Son was elected by our Legislature at their late Session, as Senator in Congress for six years commencing next March. In him you will find a close Friend to your person, & a most zealous Supporter of your administration. I have the Honor to be with the most respectful Con[s]ideration sir, Your Obedt. Servant

DAVID HOWELL

RC (DLC). RC torn. Docketed by JM. Enclosures not found, but see n. 5.

1. See Christopher Ellery to JM, 21 Dec. 1809 and 30 Sept. 1810, and Constant Taber and others to JM, 24 Sept. 1810 (*PJM-PS*, 2 : 140–41 and nn., 566–67 and n. 2, 553–54).

2. Howell referred to David Leonard Barnes, who had been serving as U.S. attorney for Rhode Island when Jefferson appointed him federal district judge in 1801 (see Barnes to JM, 14 May 1802, *PJM-SS*, 1 : 173 and n. 1).

3. JM nominated John Quincy Adams to be an associate justice of the Supreme Court on 21 Feb. 1811 (*Senate Exec. Proceedings*, 2 : 168).

4. James Fenner to JM, 3 Dec. 1810.

5. The resolutions were evidently passed in support of the Embargo, and Howell enclosed them to make the point that Gov. James Fenner and Howell's son, Jeremiah B. Howell, had been among the few New Englanders who had wholeheartedly supported that measure (see David Howell to Jefferson, 27 Nov. 1810 [DLC: Jefferson Papers]).

From Nathaniel Cutting

Tuesday morning, 27th. Novr. 1810.

Mr. Cutting has the honor to present his best respects to the President of the United States and to transmit him a *"Project for a new Organization of the Consulate, alias, Commercial Agency, of the United States in the Empire of France"*:[1] one Copy of which is also sent to the Department of State.[2]

RC and enclosures (DLC).

1. Cutting's *"Project"* was a twelve-point proposal, dated Washington, April 1810 (12 pp.), to reorganize American consuls or commercial agents throughout the French Empire into five geographical districts, all to be accountable to a single, salaried consul general in Paris. The consul general would be responsible for issuing passports, for the relief of distressed seamen, and for communicating with the French authorities. He was also to make monthly reports to the State Department, compiled from manifests that all American ship captains would be compelled to file with the consuls upon entering a French port. Among the purposes of the plan, Cutting declared, was "to identify those who have a right to the Protection of the Flag of the U. S., and to inform all whom it may concern what becomes of every Individual who sails under it."

2. Cutting enclosed a copy of a covering letter to Secretary of State Smith, November 1810 (1 p.), in which he stated that he had originally submitted his proposal in April 1810, but in the "precarious state" of relations with France it was then "thought inexpedient to bring this Subject fully on the Tapis." He was resubmitting the proposal "now that those Relations present a more agre[e]able aspect."

From Levi Lincoln

Dear Sir   Worcester Nov. 27. 1810

Your esteemed favor of the 20th of Oct. was duly recieved.[1] Such a gratifying & valuable testimonial of your confidence, & of the esteem of my other political friends, could not fail to beget a wish that it were in my power to accept of the honorable office, rendered vacant by the death of the late Judge Cushing. But my encreasing years & difficulty of sight admonish me, in a tone, which can neither be mistaken or silenced, of the propriety of confining my future action to the narrow limits of private life. But for some peculiar circumstances in the political attitude of this State, I could not have ever departed from a resolution, formed two years since, of abjuring office of every kind; & in that situation, devoting the leisure of the remnant of my life to the support of that system of government, which forms the most precious inheritance in reserve for our Descendants. The close of the present political year will, from necessity & choice, realize to me the results of such a resolution. I should want no motive of inclination or duty to unite my best official exertions with those in the administration of the General Government, whose talents, virtues & eminent services have at all times commanded my esteem, confidence, reverence, & gratitude, could my age & state of health leave to my judgement any option. Attached as I am, & always have been, to the Union & the Constitution of the United States, acquainted as I am, & impressed as I always have been, with the correctness & importance of the principles, on which you & your revered Predecessor have administered the government, & with the opposition it has met with; I could as soon forget a property of my nature, as to remit my enfeebled efforts against the enemies of that government, or withhold my diminished mites from its support. Your Administration having fallen in the worst of times, you have a claim, in the right of your Country, to demand the services of her best & ablest citizens, & of every friend whose exertions can be in any way important to her security or prosperity. Believe me, Sir, nothwithstanding [*sic*] I am compelled respectfully to excuse myself from the duties you wish to assign me, I feel the force ⟨of⟩ the foregoing sentiments, & recognize in that wish an honor to myself & an obligation to my country & its Chief Magistrate, which I shall ever most highly appreciate. Omitting to repeat to you the political situation, character, & agency of the Judicial Courts in this State, suffer me to say the friends to the Union as well in Rhode Island & New Hampshire as here feel a great solicitude on the present occasion. Would to Heaven there was some character, whose preeminent talents, Virtues, & tried services, excluding all competition, left to you only the formal, but pleasing duty of a nomination, some character, with the requisite intelligence, but both *blind* & deaf—blind to the approaches of Cabals, Factions & Party—deaf, deaf as an adder, to the suggestions of pride, ambition or prejudice & to every other voice, however attuned, except to the voice of reason, patriotism, law, truth & justice. Alas! Has such been unive[r]sally & at all times the character of Federal & State Judges. With the most sincere esteem & attachment I have the honor to be Your Hum. Servt.

LEVI LINCOLN

RC (DLC). In a clerk's hand.

1. *PJM-PS*, 2:588.

From William Pinkney

DEAR SIR   LONDON Novr. 27h. 1810.

I beg Leave to say that I wrote on the 24h. Instant a Letter to you, explanatory of my Motives for a Request, contained in my Letter of the same Date, that I may be permitted to return to America.

I mention this because, by an opportunity which now offers I send a Duplicate of my Letter to Mr. Smith, and have not Time to make a Duplicate of my Letter to you. I trust, however, that the original (sent by the Way of Liverpool) will reach you in Season, and that you will approve the Request and its Motives. Believe me to be, with affectionate Attachment and Respect—Dear sir, your faithful and Obedient Servant

WM. PINKNEY.

RC (DLC). Docketed by JM.

§ From Charles Collins and David A. Leonard. *27 November 1810, Bristol, Rhode Island.* The vacancy on the Supreme Court "has put the spirit of intrigue into quick operation." The leading Federalists of New England evidently plan to bring forward Asher Robbins of Newport, but his supporters are not "friends to the administration." The writers suggest Gideon Granger as the best candidate, although "we are not without apprehensions that Judge Howell has some honourable intentions to make interest for the office." They respect Howell's service to the nation, but his claims do not surpass those of Granger. The motives of the supporters of Robbins are those that invariably govern the conduct of the leaders of the opposition in New England. "We have nothing personal toward Mr. Robbins, . . . but our anxiety is *greater*, that the Judiciary may be filled from among the firmest friends of our republican Government."

RC (DNA: RG 59, LAR, 1809–17, filed under "Granger"). 3 pp. JM received a further letter of support for Granger from Richard M. Johnson of Kentucky on 16 Dec. 1810 (ibid.; 2 pp.).

§ From Jesse Green. *27 November 1810, Concord, Sussex, Delaware.* Encloses annual return of the militia of Delaware.

RC (DNA: RG 107, LRRS, G-96:5). 1 p. Redirected by JM to "The Secretary of War"; docketed by a War Department clerk as received 10 Dec. 1810. Enclosure not found.

§ Resolution of the Mississippi Territorial House of Representatives. *27 November 1810.* Nominates to the president Edward Ward of Madison County and Benjamin Harney of Amite County, "one of whom to be selected by him, to fill the vacancy in the Legislative Council, occasioned by the resignation of Joseph Roberts." [1]

Ms (DNA: RG 59, LAR, 1809–17, filed under "Ward"). 1 p. Signed by Ferdinand L. Claiborne as Speaker of the House of Representatives. On the verso JM noted in pencil, "Commission to make out for Ward." Printed in Carter, *Territorial Papers, Mississippi,* 6:139. JM received a recommendation in favor of Ward from Robert Williams, 4 Dec. 1810, and one in favor of Harney from Samuel Harper and Micajah Davis, 7 Dec. 1810 (printed ibid., 6:145, 152).

1. JM nominated Ward for the vacancy on 21 Jan. 1811 (*Senate Exec. Proceedings,* 2:163).

Memorandum from Albert Gallatin

[ca. 28 November 1810]

President's message[1]

Might not the introduction, including the statement of French proceedings have a stronger colour of congratulation if not exultation of the change since last session 1. by marking more pointedly the effect produced by the last law[2]—2. by hinting that the embarrassment heretofore experienced in deciding on proper measures was principally owing to the pressure from both belligerents, which being now removed leaves us at liberty to pursue without hesitation the course clearly pointed out by our present situation—3. by anticipating in consequence unanimity in the measures to be adopted or persevered in.

3d. paragraph. 2d page—the words from "and the" in 2d line to "commerce" in 4th line might I think be struck out

4th paragraph. This seems to throw rather too great a gloom on the present prospect, which might be avoided by expressing less disappointment at the non-restoration and a greater hope of its taking place. In the view I have taken of our position, the paragraph may defeat our object, by enlivening federalism & damping the spirits of our friends. I see less danger in assuming the ground that France has done & means to do us justice than in showing contrary apprehensions.

5th. paragraph May not the opinion be expressed that the orders of April being only an extensive blockade, their principle is the same with that of nominal blockades, & that the repeal of the first implies that of the last. The law under which Erskine's arrangement was made contemplated the orders of Nover. which were of a totally different character. The law of last session contemplated the orders of April and all other orders of the same nature. Does not this justify & impel a difference of conduct in the Executive under the two laws.

(NB. *alledged basis* repeated twice in two lines)

7th. paragraph "revision of commercial laws"—this may be misunderstood. What is wanted is not an alteration in the principle, but an explanation which may remove any doubt of construction, principally as relates to the definition of what shall be a revocation by Great Britain, legally producing non-importation. But either here, or in the manufactures, or in the financial paragraph, it appears to me requisite to state that as the effect will be a diminished revenue, an increase of duties has become necessary.

Last paragraph but one "Manufactures"—temporary privations are nothing, but what manufactures ought to compensate for, is the loss in the

32

price of our agricultural products. May not *losses* be substituted to *privations*. The recommendation to protect agt. importations & to foster by duties is I think too much in detail. Is not the last as it is expressed a direct recommendation to renew the Duty on salt? To this I have no objection. Will it not be said that if the impulse now given was *alone* wanted to establish, it is un-necessary to do any thing more? As I want duties for revenue purposes, I am somewhat apprehensive that a direct demand for protection of manufactures (on which Subject there will be a difference of opinion) may defeat the object.

Last paragraph—What measure should be adopted by Congress in that respect it is difficult to say; but if any is in view, it should I think be more distinctly designated. Foreign nations injure us in that respect in two ways 1st. by laying higher duties on our articles than on similar ones coming from other countries, for instance lumber in England; & this affects our agriculture and internal industry—2d by giving a preference to our articles when imported in their own vessels; & that affects our navigation. This paragraph alludes only to the last evil, which is not greater than the first & at least as difficult to repel by counter-regulations.

———

Financial paragraph will be ready in a couple of days

———

Should not the subject of licenses be introduced in the Message?

———

Is there any objection to invite on public grounds a revision of the act respecting the compensation of foreign ministers & consuls.

———

It may be stated that the land laws &a. have been arranged & printed according to law and the books waiting order of Congress. Should not at some time the orders of removal of intruders be communicated?

———

Ms (DLC: Rives Collection, Madison Papers). In Gallatin's hand. Docketed by JM. Conjectural date assigned on the basis of Gallatin's here mentioning that his "financial paragraph," which he forwarded on 30 Nov., would be "ready in a couple of days."

1. Gallatin was evidently commenting on an early draft (not found) of JM's annual message, the final version of which was delivered to Congress on 5 Dec. 1810.

2. Macon's Bill No. 2.

From David Howell

Sir,   PROVIDENCE Nov. 28. 1810.

The Letter to our mutual friend, of which copy is enclosed[1] was intended to bear on Subjects of instant concern: & lest its effect should be delayed by the Distance from Washington to Monticello I have thus far trespassed on the forms of proceeding.

That you may learn the manner in which I discharged the high trust confided to me by General Washington in his lifetime I have enclosed copy of a Letter from the late Governor Sullivan to me on that Subject.[2]

On a review of the incidents of my life I find cause of Gratitude to my fellow-citizens for their favors to me; but more abundant reason to recognize the blessings of Heaven. For the last two years I have not been sick a day, nor an hour, and have yet thirty years before I shall reach the period of my fathers life—to this I have not, however, like the Emperor of France, the assurance to file a claim. Whatever may depend on you towards rendring my future days comfortable & happy, I assure myself will receive a candid & liberal consideration & decision. I pray you to believe that I am with the highest respect, Sir, your obedient Servant,

DAVID HOWELL

RC (DLC).

1. The copy enclosed to JM has not been found, but Howell's 27 Nov. 1810 letter to Jefferson repeated at greater length the substance of his 26 Nov. letter to JM. After denouncing Asher Robbins as a monarchist by virtue of his association with Federalists, Howell urged Jefferson to write a letter in support of Governor Fenner, which Fenner and his fellow Republicans could then use to advantage in the next elections. He also hinted that Jefferson advocate the nomination of David Leonard Barnes to the vacant seat on the Supreme Court (DLC: Jefferson Papers).

2. The copy of James Sullivan's letter to Howell has not been found, but it was probably a copy of a letter written on 9 Jan. 1798 and later misidentified in the lists made by Peter Force as a letter to JM (DLC, series 7, container 2). The subject of the letter almost certainly was Howell's work on the St. Croix boundary commission, to which Washington had nominated him in May 1796 under article 5 of the Jay treaty. Sullivan at that time had acted as agent for the U.S. in the management of the commission's business (see *Senate Exec. Proceedings*, 1:210).

From James Taylor

                                    BELLE VUE NEW PORT
SIR   KENTUCKY 28th. NovR 1810

The enclosed pamphlet[1] was this day given to me by Genl. James Findlay[2] of Cincinnati. I endeavored to Obtain his opinion as to the effect it would have, he appeared unable to answer me, and said he could not make up his mind fully on the subject as he had just got hold of it; That he was of opinion it could not rise into a Matter of great mischief, but found there were men supporting it of more influence and standing than he had supposed would have medled with a thing of the kind.

Upon the whole I am of opinion he thinks the thing may do some mischief. He is of opinion it has not been printed in Pensylva., at any rate it was forwarded to the state of Ohio in Manuscript.

We were both of opinion that it would not be amiss to forward these papers to you and if you deemed them of any notice we would from time to time give you such information as might come to our knowledge, upon your signifeing that it was your wish that either of us should do so.

I can scarcely think the good sense of any quarter of the Union could be influenced to take an active part in a business of this kind, except it may be among that description of people who are immediately interested, but the language of the association appears well calculated to allure and mislead the poor and ignorant.

There is greater complaint of a scarcity of money in this part of the Western country than I have known for many years, and I find more lands of persons who have bought of the U. S. advertised for sale than had ever been since the Offices were opened, all those whose lands may be sold, and all those who are unable to purchase lands might be led away by a Mistaken interest.

I expect to be a good deal thro' the State of Ohio in Course of this Winter & shall take some pains to ascertain whether it is likely to do any mischief.

I have it in contemplation to be at the Seat of Goverment in course of two weeks & there I shall have a good opportunity of satisfying my self on the subject. I have the honor to be with great respect Sir your obedt servt

JAMES TAYLOR

RC (DLC).

1. The enclosed pamphlet has not been found, but the contents of this and other letters from James Taylor to JM suggest that it may have dealt with the question of relief for those who had purchased public lands on credit and whose lands were at risk of being forfeited if they failed to meet their payments. In January 1811 the Ohio General Assembly instructed the state's congressional delegation to seek an extension of time for the payment for public lands, including the granting of preemption rights to those who had forfeited lands for failure to make payments. These changes, it was claimed, "would perhaps, enable many good citizens to provide in a decent manner for a young and rising family" (Taylor to JM, 10 Jan. and 20 Feb. 1811; *ASP, Public Lands,* 2:252).

2. James Findlay (1770–1835) had migrated from Pennsylvania to Ohio where he had served on the legislative council for the Northwest Territory. In 1810 he was mayor of Cincinnati, and he later became a colonel and brigadier general of a regiment of Ohio Volunteers

during the War of 1812 (*Senate Exec. Proceedings*, 1:323; William T. Utter, *The Frontier State*, *1803–1825*, vol. 2 of *The History of the State of Ohio*, ed. Carl Wittke [Columbus, Ohio, 1942], pp. 68, 88).

From James Taylor

DR SIR   BELLE VUE KY 28h. Nov 1810

Be so good as to make my best respects to Mrs. Madison & inform her I have recd. her very friendly letter of the 10h inst[1] and will answer it shortly.

I am much pleased to understand that our differences may probably be adjusted with all the Billigerents.

I was at my brothers lately himself & family were well, and our fri[e]nds generally are so in this state. If Mrs. Washington is with you be pleased to mention me to her with great affection. With every wish for your health & happiness I remain Dr. sir Your fr[i]end & servt

JAMES TAYLOR

RC (DLC).

1. Dolley Madison had written to James Taylor on 10 Nov. 1810 (KyHi), conveying to him family news, including her fears that JM's nephew, Alfred Madison, was not likely to recover his health. On public matters she reported that the *Hornet* had just returned from France and "brings us nothing contradictory of the *affecti[o]nate* intentions of Napolian." The president she described as engaged in "intense study" and observed from "his constant devotion to the Cabinet, that affair's are troublesome & difficult. You see the English are stuborn yet, but we anticipate their yealding, before long—in short, the Proclamation [of 2 Nov.] gives you the state of things *now*. Genl. Armstrong is hourly expected—no successor yet decided on."

§ From Frederick Bates. *28 November 1810, Louisiana, St. Louis.* Expresses gratitude for the confidence JM has shown in him during his term as territorial secretary, during which time he twice had to assume executive responsibilities. Concedes that he probably made errors but is not conscious of having done so. Has declined to solicit reappointment "in the ordinary forms, determined to ask it only of you."[1]

RC (DNA: RG 59, LAR, 1809–17, filed under "Bates"); letterbook copy (MoSHi). RC 1 p. Printed in Carter, *Territorial Papers, Louisiana-Missouri*, 14:426.

1. JM nominated Bates for a further four-year term as territorial secretary on 9 Jan. 1811 (*Senate Exec. Proceedings*, 2:160).

§ From Harry Toulmin. *28 November 1810, Fort Stoddert.* "The situation of our country here [which] becomes every day so truly critical . . . will excuse me, I hope, if I should even communicate to you more frequently or more fully than may be deemed absolutely necessary." Has no doubt that "the alarm excited in the summer, induced the government to take the best measures" possible, but the "judicial arm is (for the want of an adequate support in the moral principles of the community) extremely feeble here." Violators of the law boast of immunity from conviction, of making war on the Spanish possessions, while the "friends of order" strive for measures to "maintain the honour of the government and repress combinations destructive . . . of the dignity of the American name."

"Three companies of militia were ordered to be in readiness some time since: but a considerable part of the officers have joined the insurgents." Has notified the Mississippi territorial governor of his apprehensions but has received no response. Refers JM to his last letter [22 Nov.] where he mentioned intimating "to an influential gentleman at Mobile" that West Florida should declare its wish to join the U.S. Has made a similar suggestion to a friend at Pensacola; encloses letters nos. 1 and 2 on the subject.[1]

The second letter was received the evening before a rendezvous between Colonel Kemper and Major Kennedy, and it was Toulmin's intention to accompany Capt. Edmund Gaines to that meeting "to represent the impolicy and rashness of proceeding in the enterprize." Gaines, however, observed that under a long-standing order from the War Department, Colonel Sparks could order him to Mobile to obtain from Governor Folch "an official declaration as to his intentions with regard to duties," which would "cut off every pretext for hostile operations on the part of our citizens." "I was myself proceeding to the meeting, to represent that Captn. Gaines was actually gone to Mobile, . . . but being unable to procure a boat large enough to take us, I merely wrote a letter stating the matter to a Justice of the peace residing in the neighbourhood, . . . which Coll. Sparks sent by two soldiers. . . . The men were immediately made prisoners of by the party at the line." Kemper wrote Sparks that he had taken his men as deserters and demanded to know the contents of the letter. "At the same time, I sent letters over the country" announcing Gaines's journey to Mobile and "the prospect of an abolition of duties." By the time information came of the arrest of the soldiers, a messenger had delivered Innerarity's letter, no. 3,[2] and two letters from Governor Folch, nos. 4 and 5.[3]

"I immediately communicated to different parts of the country the substance of No. 4. and stated the fact of the application having been made by Govr Folch to the Marquis Someruelos, nearly two months ago: and . . . forwarded Govr. Folch's letter to Govr. Holmes, and . . . I sent a copy of No: 4 to Genl. Thomas."

Sparks sent an officer to reclaim the two soldiers from Kemper and to invite him and Kennedy to Fort Stoddert. "I did not expect them to come: nor did I believe that any impression would be made on the minds of *leaders* who had gone so far." Hoped he could notify some of "their followers" of the "state of things," so he wrote to Col. John Caller and Major Buford. Caller, as chief justice of the inferior court in Washington County, "seemed from his office & his age to be under peculiar obligations to maintain peace and the laws." Does not know the effect of his letters. "The officer dispatched by Col. Sparks returned last night with the two soldiers, and brought a letter from Kemper, of which No 6. is a copy."[4]

Hears reports that the filibusters are in "high spirits" and that their leaders "breathe out vengance against their opposers, particularly myself." Believes Kennedy desires his death and "it was a fortunate event for me that I could not get a boat on Saturday, as it is probable that my life would have paid for my temerity."

"This afternoon Captn. Gaines returned from Mobile, and brought a letter addressed to him by Govr. Folch, of which No. 7. is a copy."[5] The people below "are in general consternation." "We are distributing copies of Govr. Folch's letter to Captn. Gaines." Hopes the filibustering party will not increase but has no consistent accounts of its numbers. Estimates range from sixty or seventy to over two hundred. The party reportedly consists mainly of the settlers on the public lands in the "forks of the Tombigby & Alabama." Without aid from Baton Rouge they can only "distress the inhabitants," but they expect a thousand men from there. "A person from that quarter . . . informed me that it was not from any want of their services that the [West Florida] convention invited the people here to join them, but that it had been recommended to them to adopt this step, by respectable *legal* characters in New Orleans."

RC and enclosures (DLC). RC 6 pp. Mistakenly docketed by JM, "Novr. 28. 1812," with his note: "inclosing letters from Folch & others." Printed in Carter, *Territorial Papers, Mississippi*, 6: 140–43. For enclosures, numbered by Toulmin, see nn.

1. Enclosure no. 1 is a copy of a letter written from Pensacola, 19 Nov. 1810, and headed "*Private & serious*" (2 pp.). The writer reported that "nearly 40 days have elapsed since Govr. Folch wrote to the Captain General of Havanna, impressing him with the *indispensable* necessity of entering into *immediate* negociations with the Govt. of the U. States for the cession of the Floridas." He vouched for the accuracy of his information, which he hoped would encourage Toulmin in his efforts to preserve peace. In place of the signature, Toulmin noted that he had withheld his correspondent's name but added that "it has been since stated that this 'was written by the desire and almost in the very words of Goverr. Folch.'" Enclosure no. 2 is a letter from James Innerarity to Toulmin, 22 Nov. 1810 (4 pp.; printed in *American Historical Review*, 2 [1896–97]: 703–4), reporting his conversations with Folch following the governor's arrival in Mobile the day before and relaying an offer by Folch to abolish the duties on American goods at Mobile in return for a pledge that the people of the Mississippi Territory would not aid the agents of the West Florida convention in their planned attack on Spanish soil. If such a pledge was not given, Folch declared, he would have no choice "but to oppose force with force, & the duties will remain as formerly." At the end of this letter, Toulmin included a copy of his reply, dated 23 Nov. 1810, stating that although every good citizen should be willing to "go to any length *under the authority of government*" to get rid of the oppressive Spanish duties, he feared that the leaders of the expedition were motivated by considerations of "personal preponderance and popularity" and would use any pretext for their "illegal Combinations." Nonetheless, he would try to meet with some "honest men" among them to see if "common sense" could prevail.

2. Enclosure no. 3, Innerarity to Toulmin, 24 Nov. 1810 (2 pp.), reported that Folch was making arrangements to place his province under the protection of the U.S. and asked Toulmin to persuade Lt. Col. Richard Sparks to take all necessary measures to prevent a "useless effusion of blood."

3. Toulmin enclosed copies of letters (nos. 4 and 5) from Folch to Sparks, dated 20 and 24 Nov. 1810. In the first letter (1 p.) Folch quoted his letter to Governor Holmes of the same date stating that he had requested Someruelos to address the U.S. government about delivering the Floridas "'in trust until the conclusion of a treaty in which an equivalt. to Spain shd be determind. and agreed upon.'" In the interim, he asked Holmes to make every effort to prevent "'robberies and depredations'" against the people of West Florida, who, Folch claimed, "'are on the eve of becoming American citizens.'" In the second letter (1 p.), Folch repeated this last request to Sparks and authorized Sparks to send troops anywhere "within the Jurisdiction of Florida" should it prove necessary to do so.

4. Enclosure no. 6 is a copy of Reuben Kemper's 27 Nov. 1810 letter to Sparks (1 p.), by

which he returned the two soldiers taken when they had crossed the boundary line. Kemper declined Sparks's invitation to come to Fort Stoddert, as did Kennedy, who was with Kemper at the time.

5. In his letter of 25 Nov. 1810 to Edmund Gaines (enclosure no. 7) (1 p.; docketed by JM), Folch declared that since he believed U.S. and Spanish authorities were negotiating the transfer of the Floridas, he would abolish "from this date" all duties on American goods or vessels passing to or from the Mississippi Territory.

§ From Henry Dearborn. *29 November 1810, Boston*. Notes that in his official capacity he has had many dealings with the district circuit courts. "The state of *society here* demands great firmness as well as good legal tallents in our Judges, especially in all questions that have any political bearing." Cushing should therefore be replaced by "a sound strong independant Character"; suggests that either Gideon Granger or Alexander Wolcott "would be acceptable to the friends of the Government in this vicinity." "I would not have taken the liberty of saying anything on this subject had I not have felt peculiarly interested in my official situation." In a postscript, conveys his respects to Mrs. Madison.

RC (DNA: RG 59, LAR, 1809–17, filed under "Granger"). 2 pp.

§ From Edmund Pendleton, Jr. *29 November 1810, Richmond*. Reports the death "some time today" of Joseph Scott, U.S. marshal for Virginia, and offers himself for the post.[1] Will not discuss his pretensions to office but refers JM to "our friend" Robert Taylor of Orange.

RC (DNA: RG 59, LAR, 1809–17, filed under "Pendleton"). 1 p.

1. Edmund Pendleton, Jr., was the grandnephew of Judge Edmund Pendleton. His father, Edmund Pendleton, also wrote to JM, 4 Dec. 1810, on behalf of his candidacy (ibid.; 1 p.). Between 30 Nov. and 9 Dec. JM received at least fifteen other letters relating to this vacancy. Three were on behalf of the claims of John Guerrant, William Munford, and Thomas Underwood; Brett Randolph, Jr., and Peter Johnston were the subject of two recommendations each; and ten letters were written on behalf of John W. Green (ibid.). On 10 Dec. 1810, JM nominated Andrew Moore for the position (*Senate Exec. Proceedings*, 2:156).

¶ From Joseph B. Varnum. Letter not found. *29 November 1810*. Listed as a one-page letter in the lists probably made by Peter Force (DLC, series 7, container 2).

Memorandum from William Eustis

[ca. 30 November 1810]

The fortifications for the defence of our maritime frontier (on the plan laid down in 1808) are, with some exceptions (or generally) completed, and furnished with the necessary ordnance. Those for the defence of the city of N. York, with the completing & repairing works at other posts, as will appear by a statement from the War Dept. will require a further time and an additional appropriation.[1]

The improvements, in quantity and quality, which have been made in the manufactory of small arms, at the public armories, as well as at private factories, warrant additional confidence in their competency to furnish supplies to any amount which the public exigincies may require.

The exercise of The power vested in Congress by the constitution to provide for arming & organizing the Militia, has hitherto failed to produce the desired effect of rendering them an efficient force on which to rely in case of emergency. As the object of *arming* them is already secured by Law, it remains for the wisdom of Congress to determine whether a due & proper effect can be given to their *organization* by any other means than by a provision at the public expence to call into the field, a certain portion of them, for a given time, for instruction & discipline.[2]

Ms (DLC). In Eustis's hand. Misdated 1812 in the *Index to the James Madison Papers.* Date here assigned on the basis of JM's incorporating most of the first two paragraphs as well as the substance of the third paragraph into his annual message of 5 Dec. 1810. Filed with the Ms are two other slips of paper on which Eustis wrote what appear to be drafts of parts of this memorandum (see nn. 1 and 2).

1. What seems to be an earlier version of this paragraph reads: "By a statement from the W. Dept. it will appear that the fortifications on the Seaboard are in many of the ports completed, affording the defence which was contemplated: a further time being required to finish those in the harbour of N. York and in some other places." Eustis subsequently communicated a report on the cost of completing the fortifications at New York and elsewhere to the House of Representatives on 18 Jan. 1811 (see *ASP, Military Affairs*, 1:296–97).

2. Another version of this paragraph reads:

"To give due effect to the great mass of physical and intellectual powers which distinguish the militia of the U. States it is necessary that they should be instructed and practised in the rules laid down for their government.

"*or*

"The institution of a system which shall in the first instance provide, at the public expence, for calling into the field, for a given time, certain portions of the commissioned & non commissioned officers for instruction and discipline appears to be the most effectual means of transferring thro' the whole body that practical knowlege which alone can render them an efficient force on which to rely in case of danger or alarm."

From Albert Gallatin

Dear Sir　　　　　　　　　　　　　　　　　　Nover. 30th 1810

I enclose the substance of a financial paragraph, also a statement of the receipts & expenditures of the year ending 30th Septer. last and an estimate of those of this quarter. These will supply you with all the facts on which the paragraph is founded.[1]

In the paragraph for military schools, I would place in the most conspicuous point of view (when speaking of revision of existing law) the necessity of placing them on a respectable footing. It is now worse than none. I believe that no teacher but a drawing master is allowed out of the corps & I know that Hasler[2] as professor of mathematics was discharged as not authorized by law. Respectfully Your obt. Servant

ALBERT GALLATIN

[First Enclosure]

The receipts into the treasury during the year ending on the 30th of Septer. last (and amounting to more than eight millions and a half of dollars) have exceeded the current expenses of government including therein the interest on the public debt. For the purpose of reimbursing at the end of this year 3,750,000 dollars of the principal, a loan to that same amount had been negotiated, which has subsequently, on the application of the Secretary of the Treasury, been reduced to 2,750,000 dollars. For the probable receipts of next year and other details I refer you to the statements which will be transmitted from the Treasury and which will enable you to judge what further provision may be necessary for the service of the ensuing years.[3]

[Second Enclosure]

Receipts & expenses of the year ending 30th Septer. 1810

Specie in treasury on 1st Octer. 1809			5,828.936.01
Receipts during the year			
customs	7.851.170.46		
lands	672.417.90		
sundries	165.272.81	8.688.861.17	
		14.517.797.18	

Expenditures during the year			
civil list	689.116.53		
miscellaneous civil	405.886.50		
diplomatic	145.095.37		
		1.240.098.40	
military, indians &c.	2.514.523.75		
Navy	1.674.735.50		
		4.189.259.25	
interest on public debt		2.713.526.54	
Total current expenses		8.142.884.19	
Principal of public debt reimbursed vizt.			
Debt proper	2.906.781.61		
Claims assumed by Louisa. treaty	9.101.66		
		2,915.883.27	

41

		11,058,767.46
Specie in treasury on 30th Septer. 1810	2	3,459.029.72
		14.517.797.18

Estimate of last quarter of 1810

Specie in Treasury on 30th Septer. 1810	2	3.460.000
Receipts estimated		2,500,000
Loan receivable 31st Decer. 1810		2.750.000
		8.710.000
Civil, military & naval expenses estimated	1.570.000	
Interest on public debt—estd.	650.000	
		2.220.000
Principal to be reimbursed vizt.		
annual reimbt. on six pr. cent stock exd.	670.000	
six pr. ct. exchd. stock to be reimbd.	3.750.000	4.490.000
sundries	70.000	
Probable amount of specie left in treasury on 31st. Decer. 1810		2.000.000
		8.710.000

RC and second enclosure (DLC); first enclosure (DLC: Rives Collection, Madison Papers). RC and second enclosure docketed by JM.

1. Gallatin was continuing his comments on JM's annual message, which he had begun circa 28 Nov. 1810.

2. Ferdinand R. Hassler (d. 1843), an emigrant from Switzerland, had served as an acting professor of mathematics at the U.S. Military Academy between February 1807 and December 1809 (Cullum, *Biographical Register of the Officers and Graduates of the U.S. Military Academy*, 1:78).

3. JM incorporated this paragraph as the penultimate section of his annual message on 5 Dec. 1810.

§ From John Drayton. *30 November 1810, Columbia.* "I have the honor to enclose you, a copy of my first communication to the Legislature of this State, now in Session."

RC (DLC). 1 p. Enclosure not found, but a print impression on the verso of the RC suggests that it was a broadside.

§ Memorandum from Paul Hamilton. *Ca. 30 November 1810.* Describes the instruction and students at French military academies, including those at Saint-Cyr-l'Ecole and La Flèche, the Imperial Polytechnical School, the Imperial School of Bridges and Causeways, the School of Mines, the School of Marine Engineers, the Imperial *corps du génie*, various artillery schools attached to garrisons or regiments, schools of navigation, and the "Joint Schools" of artillery and *génie* and of miners and sappers at Metz.

Ms (DLC, vol. 91). 3 pp. In an unidentified hand; docketed by JM, "Hamilton P." Headed "Military Schools in France." Undated; date assigned here on the assumption that Hamilton conveyed the notes to JM sometime before JM's annual message of 5 Dec. 1810, in which the president recommended "a more enlarged cultivation and diffusion" of the principles of military education, particularly by "Schools of the more scientific operations" of war.

§ From Zebulon Pike and Others. *2 December 1810, Washington Cantonment.* The undersigned officers have found Lt. Joel Lyon of the Third Infantry Regiment guilty of conduct unbecoming an officer and a gentleman and have sentenced him to be dismissed from the service. But they beg the indulgence of the president and recommend mercy in the belief that the prisoner "erred more from extreme youth, inexperience of mankind & want of timely advice than a depravity of heart or principle." They also state the opinion that "the charges would never have been brought against the Prisoner, had the *Note* from him to the Prosecutor (accompanying the Proceedings) never been tendered."

RC (DNA: RG 107, LRRS, L-132:5). 2 pp. Signed by Pike and seven others. Enclosed in Washington Lee to Eustis, 7 Dec. 1810 (ibid.; docketed by a War Department clerk as received 4 Jan. 1811 and with a pencil note, "Not Pardoned").

From James Fenner

Providence Decemr. 3rd. 1810

I take the liberty of addressing your Excellency on a subject of some importance to the Citizens of this State, as well as to others, and on which some diversity of opinion seems to exist.

A few, very few, of the Republicans here, have recommended Mr. Robbins, of Newport, in this State, as Successor to the late Judge Cushing of the Supreme Court of the United States. I am told that he is spoken of in the recommendations as a republican and a friend to the present Administration. Of this fact, however, I do not speak with confidence, as the recommendations which have been transmitted in his behalf, were studiously concealed from me. This was done, I presume, under an impression, that I could not join in so gross an imposition on you, as to say, that he is either a republican or a friend to the present Administration. In this Idea his friends were correct. The fact is, if I know any thing of his predilections on governmental systems, that he is in principle a Monarchist, and is friendly to federalism in proportion to its tendency to Monarchy. I can readily account for the exertions of the few republicans here, to place Mr. Robbins on the Bench. He is Brother in Law to Mr. Ellery, the present Loan Officer in this District; and has contributed more, perhaps, than any other individual, to promote the schismatical projects of that Gentleman in this State. Mr. Robbins could do this without endangering a cause which he was desirous to support; for if those projects succeeded, what the Republicans should loose the federalists would gain. These movements, to be sure, did not correspond with the *professions* of Mr. Ellery, and perhaps on some future occasion I may explain to you the real motives which governed *him*. As, however, the services were rendered, Mr. E. in gratitude for them, and from his fraternal feelings, has shewn a willingness to have them compensated by an honourable and lucrative appointment. The few adherents of Mr. E. in this Town were induced to join him in recommending his Brother, some, from the same motives which actuate Mr. E. himself, and some from a belief that Mr. Robbins has really become a convert to republicanism. But since the discovery that a part, if not the whole, of the Supreme Bench in Massachusetts, with a principal part of the Bar in Boston, and the whole in this State, have united in nominating him for the appointment, the faith in his political principles has been much shaken. Indeed, it appears to me incredible that he should receive *such* support under a belief that he is friendly to the present Administration. I can say with confidence, of the Bar in this State, that with two or three exceptions, a phalanx more zealous & malignant against the present order of things and its friends here, does not exist. Of the Court & Bar in Massachusetts I know nothing but by reputation—and from that I infer that their feelings are the same.

My object, thus far, has been to prevent an imposition (if any has been attempted) in regard to the political sentiments of Mr. Robbins. I consider him, then, as a federalist, propounded for an appointment.

I should have been much pleased had David Howell Esq consented to be nominated as Successor to Judge Cushing, as he is unquestionably the most profound Lawyer in this State; but he positively declines that nomination. He is willing, however, to accept the Office of District Judge, if Mr. Barnes shall succeed to the seat of Judge Cushing. Mr. Barnes is equal in *federalism*, and in all other respects, to Mr. Robbins; but as I hear of no other Candidate in this Circuit excepting those Gentlemen, I consider them as equal federal competitors for republican favour; and on the supposition that one of them will receive the appointment, it is of consequence to the Administration and its friends here to whom the preference shall be given. If Mr. Barnes is promoted to the Supreme Bench, and Mr. Howell supplies his place, a mischief will be removed from the District, and a great gain afforded to the republican interest. If Mr. Robbins receives the appointment, Mr. Barnes will remain where he is, and we shall be doomed to receive as salutary medicine, a compound of *Monarchical* and *federal* notions.

I am of opinion also, that a friend to the Administration on the District Bench, would have it much in his power to restrain and *curb* the insolence of the Bar; and in his charges to the Jury, to give to the Administration and our republican Institutions *at least fair play*. This is a point of immense consequence in my estimation.

I therefore wish that Mr. Barnes may be raised to the Supreme Bench, and that Mr. Howell may be appointed District Judge.[1] In this event there will be a vacancy in the Office of District Attorney, to fill which, I take the liberty to nominate John Pitman Jun Esq,[2] a young Gentleman of unblemished reputation and very promising abilities, and who has uniformly exerted himself in support of the republican Administration.

You will pardon me, I hope, for this trespass on your patience. I had determined in the first instance to say no more than might be necessary to prevent an imposition; but on further reflection, verily believing that the arrangement which I have suggested would greatly promote the republican Interest, I felt it to be my duty to propose it. I have the honour to be, with the greatest respect, Your Excellency's friend & Obt. Servt.

J. Fenner.

FC (RHi: Fenner Papers).

1. The knowledge that Fenner had made such a recommendation to JM apparently provoked other local Republicans to address the president on the subject. Sometime in December 1810, Seth and Henry Wheaton, Henry Smith, Thomas Coles, and Christopher Ellery wrote to JM (DLC; 4 pp.), criticizing Fenner for his support of David Leonard Barnes, whom they described as a man of only "secondary" legal talents and "decidedly hostile" to the administration. The five signatories to this letter traced the origins of the political disputes in Rhode Island to the lingering influence of the "remnant of the antient anti-federal or paper money party." In a postscript, they warned JM against Fenner's purposes, namely that if Barnes were appointed to the Supreme Court, David Howell would become district judge, and "Mr. Dexter, Howell's son in law, being Marshal, every thing will conspire to favour Mr. Fenner's interests, at the expense of propriety and of justice."

2. John Pitman, Jr. (1785–1864), had graduated from Brown University in 1799. After briefly residing in Kentucky in 1807–8, he returned to his native state and in 1811 was elected a member of the Rhode Island General Assembly. He held legal appointments in other New England states before becoming U.S. attorney for Rhode Island in 1820. In 1824 he was appointed U.S. district judge for Rhode Island, a position he held until his death (*Historical Catalogue of Brown University, 1764–1904* [Providence, 1905], p. 88).

From Albert Gallatin

Sir,   Treasury Department December 4th. 1810.

The situation of the arrears due on the Direct Tax and Internal Revenues, in the districts in which the Office of Supervisor has been continued, is exhibited in the enclosed Statement.

The following arrangements are respectfully submitted, to take effect from and after the end of the present year, viz:

1. That the Offices of Acting Supervisor be abolished in the States of Mas-

sachusetts, Maryland & North Carolina, leaving the collection of any arrears which may yet be recovered, to the district Attornies & Marshals.[1]

2. That the duties of the Office of Supervisor in the State of South Carolina, be transferred to the Marshal, with an annual Salary of 250 Dollars & an allowance for Clerk hire of 250 dollars for the year 1811.[2]

The situation of the Revenue in the States of Pennsylvania, Kentucky & Georgia, seems to require a continuation of the Offices of Acting Supervisor for the ensuing year. The Offices have heretofore been abolished in all the other States. I have &c

(Signed)   ALBERT GALLATIN

Tr (DNA: RG 56, Misc. Documents, ca. 1840–1906, vol. 90, Internal Revenue Direct Tax). Enclosure not found.

1. Gallatin made this recommendation under the provisions of section 2 of "An Act to repeal the Internal Taxes," approved on 6 Apr. 1802 (*U.S. Statutes at Large*, 2: 148–49).

2. Gallatin made this recommendation under the provisions of "An Act authorizing the transfer of the duties of Supervisor to any other office," approved on 3 Mar. 1803 (ibid., 2: 243–44).

From John G. Jackson

MY DEAR SIR.   CLARKSBURG Decr 4th 1810

I have for some weeks designed to write you that I may ascertain the practicability of procuring a pair of Merinos, or a Ram only, & the price; and as I know that you delight even in the midst of political engagements to turn your mind from their perplexities, to the more pleasant ones of domestic economy and have the information of all the Gentlemen now at W of that kind: I presume to make the enquiry of you. Doctor Mitchill who hailed "the Modern Jason" when landing with the golden fleece,[1] must have an *inexhaustible fund* of that kind of intelligence: & from the specimen the Doctor gave of his deep science in propagation on the trial of Alexander Whistelo[2] I apprehend he can furnish *much* curious learning on the Merinos. But in sober seriousness I should like to make the experiment of their utility & therefore want to purchase. Tho I confess my patriotism would not make me give many dollars for the means of doing so. I wont ask you for news & prospects; as your address to Congress by next mail will furnish ample scope for conjecture. Surely Florida in Louisiana will be taken possession of. But I forget it is my province to follow not advance before the Government. Dear Sir yours sincerely

J G JACKSON

RC (DLC).

1. At Chancellor Robert Livingston's annual sheepshearing at Clermont in 1810, Samuel Latham Mitchill had celebrated the role of the host in bringing merino sheep to the U.S. with the toast: "The modern Argonautic expedition, whereby our Jason has enriched his country with the invaluable treasure of the golden fleece" (*Men and Times of the Revolution; or, Memoirs of Elkanah Watson*, ed. Winslow C. Watson [New York, 1856], p. 343).

2. Jackson referred to testimony given by Samuel Latham Mitchill in *The Commissioners of the Alms-house vs. Alexander Whistelo* . . . (New York, 1808; Shaw and Shoemaker 14750), a paternity case heard before the Mayor's Court in New York City in August 1808. Lucy Williams, described as a "yellow woman," had given birth to an illegitimate child in January 1807 and stated that Alexander Whistelo, a "black" coachman in the employ of Dr. David Hosack, was the father. Whistelo denied the charge, and his position was supported by the testimony of a number of prominent New York doctors who declared that the light skin and straight hair of the child was reasonable medical evidence against his having fathered the child. Mitchill, however, seemed inclined to believe the word of the mother, and in opposing the consensus of his colleagues he argued that Whistelo's paternity by no means violated the rules of "probability" about the outcomes of interracial "propogation" as he explained them to the court. When asked under cross-examination to account for the seemingly "white" characteristics of the child, Mitchill canvassed "with much anecdote and repartee" a wide range of possibilities, including the doctrine of "maternal imagination," which held that it was possible for the physical characteristics of the fetus to be altered after conception, especially if the mother had experienced some severe shock or injury. That this might have occurred in the case of Lucy Williams was suggested to Mitchill by the fact that she admitted during her own testimony to having had sexual relations with a white man, apparently against her will and at the point of a pistol, although she also steadfastly maintained that this incident could not have led to the conception of the child and that Whistelo was the only possible father. In reaching its decision the court avoided giving an opinion on the medical and physiological issues and acquitted Whistelo of the paternity charge on the grounds that Williams had admitted that she had sexual relations with a white man.

From Paul Hamilton

NAVY DEPART. 5 Decr. 1810.

With much regret I perform the duty of laying before you for your consideration the sentence of a General Court martial on the case of Dennis Mahoney[1] a private in the Marine Corps of the United States. I have taken the liberty of adding to the papers a memorandum of the Laws, which embrace the case of this unfortunate man. Most respectfully I am Sir yr.

PAUL HAMILTON.

Letterbook copy (DNA: RG 45, LSP). Enclosures not found.

1. Dennis Mahoney had been charged in August 1810 with having run a bayonet through the body of Lt. Robert D. Wainright with the intent to kill him. A court-martial in Charleston found him guilty and sentenced him to death, but with a recommendation of mercy on account of "some symptoms of insanity." JM granted a pardon on 12 Dec. 1810, and Mahoney was discharged from the service the next day (DNA: RG 59, PPR; *National Intelligencer*, 20 Dec. 1810).

From James Taylor

Sir CHILLICOTHE OHIO Decr. 5th. 1810

I think it my duty to inform you that a man by the name of Benja. W. Lad[1] from Virginia and Genl. Duncan McArthur[2] of this state has lately made a number of entrys & surveys on lands that have been sold out by the U:States West of the line run by Ludlow from what he supposed the head branch of the Little Miami to the head of the Sciota.[3] It is beleived and I have no doubt but that Ludlow struck the Sciota some distance below the head of that river. This Mr Lad has set out from this place a few days ago for Washington in order to Obtain patents for his surveys and then it is said intends Ejecting some of the people in possession under the purchases from the UStates. It is thought that there is a variation of five degrees against the Va. Military claim, that is that the line is run that much too far to the right or East. I had a conversation with Mr. Galletine when I was last in the City, on this subject and stated to him my impression, and that I had no doubt but the Goverment would suffer the Officers & Soldiers of the Va. Cont line to locate the lands above the Indian boundary line & which might be found to lay between a true line to be run from the Source of one river to the other, and the line run by Ludlow when it was extended to the Sciota. I had under taken to locate Warrants for a number of Officers & indeed had a good many of my own, and I was much pressed by a Gentleman who was concerned with me to make locations on this land but I positively refused to suffer one to be located on any land sold by the Goverment, and I gave it as my opinion that the Goverment, if it was found had sold land that ought to belong to the Officers & Soldiers of the state of Va. would do them justice, by giving them other lands of equal value else where.

I am well informed that about 32,000 Acres have lately been located by those Men covering the U:States lands. I give this information in confidence in order that the Goverment may if they wish be ready to meet the Case when the surveys are presented to Obtain patents, if this should reach you in time.

I have notifed Genl: Jas Findley of the fact and do suppose he will give Mr. Galletine information on the subject.[4]

You must pardon this hasty scrall as I have not time to Copy it before the Mail leaves this. I have the honor to be with great respect Sir Your Obedt Servt.

JAMES TAYLOR

RC (DNA: RG 107, LRRS, T-99:5). Docketed by a War Department clerk as received 15 Dec. 1810.

1. Benjamin Ladd came from Charles City County, Virginia, and in 1814 he settled in Jefferson County, Ohio, where he was involved in Quaker efforts to resettle manumitted slaves (*Ohio Archæological and Historical Publications*, 6 [1898]: 275–76).

2. Duncan McArthur (1772–1839) was born in New York and after 1790 became a surveyor in the Scioto Valley where he rapidly acquired land. He entered state politics in 1805, rose to the rank of brigadier general in the Ohio militia, and in 1812 was colonel of one of the three regiments of state volunteers that accompanied William Hull during his Detroit campaign in the opening phase of the War of 1812. In 1813 JM appointed him a brigadier general in the Northwest Army, which force he commanded after the resignation of William Henry Harrison in 1814 (see Robert Sobel and John Reimo, eds., *Biographical Dictionary of the Governors of the United States, 1789–1978* [4 vols.; Westport, Conn., 1978], 3: 1198–99).

3. Israel Ludlow, a New Jersey land speculator who had served both as a surveyor for the Ohio Company and as deputy surveyor general of the U.S., had been appointed register of the land office in Cincinnati in 1800. The errors noted by Taylor may have arisen from problems in earlier surveys with the adjustment of magnetic compasses and "deceptions in the courses of the Scioto River." Surveyor General Rufus Putnam had reservations about accepting some of Ludlow's surveys for these reasons, but he concluded that the work had otherwise been "accurately executed" and that "no real injury could accrue either to the public or to purchasers" (Carter, *Territorial Papers, Northwest*, 3:136–37, 215; *Senate Exec. Proceedings*, 1:353, 354).

4. JM evidently referred Taylor's letter to Gallatin, who wrote a note on the cover: "This can be checked only in the War department, as patents for Virginia military lands issue there. But how can it be checked? It will not be perceived on the face of the surveys presented for patenting whether or not they are executed west of the line fixed by the 1st. section of the act of 23 March 1804 (Vol. 7. page 89). I see no other remedy than to suspend issuing the patents on late surveys & presumed to be in that quarter, & to instruct Colo. Anderson the Survr. General of those lands to certify on each survey, as a condition for obtaining patents, that the land is not surveyed west of the line first above mentioned, or on any land *previously surveyed* as land of the United States. See also 1st Section of Act of March 2. 1807 Vol. 8. page 260. 261. This is merely suggested for the consideration of the War Department. A. G."

Annual Message to Congress

WASHINGTON December 5th 1810

Fellow Citizens of the Senate, and of the
House of Representatives.

The embarassments which have prevailed in our foreign relations, and so much employed the deliberations of Congress, make it a primary duty, in meeting you, to communicate whatever may have occurred, in that branch of our national affairs.

The Act of the last Session of Congress "concerning the commercial intercourse between the United States, and Great Britain and France and their dependencies"[1] having invited, in a new form, a termination of their

Edicts against our neutral commerce, copies of the Act were immediately forwarded to our Ministers at London and Paris; with a view that its object might be within the early attention of the French and British Governments.

By the communication received through our Minister at Paris, it appeared, that a knowledge of the Act by the French Government, was followed by a declaration that the Berlin and Milan Decrees were revoked, and would cease to have effect on the first day of November ensuing. These being the only known Edicts of France, within the description of the Act, and the revocation of them, being such that they ceased, at that date, to violate our neutral commerce; the fact, as prescribed by law, was announced, by a Proclamation bearing date the second day of November.[2]

It would have well accorded with the conciliatory views, indicated by this proceeding on the part of France, to have extended them to all the grounds of just complaint, which now remain unadjusted with the United States. It was particularly anticipated that, as a further evidence of just dispositions towards them, restoration would have been immediately made, of the property of our Citizens, seized under a misapplication of the principle of reprisals, combined with a misconstruction of a law of the United States. This expectation has not been fulfilled.

From the British Government, no communication on the subject of the Act has been received. To a communication from our Minister at London, of the revocation, by the French Government, of its Berlin and Milan Decrees; it was answered, that the British System would be relinquished, as soon as the repeal of the French Decrees should have actually taken effect, and the commerce of neutral nations have been restored to the condition in which it stood, previously to the promulgation of those decrees. This pledge, altho' it does not necessarily import, does not exclude, the intention of relinquishing, along with the orders in Council, the practice of those novel Blockades, which have a like effect of interrupting our neutral commerce. And this further justice to the United States, is the rather to be looked for, inasmuch as the Blockades in question, being not more contrary to the established law of nations, than inconsistent with the rules of Blockade, formally recognised by Great Britain herself, could have no alledged basis, other than the plea of retaliation, alledged as the basis of the orders in Council. Under the modification of the original orders of November 1807, into the orders of April 1809, there is, indeed, scarcely a nominal distinction between the orders and the Blockades. One of those illegitimate blockades, bearing date in may 1806, having been expressly avowed to be still unrescinded, and to be, in effect, comprehended in the orders in Council, was too distinctly brought within the purview of the Act of Congress, not to be comprehended in the explanation of the requisites to a compliance with it. The British Government was accordingly apprized by our

Minister near it, that such was the light in which the subject was to be regarded.

On the other important subjects depending between the United States and that Government, no progress has been made, from which an early and satisfactory result can be relied on.

In this new posture of our relations with those Powers, the consideration of Congress, will be properly turned to a removal of doubts which may occur, in the exposition; and of difficulties, in the execution, of the Act above cited.

The commerce of the United States with the North of Europe, heretofore much vexed by licencious cruisers, particularly under the Danish flag, has latterly been visited with fresh and extensive depredations. The measures pursued in behalf of our injured Citizens, not having obtained justice for them, a further and more formal interposition with the Danish Government, is contemplated. The principles which have been maintained by that Government in relation to neutral commerce, and the friendly professions of His Danish Majesty towards the United States, are valuable pledges, in favor of a successful issue.

Among the events growing out of the state of the Spanish Monarchy, our attention was imperiously attracted to the change, developing itself in that portion of West Florida, which, though of right appertaining to the United States, had remained in the possession of Spain; awaiting the result of negociations for its actual delivery to them. The Spanish Authority was subverted; and a situation produced, exposing the Country to ulterior events, which might essentially affect the rights and welfare of the Union. In such a conjuncture, I did not delay the interposition required for the occupancy of the Territory West of the River Perdido; to which the title of the United States extends, and to which the laws provided for the Territory of Orleans, are applicable. With this view, the Proclamation,[3] of which a copy is laid before you, was confided to the Governor of that Territory, to be carried into effect. The legality and necessity of the course pursued, assure me of the favorable light in which it will present itself to the Legislature;[4] and of the promptitude, with which they will supply, whatever provisions may be due, to the essential rights and equitable interests of the people, thus brought into the bosom of the American family.

Our Amity with the Powers of Barbary, with the exception of a recent occurrence at Tunis, of which an explanation is just received,[5] appears to have been uninterrupted, and to have become more firmly established.

With the Indian Tribes also, the peace and friendship of the United States are found to be so eligible, that the general disposition to preserve both, continues to gain strength.

I feel particular satisfaction in remarking, that an interior view of our country presents us with grateful proofs of its substantial and increasing prosperity. To a thriving agriculture, and the improvements related to it, is added a highly interesting extension of useful manufactures; the combined product of professional occupations, and of household industry. Such, indeed, is the experience of œconomy, as well as of policy, in these substitutes for supplies, heretofore obtained by foreign Commerce, that, in a national view, the change is justly regarded as, of itself, more than a recompence for those privations and losses resulting from foreign injustice, which furnished the general impulse required for its accomplishment. How far it may be expedient to guard the infancy of this improvement in the distribution of labor, by regulations of the Commercial tariff, is a subject which cannot fail to suggest itself to your patriotic reflections.

It will rest with the consideration of Congress, also, whether a provident, as well as fair encouragement, would not be given to our navigation, by such regulations, as will place it on a level of competition with foreign vessels, particularly in transporting the important and bulky productions of our own Soil. The failure of equality and reciprocity in the existing regulations on this subject, operates, in our ports, as a premium to foreign competitors; and the inconvenience must increase, as these may be multiplied, under more favorable circumstances, by the more than countervailing encouragements now given them, by the laws of their respective Countries.

Whilst it is universally admitted that a well instructed people alone, can be permanently a free people; and whilst it is evident that the means of diffusing and improving useful knowledge, form so small a proportion of the expenditures for national purposes, I cannot presume it to be unseasonable, to invite your attention to the advantages of superadding, to the means of Education provided by the several States, a Seminary of Learning, instituted by the national Legislature, within the limits of their exclusive jurisdiction; the expence of which might be defrayed, or reimbursed, out of the vacant grounds which have accrued to the Nation, within those limits.[6]

Such an Institution, tho' local in its legal character, would be universal in its beneficial effects. By enlightening the opinions, by expanding the patriotism; and by assimilating the principles, the sentiments and the manners of those who might resort to this Temple of Science, to be redistributed, in due time, through every part of the community; sources of jealousy and prejudice would be diminished, the features of national character would be multiplied, and greater extent given to Social harmony. But above all, a well constituted Seminary, in the center of the nation, is recommended by the consideration, that the additional instruction emanating from it, would contribute not less to strengthen the foundations, than to adorn the structure, of our free and happy system of Government.

Among the commercial abuses still committed under the American flag, and leaving in force my former reference to that subject, it appears that

American Citizens are instrumental in carrying on a traffic in enslaved Africans, equally in violation of the laws of humanity, and in defiance of those of their own Country. The same just and benevolent motives, which produced the interdiction in force against this criminal conduct, will, doubtless, be felt by Congress, in devising further means of suppressing the evil.

In the midst of uncertainties, necessarily connected with the great interests of the United States, prudence requires a continuance of our defensive and precautionary arrangements. The Secretary of War,[7] and Secretary of the Navy[8] will submit the statements and estimates which may aid Congress, in their ensuing provisions for the land and naval forces. The statements of the latter, will include a view of the transfers of appropriations in the naval expenditures, and the grounds on which they were made.

The fortifications for the defence of our maritime frontier, have been prosecuted according to the plan laid down in 1808. The works, with some exceptions, are compleated, and furnished with ordnance. Those for the security of the City of New York, though far advanced towards completion, will require a further time and appropriation. This is the case with a few others, either not compleated, or in need of repairs.

The improvements, in quality and quantity, made in the manufactory of Cannon; and of small arms, both at the public Armories, and private factories, warrant additional confidence in the competency of these resources, for supplying the public exigencies.

These preparations for arming the Militia, having thus far provided for one of the objects contemplated by the power vested in Congress, with respect to that great Bulwark of the public safety; it is for their consideration, whether further provisions are not requisite, for the other contemplated objects, of organization and discipline. To give to this great mass of physical and moral force, the efficiency which it merits, and is capable of receiving; it is indispensable that they should be instructed and practised, in the rules by which they are to be governed. Towards an accomplishment of this important work, I recommend for the consideration of Congress, the expediency of instituting a system, which shall, in the first instance, call into the field, at the public expence, and for a given time, certain portions of the commissioned and noncommissioned officers. The instruction and discipline thus acquired, would gradually diffuse, thro' the entire body of the Militia, that practical knowledge, and promptitude for active service, which are the great ends to be pursued. Experience has left no doubt, either of the necessity, or of the efficacy, of competent military skill in those portions of an army, in fitting it for the final duties, which it may have to perform.

The Corps of Engineers, with the Military Academy, are entitled to the early attention of Congress. The Buildings at the Seat, fixt by law, for the present Academy, are so far in decay, as not to afford the necessary accomodation. But a revision of the law is recommended, principally with a view to a more enlarged cultivation and diffusion of the advantages of such Institutions, by providing professorships for all the necessary branches of military instruction; and by the establishment of an additional Academy, at the Seat of Government, or elsewhere. The means by which war, as well for defence, as for offence, are now carried on, render these Schools of the more scientific operations, an indispensable part of every adequate system. Even among nations whose large standing armies and frequent wars, afford every other opportunity of instruction; these establishments are found to be indispensable, for the due attainment of the branches of Military science, which require a regular course of study and experiment. In a Government, happily without the other opportunities; Seminaries, where the elementary principles of the art of War, can be taught without actual war, and without the expence of extensive and standing armies, have the precious advantage, of uniting an essential preparation against external danger, with a scrupulous regard to internal safety. In no other way, probably, can a provision of equal efficacy for the public defence be made, at so little expence, or more consistently with the public liberty.

The receipts into the Treasury during the year ending on the 30th of September last (and amounting to more than eight Millions and a half of Dollars) have exceeded the current expences of the Government, including the interest on the public debt. For the purpose of reimbursing, at the end of the year 3,750,000 dollars of the Principal, a loan, as authorized by law, had been negociated to that amount; but has since been reduced to 2,750,000 dollars; the reduction being permitted by the State of the Treasury; in which there will be a balance, remaining at the end of the year, estimated at 2,000,000 dollars. For the probable receipts of the next year, and other details, I refer to statements which will be transmitted from the Treasury;[9] and which will enable you to judge, what further provisions may be necessary for the ensuing years.

Reserving for future occasions, in the course of the Session, whatever other communications may claim your attention, I close the present, by expressing my reliance, under the blessing of Divine Providence, on the judgment and patriotism which will guide your measures, at a period particularly calling for united counsils, and inflexible exertions, for the welfare of our Country; and by assuring you of the fidelity and alacrity, with which my co-operation will be afforded.

JAMES MADISON

RC and enclosures, two copies (DNA: RG 233, President's Messages, 11A-D1; and DNA: RG 46, Legislative Proceedings, 11A-E1). Both RCs in the hand of Edward Coles, signed by JM. Received and ordered to be printed by both houses of Congress on 5 and 6 Dec. House copy referred to the Committee of the Whole (*Annals of Congress*, 11th Cong., 3d sess., 14–15, 383). Enclosures filed with House copy consist of 194 numbered pages of letters and other documents concerning U.S. foreign relations and organized as follows: 122 pages relating to relations with Great Britain; 56 pages relating to relations with France; 11 pages relating to relations with Spain; and 5 pages relating to relations with Tunis (DNA: RG 233, President's Messages, 11A-D1). Copies of the enclosures relating to U.S. relations with France and Tunis can also be found with the Senate copy (DNA: RG 46, Legislative Proceedings, 11A-E3). Message printed with eighty-three enclosures in *National Intelligencer*, 6, 8, 11, 13, and 15 Dec. 1810. Enclosures also printed in *ASP, Foreign Relations*, 3:349–72, 380–90, 394, 395–98.

1. Macon's Bill No. 2.

2. *PJM-PS*, 2:612–13.

3. *PJM-PS*, 2:595–96.

4. In justification of his West Florida policy, JM forwarded to Congress copies of the following letters and documents: John Rhea to Robert Smith, 10 Oct. 1810; Rhea to David Holmes, 26 Sept. 1810; and the 26 Sept. 1810 declaration of independence issued by the West Florida convention. He further claimed that all of this material had been enclosed by David Holmes in his 17 Oct. 1810 letter to Robert Smith (see *ASP, Foreign Relations*, 3:395–96). More than seventy years ago, Isaac J. Cox noted that JM's claim was incorrect inasmuch as the administration could not possibly have received Holmes's 17 Oct. letter in time to have used its contents as the basis for JM's 27 Oct. 1810 proclamation annexing portions of West Florida. Cox also observed that JM had omitted to communicate to Congress copies of Holmes's 26 Sept. and 3 Oct. letters to Robert Smith (see *PJM-PS*, 2:317–18), adding that the president evidently had "some reason for concealing the existence of the earlier communications from Holmes" (Cox, *The West Florida Controversy*, p. 416 n. 31). Other historians, most recently Joseph B. Smith, have asserted that JM "doctored the record" in order to establish a credible basis for Robert Smith's 31 Oct. 1810 declaration to French minister Turreau that JM and his cabinet were "strangers to everything" that had happened in the Spanish province prior to its 26 Sept. declaration of independence. On that basis Smith argued that JM's actions constituted one of the earliest uses in American history of the technique he described as "plausible presidential denial" of covert actions undertaken by the U.S. government (Joseph B. Smith, *The Plot to Steal Florida: James Madison's Phony War* [New York, 1983], pp. 66–67).

The facts relating to the documentary evidence are as follows: John Rhea's 10 Oct. letter to Robert Smith *was* enclosed in David Holmes's 17 Oct. letter to the State Department, though the administration forwarded to Congress only the last sentence of Holmes's letter and withheld the remainder, which, in contrast to the governor's previous letter of 3 Oct. 1810, declared that the West Florida convention was "now in full and quiet possession of all the country Comprehended within the jurisdiction of Baton Rouge." John Graham's docket shows that Holmes's 17 Oct. letter was received in the State Department on 8 Nov. 1810. Graham also recorded on the docket that the offer of negotiations proposed by Rhea to Robert Smith on 10 Oct. was rejected by the administration on the grounds that the West Florida convention was "not regarded as a body competent to enter into any compact—the U.S. asserting a prior right of sovereignty" (DNA: RG 59, TP, Mississippi).

John Rhea's 26 Sept. 1810 letter to Robert Smith, enclosing a copy of the West Florida declaration of independence of the same date, however, *was not* enclosed in Holmes's 17 Oct. letter to the State Department but in his earlier letter of 3 Oct. According to Joseph Gales, Jr., Holmes's 3 Oct. letter was received in Washington on 25 Oct. (see *PJM-PS*, 2:317), but the editors have subsequently been able to establish that it arrived on 22 Oct. 1810. John Graham's docket of that date, which lists both Rhea's 26 Sept. letter and the West Florida declaration of independence as being among the enclosures, has been separated from the 3 Oct. letter and is misfiled with the enclosures to Holmes's 15 Jan. 1811 letter to JM (see DNA: RG 59, TP, Mississippi).

5. Among the enclosures in JM's message was a copy of an 18 Sept. 1810 dispatch from the U.S. consul at Gibraltar, John Gavino, to Robert Smith, enclosing a 26 Aug. letter he had

received from his counterpart in Tunis, Charles D. Coxe. Coxe reported that the bey of Tunis had threatened to imprison all Americans in his realm and to sequester their property in retaliation for the seizure of one of his vessels by the American consul in Malta, Joseph Pulis. Pulis had taken the vessel on the grounds that it had originally been American property before its capture by a French privateer and subsequent sale to the bey's first minister. On being informed that the bey regarded the episode as a cause for war, Pulis withdrew his claim to the vessel, and relations were restored to "the same friendly footing on which they were before this unfortunate occurrence took place" (*ASP, Foreign Relations*, 3:394).

6. For JM's earlier advocacy of the idea of a national university, see *PJM*, 16:425–26, 436–37.

7. On 8 Jan. 1811 Eustis sent John Dawson, chairman of the House select committee on land forces and fortifications, an estimate of $131,046.30 for expenditures in 1811 on fortifications (DNA: RG 107, Reports to Congress from the Secretary of War).

8. The secretary of the navy forwarded a brief report on the state of the naval vessels to the Senate on 17 Dec. 1810 (see *ASP, Naval Affairs*, 2:229).

9. Gallatin communicated a report on the state of the finances to the Senate on 12 Dec. 1810 (see *ASP, Finance*, 2:439–49).

§ From Robert Patton.[1] *6 December 1810, Fredericksburg*. Has received JM's card advising of his draft in favor of Mr. Stone for $388.85, and the amount has been paid. Forwards him $502.50, the balance remaining per the annexed memorandum. "This remittance has been delayed a day or two that I might Avail myself of the Opportunity of the bearer Mr Maury going to the City."

RC (DLC). 1 p. A statement at the foot of the page shows a balance of £267 8s. 1½d. (including £4 4s. for two barrels of flour credited to JM's brother by mistake). JM's draft in favor of Stone was for £116 13s. 1½d., leaving a cash balance of £150 15s., or $502.50.

1. Robert Patton was a Scottish-born merchant in Fredericksburg (*PJM*, 14:273 n. 3).

§ From Harry Toulmin. *6 December 1810, Fort Stoddert*. Reports that there is no sign of any force from Baton Rouge. "The party which assembled from this district, have moved down to a bluff nearly opposite to the town of Mobile. . . . Governor Folch attempted to cross the bay with a force to disperse them; but a storm arose, and he was compelled to return. They have occasioned a general terror to the inhabitants. . . . Their numbers, however, are not sufficient to endanger the fort."

Has heard that Col. John Caller estimates this force at one hundred and expects one hundred more. Caller has said that he would "rather rely on Kemper to obtain the country than on the judge or on the United States, who had suffered themselves to be imposed upon by every power." Has been informed that one of his letters addressed to another justice was read to the group and altered to depict him as being in support of the enterprise (against Mobile) and that "they have entered into a solemn obligation to murder the public officer who shall institute a prosecution against any of the individuals concerned."

Discusses his efforts to institute proceedings against leaders of the insurgents and announces his intention to issue a warrant against Buford, the justice who is said to have misused the letter Toulmin sent him. Feels strongly the "personal danger" he is subjecting himself to and is astonished "with what effrontery the opinion is still advanced . . . that the general government have through the territorial authorities, discoverd a disposition to encourage the troubles in Florida, and thro' the agency of them to obtain possession of the country." Doubts he could obtain a conviction of the parties implicated, partly because the assembly is about to abolish the present court system.

Believes that supplies have reached the "little band of patriots" by an unexpected channel and fears that they might try to stop supplies destined for Fort Stoddert. Confesses to being at a loss to understand Kemper's object. "I have suspected that the main end proposed was to place the leading men in this district in such a situation with regard to their own government, that in case of the non-acknowledgement of the new baton rouge governt by the U. S. *this* country might easily be added to the projected state of Florida."

"This mail conveys to the Departt. of State a most interestg communn. from Govr. Folch, thro' Coll. M'Kee,[1] a gentleman, who . . . is I believe firmly attached to the interests of the U. S. . . . . Whatever mystery there was in his conduct as to the Burr conspiracy; I have never felt willing to admit that he could have taken a part in it. . . . He will set out in a day or two with the duplicate of the letter, & will be fully competent to give you a faithful picture of this country." Has no news of Colonel Cushing. Apologizes for writing too much.

RC (DLC). 5 pp. Docketed by JM. Printed in Carter, *Territorial Papers, Mississippi*, 6:149–51.

1. Toulmin referred to a 5 Dec. 1810 letter from John McKee to the secretary of war, enclosing a 2 Dec. letter from Vicente Folch to the secretary of state in which the Spanish governor offered to negotiate the transfer of West Florida to the U.S. (DNA: RG 59, TP, Orleans). Copies of McKee's letter to Eustis and an enclosed explanatory letter of 2 Dec. 1810 from Folch to McKee are printed in Carter, *Territorial Papers, Mississippi*, 6:147–48. JM forwarded the letters to Congress in his message of 3 Jan. 1811.

To Thomas Jefferson

DEAR SIR   WASHINGTON Der. 7. 1810

The letter inclosed came to me as you see it;[1] and tho' probably meant more for me than you, is forwarded according to its ostensible destination.

We have nothing from abroad, more than has been made public. The latest date from Pinkn[e]y is the 3d. of Ocr.[2] The arrival of Novr. will have been some test, positive or negative of the views of England. Her party here seems puzzled more than usual. If they espouse her Blockades, they must sink under the odium. And this course is the more desperate, as it is possible that she may abandon them herself, under the duress of events.

Lincoln does not yield to the call I made in a private & pressing letter. Still some wish him to be appointed, hoping he may serve for a time.[3] Granger has stirred up recommendations throughout the Eastern States. The means by which this has been done are easily conjectured, & outweigh the recommendations themselves. The soundest Republicans of N. England are making head agst. him, as infected with Yazooizm, and intrigue. They wish for J. Q. Adams as honest, able, independent, & untainted with such objections. There are others however in the view of the Southern Republicans; tho' perhaps less formidable to them, than Yazooizm on the Supreme Bench. If there be other Candidates they are disqualified either politically, morally, or intellectually. Such is a prospect before me, which your experience will make you readily understand.

Rodney has not yet joined us; & of course draws on himself the blame even of his best friends. And I just learn that his plan of bringing his family here, for which he has a House engaged, is broken up by the loss of his furniture, which, in coming round by sea, share the fate of a wreck on the Eastern Shore. The loss is increased by the addition of his Law Books & valuable papers. He has hopes however, of saving such articles as have been able to bear a compleat steeping in Salt water. Be assured always of my sincer[e]st affection

JAMES MADISON

RC (DLC). Docketed by Jefferson, "recd. Dec. 9."

1. JM was probably referring to a 6 Dec. letter written in Washington by Joseph Dougherty, acknowledging the receipt of a bitch from Jefferson sent "by Mr. Madison's manager some time ago." Accompanying the acknowledgment was a request to Jefferson for a loan of $130 to assist Dougherty in his efforts to go into the business of bottling porter and ale (MHi: Jefferson Papers).

2. *PJM-PS*, 2:570.

3. JM had evidently just received Levi Lincoln's letter of 27 Nov. 1810. Sometime after the commencement of Congress on 3 Dec. 1810, JM also received a two-page summary of a letter that Massachusetts Republican Ebenezer Seaver had sent to Levi Lincoln (DLC). The contents were a lengthy plea to Lincoln to overcome his preference for retirement and accept appointment to the vacant seat on the Supreme Court. The alternative, Seaver implied, was the nomination of Gideon Granger, who was unacceptable to the "Middle & Southern States" because of his support for George Clinton's presidential candidacy in 1808 as well as for his notorious sympathy toward the Yazoo claimants in Congress. Were Granger to be nominated, Seaver continued, "Mr Madisons Enimies J. Randolph at their head are ready to take every advantage of it," and he believed that the president's "popularity could not stand the shock." The Republicans would then be "like a large army scattered over an extensive country attacked by an artfull, insiduous united foe, dividing and conquering in every direction." In a postscript to the summary, Seaver stated that "the above is the substance of a letter wrote to Judge Lincoln but perhaps not the exact words as a correct copy was not preserved."

From Benjamin Rush

DEAR SIR   PHILADELPHIA Decemr 7th. 1810

Agreeably to your request I have in conjunction with my friend Dr Physick done every thing that I could for the relief of your nephew,[1] but I am sorry to add—as yet without Success. We have in vain attempted to salivate him. In consequence of the failure of that, and Other remedies, we have concluded in a day, or two to make a small puncture in his breast in order to discharge the Water from it. I have encouraged him to expect a different issue from it from that which followed a similar operation upon his brother,[2] from the consideration of its being performed by the hand of Dr Physick. You shall hear from me the result of it in a few days. In the mean while—I cannot help adding that in the most successful issue of the operation, there will be much to fear from his weakness, and perhaps from deepseated obstruction in his lungs. I sincerely sympathize with all who know and love him. I have seldom met with a more amiable and interesting young man.

I thank you for the copy of the letter to Mr Pinkney upon the Subject of the African trade carried on by the Citizens of the United States, and I rejoiced very much in reading the pointed reflection upon it in your message to Congress. It has given great Satisfaction to all who feel and think justly upon that flagitious business.

ADieu! my dear Old friend. I think of you Often, and sincerely implore the fountain of all wisdom to direct all your Acts in the present arduous State of public Affairs, to the best interests of our Country, and the continuance of that fair and just reputation which a life laboriously devoted to the noblest pursuits and employments has given you, with the most enlightned & virtuous part of your fellow citizens. From Dear Sir yours very respectfully and Affectionately

BENJN. RUSH

RC (DLC: Rives Collection, Madison Papers).

1. See JM to Rush, 29 Oct. 1810 (*PJM-PS*, 2:600).

2. Rush may have been referring to John Madison, who died of tuberculosis in March 1809 (*PJM-PS*, 1:79 and n. 1).

§ Account with St. Mary's College. *7 December 1810.* Lists charges to JM for John Payne Todd between 9 June and 7 Dec. 1810 amounting to $193.99 and a credit from former accounts of $18.66½ for a balance due of $175.32½. The charges include doctor's fees, educational supplies, postage, and money advanced to Todd to pay his washerwoman, tailor, and bootmaker as well as for travel and sundries.

Ms (MdBS: Account Book, 1809–11). 1 p. JM remitted $175.33 to pay this account to William Castel, agent of St. Mary's College, on 20 Dec. 1810 (MdBS; 1 p.).

To Peter Stephen DuPonceau

DEAR SIR   WASHIN[G]TON Decr. 8. 1810

I recd. in due time your favor of the 15th. instant[1] ⟨and⟩ with it a Copy of your translation of Bynkershoek. I am glad to find that in the midst of your professional occupations, you have compleated a work which was so much wanted, and which required that accurate knowledge of both languages which you possess. The addition of your notes will contribute to recommend both the subject & the Author of that valuable Treatise, to the attention both of our Statesmen & Students. A nation which appeals to law, rather[2] to force, is particularly bound to understand the use of the instrument by which it wishes to maintain its rights, as well as of those which, agst. its wishes, it may be called on to employ. Where the Sword alone is the law, there is less inconsistency, if not more propriety in neglecting those Teachers of right and duty. With my thanks for your very acceptable present, and my apology for the delay of them be[3] to accept assurances of my esteem & friendly respects

JAMES MADISON

RC (owned by Richard Gilder, Jr., New York, N.Y., 1990).

1. JM referred to DuPonceau's letter of 15 Nov. 1810.
2. JM evidently omitted "than" here.
3. JM evidently omitted one or more words here.

From Andrew Ellicott

DEAR SIR,   LANCASTER December 8th. 1810.

I have enclosed a communication for the secretary of the National Institute. You therefore see that I have availed myself of your kind offer to have it forwarded agreeably to the direction.

I have more to say, than could be confined to the compass of an ordinary letter, and as I do not wish to take up your time, which I am certain can, and will be more usefully employed, shall defer saying any thing for the present, except, that my conscience tells me, I could be more usefully employed to our common country on our coast, than in any other way, or place.

Your communication to congress has just come to hand, I have run over it hastily, and see nothing in it calculated to invite either cavilling, or quibbling. One or two expressions I would have altered: for instance—"To give this great mass of physical and *moral force*" &c. I should have liked it better if the words "*and moral*" had been omitted. The whole of that part respecting seminaries of learning, ought to be struck off detached from the other part of the message, and put into the hands of every citizen in the nation. On virtue, and information, we must depend for the support, and protection of our republican institutions. "Le principe" says Helvetius "le plus fécond en calamités p[u]bliques est l'ignorance. C'est de la perfection des loix que dépendent les vertus des citoyens; et des progrés de la raison humaine que dépend la perfection de ces mémes loix. Pour être honnête il faut être éclairé." [1]

The last paragraph must be placed to the account of your message. I am, with great respect and esteem yours sincerely

ANDW. ELLICOTT.

RC (DLC).

1. "The most fertile cause of public calamities is ignorance. The virtue of the citizenry depends on the perfection of the laws; and the progress of human reason depends on the perfection of the same laws. To be honest it is necessary to be informed" (editors' translation). Ellicott quoted from section 7, chapter 3, of Claude-Adrien Helvétius's posthumously published treatise, *De l'homme, de ses facultés intellectuelles, et de son éducation (Œuvres d'Helvétius* [5 vols.; Paris, 1793], 4:201–2).

From Thomas Jefferson

DEAR SIR   MONTICELLO Dec. 8. 10

I found among my papers the inclosed survey of La Fayette's lands adjacent to N. Orleans.[1] Whether it be the legal survey or not I do not know. If it is, it gives a prospect of something considerable after the 600. yards laid off round the ramparts. I inclose it to you as it may possibly be of use. With me it can be of none. I inclose you also a piece in MS. from Dupont on the subject of our system of finance when the progress of manufactures shall have dried up the present source of our revenue.[2] He is, as you know, a rigorous economist. And altho the system be not new, yet he always gives something new, and places his subject in strong lights. The application of the system to our situation also is new. On the whole it is well worth your reading, however oppressed with reading. When done with it I will thank you to hand it to mr. Gallatin with a request to return it to me when he shall have read it.

I have had a visit from mr. Warden. A failure in the stage detained him here 10. days. I suppose you had hardly as good an opportunity of becoming acquainted with him. He is a perfectly good humored, inoffensive man, a man of science & I observe a great favorite of those of Paris, and much more a man of business than Armstrong had represented him. His memoirs and proceedings in the cases of vessels seised shew this. I observed he had a great longing for his late office in Paris. I explained to him distinctly the impossibility of his succeeding in a competition before the Senate with such a man as Russell, a native, and of high standing. That failing, I endeavored to find out what other views and prospects he might have. I find he is poor, and looks ultimately to the practice of physic for an independant livelihood; that he wishes to find some means of living while he should be pursuing that study. He spoke of a secretaryship in one of the territories as desirable in that view, and I believe he would suit that office. However any appointment which would give him present subsistence. The consulships which rely on mercantile business he does not much relish, having no turn to shillings and pence. Having left Paris very hastily, he would be glad to go back there as the bearer of public dispatches, to settle his affairs there, if there should be occasion for a messenger. I collected these things from him indirectly, believing you would wish to know his views. He is an interesting man, perfectly modest & good, & of a delicate mind. His principal seems to have thrown him first on the hands of the Executive and then off of his own. We have not yet recieved your message, from which we expect to learn our situation, as well with our neighbors as beyond the Atlantic. Wishing you an easy and prosperous campaign for the winter I renew the assurances of my constant affection & respect.

TH: JEFFERSON

RC (DLC); FC (DLC: Jefferson Papers).

1. The survey has not been identified, but it may be the plat dated 1804 in the *Index to the James Madison Papers* or it may be one of a number of surveys and plats filed with the records of Lafayette's Louisiana land claims (DNA: RG 49, Special Acts, Lafayette Grant, La.).

2. The enclosed manuscript (not found) was undoubtedly the "petit Traité" that Pierre Samuel DuPont de Nemours had included in his letter of 14 Sept. 1810 to Jefferson (DLC: Jefferson Papers; docketed by Jefferson as received on 2 Dec.). DuPont was to send a second, revised version of the same treatise to JM on 4 July 1811. In these letters and manuscripts, DuPont discussed the problem of how the U.S. government might replace customs duties as a revenue source after domestic manufacturing had increased to the extent that American commerce with Europe was reduced to a few "objets de luxe" of interest to only a very small number of wealthy people. DuPont advised against recourse to excise taxes, which he criticized as unequal in their incidence and productive of civil disturbances such as the Whiskey Rebellion, and advocated instead that governments should tax only the true sources of productive wealth in the community, such as land.

¶ To the Right Reverend James Madison. Letter not found. *8 December 1810.* Acknowledged in the Right Reverend James Madison to JM, 14 Dec. 1810. Discusses the merits of an applicant. Refers to the documents accompanying his annual message to Congress.

¶ From Punqua Wingchong. Letter not found. *8 December 1810.* Described as a one-page letter in the lists probably made by Peter Force (DLC, series 7, container 2).

From Benjamin Rush

DEAR SIR,   PHILADELPHIA Decemr 9th: 1810.

I have great pleasure in informing you that the operation I mentioned in my letter of Friday was this day performed upon your nephew, and with the happiest result. I refer you to Dr Physick's letter for the particulars of it.[1] The only design of this hasty note is [to] comply with my promise, and to inform you that I shall this evening at the request of your nephew communicate the news of the safe issue of the operation, and that as yet nothing has occurred to forbid an expec[ta]tion of its being attended with good effects. From Dear Sir yours truly and Affectionately

BENJN: RUSH

RC (DLC).

1. Letter not found.

§ From James Collet. *10 December 1810, Dunkirk, France.* Refers to a letter he wrote JM's predecessor on 18 Mar. 1808 "to appoint me to one of the then vacant Consulates in this Country; Of which I have since heard nothing." Has recently learned that "many, indeed most, of the Ports of this Country are actually void of American Consuls. . . . From Holland to Bayonne there remains now hardly One American Protector Commission'd by Your Excellency." Provides some background information and references and solicits an appointment, preferably at Le Havre, Antwerp, or Dunkirk.

RC (DNA: RG 59, LAR, 1809–17, filed under "Collet"). 3 pp.

§ From Edwin Lewis. *10 December 1810, Fort St. Stephens.* Refers to his earlier letter [21 Nov.] requesting that Governor Holmes inquire into the conduct of government officials in the district. Mentions "a late occurrence of a number of the Citizens of this Country having manifested a Strong propensity to attack Mobeal when . . . robed of their hardear[n]ed wealth by a lawless exaction of duties on our trade." The people do not lack any attachment to the federal government, "but their premature Zeal to Vindicate the rights of nature are more excusable on a close examination than its likly will be represented by some people owing to a Settled personal hatred existing between Judge Toulmin & some of his party & Some who are embarked in this cause. I beg you . . . not to be alarmed by empty accusations agt. this place which is fast filling up with respectable citizens worthy of better officers to Govern us than a foreigner." Judge Toulmin's "partial administration" has rendered the laws and government contemptible. Would rejoice to see him replaced. "I beg a reference to the prosecutions agt. his countryman Capt Swain & other publick officers. . . . His residing as judge is a great means of faning up party Strife."

RC (DLC). 3 pp. Cover marked, "Fort Stoddert 2d. Jany."

§ From the Right Reverend James Madison. *10 December 1810, Williamsburg.* Recommends Joseph Prentis, son of the late Judge Prentis, for the position of port surveyor at Suffolk.[1] Praises his integrity and mentions that he has "the additional Merit of being a warm & active Friend in Favour of the present Administration." Has read "with entire Satisfaction" JM's message to Congress. "Our Vessel has a tempestuous Ocean to sail in; but I rejoice that the Helm is in Hands as distinguished for Wisdom, as for Patriotism & Firmness." Conveys his respects to Mrs. Madison.

RC (DNA: RG 59, LAR, 1809–17, filed under "Prentis"). 1 p.

1. JM nominated Joseph Prentis to the position of surveyor and inspector of the revenue at Suffolk, Virginia, on 5 Feb. 1811 (*Senate Exec. Proceedings*, 2:165).

From John Armstrong

DEAR SIR,   PHILADELPHIA Dec. 11 1810.

Some apology is, no doubt, due from me, for so long delaying my intended journey to Washington, but the truth is, that between the occupation of settling my family for the Winter in New York, and casting about here for their more permanent residence, my movements have been necessarily slow—and the more so, as, in cases of this kind, I leave something to both the taste & judgment of others, after my own have been altogether satisfied. This business however being now settled, or nearly so, I count on setting out from this place Southward on the 15th. Inst. & hope to have the honor of seeing you within a week from that time[1] and of assuring you of the very great respect and unalterable attachment of Dear Sir, Your most obedient & very humble Servant

JOHN ARMSTRONG.

RC (DLC).

1. John Armstrong arrived in Washington on 20 Dec. 1810; he remained there until 25 Jan. 1811 (*National Intelligencer*, 22 Dec. 1810 and 29 Jan. 1811).

From Robert Smith

SIR,   DEPARTMENT OF STATE December 11th. 1810.

The funds, which had been provided by law for the relief and protection of destitute American Seamen in foreign Countries, have been rendered this year inadequate to their contemplated object by the extensive seizures of our vessels in Europe, and the effect thereof on the situation of the crews.

The advances, which have been necessarily made by our Ministers and Consuls to supply the wants of these seamen and to procure them passages to the United States, have greatly exceeded the amount of these appropriated funds. Of these advances accounts, requiring immediate reimbursement, have already been rendered to the amount of 75,500 dollars, and it is apprehended that others may yet be received.

As these accounts cannot be paid under any existing law, it is respectfully proposed to submit to the consideration of Congress the propriety of passing a law, which will appropriate a sum of money for the repayment of the advances of which accounts have already been exhibited and which, at the same time, will provide for any similar expences that may have occurred or may occur during the present or the ensuing year. With this view I have the honor of laying before you the enclosed estimate.[1] With sentiments of great respect and Consideration, I have the honor to be Sir, your most Obt Sert

R Smith

[Enclosure]

Estimate

For reimbursing advances made by the Bankers under the direction of any of the Ministers of the United States, and by Consuls, for the relief of destitute American Seamen, and for discharging engagements entered into by the Consuls for their passages home, during the present year; and for defraying moreover such expences of a like nature as may be necessarily incurred during the year 1811 } Dollars 100,000

Department of State December 11th. 1810.

R Smith.

RC and enclosure (DNA: RG 233, President's Messages, 11A-D1); letterbook copy and copy of enclosure (DNA: RG 59, DL). RC and enclosure in a clerk's hand, signed by Smith; transmitted in JM's message to Congress, 12 Dec. 1810.

1. Congress passed the law sought by the administration on 7 Jan. 1811 but reduced the appropriation to $76,000 (*Annals of Congress*, 11th Cong., 3d sess., 18, 28, 29, 65, 66, 83, 390, 450, 459, 461, 487, 488; *U.S. Statutes at Large*, 2:614).

From Albert Gallatin

Sir   Treasury Department Decer. 12th 1810

The depreciation of the Russian Ruble, which had formerly been valued in our custom houses at about 55 cents, induced last spring an application from several collectors to the Treasury. The Comptroller, from the materials in his possession, judged that the ruble could not be worth less than 44 cents and gave instructions accordingly. In the course of the summer and on the arrival of the first vessels which had left the Baltic this year, other applications were made complaining of the rate fixed by the Comptroller. The subject was again taken up; and taking the medium of the contradictory information we then had, the propriety of fixing the ruble at 33 cents & ⅓ was submitted to you. This being approved has been established in the President's name and in conformity with the authority vested by the proviso to the sixty first section of the collection law.[1] (Page 379. 4th vol.)

Since that time, however, official and correct information has been received from the Consul of the United States at St Petersburg not only of the course of exchange during the present year, but also of the actual depreciation of the paper or current ruble as compared with the silver ruble. And an investigation of those data leaves no doubt on my mind that the ruble ought not, in relation to importations made in vessels which left Russia this year, be valued at more than 27 cents. The paper transmitted by Mr Harris, a new representation from the importers of Providence, and a report shewing the grounds on which my opinion of the value of the ruble has been formed are enclosed, and your decision thereon respectfully requested.

After a careful examination of the proviso above mentioned, it appears to me that the President is fully authorized to make the regulation and to give it effect so as to correct the error in the former decision in all cases where the duties have not actually been paid. In such cases Congress alone can grant relief.

I have selected the exchange on London as giving the most correct result for two reasons—1. it was understood that the exchange between Russia and other places on the continent of Europe was against Russia. The general course of exchange is also against England; and it is presumed that that between Russia & England comes nearer par than any other. 2. Goods imported from England form the greater part of our importations and are of course invoiced in £. Sterling. By taking that exchange as the rule, the importers from Russia and England are put on a par in those articles on which there is a competition.

RC (DLC). Complimentary close and signature clipped. Docketed by JM. Enclosures not found.

1. For JM's proclamation of 31 Aug. 1810 establishing the value of the ruble, see *PJM-PS*, 2:517.

From Samuel Smith

Sir,   Washn. 12th. Decemr. 1810

I have the honor to Submit to your perusal Some Notes recieved from my son on the Commerce of Russia with the U. S[1]—they may perhaps afford Some new information. I have the honor to be with the highest Respect—your Obedt. Servt.

S. Smith

RC (DLC). Enclosure not found.

1. John Spear Smith had traveled to Russia in 1809 as private secretary to John Quincy Adams. He later moved to London where he became chargé d'affaires after William Pinkney returned to the U.S. in February 1811 (John S. Pancake, *Samuel Smith and the Politics of Business, 1752–1839* [University, Ala., 1972], pp. 101–2).

§ **To Congress.** *12 December 1810.* Communicates a report from the secretary of state on expenditures from the fund for the relief of distressed seamen.

RC and enclosures (DNA: RG 233, President's Messages, 11A-D1). RC 1 p. In a clerk's hand, signed by JM. Printed in *ASP, Commerce and Navigation,* 1:821. For enclosures, see Robert Smith to JM, 11 Dec. 1810.

§ **From Thomas Elledge.** *12 December 1810.* Informs JM that "thier Can be no return made as yet Until ther is a Stop put to mobs arrising against me," especially in North Carolina, Virginia, Maryland, and Tennessee. "I know no other way to have peace With The least Confusion then to apply to Surpreme and County Courts to lay Such heavy fines As they Shall not be able to Bear Upon all Such as interrupts or mulists me on Such Occations. I want to make a return as quick as possable acording to the petetions I formly Sent to the former president I have Got the papers renued that was des[t]royed Conserning the maryland land in Baltimore County, Laying within ten or twelve miles of the Town Which may be found on Record about forty five or Six years back Bought by Thomas Cocky Decd. Also Francis Elledge Decd. Luning Burg old Court house put on Record I Supose fifty or near Sixty years back.[1] The papers will undoubtly be recorded Febreary Court next." JM may look for them "By Some Sure hand with out my Coming To Compremise" with the executors and heirs of Cocky "according to the Directions I give to Mr. Hollon and Rest of Congress." Requests he be sent directions at Statesville "to open a place in The Said County as is Suposed to be Stewards old mine fild. up &c."

RC (DLC). 1 p.

1. Francis Elledge received land in the 1732 will of John Bradford of Brunswick County, Virginia (*VMHB,* 29 [1921]: 507).

§ **From Richard M. Johnson.** *12 December 1810, Congress Hall.* "I feel it my duty to enclose you the within letter. I may be of Service. It cannot be injurious."

RC and enclosure (DNA: RG 59, LAR, 1809–17, filed under "Russell"). RC 1 p. Johnson enclosed a letter he had received from Henry Wheaton, dated 27 Nov. 1810 (3 pp.), urging that Jonathan Russell, chargé d'affaires at Paris, be nominated as Armstrong's successor as minister to France on the grounds that "as the State of New York has the Vice President—its claim to the mission to France must be considered as inconclusive." On 17 Dec. 1810 James Fenner wrote to JM on Russell's behalf (ibid.; 1 p.).

§ From Harry Toulmin. *12 December 1810, Fort Stoddert.* Reports issuing arrest warrants for Dr. Pollard and others engaged in illegal military enterprises. "Previous to the return of the Sheriff; the inclosed application for a writ of *Habeas Corpus* was made to me by Lawyer Kennedy, which I send because it exhibits the legal talents of the petitioner, & because . . . it has afforded ground for a clamour that I had denied to a citizen the benefit of the writ." Kennedy also submitted "a petition that certain negroes belonging to a Spanish inhabitant, might be seized, which had been sent above the line to prevent their being plundered, and who had originally been negroes held in this territory, till the owners moved below the line." Has given this to the attorney general.

Reuben Kemper and Chief Justice Caller "came to the fort on Sunday [9 Dec.] & I immediately had them arrested." Caller, "a good deal intoxicated," admitted the truth of the evidence in the warrant, though he later "retracted what related to Fort Stoddert." Offered to suspend determination of bail "if they had any testimony to rebut the charges, or wished to cross-examine the witnesses. . . . They informed me that they wished the testimony to be examined: and we have been three whole days engaged in the business, and may be two or three more. For the want of any other place, as there is nothing but a tavern with one public room convenient to the fort, . . . the examination has been held in Capn. Gaines' quarters." Kemper "feels perfectly at ease under the idea that he is a citizen of Florida," is convinced there is no proof against him, and maintains that the enterprise was "a laudable and an honourable one, . . . not intended to injure the United States or the citizens of Florida, & was very favourably viewed by men in the highest offices on the Mississippi." However, that he took the lead in organizing the expedition and purchasing ammunition has "all been satisfactorily established."

Caller's role was in recommending the expedition, engaging a boat for supplies, and being present with the party below the line, although he claimed "he went merely as a spectator, & took no part: and should I finally hold him to bail; it will be regarded as an outrage on justice & common sense." Buford's participation has been similarly established, while another leader, Captain McFarland—who declared that "he would have my blood"—has escaped.

"No examination, I suppose, was ever more minute or more tedious: and none, perhaps, was ever conducted with a spirit of more haughty pertinaciousness by the party accused. . . . I have promised them liberty to take a copy of the examination: & yet as from a partial exhibition of garbled extracts it is probable that the public mind may be led astray; I fear I have promised too much. Indeed I suspect that the only remedy will be to print the whole."

Admits it will be nearly impossible for him to preside at the trial and regrets that he had to act so early in the business. "But in a country where there is so much apathy, so much ignorance, . . . a judge . . . must perpetually take a more active part in the early stages of prosecutions than is customary in societies more established, and composed of better materials." And if Congress does not establish a separate government for this district, "the cause of justice for several years to come must perish in this part of the Mississippi State. . . . The new population . . . has been very far indeed from improving the state of society." The need for the presence of a governor and judges is "most impressively displayed on the present occasion: as one of the main engines employed by Kemper and his party, is the uncontradicted circulation of reports that the expedition is sanctioned by the Executive, which the distance of the Governor has precluded him from counteracting."

Does not know how to act after having taken so active a part in bringing the offenders to justice. Could not be considered impartial at a trial, but "family demands on me, seem to render a resignation ruinous."

Was consulted after the arrest of Kemper and Caller by Colonel Sparks "on a request which had been made to him by Coll. Kemper, and which he was evidently disposed to accede to." Kemper proposed to write to the authorities in Florida and Mobile for a cessation of hostilities to avoid bloodshed. Informed Sparks that compliance with this proposal would be a tacit acknowledgment of Kemper as "the representative of a power authorized to treat," which was "utterly incompatible with his standing as a violator of the laws of the United States," and that if Kemper wished to avoid bloodshed he only had to desist from his "illegal" and "needless" enterprise. Sparks seemed convinced and promised to "wave the business," though he spoke a good deal about avoiding bloodshed.

"The whole affair appeared to me to be nothing but an artful device to obtain some colour of an acknowledgement of the new goverment, from American authorities"; however, the next morning Sparks sent for Lieutenant Ware, who then started for Mobile with letters for the governor and Innerarity. Fortunately, Captain Gaines detained Ware and sent an officer to remonstrate with Sparks. Believes this was successful, and if Sparks has committed himself since, it is without the knowledge of his officers. Hopes Sparks never hears of this communication; "he is one of the best men in the world: but he has unfortunately been for some time thrown into a situation for which previous qualifications had not prepared him."

"Yesterday advice came, that Govr. Folch had the preceeding night attacked the party encamped on saw mill creek, had killed four, taken ten or twelve prisoners, and wounded and dispersed the rest. Among the prisoners is Major Hargrave a justice of our Q. S. court.[1] . . . It was this morning industriously circulated . . . that the attack was made in consequence of information given by me to Govr. Folch. The truth is that . . . till I heard of the defeat, I supposed [the party] had been on the river." Cannot judge the effects of the affair; "some no doubt will be discouraged: but more will be enraged: and should assistance come from Baton Rouge, . . . I suspect that the business will be resumed with vigour, to the destruction perhaps not only of the Spaniards but of the friends of the law in this quarter." Has written Governor Holmes requesting him to come to Fort Stoddert but hopes that there is no force on its way from Baton Rouge. Adds in a postscript that Colonel McKee set out a few days earlier. Reports in a postscript of 13 Dec. that there has been a clash on the Pascagoula, "principally between the insergents themselves, who were partly Spanish subjects & partly Americans," with eight killed.

RC and enclosure (DNA: RG 59, TP, Mississippi, vol. 1). RC 7 pp. Postscript of 13 Dec. written on a separate slip of paper. A misdated docket for the RC by John Graham, with the note "Affairs at Mobile," is filed at 12 Dec. 1811 (ibid., vol. 2). Enclosure (2 pp.) is a petition from Joseph P. Kennedy to Toulmin announcing that he had become a citizen of the state of West Florida and seeking a writ of habeas corpus to release him from his arrest by John Johnston, chief justice of Baldwin County, Mississippi Territory. RC and enclosure printed in Carter, *Territorial Papers, Mississippi*, 6:152–58, 158–59.

1. On the evening of 10 Dec. 1810, Folch had attacked a filibustering party at Saw Mill Creek near Mobile. In addition to killing four and wounding three of the party, Folch also took seven prisoners (Cox, *The West Florida Controversy*, pp. 483–84).

From Benjamin Rush

DEAR SIR,   PHILADELPHIA Decemr 13th. 1810
I have great pleasure in informing you that your nephew continues to exhibit all the marks of relief which he discovered on the evening After the Operation. His Spirits are much improved, and there is now more reason to expect his recovery, than there has been since he came to Philada: But the ultimate issue of his disease is still doubtful. His patience, and good Spirits are among the most powerful remedies upon which we rely for its being favourable. Health, Respect & Friendship! from Dear Sir yours unalterably and Affectionately

                                                          BENJN: RUSH

RC (DLC).

From the Right Reverend James Madison

DEAR SIR   Decr 14h 1810 WG.
You certainly took the right Course in your Letter of the 8h. Inst. The Applicant is unworthy of any Kind of Notice; & besides, is in the Habit of laying under Contribution every one who will yeild to her incessant Applications. Nor is she, by any Means, destitute of a sufficient Support, having not only 5 or 6 Slaves, but several Relations who are disposed to be liberal to her. I will, however, inform her of the Situation in which you are placed from similar Applications.

I am much obliged to you for your good Disposition to forward such Documents as have been laid before Congress: but, as the Newspapers do not fail to circulate them, I would, by no Means, give you that Trouble. The Measures you adopted with Respect to W. Florida, must receive the entire Approbation of all Parties. There was no Time to be lost; & you have happily blended Decision with Mildness. As to the Pretensions of the Conventionalists, I do not know whether to admire more their Impudence, their Knavery, or their Folly. They have been treated as they merited. Beleive me to be, with the highest Regard, Yrs most sincerely—

J MADISON

RC (DLC).

§ From Joseph Coppinger. *16 December 1810, No. 6 Cheapside Street, New York.* Solicits JM's assistance in establishing a brewing company in Washington as "a National object" in order to improve the quality of malt liquors and to "counteract the baneful influence of ardent spirits on the health and Morals of our fellow Citizens." "The Capital that might be made sufficient to give a begining to such an establishment need not exceed $20,000. one half of which to be allowed for buildings and utensiles the remaining half to be considered as active stock. This Capital to be raised by subscription of $500 or $1000 for each share." Is confident of a profit of 100 percent on liquor sold in casks and 200 percent on that sold in bottles. Points out that brewing is an important source of government revenue in England. "In the event of such an establishmt. taking place I beg leave through you to make the company a tender of my services."[1] Has twenty years' experience in the brewing trade. If the company is not established, offers his services in "any station or employment." Encloses a list of his "inventions and Improvements" and a copy of a letter of introduction "to convey some idea of the person who addresses you."

RC and enclosures (DLC). RC 3 pp. First enclosure (4 pp.) is a list of fourteen inventions; second enclosure (1 p.) is a copy of an 8 Nov. 1809 letter of introduction from William Du-Bourg of St. Mary's College, Baltimore, to John Couper of St. Simon Island, Georgia.

1. According to Robert Fulton, JM had a policy of never subscribing to invitations of this sort in order to spare himself from being "Innundated with applications for all kinds of projects" (see Robert Fulton to John Stevens, 20 Jan. 1811 [NjHi: Stevens Papers]).

From William Pinkney

DEAR SIR   LONDON. December 17th. 1810

The proclamation of the 2d. of November is doing good here, and may perhaps bring this Ministry to Reason. I enclose Cobbets last Number, which touches upon our Relations with this Country, & Bell's weekly Messenger of yesterday, which treats of the same Subject. My Letter to Ld. W. of the 10th. Instant[1] wd. have gone into it more fully (though I was straightened for Time) but that I was afraid of the Sin of prolixity & expected moreover to be called upon to resume the Discussion in another Letter. There is Reason to think that, though the Freedom of its Style may have given umbrage to some of the Cabinet, it will assist your Proclamation. I have never met with a State-paper to be compared with Ld. W's Note to me of the 4h. Instant.[2] To tell me gravely and dryly, after my Letters of the 25h. of August & 3d. of November,[3] that he had not been able to obtain any "authentic Intelligence" of the Repeal of the French Edicts &c!! You may perhaps suppose that in my Letter to him of the 10th. I have examined too much at large the British Construction of the French Declaration. I should not have done so but for a Conversation a few Days before with Sir Wm Scott,[4] who appeared to have a prodigious Hankering after the Nonsense about *prèalable* Conditions. It is known besides to have been the favorite Doctrine of the Court & its adherents, & of all that anti-neutral Class to which Stephen & Marryatt[5] belong, and indeed of the people in general. We shall probably hear no more of it, however; and I understood, indeed, last Night that there is a perceptible Change in the Tone of Ministers & their Friends on the whole Subject. Whether they will act wisely in the End I cannot yet say. The presumption is always against them.

I have observed in my Letter that the Convenience of relaxing the orders in Council by Licenses "seems to be no longer enjoyed." The Object of all that part of my Letter was merely to give a slight Sketch (which I should have been glad to be at Liberty to make much stronger) of that monopolizing and smuggling Scheme which has so long insulted the World & tried our Patience. The Fact is that they have not granted any Licenses for several Weeks. It is not however (as I am assured) that they are ashamed of this mean Practice, but because they hope, by abstaining from it for a Time, to get better Terms of Intercourse in this Way from their Enemy. If their orders &c should not be immediately revoked, so as to prevent the Revival of this Trick of Trade, a vigorous Tone should be used with them—and I shall be happy to be authorised to use it at Discretion. Be assured they will not stand against a shew of determined Resistance to their Injustice. But if they should, they must be resisted to the uttermost nevertheless.

There will, I incline to think, be a Regency [6]—but it is believed that the Prince will be greatly restricted at first. The Restrictions will not last; yet if he should be obliged to continue the present Ministers for any Time however short (which it is imagined will be a part of the Terms with which he will be shackled) the Mischiefs of their crooked & little policy towards the U. S., supposing that they mean to brave the Consequences of persevering in it, may become permanent & irretrievable.

There has been, I believe, some juggling in the Affair of a Minister plenepotentiary. You will see in my Letter to Mr Smith of the 14th. an Account of Ld. W's late Explanations to me on that Head.[7] I have omitted, however, to state in that Letter that he *inadvertently* remarked in the Course of the Conference that great pains had been taken by some people to persuade him "that the *British Interest in America* (I quote his words) would be completely destroyed by sending thither at this Time a Minister pleny." He soon perceived by my Comments on this Suggestion that he had committed an Indiscretion in talking of it, and he wished me I thought to consider what he had said as confidential. May we not infer that these persuasions have had an Effect, when we look to the Quality of his ostensible Reasons for not redeeming his pledge of July last? Who the *persuaders* were he did not say—but Mr. *Jackson* (who by the bye cannot be very well satisfied with his Reception here) may be supposed to be among the Number, if he is not the only one. Whether this Gentleman (if he *has* used such Instances) quotes any *American Authorities* in Support of them, can only be guessed. It would be no Breach of Charity to conjecture that he does. At any Rate there must be some secret Cause for the Delay of the promised Mission. Even the Indolence of ———, added to the Reason *assigned in Conference*, will not explain it satisfactorily. There is Cunning at the bottom; and I can imagine nothing so likely to throw a Light upon it as the unguarded Communication of Ld W. above mentioned. Believe me to be— with sincere & affectionate Attachment—Dear Sir—your faithful & Obedient Servant

W. P.

RC (DLC: Rives Collection, Madison Papers). Docketed by JM.

1. For Pinkney's 10 Dec. 1810 letter to Lord Wellesley, see *ASP, Foreign Relations*, 3:376–79.

2. For Wellesley to Pinkney, 4 Dec. 1810, see ibid., 3:376.

3. For the texts of these letters, see ibid., 3:365, 373.

· 4. William Scott (1745–1836) had lengthy careers in both politics and law. He first entered Parliament in 1790 where he held the seat for Oxford University until 1821. His true interests, however, were in admiralty and ecclesiastical law. In 1798 he was appointed to the Privy Council and to the judiciary of the High Court of Admiralty. In the latter capacity he delivered during the Napoleonic Wars many significant rulings which were harmful to American shipping interests (R. G. Thorne, ed., *The History of Parliament: The Commons, 1790–1820* [5 vols.; London, 1986], 5:113–15; Bradford Perkins, "Sir William Scott and the *Essex*," *WMQ*, 3d ser., 13 [1956]: 169–83).

5. Joseph Marryat (1757–1824) was the member of Parliament for Horsham. He was also a West India merchant, a Lloyd's underwriter, and the colonial agent for Grenada. A strong supporter of the Perceval ministry, he published several pamphlets in support of its antineutral policies, most notably *Concessions to America the Bane of Britain; or, The Cause of the Present Distressed Situation* . . . (London, 1807) and, anonymously, *Hints to Both Parties* (London, 1808) (see Thorne, *History of Parliament: The Commons*, 4:549–53).

6. The death of George III's youngest daughter, Princess Amelia, in November 1810 provoked what proved to be the king's final and permanent bout of insanity. On 20 Dec. 1810 Prime Minister Perceval introduced in the House of Commons a regency bill, based on a similar measure designed by William Pitt in 1788, and it passed into law on 5 Feb. 1811. In the event of the king's making a quick recovery, the powers of the regent were limited in certain respects for a period of twelve months (see J. Steven Watson, *The Reign of George III, 1760–1815* [Oxford, 1960], pp. 489–91).

7. In explaining the delay in replacing Francis James Jackson in Washington, Lord Welles-ley informed Pinkney that there had been "some obstacles of a personal Nature to obtaining the Services of the person whom he particularly wished to send to America; that he hoped these obstacles would soon be removed; that he had another person in View if it should be otherwise; that he had not supposed that Delay would be considered as of any moment by [the U.S.] Government after the assurance contained in his Note [to Pinkney] in July last; that these temporary Inequalities were common and when not meant to be offensive were never held to be so &c &c &c" (Pinkney to Robert Smith, 14 Dec. 1810 [DNA: RG 59, DD, Great Britain]).

From Anthony Charles Cazenove

SIR   ALEXANDRIA Decr. 18th. 1810
    I have the honour to inform you that, I am going to send a vessel to Madeira, & shall be happy to take charge of any thing you may wish to send there.
    Should you be disposed to favour me with an other order for some of Messrs. Murdoch's wine, would be glad to be able to send it by this conveyance.
    I beg leave to annex an account of the charges on the pipe received,[1] & am very respectfully Sir Your most Obedt. Servant
                                                    ANT CHS. CAZENOVE

RC and enclosure (DLC). Docketed by JM. The enclosed account (1 p.) lists $9.02½ in freight, wharfage, and customs charges on a pipe of Madeira wine and $63.22 for a custom-house bond for duties.

    1. See Cazenove to JM, 24 Sept. 1810 (*PJM-PS*, 2:553).

From Stanley Griswold

SIR,   CINCINNATI (OHIO) 18th. Decr. 1810.
    Judge Griffin, of the Michigan Territory, is solicitous for an exchange with me of our local situations. I have no objection to accommodate him, provided it be agreeable to government. Indeed, from the experience I have had of ill health in the Illinois Territory, I am induced to wish for the ex-change. I believe, that Kaskaskia to him, and Detroit to me, would be more salubrious.
    If I rightly understood my friends in the Senate last winter, they would cheerfully concur in my transfer to Michigan, in case I should desire it, and provided the government of that Territory should go into other hands.

In contemplation of the possibility, that the exchange may be effected, I shall authorise some friend of mine near you to give in my resignation as judge of the Illinois Territory, whenever he shall know, that I am transferred to the Territory of Michigan. But such resignation on my part is not in any case to be offered until after my transfer shall have been completely effected by government.

In May last I started with my family from the shore of lake Erie, with a view to proceed to the Territory to which I was appointed. Unfortunately the small pox overtook us on the way, and detained us during the fittest season to descend the river. It was mid-summer before we reached this place (Cincinnati, Ohio,) where I deemed it prudent to lodge my family, as the season had become intolerably hot, and the waters low. I proceeded myself on horseback in August, attended the whole term of the court in each of the counties, was then attacked with the ague & fever, afterwards assisted in the completion of all the necessary legislative business, and returned to my family after an absence of three months.

I had the pleasure of travelling in company with Govr. Howard, of the Louisiana Territory, on his way to take possession of his new government; as also of visiting him at St. Louis. With satisfaction I inform you, that he proves highly acceptable there, and the appointment is much applauded.

I have just had the opportunity of seeing your Message to Congress at the opening of the present session. To say nothing of its other parts, I assure you, that the portion relating to your proceedings in reference to West Florida, excites unbounded approbation as far as I can hear; and I am certain it will be peculiarly pleasing to the people whom I have visited on the Mississippi. I have the honor to be with great respect, Sir, Your most obedient and very humble servant

STANLEY GRISWOLD.

RC (DLC). Docketed by JM.

§ Robert Smith to Louis-Marie Turreau.[1] *18 December 1810, Department of State.* Acknowledges Turreau's letter of 12 Dec. in answer to his inquiries about certificates of origin and the admission to France of American agricultural products.[2] Concludes from the letter that the importation of American cotton and tobacco is "specially and absolutely prohibited." Also notes that the decree of 15 July effectively prohibits the importation of American fish oil, dyewood, salt fish, codfish, hides, and peltry;[3] and as these articles constitute the "great mass" of the exports from the U.S. to France, "no practical good, worthy of notice" has resulted from the repeal of the Berlin and Milan decrees.

Declares that the act of 1 May 1810 [Macon's Bill No. 2] was intended to bring "substantial benefit" to the U.S. as well as the recognition of a "legitimate principle," and it included the assumption that the repeal of the Berlin and Milan decrees would leave French ports "as free for the introduction of *the produce of the United States*, as they were previously to the promulgation of those decrees." The replacement of the decrees by "municipal regulations," however legal in form, is an unfriendly act, and it is inconsistent with the letter of 27 Nov. which announced the intention of the emperor to favor American commerce.[4]

If French ports are blocked, what motive has the U.S. in its discussion "with a third power" to insist on the privilege of going to France? The British edicts may be viewed in two lights—the wrong they do to the U.S. and that done to France. France may only speak to the latter condition. But what wrong can France suffer from British orders that cooperate with its own regulations? It is for the U.S. to decide what degree of sacrifice circumstances may require of it, but the inducements to these sacrifices have been reduced by France's conversion of "the right to be maintained into a naked one, whilst the sacrifices to be made would be substantial and extensive."

Hopes that instructions from the French government will soon enable Turreau to explain these measures. States that the president was satisfied to learn that French consuls had been officially authorized to issue certificates of origin to vessels bound for nations in alliance with France and that this practice did not cease in the U.S. before 13 Nov., and then only in consequence of a 30 Aug. dispatch from Cadore. Assumes that such information has been given to Denmark and that it will influence the Danish government, which had been seizing American property on the grounds that these certificates of origin were spurious. Regrets, nevertheless, that such information was not given to French functionaries in Denmark during the period when Danish authorities were committing outrages against American trade.

Printed copy (*National Intelligencer*, 1 Jan. 1811). Copy enclosed in JM to the House of Representatives, 28 Dec. 1810 (printed in *ASP, Foreign Relations*, 3:402).

1. After JM dismissed Smith from the State Department in April 1811, the former secretary included this letter among the documents he compiled for his pamphlet attacking the president over the summer of 1811 and published as *Robert Smith's Address to the People of the United States* (Baltimore, 1811; Shaw and Shoemaker 23949). At that time Smith claimed that he had written a draft of the 18 Dec. letter to Turreau himself, and he described the circumstances as follows: "Previously to the meeting of Congress last autumn, I expressed to Mr. Madison my apprehension that the Emperor of France would not *bona fide* fulfil the just expectations of the U. States—that our commerce would be exposed in his ports to vexatious embarrassments, and that *tobacco* and *cotton* would probably not be *freely* admitted into France. He entertained a different opinion, and indeed was confident that the Berlin and Milan decrees would *bona fide* cease on the first day of November, 1810, and that from that day our commercial relations with France would be encumbered with no restrictions or embarrassments, whatever." Smith claimed that after entering into correspondence with Turreau on the matter, he "was greatly checked by the . . . utter indifference on the part of Mr. Madison. Instead of encouraging, he absolutely discouraged the making of any animadversions upon Gen. Turreau's letter of December 12, 1810." Smith persisted, however, and laid the 18 Dec. 1810 letter before JM. "Perceiving upon reading it that he could not but acquiesce in the sending of it, he merely suggested the expediency of adding to it what might have the effect of preventing the British government from presuming too much upon the ground taken in the letter." This letter, Smith added, "being prominent in the catalogue of the offences that had brought upon me the displeasure of Mr. Madison, our fellow citizens will dispassionately consider whether it ought to be looked at as 'a sin beyond forgiveness' "(see *National Intelligencer*,

2 July 1811). After Smith published the letter, however, State Department clerk John B. Colvin denied that the former secretary had been its author. Colvin claimed to have written it himself, "with the exception of one paragraph" which he understood "was written by Mr. Madison" (ibid., 23 July 1811).

2. Turreau's 12 Dec. 1810 letter to Smith was written in response to a series of questions sent by the secretary of state on 28 Nov. relating to the practices of French consuls in issuing certificates of origin to American vessels (see *ASP, Foreign Relations*, 3:401).

3. In his dispatch of 18 July 1810 John Armstrong mentioned that Napoleon's recently established Council of Commerce had decided on 5 July to introduce a license system for trade in enumerated products between certain French and American ports, but he added that the necessary decrees had yet to be promulgated. He also enclosed notes of the proceedings of the Council of Commerce after 6 June 1810, the final item of which was a decree, dated 15 July 1810, allowing thirty or forty American vessels, departing from Charleston or New York and bringing with them "a gazette of the day of their departure," to import under license certain enumerated articles (Armstrong to Smith, 18 July 1810 [DNA: RG 59, DD, France]; translation of decree in *ASP, Foreign Relations*, 3:400).

4. Turreau to Smith, 27 Nov. 1810 (ibid., 3:400–401).

¶ To Benjamin Rush. Letter not found. *18 December 1810, Washington*. Offered for sale in Parke-Bernet Catalogue No. 484, "The Alexander Biddle Papers" (1943), pt. 2, item 202, which notes that the one-page letter of about one hundred words "regards his nephew who was ill, and is consoled that he is receiving the attention of Dr. Rush and Dr. Physick."

From Anthony Charles Cazenove

Sir   Alexandria Decr. 19th. 1810
I am favour'd with your letter of this date[1] inclosing your check for $63.22/100 amount of charges on your pipe of Madeira wine from Messrs. Murdoch.[2] When your stock of that article will require being replenished, will thank you to inform me of it, if you are satisfied with that received. I am very respectfully Sir Your most obedt. Servt.

                                              Ant Chs. Cazenove

RC (DLC).

1. Letter not found.

2. On 9 Jan. 1811 Cazenove informed JM that he had omitted to include payment for the freight, wharfage, and customs charges of $9.02½ (DLC; 1 p.). JM paid the outstanding balance shortly thereafter (Cazenove to JM, 17 Jan. 1811 [DLC; 1 p.]).

§ From George Joy. *19 December 1810, Copenhagen*. "I am yet unadvised of the fate of my Letters that were put on shore at Gottenburg; and such of the Duplicates that I have sent to replace them . . . save that these last have passed safely into

Sweden. I therefore give this an entirely different direction."[1] In a postscript lists the papers enclosed: Joy to JM, 8 Oct. 1810 and October 1810;[2] cabinet secretary to Joy, 27 Nov. 1810;[3] Joy to Count Rosenkrantz, 11 Dec. 1810[4] ("the last enclosed to Mr. Secry Smith, 13 Inst:"); and Joy to Robert Smith, 13 and 14 Dec. 1810.[5] Apologizes for the "slovenly Manner" of his dispatches, but he cannot afford "any regular Aid." "I am to this hour without a shilling Compensation in this business; tho' I never was more laboriously occupied by Night or by Day."

RC (DLC). 2 pp. For surviving enclosures, see nn. 2–5.

1. In a 31 Dec. 1810 postscript to the first copy of an October 1810 letter to JM (see Joy to JM, ca. 20 Oct. 1810, *PJM-PS*, 2:589–90), Joy, after mentioning that he had received neither mail nor emolument, noted: "We have a report that Mr. Smith retires. I have therefore lately covered some of my Letters, as In the pres⟨ent⟩ Case, for him to you" (DNA: RG 59, CD, Copenhagen).

2. *PJM-PS*, 2:574, 589–90.

3. See Peter Carl Jessen to Joy, 27 Nov. 1810 (1 p.; in French), stating that he had placed Joy's explanations relating to the cases of the *Ellen Maria* and the *Hannah*, condemned by a prize court, before the king. The king had taken them into consideration and referred them to the chancellor for final determination (DNA: RG 59, CD, Copenhagen).

4. See Joy to Rosenkrantz, 11 Dec. 1810 (2 pp.; in French), forwarding an extract relating to prize law and thanking him for his efforts on behalf of the *Ellen Maria*. This note may have been intended to reinforce points Joy had made in a longer letter to Rosenkrantz on 8 Dec. 1810, a press copy of which Joy had also sent to JM (DLC; 7 pp.).

5. Joy's 13 and 14 Dec. letters to Smith (4 and 5 pp. respectively) were devoted to discussions of his efforts on behalf of American ship captains before Danish prize courts and other Danish officials (DNA: RG 59, CD, Copenhagen).

From John Mitchell Mason

SIR,   NEW YORK 20th. Decr. 1810

I have the honour of acknowledging the receipt of the two notes which you were so condescending as to write me relative to a constitution for the United States drawn up by the late Gen. Hamilton.[1] I much regret that your kindness should have occasioned you so much trouble. Had I suspected it, I should have forborn a request the granting of which was to confer a favour upon me at the expence of inconvenience to yourself. Among the papers of Gen. Hamilton which have come to my hand I have not been able to discover the original draught[2] which you suppose he must have retained. Should my search among some other papers, which I expect to get in a few days, prove equally unfortunate, I shall very gratefully avail myself of your obliging offer of a copy from the one which you possess.

Permit me to tender my best respects to Mrs Madison; and to assure you of the high considera⟨tion⟩ with which I have the honour to be, Sir, your most obedt. & obliged hble servt

J. M. MASON

RC (DLC). Damaged at lower corners. Docketed by JM.

1. See JM to Mason, 5 Feb. 1810 (*PJM-PS*, 2:219–20 and n. 1). JM probably wrote to Mason again sometime after he had received John Wayles Eppes's letter of 1 Nov. 1810 (*PJM-PS*, 2:609–10). If so, his letter has not been found.

2. At a later time JM placed an asterisk here and noted in the lower left margin: "*after-wards discovered—see ⟨lett⟩er from Doc⟨to⟩r Eustis." Following this a pencil note "of April" has been added.

§ From Joseph Coppinger. *20 December 1810, No. 6 Cheapside Street, New York.* Anticipates arguments that might have been made in opposition to his letter of 15 [16] Dec. advocating the establishment of a national brewery in Washington. Believes Washington is the best place for this establishment; the production of "good Malt liquor of every Kind *there* . . . would necessarily induce a spirit of emu-lation as well as imitation in most other points of the Union" as congressmen re-ported it to their constituents. Predicts the population will soon grow to support the establishment and adds that "the more generally breweries are encouraged, . . . the more effectually health and Morals are secured. . . . Those families who are in the custom of using Malt liquor freely as their common drink all summer, Keep and preserve their health whilst their less fortunate neighbours who are deprived of it, are the victims of fever and disease." Corrects some of his earlier statements about the amounts of capital and revenue involved in the English brewing trade.

RC (DLC). 2 pp. Docketed by JM.

§ From William Thornton. *20 December 1810, Washington.* Encloses a letter from Mr. Eccleston that arrived in the U.S. some time ago.[1] Has heard rumors of a change "in the Situation of the Post Master General" and mentions that his friend Mr. Fairfax, a gentleman of integrity and "firmly attached to the Government," would be gratified to receive the appointment.

RC (DNA: RG 59, LAR, 1809–17, filed under "Fairfax"). 1 p. On 22 Dec. 1810 Ferdinand Fairfax wrote to JM announcing that he had made arrangements to reside most of the year in Washington and would gladly accept any office JM cared to give him (ibid.; 1 p.).

1. Thornton probably enclosed Daniel Eccleston to JM, 1 Oct. 1810 (see *PJM-PS*, 2:569).

§ From Dayton Leonard. *21 December 1810, Tompkins, Delaware County, New York.* "I have been sick these twenty one years Just so much strength as to be able to keep a bout and ride a bout but unable to do any labour and always very uncomfortable." Describes his plan for a perpetual motion machine conceived of in 1800. "I do now request you sir to use your influence to obtain some money of congress and for the world's sake sir I hope you will not neglect me it is out of my powr to tell what it will cost but I think three hundred dollars will facilitate the work perhaps less." If a reference is required, his neighbors may not be willing to provide one as they are "great unbelievers they argue very powrful as they imagine some say it cannot be made to go because so many skilful men have tryed and failed." Does not presume to judge the future from the past and reminds JM of the tale of the fox and the turtle. Trusts that the people will not begrudge a small sum "to oblige an unhappy fellow creature." The money can be sent by General [Erastus] Root.

RC (DLC). 4 pp.

§ From José Miguel Pey. *Ca. 22 December 1810, Santa Fe de Bogotá.* The political changes occurring in "the Capital of this New Kingdom and its Provinces since the 20th July of this year"[1] have made it possible to open communications with JM, "now that we are free from the odious restrictions, which kept us as it were insulated in the middle of the world. From this time forward we may extend our views, and offer our Ports to the other nations of the world, among whom we shall know how to distinguish the Inhabitants of New Albion, who have presented to us the form of a New Government, which perhaps may lead to the Happiness of the whole American Continent."

JM knows "the necessity we are under of counting on our own proper resources in this unhappy period" following the removal of the sovereign from his throne and with the imminent prospect of Spain yielding to the emperor of France, there being blockaded in Cadiz a government without popular support and unable to provide security to these remote dominions. "It will not be possible to keep ourselves in apathy and indif[f]erent in this dangerous situation, liable to be involved in the ruin of the Mother Country." The people have therefore agreed "to form for themselves a Gov[e]rnment which might save them under such terrible circumstances."

Santa Fe has created a Supreme Junta which has invited the provinces of the kingdom to send representatives to the capital and which anticipates the honor of offering respects to JM and the "illustrious Congress in the United States over which Y[our] E[xcellency] worthily presides with whom this Government desires to establish the most friendly correspondence." They will be fortunate if they can follow the example set by the U.S. and adopt a "political form which founded in equity, may make us worthy of being the allies of that Great Republic." Hopes that JM will assist in this difficult undertaking and that "in conformity to the liberal and wise principles which govern these States Y E will condescend to contribute to the Happiness of all the Continental People of America who fix their Eyes on your Exy and rest their hopes on the reciprocal ties of the new governments which . . . are about to be established in this part of the world, of which, that formed by your illustrious Nation is the root & foundation."

A "Brilliant field" is opening on which JM may display "the resources of your great mind—for the benefit of al⟨l⟩ the People of America who are about to ar[r]ive from the political abasement in which they have until now been kept: for these holy purposes they promise themselves the powerful assistance of the People who opened the way to Happiness for america."

"Y E having gone over the Road which we are about to travel may illumine for us our path and teach us to avoid those Precipices, which from want of experience, we might not be aware of." Assures JM of their respect for him and the U.S. Congress, with whom they wish "to strengthen the ties of Friendship & political relations which may lay a foundation for the stability of this new government which will always profess the closest adhesion to the Mother Republic."[2]

Translation of RC (DNA: RG 59, NFL, Colombia). 4 pp. In the hand of John Graham. Undated; conjectural date here assigned on the basis of internal evidence (see n. 1). RC (ibid.) in Spanish; docketed by Graham with the note, "An Address from the Junta of Santa Fe to the President of the United States." Translation printed in Manning, *Diplomatic Correspondence of the United States concerning the Independence of the Latin-American Nations*, 2:1165–66.

1. After some popular disturbances against the Spanish viceroy, the *cabildo* of Santa Fe de Bogotá on 20 July 1810 established the Supreme Junta of the New Kingdom of New Granada as a temporary ruling authority in the name of Ferdinand VII, pending the drafting of a constitution to protect the public welfare. At that time José Miguel Pey was elected vice president of the junta, which in September 1810 issued an invitation to the provinces of New Granada to send delegates to a congress to organize a federal system of government. That congress met in Santa Fe de Bogotá on 22 Dec. 1810, and José Miguel Pey addressed its members in a speech celebrating the events of 20 July 1810. The congress then formally rejected the authority of the Supreme Council of the Regency in Spain (Jesús María Henao and Gerardo Arrubla, *History of Colombia*, trans. J. Fred Rippy [Chapel Hill, N.C., 1938], pp. 199–211).

2. It is uncertain when JM received this letter. William R. Manning and Raimundo Rivas suggest that it was enclosed in an undated note, probably written in November or December 1811 and sent by Pedro de la Lastra to Secretary of State Monroe (see Manning, *Diplomatic Correspondence of the United States concerning the Independence of the Latin-American Nations*, 2:1165; Raimundo Rivas, *Historia diplomatica de Colombia, 1810–1934* [Bogotá, 1961], p. 19). However, since Onís reported to his superiors that Pedro de la Lastra departed the U.S. for Cartagena in August 1811, it is possible that JM received the letter, along with other correspondence from Santa Fe de Bogotá, in mid-August 1811 (see Griffin, *The United States and the Disruption of the Spanish Empire*, p. 64 n. 118; JM to Monroe, 15 Aug. 1811, and n. 1).

From Erick Bollmann

Sir,   PHILADELPHIA Dec. 23d. 1810

I take the liberty of sending Your Excellency a Copy of a trifling Production which may perhaps derive some Interest from the Circumstances of the Moment.[1]

If You will receive it with Indulgence and on Perusal should think well of it I shall be highly gratified. I have the Honour to be with great Respect Your Excellency's most obedient St.

ERICK BOLLMANN[2]

RC (DLC).

1. Bollmann probably enclosed a copy of his recently published pamphlet *Paragraphs on Banks* (Philadelphia, 1810; Shaw and Shoemaker 19584). The following day, 24 Dec. 1810, the Philadelphia Chamber of Commerce sent Congress a lengthy petition calling for the recharter of the Bank of the United States (see *ASP, Finance*, 2:453–54).

2. Justus Erick Bollmann (1769–1821) was a physician, born in Hanover, who, in 1796, came to Philadelphia where he established a business house with his brother, Ludwig. He

remained in the U.S. until 1814, engaging in a variety of commercial and speculative enterprises. His interests in New Orleans and Mexico made him a suitable agent for the schemes of Aaron Burr in 1806–7, but Brig. Gen. James Wilkinson arrested him and dispatched him to Washington in January 1807 to inform the administration about Burr's activities. JM was present, taking extensive notes, during Bollmann's interview with Jefferson where he divulged information in his possession about the Burr conspiracy (Fritz Redlich, "The Business Activities of Eric Bollmann," *Bulletin of the Business Historical Society*, 17 [1943]: 81–91, 103–12; "Burr's Conspiracy: Bollman's Communication," 23 Jan. 1807, Madison, *Letters* [Cong. ed.], 2:393–401).

From William Madison

DEAR BROTHER   25th Decr. 1810

    I return you the inclosed. We have recd letters from Doctr Buckner,[1] who is Alfred's room mate & constant attendant, which continue to cherish hopes of his recovery: the Doct informs us that the wound was nearly healed—& the cough nearly left him. As soon as I was advised of the Operation on Alfred—I came home with a view of visitg him. He had previously written for his brother Robert—but afterwards forbid it as Doctr Buckner acted the part of a friend & Relative. Unless some unfavourable accounts should be ⟨r⟩ecd. I shall return to Richmd the latter end of next ⟨week⟩. With much difficulty I have obtained from the Mill 92 Bls of your Flour—82 of which are sent down. The holladays will interrupt the Waggons a few days. Every effort shall be used to get the Flour to Market as fast as possible. My Mother has lost Phil. He died with a mortification in his throat. Give our Affectionate Regards to my Sister & accept them yourself.

                                               WM. MADISON

RC (NjP). Damaged by removal of seal. Cover dated 25 Dec. at Orange Court House. Enclosure not found.

    1. William Madison may have been referring to Dr. Horace Buckner of Culpeper County, Virginia, who was also a neighbor of Isaac Winston, Jr. (*VMHB*, 30 [1922]: 68; Torrence, *Edward Pleasants Valentine Papers*, 3:1627).

From Enoch Parsons

SIR   MARYVILLE 25th December 1810

    As it is contemplated to attempt bringing before you for decision an occurrance between the creek and cherokee Nation of Indians which transpired in the spring of 1809[1] Candour impels me to communicate an attempt of the injured Party for redress through me as their agent to Col Benjamin Hawkins principal agent of Indian affairs South of Ohio.

Sir the vouchers which will be submitted to you will explicitly evince that a large quantity of spirits and other property was owned by James McIntosh a son of quotiquisque and others was intended to be conveyed by McIntosh a cherokee to the Mobile market by way of the Coose river one of natures highways And that the enterprize was sanctioned by Col Meigs the agent of the cherokees and not intended to dispose of any of the cargo to the Natives. That McIntosh had proceeded as far down the Coose as the Pathkillers the principal Chief of the Cherokee Nation when he was intercepted by a number of creek Indians and robbed of his cargo entirely. It clearly appears that McIntosh was at the time on cherokee ground by settlement and that there will be no other criterion for the asscertainment of boundary but settlement and that McIntosh and his property was justly protected by the principal cherokee and the taking was a wanton violation of the rights of the Cherokee Nation and that the offer of the banditti to share the spoil with the cherokee Nation was only equaled by the outrage.

Sir In April last Messieurs Houston & Blackburn who originally owned the property and whom had Interested young McIntosh in the same and made him supercargo prevailed on me as I was passing through the southern Country to visit Col Hawkins and deposit with that Gentleman their Vouchers and require him to decide and report thereon with all the expedition convenience would permit. On my arrival I found Col Hawkins just recovering from a strong indisposition & unable to do business except verbally. But Col Hawkins promised to decide on the subject in a few days and to report forthwith to the proper department and for the information of the Parties concerned to forward to me by mail a copy of his proceedings (immediately). In conversation Col Hawkins alledged that the sale of a small portion of the property to the hands who aided McIntosh where he first embarked on the Coose and in transporting the same from the Highwasse river to the Coose was exceptionable and made the property legal prize by the intercourse Laws which was insisted did not apply against a Cherokee and if so did not make the property legal prize to the creeks as the transaction was without their boundary and could not have confiscated it to any other than the Nation within whose boundary it was done. More over the act of Congress prescribed a penalty for certain trespasses on Indian territory and that in that case if any thing nothing more than the penalty could be incurred. But inasmuch as McIntosh was a cherokee and part owner of the property and the act authorized by the cherokee agent as he admits a passport and observes the enterprize was both laudable and just there was no colour for the idea moreover to compare McIntosh to a common carrier by the laws of England the owners would have an undoubted right to the property or the value from the Robbers and McIntosh and the Cherokee Nation upon that principal fairly entitled to pay and that the most remote Tribe of Indians within the U S would have been as well justified in the seizure as the Creeks as when they transcended their bounds they had no line at which they shou'd cease. Col Hawkins said he had given the creeks in the quarter the mischief was done instruction to stop the boats and prevent their descending the Coose river and to allow the owners to return with the whole of their property and by all means to allow them Sufficient time for that purpose but that they had evidently transcended his orders and that the Chief who commanded that party of the Creeks was a rash man and had been cashiered since and the creeks had certainly exceeded all bounds on that occasion Col Hawkins added a Passport purporting to be signed by him had been Forged and McIntosh admitts some irregularity by him relative to the same. But Col H. also observed it had not been done by any one of the Party that it was so well executed that none of the party were capable of the act (But it is certain the passport which was spurious had not been used as they had not reached the creek Territory and had no occasion for it before) and that it must have been imposed on McIntosh probably by some artfull or designing person.

Col Hawkins expressed a degree of surprize that he had not at an earlier period heard of ⟨the⟩ transaction and been furnished with the information afforded by the vouchers I deposited with him and a copy of which will be submitted to you But seemed well pleased to have them as they had removed the greater part of the suspicion he anterior to that entertained against the persons concerned in the affair and that he might be enabled to do justice to the parties and although it seemed to me impossible that the penetration of Col H should conceive justice could be attained other than by the Creek Nation remunerating the Cherokees for the loss of their property Yet no account of the decision of Col Hawkins can be obtained nor in what light that gentleman has viewed the transaction can I say. I have addressed Col Hawkins two letters on the subject but receive no answers from what motives I know not. Sir As the parties will attempt to bring the subject before you or the proper Department in quest of the justice they think they are entitled to I trust this statement will find an apology And that our members of Congress will manifest to you the great redundancy of produce of the Western Country which surcharges the home market and will not bare land carriage to the eastern markets and the difficulty of passing the mussle shoals on Tennessee and glutted situation of the Orleans market and the necessity of a passage by the mobile and its branches more especially at this crisis. Sir Please to accept the Esteem of your well wisher and humble Servant

ENOCH PARSONS[2]

RC (DNA: RG 107, LRRS, M-245:5). Enclosed in Pleasant M. Miller to Eustis, ca. 22 Jan. 1811 (ibid.). Cover dated 1 Jan. 1811 at Maryville. Docketed by a War Department clerk as received 22 Jan. 1811, with the notation "file."

1. The episode narrated by Parsons arose from the efforts of Samuel Blackburn, brother of the Presbyterian missionary Gideon Blackburn, to transport whiskey from stills in Maryville, Tennessee, to the Gulf Coast in March and April 1809. It is possible, however, that the purposes of this venture also comprehended an attempt to evade federal prohibitions on whites selling liquor to the Indians. There were no laws to prevent Indians from selling liquor to other Indians, and this may have been the reason why Samuel Blackburn and one of his partners, Robert Houston, decided to consign a cargo of some 2,200 gallons of whiskey to a young half-breed Cherokee, James McIntosh, the son of a white "countryman," John McIntosh (Quotaquskee), and formerly a pupil in Gideon Blackburn's Indian school.

After traveling through the Cherokee Nation, however, McIntosh and his party were stopped by Big Warrior as they were on the point of entering the Creek Nation on the Coosa River. Since the Creek were already disputing with the U.S. government the right of trading parties to cross their territories, they were unwilling to let McIntosh and his boats pass. They also confiscated his whiskey on the grounds that it was being illegally sold en route. Samuel Blackburn and his Tennessee supporters, who included not only Parsons but also Cherokee agent Return Jonathan Meigs and Gov. Willie Blount, then appealed to the administration for restitution of the whiskey. Their arguments included the claim that American citizens had a "natural right" to use the rivers flowing down to the Gulf Coast and that both the president and the secretary of war had tacitly condoned the efforts of Blackburn and the Cherokee to open up a trade with Mobile. On behalf of the Creek, Indian agent Benjamin Hawkins maintained that they had been within their rights to stop McIntosh's party. The dispute was never resolved (see William G. McLoughlin, "Parson Blackburn's Whiskey and the Cherokee Indian Schools, 1809–1810," *Journal of Presbyterian History*, 57 [1979]: 427–45; idem, *Cherokees and Missionaries, 1789–1839* [New Haven, 1984], pp. 79–81).

2. Enoch Parsons was the attorney general for eastern Tennessee.

From the Right Reverend James Madison

MY DEAR SIR,   WILLIAMSBURG Decr 26h 1810

To the Multitude of Addresses, which you will, no Doubt, receive in Consequence of the Death of Judge Griffin,[1] I feel great Reluctance in making an Addition; but, persuaded as I am that your Selection of a Successor will be guided by no other Consideration, than the relative Fitness of the different Characters, which may pass in Review before you, I take the Liberty of mentioning, that Judge Tucker would willingly accept of the office held by Mr Griffin. The Talents of Mr. Tucker, I beleive, are known to you; they, certainly, are inferior to those possessed by few, if any, in this State, especially, if we take our Comparison from the Bench. In Application to Official Duties, in the excellent Qualities of his Heart, and in the Soundness of his republican Principles, he is inferior to none. Of the present Administration he is a warm & decided Friend.

Mr. Tucker knows Nothing of this Communication; nor would I have made it, did I not think, that you only want to know who is the most fit Person to sit on the same Bench, & at the same Time, with Judge Marshall: such Mr. Tucker appears to be. With the highest Respect & Esteem I am, Dr sir Yrs truly & affy

J MADISON

RC (DNA: RG 59, LAR, 1809–17, filed under "Tucker").

1. Cyrus Griffin, the federal district judge for Virginia, died on 14 Dec. 1810. JM nominated John Tyler as his successor on 2 Jan. 1811. After Tyler died, JM then named St. George Tucker to the position on 18 Jan. 1813 (see Jefferson to JM, 25 May 1810, *PJM-PS*, 2:356–57 and n. 1; *Senate Exec. Proceedings*, 2:316).

§ From Robert Gardner. *26 December 1810, Boston.* Assuming that trade with France will be renewed, he offers himself as a candidate for any consular vacancy in that country. "I am a native American—educated to Mercantile Business, & have been much employed in its most intricate parts." Refers JM to his friend Mr. Cutts, who will present this application.[1]

RC (DNA: RG 59, LAR, 1809–17, filed under "Gardner"). 1 p.

1. On 22 Apr. 1811 Richard Cutts wrote to James Monroe, reminding him that the previous winter he had deposited in the State Department several recommendations of Gardner for a French consulship. Cutts recalled that "the Situation of our affairs with that Country, then, seemed to preclude any new appointments" (ibid.).

§ From John Mullowny.[1] *26 December 1810, Philadelphia.* Sends JM a pitcher made at the Washington Pottery in Philadelphia, a business he opened on 4 Mar. with an Englishman, James Charleton. The pottery has about $15,000 in capital and makes about $150 per week. It will be extended when workmen and boys who can be "taught the art of manufacturing as in England" are obtained. Solicits JM's support for the enterprise.

RC (DLC). 1 p. Misdated 26 Oct. 1809 in *Index to the James Madison Papers.*

1. Mullowny, who had served as a lieutenant in the U.S. Navy, 1798–1801, was a merchant and shipowner in Philadelphia. He had corresponded earlier with JM about captures made during the Quasi-War with France. The pitcher was delivered by Capt. Caleb Hand (Callahan, *List of Officers of the Navy*, p. 397; JM to Mullowny, 7 Dec. 1804 and 5 Feb. 1807 [DNA: RG 59, DL]; receipt from Caleb Hand, 21 Dec. 1810 [DLC]).

From Benjamin Rush

DEAR SIR,   PHILADELPHIA, Decr: 28th. 1810.

I write to you at the request of your nephew to acknowledge for him the receipt of your letter sent under cover of mine.[1] He is upon the Whole better, but as yet not in a condition to employ his pen. There has been a second discharge of a fluid from his breast induced by a spontaneous opening of the puncture made by Dr Physick. He has been releived by it. We are using remedies to prevent a reaccumulation of it. He begs to be rememberd Affectionately to you and all the branches of your family. Health, respect & friendship! from Dear Sir yours truly

BENJN: RUSH

PS: I attended the late General Peter Muhlenberg in his last illness.[2] During my Attendance upon him he informed me that while the funding System was the Subject of discussion by Congress, a Gentleman came to his lodgings and offered him two hundred thousand dollars upon a Credit of a whole year at ten Shillings in the pound upon his single note without an endorser. He instantly rejected the offer. Before the year expired, he added that the funded Certificates sold at 25 shillings in the pound. This I recollect was the case. I wish this fact may be preserved with the history of that most flagitious Act of national Swindling. It was the prolific Source of all the Vices that have been introduced into our country by Banks, and lotteries and land Speculations. In short it was a national precedent, for private injustice. It was a bold and profligate violation of the first words in the Constitution of the United states which was "to establish justice." Cooled and indifferent as I have been for many years to public objects and events, I cannot think for a moment of that Act of national robbery without feeling the same indignation which I expressed to you in my letters while the Act was under litigation.[3] All this is inter nos. The communications from Genl. Muhlenberg may be mentioned, but without my name.

RC (DLC: Rives Collection, Madison Papers). Docketed by JM, "Bribe offered to Genl. P. Muhlenberg for his vote in favor of funding system."

1. JM's letter to Alfred Madison has not been found. His letter to Benjamin Rush was probably that written on 18 Dec.

2. Gen. John Peter Gabriel Muhlenberg, who had served in the First and Third Congresses, died in 1807.

3. See *PJM*, 13:45–47, 67–70, 97–99, 145–46, 188–89, 279–80.

§ To the House of Representatives. *28 December 1810.* Communicates a report from the secretary of state in compliance with the House resolution of 21 Dec. 1810.[1]

RC and enclosure (DNA: RG 233, President's Messages, 11A-D1). RC 1 p. In a clerk's hand, signed by JM. Enclosure (21 pp.) is a 28 Dec. report with three sections, marked A, B, and C, on the duties imposed by France on imports carried in American vessels (printed in *ASP, Foreign Relations*, 3:400–403). The report was received by the House on 31 Dec. and referred to the Committee on Commerce and Manufactures and the committee on foreign relations (*Annals of Congress*, 11th Cong., 3d sess., 478).

1. On 21 Dec. the House of Representatives adopted a resolution proposed by Jacob Swoope of Virginia requesting the president to forward information "relative to the duties as at present imposed by the Emperor of France, on all articles, the importation of which into the dominions of France is permitted on board of American vessels; and whether *all* articles, the *produce of the American soil*, will, on their exportation from the United States, obtain a free admission into the ports of France; and, if not, what articles of said produce are prohibited" (*Annals of Congress*, 11th Cong., 3d sess., 459).

The 28 Dec. report submitted by the secretary of state established that France, under an imperial decree of 15 July 1810, only allowed the importation of certain enumerated American products under highly restrictive conditions and, as Robert Smith observed in his correspondence with Turreau on the subject, that "the importation into France of cotton and tobacco, the produce of the United States, is, at this time, specially and absolutely prohibited" (*ASP, Foreign Relations*, 3:402).

From Henry Middleton

SIR,   CHARLESTON SOUTH CAROLINA 31st. Decr. 1810.

The Legislature of this State has directed me by resolution, a certified Copy whereof I have the honour herewith to transmi⟨t,⟩ "To request the President of the United States to apply for and purchase by Treaty from the Cherokee Nation of Indians, all the Lands which they claim within the limits of this State."

On the subject of this request, I beg leave to state in explanation, that the territory in question lies in the northwestern corner of our State, and was reserved as hunting ground for the Cherokee Nation in the Treaty entered into with them in the year 1777.[1]

Your early attention to this request will be highly gratifying to our citizens, and the success of such negotiation as you may judge proper to commence cannot but redound to the benefit of the agricultural interests of the State—part of these lands to which the Indian title has not been yet extinguished is cultivable, and they form collectively one of the most elevated and healthful portions of our Country. I have the honor to be, Sir, with sentiments of the highest consideration & respect, Yr. most obt. Sert.

HENRY MIDDLETON.[2]

RC (DNA: RG 75, LRIA). Enclosure not found.

1. The Cherokee finally ceded this tract of some 94,000 acres for $5,000 in a treaty signed at Washington, on 22 Mar. 1816 (see *ASP, Indian Affairs*, 2:88–91).

2. Henry Middleton (1770–1846) had been elected governor of South Carolina on 8 Dec. 1810. He served through 1812 (N. Louise Bailey et al., eds., *Biographical Directory of the South Carolina Senate, 1776–1985* [3 vols.; Columbia, S.C., 1986], 2:1102–3).

§ To the House of Representatives. *31 December 1810*. Communicates a supplemental report from the secretary of state with information received since his message of 28 Dec. 1810.

RC and enclosure (DNA: RG 233, President's Messages, 11A-D1). RC 1 p. In a clerk's hand, signed by JM. Enclosure (5 pp.) is Robert Smith to JM, 31 Dec. 1810, forwarding a letter from John Armstrong to Robert Smith, 29 Dec. 1810 (marked D), which enclosed a translation from the minutes of the French Council of Commerce, 12 Sept. 1810, including the listing of duties on various articles of American produce to be imported into France (printed in *National Intelligencer*, 1 Jan. 1811).

§ From Benjamin Henry Latrobe. *31 December 1810, Washington.* Encloses a copy of his report on the public buildings. Will call on JM in a few days to see if any part of the report appears improper to lay before Congress or requires further information.

FC (MdHi: Latrobe Letterbooks). 1 p. Latrobe apparently enclosed a draft of his 28 Dec. report, the final version of which was enclosed in his 11 Jan. 1811 letter to JM.

From William Tatham

Sir,   January 1st. 1811.

Observing that Government are now occupied on the claim of the United States to West Florida,[1] & having some idea of that subject through my researches in London, at the instance of our late Minister Mr. Monroe, I shall be pardoned for offering to the executive aid certain evidences tending to strengthen our pretensions—viz.

1st. An old Map (heretofore mentioned to you)[2] procured by me at the request of Mr. Monroe, and most probably deposited in the London office of our legation.

2dly. An old Map published by Emanuel Bowen[3] Geographer in London, in political reference to European claims, wherein the French claim to "New France," or Louisiane, is distinctly coloured—from Rio Perdido to the river Guardalope; which is the river eastwardly of the river St. Mark, in the bay of St. Louis, Mexico, comprehending the 29th. degree of latitude—north.

This map will be put into my hands by a friend, when he is assured that you want it.

3dly. An official Copy, by one of the French Engineers employed at New Orleans in the national transactions of France and Spain. This document fell into my hands in the official collection of General Montresor,[4] Engineer general of the British forces in America; and corresponds with the two former.

89

You will, I doubt not Sir, recollect the valuable collection of Florida Charts & Surveys which you have seen in my library; and the value a Report in Congress (1806)[5] has stamped on them: may I also hope that while a suffering Soldier of the Revolution is entering his sixtieth year under misfortunes which that revolution has heaped on his eve of life, (and wishes you many happy returns of the season) that you may recognize in his services, or acquisitions, enough to keep him & his infants from Starving?[6]

It will only remain to address your commands, through the Post office, Norfolk, to your well known friend & H: Servt.

WM TATHAM

RC and duplicate (DLC). RC docketed by JM. Duplicate has a postscript not on the RC: "P. S. Dated August 18th. 1809, I wrote you on this & other subjects; it may now, be well to refer to that letter. W. T." (see n. 2).

1. On 18 Dec. 1810 William Branch Giles had introduced in the Senate a bill to extend the laws in force in the Orleans Territory to that part of West Florida up to the Perdido River annexed by JM in his proclamation of 27 Oct. 1810. The Senate began debate on the measure on 27 Dec. 1810 (*Annals of Congress*, 11th Cong., 3d sess., 25, 37ff.).

2. Tatham had already offered JM much of the material relating to Florida and Louisiana in his 18 Aug. 1809 letter (calendared in *PJM-PS*, 1:332; printed in McPherson, "Letters of William Tatham," *WMQ*, 2d ser., 16 [1936]: 383–87).

3. Emanuel Bowen (d. 1767) was a map engraver to both George II and Louis XV. His "Accurate Map of North America: Describing and Distinguishing the British, Spanish, and French Dominions on this Great Continent" was first published in 1755.

4. John Montresor (1736–1788), like his father James Gabriel Montresor, had extensive experience as an engineer and a draftsman with British forces in North America. He was appointed chief engineer in America in 1775 and was actively involved in many campaigns in the American War for Independence until his retirement in 1779.

5. For the House report of 1 Apr. 1806 recommending an appropriation for the purchase of books, maps, and charts from Tatham's collection deemed to be of "public use" by the secretary of war, see *ASP, Miscellaneous*, 1:456–61.

6. The secretary of the navy expressed some interest in acquiring Tatham's maps, but after examining them he decided that, although "well executed," they were "drawn upon a scale too small for a public Department" (Paul Hamilton to Tatham, 18 Mar. 1811 [DNA: RG 45, Misc. Letters Received]).

§ From Robert Patterson. *1 January 1811, Philadelphia.* Forwards annual report on the operation of the Mint. Enumerates gold, silver, and copper coins struck, amounting to $1,155,868.50 in value. The Bank of the United States continues to furnish an ample supply of bullion for coinage.

RC and enclosures, two copies (DNA: RG 233, President's Messages, 11A-D1; and DNA: RG 46, Legislative Proceedings, 11A-E5); FC (DNA: RG 104, Letters Sent by the Director). Each RC 1 p. Enclosures (2 pp.; signed by Benjamin Rush) are quarterly statements of coinage struck in 1810 and an expense account of the Mint for 1810 totaling $20,753.85. RC and enclosures forwarded in JM to Congress, 7 Jan. 1811.

To Levi Lincoln

[ca. 2 January] 1811

... You will see by the commission which will be forwarded from the Department of State, that I have taken the liberty of nominating you to the Senate as successor to Judge Cushing, notwithstanding your remonstrances against a recall into the national service. I was induced to this step, not only by my personal wishes, but by those of others, between whom and yourself exists all the reciprocal respect that can add weight to them, and particularly by their persuading themselves, that your patriotism would acquiesce in an appointment, however contrary it might be to your previous inclinations. I venture to flatter myself that in this we may not be disappointed; and that, in every event, you will regard the liberty I have taken in imposing the dilemma upon you, with the indulgence due to my motives, and to the great esteem and sincere friendship of which I pray you to accept my renewed assurances. . . .

Printed extract (Benjamin Thomas Hill, ed., *The Diary of Isaiah Thomas, 1805–1828*, Transactions and Collections of the American Antiquarian Society, vols. 9–10 [2 vols.; Worcester, Mass., 1909], 1:43–44 n. 1). Printed extract dated 1811. Conjectural date here based on JM's 2 Jan. 1811 nomination of Lincoln to the Senate for appointment to the Supreme Court. The Senate confirmed the appointment the following day (*Senate Exec. Proceedings*, 2:159).

From Jonathan Russell

SIR   PARIS 2nd January 1811.

The inclosed is a sketch of a treaty and convention which, after much conversation between the Marquis of Almanara[1] his agents and myself, was drawn up & contains in my opinion the most favourable terms on which can be obtained an extinguishment of the title claimed by the actual king of spain to the whole of the territory therein mentioned. The Marquis of Almanara appeared in this business to act from a conviction that this territory was beyond the reach of his master & that it was no longer in his power to maintain its dependence on the Spanish throne. Pride & perhaps poverty, forbid him however to abandon it without a valuable consideration & the end of his conferences with me was evidently to ascertain what in my opinion was the *maximum* which the United States would be willing in existing circumstances to allow for it. On my part I endeavoured to depreciate its value—& the title which King Joseph could give to it. From the first I adhered to two leading principles—vizt—that the right of the United States to the territory between the Perdido & the Sabine should not be called in question & that for the cession of Florida to the Eastward of the Perdido an equivalent should be found in the vacant lands of the territory thus ceded and in the vacant lands of the disputed territory laying between the Sabine & the Rio Bravo. This basis being settled the quantity & location of the land to be reserved by the King of Spain formed the principal subject to be discussed. The result of this discussion will appear in the plan of the convention herein inclosed.

I have reason to beleive that the Marquis of Almanara proceeded in this business with the knowledge of the Emperor. In the course of it I was sorry however to perceive the agency of two men whose established character for extensive speculation might render suspicious the fairest negociation. These two men were David Parish & Daniel Parker.[2] The reputation of the first I beleive to be unblemished but it is said the second has sometimes made those sacrifices to interest which honest men avoid. This man had the indiscretion to observe to me one day that he expected a handsome share in the transaction & looking at me significantly "I intend" says he "that all my friends who aid in the operation shall be provided for." I felt too well his meaning but passing coldly to another part of the subject I endeavoured to appear to disregard it. I am however to this moment puzzled to decide whether the Marquis of Almanara originated at this time the discussion and sought these men for agents to raise funds out of the reserved lands—or whether they originated it & brought him forward merely to aid in their purposes of speculation. To decide this however cannot be important as far as it does not affect the terms of the bargain. I satisfied myself that the twenty-five millions of acres were to be converted into money for the spanish Government but that the seven millions were to be used as a *bonus* for Almanara & his coadjutors at court in obtaining the ratification of the treaty & for the Gentlemen above mentioned. The loan was partly also to be distributed in this way & partly to be appropriated to surveying the lands. I have no doubt that *two millions* of dollars *down* would procure all the title which King Joseph can give to the Floridas & run our boundary line from the mouth of the Bravo to the mouth of the Cumberland.

It does not become me to give an opinion upon the propriety of treating with him & thereby recognizing him as king of Spain & in doing so provoke perhaps hostilities with the Regency & its allies but I have felt it my duty to lay before you either directly or indirectly all that I may learn or in which I may be concerned while I am charged with the affairs of the American legation here. In my conversations with the Marquis of Almanara I distinctly & repeatedly declared to him that I was without the shadow of authority to treat for the Floridas or any other territory & that whatever I might agree to would not even be entitled to the notice much less to the sanction of my government. On his part also he avowed that he was without authority but he said that he would take the project of the treaty & convention to Madrid and lay it before his King. He left here a few weeks since & we have already heard of his arrival at Valadolid.

I should have written on this subject by the Commodore Rogers but I feared, should she fall into the hands of the English, that the discovery of my conversations with Almanara might lead to unpleasant consequences. I do not address myself to the secretary of state as I do not wish to give to what I have done an official character—but I communicate it to you, & to you only, knowing it to be my duty during my brief residence here to reveal every circumstance of my conduct & hoping, if I be guilty of any indiscretion, that I shall be judged with indulgence. I am Sir with the highest respect Your faithful & Obt Servt.

Jona Russell

N.B. I ought to have said to you that the marquis of Almanara is Minister of Interior to King Joseph.

RC (DLC); FC (RPB-JH: Russell Papers). RC docketed by JM. FC misdated 1810 by Russell. Enclosure not found. Minor differences between the RC and the FC have not been noted.

 1. Joseph Bonaparte, king of Spain, had sent the marquis de Almenara to Paris in mid-1810 in an unsuccessful attempt to dissuade Napoleon from imposing direct military rule on the northern regions of the kingdom in order to pay the costs of supporting the French army (Lovett, *Napoleon and the Birth of Modern Spain*, 2:530, 532–33).
 2. For a discussion of Daniel Parker and his long-standing interest in the Floridas, see Egan, *Neither Peace nor War*, pp. 63–65.

To Congress

Confidential
Washington January 3d 1811

I communicate to Congress, in confidence, a letter of the 2d of December, from Governor Folch of West Florida, to the Secretary of State;[1] and another of the same date, from the same, to John McKee.[2]

I communicate, in like manner, a letter from the British Chargè d'affaires, to the Secretary of State, with the answer of the latter.[3] Altho' the letter can not have been written in consequence of any instruction from the British Government, founded on the late order for taking possession of the portion of West Florida, well known to be claimed by the United States; altho' no communication has ever been made by that Government to this, of any stipulation with Spain, contemplating an interposition which might so materially affect the United States, and altho' no call can have been made by Spain, in the present instance, for the fulfilment of any such subsisting engagement; yet the spirit and scope of the document, with the accredited source from which it proceeds, required that it should not be withheld from the consideration of Congress.

Taking into view the tenor of these several communications, the posture of things with which they are connected, the intimate relation of the country adjoining the United States Eastward of the River Perdido to their security and tranquility, and the peculiar interest they otherwise have, in its destiny; I recommend to the consideration of Congress, the seasonableness of a declaration, th⟨at⟩ the United States, could not see, without serious inquietude, any part of a neighbouring territory in which they have, in different respects, so deep and so just a concern, pass from the hands of Spain, into those of any other Foreign power.

I recommend to their consideration, also, the expediency of authorizing the Executive to take temporary possession of any part or parts of the said territory, in pursuance of arrangements, which may be desired by the Spanish authorities; and for making provision for the Government of the same, during such possession.[4]

The wisdom of Congress, will at the same time determine, how far it may be expedient to provide for the event of a subversion of the Spanish authorities, within the territory in question, and an apprehended occupancy thereof by any other foreign power.

JAMES MADISON

RC and enclosures (DNA: RG 46, TP, Florida). RC in the hand of Edward Coles, signed by JM. For enclosures, see nn. 1, 2, and 3.

1. JM enclosed a translation of Vicente Folch's letter to Robert Smith, 2 Dec. 1810 (2 pp.; printed in *ASP, Foreign Relations*, 3:398), offering to deliver West Florida to the U.S. "provided I do not receive Succour from the Havanna or Vera Cruz during the present month; or that His Excellency, the Marquis of Someruelos, . . . should not have opened directly a negociation on this Point." Folch declared he had no alternative to this step to spare his province "from the Ruin which threatens it," but he urged the U.S. government to order its forces at Fort Stoddert to compel the "Party under the command of Reuben Kemper to retire within the Limits of the District of Baton Rouge; intimating to him that if, in future, he should repeat his Incursions in the Districts of Mobile & Pensacola, the Troops of the United States, joined to the Spanish Troops, will use force to keep them back." Folch also pointed out that Kemper's party had been "recruited, armed and provisioned" within the U.S. Should his proposition be accepted, the governor concluded, he would treat with some authorized person to arrange for the evacuation of West Florida.

2. In his 2 Dec. 1810 letter to John McKee (2 pp.; printed ibid., 3:399), Folch explained his reasons for writing to Robert Smith with a proposal to deliver West Florida to the U.S., and he requested McKee to convey duplicates of his letter to Washington—one copy by mail and the other in person with an "eye witness" account of the situation. Also filed with the RC is a copy of McKee's 5 Dec. 1810 letter to Eustis (1 p.; printed ibid.), in which McKee enclosed Folch's letters to Smith and himself and announced his intention to proceed to Washington immediately.

3. In a 15 Dec. 1810 letter, John Philip Morier had protested to Robert Smith the American decision to take possession of West Florida (3 pp.; printed ibid.). Describing the U.S. claim to the province as "manifestly doubtful," Morier asked why the administration had re-

sorted to force rather than to negotiations with Spain, and he dismissed those Americans who were attempting to subvert Spanish authority in the region as "a band of desperados who are here known by the contemptuous appellation of Land-jobbers." Morier declared that his sovereign had a "deep and lively interest" in Spain's affairs and that he could not "see with indifference any attack upon her interests in America." On that basis, he requested the U.S. government to make such explanation of its conduct "as will at once convince His Majestys Government of the pacific disposition of the United States towards His Majesty's Allies the Spaniards." The British chargé repeated this request on 22 Dec. 1810 (1 p.; printed ibid., 3: 400), and on 28 Dec. Robert Smith responded that documents before the public made it clear that "no hostile or unfriendly purpose is entertained towards Spain" (1 p.; printed ibid.). Smith declined any further discussion of Morier's letter with the remark that the American minister in London had "been enabled to give to your Government whatever explanations may comport with the frankness and the Spirit of Conciliation, which have been invariably manifested on the part of the United States."

4. After several days' debate behind closed doors, both houses of Congress, on 15 Jan. 1811, agreed on a resolution that the U.S., "under the peculiar circumstances of the existing crisis, cannot, without serious inquietude, see any part of the said territory pass into the hands of any foreign Power; and that a due regard to their own safety compels them to provide, under certain contingencies, for the temporary occupation of the said territory." On the same day, Congress also approved an act authorizing the president to "take possession of, and occupy" Spanish territory east of the Perdido River in the event of an arrangement being made with the local authorities to deliver the region to the U.S., or in the event of an attempted occupation by any foreign power. The president was authorized to employ any part of the U.S. Army and Navy he deemed necessary, and $100,000 was appropriated to cover the costs. Should the territory come into the possession of the U.S., the president was also authorized to establish a temporary government until Congress made other provisions. On 3 Mar. 1811, Congress passed, and JM signed, a further act stating that neither the resolution of 15 Jan. 1811 nor the act of the same date be "printed or published, until the end of the next session of Congress, unless directed by the President of the United States" (*Annals of Congress*, 11th Cong., 3d sess., 370–80, 1117–48; *U.S. Statutes at Large*, 3:471–72).

From Benjamin Henry Latrobe

SIR,   WASHINGTON January 3d. 1811

In obedience to your directions that I should furnish to You all the information on the subject of the expenditure of the appropriation of May 1t. 1810, in my possession, I have to report to you as follows:

In my report d. Decr. 11th. 1809,[1] I stated, that although the estimate submitted by me on Decr. 1st. 1808, of the sum requisite for the court room and Library has not been considered in the appropriation, it had been absolutely necessary to carry up the court room & offices on the East side of the North wing of the Capitol in order to support the Senate chamber & committee rooms which are immediately over them. This expenditure is stated to have been taken into consideration in the estimate* of 40.000$ *necessary for defraying the expense of completing the courtroom and the Offices of*

*In my report d. Decr. 11h. 1809

the Judiciary on the East side of the North wing, completing the Senate chamber, & for the Library. The Courtroom & the offices of the Judiciary on the East side, were then completed, the Senate chamber required to its completion a sum not exceeding, 2.500$.—and the Library was not begun. I hoped to have carried up the solid work under cover of the present roof during the Season of 1810. 20.000$ however only were granted, and the whole appropriation for the public buildings was made liable to the expenses already incurred. The principal part of these expenses were created by the necessity of constructing the Courtroom & Offices under the Senate chamber.

The expense of fitting up, & furnishing the court Room having never been estimated by me, or contemplated by the words of any Law making appropriation for the public buildings, I took no steps whatever to fit up & furnish the room, untill the propriety of so doing was urged by the Judges of the courts who had been obliged to hold their sittings at a Tavern. I then understood that the contingent fund of the Judiciary was liable to this expense, the accounts being properly certified by the Judges.

Under these impressions the Courtroom was fitted up & furnished, & the accounts being made up were submitted to the Chief Justice of the U. States, whose letter & certificate is enclosed.[2] On submission however to the Officers of the Treasury it was decided that these accounts should be paid out of the appropriation of May 1st. 1810, and their amount as appears by the books of the Superintendant of the city has accordingly been paid out of that fund.

This decision wholly unexpected by me, reduced the sum applicable to the public works so much that I immediately discharged all the workmen and Laborers excepting those that were necessary to render the Hall of Representatives and the Senate Chamber—which had been dismantled, capable of being occupied by the Legislature during their present session, and excepting the Artists, who being engaged under special contracts, could not be discharged by me, but who were fully apprized of the State of the funds of the public buildings. These persons therefore continue to be employed.

To these circumstances it is owing that the expenditures on the public buildings have been confined to the objects stated in my detailed report of the 28h. of Decr. 1810. I am very respectfully &c

B HENRY LATROBE, surveyor
of the public Buildings.

RC and enclosure (DNA: RG 233, President's Messages, 11A-D1); FC (MdHi: Latrobe Letterbooks). JM subsequently forwarded the RC and its enclosure to the House of Representatives in his first message of 14 Jan. 1811. For enclosure, see n. 2.

1. *PJM-PS*, 2:128.

2. Latrobe enclosed an itemized account of the sums due for furnishing and fitting up the courtroom and judiciary offices in the Capitol, to which John Marshall had added a note dated

9 June 1810 attesting to the necessity of these expenses (2 pp.) (see Van Horne, *Papers of Latrobe*, 2:865 n. 6).

§ From James Gartland. *3 January 1811, Philadelphia.* As a naturalized citizen who emigrated from Dublin because the U.S. laws and constitution were "more congenial to my feelings," thinks himself duty bound to submit a statement on the renewal of the charter for the Bank of the United States. Believes the public has not reflected on this matter, otherwise it would not support a petition "which has such a tendency of draining the Country of its Treasure & Wealth." Calculates that the bank stockholders under the last charter have averaged profits of 8 percent over and above the expenses of obtaining the charter. If the charter were to be renewed for a further twenty years, the net gain to the stockholders, at 8 percent interest compounded, would amount to $124,800,000 over the forty-year period. This is a bounty in favor of the English, which neither the English nor the French would suffer in favor of Americans.

Advocates a different banking system by which the 8 percent would benefit the U.S., with each state's capital to be invested in the legislature and to increase in proportion to its population every seventh or tenth year. This would make "one of the greatest Establishments that ever appeared" and could also provide the government with paper money in time of war. Describes a method he devised using transparent ink to prevent enemies from forging this paper. His plan supposes that eighteen states have a capital of $30 million, compounding at 8 percent annually, from which Congress could borrow $6 million at 6 percent per annum. At the end of twenty years, the government would have a net gain of $10,640,264.20 after liquidating the loan and its interest. At the renewal of the bank charter, the government would have a "respectable Capital" in new funds on which it would have to pay no interest. At 8 percent compound interest, at the end of the second twenty-year charter the government would have $27,664,686.92.

Calculates the portion the states would have in this capital according to their population and estimates that $24 million at 8 percent compound interest would increase to $62,400,000 in the first twenty years and to $162,240,000 in the second twenty years, resulting in a net gain for the states of $138,240,000. "This is the favour that those who prefer the Interest of England to that of this Country prays Congress to grant in favour of England & English Agents." Offers to convey further details of his scheme through his son, Simon Gartland, who is at Georgetown College. Describes the proposed recharter plan as "similar to that which had been advocated by the corrupt Legislatures of the Irish Parliament, that Ireland would become more powerful, rich & happy by having the whole income of the landed Property of Ireland spent in London, than by having it spent in Dublin." Argues that the plea of "necessity" to justify recharter of the present bank will always exist and will increase "at the lapse of every Cycle of 20 years which may revolve forever." If the world continues for about another three thousand years, the bank stockholders, at their present rate of earnings, would make $5,446,801,905,834,287,424 million by March 2561, "and all this would be raised on the Country without the present stockholders having one single Dollar of English Capital in the fund."

RC (DLC). 3 pp. Cover bears Gartland's note, "in Person."

§ From John Kilty. *4 January 1811, Adjutant General's Office, Annapolis.* Transmits a return of the Maryland militia for 1810 as required by the uniform militia act.

RC (DNA: RG 107, LRRS, K-27:5). 1 p. Enclosure not found.

From Ebenezer Cooley

Sir,   PARISH OF POINTE COUPÉE, Jan. 5 1811.

I have been informed that you are the Agent of Major General la Fayette in the U. States & that you have appointed Mr. Duplanty to conduct the location of the land that was assigned to him for his services in the U. States during the revolutionary war.[1]

My object therefore in writing to you is to let you know that I have been for a considerable time in actual possession of a tract of land which has been lately located by Mr. Duplanty in behalf of Major General la Fayette & that as my claim to it has always been considered as good as any in the country if it Should appear in the same light to you, any unnecessary trouble or expence relative to that location, may be saved.

I am not willing to believe that you have directed or incouraged Mr. Duplanty or any other person to indeavour to remove from thier [*sic*] plantations any of the old inhabitants who have with great difficulty & indefatigable industry improved wild lands under a full belief of having good titles.

It appears however that no exertions is wanting on the part of Mr. Duplanty to accomplish this purpose. His first attempt was to procure a rejection of my claim by the commissioners. In this he has proved successful & that too before any legal evidence of my claim was received & before any other claims of the same or a simular nature had been acted on by them.

I now beg leave to lay before you a brief account of the origin and nature of my claim.

The plantation or tract of land that I live on was rejected by the commissioners on the 16th. of April last without my being present or assigning me any reasons, & since that period Surveyed by Mr. Duplanty. This plantation I purchased on the 15th day of April 1806. of Margaret Bourgeat of the parish of pointe Coupée Widow of Doct. Joseph Bourgeat to whom it is said to have been conceded about the year 1767.

This tract of land is situated ten miles below the chafiliate fronting the Mississippi and containing 677. Acres. In the above mentioned year Docr. Bourgeat Settled and improved the said tract of land and cultivated it for five years, afterwards as an Indigo plantation then he left his Overseer on it who continued to cultivate it for Seven years afterwards; then in consequence of the unusual hight of the spring floods he was entirely driven off. The same reasons prevented him from returning for Several years and he finally concluded that it would be in vain to return untill he could procure more help to make the levée. He therefore continued on a Small plantation that belonged to his wife, in pointe Coupée untill he died, but he uniformly declared an intention of returning as soon as he could get more help to keep up the levées and open the roads above & below him.

This 677 Acres with a cypress swamp adjoining to furnish it with timber, is all the land that was ever conceded to that family consisting of the first proprieter his wife & nine children.

That this plantation always was considered and known under the former government to be the property of the said Doct. Bourgeat and his wife & that his right to it was acquired agreeable to the customs of the country & likewise that the above statement with respect to it is correct, I beg leave to refer you to Mr. Julian Poydras the delegate in congress from this Territory.

I settled on this place on the 7th. of july 1806. with full confidence of having as good a title as any in Louisiana and have cultivated it ever since as a cotton plantation and besides a clearing made by the first proprieter of Sixty acres I have added about a hundred more and have built about twenty different houses all of which are now in good repair.

If the above statements should be confirmed to your sattisfaction I am confident you would not wish to have any troublesome exertions made to deprive an individual with a young and growing family of his principle support. If however they should be persisted in by Mr. Duplanty, I beg to inform you that an attention to the interest of my family & a firm belief that my claim is such a one as aught to be confirmed agreeable to the antient customs of the country & to the acts of congress will urge me to use all the exertions in my power to retain it.

What induced the commissioner⟨s⟩ to act on & reject my claim so long ago as last April and before such evidence had been received as I had repeatedly informed them that the confirmation of my claim depended on, I am not able to say, but the general report is that it was done because I had writen unfavourably of thier proceedings to some of the officers of the general government.

I shall not trouble you with any remarks on the proceedings of the commissioners of the E. District but shall only observe that thier decision in ma[n]y cases & perticularly such as one founded on a possession of ten consecutive years (*which* were always thought to constitute as good a claim as any that could issue from the crown) have been so notoriously contrary to the antient laws General usages and customs of the former governments that it is generally believed that the assembly will at thier next meeting give some information to the general government of thier proceedings. I have the honour to be very respectfully—Sir, your most Obedient & very humble Servant

EBENR. COOLEY[2]

RC (DNA: RG 59, ML). A separate address sheet filed with the RC is postmarked Pinckneyville, 30 Jan.

    1. For the background to JM's activities as agent for Lafayette, see Madison and Lafayette's Louisiana Lands, 26 Oct. 1809, *PJM-PS*, 2:35–38.

    2. Ebenezer Cooley had been a justice of the peace at Pointe Coupee since May 1805 and a clerk of the court there since January 1806 (Carter, *Territorial Papers, Orleans*, 9:598–99, 776).

From Albert Gallatin

DEAR SIR   Saturday 5 Jany. 1811

At request of Mr Astor, I beg to be informed whether his son in law Mr Bentson can be permitted to have a passage on board the public vessel which is to take Mr Erving to Europe. I told Mr B. that I would try to ascertain the fact before Monday. I have thrown some notes on the back of Mr Astor's letter;[1] be pleased to return his English passport.

Mr Astor sent me a verbal message that in case of non renewal of the charter of the Bank U. S., all his funds & those of his friends to the amount of two millions of dollars would be at the command of Government, either in importing specie, circulating any Govern^t. paper, or in any other way best calculated to prevent any injury arising from the dissolution of the Bank. Mr Bentson told me that in this instance profit was not his object, and that he would go great lengths, partly from pride & partly from wish to see the Bank down. As there will be no time to be lost, I think that I had better open a correspondence with him on the Subject.

My cold has prevented my calling on you on both subjects. Respectfully Your obt. Servt.

ALBERT GALLATIN

RC (DLC). Docketed by JM.

    1. Gallatin evidently enclosed a letter he had received from John Jacob Astor, dated 27 Dec. 1810 (*Papers of Gallatin* [microfilm ed.], reel 22), in which Astor had requested a passage on the *John Adams* for his son-in-law, Adrian Benjamin Bentzon. Bentzon was bound for Russia on business for Astor's American Fur Company, but Astor believed that his son-in-law, who was a Danish national, could also provide George W. Erving with useful information for his mission to Denmark (see Gallatin to JM, 5 Sept. 1810, JM to Gallatin, 12 Sept. 1810, *PJM-PS*, 2:526, 527 n. 1, 536 and n. 2). On the cover of Astor's letter, Gallatin summarized

his request and raised the following questions: "Is it proper at all to grant this? Is it eligible that he should go; the object of his voyage being Russia on Mr Astor's business? Will the granting a passage be as a piece of civility to a Danish officer or of any use to Erving? If he goes, will it be better to apprize Mr Adams of his views. If we do not want him to go, I think that Astor will abstain from sending him." JM's response has not been recorded, but Bentzon not only obtained a passage on the *John Adams* but also deprived Erving of the only spare cabin on the vessel (Astor to Gallatin, 17 Jan. 1811, *Papers of Gallatin* [microfilm ed.], reel 22; James Ronda, *Astoria and Empire* [Lincoln, Nebr., 1990], pp. 76–81).

From James Neilson

SIR   BATON ROUGE 5th. Janry. 1811

In complyance with the duties which are incumbent on me, having been chosen a guardian of the rights of the People in the late State of West Florida; I deem it my duty to address you as the chief M[a]gistrate of a Great and Prosperous Nation, and who was pleased to extend the hand of friendship to a People Struling for Liberty. That being gained and Secured to us. You will please be so good as to use your Influance in Secureing to Us the rights of our lands which has been created Since the year 1803 for I can assure you that at least two thirds of the People of this Territory is concerned in what is called Grand Pré's Titles (not Moraleses Titles) for land,[1] those Titles has been created Since the year 1803 most of them in the year 1806 and 1807 by Governor Grand Pré who was then the acting Governor, and the good Subjects had the fullest confidence in all his acts, and I do not recollect that he ever granted any but to the Subjects, and many of them have been Sold from one to another Several times for a valuable consideration Some of the original owners dead, and Some of them gone away, Some of those lands which was Sold was emproved, others were not, the People were in the habit of buying and Selling, to Suit each others convenience, as they do in all other parts of the Country. The Title was simply a réquité or order of Survey Some of them Specifying the Spot of land where the warrant was to be layed—others where ever they could get vacant land; the Surveyor—Surveyed the land and put the Man in Peacable Possession— many made emprovements, and perhaps the one third or near the one half of the People of this Territory are Settled on lands of this description.

Now the Country is taken Under the purchase of Louisiana which Sweeps all those Title⟨s⟩ off at once and leaves the poor People of the country without a home or Place of refuge—or in other words destroy those Titles and you destroy the happiness of they [*sic*] People.

Secondly Public Faith and Public contracts was all destroyed by the taking of the Country, and there is upwards of Twenty thousand Dollars due from the Government to the different Individuals of the country in this

Place exclusive of what is due at two or three other Places many of the crediters are Poor and actually Stands in need of the Money—but in this case the United States will be Just for the Public Property put into their hands is worth much more than all the State Debt.

And although the Inhabitants of Florida are Generally warm friends to the Government of the United States—it can not be expected but they will look to be Secured in their Just rights and Property—let that be done, then there may be as much confidence placed in them as in any Such numerous branch of the United States. Believe me Sir to be a sincere friend and Huml. St.

JAMES NEILS⟨ON⟩[2]

RC (DLC). Docketed by JM.

1. In the period between the retrocession of Louisiana by Spain to France in 1800 and its cession to the U.S. by France in 1803, the Spanish intendant at New Orleans, Juan Ventura Morales, authorized land grants, often to large-scale speculators, in the regions of West Florida subsequently claimed by the U.S. under the terms of the Louisiana Purchase. Morales continued this policy even after the cession of Louisiana to the U.S., and the Spanish crown, refusing to recognize the American claim to West Florida, confirmed the validity of the titles. Carlos de Grand Pré, the Spanish commander at Baton Rouge until his death in 1808, also exercised the traditional prerogative of colonial executives to make land grants subject to confirmation by the crown. Generally, however, he appears to have granted small quantities of land to actual settlers, most of them Americans. As Neilson pointed out to JM, the American occupation of parts of West Florida in 1810 seemed to require a settlement of the issue of land titles, but the U.S., much to the distress of many American settlers in the region, was reluctant to recognize any Spanish land titles after 1803 for fear of undermining its own claims to West Florida. JM had long been aware of the problem, but it was not settled until after his retirement from the presidency when Congress, in 1819, finally recognized Spanish titles to land that had been both occupied and improved in the years between 1800 and 1813 (see Carter, *Territorial Papers, Orleans*, 9:67, 333, 405, 489, 492, 509, 898, 967–68; Cox, *The West Florida Controversy*, pp. 162, 174, 602, 642–43).

2. James Neilson was a settler in the Feliciana District of West Florida. When the forces of the West Florida convention seized the Spanish fort at Baton Rouge on 22–23 Sept. 1810, Neilson made an inventory of the property that had come into their possession. A week later, the convention appointed him as commissary to its armed forces, and he also served as a member of the short-lived General Assembly of the state of West Florida which had held meetings between 20 Nov. and 6 Dec. 1810 (see "Journal of the Committee of the Convention of Florida," entries for 29–30 Oct. 1810, and "Journal of the House of Representatives of the Republic of West Florida," entry for 20 Nov. 1810 [DLC: West Florida Miscellany]).

From Benjamin Henry Latrobe

SIR,   WASHINGTON, Jany. 6h. 1811

I herein enclose the letter you did me the favor to write on the 29h. septr. 1809.[1] The point which I wished to impress by quoting it is only that of the

Jury boxes, to preoccupy the ground of objection to the manner of fitting up the court room. With high respect

B Henry Latrobe

RC (DLC); FC (MdHi: Latrobe Letterbooks).

1. Letter not found.

§ From William Sinclair. *6 January 1811, Baltimore.* "You will be surprised that a stranger in a strange land presumes to address you. . . . The object of my letter is the case of Mr. [David Bailie] Warden late consul General in Paris. . . . The private history of his life, manners and character previous and subsequent to his arrival in this Country, may not have Come accurately within the sphere of your knowledge. . . . He & myself were banished together from the Country of our birth." Describes Warden's educational attainments, his study of maritime law, his acceptance into leading literary circles in France, and his authorship of several essays. States that Warden has been a U.S. citizen above five years and that his being an alien cannot be an obstacle. "Republican freedom is a charter from Nature not a boon of municipal law or National prejudice. . . . But what is his present situation—degraded from a high appointment without any alledged charge or even the suspicion of criminality." Requests that Warden's claims be fairly investigated "& if pure, to be supported."

RC (DNA: RG 59, LAR, 1809–17, filed under "Warden"). 4 pp. Addressee not indicated.

From John Quincy Adams

Sir   St: Petersburg 7. January 1811.

I have received from the Secretary of State a letter, dated 15. October last, enclosing a letter of leave for the Emperor of Russia, with an optional power to me to present it immediately, and suggesting your obliging permission to me to return to the United States, to avoid the ruinous expences to which it had been intimated to you by a person particularly attentive to my interest,[1] a longer continuance here must necessarily subject me.

As I have determined to avail myself of the discretionary power contained in the Secretary of State's letter, to postpone the delivery of the letter to the Emperor, untill I shall be honoured further with your orders on the subject, and as the motives for your acquiescence in what you understood to be my wish, are entitled to all my acknowledgments and gratitude, I consider it incumbent in duty upon me to state explicitly to you the grounds upon which I shall reserve the letter of leave, untill your definitive Instructions in regard to it shall come to my hands.

Previously to my departure from the United States, I had understood from you that the time destined to the mission to Russia would probably be three or four years; a period which the more readily engaged my acceptance of the trust which you was pleased to confide to me, as a shorter term seemed scarcely the suitable object of so long and distant a voyage, and as a longer one would have been a contemplation too painful of separation from my Country and from the objects of my particular affections whom I was to leave behind.

On my first arrival here, I had reason to suppose that the expences of absolute necessity to the station which I held would require a sacrifice of a considerable portion of my own property and I made the arrangements necessary for rendering it disposable at my order; but it was never my intention to trouble you or the Secretary of State on a subject which was merely my private concern. I considered myself bound in duty to my Country on one side, and to my family on the other to proportion if possible my establishment to the legal allowance and to limit my expenditure by the bounds which the Government of the United States have judged sufficient for the compensation of their Ministers abroad. Circumstances upon which I had not calculated have contributed to assist me in the execution of this Resolution, and although it has forbidden me the exhibition of magnificence which the example of other foreign Ministers here has made customary, it has allowed every arrangement of a domestic nature which decency requires, and which from the representative of a frugal Republic, ought to be expected. After an experience of fifteen months, and a full knowledge of the expences incident to my situation I have ascertained that whatever my continuance here may be, my expences will not exceed the compensation allowed me by law, provided it shall be possible for me to embark for the United States immediately upon the cessation of my public character. But if after taking leave here, for one Quarter's compensation which the usage allows, I have to remain here without occupation or character, at my own cost, six, nine, or even fifteen months as might be the case should I now take leave, I should indeed find it ruinous, and must make a sacrifice as impossible to avoid as it was to foresee.

For more than four months to come, and probably for more than five the Season of this Latitude has interposed a barrier, which makes it impossible for me to embark; and from the peculiar situation of my family it is very uncertain whether it will not be equally impracticable to embark for *such* a voyage, during the next Summer. Should I take leave in my Official character, I should in the present state of things be compelled to stay here the remainder of the present Winter and the whole of the next. The question is only between remaining in my public character, and remaining as a private individual; and although I should not hesitate a moment to divest myself of my official station, if your instructions had hinted at such an intention in you, I flatter myself that the very inducements upon which you had the goodness to furnish me the letter of leave will operate as a justification to me for keeping it untill its presentation can be speedily followed by my actual departure, or untill your express instructions shall make its immediate delivery my duty.

As the letter to the Emperor itself mentions considerations of a private nature as the motives for my departure, there would be obviously an inconsistency in my presenting it, and still remaining here without character— Nor would any explanation which I could give probably remove an unfavourable impression which would result from it at this Court.

I have been the more particular in these observations, because it has occurr'd to me that there may have been motives of a public nature which concurred in leading you to the adoption of this measure. In that case I would intreat that all reference to my convenience or advantage may be put entirely out of the question. From the Communications which you must before this have received from me you will perceive that *the emperor and his principal minister are not only particularly attached to the idea of regular and permanent diplomatic intercourse of ministers between United States and Russia but that repeated indirect intimations have been given to me of a wish to cement the relations between the two countries by a commercial treaty.* On the 5th: of September last I had the honour of writing on this subject to the Secretary of State,[2] and I hope soon to be favoured with your Instructions in answer to that letter. *Should the proposition for a treaty* meet your approbation it may furnish the means of securing a protection and favour to our Commerce which it will be difficult to obtain without it. *Should you ⟨deem⟩ it inexpedient to enter into any con⟨tractu⟩al stipulations with Russia* as my continuance here in a public character is constitutionally dependent upon the pleasure of the President, I shall in all Events cheerfully acquiesce in your dispositions concerning it, as founded upon considerations of the public interest alone; and in repeating my thanks to you Sir, for the regard to my personal convenience which has on this occasion influenced you, I beg you to be assured of the Sentiments of sincere respect and attachment with which I have the honour to be, your very humble and obedt: Servt:

JOHN QUINCY ADAMS.

RC (Forbes Magazine Collection, New York, N.Y.); FC (MHi: Adams Family Papers). RC marked duplicate. Docketed by JM. FC dated 5 Jan. 1811; written in shorthand. Italicized passages are those encoded by Adams using a code provided by the State Department to John Armstrong in France and to both William Short and Adams for the purposes of their missions to Russia (see Ford, *Writings of J. Q. Adams*, 3:328). Key not found. Decoding here is supplied from a partial key on file at the Madison Papers offices, with angle brackets indicating conjectural readings.

1. See Abigail Adams to JM, 1 Aug. 1810 (*PJM-PS*, 2:455–56).

2. Adams had concluded his 5 Sept. 1810 dispatch with the news that Russia desired a commercial treaty with the U.S. He requested powers and instructions for this purpose if the president had no objections. Sometime early in February 1811 JM decided to authorize Adams to negotiate a treaty with Russia, and he had the secretary of state draft the heads of an agree-

ment between the two nations. The most significant clause in the proposed treaty was the seventh head, which stipulated that no place or port should be considered blockaded "unless in respect of particular ports which may be actually invested by a competent naval force, and vessels bound to such ports are not then to be captured unless they shall have been previously warned not to enter them" (Adams to Robert Smith, 5 Sept. 1810, Ford, *Writings of J. Q. Adams*, 3:496; Smith to Adams, February 1811 [DNA: RG 59, IM]). This was the same definition of blockade that JM believed Great Britain had adhered to as recently as 1804 and that he still hoped Great Britain might accept in negotiations with the U.S. over the orders in council (see JM to Jefferson, 19 Oct. 1810, *PJM-PS*, 2:585–86 and n. 1).

From Horatio Gates Spafford

HOND. & ESTEEMED FRIEND—   ALBANY, N. Y., 1 Mo. 7. 1811.

I ought, perhaps, to apologize, for troubling thee with a subject of so little direct concern to thyself, as that I am now about to propose, for thy consideration.

The details, which the 3rd Census will afford, aught to be embodied, in a Volume of convenient size, & published for general use; & unless some other person shall have effected this previous to next 6 Mo., (June,) I contemplate proposing to do it. At about that time, I can repair to Washington for that purpose; & if the public officers encourage my doing so, I shall certainly do it, unless it be likely to interfere with the intentions of some other person.

Had I not thoughts of removing to Washington, I should certainly not contemplate a journey thither, solely on account of gaining access to the public records & papers collected by the late Census. But I have in contemplation to fix my residence there, after I shall have published the Gazetteer of this State;[1] & to prosecute my plan of authentick Gazetteers of the several States, & of the United States.

If thou canst find time to favor me with thy advice on these subjects, thou wilt confer a great favor. And I should be gratified if my friend Dr. S. L. Mitchill, were also consulted; & to whom I refer thee for any information relative to myself, on which to ground thy advice. With sentiments of gratitude & esteem, thy friend,

H. G. SPAFFORD.

Of whom am I to get permission, to send a small packet to some Correspondents in France & England, in the next Vessel that sails under the protection of Government? Or can I get such permission?

H. G. SPAFFORD.

RC (DLC).

1. See *PJM-PS*, 2:413–14, 436 n. 2.

From John Tyler

Dear Sir;   In Council Chamber Jany 7th. 1811

Your confidential communication[1] has been duly receiv'd and attended
to, and all the papers we have I beg leave to send you by Consent of the
Cou[n]cil. It is believ'd there is a mistake as to the Name, Logwood being
the only person who has made any discoveries on the Subject you mention.[2]
Nothing was put on the journals, but the papers put away under the necessary caution. Longcocke's name is nowhere to be found at present. There
shall still be further examination made, and the result will be made known
if it shall be such as to be worthy of your Attention.

You will not be able to discover any thing in the papers sent I believe wh.
can lead to detection. In the state of Tennessee severy [*sic*] Culprits have
been apprehended for forging the Bank Paper of this City. This has been
produced by the vigilance of the Govr: of that State & many other Citizens
in consequence of several communications made by me and the cashier of
the Bank of Richmond requesting his aid. I am with considerations of high
Respect and esteem Yr very obt. Servt.

JNO: TYLER

RC (DLC). Enclosures not found.

1. Letter not found.
2. Tyler probably had in mind the Buckingham County planter Thomas Logwood, who
had been sentenced to ten years' imprisonment on four charges of counterfeiting bank notes
by Chief Justice John Marshall in the U.S. Circuit Court for Virginia on 1 June 1804 (see
Herbert A. Johnson et al., eds., *Papers of John Marshall* [6 vols. to date; Chapel Hill, N.C.,
1974—], 6:287 and n. 1, 290–91).

§ To Congress. *7 January 1811, Washington.* Transmits the director of the Mint's
annual report for 1810.

RC and enclosures, two copies (DNA: RG 233, President's Messages, 11A-D1; and DNA:
RG 46, Legislative Proceedings, 11A-E5). Each RC 1 p.; in a clerk's hand, signed by JM. Read
and tabled by the Senate on 7 Jan. and by the House on 9 Jan. (*Annals of Congress*, 11th Cong.,
3d sess., 89, 510). Printed in *ASP, Finance*, 2:458–59. For enclosures, see Robert Patterson to
JM, 1 Jan. 1811, and n.

¶ To Bossange & Masson. Letter not found. *7 January 1811.* Acknowledged in Bossange & Masson to JM, 5 July 1811. Accepts the offer of a translation of the *Iliad*
(see *PJM-PS*, 2:474).

§ From Gideon Granger. *8 January 1811.* "He does not interfere as to the appointment of Marshall but he feels it due to his kinsman, Ebenezer Granger, to submit
the enclosed letter to the Presidents perusal."

RC (DNA: RG 59, LAR, 1809–17, filed under "Granger"). 1 p. Enclosure not found, but it probably related to the vacancy for the office of U.S. marshal for Ohio.

To Congress

Confidential

January 10th 1811

I communicate to Congress, in confidence, the translation of a letter from Louis de Onis, to the Captain General of the Province of the Caraccas.[1]

The tendency of misrepresentations and suggestions, which, it may be inferred from this specimen, enter into more important correspondences of the writer, to promote in foreign Councils, at a critical period, views adverse to the peace and to the best interests of our Country, renders the contents of the letter of sufficient moment, to be made known to the Legislature.

JAMES MADISON

RC and enclosure (DNA: RG 46, Executive Proceedings, 11B-B1). RC 1 p. In a clerk's hand, signed by JM. For enclosure, see n. 1.

1. JM forwarded a translation of a 2 Feb. 1810 letter from Onís to the captain general at Caracas (3 pp.; printed in *ASP, Foreign Relations*, 3:404), which had been sent to Washington by Robert K. Lowry, whom JM had dispatched as an agent to Venezuela in the summer of 1810 (see *PJM-PS*, 2:311–12). The Spanish diplomat reported a debate in the House of Representatives on 31 Jan. 1810 over whether to make an appropriation for an American minister to Spain. Although the outcome had been against sending a minister to the court of Joseph Bonaparte, Onís noted that friends and relatives of JM, principally John Wayles Eppes and Richard Cutts, were in favor of the proposal. He concluded from the episode that nothing useful could be obtained from the U.S. *"but by Energy, by force and by chastisement."* Onís further complained of American efforts to obtain access to Spanish colonial ports, and he assumed that the administration supported Joseph Bonaparte in order to advance this goal. He also believed that the U.S. was determined to make war on Great Britain and its Spanish ally and that John Quincy Adams had been sent to St. Petersburg for the purpose of forming an alliance with France, Russia, Denmark, and Sweden. Onís therefore suggested that Great Britain and Spain should counter this strategy by sending ships and troops to the Louisiana area in order to divide the U.S. into two or three republics, which would "remain in a state of perfect Nullity. We should soon have from the Republic of the North, which would be our friend, all the supplies which are now drawn from the others—who would perish, from Poverty and quarrels among themselves."

The letter continued with an assessment of American financial and military weakness: the country "is now without a cent"; the army had no more than "6000 despicable men"; and the navy "is for the most part disarmed." He concluded with an anecdote suggesting that Gallatin and other members of the administration assumed that any Spaniard who happened to be in the U.S. was a Bonapartist agent fit to be employed for the goal of inducing Mexico and Havana "to unite themselves to this Republic."

From Charles Jared Ingersoll

PHILADELPHIA 10 January 1811

The author of Inchiquins Letters on the United States,[1] who has the honor of being known to the President,[2] begs his acceptance of one of the earliest published copies of that work; which, as it was undertaken with a view of putting this country in good humour with itself, by endeavouring to expose the prejudices that prevent its proper estimation, the author hopes will not be unacceptable, in design, however imperfect the execution may be thought, to the person, who, with so much credit to himself and advantage to the community, fills the chief magistracy.

As for the present, at least, the author's name is not to be made known, if ever, he requests the President not to communicate his knowledge that the Letters were written here, and not, as they purport, abroad.

The copy for the President will be forwarded by the same mail that carries this note.

RC (DLC). Unsigned. Docketed by JM, "Ingersoll C. J."

1. [Charles Jared Ingersoll], *Inchiquin, the Jesuit's Letters, during a Late Residence in the United States of America. . . . By Some Unknown Foreigner* (New York, 1810; Shaw and Shoemaker 20436).

2. See Jared Ingersoll to JM, 28 Jan. 1810 (*PJM-PS*, 2:210).

From James Taylor

SIR   ZAINESVILLE, OHIO Jany. 10th. 1811.

I promised to drop you a line on the subject of the petition &c. I did my self the pleasure to address to you some time since.[1] I am happy to inform you that I am of opin[i]on there is nothing to be apprehended from this association. Indeed I am informed it is very unpopular among the land holders in that quarter of the state where it has met with the most countenance.

The Legislature of this state have done nothing of importance as yet except to elect a senator to the U:States.[2] I do imagine they could not have done better out of those they had to make choice out of.

The question of a Spot for the permanent Seat of Govement is to come on tomorrow. I think the report of the Commissione[r]s will be confirmed. They reported in favor of a Spot on the bank of the Sciota about 55 Miles above the Town of Chillicothe. There will be great exertions made to remove the seat of Goverment back to Chillicothe until the buildings are completed for the reception of the Legislature & Officers of Govrment & I think it will be done.

I am at this place attending to my land business & expect to return home or rather set out in about two days. I have the honor [to] be with great respect sir Your Obedt servt.

JAMES TAYLOR

RC (DLC).

1. See James Taylor to JM, 28 Nov. 1810 (first letter), and n. 1.

2. Thomas Worthington was elected to the U.S. Senate on 15 Dec. 1810 to fill the vacancy caused by the resignation of Return Jonathan Meigs, Jr. (Alfred Byron Sears, *Thomas Worthington, Father of Ohio Statehood* [Columbus, Ohio, 1958], p. 153).

From Harry Toulmin

DEAR SIR   FORT STODDERT 10th. Jany 1811

When I last took the liberty of addressing you,[1] I was engaged I believe in the examination of Reuben Kemper and John Callier. Col. Kennedy of the conventional army had been arrested and held to bail, and had thereupon applied to me for a writ of *habeas corpus*, to *bring up the recognizance*; in consequence of which I stand charged before the public of denying to a freeman the sacred writ of liberty.

Captn. M'Farland had been arrested, and had assured the sheriff that he would have the blood of the judge, & had escaped. Major Hargrave, had been notified of the Sheriffs approach, & had joined the little band below the line, & was the same night made prisoner, & is now confined in Pr near Pensacola. The examination of Kemper and Callier continued from Sundy Evg till Thursday eveng.

It took place at their own request, as I offered to admit them to bail at once: but I suspect that, in fact, they found that they could not raise so great a force as they expected, and being also disappointed in their expectations of succour from Baton Rouge, they were rather glad to have some excuse for keeping themselves out of danger. Certain it is, that my embracing the first moment of their coming above the line, to issue process against the leaders; gave a discouragement to their enterprize, of the effects of which they were undoubtedly sensible. On the evening of the last day of their examination, our representatives in Assembly came with the Presidents Proclamation, full of vehement indignation at the check which had been given to the conspirators, forward to bail them, and eager to assure us that the whole of the Baton Rouge business was fully understood by the general government, that every thing was done in concert with it, and that Mr Skipwith was elected governor at their particular instance.

Callier (who had been appointed Coll. to command the militia detatch-

ment) brought orders from Govr. Holmes & Govr. Claiborne (founded no
doubt on the presumption that Col. Cushing had arrived with the troops
& the gun boats) addressed to Coll. Cushing the commanding officer, at
Fort Stoddert, authorizing him to order such portions of the militia as he
may deem necessary to be *ready* for actual service. Callier immediately acquired a perfect ascendancy over the mind of Coll. Sparks: Kemper was
taken into favour and was in habits of constant, daily, familiar and confidential intercourse with Col. Sparks, his officers, of whom some had actually
renounced the U. States, & all had subscribed an oath of allegiance to the
Convention, were adopted and authorized by Callier, as officers to command the Militia, and the idea was thrown out and circulated that Col.
Sparks had full authority to call the Militia into actual service & to proceed
instantly, without waiting for Coll: Cushing to take possession of Mobile.

Kemper had had the hardihood even to tell me, after your proclamation
was recd. that the Conventional Flag should fly on the fort of Mobile, before that of the U. States: and I had heard from other quarters of his holding up the pretension, (seriously and as if he had authority to enforce it) to
640 acres of land for each of his followers, as well as the more important
one, (which has probably given birth to this famous revolution, & procured
for it so many patrons in Orleans & the Mississippi Territory) that a confirmation of all grants made by the Spanish government since the cession
of Louisiana, woulld [*sic*] be a necessary requisite to their acquiescence in
the occupation of Florida by the United States. I will confess therefore that
I was alarmed when I beheld the open and undisguised patronage given to
Kemper, the ground of whose defence itself seemed to rest on his disclaim-
ing the character of an American citizen, and more especially when I saw
the privates who had served under him, incorporated with the militia, to be
armed, fed & paid by the U. S. and the Command of the detatchment given
to the men who had either acted as his officers or been his avowed advocates
and partizans. Orders (it also lately appears) were sent by Col. Callier &
Col. Sparks to Pascagola, directing one Dupree[2] (who had been at the head
of a band of plunderers under the name of patriots) to take possession of
that part of the country in behalf of the United States, and it is reported by
some who have come from thence that, the best friends of the United
States, who had opposed the plundering system, had on his a[c]quiring this
new power been denounced as enemies, and that he had given orders to
shoot them down, if found at large, as wild beasts. Some allowance, perhaps, ought however to be made on both sides for the violence of party
spirit. As to Kemper himself, whether he really expected to establish his
extravagant pretensions or merely wished, by associating his men with the
militia, to hold up the idea of a connection between him and the federal
government, and to pave the way for his personal influence and for the
advancement of his followers under the new order of things to be estab-

lished by govr. Claiborne, I do not know & can scarcely conjecture: but as there unquestionably have been foreign parties, both British & French, in the settlements on the Mississippi, it is possible that Kemper might have belonged to one of them and might have calculated, on finally establishing a government in Florida independent of the U. S. or at least of obtaining such a hold in the country as would completely have procured success to their favourite land speculations.

He had not patience, however, to wait till the militia could be collected, but determined to try his fortune with a little band of his own. On Friday the 21st. Decr. he set out (himself I believe from the house of Col. Sparks, tho' I do not know that the latter was aware for what purpose) with between 30 and 40 men mostly on horseback.

I knew nothing of this till after dark, when Mr Darling (the Collector) informed me of what was going on and that they meant to enter Mobile next evening before the commandant had retired to the fort, & by seizing & carrying off him and Mr Innerarrity, to compel him to deliver up the Fort. I sent in, to the fort, to inform Captn Gaines and it was agreed that he should acquaint Colo Sparks with it, in order that proper measures might instantly be taken to defeat a project so incompatible with the dignity & probably with the interests of the U. States. Coll. Sparks seemed to have great doubts about it, but on learning that the information came from a person actually residing in his family, he no longer disputed the fact, but expressed his belief that Kemper was countenanced by the general government. However, upon sending for some of his officers, & learning their opinion he determined to send Capn Gaines down that night with the greater part of the troops to oppose Kemper in any illegal attempts on the fort: but at the same time he sent two messengers in the night after Kemper to apprise him of the steps which had been taken and to induce him to return. He gave to Captn Gaines full power to demand the fort. The latter step he took, by the advice of his officers, under the presumption that he was authorized by instructions which they had not seen, & which I believe they are since convinced never existed.

Finding that the detatchment had taken scarcely any provisions I went down (as the contract is in my hands) with a small supply on the sunday following: & as I did not notify Col. Sparks of my departure, (as to notify him would have been to notify Kemper whose disappointed followers were on the road) it has been since alledged that I went down at midnight to correspond with the enemy. When at Mobile I learnt by a letter from Coll. Sparks to Captn Gaines, that in four days he meant to follow with from three to 4 hundred militia. I knew that the necessary consequence of their arrival would be the utter demolition of the town from the guns of the fort, and that it could be productive of no good, inasmuch as a place of that strength never could be taken by small arms.

I was satisfied besides, that if they could succeed, nothing but confusion would follow, as no arrangements had been made for the civil government of the province. Indeed this consideration was in my mind decisive, that no such powers had been communicated as were assumed by Col Sparks and Col. Callier. I deemed it essential that Col. Cushing should be apprised of the existing state of things. A messenger had been sent to him, but he had not returned. He was a Spanish subject: he might have been careless, or he might have been unfaithful. I offered to go myself. I sailed in a canoe down the bay, and in 28 hours I found Col. Cushing, detained by contrary winds, about 20 leagues from Mobile. He was astonished at the precipitancy of Col. Sparks: he did not think that he seriously intended what he promised: but lest he should be so far overcome by the influence of others, he wrote a letter to him to suspend calling out the militia or to dismiss them if they had been called out. Contrary winds & boisterous weather rendered my return dangerous & tardy: and much did I suffer from the apprehension of a destruction in the mean time of the property of unoffending individuals and the loss of valuable lives. Happily only a few of the militia had arrived at Mobile: the rest, amounting to about 250 I found at fort Stoddert. Many of them had been two or three weeks drawn from home: but they had only recently reached this place, and were to march for Mobile the next morning. They were discontented with me for not having a full supply of provisions, tho' there was enough for the current demands of the place, and I had received no intimation of the necessity of any extraordinary supply.

Coll. Sparks did not communicate to them the orders he had received from Col. Cushing: but sent to Col. Cushing with copies of the instructions recd from Govr. Claiborne, and with representations, as it was said, of the necessity of calling out the militia, a young man of the name of Carson, a partizan or at least an advocate of the Kemper expedition, and a militia Colonel whom he had made commandant at Fort Stoddert. Carson came back with a renewed order from Col. Cushing to permit the militia to return home. Callier on saturday last, when this order was to be made public, read to his men, formed in a hollow square, a most vehement invective on the measure, and concluded with denouncing *me* by name, as a traitor, an intriguer &c &c. I had the moment before heard of the projected attack, and attempted a public defence: but the moment I came to any material or impressive observation, my voice was drowned by his incessant bellowing of traitor, liar, dam——d saltwater son of a b——h, British emissary, & other epithets of the same elegant and gentlemanly description, familiar, from daily use, in his vocabularly [*sic*]; but such as I cannot even recollect: and all this from a man who has repeatedly observed to me that there was not one single act of mine, which my enemies could lay hold of, anxious as they were, to found a charge against me.

Having thus represented me, and having as I have been informed by others, been for three days assisted by M'Farland, Kemper, Kennedy & Pollard, in holding me up to the men, as a person who had abused them to Col. Cushing, and prevented the glorious prize from reaching their hands at the moment that they were ready to grasp it; it is no wonder that their soldiers, friends of Kemper & his plans, most of them new comers in the country and strangers to me and to my incessant exertions for its prosperity, & indeed for the most part mere birds of passage, who are here to-day, & will be perhaps in some other part of the uncivilized world to-morrow; it is no wonder that a large majority of such men should without knowledge & without reflection, put their hands to a statement of facts, addressed to congress as a ground for my impeachment, which none of them could possibly know any thing about. This petition was brought forward by J. P. Kennedy, and charged me, as far as I cd hear it, 1st with partiality in giving or refusing bail, 2dly. with carrying on for three months a secret negociation with the spanish authorities, 3dly. with going from my post at midnight to Consult with the enemy below the line, and proceeding from thence with misrepresentations to Col: Cushing. As to the first, I know not what cases are alluded to and can only say that I have always ingenuously followed the light of my own understanding: as to the 2d. you, Sir, are acquainted with every thing I have said or done. I have held no correspondence with Spanish officers: and if I have with earnestness & anxiety expressed my ideas & wishes to persons residing below the line, it has only been, that their government would save their people from the anarchy and ruin portended by Kemper, by making a surrender to the U. States of the disputed territory: and as to the 3d. I fortunately had a friend with me (a stranger in the country, Mr Lewis of Athens) during the whole time alluded to, who can certify every tittle of it to be false.

There was, indeed, a 4th. charge, which I had forgotten. I had examined the witnesses in the case of Kemper and Callier in a federal garrison. It is true I did examine them in the dwelling house of Captn Gaines; which is within the pickets, but I believe not within the chain of centinels. As to the latter however, I am not sure. I live about one mile and a quarter from the fort. Woods only intervene. Hargrave had escaped. M'Farland had broke custody: and from one to 200 men were expected to assemble at the same time not far from us below the line. Col. Kirby, my predecessor, had transacted similar business in the same place. The court of land claims was held there. No other house could be got any way convenient. No duress, no restriction, no exhibition of military force was used or thought of.

I doubt much, after all, whether it be really intended to forward this petition to congress. I suspect that the main use contemplated may be an effect to be produced by it on Governor Claiborne, for the purpose of throwing the practical power of making appointments in the district below, into the hands of the same faction which has obtained the ascendancy on this side of the line. If it should have this effect, this will be completely a ruined country.

Mr Darling the collector, a worthy man, attentive to his duties, and a firm supporter of the laws, is attempted to be displaced as collector of the district of Mobile, in favour of a young man of the name of Carson, whose negative qualities induced Captn. Gaines four or 5 years ago to recommend him but whose positive ones since exhibited as the patron and supporter of an abandoned faction, have fully satisfied him, to be a very improper person. Mr Darling has removed to this place on acct. of his office, & is ready to remove to Mobile, & certainly will with a little experience become a very accurate & respectable officer.

As to myself, I hardly know how to act. I cannot obtain a sight of the petition. The facts are of such a nature, that the petitioners who are generally poor ignorant strangers, who live at a distance from me, could know nothing about: and Callier encouraged them to sign by stating that its object was merely to ask an enquiry. By his abusive and outrageous treatment of me, he incited his followers to personal violence, & when he stopped the arm of one of his captains who offered to cleave me down with his sword, it was only to have an opportunity of boasting the next day "that he had saved one old, damned rascal from being murdered": and the "damned cowardly villain Col. Cushing" is in his elegant declamation coupled with the damned traitor of a judge. I pray, Sir, that you will grant me pardon for this style of writing so offensive to myself as well as to you: but in many cases one can never give an accurate idea of the spirit of a writer but by literal quotations. As to the address itself, I am at a loss how to act. An acquittal would be no triumph where such men are the adversaries: and to do any act which would produce suspence, either in the public mind or in my own destiny, would be to afford them all the success which their most extravagant expectations can dream of. In the mean time all the arrangements for the future organization of the government of this country wd be completed, and in the defeat or even temporary adumbration of one man who had stood foremost in defence of the laws and of the security of property whether of a friend or an enemy, they will see all the success and triumph which their hearts can desire or anticipate, and erect an aweful monument as a warning to future officers of government on the waters of the Mobile, not to dare to encroach on the sacred, sovereign right of plunder & desolation.

I doubt, therefore, whether to adhere to the idea which first struck my mind, of petitioning for an enquiry. I shall consult my friends & determine accordingly. I think I shall write a line to Mr Rhea, & Mr R. M. Johnson, but have not time to write fully. Coll. Cushing is now at Mobile waiting for orders. He finds none to justify the measures already taken. Govr. Claiborne is to be there in ten days. I am dear sir very respectfully your faithful and obedt Sert

H. Toulmin.

RC (PHi: Daniel Parker Papers). Postmarked Philadelphia, 17 Feb. Redirected by JM to the secretary of war.

    1. Toulmin to JM, 12 Dec. 1810.
    2. Sterling Dupree was one of a group of settlers on the Pascagoula River who, in November 1810, decided to emulate the West Florida convention at Baton Rouge by electing local officials to displace the Spanish authorities. Dupree, with the sanction of Reuben Kemper and Joseph P. Kennedy, subsequently organized a military force to seize a small Spanish garrison at the mouth of the Pascagoula. This force, however, also preyed on the local inhabitants, from whom, according to one account, it seized $10,000 to $12,000 in property (Cox, *The West Florida Controversy*, pp. 422–27; Edwin Lewis to James Monroe, 15 Feb. 1812, Carter, *Territorial Papers, Mississippi*, 6:266–67).

To William Madison

DEAR BROTHER   WASHINGTON Jany. 11. 1811.

    I observe that a parcel of Merinoes are to be sold at Amphill on the 17th. inst.[1] From the numbers latte⟨r⟩ly imported, & the little demand as yet excited in Virga. it is not unlikely they may go off at very low prices, say 20. 30. or 40 dollars for Ewes. In this case I shd. wish you to have 8 or 10 of the younger ones bought for me, & sent up to Orange, taking for granted that their pedigree is well authenticated, or evinced by their external characters. Having eno' already to require a separate estabt. such an addition wd. not be felt in the trouble &c. I should even be willing to buy a greater than the above number, in case the price shd. not exceed 20 or 25 dollrs. If the Rams shd. be good, & sell for less than $100 dollars I advise you to purchase one for yourself. This with mine wd. be an ensurance for both of us. I hear nothing from Philada. since my last.[2] Yrs. affey

J. Madison

RC (courtesy of an anonymous collector). Addressed by JM to William Madison at the House of Delegates in Richmond. Below JM's address "Orange C H" was added, then crossed through and the letter redirected to Richmond.

    1. On 8 Jan. 1811 the *National Intelligencer* had advertised a sale of merino sheep to be held at Ampthill, the seat of Robert Temple, in Chesterfield County, about seven miles south of Richmond.
    2. JM had presumably been corresponding with his brother about the health of Alfred Madison. His letters have not been found.

From Benjamin Henry Latrobe

Sɪʀ,   Jany. 11h. 1811

I herewith transmit to you two reports. The first my annual report of the public Building[1] the other that called for by a resolution of the House of representatives.[2] I am sorry that I have not found it possible to send them sooner, especially as the friends to the completion of the buildings, in congress have pressed me on the subject. With high respect Yrs.

B Henry Latrobe

FC (MdHi: Latrobe Letterbooks).

1. For Latrobe's 28 Dec. report on the state of the public buildings, see JM to Congress, 14 Jan. 1811 (second message), n.

2. Latrobe to JM, 3 Jan. 1811. On 28 Dec. 1810 Willis Alston of North Carolina had presented a resolution requesting the president to lay before the House an account of the expenditure of the money appropriated on 1 May 1810 "for completing the Capitol, and for other purposes, distinguishing the sums expended for each item of appropriation, and the sums expended in payment of debts previously incurred" (*Annals of Congress*, 11th Cong., 3d sess., 473).

§ To Congress. *12 January 1811*. Transmits a copy of a letter from the U.S. minister in London to the secretary of state[1] and a copy of a letter from the same to the British secretary of state for foreign affairs.[2]

RC and enclosures (DNA: RG 233, President's Messages, 11A-D1); RC (DNA: RG 46, Legislative Proceedings, 11A-E3). Each RC 1 p.; in a clerk's hand, signed by JM. For enclosures, see nn.

1. JM forwarded a copy of William Pinkney's 5 Nov. 1810 dispatch to Robert Smith (2 pp.) reporting that the state of George III's health was such that the British cabinet was unlikely to withdraw the orders in council in the near future. Pinkney declared that the date for the effective repeal of the Berlin and Milan decrees had passed and complained that he had received no indication that Great Britain would repeal the orders. Lord Wellesley's last communication on the subject on 31 Aug. 1810 had been "vague and equivocal," Pinkney wrote, and it was "highly important . . . that this ambiguity should be cleared away with all practical expedition." If this could not be done, "no presumption should be afforded of a disposition on the part of the United States to acquiesce in it" (printed in *ASP, Foreign Relations*, 3:372–73).

2. In a note dated 3 Nov. 1810 (7 pp.) Pinkney reminded Lord Wellesley that the Berlin and Milan decrees had ceased to have any effect after 1 Nov., and he therefore requested a response to his previous note calling for the repeal of the orders in council. The trade of the U.S. now required a statement of British intentions, Pinkney declared, adding that he anticipated a "speedy recall" of British orders and blockades restricting American shipping. If the British government did not intend to remove its orders in council, Pinkney asked that the U.S. government "be apprized, with as little delay as possible, of a determination so unexpected and of such vital concern to its rights and interests, and that the reasons upon which that determination may have been formed not be withheld from it" (printed ibid., 3:373).

To the Chiefs of the Creek Nation

My Children,   [14 January 1811]

Your father the President of the United States takes you by the hand. He has received from Colo: Hawkins your Talk of the last Autumn.[1] Either you have not been sufficiently informed, or you have not rightly understood his design in sending out the two parties from Fort Stoddert. Good path ways and roads are equally useful to his White and to his Red Children. Rivers & Water courses are made by the Great Spirit, to be used by the Nations to and thro' which they run. If his Red Children want to use the roads and rivers on which his White Children live they are open to them.

His white Children, particularly those in Tennessee, have to go a great way to carry their produce and to bring home necessaries from the sea. Now, if a shorter way by land, and good passage ways by the waters from Highwassee to the Mobile can be found for them, they ought to have them. The way lies thro' your nation. When his White Children want to go by the roads & rivers thro' the seventeen fires, the roads and rivers are all common. They pass without enquiry being made to what tribe they belong. His red Children have never been refused the same privilege. Colo: Hawkins will attend at your Council. He will explain to you that the two parties were sent to measure the distances and to go down the Alibama in order to find out the shortest way by land and the best way by Water. He would have done it before but Capt: Gaines's letter to him was delayed by the freshes or by some other accident. He will inform you that the object of the President was not to take away your lands, or any of your rights but to prepare the way for opening a road and using the rivers, which will be good for his red as well as his white Children.

He will satisfy you of this, and then he will acquaint you that next Summer Capt. Gaines & Lieut. Luckett will begin the survey anew.

As the purpose is both just and reasonable, so your father the President will expect that his Officers and Men will be treated with the hospitality and kindness which he has always manifested towards your Nations, and which he hopes will forever distinguish the friendship subsisting between the United States and the Creek Nation. Done at the City of Washington this fourteenth day of January 1811.

(signed)   James Madison.

Letterbook copy (DNA: RG 75, LSIA).

1. See Hobohoilthle to John Roger Nelson Luckett, 24 Oct. 1810 (*PJM-PS*, 2:592–93 and n.). In his 5 Nov. 1810 letter to Eustis which conveyed Hobohoilthle's speech to Washington, Benjamin Hawkins stressed the importance to the U.S. of gaining access to the rivers running through the Creek Nation. He recommended that the president's answer "in a plain,

firm, paternal tone should occupy at least the ground I have taken" (Grant, *Letters of Benjamin Hawkins*, 2:576).

From Thomas Leiper

Dear Sir   Philada. Janry. 14th. 1811

This evening I was informed by John Smith[1] the Mar[s]hall of this district that their has been a charge brought against him for not acting properly in the line of his Office in the Case of Olmstead.[2] I beg leave to relate what has come within my own knowledge in that case. I was One of the Grand Jury and heard the Marshalls Testimony and his Two deputies against General Bright and his men who opposed them in the serving of the process. The Marshall certainly did not desert 'till the Guns & Bayonets were at their breast and were given to under[s]tand if the[y] advanced they would be run through. Now Sir the Grand Jury found a Bill against Bright & Co the Petty Jury found them guilty and the Judge sent them to Prison. I am of the opinion had their been any thing improper in the Marshall's conduct it would have made its appearence on the Trial. If this is the only charge I have no doubt but the marshall will clear it up to your satisfaction indeed he says himself and I can believe him if he ever had any Merit in the line of his Office he had it in the case of Olmstead. My opinion of Pennsylvania at present is not the most favorable. To speak in a General sense we all want office or if you like it better Office hunters and if the truth was known the person who is at the bottom of this charge wants the Office himself. Bright got a fat Office from Snyder for opposing the Laws of the United[3] in Smith the Marshall and Smith is to be Turned out of Office for doing his duty. Wilkinson is to be persecuted for preventing Burr Treason where will this end you who sit higher may see further. I saw Wilkinson at his post on Plouden Hill when the British were on Bunkers hill. These men and these only are to be Trusted to command a Republican Army. The United States are in a State of Fermentation and it requires some Skill to prevent the Scum getting uppermost. It has already get uppermost in Pennsylvania and if I am correctly informed they would put you undermost. But I think it is impossible we should remain long in our present State. I am with esteem & respect Your most Obedient St.

Thomas Leiper

RC (DLC). Docketed by JM.

1. John Smith's term as marshal of Pennsylvania was due to expire on 25 Jan. 1811. On 10 Jan. 1811 Gallatin had written, evidently with JM's knowledge, to Alexander James Dallas, the U.S. attorney for Pennsylvania, warning that Smith's reappointment would be opposed. In his

reply several days later Dallas defended at length Smith's conduct throughout the Olmstead affair, stressing that the marshal had at all times acted under his orders. The impression conveyed in the charges, made by U.S. senator Michael Leib and other opponents of Pennsylvania governor Simon Snyder, that Smith had neglected his duties by colluding with the state authorities to avoid confrontation, Dallas believed, was more apparent than real. He mentioned that Smith was grateful to the president for the "hint" and added that Smith himself would write to JM on the subject. Smith's letter to JM has not been found, but he evidently enclosed it in a 14 Jan. 1811 letter to Robert Smith in which he explained that he sought both to be reappointed as marshal and to "refute some unfounded complaints against my official proceedings in Olmsteads Case." JM received one other letter in defense of Smith's conduct as marshal, and he nominated him for a further four-year term on 22 Jan. 1811 (Gallatin to Dallas, 10 Jan. 1811, Dallas to Gallatin, 13 Jan. 1811, *Papers of Gallatin* [microfilm ed.], reel 22; John Smith to Robert Smith, 14 Jan. 1811 [DLC; docketed by JM]; W. Lewis to JM, 14 Jan. 1811 [DNA: RG 59, LAR, 1809–17]; *Senate Exec. Proceedings*, 2 : 163–64; Higginbotham, *Keystone in the Democratic Arch*, p. 230).

2. For the background to the Olmstead affair, see Madison's First Public Crisis: *Olmstead v. the Executrices of the Late David Rittenhouse*, 6 Apr.–6 May 1809 (*PJM-PS*, 1 : 102–4).

3. Leiper appears to have omitted the word "States" between the second and third pages.

§ To Congress. *14 January 1811*. Transmits an account of the contingent expenses of government for 1810.

RC and enclosure, two copies (DNA: RG 233, President's Messages, 11A-D1; and DNA: RG 46, Legislative Proceedings, 11A-E4). Each RC 1 p.; in a clerk's hand, signed by JM. Enclosure (1 p.) is an account signed by Joseph Nourse, 4 Jan. 1811, showing a balance carried forward of $14,110, "there not having been any Expenditures on account of this fund in the year 1810."

§ To Congress. *14 January 1811*. Transmits a report from the surveyor of the public buildings "relative to the progress and present State of them."

RC and enclosure, two copies (DNA: RG 233, President's Messages, 11A-D1; and DNA: RG 46, Legislative Proceedings, 11A-E2). Each RC 1 p.; in a clerk's hand, signed by JM. Enclosure (9 pp.) is Latrobe's "Report on the public buildings," dated 28 Dec. 1810 (printed in Van Horne, *Papers of Latrobe*, 2 : 945–49).

§ To the House of Representatives. *14 January 1811*. Transmits reports of the superintendent of the city[1] and the surveyor of the public buildings[2] on the subject of the House resolution of 28 Dec. 1810.

Printed copy (*Message from the President of the United States, Transmitting Reports of the Superintendent of the City, and of the Surveyor of the Public Buildings . . .* [Washington, 1811; Shaw and Shoemaker 24231]); enclosures (DNA: RG 233, President's Messages, 11A-D1). For enclosures, see nn. 1 and 2.

1. JM enclosed an "Account of the Expenditure of the money appropriated on the 1st. of May 1810 for compleating the Capitol, and other purposes," including a list of the expenditures on the north and south wings of the Capitol and also the President's House, totaling $31,466.60 (2 pp.). Attached to this is a receipt for the salaries of the surveyor of the public buildings and Italian sculptors, totaling $1,033.40 (1 p.; signed by Thomas Munroe, superintendent of the city, 4 Jan. 1811).

2. See Latrobe to JM, 3 Jan. 1811, and n. 2.

§ To the House of Representatives. *14 January 1811*. Transmits copies of the documents requested in the resolution of 4 Jan. 1811.[1]

RC and enclosure (DNA: RG 233, President's Messages, 11A-D1); Tr (DNA: RG 46, Legislative Proceedings, 11A-E3). RC 1 p. In a clerk's hand, signed by JM. For enclosure, a printed copy of JM's proclamation of 2 Nov. 1810 and a Treasury Department circular to customs collectors dated 2 Nov. 1810, see *PJM-PS*, 2:612–13 and n. RC and enclosure printed in *Annals of Congress*, 11th Cong., 3d sess., 546–47, with the date of the Treasury Department circular as 5 Nov. 1810.

1. On 4 Jan. 1811 the House of Representatives adopted a motion presented by Lewis Sturges of Connecticut requesting from the president copies of his 2 Nov. 1810 proclamation and the Treasury Department circular issued "in pursuance of said Proclamation" (*Annals of Congress*, 11th Cong., 3d sess., 487).

§ From Ezekiel Pattee. *14 January 1811, Winslow, District of Maine*. As an officer who served in the American Revolution and is now "advanced in age," solicits an appointment to command one of the forts in the District of Maine.

RC (DNA: RG 107, LRRS, G-113:5). 1 p. In an unidentified hand, signed by Pattee. Witnessed by James Stackpole and David Pattee who testified as to the facts in the petition. Docketed by a War Department clerk as received 18 Feb. Enclosed in Barzillai Gannett to Eustis, 15 Feb. 1811 (ibid.), with the observation that Pattee "*has been* a respectable and useful citizen."

§ From David Holmes. *15 January 1811, Washington, Mississippi Territory*. "The inclosed letter from Mr. Joseph Robert resigning his Commission as a Member of the Legislative Council was received while the Legislature of the Territory was in session. I thought it proper therefore to communicate the information to the House of representatives in order that they might proceed to nominate Conformable to the ordinance." Is aware it would have been "more regular" to have submitted the matter to JM before sending it to the House, but "this course in all probability would have occasioned a delay of near twelve months." Encloses the nomination made by the House and recommends "the Gentln. first named," Edward Ward of Madison County, a respectable man from a county that had no voice in the appointment of the legislative council.

RC and enclosures (DNA: RG 59, TP, Mississippi). RC 3 pp. Enclosures are Joseph Robert to Holmes, 5 Oct. 1810 (1 p.), and a resolution signed by Speaker Ferdinand L. Claiborne and clerk William O. Winston, 27 Nov. 1810 (1 p.), nominating Edward Ward and Benjamin Harney for the vacancy.

From Albert Gallatin

SIR   TREASURY DEPARTMENT January 17th 1811
    I have the honor to transmit two copies of the "Laws, treaties & other documents relative to the public lands" as collected and arranged pursuant to the act of Congress passed April 27, 1810.[1]

The marginal notes and index were prepared by Judge Thruston who also assisted in selecting the documents inserted in the collection.

It is provided by the above mentioned act that the residue of the printed copies, after supplying the land officers, shall be reserved for the future disposition of Congress. I have the honor to be with the highest respect Sir Your obedient Servant

ALBERT GALLATIN

RC (DLC). JM forwarded copies of Gallatin's letter in his message to Congress of 30 Jan. 1811.

1. See *U.S. Statutes at Large*, 2:589. The volume was printed in 1810 in Washington by Joseph Gales, Jr. (Shaw and Shoemaker 21674).

From Paul Hamilton

SIR   NAVY DEPARTT. Jany. 17th. 1811

I beg leave to submit to your perusal the papers sent herewith, which detail the loss of the U. S. schooner Revenge,[1] which was on her way from Newport to New London, the harbour chosen for it's superior security as a Rendezvous, during the winter and equinoctial gales.

However unpleasant this occurrence, at first sight may appear, as the crew, the arms and furniture are saved, I do not think that the loss of the mere hull of the vessel is much to be regretted, as it was very unsound, and but for this accident, might at some other time have foundered under circumstances much more calamitous. I have the honor to be, Sir, with the greatest respect yrs.

PAUL HAMILTON

RC (DLC).

1. Hamilton probably enclosed two letters, dated 9 and 10 Jan. 1811, he had received from Commodore John Rodgers describing the loss of the *Revenge* (DNA: RG 45, Captains' Letters). The schooner, under the command of Lt. Oliver Hazard Perry, had run aground on Watch Hill Reef, six leagues east of New London in Long Island Sound. The deck of the vessel had broken loose from the hull, but salvage parties saved the sails, rigging, boats, and small arms.

From Robert Smith

SIR,   Thursday. [17 January 1811]

I have this moment seen Col McKee. He says he will immediately proceed to the Country in question and will be happy in affording to his Country any services in his power[1] but that he cannot go thither in the Character of a Secretary.[2] I hasten to give you this information in order that arrangements may be made for fixing upon a proper person as Secretary to Matthews.[3] Respctfy

R SMITH

RC (DLC). In pencil. Undated. Dated ca. 17 Jan. 1811 in the *Index to the James Madison Papers*, a date based on the assumption that Smith met with McKee shortly after the passage of the law of 15 Jan. 1811 authorizing the administration to take possession of East Florida and before Smith's 26 Jan. 1811 instructions appointing both McKee and George Mathews commissioners to implement the law (see n. 1).

1. On 26 Jan. 1811 McKee and Mathews were instructed as to how to receive the transfer of those parts of West Florida still under Spanish rule (i.e., Mobile) should Vicente Folch or any other local authority be disposed to surrender them to the U.S. Similar instructions were given relating to Florida east of the Perdido River, but their execution was left to the discretion of Mathews and McKee, depending on circumstances and the disposition of the Spanish authorities in the region. Mathews and McKee approached Folch on several occasions in the early months of 1811, but their discussions were fruitless. The Spanish governor, after stating that he had received orders from his superiors to retain his province at all costs and then pointing out that American intervention in the region had reduced the threat of filibustering expeditions anyway, told the Americans that circumstances had changed since he had made his offer to the U.S. in December 1810.

By June 1811 JM concluded that Folch was unlikely to deliver those portions of West Florida under his control to the U.S., and he instructed the secretary of state to terminate the mission of Mathews and McKee with respect to that territory. Their powers were then transferred to Governor Claiborne in New Orleans. At the same time, however, JM explicitly left in force those parts of the 26 Jan. 1811 instructions to Mathews that related to East Florida, and the general was told to continue his mission if he thought he had reasonable prospects for success (Robert Smith to Mathews and McKee, 26 Jan. 1811, James Monroe to Mathews and McKee, 29 June 1811, Monroe to Claiborne, 29 June 1811, Monroe to Mathews, 29 June 1811 [DNA: RG 59, DL]; Patrick, *Florida Fiasco*, pp. 32–39).

2. Ralph Isaacs was appointed secretary to George Mathews (Patrick, *Florida Fiasco*, p. 16).

3. George Mathews (1739–1812), a Revolutionary War veteran, a two-term governor of Georgia, and a former member of the House of Representatives, had been selected by Georgia senator William Harris Crawford in the summer of 1810 as an agent to advance the administration's policy of mobilizing support in the eastern section of West Florida for its incorporation into the U.S. (see ibid., pp. 4–6; *PJM-PS*, 2:310–13). After traveling through the region between Mobile and Pensacola, Mathews came to Washington in January 1811 and met with JM for discussions on the situation in the Spanish Floridas. At this time he also appears to have submitted a report to the State Department on the "Affairs of E & W Florida." The military force of West Florida, he wrote, "is about three hundred and fifty soldiers, Sixty of which are Stationed, at Mobiel, the remainder at Pensecola, and a fort at the inlet into the bay. Agreeable to my letter to Mr. Crawford, I persued my Journey to East florida. I found the people there in expectations of soon declareing for themselves; they appeared only to be waiting to hear the fate of Cadiz."

"A large majority, of them," Mathews continued, "are disposed to become a part of the United States; but they will expect some arrangements on the part of our Goverment with respect to debts due to individuals from the Goverment of Spain. The Officers & Soldiers will likewise expect, if they become a part of the United States that the debts due them will be paid; and some provision in land for each family; how far these expectations are Just, our goverment will determine. The Military force of East Florida consists of about two hundred and fifty Soldiers, all most the whole of which are stationed, at Augusteen, should the people declare for themselves those who will be foremost in it expect to get possession of the fort by surprise. To those most favourable to our goverment, it would be grateful to see some Military force, of ours on that frontier, it would have a tendancy to awe what British influence there is in the province and give confidence to those friendly to us."

"With the different persons with whome I conversed, I end[e]avoured to impress them with the friendly disposition of the United States towards them and how much more it would be to there intrest to be connected with us than any forreign power; and if the Spanish nation was established in North and South America them and us ought to act as one nation in preventing every European nation from getting possession of any part of the Continent and I told them that the united States was two much interested in this event to permit either france or Great Brittain to get possession of either of the Floradys this was recived as I wished it they fully acquiessing in the same centiment. It will rest with the President whether it may not be advisable to have some person on whome, he can depend near the Governments of the Floridys to avail themselves of any occurrence that may offer. The Gentlemen of influence in East Florada in our intrest, donnot wish there names commited to paper—but I am at liberty to mention them in a conferrence with the President or you" (Mathews to Robert Smith, n.d. [DNA: RG 59, Undated Misc. Letters, ca. 1807–20]).

Filed with this letter is a small slip of paper listing, in an unidentified hand, "Gentlemen in Florida": "John H. McIntosh / Mr Amasa Areadonde / Andrew Atkinson on St. Johns / George Fleming St. Augustine / Don Lopes Comandant Amelia with about 12 Soldiers / 150 Soldiers compose the Garrison of St. Augustine / 30 in Detarchments [sic] on St: Johns / Not any Navil force in the Province."

From Jenkin Whiteside

SIR.   SENATE CHAMBER 17th. Jany 1811
    I received the Commissions for taking the Testimony of Messrs Miller, Rhea, Weaklay &c with a memorandum of the points to which the examination is to be directed by Mr Coles. I have also received a line from R. J. Taylor esqe of Alexandria requesting me to inform him whether the persons named would attend at the place specified in the Notice on the 19th. Inst: and applied to Messrs Rhea & Miller on that subject. I believe that Colo Weakley knows nothing material to depose. Mr. Rhea will not attend. Mr Miller, who can give Material testimony informed me that he would chearfully attend, if furnished with a horse or conveyance of some kind, having none of his own here. I shall procure a horse & attend, if the day is not very inclement. I have given the information above to Mr Taylor. I believe Mr Miller & I can give all the information requisite on the points proposed, & that the attendance of Mr Rhea will not be very material. You probably can have a horse furnished for Mr Miller, which will Secure his attendance. I am Sir with much respect & consideration Your Most Ob⟨t.⟩

                                        JENKIN WHITESIDE[1]

RC (DLC). Addressee not indicated. Docketed by JM.

1. Jenkin Whiteside was a U.S. senator from Tennessee, 1809–11.

From Benjamin Henry Latrobe

Sir,   Washington, January 18h. 1811

In obedience to your directions conveyed to me by Mr Munroe, & contained in the resolution of the House of Representatives of the 14h. of January transmitted to me,[1] I shall without Loss of time comply with that part of it which relates to the outstanding Claims.

But to make an estimate of the sum necessary to finish the Capitol, it is impossible for me to proceed without Assistance especially as the time remaining of the Session is so short, and the Clerk of the works is absent. I therefore solicit leave to employ, one or more Clerks to assist me in so extensive & laborious a task it being understood that the Salary of the Clerk of the works during the time be appropriated towards payment for this assistance. As the parts of the work cannot be estimated without being drawn, it is evident that I cannot possibly go thro' this labor myself, even if [I] had not any other business to do. But having at present more work to design; & direct at the Navy Yard than my whole time will easily accomplish, the resolution of the House cannot possibly be complied with unless I can obtain the assistance asked, of which, I beg leave to assure you, I will not employ any more than is indispensibly necessary. I have already made some Years ago all the general drawings, but the details which are essential necessary are untouched.

I solicit your attention to this request as early as possible, and am with high respect Yours

                                        B H Latrobe
                                        Surv. p Bldgs UStates

P.S. I presume there cannot be any doubt of the appropriation necessary to carry the resolution of the house into effect.

RC (DLC); FC (MdHi: Latrobe Letterbooks). RC docketed by JM. Filed with the RC is a one-page note: "Mr. Latrobe has drawn on Accot. of the fund for furnishing the Presidents House—13.800.—of which there remains unaccounted for [in] his hands Ds. 1130..96, exclusive of the proceeds of old Furniture which may have been sold by him."

1. On 14 Jan. 1811 Nathaniel Macon of North Carolina had presented a resolution calling on the president to lay before the House "an estimate of the sum necessary to finish the Capitol, designating what may be necessary to finish each wing, and the main building, and what time may be required to finish the whole building." After some debate the resolution was amended at the suggestion of Benjamin Tallmadge of Connecticut to include a call for an

account of the debts due to individuals for work on the Capitol and of the "whole moneys expended on the public buildings" (*Annals of Congress*, 11th Cong., 3d sess., 517–18).

§ From Thomas Munroe. *19 January 1811, Superintendent's Office, Washington.* Gives an account of the moneys expended under the act of 28 Apr. 1810 for the better accommodation of the Post Office and the Patent Office.[1] Reports that on 28 May 1810 the building "commonly called the Hotel" and several accompanying lots were purchased for $10,000 and that the attorney general duly executed the deed of conveyance to the U.S. Since the purchase, the sum of $3,268.26 has been expended on the said building; a further sum of $1,360.82 has been spent on the office west of the President's House. Of the sum of $20,000 appropriated by Congress, there remains unexpended $5,370.92.

RC (DNA: RG 233, President's Messages, 11A-D1). 2 pp. Printed in *ASP, Post Office,* p. 44. JM forwarded the letter to the House of Representatives in his message of 25 Jan. 1811.

1. For the background, see Robert S. Bickley to JM, 8 and 18 May 1810 (*PJM-PS*, 2:336–37 and nn. 2 and 3, 343–44 and n. 2).

§ From Thomas Munroe. *19 January 1811, Superintendent's Office, Washington.* Transmits an account of the moneys expended on the Capitol from its commencement until 14 Jan. 1811 as required by the resolution of the House of Representatives of that date.

RC and enclosure (DNA: RG 233, President's Messages, 11A-D1). RC 1 p. Enclosure (1 p.) is a statement showing that the sum of $761,485.04 had been spent on the Capitol since 1801. JM forwarded the RC and enclosure to the House of Representatives in his message of 25 Feb. 1811.

From Levi Lincoln

DEAR SIR   WORCESTER Jany. 20. 1811

I feel myself much honored by your favor & the Commission accompanying it, appointing me a successor to the late Judge Cushing.[1] Among the various sensibilities, awakened on this occasion, I should express to you my anxiety, gratitude & encreased public devotedness, were it in my power to make the return called for by my sense of the obligation conferred. Yourself & my other friends did me but justice in believing, that, under the existing political circumstances of our country, a selfish & obstinate adherence to favorite private arrangements was not the most prominent feature of my character. The recollection of many of my friends can vouch for my yielding compliances. Be assured that such are now my sentiments that your wishes for the services of a citizen ought to influence with the authority of a public command where there is the ability to obey & that if my situation would permit the discharging the duties of a Judge I would hold the office at least for one or two years, untill, by looking around, you should be enabled to make a more permanent & satisfactory appointment. The difficulty of my sight although it has latterly so encreased as to compel me to abandon the use of pen & the examination of books & papers, which is indispensable to the office of a Judge yet it has become less formidable than I had apprehended & promises to yield to the hand of the skilful oculist when it shall have sufficiently progressed. Notwithstanding promptly declining or resigning (whichever term may be deemed most proper & respectful,) the office with which you have been pleased to honor me, was, in my own mind a matter of duty & necessity; yet from a possi[bi]lity that a second consultation with Dr. Smith,[2] a Professor at Darthmouth Colledge [sic] & a successful & celebrated operator in cases of cataracts, might have changed my opinion if not the state of my sight I defered this answer. He was to have been in the Town of Boston last week, but failed. It ⟨wo⟩uld have been my pride to have shared with my political friends, the labors, troubles & even the odium which the firm & decisive measures called for by the present crisis may subject them to. It is mortifying to be separated from them when the situation of our country is peculiarly trying, difficult if not dangerous, calling for personal sacrifices, & the utmost efforts of all its friends. I feel a further regret lest the partiality expressed by the present appointment shall embarrass a subsequent selection.

I have been thus particular from a solicitude to satisfy those of the correctness of my conduct whose esteem & confidence I cannot too highly appreciate. With the highest Consideration Esteem & Friendship, I am most respectfully Your most Obdt.

LEVI LINCOLN

RC (DLC). In a clerk's hand.

1. See JM to Lincoln, ca. 2 Jan. 1811. In a letter of 25 Jan. 1811 to Robert Smith (DNA: RG 59, LOAG), Lincoln acknowledged receipt of a letter from Smith enclosing a commission appointing him to the U.S. Supreme Court and informed the secretary of state of his unwillingness to serve.

2. Nathan Smith (1762–1839) studied medicine with Benjamin Waterhouse at Harvard College and in 1798 was elected professor of medicine at Dartmouth College. He resided in Hanover until 1817 but also traveled extensively as a physician and surgeon. He then moved to New Haven and taught at Yale College until his death.

§ From Aaron H. Palmer. *20 January 1811, New York.* Is contemplating a visit to Spain in the spring "in the event of the re-establishment of peace and tranquility" in that country and offers his services as chargé d'affaires, since the U.S. has no diplomatic representation at Madrid.

RC (DNA: RG 59, LAR, 1809–17, filed under "Palmer"). 2 pp.

§ From Elizabeth Parke Custis.[1] *Ca. 22 January 1811.* Wishes to be "the humble instrument to serve my country; and you, Sir, by telling you the claims of a good Man, and securing to you an honourable Agent in a foreign land." Is not "so vain as to imagine that the President of the United States will let me dictate who he shall depute to serve him" but wishes to seek his "protection and patronage" for David Bailie Warden. Observed Warden as a stranger in JM's drawing room and believed that his "countenance denoted a man of Sorrow." Learned that he had been displaced from his post by Armstrong in favor of Alexander McRae and resolved to obtain information from those who had known him in France. Wrote to Captain Fenwick for this purpose and encloses his reply [not found]. "His letter speaks for itself. I fervently pray that it may influence you in favour of his friend." Praises Fenwick as a man of truth and honor and begs JM to hear the voice of "the adopted Child of Washington who knows and esteems you—who prays that you may live long possesed of the love and gratitude of our Country. When my voice ascends to the throne of God, this is one of its most fervent prayers."

Tr (MdHi: Warden Papers). 3 pp. In the hand of David Bailie Warden. Undated; conjectural date assigned on the assumption that Elizabeth Parke Custis wrote the letter shortly before Warden had his conversation with JM on 26 Jan. (see Account of a Conversation with David Bailie Warden, 26 Jan. 1811). Following the account of this conversation in Warden's letterbook is a note recording that "M Custis" had interceded on his behalf.

1. Elizabeth Parke Custis (1776–1832) was a daughter of John Parke Custis and a granddaughter of Martha Washington. In 1796 she had married Thomas Law but was later divorced from him (Donald Jackson and Dorothy Twohig, eds., *The Diaries of George Washington* [6 vols.; Charlottesville, Va., 1976–80], 4:72, 6:239).

From John Armstrong

SIR,   WASHINGTON 23d January 1811

Understanding that Mr. James Bowdoin while residing in France, had transmitted to the President of the United States a deposition made in Paris, in the Year 1807, by Chs. M. Somers of that City, and being possessed of a second Deposition, made by the said Somers on the subject of the former, I have conceived it to be my duty to forward to You this last & with it sundry other papers numbered, on their margins, 1, 2. 3. 4. 5. 6. 7. 8.[1]

On these communications I forbear all remark, excepting to express a degree of surprize, that Mr. Bowdoin should have placed any confidence in the declarations of a man so entirely destitute of principle & character as Chs. M. Somers who had been ejected from the Office of Sworn Interpreter to the Council of liquidation, for a false & fraudulent exercise of his public functions. I have the honor to be Sir with very high consideration Your most obedient & very huml Sert.

JOHN ARMSTRONG

RC and enclosures (DNA: RG 59, DD, France). RC in a clerk's hand, signed by Armstrong. For enclosures, see n. 1.

1. The enclosures concerned a subject Armstrong had previously raised with JM in his letter of 6 May 1810, namely the suspicion voiced by James Bowdoin that Armstrong had been engaged in land speculation while negotiating for the purchase of the Floridas in 1806 (see *PJM-PS*, 2:332–33 and n. 1). The enclosures, numbered by Armstrong, are (1) Charles Somers to Armstrong, 20 May 1810 (2 pp.), explaining his deposition relating to Armstrong and attaching to it (2) a copy of his deposition to James Bowdoin of 5 Feb. 1807 (4 pp.; in French) and (3) Somers to Armstrong, 20 May 1810 (4 pp.; in French), with a postscript in Armstrong's hand stating that Leonard Jarvis had sworn that nos. 1 and 3 were in the hand of Somers and that no. 2 was a true copy of a document referred to in nos. 1 and 3; (4) a copy of Armstrong to T. Nancrede, 20 Apr. 1810 (1 p.), requesting a written statement of a conversation held the previous day; (5) a copy of Armstrong to Somers, 15 May 1810 (1 p.), submitting to him a copy of Nancrede's letter of 1 May 1810 and requiring from him an explanation of his conduct in implicating Armstrong in land speculation schemes; (6) T. Nancrede to Armstrong, 1 May 1808 [1810] (2 pp.), affirming that Somers had given an affidavit to Bowdoin containing material harmful to Armstrong's reputation; (7) a copy of Armstrong to Daniel Parker, 24 May 1810 (1 p.), sending him the deposition by Somers; and (8) Parker to Armstrong, 25 May 1810 (2 pp.), stating that there was no truth in the deposition by Somers.

From Harry Toulmin

Dear Sir   Fort Stoddert 23d. Jany 1811

As I have observed in the instructions from the Secretary of State to Govr. Claiborne, which have lately reached this Country;[1] that weekly communications from him were expected relative to the State of things in West Florida; I feel less apprehensive of being considered as guilty of intrusion, in the frequent reports which I have thought it proper to trouble you with, relating to events more immediately under my own observation. I came from Mobile yesterday morning. Govr. Claiborne had not then arrived at that place: nor did there appear to be any sufficient ground for expecting him immediately.

Indeed it is not likely that he would leave Orleans till the answer from Govr. Folch to his communications,[2] (which I think went on to Orleans from this office only 9 days ago,) should be received by him: and as it is hardly to be expected that this answer will be perfectly and decisively satisfactory, if we make a reasonable allowance for the effect produced, probably, on the mind of the Spanish governor by the threatening attitude which has been assumed in this country and neighbourhood, and by the strong manifestation of a spirit of cordiality and co-operation between our public officers here and the agents of the conventional party; *my* only hopes of our obtaining possession of the residue of Louisiana, rest on those arrangements which, under a full knowledge of the present actual posture of affairs, will be made at the seat of the general government.

The late step taken by the Governor of Orleans of laying off parishes as far as the Bayou Battrie (12 or 15 miles east of Pascagola, and where the only family between that river and the Mobile resides)³ and sending a parish judge to Pascagola has been a wise and happy one, as it will strengthen the confidence of the inhabitants in the American government, and restrain those outrages which the tyrannical officers of the Baton rouge party, lately pretending to federal authority, have been practising in that unfortunate country. The judge, I understand, entered upon the work of endeavouring to compel a restitution of stolen property, immediately on his arrival: but as a good deal has been consumed, and some divided among the partizans above the line; he will be only partially successful.

The appearances of war exhibited in this settlement, have put our cattle in jeopardy. Two men were lately detected near this place, in driving off about 100 head belongg to me and my neighbours: and prudent persons I find are cautious of sending their negroes far from home, alone; lest they should be taken off, on the pretence of their being Spanish property.

Col. Cushing proposes continuing at Mobile with three companies till he receives farther orders; & he has taken a house in the town for himself & family. This step has given much confidence to the inhabitants, who having again been confirmed in their fears of remaining in town, by the assembling of the Militia, have now begun to return once more. Their fears indeed have been grounded as much on the resentment of the Spanish authorities, as on the violence of the adherents of Kemper: and on the appearance of the Presidents proclamation, understanding the promise of protection in their rights & property, to have instant operation & not to have relation to the state of things which should take place after the actual occupation of the country by the U. S. many men expressed themselves more freely concerning the existing government & its ministers, than they would have deemed it prudent to do, had they calculated on the possibility of their being afterwards abandoned to the exercise of Spanish power.

It is true that Col. Cushing neither exercises nor indicates a wish to exercise any authority beyond the limits of his camp: but whilst he is there the people feel satisfied that the Spanish officers will not venture to molest them; and possibly the Spanish officers themselves, may be impressed with the apprehension, that the sword which hangs over them is really suspended by a hair. They were at first extremely shy and suspicious. They confined themselves entirely to the fort; and cut away the embrassures of the fort, so as to enable them to bring the guns to bear on the gun boats in the river. But on Col. Cushings paying a visit to the commandant in the fort, about a week ago, their hostile or rather suspicious feelings, seemed to wear away: the commandant returned the visit next day, and indicated much ease of mind, and since that time a friendly intercourse seems to have prevailed between the Spaniards and Americans. The commdt readily permitd me to land provisions for the American troops at the Bay's warf.

Mr. Kemper left this place for Baton Rouge on Thursday last, after having, as I am informed, held during the 3 preceeding days at different places, high courts of impeachment, against the judge who had the presumption to doubt the authority of the plenipotentiary of the Floridian republic, within the U. S., and to arrest the military career of him & his patriotic adherents. The result, I suppose, will be laid before Congress.

The apology, I am informed, which is now given by Coll Callier for calling out, or inducing Col. Sparks to Call out the militia to make an attack on Mobile, so contrary to the evident intentions of govt. is that it had been intimated to him by Col. Claiborne at Natchez, as if in the name of his brother, (whose official station prevented his saying it) that if he could hurry down the militia and take Mobile, the proclamation, would bear him out: but that if it was left to the ordinary operations of governt. not a blow would be struck. I mention this as I received it: without giving any credit to the suggestion, as it relates to the governor. I am dear Sir very respectfully your faithl. & obedt sert

Harry Toulmin

RC (DLC). Docketed by JM.

1. Robert Smith's 27 Oct. 1810 letter to Governor Claiborne had been included in JM's 5 Dec. 1810 message to Congress and was subsequently reprinted in newspapers throughout the nation (*ASP, Foreign Relations*, 3:396–97).

2. Toulmin was probably referring to two letters from Claiborne to Vicente Folch. The first, sent on 20 Dec. 1810, informed Folch of JM's 27 Oct. proclamation annexing portions of West Florida and expressed the wish that the Spanish governor would not oppose Claiborne's implementation of the president's policy. Claiborne sent a duplicate of this letter to Folch on 27 Dec. 1810, and on 7 Jan. 1811, after hearing a report that Folch had entered West Florida with an armed force, he warned him that such conduct would be viewed as evidence of "hostile intentions" toward the U.S. Claiborne did not receive a response from Folch until 27 Jan. 1811 (see Rowland, *Claiborne Letter Books*, 5:78, 93, 120).

3. For Claiborne's ordinance of 4 Jan. 1811 establishing parishes in West Florida, see Carter, *Territorial Papers, Orleans*, 9:914–15.

§ From William Eustis. *23 January 1811, War Department.* Transmits a return of the army with a letter from the adjutant and inspector general containing the information requested by the House of Representatives in the resolution of 21 Jan. 1811.[1]

FC (PHi: Daniel Parker Papers); letterbook copy (DNA: RG 107, LSP). FC 1 p.

1. On 21 Jan. 1811 William Helms of New Jersey presented a resolution requesting the president to lay before the House a return of the army "with the stations at which the garrisons are fixed, and the strength of each garrison; also the state of the recruiting service, and the progress that has been made therein since the last session" (*Annals of Congress*, 11th Cong., 3d

sess., 673). JM forwarded the information requested to the House in his message of 31 Jan. 1811.

§ From Albert Gallatin. *24 January 1811, Treasury Department.* On the subject of the Senate resolution of 21 Jan. 1811,[1] reports that the treasury has no documents showing the amount of British or French property confiscated under the Nonintercourse Act of 1809 and the act of 1 May 1810.[2] A circular letter was written on 22 Jan. to the several district attorneys to obtain this information. Encloses a letter from the register of the treasury to show that the information requested on imports for 1810 cannot be prepared during the present session of Congress. Will prepare and transmit the information for the last three quarters of 1809.

RC and enclosure (DNA: RG 46, Legislative Proceedings, 11A-E4). RC 2 pp. In a clerk's hand, signed by Gallatin. Enclosure (1 p.) is a copy of Joseph Nourse to Gallatin, 23 Jan. 1811, explaining why the treasury could not at that time provide the information for 1810 sought by the Senate. RC and enclosure printed in *Annals of Congress*, 11th Cong., 3d sess., 105–6. JM forwarded Gallatin's letter and its enclosure to the Senate in his message of 26 Jan. 1811.

1. On 21 Jan. 1811 the Senate passed a resolution, introduced by James Lloyd of Massachusetts on 18 Jan., requesting JM to forward an account of British and French property confiscated under either the Nonintercourse Act or the law of 1 May 1810 and also to forward an account of the goods, wares, and merchandise imported from foreign countries between 1 Apr. 1809 and 31 Dec. 1810, "distinguishing between the amount imported in American and foreign vessels, and specifying the countries to which the latter belonged" (*Annals of Congress*, 11th Cong., 3d sess., 98–99, 100).

2. Macon's Bill No. 2.

§ From Fontaine Maury. *24 January 1811, Georgetown.* Called on JM "this Morning" but found him engaged with Secretary of State Smith. Offers himself as a candidate for the collectorship vacated by the removal of Laurence Muse. Has no testimonials ready; "I presume however that your own knowledge of me may be Sufficient to Judge in that respect." If documents are needed he can have them in four or five days.

RC (DNA: RG 59, LAR, 1809–17, filed under "Maury"). 2 pp. Maury wrote a further letter to JM on this subject on 3 Feb. 1811 (ibid.; 1 p.), mentioning that he was obtaining testimonials and concluding that "although I have been unfortunate in Commercial persuits . . . I am totally Free from any embarrassments arising out of them."

§ To the House of Representatives. *25 January 1811.* Transmits a report of the superintendent of the city stating the expenditures under the act of 28 Apr. 1810 for the better accommodation of the Post Office and Patent Office and for other purposes.

RC and enclosure (DNA: RG 233, President's Messages, 11A-D1). RC 1 p. In a clerk's hand, signed by JM. Printed in *ASP, Post Office*, p. 44. Enclosure is Thomas Munroe to JM, 19 Jan. 1811 (first letter).

From Alexander McRae

DEAR SIR,   PARIS 26. Jan 1811.

The change which it was General Armstrong's pleasure before he left France to make in the American Consulate at Paris,[1] gave me the honor to receive your communication of Judge Cooper's patriotic wishes, to obtain the publications &c. indicated by the copy of his Letter which was enclosed to Mr. Warden.[2] A Stranger, & almost entirely ignorant of the language even of the Country, I have been obliged to avail myself of the aid of Doctor Patterson a young American Patriot of distinguished merit, (Son of the Director of the Mint at Philadelphia) to procure a partial supply, the best we could obtain, of such books as Judge Cooper's Letter described; which are forwarded to L'Orient for the purpose of being conveyed by the Essex to Mr. John Vaughan, whom the Judge has named as his friend. These books were purchased at so cheap a rate, as to render it entirely unnecessary that I should trouble you with the draft which your friendship for Judge Cooper had invited. I regret very much that it is not in our power at this moment to procure for Judge Cooper the Abbe Hany's Porcelain illustrations of Chrystallography; but hope we shall be able to forward them by the next suitable conveyance. As to a new Edition of Loysel sur l'art de la Verrerie, Doctor Patterson assures me that the Judge is misinformed: He says that after strict enquiry he has ascertained, that there is only a single Edition of that Work.

Excuse the liberty to which this incident has led, of observing that accident has produced an absence from my Family of much greater duration than I had anticipated, & that I shall hope the arrangements I have made to return to my Country for a short time, will not in any event be regarded as improper. If I were to remain, I would spare no pains to obtain for Judge Cooper, every publication extant on the Sciences to which his Patriotism devotes his mind; and the gentleman who may represent me during my absence, will I hope attend with equal pleasure to the Judge's wishes in this respect.

Enclosed I have the pleasure to send you a small Work (concerning the merits of which from my ignorance of the French language I can say nothing) on a subject which has at a former day, very greatly to the advantage of the Public received your attention—and with the highest respect & esteem I have the honor to be sincerely Dear Sir, Your friend & obedient Servant

AL: MCRAE.

RC (DLC). Docketed by JM. Enclosed work not identified.

1. See McRae to JM, 8 Dec. 1809 (*PJM-PS*, 2:118–19 and n. 2).

2. See Thomas Cooper to JM, 19 Aug. 1810, and JM to David Bailie Warden, 1 Sept. 1810 (*PJM-PS*, 2:495–96, 518).

Account of a Conversation with
David Bailie Warden

WASHINGTON [26 January 1811]

Conversation with the President observed respecting My appointement that he would be as open to my [*sic*] as I had been to him that the place was given to my [*sic*] by general A[r]mstrong—that it was only ⟨precarious?⟩ that he had appointed another—that by reappointing Me he might offend G. as a friend—Besides the place was destined for Mr. Russel who May wish to occupy it when appointed by a Minister—that he could not decide for the moment[1]—that he would wait for further information that he had personal feelings toward me that he was pleased with the discharge of my official duties.

Letterbook copy (MdHi: Warden Papers). Dated "26 1811 Janvier."

1. In reporting this conversation to Jefferson, Warden wrote that JM "informed me today that he cannot nominate me at present. I propose to remain here a few weeks in hopes that he will decide in my favor, tho' he does not give me much encouragement. He mentioned that Mr Russel had been destined as Consul for Paris, and that perhaps he will wish to occupy that place when supplanted by a Minister." Warden added that his friends in New York, Philadelphia, and Baltimore had written to many senators and representatives on his behalf and he believed that Congress would support his nomination. "The mass of Republican Irishmen, established in this Country," he continued, "are interested in my success, and have declared that they will feel obligations to the President if he nominates me as Consul to Paris" (Warden to Jefferson, 26 Jan. 1811 [DLC: Jefferson Papers]).

§ To the Senate. *26 January 1811.* "I transmit to the Senate a Report from the Secretary of the Treasury on the subject of their Resolution of the 21st. instant."

RC and enclosures (DNA: RG 46, Legislative Proceedings, 11A-E4). RC 1 p. In a clerk's hand, signed by JM. For enclosures, see Gallatin to JM, 24 Jan. 1811, and n.

§ From Thomas Hazard, Jr. *26 January 1811, Boston.* Informs JM that his son Samuel is now in Russia where he intends to remain for several years on business. Requests he be appointed consul at Archangel, "a place of Considerable trade with the United States, Several hundred American vessels it is said, loaded there the last summer, and . . . the probability I presume is, that our trade will increase to that Country."[1]

RC (DNA: RG 59, LAR, 1809–17, filed under "Hazard"). 2 pp.

1. On 1 Mar. 1811 JM nominated Samuel Hazard to be consul at Archangel. At that time JM may have been unaware that Levett Harris, American consul at St. Petersburg, had already appointed Francis Dana to be vice-consul and agent at Archangel and that the Russian government had recognized Dana in that capacity (*Senate Exec. Proceedings*, 2:173; Harris to Robert Smith, 18/30 May 1811, Bashkina et al., *The United States and Russia*, pp. 755–56).

§ From Mariano Velazquez de la Cadena. *26 January 1811, New York.* Encloses a copy of his *Elements of the English Language,*[1] written during his residence in the U.S. "for the benefit of my countrymen, who are desirous of acquiring that language."

RC (DLC). 1 p.

1. *Elementos de la lengua inglesa para uso de los españoles* (New York, 1810; Shaw and Shoemaker 21891).

From Benjamin Henry Latrobe and George Murray

SIR,   WASHINGTON, January 27th. 1811

The Society of Artists of the United States established at Philadelphia,[1] have committed the immediate management of the institution to a President, & four Vice-presidents. But for that Patronage which shall give to it, in its very infancy, the character of public usefulness, and secure to it public encouragement, the Society look up to You: to You, who while your life has been devoted to the great and permanent interests of Your country, have exhibited in all your labors the polish & refinement of a highly cultivated taste. In the name & on behalf of the Society we therefore solicit you to accept of the highest distinction of the institution, by becoming the *Patron* of an establishment, the object of which is, to give to native Genius those means of attaining excellence in the Arts, for which we have hitherto been indebted to foreign instruction.

B. HENRY LATROBE
GEO. MURRAY
}Vice presidents

RC (DLC); draft (MdHi: Latrobe Letterbooks). RC docketed by JM. Draft dated 26 Jan. 1811. Minor variations between the RC and draft have not been noted.

1. For a discussion of the origins and history of the Society of Artists of the United States, established in May 1810, see "Latrobe and the Society of Artists of the United States" in Van Horne, *Papers of Latrobe,* 3:65–67.

To Lafayette

MY DEAR SIR,   WASHINGTON Jany 28. 1811

Your favor by Genl. Armstrong[1] & that of Sept 26,[2] have been duly received. My last to you, went by the Essex frigate.[3] I wish it could have rendered an account of your interests on the Mississipi more correspondent with your favorable calculations. The view it gave of them nevertheless indicated a great intrinsic and even venal value. Should our efforts in the vicinity of N Orleans finally disappoint us on this prospect I can say nothing in addition to the contents of my last, more than that the auxilliary to Mr Duplantier has lately received fresh exhortations to do the utmost for you that may be possible and he is intelligent active and the best dispositions for the purpose.

Tr (CSmH).

1. Lafayette to JM, 20 Sept. 1810, *PJM-PS*, 2:547–49.
2. *PJM-PS*, 2:559–60.
3. JM to Lafayette, 1 Nov. 1810, *PJM-PS*, 2:609.

From Vincent Bramham

DEAR SIR,   Monday Evening January 28th. 1811

Not until last night did I receive your letter[1] owing to my absence from home. Few can lament your Ill health more than I do, and few very few wou'd rejoice more were your health perfectly restored.

The Collectors office[2] to which your friendly confidence calls my attention occasioned me to day to make some enquiries as to the duties and lucre thereto attached. Poor Muse (who seems extremely unhappy at the distracted state of his affairs) gives me no information calculated greatly to rouse my Anxiety: he says the profits at present, after deducting incidental and unavoidable expences, are very inconsiderable; And I think the lowering appearences of the Multiform restrictions on neutral commerce betoken no hope of a Speedy change. The Sacrifice of my accustomed habits for a Town residence cou'd not be prudently warranted for a much less sum than $1.000 ℗ Annum.

You my dear Sir are contiguous to that department of State where a correct knowledge as to the profit can be satisfactorily obtaind; and your Superior discernment in the probable state of our future commerce whereby the Emoluments of the office may be encreased render you more competent than I am to decide, therefore I most willingly confide to your better Judgment to propose me or not: and in the event of my appointment be well assured your friendship and preference of me Shall not be abused.

I have not been inattentive to your request as it respects your little Kentuckey friend, and am informed by Thompson he certainly will not start earlier than about the 1st. of April. At any time to hear from you will afford the sincerest pleasure to Dr Sir yours very truly

VIN BRAMHAM[3]

RC (DLC). Docketed by JM.

1. Letter not found.

2. JM was seeking to fill the position of collector for the district of Tappahannock after the removal of Laurence Muse, who had held the position since 1794 (see *PJM*, 15:244 and n. 1). On 30 Jan. 1811 John Tayloe sent JM letters he had received from Thomas Brockenbrough and John Haile, dated 26 and 27 Jan., requesting that Haile be appointed to the post. JM nominated Haile on 5 Feb., and after Senator William Branch Giles of Virginia had the nomination referred to a select committee, the appointment was confirmed on 19 Feb. (Tayloe to JM, 30 Jan. 1811, and enclosures [DNA: RG 59, LAR, 1809–17, filed under "Haile"]; *Senate Exec. Proceedings*, 2:165, 167).

3. Vincent Bramham represented Richmond County in the Virginia House of Delegates, 1801–5 and 1818–26 (Swem and Williams, *Register*, p. 350).

From Samuel Carswell

DEAR SIR,   PHILADA. Jany. 28th. 1811

I last had the pleasure to address you in March 1810, since which time I have had nothing interesting to communicate.[1] I beg leave to congratulate you, on the decision of the US Bank question,[2] as it is so favorable to the future welfare of this Country, & is another triumph of American Virtue, over British corruption & intrigue. It must be obvious to every one, who has the least knowledge of that Bank & is not wilfully blind, that it has always been under the influence of those who are inimical to the Republican principles of this Government—that it has been partial in the distribution of its favors & more disposed to withold, than to bestow them, on such persons, as were active to diffuse those principles. An Institution that can receive into it's bosom, a friend & fellow conspirator of Burr, & in favor of which, another notorious traitor, openly & impudently appears, cannot, in it's operation be friendly to this Republic.[3]

I am glad, since the majority opposed to it, was so small, that the decision took place early enough to prevent the effect, which the uncommon exertions of it's friends here, might have had. They had two public meetings in this place last week. One, of the Merchants:[4] The other, of the Mechanics.[5] At those meetings many appeared & approved of their object, who hitherto stood in the Republican ranks, some through ignorance, some thro apostacy, but more from motives of fear. This last reason, is a strong argument, in favor of it's dissolution. No institution, capable of extending it's influence so greatly, as the US Bank was & of establishing that influence, by so powerful a motive, as a sense of dependence in those connected with it, should be suffered to exist in this Country. If we must have monied institutions, Congress cannot use too much care to render them harmless; that the people may enjoy the benefits arising from them, without having their independence shackled & this can be effected in no other way, than by preventing any one, from having a superiority to the rest, in point of privelege & power. It is to the advantage which the US Bank possessed in this respect, that the distress of our Citizens ought to be attributed, & not to a great scarcity of money, for the defered 6 ₱ Ct. Stock cannot be had under 104 & the 3 ₱ Ct. Stock is from 62½ to 65. It is true, the Bank paid on the first of the Month, $1.700.000 Dolls. on Acct. of Government, but that did not throw much money into circulation, as $1.100.000, was due to her. It is, her almost unbounded influence, then that has occasioned the great cry of distress, you have heard.

I understand that Doctor Bache will be removed from the Office of Surveyor of this Port. In prospect of such an event, I take the liberty, to submit to your consideration for that Office, William J. Duane.[6] You are, doubtless, acquainted with his public character; with his integrity & correctness as a politician & the ability with which he discharged his Duty, as a Representative of this District, in our Legislature. I believe, his private character, stands equally fair, at least, I have never heard any thing alleged against it. I do not know any person, better calculated, to fill that Office & as he is Brother-in-Law to the Doctor, it will be keeping the Office in the family. With Sentiments of Respect I have the honor to be Your Obdt. Hble. Sert.

SAML CARSWELL

RC (DLC). Cover marked "Private" by Carswell. Docketed by JM.

1. Besides his letter of 29 Mar. 1810, Carswell had written to JM on 16 June 1810 (*PJM-PS*, 2:291–92, 382–83).

2. On 4 Jan. 1811 William Burwell of Virginia introduced in the House of Representatives a bill to continue in force the 1791 act incorporating the subscribers to the Bank of the United States. After much debate, the House voted on 24 Jan. by 65 to 64 to postpone the bill indefinitely (*Annals of Congress*, 11th Cong., 3d sess., 488, 826).

3. The presence of foreigners, former Loyalists, and the associates of Aaron Burr—such as Mathew Carey, Tench Coxe, and Erick Bollmann—in the ranks of those favoring the recharter of the Bank of the United States drew much hostile comment from those Republicans opposing recharter. The Philadelphia *Aurora General Advertiser* remarked on 19 Jan. 1811 that if Burr's adherents were friendly to the Bank of the United States, *"the bank cannot be friendly to the country."*

4. Carswell referred to a meeting held at the Merchant's Coffee House on 23 Jan. 1811 and chaired by Joseph Grice. A committee of five was formed to draft a petition in favor of rechartering the Bank of the United States and to convey it to Washington (*Poulson's American Daily Advertiser*, 25 Jan. 1811).

5. The Master Mechanics and Manufacturers of Philadelphia held a meeting at the Shakespeare Hotel on 24 Jan. 1811 to memorialize Congress on behalf of the Bank of the United States. The meeting was chaired by Gen. John Barker (ibid., 26 Jan. 1811).

6. William John Duane (1780–1865) was the eldest son of William Duane, editor of the Philadelphia *Aurora General Advertiser*. Between 1809 and 1820 he served three terms in the Pennsylvania House of Representatives. In 1833 President Andrew Jackson appointed him secretary of the treasury but dismissed him after he refused to remove the deposits of the

Second Bank of the United States (Higginbotham, *Keystone in the Democratic Arch*, p. 355 n. 74).

§ To Benjamin Henry Latrobe and George Murray. *28 January 1811, Washington.* Accepts their invitation of 27 Jan. to serve as patron of the Society of Artists in Philadelphia. Supports the "laudable objects" of the society but regrets that his services "will consist more in favorable inclinations, than in the usefulness, which would be the best title to the distinction." Conveys his thanks and an assurance to the society that "regarding the Arts which it cherishes, as among the endowments & enjoyments, which characterize human Society, under its highest & happiest destinies; it is one of my ardent wishes, that the tendency of our free system of Govt. may be pourtrayed as well in what may contribute to embellish the mind & refine the manners, as in those primary blessings, of which it already affords so many grateful proofs & presages."

Draft (DLC). 1 p. RC printed in *National Intelligencer*, 14 Feb. 1811, where it is misdated 11 Jan. 1811.

§ From Joseph Woodman and Others. *28 January 1811, Boston.* The subscribers, members of the legislature of Massachusetts, "having Understood that there would probably be a District Attorney soon Appointed for the District of Maine in room of the Hon. Silas Lee, . . . recommend Benjamin Green Esquire of Berwick in the County of York as . . . well Qualified to discharge the Duties of that Office."

RC (DNA: RG 59, LAR, 1809–17, filed under "Green"). 2 pp. Signed by Woodman and thirty-nine others.

From George W. Erving

Private

Dear Sir   Boston Jany 29. 1811

I was in hopes that I shoud have learnt in my communications with Senr Onis, on my passage thro' Phila something of sufficient importance to have been communicated to you; but his conversation on every point of interest, was so extremely, & even more than usually Extravagant, that I coud not presume to trouble you by any mention of it, the less necessary since (as I presumed) the then actual state of affairs with regard to the Floridas, rendered whatever utility I had hoped to derive from him (in your view always questionable) of less importance: a friend there furnished me with a copy of his secret instructions to the captain of the schooner "Ramona";[1] (the vessel which was taken by the english) tho' these do not contain any thing of political consequence, they are interesting as they shew his mode of operating, & therefore I take the liberty of inclosing them herewith: the loss of that vessel has not failed to irritate him; but the landing of Miranda,[2] a proceeding so wholly unequivocal in its character, & so utterly without palliation, this has completed his disgust with his former friends, & he begins to express himself openly in this new sense.

As relates to the character of Mr Skipwith, & those late proceedings of his which have so surprized & disappointed his friends,[3] I cannot refrain from taking the liberty of inclosing herewith, an extract of a letter from him to Col Skipwith[4] which has fallen in my way; it seems to afford room to hope that he has been directed in his late extraordinary conduct, by causes which may be susceptible of an explanation, in some sort satisfactory.

I wrote to Mr Smith from Phila suggesting a wish that something may be added to my instructions as to the conclusion of my mission; stating that unless I shoud completely succeed in the object of it, it woud be impossible for me (according to the present form of the instructions) to quit Copenhagen without your express order, & adverting to the obvious objections to my being left on that footing: I hope Sir that he has submitted to you this matter,[5] which I was the more encouraged to mention to him, knowing from himself that it had also occurred to you. Dear Sir with the most sincere Respect & attachment Your most obt & obliged Servt

GEORGE W ERVING

PS.

Having accidentally heard at N. York that a person whom I have had an opportunity of becoming sufficiently acquainted with to know that he is unfit for, has hopes of obtaining the Consulate of Gibraltar, I think it a duty to mention with respect to the present occupant Mr Gavino, who personally & officially I am particularly well acquainted with, that I have not seen any thing exceptionable in his conduct, but on the contrary beleive him to be a very faithful & useful public officer.

RC (MHi: Erving Papers). Docketed by JM. Enclosures not found.

1. The schooner *Ramona* had been fitted out by Onís with arms and munitions over the summer of 1810 in response to a request from the governor of Maracaibo for assistance and supplies. Both the vessel and its cargo were condemned and sold in Philadelphia in the first week of September for violation of the neutrality laws, and Onís was accordingly compelled to purchase the vessel and its supplies at a public auction before it could commence its voyage on 6 Oct. 1810. Onís gave the *Ramona*'s captain, Francisco Sanchez Crespo, instructions that he was to put into Curaçao in order to ascertain the political situation at Maracaibo before proceeding to his destination, but when the captain did so the British authorities on the island, whose suspicions seem to have been aroused by the facts that there were very few Spaniards in the *Ramona*'s crew and that the vessel was carrying munitions of war, also seized and detained the vessel. The episode led Onís to conclude that the British were secretly aiding the Caracan rebels. He subsequently had to appeal to his superiors in Spain to intercede with the British government in what proved to be a lengthy and protracted campaign to get the *Ramona* released from detention (Onís to Don Eusebio de Bardaxi y Azara, 20 Sept. 1810 and 4 Jan.

1811 [AHN: Archivo de Ministero de Estado, legajos 5636 and 5553, photocopies in DLC]).
The last-cited source contains three folders of documents relating to the case of the *Ramona*.

2. In September 1810 the Venezuelan rebel Francisco de Miranda sought permission to
return to his native land on board a Royal Navy vessel in the company of the delegates who
had been dispatched to London earlier in the year by the ruling junta in Caracas. Lord Wellesley would neither grant nor deny his request, with the result that Miranda departed Great
Britain for Curaçao, then took passage for La Guaira on a British vessel, HMS *Avon*, on 4 Dec.
1810. After arriving at La Guaira one week later, Miranda proceeded in triumph to Caracas
and thereafter played a prominent role in the events leading to the Venezuelan declaration of
independence from Spain on 5 July 1811 (William Spence Robertson, *The Life of Miranda*
[2 vols.; Chapel Hill, N.C., 1929], 2:71–124).

3. After traveling to Baton Rouge late in 1809, Fulwar Skipwith had settled in West Florida
where, on 22 Nov. 1810, he was elected governor of the republic that had just declared its
independence from Spain. His term of office was interrupted one week later by the arrival of
the Orleans territorial governor, William C. C. Claiborne, bearing JM's proclamation annexing West Florida as far as the Perdido River to the U.S. In the days that followed, Skipwith
seemed reluctant to accept the American annexation. He attempted, albeit unsuccessfully, to
negotiate conditions on which the government of West Florida might agree to enter the U.S.,
and he also protested what he regarded as Claiborne's overbearing manner in carrying out
JM's orders. Skipwith even went so far as to draft two letters to JM, dated 5 and 9 Dec. 1810,
on these matters. On reflection, however, he changed his mind, did not send the letters to JM,
and was eventually reconciled to the new order (DLC: West Florida Miscellany).

4. Henry Skipwith (1751–1815) had served as a lieutenant colonel of Virginia forces during
the Revolution and in 1782 had represented Cumberland County in the Virginia House of
Delegates. By virtue of his marriage to Anne Wayles in 1773, he was also Jefferson's brother-
in-law (*DAR Patriot Index*, p. 620; Swem and Williams, *Register*, p. 15; Malone, *Jefferson and
His Time*, 1:433).

5. On 20 Dec. 1810 the Senate had confirmed Erving's appointment as special minister to
the court of Denmark. His instructions of 3 Jan. 1811 were silent about the termination of his
mission beyond specifying that his salary was to cease at the time he received permission to
return. On 8 Feb. 1811 Robert Smith issued a supplementary instruction allowing Erving to
return to the U.S. as soon as he had accomplished the object of his mission or as soon as he
had satisfactorily ascertained that further efforts to assist American merchants in Denmark
would be "ineffectual" (DNA: RG 59, IM).

From Benjamin Rush

DEAR SIR,   PHILADELPHIA Jany 30. 1811.

With sincere Sympathy I sit down to inform you that this evening your
amiable nephew expired. His Sufferings from the last Symptoms of his disease were much less than is common in similar Cases. I write this note in
great haste, as the post office will close in a few minutes, and with a View
that your brother may be stopped on his Way to Philadelphia. From Dear
Sir yours truly and respectfully

BENJN: RUSH

RC (DLC). Docketed by JM.

§ To Congress. *30 January 1811.* "I transmit to Congress Copies of a letter from the Secretary of the Treasury accompanied by copies of the 'Laws, Treaties and other documents relative to the public lands' as collected and arranged pursuant to the Act passed April 27th 1810."

RC and enclosure, two copies (DNA: RG 233, President's Messages, 11A-D1; and DNA: RG 46, Legislative Proceedings, 11A-E2). Each RC 1 p.; in a clerk's hand, signed by JM. In addition to copies of the volume Gallatin had sent to JM on 17 Jan. 1811, JM also forwarded to each branch of Congress a copy of Gallatin's letter to him of that date.

§ From J. A. P. Poutingon.[1] *30 January 1811, Philadelphia.* Submits to JM several "reflexions" originally published in the Philadelphia *Tickler,*[2] the Boston *Columbian Centinel,*[3] and the Boston *Democrat,*[4] the last two dealing with coastal fortifications and flying artillery. Asserts that no one can prove that a successful invasion of Great Britain is impossible or that invasion forces prepared by Napoleon might not be used against the U.S. Argues that the U.S. has no reason to believe that it will be treated differently from any other nation and that no one has ever proved that harbor fortifications are a waste of money. Points out that these publications show his desire to serve the U.S. and suggests that it is customary to reward such services. Asks JM to take into consideration that he is a foreigner, blind in one eye, without property, "and without any other capacity, than my professional of a military man of Cavalry." Seeks JM's support for his scheme to establish a military academy in Boston, for which he encloses a prospectus requesting payment of $10.[5]

RC and enclosures (DNA: RG 107, LRRS, P-208:5). RC 2 pp. Docketed by a War Department clerk as received 8 Feb. 1811. For enclosures, see nn. 2–4.

    1. J. A. P. Poutingon, who signed his letter as "Riding Master / Philadelphia," was probably the same person as the Peter Poutingam who had opened a riding school in July 1810 at Tenth and Arch Streets in Philadelphia (*Pa. Magazine of History and Biography,* 47 [1932]: 372).
    2. Poutingon enclosed an undated newspaper clipping (1 p.), written under his signature, which argued that an invasion force being prepared in French-controlled harbors was destined for North America. The argument assumed that the only way for Napoleon to destroy Great Britain was by producing a "civil commotion or revolution" and this could best be achieved by the bankruptcies that would result from the loss of American provisions and markets.
    3. The enclosure (1 p.) is a handwritten copy of a note by Poutingon, headed "for *the Centinel,*" addressed to the American government, and posing the question: "If the British navy passed the strong forts of the *Dardanelles,* what then can be the use of fortifications at the entrance of harbours?"
    4. Poutingon enclosed a handwritten copy of an essay headed *"for the Democrat"* (2 pp.), on flying, or light, artillery.
    5. "Prospectus of a Military Academy, for Artillery, Infantry, and Cavalry to be established in the City of Boston" (2 pp.). Poutingon sent JM a similar letter on 15 Feb. 1811. On that occasion, however, he asked JM to return the prospectus sent earlier, regardless of whether JM chose to subscribe (DNA: RG 107, LRRS, P-213:5; 1 p.).

From John Wayles Eppes

Thursday. [31 January 1811]

Jno W Eppes presents his respects to the President. He considers the subject on which he conversed with him today as of so much importance as to merit a deliberate decision of the question whether it is better for the public interest that the non importation law should be at present pushed in the House of Representatives or whether it should be suffered to lie until we asscertain with more certainty the actual situation of our relations with France.[1] A discussion of the Bill at the present time "clogged with the official communication of General Turreau that Tobo. and cotton are excluded["][2] "with the official opinion of the Secretary of State that France has not executed with good faith her agreement"[3]—"with information from private sources that American vessels have been seized and condemned under the Berlin and Milan decrees since the first of November"—will afford to our adversaries powerful weapons. Under such circumstances the Bill like the Sloath will drag through the house with groans at every step & be opposed by many of our own friends. If passed at all it will be with a feeble majority & connected with a discussion calculated to give to France a very erroneous view of the standing of our Government.

If any provisions for the relief of our own citizens shall be considered necessary—Que—if it would not be better to continue for the present our legal provisions to that object & leave the provisions necessary for the Execution of the Measure until it shall be asscertained, whether such provisions are absolutely necessary.

RC (DLC). Dated 1810 in the *Index to the James Madison Papers.* Date assigned here on the basis of the evidence discussed in nn. 1 and 3.

1. As chairman of the House committee on foreign relations, Eppes had introduced on 15 Jan. 1811 a bill to supplement the provisions of Macon's Bill No. 2 by excluding all British vessels, goods, and merchandise from American ports after 2 Feb. 1811, three months after JM's proclamation of 2 Nov. 1810. The bill was delayed while the House debated the renewal of the charter for the Bank of the United States, but in the interval doubts about the extent to which France had repealed the Berlin and Milan decrees were voiced in several quarters. The contents of JM's message to Congress on 31 Jan. 1811 confirmed the validity of these doubts and was evidently the occasion for Eppes's conversation with the president (see n. 3). Two days later, on 2 Feb. 1811, Eppes moved that the bill he had introduced on 15 Jan. be recommitted, a step he justified as prudent "until the doubts hanging over our foreign relations were dissipated." The motion for recommittal was carried, 82 to 9 (*Annals of Congress,* 11th Cong., 3d sess., 547–51, 863–96).

2. See Robert Smith to Turreau, 18 Dec. 1810, and n. 2.

3. No "official" declaration to this effect by the secretary of state has been found, but it was common knowledge in Washington by the end of January 1811 that the president and Robert Smith were in serious disagreement over the issue of the repeal of the French decrees. After attending the president's drawing room on 30 Jan. 1811, Joseph Gales, Jr., recorded in

his diary that the views of JM and Smith "on the subject of our relations with France, differ essentially—the President being in favor of suspending the Non-intercourse law, as to France, notwithstanding the news from France to January 1st, and the Secretary of State being in favor of postponing the decision of that question until we learn that France has actually revoked her Decrees. The President explained his ideas, at length, and appeared to be afraid *to think* that France would not fulfil her engagement. The Secretary of State differed from him, upon this point." On 1 Feb. Gales wrote: "On consulting Mr. Eppes, I find that he is of the same opinion as the Secretary of State; and, before the documents, yesterday brought to the House, and the letter from Mr. Russell, he had addressed a letter to the President, informing him that, under present circumstances, a Bill upon the subject, if carried through the House of Representatives, at all, of which he was very doubtful, would be carried by a feeble majority." At about the same time Robert Smith also informed the British chargé d'affaires, John Philip Morier, that in his opinion the French decrees "were not repealed, and that, before the rising of the present Congress, the whole of their restrictive commercial System would be entirely done away" ("Recollections of the Civil History of the War of 1812," *Historical Magazine*, 3d ser., 3 [1874–75]: 161; Morier to Lord Wellesley, 4 Feb. 1811 [PRO: Foreign Office, ser. 5, vol. 74]).

From Benjamin Henry Latrobe

SIR,   WASHINGTON January 31st. 1811

I herewith transmit to you the account of monies expended on the furniture of the presidents house since March 1809. The original Account and Vouchers have been lodged with the Accounting Officers of the Treasury. Besides the Sums put down in this account, I have disbursed others for which I have not yet obtained proper Vouchers the principal part of them being for the minor utensils of Housekeeping as buckets, brooms, &c &c, to defray which & for the sake of having Vouchers I deposited a Sum in the Hands of Mr. Deblois, part of which remains unexpended. Having collected all the outstanding balances, I have now to request a further advance to enable me to defray the same. There remains in the Treasury the Sum of 1.500 Dollars, and in the hands of Andrews & Jones for furniture sold, the further sum of near 500$, which will become due in the course of a Month, the furniture having chiefly been sold on credi⟨t.⟩

I therefore in order to be enabled to answer the⟨se⟩ demands ask you to grant me a warrant for 1.000⟨$⟩ which will leave in hand a sum equal to near⟨ly⟩ 1000$ more.

I take the liberty of enclosing the form in which you have usually drawn on the Treasury, & am with high respect Yr

B H LATROBE.

RC and enclosure (NN). Surviving enclosure (2 pp.) is an account of moneys spent by Latrobe between April 1809 and January 1811 on furniture for the President's House, totaling $12,670.13. The enclosed form has not been found.

§ To Congress. *31 January 1811.* Transmits letters written by the U.S. chargé d'affaires at Paris to the secretary of state and to the French minister of foreign relations; also transmits two letters from the agent of the American consul at Bordeaux to the secretary of state.[1]

RC and enclosures, two copies (DNA: RG 233, President's Messages, 11A-D1; and DNA: RG 46, Legislative Proceedings, 11A-E3). Each RC 1 p.; in a clerk's hand, signed by JM. Enclosures 9 pp. (see n. 1). RC and enclosures printed in *ASP, Foreign Relations,* 3:380, 390–92.

1. JM enclosed copies of letters written by Jonathan Russell to Robert Smith and to the duc de Cadore, dated 11 and 10 Dec. 1810, respectively. Both letters reported the seizure of an American vessel, the *New Orleans Packet,* at Bordeaux under the Berlin and Milan decrees. Russell also mentioned that the frigate *Essex* had been put under quarantine unnecessarily on its arrival at Lorient, delaying the delivery of dispatches from the U.S. government. The two letters from Christopher Meyer at Bordeaux, dated 6 and 14 Dec. 1810, conveyed the same information as well as a report that another American vessel, the *Friendship,* had been seized.

§ To the House of Representatives. *31 January 1811.* Transmits a report of the secretary of war in compliance with the House resolution of 21 Jan. 1811.[1]

Printed copy and enclosures (*Message from the President of the United States, Transmitting a Return of the Army* . . . [Washington, 1811; Shaw and Shoemaker 24224]). For enclosures, see n. 1.

1. JM forwarded seven enclosures, including a covering letter from Secretary of War Eustis, dated 31 Jan., the contents of which repeated the information Eustis had sent to JM in his 23 Jan. letter (see Eustis to JM, 31 Jan. 1811 [FC, PHi: Daniel Parker Papers; letterbook copy, DNA: RG 107, LSP]). The second enclosure is a 31 Jan. letter from Abimael Y. Nicoll to Eustis, transmitting a general return of the army showing "the several stations at which garrisons are fixed, and the strength of each garrison," compiled from reports received up to 30 Nov. 1810. Nicoll also reported troop movements since that date and added that throughout 1810 "recruiting rendezvous have not, generally, been opened in the different states." Commanding officers had, however, been instructed "to enlist such men as offered," and Nicoll stated that 436 men had been recruited since the last session of Congress. Measures had also been adopted to extend the recruiting service by opening additional rendezvous.

The third enclosure, a "Statement of Expenditures for relief of sick seamen, during the year 1809; their amount, and in what manner made," shows a total expenditure of $48,058.06. The fourth enclosure is "A General Return of the army of the U.S.," showing a total of 5,685 officers, enlisted men, artificers, cadets, and musicians in the several posts and garrisons. This return of the army was submitted in the form of a large folio sheet (DNA: RG 233, President's Messages, 11A-D1). The fifth enclosure, a return of the troops in the "Military Peace Establishment," shows a total of 2,576 officers and enlisted men. The sixth enclosure is a return of the "Additional Military Force," showing a total of 3,217 officers and enlisted men. The seventh enclosure consists of accounts of absentees and lists 342 officers and men as absent from the several posts and garrisons.

§ From John Coburn. *31 January 1811, Mason, Kentucky.* Reminds JM that he accepted a judgeship in the Louisiana Territory and claims that he has faithfully performed his duties, despite the fact that he has not yet moved to the territory because of "the reluctance of my family to abandon their relatives and connexions in Kentucky." Since he has been employed in judicial positions for about twenty years and therefore lacks "the ordinary means of acquiring that competency sought for by most men," he is willing to serve for a further four years if JM approves. Points out that his commission will expire during the next recess of Congress and therefore suggests the propriety of renewing his commission during the current session.[1]

RC (DNA: RG 59, LAR, 1809–17, filed under "Coburn"). 2 pp. Cover dated Maysville, 8 Feb. 1811. Printed in Carter, *Territorial Papers, Louisiana-Missouri,* 14:437.

1. JM nominated Coburn for a further four-year term as judge in the Louisiana Territory on 20 Nov. 1811 (*Senate Exec. Proceedings,* 2:191).

§ From Ezra Davis and Others. *31 January 1811, Boston.* The memorialists, "Merchants & native citizens of the United states, engaged in a lawfull Commerce, with ports & places in the West Indies," complain that Henri Christophe, the "present Military & civil chieftain of Cape Henry" in Saint-Domingue, has seized and detained "a large amount" of their property. They enclose a copy of Christophe's 3 Jan. 1811 general order under which the seizures were made and declare that there is no justification "for this plunder of private property." They also state that on 6 Oct. 1810 Christophe ordered the arrest of the officers and crews of the eleven American vessels then at Cape Henry and would not permit their departure until 4 Jan. 1811. During this period of detention, many of the vessels were damaged and their crews "arbitrarily detained in consequence of which great numbers sickened, & many of them died." As "Native Citizens," they look to their government for redress; but since neither the U.S. nor other nations recognize a legitimate government in Saint-Domingue, the "ordinary course of demanding & obtaining redress for wrongs seems to be impeded." Such a situation "appears to afford just cause for granting Letters of Marque & Reprisal." The memorialists also suggest that "the presence of a few Frigates" from the U.S. Navy would be "the means of obtaining indemnity" and preventing future violations.[1]

RC and enclosure (DNA: RG 76, Haiti, Misc. Claims). RC 3 pp. Signed by Davis and thirteen others. Enclosure is a four-page printed *Ordre général de l'armée* (in French).

1. It is uncertain whether JM received this memorial in 1811. On the supposition that he did not, another version of it was submitted to him in November 1816, supported by documents specifying the extent of the damages suffered by the memorialists and seeking compensation for those damages (William Patterson to James Monroe, 1 Nov. 1816, Jabez Boothroyd to Monroe, 13 Nov. 1816 [ibid.]).

§ From an Unidentified Correspondent. *February 1811.* Forwards to JM "parts of a letter written to a friend on the 27. of July last which has lately returned to my hands." Hopes it may contain some ideas of benefit to the country.

RC (DNA: RG 107, LRRS, R-103:5). 1 p. Signed "A Republican." Docketed by a War Department clerk as received 9 Feb. 1811, with the notation: "Reflections on the situation of the U. S. with regard to S. A. & the views of the European Beligerents." Enclosure not found.

§ From Alexandre DuVernet. *1 February 1811, Castries, Saint Lucia, West Indies.* Mentions having sent copies [not found] of his complaints to the authorities on Guadeloupe to JM under cover of the minister at London two years ago and having omitted his last protestation. Taking the secure opportunity he finds here for this letter under the cover of Judge Bertholio, he adds to it a copy of the letter that he requested Judge Bertholio to send to General Ernouf[1] on 1 Jan. 1809. The response of 9 Jan. was flattering to the energy with which he claims the rights of an American citizen. The English translation, intended for a lawyer, conforms perfectly to the French original. Has learned that there is an American agent at Martinique, and he hastens there to make the acquaintance of this Mr. Cock. Claims JM's protection for justice from General Ernouf, who has completely ruined him, from whom he demands 80,000 gourdes, and who is presently a prisoner in England.

RC and enclosure (DNA: RG 59, ML). RC 1 p. In French. Enclosure is a copy of Du-Vernet to Bertholio, 20 Feb. 1810 (4 pp.), complaining of the treatment he received from General Ernouf.

1. Jean-Augustin Ernouf had been appointed captain general of Guadeloupe in 1803. He held the office until the British occupation of the island in 1810.

§ From Albert Gallatin. *1 February 1811, Treasury Department.* Encloses a copy of the departmental correspondence respecting the act to provide for a survey of the coasts of the U.S.[1] Reports that Mr. Hassler, "who has been designated to proceed to England in order to have the necessary instruments executed under his immediate care," is still willing to perform the service.

RC and enclosures (DNA: RG 46, Legislative Proceedings, 11A-E4). RC 1 p. In a clerk's hand, signed by Gallatin. Enclosures (67 pp.) are copies of Gallatin's correspondence with Isaac Briggs, Robert Patterson, Andrew Ellicott, F. R. Hassler, John Garnett, the Right Reverend James Madison, Joshua Moore, and John Vaughan between 25 Mar. and 24 Sept. 1807 on surveying the coasts of the U.S. Printed in *ASP, Commerce and Navigation,* 1:828–39. JM forwarded the RC and enclosures to the Senate in his message of 4 Feb. 1811.

1. On 20 Dec. 1810 the Senate had passed a resolution proposed by Samuel Dana of Connecticut directing JM to forward a statement of the proceedings made under the act of 10 Feb. 1807 "to provide for surveying the coasts of the United States" (*Annals of Congress,* 11th Cong., 3d sess., 27).

§ Receipt from Benjamin Henry Latrobe. *1 February 1811.* "Recd. of the President of the U. States his letter to the Secretary of the Treasury U.S. [not found] directing a Warrant for 1.000 on account of the fund for furnishing the President house to be issued in my favor."

Ms (DLC). 1 p. In Latrobe's hand.

¶ To George W. Erving. Letter not found. *1 February 1811.* Acknowledged in Erving to JM, 10 Mar. 1811. Discusses events in Florida and the policy of France toward the U.S. Also encloses five letters.

From Samuel Smith

SIR,   [ca. 4 February 1811]

I have the honor to send you herewith information recieved by the Schooner mentioned in Mr. Russell's letter—which will Shew that Mr. R. has been misinformed.[1] I have the honor to be your Obedt. servt.

                                                                    S. SMITH

[Enclosure]

                                                          BALTE. 4th. Feby. 1811.

The Supercargo of the Schooner Friendship, Captn. Snow of Baltimore, writes his owners under date of the 13th. Decemr. of his arrival at Bordeaux on the   [2] and that the vessel was obliged to perform quarantine. In a postscript to this letter of the 14th. he states, that he had received an order to land his Cargo on the first fair day and deposit it in the public stores— at this he felt much alarmed, apprehensive it amounted to a seizure, but adds, that on enquiry his fears abated as he was informed it was the customary mode and practised in all cases—he says nothing about the vessel's being sequestered as reported. The friendship sailed from this port on the 15th. Octr. & left the Capes on the 17th. She had cleared out for Gottenburgh (to elude detention from British Cruisers) but was bound to port in France in the Bay of Biscay—her cargo was principally Coffee & a little logwood—she had no licence. Her papers were sent on to Paris, his expectations of a favorable result were sanguine.

RC and enclosure (DLC). RC undated; docketed by JM "Feby. 4. 1811." Date supplied on the basis of JM's docket and the date of the enclosure.

1. Smith was probably referring to Russell's report of the arrival of the *Friendship* in Bordeaux in a postscript to his 4 Dec. 1810 letter to the secretary of state (DNA: RG 59, DD, France). Russell declared that he did not know how French authorities would receive the vessel, although he doubted that it would come within the provisions of the Berlin and Milan decrees. He did predict, however, that the case would determine whether colonial produce would be admitted into France from American vessels without "a special permit or licence." His conclusion was "that it will not be so admitted."

2. Left blank in enclosure.

§ To the Senate. *4 February 1811*. Transmits a report from the secretary of the treasury in compliance with a Senate resolution of 20 Dec. 1810.

RC and enclosures (DNA: RG 46, Legislative Proceedings, 11A-E4). RC 1 p. In a clerk's hand, signed by JM. For enclosures, see Gallatin to JM, 1 Feb. 1811.

§ From Robert Smith. *4 February 1811, Department of State*. Forwards copies of the latest census and militia returns from the Orleans Territory in compliance with a Senate resolution of 1 Feb. 1811.[1]

RC and enclosures (DNA: RG 46, TP, Orleans); letterbook copy (DNA: RG 59, DL). RC 1 p. In a clerk's hand, signed by Smith. Enclosures are copies of the census return for the Orleans Territory, 31 Dec. 1806 (1 p.), and the militia return for the Orleans Territory, 30 June 1810 (1 p.). Printed in Carter, *Territorial Papers, Orleans,* 9:886–87, 923–24. JM forwarded the RC and enclosures to the Senate on 5 Feb. 1811.

1. On 1 Feb. 1811 the Senate had passed a resolution proposed by James A. Bayard of Delaware requesting the president to forward copies of the latest census and militia returns from Orleans Territory (*Annals of Congress,* 11th Cong., 3d sess., 114).

¶ To Benjamin Rush. Letter not found. *4 February 1811.* Offered for sale in Parke-Bernet Catalogue No. 499, "The Alexander Biddle Papers" (1943), pt. 2, item 169, which notes that the one-page letter of about seventy-five words reads in part: "I have just recd. your favor of the 7th inst. [not found] as I had before that communicating the death of my nephew [Rush to JM, 30 Jan. 1811]. In thanking you for your kind attention, which followed him to his grave, I express the grateful feelings of his parents as well as myself." Apparently, either the date of JM's letter or the date "7th inst." is rendered incorrectly in the catalogue.

From John Armstrong

DEAR SIR,   NEW YORK 5 feb. 1811.
  I yesterday, on my return to this city, received from M. Russel a letter, from which I make the following extract.[1] It's enclosures are sent entire. It would be injustice, as well to M. Russel, as to a suggestion which fell from you when I had lately the honor of seeing you, were I to withold a testimony of his very respectable standing in the place which he now fills, & which removes every doubt of his future usefulness in a higher office, were it conferred upon him.[2] This testimony comes from one of the oldest and ablest diaplomatists in France, and is sub-joined to one of the annexed papers. Permit me to assure you of the very great respect & attachment of, dear Sir, Your most Obedient, & very humble Servant,

                                                  JOHN ARMSTRONG.

RC (DLC). Docketed by JM. Enclosures not found, but see n. 1.

1. In his 19 Feb. letter Armstrong mentioned that he had sent JM a letter about Alexander McRae, and in his 3 Mar. letter to JM Armstrong again referred to a letter he had received from Jonathan Russell containing references to McRae. On that basis it is possible to suggest that Armstrong sent the president an extract from a 6 Nov. 1810 letter he had received from Russell in Paris (RPB-JH: Russell Papers). This was a lengthy and damning indictment of McRae's conduct in Europe. Russell accused the Virginian, among other things, of being a spy for James Monroe, of having engaged in speculation in "English licences," and of having attempted to engage in improper negotiations with the duc de Cadore on the future of Spain's American colonies.
2. On 5 Feb. 1811 Armstrong informed Russell that in his recent meeting with JM in

Washington "you were mentioned as my successor at Paris." JM was, Armstrong continued, "much embarrassed on this, as on many other points & there is no knowing what may be the result. It does not appear to me to be his intention to take any one from this state [New York]—but as B. L. [Brockholst Livingston] is now at Washington & as his presence may revive his pretensions, even this pre-disposition may be got over. In a letter of this day to him, I have mentioned you again & have given him an extract of a letter received from france . . . which speaks in a very friendly & respectful way of you" (RPB-JH: Russell Papers).

From Henry Dearborn

DEAR SIR,　　　　　　　　　　　　　　　BOSTON Febrry. 5th. 1811

I consider it my duty to give you the following information in relation to the conduct of our Consul Dabney at Fayal.[1] I have received Mr. Dabneys official certificates to two facts which are contradicted by two witnesses on oath, one certificate is to verify the landing of a cargo at that Island, the other, certifying that the crew of the vessel from which the said cargo was landed, were there discharged and paid of[f] according to the law of the U. S. The vessel, was the Brig Mount Etna from this port, cleared out for the Brazils, under bonds not to violate the nonintercourse laws, but by the testimony of two of her crew and the declaration of a third, whose testimony on oath has not yet been ta⟨ken⟩ by reason of his absence, is to the following purport, that the Brig, with one of the owners on board, went direct to Fayal, and there changed her na⟨me⟩ & Flag, and took on board a young Portugese lad as a nominal Master, and by threats & force compeled the crew to continue the voyage to the coast of africa, without discharges or pay, as the law directs, that at Goree, a British establishment near the mouth of the River Gambia, the cargo was principally sold and discharged, and measures were then pursued for procuring a cargo of Slave⟨s⟩ and that after having obtained from twenty to thirty, the Brig was taken and condemned. What gives weight to the testimony of those men, is their having found their way home by different vessels at different times, and were examined seperately without any means of making up their story here together, and if their testimony is to be credited, the certificates of Mr. Dabney must be incorrect, at least, and from my own examination of two of the witnesses, I am strongly inclined to believe that their stories are substantially true. I am Sir with the highest respect Your Humbe. Servt.

H. DEARBORN

RC (DNA: RG 59, ML).

1. John B. Dabney had been appointed consul at Fayal (in the Azores) in December 1806. He remained in office until his death in 1826, when he was succeeded by his son (*Senate Exec. Proceedings*, 2:44–45, 3:544).

From Samuel Smith

SIR,
                                                    [ca. 5 February 1811]
    I do myself the honor to send you a Copy of the letter of the supercargo
of the Schooner Friendship to his Owners & am your Obedt. servt.

                                                    S. SMITH

[Enclosure]

DEAR SIR
                                            BALTIMORE 5th Feby. 1811
    Apprehensive that the statement I hastily furnished you last evening, re-
specting the Schooner Friendship, Captn. Snow, might be incorrect in
some particulars, I this day procured from Mr. Wilmott* the Supercargo's
letter to him, dated Bourdeaux December 13. 1810. The following are extracts, which I presume will not be found to differ materially, if at all, from
the hasty sketch already in your possession.[1]

                            Extracts.
"We arrived here on the 29th November, all in good health, and had to
perform a quarantine of 7 days, in which time, *two American vessels which
had* been *here with a Cargo of fish,* from the Banks, passed us, it was not
possible to write, and it was with difficulty that we only could tell them to
report the vessel. The strictest examinations have been made, and all, so far
as I can inform myself, is in our favor. Some of the first and best informed
merchants have no doubt, that after the papers have been sent to Paris, that
we will get permission to sell the Cargo, and to take one in return. It will
take about 4 or 6 weeks, and in this time nothing can be done than to wait
patiently the decision of the Emperor." In a post[s]crip[t] of the 14th Decr.
he adds, "An order from the director of the custom house has been given to
land the cargo the first fair day, and to put it in the public stores; I felt rather
a little alarmed, but I understand that it is the usual way in which all those
Americans [who] had obtained permission to sell have been treated."

    The foregoing are extracted verbatim from the letter now before me, and
from which it would appear that altho the cargo was ordered to be landed,
and placed in the public stores, yet that the vessel remained free from seizure or sequestration.[2]

    There is nothing new to day. Flour 8¾ to 9$. Very truly Yr. friend &
He. Servt.

                                            JERE: SULLIVAN[3]
Solomon Etting Esqr.

*Mr. Wilmot is one of the owners of the Schr. Friendship.

Mr Sullivan the writer of this extract, is another of the owners. Mr. Eppes
will notice that in the sketch delivered him yesterday, Mr Sullivan says the

151

vessel was laden with colonial produce, and that she had no licence. That circumstance is omitted in the foregoing extract, but may notwithstanding be relied on.

A. McKim[4]

RC and enclosure (DLC). RC undated; written at the foot of the enclosure.

    1. See Samuel Smith to JM, ca. 4 Feb. 1811, and enclosure.

    2. On 7 Feb. 1811 the *National Intelligencer* reported that letters recently received from Baltimore indicated that the cargo of the *Friendship* had not been seized but merely "placed in depot" and that the details of the case had apparently been misreported.

    3. Jeremiah Sullivan was a partner in the Baltimore mercantile firm of Hollingsworth and Sullivan. He also held offices in a Baltimore bank, fire company, and the local militia (Jerome R. Garitee, *The Republic's Private Navy: The American Privateering Business as Practiced by Baltimore during the War of 1812* [Middletown, Conn., 1977], p. 269).

    4. Alexander McKim (1748–1832) was a Republican member of the House of Representatives from a Baltimore district from 1809 to 1815.

§ To the Senate. *5 February 1811.* Forwards a report from the secretary of state in compliance with a Senate resolution of 1 Feb. 1811.

RC and enclosures (DNA: RG 46, Legislative Proceedings, 11A-E3). RC 1 p. In a clerk's hand, signed by JM. For enclosures, see Robert Smith to JM, 4 Feb. 1811, and n.

From John Armstrong

DEAR SIR,   NEW YORK 6th. feb. 1811.

    I have but two motives in transmitting to you the enclosed papers: 1st. to prevent you from suffering, as I have done, by a mis-placed confidence; & 2d. to justify myself against the insinuation that I acted, in the case of Mr. W.[1] with unreasonable severity. Beyond yourself however I do not wish this evidence to go, because I do not desire to take from him that degree of character which may be necessary to the successful persuit of some private calling.[2] I am, dear Sir, with the highest respect, Your most obedient & very humble servant

JOHN ARMSTRONG.

RC (PU). Enclosures not found.

    1. At a later time someone, possibly JM, interlined "Warden" here.

    2. Warden had long been seeking a permanent consular position in Paris, but Armstrong, during his tenure as minister to France, refused to support his pretensions and offered him lesser positions at Le Havre and Bordeaux instead. Warden declined these offers and returned home to lobby on his own behalf. He succeeded in obtaining the endorsement of former

president Jefferson for his claims to office, and he also actively cultivated the support of Dolley Madison (Skeen, *John Armstrong*, pp. 113–15, 118; Jefferson to JM, 8 Dec. 1810; Warden to Dolley Madison, 19 Jan. 1811 [ViU]).

§ **From Albert Gallatin.** *6 February 1811, Treasury Department.* Transmits a statement of importations in American and foreign vessels from 1 Apr. to 31 Dec. 1809, prepared by the register of the treasury, in compliance with a Senate resolution of 21 Jan. 1811.[1]

RC and enclosure (DNA: RG 46, Legislative Proceedings, 11A-E4). RC 1 p. Enclosure (10 pp.) is a statement in two parts—imports in American vessels and those in foreign vessels—signed by Joseph Nourse on 5 Feb. 1811. JM forwarded the letter and its enclosure to the Senate on 7 Feb. 1811.

    1. See Gallatin to JM, 24 Jan. 1811, and n. 1.

§ **From Harry Toulmin.** *6 February 1811, Fort Stoddert.* Writes that "nothing material has occurred" since his last letter other than the failure of the judge sent by Claiborne to establish civil government in the settlement on the Pascagoula River. Quotes from a 27 Jan. letter written to him by Judge Cumming[1] describing "'the state of anarchy and confusion'" on the Pascagoula and the refusal of Dupree to permit the rule of law. Cumming "seems fearful that a number of slaves taken by Dupree, might be carried off, and wishes me to have any answering to the description he gives, stopped in this country, if carried this way." The individual who owns the slaves has reportedly "been plundered to the amount of 30,000 dollars," and Dupree has harassed smaller property owners as well, alleging that he has been directed by Col. James Caller "to maintain his authority." Chief Justice John Caller of Washington County "has gone, I am told to pay him a visit," which Toulmin trusts will produce "submission to the laws."

"As to the Spaniards, it is said that a talk has lately been given to the Indians at Pensacola, creating an expectation of a war with the U. States. I cannot satisfy myself of the truth of the report." Nor does he give much credit to rumors that a British force is expected at Pensacola. Declares that the U.S. has lost standing with Spanish officials, who believe that the U.S. "countenanced and abetted" the revolt of their subjects. "Hence it is probable that difficulties may arise in the arrangements with the Governor of Florida, which there was not the smallest reason to apprehend when Col. M'Kee left this place." Gives credit, however, to JM's proclamation for effecting some "releasement from revolutionary dangers." Adds in a postscript that a letter just received from Cushing states that Hampton has ordered the troops to be removed from Mobile and sent to Fort Stoddert.[2] "I regret this step, as I fear that many of the citizens at Mobile have so far *committed* themselves with the Spanish officers, that they may now feel their displeasure."

RC (DLC). 4 pp. Docketed by JM. Printed in Carter, *Territorial Papers, Mississippi*, 6:175–77.

    1. Fortescue Coming (Cumming) (1762–1828) was a justice of the peace and sheriff in the St. Helena Parish of Orleans Territory. He was also the author of *Sketches of a Tour to the*

Western Country, through the States of Ohio and Kentucky . . . and a Trip through the Mississippi Territory, and Part of West Florida (Pittsburgh, 1810; Shaw and Shoemaker 19902). In January 1811 Claiborne commissioned him as a justice of the peace for the Pascagoula region of West Florida (Carter, *Territorial Papers, Orleans,* 9:985, 986; Claiborne to William Flood, 5 Jan. 1811, Rowland, *Claiborne Letter Books,* 5:82).

2. On 24 Dec. 1810 Lt. Col. Richard Sparks had ordered a force of territorial militia and regulars under Capt. Edmund P. Gaines to take possession of Mobile in pursuance of JM's 27 Oct. 1810 proclamation annexing West Florida. Col. Thomas Cushing counter-manded Sparks's order to seize Mobile on 4 Jan. 1811, but the troops under Gaines's command remained in the vicinity of Mobile awaiting further developments. On 19 Jan. Brig. Gen. Wade Hampton directed Cushing to withdraw the force to Fort Stoddert, an order that Cushing, for reasons similar to those indicated by Toulmin to JM, obeyed with some reluctance (see Cushing to William Eustis, 15 Jan. 1811, and enclosures [DNA: RG 107, LRRS, C-335:5], and 27 Feb. 1811, and enclosures [ibid., C-362:5]).

From Michael Leib

SIR,   WASHINGTON February 7th. 1811

A gross and calumnious attack has been made upon me in a Philadelphia print,[1] for having, under an impression of duty, submitted objections to you, against the nomination of Mr. John Smith as Marshal for the district of Pennsylvania; and it is alledged, that I was an applicant for that office.[2] Allow me to request of you to say, whether I, or any of my friends in my behalf, made any application to you for that office. I am Sir Your obedient Servant

M LEIB

RC (DLC).

1. This attack very probably appeared in the Philadelphia *Democratic Press* published by John Binns, but the editors have been unable to obtain copies of any issues for the first week in February 1811.

2. See Thomas Leiper to JM, 14 Jan. 1811, and n. 1.

§ To the Senate. *7 February 1811.* Transmits a report of the secretary of the treasury in compliance with a Senate resolution of 21 Jan. 1811.

RC and enclosure (DNA: RG 46, Legislative Proceedings, 11A-E4). RC 1 p. In a clerk's hand, signed by JM. For enclosure, see Gallatin to JM, 6 Feb. 1811, and n.

§ From John Melish.[1] *7 February 1811, New York.* Offers JM his opinions on trade and political economy, prompted by a consideration of the "Pecul[i]ar manner in which the Government of the United States is situated regarding the Bank Charter." Summarizes the state of U.S. trade with Europe, which has been interrupted for a number of years by the injustices of the belligerent powers. The continent is "almost compleatly sealed up" and the British market is glutted with American produce, creating a decline in revenue "which has afforded matter of triumph to the political oponents of the Government; and these oponents, in conjunction with a foreign faction, have unceasingly villified the party in power as the cause of evils which they have laboured incessantly to prevent." Manufactures have sprung up, but they have not advanced since the country cannot actively support them.

Believes America's foreign trade will not soon improve and claims "the chief cause is to be found in the rapacity of the British Fleet, and the Violent hatred which the British Court bear to Republican principles." Surmises that "in the course of this spring a change of councils may take place in Britain" and that this could "bring about a General peace." But this is uncertain. The "Revolution of Commerce" will continue, and the American government "will render an essential service to their Country, by making it really independant; and to Republican principles, by fixing them upon a Rock never to be shaken."

Advocates that the American government pursue the following course of action. First, free the revenue from dependence on foreign commerce; second, reorder "monied institutions" so they do not harm Republican principles and establish a bank that will benefit commerce generally; and third, organize the "National property" to create a fund for internal improvements. Discusses each proposal in detail, particularly the plan for "*a new National Bank;* calculated to Consolidate and strengthen Republican principles; to encourage and support Manufactures, and internal Commerce; and to bring a large revenue to the public, to whom the profits of a paper circulation should exclusively belong." Also notes "a few objections which may be urged against establishing such a Bank." The "popular" argument— that " 'the Bank should be unconnected with the Government' "—is applicable to Great Britain but not to the U.S. The plan to establish banks independent of the government is "dangerous to Republican principles, as it has an evident tendency to raise up a monied Aristocracy." Believes also that state governments should establish state banks and not grant charters and "peculiar priviledges" to "monied Men." "The Constitutional objection of the right of the United States to establish branches, is done away by the plan of establishing them with Consent of the State Governments." The next objection, "the want of Capital," is "a very weak one" and can be met by issuing paper money. "No paper Currency, in this Country, could be so Substantially backed as that issued by a Bank belonging to the United States; for it would actually be the representative *of the whole property in the Country.* . . . A very small sum of the precious Metals is sufficient as a basis." Admits there may be danger in changing an existing system for a new one, but these arguments have their limits and can be "set up as mere bug-bears . . . to put a stop to all improvement in the State of Society. The Arguments against renewing the old Charter are insuperable." Asserts that the old bank can easily "wind up its affairs" and that the new bank, established at Washington, could realize annual profits in excess of $2 million. The revenue from import and tonnage duties will probably exceed $10 million, and this revenue, augmented by "a judicious application of the Public Lands," will create an "ample fund" for internal improvements. Mentions that he has seen and conversed with Jefferson, to whom he has sent a copy of this letter. Adds in a postscript that his address is "John Melish New york."

Tr (DLC: Jefferson Papers). 12 pp. Marked "Copy." In Melish's hand. Sent as enclosure in Melish to Jefferson, 16 Feb. 1811 (ibid.). Misdated 7 Feb. 1810 in *Index to the Thomas Jefferson Papers.*

1. John Melish (1771–1822) emigrated from Scotland, traveled widely in the U.S. and Canada, and settled in Philadelphia in 1811. In 1813 JM purchased a copy of Melish's *Travels in the United States of America, in the Years 1806 and 1807, and 1809, 1810, and 1811* (2 vols.; Philadelphia, 1812; Shaw and Shoemaker 26062) (Melish to JM, 5 Jan. 1813 [DLC]).

From John Quincy Adams

SIR.   ST: PETERSBURG 8. February 1811.

I had the honour of writing you, on the 7th: of last Month, immediately after I received a letter from the Secretary of State of 15. October, with the letter of leave to His Majesty the Emperor of Russia; and of informing you that I should not deliver that letter, untill the receipt of further Instructions from you. It was not untill last Evening that I had the pleasure of receiving your very obliging private letter of 16. October;[1] which has relieved me from some concern which I felt, lest in withholding the letter for the Emperor, I should have incurred a delay in the execution of your intentions, and has at the same time explained to me, what the general terms of the Secretary of State's letter had left me to conjecture; *the Source,* of the application to you, for your permission to me to return home.

My Mother, who during the whole course of my life, has been as much my guardian Angel, as my earthly Parent, had probably been informed of dispositions, which on my first arrival here, I had thought it necessary to make, to draw upon my property in America, to meet the expenditures which I expected to find indispensible. Alarmed at the prospect which these arrangements might open to futurity, for my rising family, she must have concluded that delicacy alone had restrained me from asking an immediate recall, and that in expressing this wish to you, without my knowledge, she was sparing that delicacy, and at the same time saving me from a sacrifice which might reach beyond the extent of my means.

I have already had the honour to inform you, that my experience here, has proved much less burdensome than my Expectations—and that whatever my continuance here may be, my expenditures will be adapted with sufficient accuracy to the allowance made me by my Country—That the Season for some months, and the Circumstances of my family, for the remainder of this year, will in all probability, make it impracticable for me to embark for such a voyage as that to the United States, and that I shall thus have ample time to receive your definitive Instructions, with respect to the letter of leave to the Emperor. And I have expressed the wish, which I now beg leave to repeat, that in the exercise of your pleasure with regard to my continuance here, or to my recall, you would have the goodness to consult considerations of a public Nature, alone; with the most explicit assurance, that I shall not only cheerfully acquiesce, but shall find my strongest gratification, either in remaining here, or in returning to the United States, as you shall deem either alternative most conducive to the public interest. If indeed I should receive my recall at a time, when I could not immediately embark, it would subject me to some inconvenience, to which however I should willingly submit under the consideration that it would be compensated by an equivalent benefit to the public.

Though I have not delivered to the Emperor the letter of leave, I thought it most respectful and proper to give notice to the Chancellor Count Romanzoff that I had received it; with an intimation that as it had been prompted by considerations relating altogether to my personal affairs, and as they would for some time prevent my departure, I should with His Majesty's Approbation reserve the letter for the present, and probably untill I should receive your further orders. The Count not only approved of this course, but was pleased to express in flattering terms, his own regret and that of His Majesty's Government in general at the prospect of my departure. The Emperor himself, whom I have had the honour of seeing twice since the receipt of the despatches, and who had doubtless been informed by Count Pahlen, of my probable return, was pleased both times to express himself in the most gracious manner to the same effect. I have indeed during the whole course of my residence here, both in respect to myself and to my family, received from the Emperor, as well as from Count Romanzoff, marks of distinction, and of attention, calculated to render my situation as agreeable as the nature of things will admit; but which in my public Correspondence with the Secretary of State, I have not noticed in detail; to avoid deriving a self-importance which might be ridiculous, from Courtesies altogether personal.

I am conscious, Sir, that an apology is due from me, for occupying so much of your time, with an object which belongs so essentially to my particular affairs—And I cannot but regret, although it was from motives of the most affectionate concern for me, that the subject was brought before you for consideration at all. Yet, as it has given the occasion upon which you have the goodness to express the sentiments relating to me, contained in your favour of 16 October, I ought perhaps rather to consider it as fortunate. The reasons which you suggest against my immediate departure are so entirely in unison with my own opinions, that had my continuance here been as inconvenient even as my first expectations had anticipated, I should have considered it my duty to remain untill your further pleasure should be known: but under the present Circumstances when I could not without more than inconvenience embark for America, with my family, your perswasion that my remaining here some time longer will be of public advantage is the more gratifying to me, as, however inconvenient it might prove to myself to go, I should be unwilling to stay here an hour, after you should judge that the public expediency would advise my recall. With great respect and attachment, I am, Sir, your very humble & obedt: Servt:

JOHN QUINCY ADAMS.

RC (ICHi); FC (MHi: Adams Family Papers). RC docketed by JM. FC written in shorthand.

1. *PJM-PS*, 2:582–83.

From Lafayette

MY DEAR SIR   PARIS 8 february 1811

It is to me a particular Gratification, in Remembrance of old times, and in Justice to a Very Respectable Gentleman, to Recommend the Concerns of M. de Rayneval.[1] He Has Been the first European diplomate Whose Negociations Have Met American independance, and None of them Has Been, in personal Exertions, More zealous and Useful. These Considerations Join With the Very Great Regard due to His private Character, and While the Merits of His Claim are laid Before You, I think it Both a duty and a pleasure to Express My Wishes in His Behalf. With Most affectionate Respect I am, My dear friend Yours

LAFAYETTE

RC (InU: Lafayette Collection).

1. Joseph-Mathias Gérard de Rayneval was claiming land that had been granted to his brother, the late Conrad-Alexandre Gérard, during his tenure as French minister to the U.S. (see George Joy to JM, 28 Apr. 1810, *PJM-PS*, 2:327, 328 n. 1).

§ From Landon Carter. *8 February 1811, Cleve, Virginia.* Apologizes for the intrusion but assumes JM has clerks "who can, by your direction, give me the information which I ask." Has invented a machine that "in practice promises to gather wheat from the field in such a manner as to save all the waste attendant upon the usual modes used in harvest." Wishes to know the probable quantity of wheat sown annually in the U.S. in order to estimate the machine's value.

RC (DLC). 1 p.

§ From Albert Gallatin. *8 February 1811, Treasury Department.* Transmits in compliance with the Senate resolution of 7 Feb.[1] a copy of George W. Erving's account in relation to awards under article 7 of the British treaty. A commission of 2½ percent is being charged on £217,009 3s. 9d., this being the amount Erving received for claimants who had not appointed agents to prosecute their claims and receive the awards.[2] The accounts, which have passed the offices of the auditor and comptroller, are voluminous and "correct in every respect." Another account of Erving's for over £55,000 is not sent as it is not finalized and no commission is being charged on it. That sum consists of deductions the commissioners made from the awards in order to reimburse the U.S. for expenses incurred in prosecuting the claims. Part of this was applied by Erving to discharge proctors' accounts for which the U.S. had become responsible, and the balance (over $160,000) was paid by him into the treasury. The president should have deducted Erving's compensation from this fund, but instead the unexpended balance was applied to the surplus fund, making a new appropriation necessary to settle the account and repay the award fund. Adds that the Treasury Department has no information respecting Erving's services other than what is in the accounts and enclosed letter and that the services were performed in accordance with instructions.

RC and enclosures (DNA: RG 46, Legislative Proceedings, 11A-E4). RC 2 pp. For enclosures, see n. 2. JM forwarded the RC and enclosures to the Senate in his message of 11 Feb. 1811. Printed in *ASP, Finance*, 2:484–86.

1. On 7 Feb. 1811 the Senate had approved a resolution proposed by Jesse Franklin of North Carolina requesting JM to forward such information as he possessed on the accounts of Erving "for his services and compensation for attending the Board of Commissioners" established under article 7 of the 1794 Jay treaty with Great Britain (*Annals of Congress*, 11th Cong., 3d sess., 128).

2. Gallatin enclosed a copy of Erving's account with the U.S. "in relation to Awards under the 7th Article of the British Treaty," dated 24 Sept. 1808 at the auditor's office, 30 Sept. 1808 at the comptroller's office, and 7 Nov. 1810 at the Treasury Department (one large folio page). The account shows a balance of $22,392.67 claimed by Erving for his commission "but which cannot be allowed until duly Authorized." On 1 Dec. 1810 Robert Smith endorsed the account: "The above balance heretofore suspended is to be admitted to Mr. Ervings credit." Accompanying the account is a 25 Nov. 1810 letter from Erving to Robert Smith (5 pp.), explaining that he had been authorized to retain the sum of $22,392.67 for his services by charging 2½ percent of the sums paid to him as agent for claims to compensate him for his extraconsular duties while he was in London. This letter included an extract from an "order the Secretary of State wrote to [Erving], in the month of November, 1805," authorizing the retention of the commission after JM had laid before the president representations Erving had made to him on the subject in 1804.

§ From Josiah Smith and Levi Smith. *8 February 1811, Stanstead.* The petitioners, brothers now in Stanstead, Lower Canada, state that Josiah Smith, aged thirty-two, has a wife and five children in Chichester, New Hampshire, who are unable to support themselves. He enlisted in the U.S. Army for five years at Fort Constitution, served about eighteen months there, and then deserted. Levi Smith, aged twenty-four, enlisted for five years at Fort Constitution in May 1810 and deserted after two months. "We are now Both of us in the Province aforesaid . . . and we feel Anxious and a Desire to return to our Native Country and becoming your Royal [*sic*] Subjects and Citizens of the United States of America." They request JM to grant them discharges and in a postscript ask JM to direct his response to Capt. John Masson of Stanstead, "to be left at Derby Post office Vermont."

RC (DNA: RG 107, LRRS, S-309:5). 2 pp. Docketed by a War Department clerk as received 28 Feb. 1811.

¶ To Joseph Hopkinson. Letter not found. *8 February 1811*. Offered for sale in Anderson Catalogue No. 1912 (19–21 Jan. 1925), item 406, where it is described as a one-page letter to Hopkinson in Philadelphia thanking him for a copy of a discourse (see Joseph Hopkinson, *Annual Discourse, Delivered before the Pennsylvania Academy of the Fine Arts. On the 13th of November 1810* [Philadelphia, 1810; Shaw and Shoemaker 20379]).

§ From Samuel Latham Mitchill. *9 February 1811, Washington.* "At the request of Mr. Charles Sherry, one of my constituents, . . . I inclose for the President's consideration a letter from him to me, and a letter from Mr. Dabney, our Consul in the Azores."[1]

RC and enclosures (DNA: RG 59, LAR, 1809–17, filed under "Dabney"). RC 1 p. For enclosures, see n. 1.

1. Mitchill enclosed a 6 Feb. 1811 letter he had received from Charles Sherry in New York (2 pp.) relating circumstances that occurred after a vessel in which Sherry had shipped thirty bales of cotton put into Fayal the previous spring for repairs. The captain had placed the cargo under the care of John B. Dabney, the American consul there, but since the vessel was beyond repair another ship had to be sent to pick up the cargo and deliver it to its destination. Sherry authorized the captain to pay Dabney for "Carting Storing repairs &C.," which he expected would amount to $30 or $40. He enclosed to Mitchill a 15 Nov. 1810 letter Dabney had written to him outlining the charges (1 p.), noting that Mitchill would be "Surprised" to find that the captain had to pay $588 in order to regain the cotton. Sherry denounced Dabney and threatened to "publish his conduct to the world" if no redress could be obtained. He enclosed his certificate of naturalization [not found] and requested three certificates signed by JM if possible, "as with his signature they are more respected in a foreign country."

From William Jones

SIR   PHILADA 11 Feb. 1811

The enclosed circular is I believe the only one of the kind received here this day and as none of our papers have published it although it was here before noon, I deemed it of some importance to put it in your possession as soon as possible.[1] I know not whether the translation be correct, but it appears to me necessary to enclose in a parenthesis the words "the vessels taken or detained before being alone under Sequestration" in the last paragraph, in order to render the sense complete, otherwise the class of Prizes most obnoxious would be the first restored, and the other remain suspended. With the most sincere respect And regard I am Sir Your Obdt Servt

                                                                      WM JONES

RC (DLC). Enclosure not found, but see n. 1.

1. Jones evidently enclosed a copy of a circular sent by the French minister of justice to the president of the Council of Prizes, dated at Paris on 25 Dec. 1810. This circular consisted of copies of the duc de Cadore's 5 Aug. 1810 letter to John Armstrong and JM's 2 Nov. 1810 proclamation. It also included instructions from Napoleon to the following effect: that all cases before the Council of Prizes respecting American captures dating from 1 Nov., and those that might be brought afterward, should not be decided according to the principles of the Berlin and Milan decrees but should remain suspended, the vessels previously seized being only placed under sequestration, and reserving to the proprietors their rights until 2 Feb. 1811, when, in consequence of the U.S. fulfilling its engagement to make its rights respected, the captures must be declared null and the vessels restored to their owners. Translations of the circular appeared in several American newspapers (see *Aurora General Advertiser*, 12 Feb. 1811; *National Intelligencer*, 14 Feb. 1811; JM to Jones, 13 Feb. 1811).

From Benjamin Henry Latrobe

SIR   WASHINGTON Feby. 11h. 1811

I saw Mr. Bacon[1] this morning who informed me that the letter I mentioned to you is now in possession of the Committee. I entreated him to transmit it to You, which he appeared to think would not be improper as one or two expressions might be considered as equivocal and authorize a communication to You by the members as individual members of the Legislature. Whatever those expressions may be, as it is utterly impossible that a Knowledge of facts can be indicated of which facts the writer was wholly ignorant, not the most distant apprehension is felt on that point, however he may regret the exposure of his weakness, & indiscretion. With the highest respect I am &c

B HENRY LATROBE.

RC (DLC); copy (MdHi: Latrobe Letterbooks). RC docketed by JM. Copy in Latrobe's hand, dated 12 Feb. 1811, and filed after Latrobe to Robert Fulton, 16 Feb. 1813 (ibid.); on the verso is a copy of Latrobe to JM, 19 Feb. 1811.

1. Latrobe was probably referring to Ezekiel Bacon of Massachusetts, a member of the House Ways and Means Committee. The letter he mentioned has not been identified.

From William Lee

SIR   NEW YORK Feby 11: 1811

A friend of mine writes me, it has been represented at Washington, that I brought with me from France "a number of licenses, under which I have been expediting a number of Vessels." As I have pointedly, and uniformly, refused to have anything to do with the French & English system of licenses, and as this insinuation is calculated to make impressions injurious to me, I hope Sir, you will not think it improper in me to declare to you in this formal manner, that I never owned, or made use of a French, or English license, in my life, and that all the Vessels, which have been sent to the address of my house, at Bordeaux by the merchants of this City, have been sent without licenses. With great respect & attachment I have the honor to remain the Presidents obedient Servant.

Wm Lee

RC (DLC). Docketed by JM.

§ To the Senate. *11 February 1811.* Transmits a report from the secretary of the treasury in compliance with a Senate resolution of 7 Feb. 1811.

RC and enclosures (DNA: RG 46, Legislative Proceedings, 11A-E4). RC 1 p. In a clerk's hand, signed by JM. For enclosures, see Gallatin to JM, 8 Feb. 1811, and n. 2.

§ From the Junta of the Provinces of the Río de la Plata.[1] *11 February 1811, Buenos Aires.* The members of the junta recall JM's magnanimous conduct toward the province of Caracas as proof of his interest in the rights of humanity. As their situation and its causes are the same as those of the "Noble Caraquans," they have an equal right to hope that the U.S. will express a cordial friendship for the provinces on the Río de la Plata. The people of these provinces, though long oppressed, have loyally performed their duties and were persuaded that "the Re-union of the whole Spanish monarchy was the only thing that could save it from Ruin." "Every thing was put in contribution" to save these dominions and the kingdom from "this assassinating orde[2] which now crams itself with the carcass of Europe." But matters have changed. "Almost the whole of the Peninsula fell under the Dominion of the common oppressor and that Body of Ambitious Egotists, of which was composed the Central Junta, was dissolved. . . . The same Principles of Loyalty which had until then retained us in Union with Spain authorised our separation. Our security being threatened, there was no obligation to prostitute ourselves to the ephemeral authorities which had lost the Character of Dignity & Independence."

The viceroy and the "Club of proud oligarchists composing this 'audiencia,'" moreover, "endeavor'd to keep us in a torpid state." "Their re-iterated attempts to subvert the state . . . obliged us to depose them." Such are the reasons that have led to the installation of the junta now ruling these provinces. Towns in the interior are freed from their ancient tyrants and have reestablished the rights with which nature endowed them. The junta, wishing to comply with the wishes of the provinces for a national congress, redoubles its efforts, and the assembly will meet shortly. Some will oppose these proceedings, but the junta appeals to "the Tribunal of Reason" for the "purity of [its] Intentions." The junta does not doubt the equity of the decisions of the U.S., believes that JM is friendly to its cause, and believes that he will receive with pleasure these statements of friendship.

Translation of RC (DNA: RG 59, NFL, Argentina). 3 pp. In the hand of Daniel Brent, who noted that the letter was "signed by the Members of the Junta." RC (DNA: RG 59, ML) in Spanish; filed with a covering letter to Monroe from Telésforo d'Orea in Philadelphia, 18 June 1811, who noted that he was enclosing two letters from the Supreme Junta to JM that he had received from a gentleman who had just arrived from Buenos Aires. A translation of Orea's covering letter (DNA: RG 59, NFL, Colombia) is in the hand of John Graham. Translations of RC and covering letter printed in Manning, *Diplomatic Correspondence of the United States concerning the Independence of the Latin-American Nations*, 1 : 319–20.

1. During the days of 22–25 May 1810 the *cabildo* of Buenos Aires established a provisional popular junta to govern as a "mask" for Ferdinand VII following the arrival of the news of the demise of the Supreme Central Government Junta in Spain. In the ensuing months, the Buenos Aires junta was preoccupied with the problems of extending its authority to the other provinces of the La Plata area and obtaining some form of recognition from Great Britain of the legitimacy of its status. To accomplish the former goal, the junta, between 18 Dec. 1810 and 10 Feb. 1811, made a number of decisions to incorporate the provincial juntas of La Plata into its organization pending the meeting of a general congress. To achieve the latter, the junta sent diplomatic missions, first to Great Britain and Chile and subsequently to the U.S. (Ricardo Levene, *A History of Argentina*, trans. William Spence Robertson [Chapel Hill, N.C., 1937], pp. 208–70; Eugene R. Craine, *The United States and the Independence of Buenos Aires* [Hays, Kans., 1961], pp. 26–33, 77–80).

2. Brent inserted an asterisk here in his translation and noted at the foot of the page: "*This word is not to be found in the Dictionary." JM's correspondents probably intended to write "horda," meaning tribe or clan.

§ From Benjamin Henry Latrobe. *11 February 1811, Washington.* Submits at JM's direction a list of outstanding claims against the public buildings. "The two first items arise from engagements which have subsisted for some years, and have not been closed. The latter exhibits the amount of the demands against the public for Labor & for materials delivered: the certified vouchers of which are deposited with the Superintendent of the city."

RC and enclosure (DNA: RG 233, President's Messages, 11A-D1). RC 1 p. Enclosure (2 pp.) is a "List of Claims outstanding against the public Buildings of the U.S. Feby. 1st. 1811." The three categories of claims—"Sculptors & their Assistants," "Salaries," and "Labor & Materials"—amounted to a total of $6,502.92½. Latrobe evidently enclosed the RC and list of claims to JM on 23 Feb. 1811 (first letter), and JM forwarded them to the House of Representatives in his message of 25 Feb. 1811.

To William Jones

DEAR SIR   [13 February 1811]
I return with my thanks the printed document you were so good as to send.[1] There is an obscurity in the passage which you note, that calls for some such emendation as you suggest; unless the term sequestration has a meaning in the French Code, different from that generally attached to it. The translation may also be inaccurate; the more probably so, as there are

two in the Newspapers not entirely consistent with it. Whatever the true construction may be, the letter presents several interesting points for consideration. Perhaps Mr. Serrurier[2] who is hourly expected here, may tho' it is very doubtful considering the time & place of his departure be able to throw light on the difficulties. Accept my friendly respects

JAMES MADISON

RC (PHi: William Jones Papers). Undated, but postmarked in Washington on 13 Feb.

1. See Jones to JM, 11 Feb. 1811, and n. 1.
2. Louis-Barbé-Charles Sérurier (b. ca. 1775) had held diplomatic posts in Cassel and Holland before Napoleon appointed him minister to the U.S. in September 1810. Sérurier had left Paris on 19 Nov. 1810, sailed for the U.S. on 30 Dec., and arrived in Washington on 14 Feb. 1811. He was presented to JM two days later (Egan, *Neither Peace nor War*, pp. 137–38; Edward A. Whitcomb, *Napoleon's Diplomatic Service* [Durham, N.C., 1979], pp. 68–69; *National Intelligencer*, 16 Feb. 1811).

§ From Jonathan Jennings.[1] *13 February 1811, Representatives Chamber.* "I have again to lay before your Excellency testimony additional to the former [not found], relative to the Governor of the Indiana Territory."[2]

RC and enclosures (DNA: RG 59, LAR, 1809–17, filed under "Harrison"). RC 1 p. For enclosures, see n. 2. RC and enclosures printed in Carter, *Territorial Papers, Indiana*, 8:108–11.

1. Jonathan Jennings (1784–1834) was the delegate from the Indiana Territory in the Eleventh through Fourteenth Congresses, 1809–16.
2. By the end of 1810 a sizable opposition had arisen in the Indiana Territory to the administration of William Henry Harrison over such issues as the use of blacks as indentured servants or slaves, land grants, the territorial governor's appointment powers, apportionment in the territorial legislature, and the location of the territorial capital. In January 1811 Harrison forwarded documents to both the secretary of state and his old school friend John Wayles Eppes to acquit himself of charges made by his opponents that he was a land speculator, that he misused his authority, and that he was an associate of Aaron Burr—allegations which the governor declared were based on "perjury and forgery" (see Harrison to Robert Smith, 10 Jan. 1811, and enclosures, Eppes to Smith, Jan. 1811, and enclosures, and Harrison to Eppes, 22 Jan. 1811, and enclosures, in Carter, *Territorial Papers, Indiana*, 8:72–75, 76–85, 87–102). The documents forwarded to JM by Jennings, whose election as territorial delegate had been opposed by Harrison, included a transcript from the book of locations for Knox County, Indiana Territory, recording an 1804 entry for a tract of land opposite the "Grand rapids" on the Wabash River in the names of Henry Vanderburgh and William McIntosh (1 p.); and two depositions, sworn by Toussaint DuBois and William McIntosh, describing Harrison's efforts to dispute the ownership of parts of the tract (3 pp.). Jennings also circulated copies of these and other documents among members of Congress in the hope of laying "the ground work of an impeachment" to end Harrison's political career (Jennings to Solomon Manwaring, 22 Jan. 1811, Esarey, *Letters of Harrison*, 1:501–3).

§ From the Junta of the Provinces of the Río de la Plata. *13 February 1811, Buenos Aires.* Declares that "Don Josef R Poinsetts has just presented himself to this Junta" with his credentials as commercial agent of the U.S. and that "this Government conformably to the cordial and friendly intentions which it made known to Y E in its official Letter dated yesterday,"[1] has admitted him to the full exercise of the powers of his agency. Regards this agency as "a preliminary to the Treaties between Nation and Nation which will be formed to point out the Rules of a permanent Commerce and of the greatest amity and Union between the two States."[2]

Translation of RC (DNA: RG 59, NFL, Argentina). 1 p. In the hand of John Graham, who noted that the letter was "signed by the Members of the Junta." Printed in Manning, *Diplomatic Correspondence of the United States concerning the Independence of the Latin-American Nations*, 1:320–21. RC (DNA: RG 59, ML) in Spanish; filed with Telésforo d'Orea to Monroe, 18 June 1811 (see Junta of the Provinces of the Río de la Plata to JM, 11 Feb. 1811, n.).

1. Junta of the Provinces of the Río de la Plata to JM, 11 Feb. 1811.
2. Joel Roberts Poinsett had arrived in Buenos Aires on 13 Feb. 1811 and he lost no time in presenting his letter of appointment as agent for commerce and seamen to the junta. When it was translated, he recorded in his journal, "it produced a sensation of disappointment and irritation." The members of the junta apparently had hoped to receive the credentials of a representative of the U.S. government who had been sent directly to them by the president. Poinsett explained that JM was unaware of the magnitude of the changes that had occurred in Buenos Aires and that his letter of appointment had followed the forms used by the administration in sending unofficial agents to Havana. He requested, however, that JM send him a letter of credence which, he believed, would give him "a decided advantage" with the junta, whose members he wished to persuade to declare the province's independence from Spanish rule. In response, the president elevated Poinsett's status to consul general for Buenos Aires on 30 Apr., but he did not otherwise alter the administration's earlier instructions respecting Poinsett's duties (Joel Roberts Poinsett, "Journal to Rio de Janeiro, Buenos Ayres & Chile, 1810–11" [DLC]; Poinsett to Robert Smith, 13 and 23 Feb. 1811, Monroe to Poinsett, 30 Apr. 1811 [PHi: Poinsett Papers]).

From Levi Lincoln

DEAR SIR   WORCESTER Feby 15th. 1811.

The last papers announce the nomination of Alexander Wolcott Esqre.[1] as an associate Jud⟨ge o⟩f the Supreme Court of the United States, & that the nomination ⟨has⟩ been submitted by the Senate to a Committee for inquiry & consid⟨eratio⟩n. It is conceived, as this commitment was not of course, that ⟨it is?⟩ indicative of opposition & delay, if not of obloquy to be heaped on ⟨the?⟩ Candidate, & the advocates of the appointment. Resistance ⟨is to?⟩ be expected from political opponents, in proportion as the nominated ⟨mi⟩ght appear to them, capable, decided, independent, firmly attached ⟨to the⟩ administration of the General Government, & devoted to the suppor⟨t of⟩ its general policy & its particular system of measures. For years, ⟨I hav⟩e been acquainted with Mr. Wolcott, & have met with few men of ⟨firm?⟩er mind, of greater perceptive & discriminating powers, of more ste⟨ady⟩ & uniform adherence to the principles of the Union & the arrangemen⟨ts o⟩f the general government. His literary acquisitions are known to many ⟨of o⟩ur friends at Washington. Of his professional merits & standing as ⟨a⟩ Lawyer, I am unacquainted. His pride, patriotism & sense of dut⟨y w⟩ill be pledges of his exertion. He will have in Custody, not only his ow⟨n, b⟩ut the reputation of his friends. Whatever therefore may be his present ⟨attai?⟩nments & legal habits, an industrious application to professional stud⟨ies &⟩ official duties will soon place him *on a level, at least,* with his As⟨soci⟩ates. His independence firmness & patriotism, in being thus a valuab⟨le ac⟩quisition to the Bench, will, I conceive, be peculiarly useful & satisfact⟨ory⟩ to the friends of the National Administration, in this section of the Union. I have thus early volunteered my opinion, not only from the int⟨er⟩est I feel, in countenancing an useful measure, against which Calumny has already commenced her common place whispers, but from a general preference to that explicitness, which subjects to responsibility, than to that timid & cowardly reserve, which ultimately joins in the Chorus, refuted by the experiment.

My son Daniel Waldo Lincoln, journeying from Boston to the Seat of government on business, & desirous of paying his respects to the President of the United States will avail himself of the delivery of this letter as an introduction for that purpose.

Please to present me respectfully to the recollections of Mrs. Madison & accept the assurances of the high esteem & friendship, with which I am your most obedt servt.

LEVI LINCOLN

RC (DLC). Damaged at fold. In a clerk's hand. Docketed by JM.

1. Alexander Wolcott (1758–1839) was born in Windsor, Connecticut, and graduated from Yale College in 1778. Strongly Antifederalist and Republican in his politics, he served in the Connecticut General Assembly from 1796 to 1801, and in 1802 Jefferson appointed him customs collector at Middletown. JM nominated him as associate justice of the Supreme Court on 4 Feb. 1811, but the Senate rejected the nomination on 13 Feb. (Franklin Bowditch Dexter, ed., *Biographical Sketches of the Graduates of Yale College* [4 vols.; New York, 1885–1912], 4:80–82; *Senate Exec. Proceedings*, 2:165–67).

From Stanley Griswold

SIR,   CINCINNATI 16th. Feby. 1811.

Aaron Greely, Esquire, the bearer of this, has been employed by the Surveyor General as his Deputy in the Michigan district, and now makes his returns to the proper offices, which do him great credit. His maps of that country are no less accurate than elegant. I have given them a close examination and find them entirely correct so far as my personal knowledge extends. They may well be considered an acquisition to our geographical science, as well as a valuable article in the department of the public lands. The Surveyor General is highly pleased with his performance, as are also those now in office in the Michigan territory. I have the honor to be with great respect, Sir, Your most obedt. servant,

STANLEY GRISWOLD.

RC (DLC).

From Timothy Pickering

SIR,   WASHINGTON Feby. 16. 1811
The two nominations of an associate judge of the supreme court to fill the seat vacated by the death of Judge Cushing, having failed; will you permit me to bring to your recollection a man whom you knew in the House of Representatives, in Philadelphia—Jeremiah Smith of New Hampshire?[1] He is a federalist; but one of great distinction as a lawyer; at the same time, amiable, moderate & conciliatory as one of a political party. Since he left Congress (fourteen years ago) he resumed the study of the law, with increased and indefatigable application, and practised it successfully. The state of New-Hampshire, desirous of availing itself of his superiour endowments, appointed him its chief-justice of the supreme court; in which he presided with such ability and impartiality, that the legislature, all parties (as I have been informed) concurring, made an *addition* of five hundred dollars to his salary, to continue so long as *He* should hold the office of chief Justice: it was appropriate to *him*, and not to the *Office.*

Mr. Smith is, confessedly, one of the most distinguished lawyers in New-England. In questions merely political, parties will prefer those of their own sect: but *all* are equally concerned in the able and upright administration of justice. If the want of suitable qualifications cause erroneous judgements, it will be no consolation to a man that he suffers by the hand of a political brother.

In one word, the dignity of the supreme court of the United States (hitherto maintained in the appointments of Judge Johnson & Judge Livingston)—the confidence of the citizens in the wisdom and rectitude of its decisions—and the welfare of the Union, require such an appointment: and allow me to add, that it is not a matter of indifference to your own reputation.

Mr. Gilman, senator from New-Hampshire, perfectly well knows Judge Smith; and I am persuaded his candour will confirm all I have said of his character & merits. I verily believe that New-Hampshire, without distinction of parties, with the exception, perhaps, of a few individuals, will feel herself honoured by the preference of a citizen of whom she has reason to be proud. While the whole circuit, containing near a million of freemen, will be, to say the least, greatly dissatisfied, should a candidate be selected from a state not comprehended within its limits. It will be saying to the whole body of the people, Republicans as well as federalists, "You have not a man among you, qualified for this high Office." I am respectfully, sir, Your obedt. servt.

TIMOTHY PICKERING

FC (MHi: Pickering Papers).

1. Jeremiah Smith (1759–1842) had served in the House of Representatives from 1791 to 1797 when he resigned to take up the position of U.S. attorney for New Hampshire. In February 1801 he received a "midnight" judicial appointment from President John Adams. Thereafter he served as chief justice of the Superior Court of New Hampshire, 1802–9 and 1813–16, and in 1809–10 he was governor of New Hampshire. In 1808 he had been a presidential elector on the Federalist ticket headed by Charles Cotesworth Pinckney of South Carolina (*Senate Exec. Proceedings*, 1:249, 381).

§ To Congress. *16 February 1811.* Transmits "the Treaty concluded on the 10th of November 1808 on the part of the United States with the Great and Little Osage Tribes of Indians; with a view to such legal provisions as may be deemed proper for fulfilling its stipulations."

RC and enclosure (DNA: RG 46, Legislative Proceedings, 11A-E2). RC 1 p. In a clerk's hand, signed by JM. Enclosure (13 pp.) is a printed copy of the *Treaty between the U. States and the Great and Little Osage Nations of Indians, Concluded and Signed at Fort Clark, on the 10th Nov. 1808* (see *ASP, Indian Affairs*, 1:763–64). Another copy of the treaty may be found in the House records (DNA: RG 233, President's Messages, 11A-D1). See also JM to the Senate, 15 Jan. 1810 (*PJM-PS*, 2:179, 180 n.).

§ From William Eustis. *16 February 1811, War Department.* Forwards a general return of the militia of the U.S., made from the latest returns from the several states and territories.

Letterbook copy (DNA: RG 107, LSP); enclosure, two copies (DNA: RG 233, President's Messages, 11A-D1; and DNA: RG 46, Legislative Proceedings, 11A-E6). Letterbook copy 1 p. Enclosure (one large folio sheet) is a "Return of the Militia of the United States," 15 Feb. 1811 (printed in *ASP, Military Affairs*, 1:298–301). JM forwarded the enclosure to Congress in his message of 19 Feb. 1811.

§ Louis-Barbé-Charles Sérurier to Robert Smith. *17 February 1811, Washington.* The effort of being presented yesterday to the president and at the State Department has worsened his indisposition to the extent that he cannot pay his respects to

Mmes Madison and Smith and to others as he had proposed. Offers his apologies; will make the visits his first duty and he is eager to fulfill it. Still hopes to be able to come to the State Department tomorrow morning; if he is too indisposed to do so, M. de Caraman¹ will advise Smith.

RC (DLC). 2 pp. In French. Docketed by JM.

1. Georges de Caraman was secretary of the French legation (see Georges de Caraman, "Les Etats-Unis il y a quarante ans," *Revue contemporaine*, 3 [1852]: 209).

From William McKinley

Sir,   Capital 18th feby 1811
  I am prepairing a circular. I do not know what information to give, relative to our foreign afairs. You will do me a grat favour by furnishing me with the information requ[i]site, in such way as you may deem proper. Accept my best respects
                                        Wm. Mc.Kinley

RC (DLC).

§ From David Boudon.¹ *18 February 1811, Georgetown.* Offers his services as a teacher of drawing for the military academy in Washington proposed in JM's message to Congress. Mentions that he has had the honor to know JM, lists his credentials, and gives his reasons for seeking the post. In a postscript mentions that the previous summer he had shown Dolley Madison part of his collection of paintings by old masters and adds that he also owns a *Holy Family* by Michelangelo da Caravaggio, which he was obliged to cut in order to put it in his trunk for fear that, if rolled up, the colors would shred as paint on a too brittle canvas.

RC (DLC). 2 pp. In French. Docketed by JM.

1. David Boudon was a Swiss-born miniaturist who had resided in Philadelphia in 1797. By 1816 he had moved to Chillicothe, Ohio (George C. Groce and David H. Wallace, eds., *The New-York Historical Society's Dictionary of Artists in America, 1564–1860* [New Haven, 1957], p. 68).

§ From Nathaniel G. Ingraham. *18 February 1811, New York.* "It would be highly gratifying to me if my son Nathl. G Ingraham Jr who resides in England could be honor'd with a Consular appointment in that Country. My friend Mr Phoenix informs me that he made an application to your Excellency thro the Secretary of State for an appointment at Plymouth at which place the Interest of the United States would be much promoted by having an American, in the place of the present consul Mr Hawker, who is not only an Englishman but is agent for British men of war

& privateers."[1] Forwards letters from Mr. Shaler to the secretary of state.[2] "In my letters by the same arrival Mr Shaler mentions that all is quiet at the Havanna, and likely to continue so."

RC (DNA: RG 59, LAR, 1809–17, filed under "Ingraham"). 2 pp.

    1. Alexander Phœnix to Robert Smith, 18 Jan. 1811 (ibid.).

    2. Among the letters Ingraham mentioned was a report that the American annexation of West Florida had caused "very little sensation" in Cuba. To this news Shaler added a brief description of the defenses and military strength of the island and also mentioned that a British vessel had taken delegates from Veracruz, Guatemala, and Cuba to the *cortes* in Cadiz. He concluded with an account of events in Mexico to the effect that the rebels were in control of the country and the revolution was about to be "consummated" (William Shaler to Robert Smith, 15 Jan. 1811 [DNA: RG 59, CD, Havana; docketed as received 20 Feb. 1811]).

§ From Henry J. Knox.[1] *18 February 1811, Windsor, Connecticut.* Seeks reappointment to the navy. Received a midshipman's warrant in April 1798 and was promoted to lieutenant in June 1799, but the nomination was rejected in Senate "in consequence of a fracas, in which I was concerned at Boston." He then left the service. These circumstances are well known to the secretary of war, who will present this letter. Wishes to serve his country again and "would immediately accept of a Commission as after the first of September next, I shall be at perfect liberty to act, wherever I may be ordered."

RC (DNA: RG 45, Misc. Letters Received). 2 pp.

    1. Henry Jackson Knox (1780?–1832) was the son of the former secretary of war, Henry Knox. He apparently had problems with gambling and dissipation and in 1809 was reported to be in debtors' prison in Boston (North Callahan, *Henry Knox: General Washington's General* [New York, 1958], pp. 375, 377, 381–82).

From John Armstrong

DEAR SIR,   NEW YORK 19 Feb. 1811.

    The enclosed letters having some relation to public business & one of them solliciting for its object a direct reference to you,[1] I have thought it proper to transmit them & to request, that M. Coles may be instructed to acknowledge their receipt. Permit me to enquire, whether two other letters which I have had the honor of writing to you, since my return to this City, have been received? One of these related to M. Warden,[2] the other, to Mr. Mc.Crae.[3] I am, Sir, with very great respect, Your faithful & Obedient Servant,

JOHN ARMSTRONG

RC (DLC). Docketed by JM. Enclosures not found, but see n. 1.

1. Possibly Armstrong sent JM a 1 Nov. 1810 letter he had received from Jonathan Russell in Paris (RPB-JH: Russell Papers), complaining about the abuse of U.S. passports abroad by "unprincipled foreigners" claiming to be naturalized American citizens. Russell requested Armstrong to make "an application to the President upon this subject."

2. Armstrong to JM, 6 Feb. 1811.

3. See Armstrong to JM, 5 Feb. 1811, and n. 1.

From Benjamin Henry Latrobe

SIR   WASHINGTON Feby 19h. 1811

In order to furnish some apology for the writer of the anonymous letter, I enclose a letter [*illegible*] written in 1797.

A Member of the committee informs me that all the equivocal passages are underlined, ⟨& that⟩ if they were not so that they could make no impression. With high respect I am &c

B H LATROBE

Copy (MdHi: Latrobe Letterbooks). In Latrobe's hand; written on the verso of a copy of Latrobe to JM, 12 [11] Feb. 1811. Filed after Latrobe to Robert Fulton, 16 Feb. 1813 (ibid.).

§ To Congress. *19 February 1811.* Transmits a return of the militia of the U.S. as received by the War Department.

RC and enclosure, two copies (DNA: RG 233, President's Messages, 11A-D1; and DNA: RG 46, Legislative Proceedings, 11A-E6). Each RC 1 p.; in a clerk's hand, signed by JM. Printed in *ASP, Military Affairs*, 1:297. For enclosure, see Eustis to JM, 16 Feb. 1811, and n.

§ From Robert Smith. *19 February 1811, State Department.* Transmits in accordance with the House of Representatives resolution of 18 Feb. 1811 the papers marked A and B,[1] which contain all the information, not heretofore communicated, concerning the "repeal or modification as well as the practical operation of the orders and decrees affecting our neutral commerce" since 1 Nov. 1810.[2]

RC and enclosures (DNA: RG 233, President's Messages, 11A-D1); letterbook copy (DNA: RG 59, DL). RC 1 p. In a clerk's hand, signed by Smith. For enclosures (59 pp.), see n. 1. JM forwarded the RC and enclosures to the House of Representatives in his message of 19 Feb. 1811.

1. The papers marked A include copies of five documents relating to the status of American commerce with France: Jonathan Russell to Robert Smith, 4 Dec. 1810; Russell to William Pinkney, 1 Dec. 1810; Christopher Meyer to Robert Smith, 31 Dec. 1810; duc de Massa to the president of the Council of Prizes, 25 Dec. 1810; and duc de Gäete to the director general of the customs, 25 Dec. 1810 (printed in *ASP, Foreign Relations*, 3:390, 393). The papers marked B include copies of Pinkney to Russell, 7 Oct. 1810, requesting "decisive proof" of the repeal of the Berlin and Milan decrees; and six letters from Pinkney to Robert

Smith between 7 Nov. and 23 Dec. 1810, including Pinkney's correspondence with Lord Wellesley between 4 and 10 Dec. 1810 on the appointment of a British minister to the U.S., the settlement of the *Chesapeake* affair, and the conditions for the repeal of the orders in council (printed ibid., 3:389, 373–79).

2. For the House of Representatives resolution to this effect, see *Annals of Congress*, 11th Cong., 3d sess., 975. According to Joseph Gales, Jr., the author of the resolution, Pleasant M. Miller of Tennessee, "had previously shown it to the President of the United States, who had suggested modifications of it, etc." ("Recollections of the Civil History of the War of 1812," *Historical Magazine*, 3d ser., 3 [1874–75]: 161–62).

§ To the House of Representatives. *19 February 1811*. Transmits a report of the secretary of state in compliance with the resolution of 18 Feb. 1811.

RC and enclosures (DNA: RG 233, President's Messages, 11A-D1). RC 1 p. In a clerk's hand, signed by JM. For enclosures, see Robert Smith to JM, 19 Feb. 1811, and n. 1.

§ From Christopher Greene, Jr. *19 February 1811, Warwick, Rhode Island.* Introduces himself as a nephew of Nathanael Greene and solicits the consular position at Marseilles held by Stephen Cathalan. Knows that Jefferson was partial to Cathalan; "but Sir, has not the debt of gratitude that was due the Father of Mr Cathalan for his Services to this Country during the Revolution, been fully cancelled in the person of his Son?" Declares that American consuls in France should be citizens of the U.S.; otherwise, they "cannot at all times act with boldness and impartiality in defending the rights and privileges of those, who have a claim to Consular protection." States that Cathalan is incapable of performing the duties of the office. Refers JM to Jacob Morgan for confirmation of this claim. Notes that this is the first request his family has made to the government since the death of his uncle.

RC (DNA: RG 59, LAR, 1809–17, filed under "Greene"). 3 pp.

From James Taylor

DEAR SIR   NEW PORT KY February 20th. 1811.

Judge Coburn informs me his commission as Judge of Louisiana expires in November next during the recess of Congress; that under similar circumstances a Commission was renued (before it had expired) so as to prevent a failure of an important term of that Court. I expect the Judge will write to you on this subject and state to you the reason why it would be proper to renew his commission during the present session.[1]

I am assured that Judge Coburn has performed his duty to the utmost extent, and I am sure he will continue to do so as long as he may be honored with the Confidence of his goverment.

His removal to that country is as yet uncertain, but I am well informed his want of residence is no Objection by the people of the Territory. I am convinced they are perfectly satisfied that he should hold the Office under the Circumstances he now holds it. Of this I am sure abundant proof could be produced.

I know of my own knowledge that he has not missed a meeting of the Legislature or a Term of the Court since his appointment.

Mr Coburns want of residence may by some who wish to get him out of Office, be made use of, but it is really a doubt with me whether in the agitated state of a New Territory: a Judge who is far removed from popular influence is not to be prefered to a resident, on whom the local impressions are sure to produce unpleasant effects.

But should you have any doubts on this subject I am well informed you can be furnished with abundant evidence of his standing in that Country; and if you would be so good in such case to signify your wish of such evidence I will venture to say it shall be furnished you. The Judges politics has been the same since my first acquaintance with him which has been for eighteen years.

He has been always popular as a Judge without ever appearing to take any pains to be so. He is firm and dignified, and I declare that I think he commands as much respect and presides with as much dignity as any Judge I ever saw.

I am sure Govr. Howard thinks well of him and no doubt but you & him have had some conversation on this subject.

On the subject I took the liberty of saying some thing some time since,[2] I have now to Observe, that I have lately been informed that the Petition has been industr[i]ously circulated & a number of signatures procured. I am informed that great numbers of signatures were procured at the Market at Cincinnati a few days ago. I confess I do not for my own part apprehend much danger, but I submit it to your super[i]or judgment, the propriety of convincing the people the injury that the leaders of this improper course may do to those people who may be in arrear to the Goverment for lands purchased in the state of Ohio.

This arrangment perhaps could be made thro' the representation of that state when they return. This business has been set on foot by some designing persons to answer some design. It is possible you may be much better informed on this subject than I can do it, but feeling an interest in every thing that concerns my Country & particularly your administration, I think it my duty to give you information from time to time of every occurrence that I may think may effect my beloved Country. If the information should be unimportant I am convinced yourself and all composing the Administration will appr[e]ciate my intentions. My family, my property, my all, is in this country. I am therefore deeply interested in every thing that concerns the Western country, and I think all of us who have it in our power ought to set our faces against any act or measure that may have a tendency to create jealousies in the Eastern states. I have the honor to be with the greatest respect Sir Your Obedt. Hble servt

JAMES TAYLOR

RC (DLC).

1. See John Coburn to JM, 31 Jan. 1811.
2. See Taylor to JM, 28 Nov. 1810 (first letter), and n. 1.

Draft of Robert Smith
to Louis-Charles-Barbé Sérurier

SIR,   DEPARTMENT OF STATE February 20th. 1811.

Desirous of laying before the President, with the utmost precision, the substance of our conference of this day,[1] and knowing that verbal communications are not unfrequently misunderstood, I consider it proper to propose to you in a written form the questions, which I have had the honor of submitting to you in conversation,[2] namely;

1st   Were the Berlin and Milan Decrees revoked in whole or in part on the first day of last November? Or have they at any time posterior to that day been so revoked? Or have you instructions from your Government to give to this Government any assurance or explanation in relation to the revocation or modification of these Decrees?

2d   Do the existing Decrees of France admit into French ports, with or without licences, American vessels laden with the produce of the United States? and under what regulations and conditions?

3   Do they admit into French ports with or without licences, American vessels laden with Articles not the produce of the United States, and under what regulations and conditions?

4   Do they permit American vessels, with or without licences, to return from France to the United States, and upon what terms and conditions?

5   Is the importation into France of any articles the produce of the United States absolutely prohibited? and if so, what are the articles so prohibited, and especially are Tobacco and Cotton.

6   Have you instructions from your Government to give to this Government any assurance or explanation in relation to the American vessels and cargoes seized under the Rambuillet Decree?[3]

FC (MdHi). In a clerk's hand, with Smith's note: "NB. The sending of this letter not approved by the President / RS."

1. State Department clerk John Graham was present at this conference and made a record of the conversation, which, he wrote, "turned principally upon three subjects viz 1st. The

Repeal of the French Decrees. 2d. The Restoration of the american Property seized under the Rambouillet Decree. 3d. The commercial Regulations of France having relation to the Trade of the UStates." In reply to Smith's inquiry on the first subject, "Mr Serurier observed that he was authorised to assure this Govt. that the Emperor would fully comply with his Engagements. That he could not say precisely what measures had been adopted subsequent to the 1st Novr as he had left Paris prior to that day to embark at Bayonne for the UStates and that altho he had been detained a long time at Bayonne he did not hear from his Govt. as they must have supposed he had sailed, for he was from day to day detained, by circumstances of which they could not have been aware."

On the second subject the minister "replied that the Duke de Cadore had told him that he considered that as an affair finished or fixed (and that he might say so to this Government[)]. He gave it however as his own opinion, that decisive Measures on the part of this Government in relation to England might not only ensure the restoration of that Property—but lead to great commercial advantages on the Continent of Europe." On the last subject Sérurier "seemed to be entirely uninformed but professed a readiness to transmit to his Government any enquiries Mr Smith might think proper to make. He only knew that the Emperor was much disposed to encourage a Trade between France & the UStates and that American vessels would be received in the Ports of France and if I mistake not he gave it as his Opinion that they might carry there any of the Productions of this Country except Tobacco—and if there was a difficulty it would simply be a difficulty of the Custom House, which could be gotten over." "It may be proper to remark," Graham concluded, "that Mr Smith confined himself to making enquiries" (DNA: RG 59, Undated Misc. Letters).

2. This letter was subsequently published by Robert Smith in his *Address to the People of the United States* after JM had dismissed him from the cabinet in April 1811. According to Smith, he had concluded his conference with Sérurier by informing him that he would send him a note "propounding the several questions, that I had just had the honor of putting to him in conversation, and that thus by his answer I should be enabled to lay before the President with the utmost precision his communications to me. I accordingly immediately prepared the following draught of a letter, and considering the President's sanction a matter of course, I had it in due official form copied by the appropriate clerk. But waiting on the President with it, and after having reported to him verbally the result of the conference, I was, to my astonishment, told by him that it would not be expedient to send to Mr. Serrurier any such note. His deportment throughout this interview evinced a high degree of disquietude, which occasionally betrayed him into fretful expressions" (*National Intelligencer*, 2 July 1811).

3. Two days before the meeting of 20 Feb. 1811, Robert Smith, according to Joseph Gales, Jr., had come to the conclusion that Sérurier "has nothing to say; that he is a young man, obscure, and not trusted with the secrets of Buonaparte; that he had seemed much surprised at the position in which he found himself, here; that he seemed to have no idea that he had come here to be *questioned*" ("Recollections of the Civil History of the War of 1812," *Historical Magazine*, 3d ser., 3 [1874–75]: 161).

§ From Matthew Lyon and Others. *20 February 1811, Washington.* Encloses a resolution of the General Assembly of Kentucky "respecting the extinguishment of the Indian claim to the Territory lying South of River Tennessee, & within the limits of the Southern boundary of Kentucky."[1] Expresses confidence that the executive will make "reasonable exertions" to extinguish the claim.

RC and enclosure (DNA: RG 107, LRRS, L-147:5). RC 1 p. Signed by Lyon, Joseph Desha, Samuel McKee, and Richard M. Johnson. Docketed by a War Department clerk as received 21 Feb. For enclosure, see n. 1.

1. The four members of the Kentucky congressional delegation enclosed a printed copy of a resolution approved by Gov. Charles Scott on 31 Jan. 1811 (1 p.), which stated that the interest of the commonwealth "does imperatively require" the extinguishment of the Indian claim to the territory.

To the House of Representatives

February 21st 1811

Having examined and considered the Bill, entitled "An Act incorporating the protestant Episcopal Church in the Town of Alexandria in the District of Columbia," I now return the Bill to the House of Representatives, in which it originated, with the following objections:

Because the Bill exceeds the rightful authority, to which Governments are limited by the essential distinction between Civil and Religious functions, and violates, in particular, the Article of the Constitution of the United States which declares, that "Congress shall make no law respecting a Religious establishment." The Bill enacts into, and establishes by law, sundry rules and proceedings relative purely to the organization and polity of the Church incorporated, and comprehending even the election and removal of the Minister of the same; so that no change could be made therein, by the particular Society, or by the General Church of which it is a member, and whose authority it recognizes. This particular Church, therefore, would so far be a religious establishment by law; a legal force and sanction being given to certain articles in its constitution and administration. Nor can it be considered that the articles thus established, are to be taken as the descriptive criteria only, of the corporate identity of the Society; in as much as this identity, must depend on other characteristics; as the regulations established are generally unessential and alterable, according to the principles and cannons, by which Churches of that denomination govern themselves; and as the injunctions & prohibitions contained in the regulat⟨ions⟩ would be enforced by the penal consequences applicable to a violation of them according to the local law.

Because the Bill vests in the said incorporated Church, an authority to provide for the support of the poor, and the education of poor children of the same; an authority, which being altogether superfluous if the provision is to be the result of pious charity, would be a precident for giving to religious Societies as such, a legal agency in carrying into effect a public and civil duty.[1]

JAMES MADISON

RC (DNA: RG 233, President's Messages, 11A-D1). In a clerk's hand, signed by JM.

1. The vestry of the Protestant Episcopal Church of Alexandria had petitioned Congress for an incorporation bill on 12 Jan. 1808. On 20 Dec. 1810 Burwell Bassett of Virginia introduced the petition, and the bill passed both houses of Congress by 8 Feb. 1811 (for the text, see *ASP, Miscellaneous,* 2:153–54). Following JM's veto, the House of Representatives debated at some length both the constitutionality of the bill and the means of reconsidering it before voting, on 23 Feb. 1811, against its passage (*Journal of the House of Representatives,* 7:454; *Annals of Congress,* 11th Cong., 3d sess., 129, 453, 828, 832, 983–85, 995–98).

From William Jones

DEAR SIR   PHILADA. 21 Feb 1811.

As information from respectable private sources may in the absence of Official intelligence serve to throw some light upon the equivocal policy of france in her professed cessation from the violation of our neutral commerce, I take the liberty of enclosing an extract from a letter recd by a gentleman in this city, by the Osmin lately arrived here from Rochelle, which letter was not delivered 'till tuesday last.[1] The writer of the letter is a Mr Jonathan Jones of Bordeaux, an American whose residence in France was anterior to the revolution. He is a Merchant of the first standing and a gentleman of intelligence probity and sound judgement; upon which from my knowledge of his character I should place much reliance.

I confess, my impressions as to the sincerity of france have been very unfavorable ever since the iniquitous seizure of the American property under the Rambou[i]llet Decree, and particularly the property at St Sebastians, than which a purer property never entered any country, as the owners encountered a War risk and war premiums to get it there uncontaminated, and were never charged with violating any Decree or municipal law of france—this property has been sold and the proceeds deposited in the Imperial treasury since the declared repeal of the Berlin & Milan Decrees.

Notwithstanding these impressions I should hail with pleasure any evidence of her sincerity and justice, and although the letter of Mr Jones furnishes nothing conclusive yet the general opinion there of a favorable termination bids us hope for a better state of things.

I pray you not to give yourself the trouble to acknowledge the receipt of this, as I wish to avoid intruding on your time at a moment which must require so much of your attention. With Sincere respect and regard I am Sir Your Obdt

WM JONES

RC and enclosure (DLC). RC docketed by JM. For enclosure, see n. 1.

1. Jones forwarded an extract (1 p.) of a letter dated at Bordeaux, 12 Jan. 1811, which stated that "no new Decree has been published concerning American affairs except it be two circular

letters from the Grand Judge and Minister of finances." The first, the writer continued, ordered the prize tribunal to suspend proceedings respecting American property; the second exempted vessels from formalities previously required by the Berlin and Milan decrees as those decrees were withdrawn. Both circulars indicated that new instructions would be issued by 2 Feb.; "thus the great question will ultimately be pronounced in a very short time and the general opinion is that it will terminate finally advantageous to the American interest." The writer added that there was no news of the *Essex* having returned from England. "As there is every appearance of a total change in the English Ministry perhaps new dispositions will be adopted by that government."

From David Bailie Warden

SIR,   WASHINGTON 21 february, 1811.

In consequence of the enquiry which you were pleased to make last evening, with respect to my conduct in a certain affair, I beg leave to present you the following statement of facts. A french vessel, by the particular permission, or instruction of General Armstrong was purchased by Captain Haley, in the name of Captain Banks, an american, to sail as a *Parlementaire* or flag vessel for the United States, with passengers, and was advertised as such in the commercial journal of Paris. Haleys' presence was required at Dieppe, and he, for certain reasons, not wishing to be known as the real agent in this affair, with regard to the receipt of monies for the passage, requested me to act in this capacity, and I permitted my name to appear, agreeably to General Armstrongs' wishes, in the newspaper advertisement. A Mr. Auguste, who had been watchmaker to the Emperor, was recommended to me, by Mr. Bonpland, the fellow-traveller of Humboldt, as an able artist, or mechanician who proposed to embark for the United States, with a large collection of mathematical, and other Instruments, and machines for making them; and he—Auguste—stated to me that he had obtained a passport to enable him to embark with the said articles, and this thro the medium of a distinguished personage, the Governor of the Palace. I, at once offered to favor his project, believing with Baron Humboldt, Bonpland and several americans, that the machines would be infinitely useful to the United States, and that the President would grant permission for their entry. I mentioned this to Captain Haley, who had returned to Paris, and who proposed to put them in the hold of the said vessel as ballast; and he requested me to write a note to his friend Mr De La Rue, at Dieppe, whom I never saw, to receive the cases containing them, which I did, according to a written statement, furnished by Auguste, indicating their weight. He, for some reason, of which I did not ask an explanation, requested me not to mention, in my note, that they were his property, or that

he was to embark, which I observed. Auguste, by my advice, was to make
his arrangement with Captain Haley, at Dieppe, for the amount of his passage and freight of the machines which I refused to arrange not knowing
Haleys' terms with respect to the latter. I sent him, by Capt Haley, a note
of introduction to Mr Bullus, navy agent, at New York, in which I mentioned the machines, and asked his intercession with the President for their
free entry. I heard no more of Auguste untill after the departure of the
vessel, and the return of Captain Haley to Paris, who informed me that the
cases forwarded to Dieppe by Auguste had been seized by his Creditors,
and that they contained not only machines but silks and other articles of
merchandise. I was deeply mortified at this deception, tho, I never, for a
moment, suspected, that I would be accused, even by an enemy, of conniv-
ance in this Affair, as I had no interest whatever in the vessel, which was
under the particular direction of General Armstrong and Captain Haley
with respect to what might be taken on board. It was during the embargo,
and it was impossible that I could be employed in evading its execution. My
letter to Mr. Bullus was the best proof of this. Besides, there was no invoice,
no letter of instruction, or of consignment to shew that I had any interest
therein. When every means had failed to injure me, which art and wickedness could contrive, this was resorted to after the annulment of my appointment, and being apprised of it, I communicated all the circumstances of the
case to several americans to Baron Humboldt, Mr. Bonpland, and Mr. Gay
Lussac of the Polytechnic school, who had been long acquainted with the
project of Auguste to export the machines &c which were considered by
them as of great value. All of them, knowing my innocence, said that it was
impossible to represent this affair to my disadvantage. Colonel Taite, who
is now in this Country, had often spoken of the said machines to General
Armstrong; and had proposed several times, when at Paris, to aid Auguste
in transporting them to this Country. Permit me, Sir, to declare to you, in
the most sacred manner, that the above statement is correct and true—that
I knew nothing directly, or indirectly, of the purchase of the said silks, or
other merchandise, or of their transportation, before it was communicated
to me by Captain Haley after the departure of the vessel; and that I had
neither interest, nor profit, nor concern therein—nor in the said vessel—
that I acted merely as agent to receive monies from Individuals, permitted
by General Armstrong to embark as passengers, of which I gave him a list
as he had instructed me. It is well known to all the american consuls in
France, to the Bankers and merchants of Paris, and to the americans who
resided there that I never was concerned in any mercantile speculation, the
whole time that I acted as Secretary and as Consul.[1]

General Armstrong told me, several months before he made known Mr.
Russels' appointment, that there was a person on the European continent,

who was destined to take my place. I asked his name, which he refused to reveal; but observed that it was an arrangement made thro the influence of General Smith, with which he had nothing to do. He spoke to me with the appearance of friendship on the subject, and offered me the Consulship of Nantes, or of Havre, which I refused for two reasons, viz 1e. Because the acceptance of a place inferior to that which I held would be considered as a degradation; and, 2e. That as there was no commercial business in either of these ports, and as I had no fortune, I could not there find means of existence corresponding to my education, and situation in life. He afterwards offered me his influence to procure me an appointment in South america, and as I placed entire confidence in his friendship, I accepted this offer, and resolved to accompany him home, convinced that Mr. Russel was to take my place. In the mean time, he arrived at Paris, and refused to accept it; and some days afterwards my letters from Doctors Bullus, Mitchill and others, received by the *Hornet* Brig of War, informed me that there was no question of the Government annulling my appointment but, on the contrary, that there was every reason to believe, that the President of the United States would continue me in office. I then called on general Armstrong, and requested him to allow me to remain in office for some short time to enable me to arrange my affairs, and to aid americans in the prosecution of claims which they had committed to my care. He replied, that he would speak to Mr. Russel on the subject; and the next day, the Minister informed me, as well as Mr. Parker, that I was to remain in my situation till the ensuing spring. A day, or two afterwards I was informed by a friend that he proposed to nominate Mr. McCrae as Consul. In the mean time he sought a pretext for this conduct; and the correspondence took place of which I had the honor to present you a Copy:[2] and three days after the date of my second note he annulled my powers because I refused to give him the certificate, or declaration respecting him which he demanded and mr. Deverux informed me that if I gave the declaration he expected General Armstrong would continue me in office, and would write me a friendly letter from Bordeaux. I never gave him any reasonable cause of displeasure. General La Fayette, Colonel de T⟨orn?⟩ant, General O Conner, Mr. Parker and other Gentlemen assured him that during several years acquaintance they never heard me speak of him but with respect, and that the whispers of enemies were false. He gave me an opportunity of declaring the same. My disposition was best manifested by my daily visits to him, by my prompt attendance at his cabinet when asked, and my constant readiness to do him every possible service. Captain Haleys rage against me was owing to the circumstance of my refusing to associate intimately with him. On account of his employment from General Armstrong, I always treated him in a civil manner. I have, Sir, offered this statement of facts for your satisfaction, and regret that I am obliged to trouble you with it at a moment when you are occupied with such important affairs. It is mortifying to my feelings of self-respect to be reduced to the necessity of noticing the calumnies and insinuations of slanderers, but I know what is due to the high station and eminent character of the chief magistrate of the United States, whom I have the honor to address. I am willing that every act of my life be examined with the strictest scrutiny, for I am convinced that I can bid defiance to the malice of my greatest enemy. I have the honor to be, Sir, with profound respect, Your very obedt and very humbe Sert

DAVID BAILIE WARDEN

RC (DLC); letterbook copy (MdHi: Warden Papers); partial copy (DLC: Jefferson Papers); Tr (DNA: RG 84, France, Misc. Correspondence Received). Letterbook copy misdated 20 Feb. 1812. Partial copy and Tr dated 20 Feb. 1811. Tr marked by Warden as "a true copy of the original . . . Paris 4 Sept. 1813." Minor differences between the copies have not been noted.

1. The remainder of the RC is not in the partial copy, which includes instead a paragraph providing further details of Warden's conduct regarding the shipment on the *Happy Return*. Warden incorporated this paragraph in his 26 Feb. letter to JM and in a later transcript (see Warden to JM, 26 Feb. 1811, and nn. 2 and 4).

2. Warden referred to copies of letters from John Armstrong to Warden, 6 and 10 Sept. 1810, and Warden to Armstrong, 7 and 10 Sept. 1810 (DLC; docketed by JM). The correspondence arose from Armstrong's belief that Warden had promised to provide Seth Hunt with material for a "future attack" on him in the U.S. The minister demanded a written denial and challenged Warden to name any occasions "in the eight years of acquaintance and intimacy in which we have lived, [when] you have . . . found my conduct inconsistent either with private morals, or public duty." Warden replied "in the most solemn manner" that he had "neither promised, nor furnished materials of accusation" to Hunt and that he had "neither the cause, nor the right" to censure Armstrong's private conduct. But he insisted that he had nothing to do with Armstrong's "ministerial acts, . . . except those which may regard me in my present delicate situation," and he was not obliged to explain his views on the minister's conduct (see Skeen, *John Armstrong*, pp. 114–15).

§ From John H. Hall. *21 February 1811, Portland.* Claims to have made an improvement in the construction of firearms which will increase the strength of the militia. "This improvement I wish to introduce to the notice of the American Government & that those to whose cognizance it more particularly belongs may properly investigate & ascertain its value. . . . Presuming upon the interest which you appear to take in every thing tending to promote the improvement of the militia I have address'd this letter to you requesting your assistance." Requests a response. [1]

RC (DNA: RG 107, LRRS, H-291:5). 1 p. Docketed by a War Department clerk as received 4 Mar. 1811.

1. JM forwarded the letter to the secretary of war, who wrote to Hall on 4 Mar. 1811, asking him to communicate examples of his improvement to gentlemen acquainted with firearms and, if their opinions were favorable, to send them to the War Department for consideration (DNA: RG 107, LSMA).

From Benjamin Henry Latrobe

Sir,   Washington Feby. 23d 1811

Notwithstanding the exertions I have made to complete the estimates required by the resolution of the House of Representatives of the 14h. of January,[1] devoting a considerable part of every night to that object I have only been able to accomplish it *now*. At the same time I submit a list of outstanding claims.[2]

The drawings to which I allude in my letter are upon such large & heavy boards that I cannot, I fear, bring them to the President's house before tomorrow morning.[3] But as the view alluded to is very nearly a copy of that which you have seen, if you could dispense with its being brought to You & permit it to be hung up in the house of Rep., I would place it there tomorrow or Monday morning, provided it may be convenient to send in your Message on that day, which owing to the late period of the session, & the dependence of the appropriation on this report, I should with great deference to you, solicit.

The Estimates for the Wings are so correct that I am very confident they will not be exceeded. That for the Center appears to me to be ample.[4] It has been made with great care. I am with high respect Yrs &c

B Henry Latrobe

RC (DLC); FC (MdHi: Latrobe Letterbooks). RC docketed by JM.

1. See Latrobe to JM, 18 Jan. 1811, and n. 1.
2. See Latrobe to JM, 11 Feb. 1811 (second letter).
3. No letter alluding to drawings has been found, but Latrobe was evidently referring to some drawings of the Capitol in a series of sketches he made between 1803 and 1812, very probably the perspectives of the east front drawn in 1806 and 1810 (see Van Horne, *Papers of Latrobe*, 3:36–37 n. 5).
4. For these estimates, see Latrobe to JM, 23 Feb. 1811 (second letter). This letter, however, contains no estimate for the center of the Capitol, suggesting either that Latrobe revised it before sending it to the president or that JM or Latrobe decided to omit the estimate before sending the report to the House of Representatives on 25 Feb.

§ From Benjamin Henry Latrobe. *23 February 1811, Washington.* Makes the following statement in compliance with JM's direction that he submit information required by the House of Representatives resolution of 14 Jan. "Of the Center of the Capitol, no estimate can be presented without a more definite plan than I possess of that part of the building. I have therefore transmitted only an estimate of the Wings." Provides estimates for the expense of completing the north wing totaling $85,000 and for the south wing totaling $61,000. "The Work may be compleated in two Years from the 1st. of Augt. next, the intermediate time being required for preparatory arrangements." To these figures he adds an estimate of $17,000 for the platforms for the north and south fronts.

RC (DNA: RG 233, President's Messages, 11A-D1). 3 pp. Forwarded by JM in his message to the House of Representatives on 25 Feb. 1811.

§ From John Nicholson.[1] *24 February 1811*. Seeks employment in the "contemplated new territory of Mobile." Would request the position of secretary but does not wish to stand in the way of his friend Thomas Gales, who is already a candidate. Considers himself qualified for a judgeship but would accept a position inferior to that. "I have for several years past been troubled with a pulmonary complaint, and I find it gains ground on me so fast that I am convinced I never shall get rid of it unless in a southern climate. . . . Prudence requires my keeping within doors more than is compatible with the duties of a representative." Has some knowledge of the law but his health has prevented him from practicing much over the last three years. Promises to call on JM in a day or two for information.

RC (DNA: RG 59, LAR, 1809–17, filed under "Nicholson"). 3 pp.

1. John Nicholson (1765–1820), of Herkimer, New York, was a Republican representative in the Eleventh Congress, 1809–11.

§ From Alexander Taylor. *24 February 1811, 59 Williams Street, New York.* "Some time after I wrote to you of an instrument which I proposed to be used to level a gun with[1] Captn. Bumstead called desiring to see it & recommended to me to make a larger one saying he would call & see me again which he has not yet done." After making a glass nearly three feet long and more simply constructed, called on Bumstead to tell him it was finished; "he said . . . that being liable to refraction it could not be depended on to level a gun with." Believes this view to be based on "false premises." Refers JM to the "enclosed opinion and Sugestion of Mr Chilton for a knowledge of whom I refer you to Samuel L. Mitchill senator from this State."

Recounts his discussion of submarine and torpedo warfare with Bumstead. Has also discussed the subject with the governor of New York, who wishes to try the instrument with a gun at the battery on Staten Island. Proposes that the U.S. and New York "join to introduce submarine Navigation & appoint proper persons to superintend and direct the business." Suggests engaging five men on Staten Island. Wishes to participate in the enterprise himself. "If however it were judged improper to employ me it would have my warmest wishes for its success for . . . altho I have a portion of pride & avarice and know an agent of another government in this town and have heard that Monarchies are more gratefull than Republics yet these feelings . . . [have] not led me to mention the business to ———." In future dealings would prefer JM's "taking a different channel of conveying it than the last."

RC and enclosure (DNA: RG 107, LRRS, T-127:5). RC 3 pp. Docketed by a War Department clerk as received 1 Mar. 1811. Enclosure (1 p.) is an endorsement by George Chilton, dated 6 Feb. 1811, of an optical instrument constructed by Taylor, noting that "as the instrument is constructed with reflectors of glass, objections might be furnished from the refractions of the glass, and the concussion arising from the report, which may be easily obviated by substituting metalic reflectors."

1. No previous correspondence between Taylor and JM has been found.

¶ To John Armstrong. Letter not found. *24 February 1811*. Mentioned in Armstrong to JM, 3 Mar. 1811, as discussing the character and conduct of David Bailie Warden in relation to the American consulate in Paris. Also mentioned in Armstrong to Jonathan Russell, 5 Mar. 1811, as JM's answer to Armstrong's suggestion that Russell be appointed as minister to France. "You had," Armstrong wrote Russell, "no friends in the administration," and he added that Warden "will probably return private Secy. to the New Minister (Barlow) or, it may be, Secy. of legation" (RPB-JH: Russell Papers).

§ To Alexander I. *25 February 1811, Washington*. "John Quincy Adams who has for some time resided near your Majesty in quality of Minister Plenipotentiary of the United States, having been selected to fill a distinguished and important office at Home,[1] we have desired him to take leave of your Majesty, and to embrace that occasion to assure you of our continued friendship and sincere desire to preserve and strengthen the harmony and good understanding so happily subsisting between the two nations, and which will be further manifested by his Successor."

RC (MHi: Adams Family Papers). 1 p. In a clerk's hand, signed by JM and Robert Smith. Enclosed in Smith to Adams, 26 Feb. 1811 (Ford, *Writings of J. Q. Adams*, 4:18–19).

1. On 21 Feb. 1811 JM had nominated John Quincy Adams to be an associate justice of the Supreme Court. The Senate confirmed the nomination the next day (*Senate Exec. Proceedings*, 2:168).

§ To the House of Representatives. *25 February 1811*. Transmits reports from the superintendent of the city and the surveyor of the public buildings in compliance with the resolution of 14 Jan. 1811.

RC and enclosures (DNA: RG 233, President's Messages, 11A-D1). RC 1 p. In a clerk's hand, signed by JM. For enclosures, see Thomas Munroe to JM, 19 Jan. 1811 (second letter), and Benjamin Henry Latrobe to JM, 11 Feb. 1811 (second letter) and 23 Feb. 1811 (second letter).

From Albert Gallatin

SIR   TREASURY DEPARTMT. Feby. 26th 1811

As the Charter of the Bank of the United States will expire on the 3d of March,[1] it became necessary, until permanent arrangements should be made, to provide immediately for the collection of the revenue bonds falling due after that day. The object of primary consideration being at this critical moment to ensure as far as practicable punctuality of payment of such bonds, the only condition, annexed for the present to the deposits arising therefrom, has been that the Bank thus selected should give facilities to the collection, by discounting in favor of persons indebted to Govt. on acct. of such bonds. And for that purpose the letter, of which copy is enclosed, has been written to the principal collectors. Other officers of Government having public monies in their hands & who are under the superintendence of the Treasury have also been instructed to withdraw their deposits from the Bank of the United States and its branches and to place such monies in the Bank which shall have thus been selected by the Collector. The object of that instruction is to afford to Such Bank additional inducements to afford the facilities required for ensuring punctuality in the payment of revenue bonds. That consideration is at this moment of such vital importance, that I feel it my duty to submit to your consideration the propriety of a similar instruction being given to those agents who, by the 4th Section of the Act of March 3d 1809 (9th vol. page 265)[2] are directed to keep the public monies in their hands in a bank to be designated by the President of the United States. The instruction may be suspended in relation to the paymaster general of the army & to the pursers & other agents residing at the seat of Government until a general arrangement shall have been made with the Banks here. But it would be very desirable that all such agents as keep the public monies at either of the ports of Boston, New York, Philada., Baltimore, Norfolk, Charleston & New Orleans should immediately be directed to place *for the present* all public monies coming into their hands after the 3d of March, in the same Bank with the collector of the port. As to any balance in their hands on 3d of March, it may be left optional to the officers to transfer the balance from the Bank (or Branch) of the U. States to the other Bank, or to leave that balance in the Branch or Bank of the U. States, drawing on it as usual until said balance be exhausted. I have the honor to be with the highest respect Sir Your obedient Servant

ALBERT GALLATIN

RC and enclosure (DLC). RC docketed by JM. Enclosure (2 pp.) is a copy of a 25 Feb. 1811 letter from Gallatin to David Gelston with instructions on how to handle the financial transactions of the customhouse after 3 Mar. 1811.

1. The third session of the Eleventh Congress, after a lengthy debate supplemented by a lobbying campaign that began on 18 Dec. 1810, failed to make any provision for renewing the charter of the Bank of the United States. On 24 Jan. 1811 the House of Representatives had voted, by a margin of one, to postpone indefinitely a bill to extend the charter, while the Senate, on 20 Feb., divided evenly on the same issue. Vice President George Clinton then used his casting vote to defeat the measure on the grounds that Congress lacked the constitutional authority to create corporations. Following the decision in the Senate, the House, on 21 Feb., took up a bill to repeal the section of the act that had incorporated the bank's stockholders (*Annals of Congress*, 11th Cong., 3d sess., 21, 329–47, 431, 791–826, 982).

2. Section 4 of "An Act further to amend the several acts for the establishment and regulation of the Treasury, War and Navy Departments" directed that "the paymaster of the army, the military agents, the purveyor of public supplies, the pursers of the navy, and the agents appointed by [the president], shall, whenever practicable, keep the public monies in their hands, in some incorporated bank, to be designated for the purpose by the President" (*U.S. Statutes at Large*, 2:535–37).

From Thomas Lightfoot Griffin

CITY OF WASHINGTON Feby. 26. 1811

Mr. Thomas Lightfoot Griffin by way of subjunction to his Letter of the 20th. Inst.[1] addressed to His Excellency James Madison President of the United States of America presents his most respectful compliments and respectfully solicits an answer in regard to the subject matter contained therein; and is ready & willing now and at all times hereafter to make reply to any Interrogatories that may be propounded him by the President himself should such a measure be adopted or deemed in the least degree necessary. He has other Letters in his possession at the service of the President which he will transmit him at any time. With the most profound respect He subscribes himself

THO: L: GRIFFIN[2]

RC (DLC).

1. Letter not found.
2. Thomas Lightfoot Griffin was a clerk in the register's office of the Treasury Department (*Records of the Columbia Historical Society*, 9 [1906]: 230).

From Charles Jared Ingersoll

SIR   PHILADELPHIA 26 February 1811

Some weeks ago I took the liberty to trouble you with a pamphlet lately published, without communicating my name as the writer.[1] But as this concealment will soon be no longer necessary, and I am very desirous of ascertaining your sentiments on the subject, I beg leave to make it known to you, that with a design, which I am confident ought to be approved, whatever imperfections may appear in the performance, I published the Jesuits Letters, in defence and vindication of this happy and great republic, against the detraction and insidious hostility of the nations of Europe, particularly France and England, the two with which it is our misfortune to be most intimately connected. As my object was patriotic, much minor matter was cast aside in the course of preparation for the press, in order that nothing might be published which would be objectionable as personal or political— so that the work, at best but a skeleton, came forth mutilated and imperfect. I presume however that enough remains to exhibit the moral intended— an epitome of the miseries and prejudices of France and England, their detestation of each other and coincidence in contempt jealousy, and hostility toward us, contrasted with a sketch of our prosperity, national character, resources and virtue, with a transient outline of our policy. Want of selfrespect, an unjust self appreciation has always struck me, since my return from Europe, as a defect in the American people—and tho I felt my own want of capacity and of time for the task, yet, as no one else seemed disposed to undertake it, I determined to make such an essay as might perhaps excite abler pens, and tend, however faintly, to shew our inestimable advantages.

Your approbation, not only as chief magistrate of the country, to which I am grateful and proud to belong, but likewise as a man of letters and extraordinary attainments in the provinces I have ventured to explore, would be one of the highest gratifications I could flatter myself with—and I presume, with much anxiety for the result, to ask your opinion. I remain with the greatest respect and consideration your most obedient servant

C. J. Ingersoll

RC (DLC). Docketed by JM.

1. See Ingersoll to JM, 10 Jan. 1811, and n. 1.

From Samuel Latham Mitchill

Capitol hill 26th. feby. 1811

Saml L Mitchill ventures to submit to the President, the petition of Capt John OBrien who is now charged in execution for a penalty incurred in consequence of a violation of the embargo-laws; and therewith to express his own wishes, that the President would extend to the petitioner, all the clemency that he can.[1]

RC and enclosure (DLC). RC docketed by JM. For enclosure, see n. 1.

1. Mitchill enclosed a petition addressed to JM by John O'Bryan, 23 Feb. 1811 (3 pp.; docketed by JM), written from debtors' prison in New York where he was being held after his failure to pay a $4,000 fine that had been imposed in May 1809 for his violation of the embargo laws. O'Bryan maintained that he had been misled into an "involuntary infraction" of the laws by the owners and agents of the vessel that was implicated, and he argued that since he had departed on his voyage from New York on 11 Jan. 1809—before the law passed on 9 Jan. 1809 at Washington could have been in operation there—the "penalties of said additional Law" should not have been imposed. He also mentioned that he had a wife and ten children who were dependent on him for support and who were in distress. O'Bryan's wife, Jane, had petitioned Dolley Madison earlier for a pardon for her husband (Jane O'Bryan to Dolley Madison, 27 Jan. 1811 [DLC: Dolley Madison Papers]). On 30 Mar. 1811 JM granted the pardon on the grounds that poverty had prevented O'Bryan from paying the fine and thus made him "a fit object of mercy" (DNA: RG 59, PPR).

From David Bailie Warden

Sir,   Washington, 26 february, 1811.

I beg leave to offer you the following explanation concerning my conduct as Agent of Prize Causes, which has been, as you are pleased to inform me, represented to you, in an unfavorable manner. It gratifies me much to be permitted to expose the false charges secretly made for the purpose of disappointing my views. Without this favor, I could find no security against the shafts of malice. If I were acquainted with the particular case, for which I have been accused of receiving improperly a sum of thirty, or forty Louis for its defence, I could give the most satisfactory proofs of my innocence, by an exposition of documents and particular facts. It is fortunate for me, that my conduct, in this business, was never influenced by pecuniary motives. It was the custom of my predecessor,[1] (as it is that of all Bankers, merchants, and agents), to charge a regular commission on claims specially committed to his care. Contrary to this usage, I commenced my agency by writing a circular, which stated, that I claimed no commission: and this engagement I faithfully observed. I was accused by my friends, and laughed at by merchants and agents, for this act, which, they observed, would procure me no thanks. I found an ample recompence in the friendship and confidence of americans, which it contributed to inspire. It may be useful to remark, that the usual sum of money given to a lawyer for defending a Prize Cause, is fifty Louis, and sometimes he receives a hundred and upwards. The Captains, or supercargoes of american vessels are usually instructed to commit their case to the particular direction of some Banker, or merchant, who is authorised to pay the necessary fees and expences for its prosecution. General Armstrong, by whose advice, or suggestion, I was guided in all this business, recommended Mr. Pichon as a lawyer to be employed by me in cases specially committed to my Management. I made an agreement with him, on the part of the americans, by which he was to receive no more than thirty Louis, instead of fifty, for the defence of each case, of which I had the particular direction. I was instructed to pay him this sum, for which I took his receipt, a duplicate of which I retained; and the americans were pleased with this arrangement. He complained to General Armstrong and to myself that the sum was too little, and he demanded more, with which demand I could not comply, as it was contrary to the above mentioned engagement. After Mr Pichons' departure from Paris, I was permitted to go daily to the Prize Court, where I became intimately acquainted with its proceedings, and I was authorised, in virtue of instructions and special procurations, by Mesrs Willink and van Staphorst, by Hope & Co, and by Crommelin & Sons, Bankers, at amsterdam, and by Messrs Hottinguer and other Bankers, at Paris, to make defences in certain cases. The memoirs, written by myself, in a style and manner, which none but a public Agent could dare to assume, were presented with those of the Lawyers I employed, who co-operated with me in the prosecution of the Claim. In all these cases, they voluntarily furnished me with the sum of thirty, or forty Louis to pay the Lawyers' fee, the printing of the memoir & legal fees of the Council of Prizes, for which I transmitted them regular receipts. Every thing executed by me, was in virtue of their instructions, or of those of the Agent of the vessel and Cargo. In no case did I receive a Commission. This fact is well-known to all who are acquainted with my agency in this business. I could easily prove, that I have lost upwards of two hundred Louis advanced to Lawyers for defending cases before the Prize Court, which, not being represented by any Agent, I thought it a duty not to permit them to be adjudged without a defence. The cases were insured, and the underwriters despairing of the restoration of their property, refuse to reimburse the sums advanced. I regret to be under the necessity of saying so much in my own behalf. All the acts of my public conduct were intimately known to General Armstrong and to the american Captains and agents who visited me daily. Federalists and Republicans, of this description, have certified that I acted according to my duty. If necessary, I could furnish a particular account of every case of which I had the management. I defy any Individual to prove that I ever asked, or received a Commission, or improper compensation. I felt an enthusiasm to act so as to be worthy of the trust confided to me.

I[2] was induced, Sir, by a certain circumstance, to write, in great haste, the letter which I last had the honor of addressing to you:[3] and I forgot to state, that the vessel, to which I alluded, named the *Happy Return*, sailed from Dieppe, for the united States, in the month of October, 1809. The art, employed by Auguste, was made known to General Armstrong, and to several americans; and so particular were its circumstances, that suspicion herself could not accuse my motives and conduct. To be useful to the united States, to M. Auguste, and to his friends was all that I had in view. If there had been any room for accusation against me, it would have been circulated by enemies, or mentioned by friends in the course of the year which elapsed between the sailing of the said vessel, and the annulment of my powers as Consul. M. Auguste had been introduced to me as an excellent artist: I saw him often at my office, and at the house of a friend, and he never failed to introduce into conversation his favorite project of transporting himself, his machines and machinery to the united States, of whose Government he expressed great admiration. I was quite ignorant that his affairs were in a deranged state: on the contrary, I was led to believe, that he was very independent. Having no suspicion concerning articles of merchandise, the positive prohibition of which I mentioned to him and to all other passengers, I did not reflect on the weight of the cases, owing perhaps to the hurry of business, and to the circumstance of his stating, that he proposed to embark models of brass cannon, and machinery of great weight. He had invited me to see the said articles, but I was prevented by the business of my office. I am conscious that my motives were just, and my intentions good in every act of my public conduct.[4] If I am reinstated, as I fondly hope, in the situation I filled at Paris,[5] I will labor, with all possible zeal and industry, to discharge faithfully the duties of my office, and to promote the views of the administration of the United States to which I feel sincerely attached. I regret, Sir, to give you so much trouble, at a moment, when your labors are more than usually great. I have the honor to be, Sir, with the greatest respect, Your most obedient & very humble Servt.

DAVID BAILIE WARDEN

RC (DLC); letterbook copy (MdHi: Warden Papers); partial Tr (DNA: RG 84, France, Misc. Correspondence Received). Partial Tr marked by Warden as "a true copy of the original . . . Paris, le 4 Sept. 1813." Minor differences between the copies have not been noted.

    1. Fulwar Skipwith.
    2. Partial Tr begins here.
    3. Warden to JM, 21 Feb. 1811.
    4. Partial Tr ends here.
    5. JM nominated Warden to be consul at Paris on 1 Mar. 1811. The Senate consented to the nomination two days later (*Senate Exec. Proceedings*, 2:173, 175).

From Robert Smith

DEPARTMENT OF STATE February 27. 1811.

The Secretary of State respectfully represents to the President, that agreeably to the several Acts of Congress authorizing the third Census or enumeration of the Inhabitants of the United States and the Territories thereof, instructions were issued to the several Marshals and Secretaries, conformably to the provisions of the Law; in consequence of which, regular returns of the population of the following Districts and Territories have been received at the Department of State; to wit: Maine, Massachusetts, New Hampshire, Vermont, Rhode-Island, Connecticut, New York, New-Jersey, Pennsylvania, Delaware, Maryland, Ohio, Kentucky, North Carolina, Georgia, West Tennessee, the Territory of Louisiana, the Territory of Indiana, the Territory of Illinois, the Mississipi Territory, and the ⟨District of Columbia; And that returns remain to⟩ be received from the District of East Tenessee, the Territory of Orleans, the Territory of Michigan, the District of South Carolina, and from the District of Virginia: That with respect to the latter, a Letter has been this day received from Andrew Moore Esqe. Marshal of the District of Virginia dated "Richmond Feby. 20th. 1811" informing that "no return has been received from Norfolk County, Norfolk Borough, or Petersburg"; that he had pressed his assistants in those divisions of his District by "repeated Letters"; and that "from their silence he doubts whether they have done any part of the business." The Secretary of State further represents to the President that the first of March 1811, is the time limited by Law for the Marshals and Secretaries to complete their returns to this Department and as that period is now at hand, he suggests the propriety of recommending to Congress the consideration of the subject in order that timely provision may be made by the competent authority for obviating such doubts and difficulties as may occur accidentally, or thro' negligence to prevent the perfection of the enumeration or returns of the inhabitants of any District or Territory, or divisions thereof, within the time prescribed by the several acts authorizing the third Census. All which is respectfully submitted.

R SMITH

RC, two copies (DNA: RG 233, President's Messages, 11A-D1; and DNA: RG 46, Legislative Proceedings, 11A-E3); letterbook copy (DNA: RG 59, DL). Each RC in a clerk's hand, signed by Smith. Angle brackets enclose words trimmed from lower margin of House copy and supplied from Senate copy. JM forwarded the RC to Congress in his message of 28 Feb. 1811.

From Jonathan Williams

SIR   Wednesday morning Feb. 27. 1811

The momentary, although faint, hope that the Military Academy Bill will be called up,[1] induces me to attend in the House all day, and prevents me from stating to you verbally its almost forlorn situation. I am convinced that there is a sufficient Majority in the House to pass the Bill without Amendment, which is now the only way it can pass, for should it go back to the Senate the session would close before it could be acted upon. The only thing wanting is sufficient zeal to get it up, and here I find the weakness of my influence, although I keep the little I have in constant action.

I should be sorry to appear too officious, but my motives cannot be condemned, for although it may be found that I seek for additional care, anxiety & responsibility in the new organization, it will not be seen that I can enjoy any additional rank or emolument; I therefore hope you will pardon my suggesting to you the expediency of impressing upon the minds of a few leading members of the House, as you occasionally see them, the same sentiments as to the public importance of this Institution that you have been pleased to express to me. This coming from you will produce a call for the Bill from various Quarters and so force it up; The amendment as to site will doubtless fail, and the friends to the Bill had better let the other as to increase of appropriation fail also, then the vote on its passage would be conclusive. I have the honour to be with the most perfect respect Sir Your devoted servant

JONA WILLIAMS

RC (DLC).

1. In his annual message on 5 Dec. 1810, JM had called for the establishment of an additional military academy at Washington, D.C., or elsewhere. On 7 Dec. the Senate referred the matter to a select committee of five whose members reported a bill that passed the Senate in amended form on 11 Feb. 1811. The House took up the Senate bill on 15 Feb., reporting it with amendments: "among others, the power of locating an academy is proposed to be taken from the President of the United States, and the academy fixed at Staten Island; the appropriation for buildings is raised from twenty-five to forty thousand dollars." On 3 Mar., however, the House postponed consideration of the bill indefinitely (*Annals of Congress*, 11th Cong., 3d sess., 16, 87–88, 89, 94, 104, 117, 121, 125, 128–29, 130, 967, 1110).

§ From Harry Toulmin. *27 February 1811, Fort Stoddert.* Acknowledges having received JM's letter of 22 Dec. [not found] "about three weeks ago." "Since that was written you will have seen that the authority given to governor Claiborne, instead of having the effect . . . to extinguish illegal enterprize, has only given a new direction to it: and that nothing probably but the timely, tho' barely timely, arrival of Col. Cushing with a competent force, has really saved this country from becoming a scene of plunder and desolation."

"The court at which the trials of the offenders, or at least a part of them, should come forward, commences on Monday next: but . . . I doubt, if any material business can be done. Indeed, I have no idea that any indictment will be found. . . . Nor indeed, will an exposure of their guilt, produce any odium in this country: whilst their continuance in office, (for almost all the leaders of the insurrection are public officers) will . . . perpetuate and strengthen their ability to do evil." The evidence from his examination of Reuben Kemper and John Caller fills more than half a quire of paper, "& yet I suppose that more striking testimony of the objects of the accused might be obtained."

"I have heard nothing lately from Pascagola, but that after the visit of John Callier, to Dupree, . . . the latter had taken refuge, with some of the plundered negroes, in Washington county, and that the former had stationed himself at the mouth of the Pascagola." Refers to an earlier "report . . . of a talk, unfriendly to the U. States, having been given by Govr. Folch to the Creek Indians" and adds that persons residing in the Creek Nation had not heard of it. Speculates that the report was "a mere device to irritate the minds of the French against the Spaniards, & eventually against the American governmt. for not expelling them."

All appears quiet below the line. Has no news of any recent arrivals from Havana, but it is reported that prisoners taken by Folch have been sent to Cuba for trial.[1] Hopes matters remain quiet at Fort Stoddert, "tho' considerable threats of personal violence, have been thrown out against me, in case I should presume to hold a court."

RC (DLC). 3 pp. Docketed by JM. Printed in Carter, *Territorial Papers, Mississippi*, 6:179–80.

1. Toulmin referred to the prisoners taken at Saw Mill Creek (see Toulmin to JM, 12 Dec. 1810, and n. 1). JM had been kept informed about the prisoners by Orleans territorial governor Claiborne, who reported to the secretary of state on 20 Jan. 1811 that "throughout the whole District of Baton Rouge, there is a lively interest ⟨ex⟩pressed as to the fate of these unfortunate men." The governor mentioned that he was frequently requested to intercede on behalf of the prisoners but he declined to do so without the sanction of the administration (DNA: RG 59, TP, Orleans, vol. 12). In a pencil note filed with Claiborne's 20 Jan. letter, JM wrote: "Might not Matthews or McKee, verbally & unofficially, promote a liberation of the prisoners." He subsequently authorized Claiborne to apply to the Spanish authorities in Havana for the release of the Americans (Monroe to Claiborne, 9 May 1811 [DNA: RG 59, DL]).

To the House of Representatives

February 28th 1811

Having examined and considered the Bill entitled "An act for the relief of Richard Turvin, William Coleman, Edwin Lewis, Samuel Mims, Joseph Wilson, and the Baptist Church at Salem Meeting House, in the Mississippi Territory" I now return the same to the House of Representatives in which it originated, with the following objection:

Because the Bill, in reserving a certain parcel of land of the United States for the use of said Baptist Church, comprizes a principle and precedent for the appropriation of funds of the United States, for the use and support of Religious Societies; contrary to the Article of the Constitution which declares that Congress shall make no law respecting a Religious Establishment.[1]

JAMES MADISON.

RC (DNA: RG 233, President's Messages, 11A-D1). 1 p. In a clerk's hand, signed by JM.

1. The bill had been introduced in the House of Representatives by Jeremiah Morrow of Ohio on 7 Jan. 1811 and had passed both houses of Congress by 20 Feb. The first five sections entitled its beneficiaries either to receive preemption rights to land in the Mississippi Territory upon their producing proof of their entitlement or, in the case of Edwin Lewis, to receive preemption rights to five acres of land in return for land that had been used as an encampment by U.S. troops. Section 6 reserved five acres of land, including the Salem Meetinghouse, for the use of the Baptist church (see *ASP, Miscellaneous*, 2:154). On 2 Mar. both houses of Congress reconsidered the bill. The House of Representatives failed to override JM's veto, then passed the bill after removing section 6. The Senate concurred on 3 Mar. (*Annals of Congress*, 11th Cong., 3d sess., 125, 127, 150–51, 329, 508, 900, 906, 1098, 1103, 1105, 1106).

§ To Congress. *28 February 1811*. Transmits a report of the secretary of state relative to deficiencies in the returns of the census.

RC and enclosure, two copies (DNA: RG 233, President's Messages, 11A-D1; and DNA: RG 46, Legislative Proceedings, 11A-E3). Each RC 1 p.; in a clerk's hand, signed by JM. Enclosure is Robert Smith to JM, 27 Feb. 1811.

To Charles Jared Ingersoll

SIR   WASHINGTON Mar. 2. 1811

I have recd your letter of the 26. Ult: referring to a pamphlet previously sent me; and for which now that I know to whom I am indebted, I return my thanks.

Having recd. the pamphlet at a moment, which permitted a very hasty perusal only, my judgment of it ought to have the less value even with those most partial to it. I am able to say, however, without compliment, that the perusal of the work afforded me pleasure, as being a seasonable antidote to t⟨he⟩ misconceptions & perversions which prevail agst. the true character of our nation & its Republican polity; and as presenting features of lear[n]ing, reflection & discrimination, doing credit to the Author; a credit which seems to be the greater when it is known that he is a young one. In expressing this opinion, I must at the same time do it with a reserve as to some views of characters & things,[1] which I can not but ascribe to errors which time will remove from all candid & discerning minds. Accept my esteem & friendly respects

JAMES MADISON

RC (NjP: Crane Collection).

1. One can only speculate about JM's initial reactions to Ingersoll's attempts to satirize certain European misconceptions about the U.S., namely the report in Charlemont's first letter to Inchiquin that "the reigning president, unless fame belies him, is much addicted to gallantry, and not very fastidious in his loves." In Inchiquin's fourth letter to Pharamond, this report was corrected to the extent that the president was said to have "no harem, and but one wife." In Inchiquin's sixth letter discussing the merits of the first four presidents, Ingersoll's remarks about JM were more circumspect. After penning some frank, and even severe, criticisms of the presidential conduct of John Adams and Thomas Jefferson, Ingersoll, writing in 1809, declared that "as Mr. Madison has but just entered on the chief magistracy, his probation is to come, and his estimate can be conjectured only. . . . Mr. Madison having distinguished himself as an accomplished speaker, and an able writer, it remains to be seen whether he will prove himself an enlightened executive statesman." The difficulties facing JM, Ingersoll noted, were many, and his country expected much from "his zeal, moderation and abilities" (see *Inchiquin, the Jesuit's Letters*, pp. 6, 35, 78–79).

From Richard Forrest

                                              CAPITOL HILL
DEAR SIR,   Saturday Night. [2 March 1811]

Judge Anderson seems to think that, some doubts exist respecting the situation of my nomination.[1] Some of the Members think it still in the possession of the Senate, and others that a new one must be made, and as tomorrow is the last day, he conceives it would be well to have it ready in case it should become a question, for the new one to be used only in case of need. I think there is no doubt of the result.

I have sent my Son up to inform ⟨you⟩ of the real state of the case, and beg you to stand by me in this last extremety. I remain most sincerely Your obt. Servt.

RICHD. FORREST

RC (NN). Damaged by removal of seal. Date assigned on the basis of internal evidence (see n. 1).

1. JM's nomination of Forrest to be consul at Tunis on 22 Dec. 1809 had been the subject of hostile editorial comment in the Baltimore *Whig*, and on 1 May 1810 the Senate had resolved that the appointment was neither necessary nor expedient. On 3 Mar. 1811 JM responded to Forrest's request by nominating him to be consul at Tripoli and replacing his nomination to Tunis with that of George Davis of New York. The Senate refused to give the president's message a second reading and ordered it to lie on the table (*Senate Exec. Proceedings*, 2:132, 139, 140, 147, 154, 174; see also *PJM-PS*, 2:248, 325).

§ From Samuel McKee. *2 March 1811, Washington.* Solicits an appointment as secretary or judge in one of the territories for Craven Peyton Luckett.

RC (DNA: RG 59, LAR, 1809–17, filed under "Luckett"). 1 p. JM received similar letters on Luckett's behalf from Henry Clay, William T. Barry, Nicholas Ruxton Moore, Benjamin Howard, Samuel Smith, George Poindexter, Buckner Thruston, and John Pope, all dated between 3 and 25 Mar. 1811 (ibid.). Luckett apparently presented these credentials to JM when he called on the president some time in April, on which occasion JM told him his letters were "entitled to respect" (Luckett to JM, 11 Nov. 1811 [ibid.]).

From Joseph Anderson

SIR   SENATE CHAMBER 5 OClock PM [3 March 1811]

The nominations you Sent in to day—will not be finally acted on for want of time.[1] By a rule of Senate, they must lie one day for consideration—an attempt has been made to Suspend the rule but without Success. If therefore—you consider those nominations of Suffic[i]ent importance—to require the attendance of Senate to morrow—we meet again at Six OClock—and I have taken leave to give you this information. With verry high respect

JOS: ANDERSON

RC (DLC). Date based on internal evidence (see n. 1).

1. Anderson was referring to the nominations of Richard Forrest and George Davis (see Forrest to JM, 2 Mar. 1811, and n. 1).

From John Armstrong

Sir,   New York 3d. March 1811.

The first paragraph of your letter of the 24th. Ult. on the subject of Warden's character & conduct, makes it a duty on my part to speak fully and freely to you with regard to this Adventurer. He is an impostor in every thing, and as deficient in capacity, as he is in fidelity. He has not written a single page of those memoirs, which have been so ostentatiously published as his, and on which is founded, whatever degree of reputation may be imputed to him, for zeal—for industry and for talent. They are by his own acknowledgment & without exception, the productions of French lawyers, & particularly of a Mr. Darchey an indigent man of letters & of law, to whom Warden gave *five* louis for each Memoir, while for each, his regular charge against the American Sufferer, was *thirty* louis. Like other traders however of small capital and bad morals, he had more than one price for his wares. Their value rose, or fell, according to the temper, or the means of the person employing him. Hence it was, that in the case mentioned by Mr. Russel, he actually charged and received *fifty* Louis for doing nothing; while in that of Capt. Merrihew, he brought himself down to accept a doceur of *five*, (over and above the expences of the process) for doing all, that it was in his power to do for any man. The truth is, that taking one case with another, ten louis may be regarded as the Amt. necessarily expended for copying and printing &c. &c. and when it shall rise above this sum there is room to suspect the existence of extortion. To this therefore M. Warden was fairly entitled, but not to a single shilling beyond it. His personal services, as agent of Prize Causes, were compensated by the public, and for *these* he received a sallary of 2000$ per An. from the Diaplomatic fund, as you know.

In the case mentioned by M. Russel, Warden has pledged himself, as you inform me, that he will give an explanation which shall be satisfactory. Does this also turn on mere inexperience and want of caution? With what propriety can a man of his age, who has been six years in public Service, set up a defense like this? The apology itself is an admission of incompetency, as well as of wrong-doing; and in what country on earth, are the claims of either, deemed a sufficient pass-port to public confidence and public office? But, Sir, permit to say, that any explanation of the case of the meditated shipment, which shall have the effect of leaving him subject only to imputations of inexperience and want of caution, is a false one. Did he know that the non-intercourse law existed? Did he know that the introduction of French merchandise into the United States, was forbidden by this law? Did he know that Capt. Freeman was specially prohibited from carrying with him such merchandise? He knew all these circumstances, yet in defiance of all, he presses his friend Haley (Who was part owner of the vessel) to take on board twenty thousand pounds weight of *merchandise*, to which he gives the name of *machines*, and which turns out to be silk stockings, millenery, Clocks and their Ornaments, house-hold furniture Chymical & surgical instruments &c. &c. and all destined for the Philadelphia market. And how does this up-right servant of the public, propose to get over the inhibitions of the law? "Why" says he *"you may take them as private property"*—not as *merchandise*. And what temptation does he offer to the ship owner to bring about his concurrence in the business? One, not badly calculated to produce the effect. *"He* (the Shipper)" says Warden *"will pay you well for it."* That this carries with it abundant proof of a want of caution, will be readily admitted. But does it prove nothing else? Does it look like the blunder of mere inexperience? Is it not evident that he knew what he was doing? that he labored both corruptly and cunningly? that he not only saw that a law was to be violated, but that the risk of that violation was to be compensated also, and that his measures must be adapted to both purposes?

It is your opinion in the case of Mc.Rae, that the single fact of his bringing with him from England, two British licences, would be sufficient ground to dismiss him from office, provided, the proof of the fact, could be clearly made out. But between this offense, taking the fact for granted, and that of Warden, how substantial is the difference? At the time of taking these licences, Mc.Rae was not in any public office, and there is neither proof of his using, nor of his attempting to use them, after his arrival in France—Nay the very reverse is the regular conclusion from M. Russel's letter, for he says, (somewhere about the middle of November) that Mc.Rae still had these licenses in his pocket.[1] Warden, on the other hand, a consul of the U. S. deliberately and in writing, proposes to another citizen of the said states, a violation of a known and acknowledged law of his Sovereign and employer, and offers a mercenary motive, to draw him into the commission of the offense. Nor is there in this case, as in the other, any deficiency of proof—the fact is established by Warden's own hand-writing. It is found in a letter from himself to Nathan Haley—the genuiness of which, is admitted by you. Between these cases then, there is certainly a very wide difference, and if Mc.Rae's conduct merits dismissal from office, Warden's is not such, as will entitle him to a new, & perhaps to higher appointment.

With regard to his general character and habits, (of which you appear to think favorably) were they much better than they are, they cannot outweigh conclusions drawn from a specific Charge, clearly and distinctly made out against him. Mal-conduct in office, like other things, has it's beginnings, and I know not that the best method to check these, is to bestow upon the person guilty of it, new marks of confidence & favor. Amendment, if it ever come, will be preceeded by repentance, and this is not a fruit likely to be produced by fresh hopes & encreasing patronage.

That some respectable men may favor his re-appointment, is no doubt true, since you assert it—but do these Men know, what has been Mr. War-den's conduct in France? If they do not, their warmth and their wishes ought to go for nothing, because the regular presumption is, that their opinions of him would change, as mine have done, on a nearer view of him and of his conduct. But who Sir, of these respectable men, can know his Character and habits better than myself? With me he has lived nearly eight years in an intercourse of daily business—six of these under my roof and at my table, and I scruple not to declare it as my solemn conviction, that he is unworthy of both public and private trust. Of this fact I have proofs, not yet submitted, but which shall be submitted, the moment they can be copied. I shall then shew (in his own hand-writing) an insinuation that he was the depositary of a secret which gave him a powerful hold of Me & which he must retain for the purposes of self-defense. Exonerating as he does my private morals, it follows that the offense he would impute to me, has been of a public or official character—but when pressed to come out with a direct charge, he makes to me substantially the following infamous proposition: "Keep me in place—& I will keep your secret. I will do more—I & my friends will strain every nerve to promote your views, what-ever they may be." What, I ask, ought to have been my answer? What was my answer? I instantly dismissed him from office: "go Sir, and carry your secret to the best market you can find. You may get bidders for it, but their deception will be that of a moment. If you tell truth, you will do me honor, and if you lie, I will certainly detest you." Such was our parting, and I have not seen him since. When I went to Washington he had disappeared from that place. When I returned to the North, he was no longer there. Traces of him I did find, that is, abundance of falsehoods scattered up and down, and all communicated under the severest injunctions of secrecy. But I will not trouble you with a detail of these—nor will I do more at present than merely state, that to this Country he has not, he cannot have, a Shadow of Attachment. He was neither born nor bred in it—nor has he a shilling of property nor a single connexion either of blood or of affinity within it's limits. He is not even a resident of it by election, for he was deported hither against his will & in commutation of a punishment of a different kind—nor did he seek to be naturalised amongst us untill the eve of his departure for France and as a protection on his passage thither. What tie then can bind him to us? not a sense of duty, for we have proof before us, of his want of reverence for the laws; not pecunary interest, for he has none of it; not natural affections, for they have no object here. According to his own ac-count, it is the civil & political liberty to be found in the U. S. and if so, why not stay & enjoy them? Why such eagerness—such anxiety to be gone?—to get back to Europe & to an empire of Europe, certainly not much distinguished by the resemblance between it's institutions & those of our own Country? Truth does not in this case lie at the bottom of the well:

though without a single grain of attachment to the U. S. M. Warden has a most sincere & affectionate regard for their public offices & for the honors & emoluments they confer. And well he may, for they have already enabled him to live longer in France, then he ever lived in America. But Sir, are these circumstances of a nature to favor new claims upon us? Are they not dissuasion against such claims? Does our own country furnish no native citizen willing & able to fill the consulate at Paris? Does it furnish none such of at least equal pretensions with this Mr. D. B. Warden? If it does not, God help us, for our national intellect must, in that case, be smitten with barrenness. But I have done. I have written thus far in the frankness which has characterised all my intercourse with you, public and private, and which I cannot lay aside without remarking, that if M. Warden be re-instated, you pass an indirect censure on my conduct in removing him, and, of course, impose upon me the necessity of shewing the grounds on which I acted. At whatever time, or in whatever way I may do this, I shall not cease to remember the very high respect, with which I have the honor to be, Sir, Your most Obedient & very humble servant

J ARMSTRONG.

RC (DLC). Docketed by JM.

1. In his 6 Nov. 1810 letter to Armstrong, Russell had described Alexander McRae's second visit to France "with his *two licences* in his pocket" but noted that McRae's real concern appeared to be not so much with illegal trade as with "making his fortune from the sale of the inestimable estate in which he was interested near Richmond" (RPB-JH: Russell Papers).

§ From Samuel Smith. *4 March 1811, Washington.* "My excellent young friend Mr. John Skinner of Annapolis, (who I believe was presented to you by Mr. Duvall) intends going to the Western Country. He wishes to commence his Career there in Some public Employ." Skinner's legal studies and service as a clerk in the state legislature qualify him for a secretary's position, and his "connections & family are among the most respectable in Calvert County."

RC (DNA: RG 59, LAR, 1809–17, filed under "Skinner"). 1 p. Addressee not indicated.

§ From William Tatham. *4 March 1811, Norfolk.* "Perhaps there never was a period when speedy communication was more important to the safety and prosperity of the United states than the present; especially when we consider how difficult it must be to manage a population so far and widely expanding itself." Encloses a sketch to demonstrate a method of telegraphic communication "whereby I deem it practicable to pass a question & answer to and from the President, or heads of department, by a confidential Officer at Cape Henry, in one hour." On the supposition that each glass could cover a distance of six miles, it would require fifty telegraphs, at $300 each, to communicate between Washington and Cape Henry, for a total cost of $15,000. A rate of $5,000 for one hundred miles gives "a rough estimate for any extent of country," but believes that "double the distance may be accomplished for that Sum" in the area between Washington and Georgia. If this matter is given to the War Department, there would be little additional cost, as three hundred soldiers and their officers could do the duty while also serving as "an useful line of patrole." Requests assistance to try the experiment "between the Capitol and College in Williamsburgh, procuring the aid of the Professers there," in order to perfect the system. Concludes by observing that "peace is the time for the operations required in preparation for war."

RC and enclosure (DNA: RG 107, LRRS, T-130:5). RC 2 pp. Docketed by a War Department clerk as received 11 Mar. 1811 and marked "file." Enclosure (1 p.) is a diagram of a house with a flagstaff, seventy-five feet high, bearing telegraphic signals.

§ From Bryan McDonogh. *5 March 1811, Malta.* "From many years residence in Tripoli, and the knowledge that Mr. Davis and Mr. Payne have of my acquaintance with all the affairs of that Regency, I am in consequence of which left by the latter Gentleman (who is obliged by ill health to go from hence to his Native Air) as charged with the affairs of America, untill the pleasure of the Government of the U. S. is known." Recalls that he has performed similar duties in the past at Tripoli and received a letter of approval from Mr. Pickering for doing so. Refers JM to Davis and Payne to counter the "malicious insinuations" made on his character by a former American consul.[1]

RC (DNA: RG 59, LAR, 1809–17, filed under "McDonogh"). 2 pp.

1. McDonogh, who was British consul at Tripoli, was probably referring to William Eaton, who had been critical of McDonogh's conduct (see Eaton to JM, 5 Sept. 1801, and Rufus King to JM, 14 Dec. 1801, *PJM-SS*, 2:88 n., 316, 317 n. 2).

§ From Joseph Thomas. *5 March 1811, Malta.* "During a residence of ten Years, in this Island, as Garrison Surgeon I have had frequent opportunities of knowing & attending professionally, many of your Excellencys Countrymen. . . . The purport of my writing to your Excellency, at this time is to acquaint of Mr. Payne's state of health."[1] For some time Payne has been in "a most dangerous state, of nervous instability, attended with great general debility." Mr. Moore, in whose house Payne has resided, has done all he could, and "the only alternative left, was the sending him home to his native Country, & air, for a change." Makes this statement in justice to Payne and to explain why he leaves his public post without first communicating with his government, "a delay which in this instance might be attended with fatal consequences."

RC (DNA: RG 59, ML). 2 pp. Filed with the RC is the report of a medical board on the health of John C. Payne, dated 3 Mar. 1811 and signed by Joseph Thomas and W. T. Iliff (1 p.).

1. Since 1807 John C. Payne, brother of Dolley Madison, had been serving as secretary to the U.S. consul in Tripoli where he had been sent after experiencing problems with alcohol. Sometime in 1809 Payne apparently took up residence in Malta, but in March 1810 the consul in Tripoli, George Davis, turned over the affairs of the consulate to Payne so that Davis could

return with his family to the U.S. It had been JM's intention to replace Davis in Tripoli by appointing Richard Forrest and at the same time to send Payne to Paris as secretary to Joel Barlow, minister-designate to France. Payne, however, returned to the U.S. in June 1811, suffering from fever, possibly malaria, and in embarrassed financial circumstances. He did not accompany Barlow to France as his secretary because he had borrowed money in Malta, and as Dolley Madison wrote, "if he went to france without it, he would be liable to arrest there." She despaired for her brother, who seemed to be incapable of supporting himself independently (Davis to Payne, 15 Mar. 1810 [DNA: RG 59, CD, Tripoli]; Forrest to JM, 2 Mar. 1811; Dolley Madison to David Bailie Warden, 8 Mar. 1811 [MdHi: Warden Papers]; Dolley Madison to Anna Cutts, 15 July 1811 [owned by Mr. and Mrs. George B. Cutts, Brookline, Mass., 1958]; JM to Richard Cutts, 6 Oct. 1811).

From Harry Toulmin

DEAR SIR   FORT STODDERT, March 6. 1811
    When I had last the honour of addressing you, I did not think it probable that any event would speedily occur which would render it proper for me again to intrude upon your attention: nor am I certain at the present moment that any will occur which will absolutely require the interference of the chief magistrate of the Union: but so great is our distance from the seat of government, and so impracticable is it that any measures should be taken by the Executive authority to restore the public peace after it is actually violated, that even distant and incipient symtoms of disease ought probably to be noticed, as no effectual remedies can possibly be applied after it is actually formed.
    Intimations have been given to me that a new plan is actually forming for the purpose of making war on the Spanish possessions, and although I know but little of the character of my informant who has been applied to, to join in it, yet the information which he gave me is strengthened by a declaration which I understand on good authority, has been made by a leader in the business, that they will now have ten men to support them in the expedition to one that they had before. Other promoters of the late enterprize have also, as it is said, been lately making purchases of all descriptions of land claims on the Pascagola, and have been industriously encouraging the new settlers in this district who served under Kemper, to go to that river and take possession of their 640 acres of land guarranteed to them by the convention: and I must confess that I can see nothing in this step but an attempt to form a party who may be bound by a community of interests to carry into operation any new projects of unlawful ambition.
    A neighbour, also, who has just returned from the settlements near Baton Rouge, gives me no very favourable picture of the temper of mind prevailing in that part of the Country.
    A general spirit of murmuring and discontent he represents as predomi-

nant. They regret extremely that they gave up the country so readily to the United States, talk of a dissolution of the Union and a new western Confederation, and (tho' to[t]ally inconcerned in the affairs of this part of Florida, and tho' never before taking any part in them) declare that if the United States do not take possession of the country in the hands of the Spaniards, they will again assert their independence and maintain it at every risque.

They propose, however, to wait till Congress adjourns, and if they then find that no effective steps have been taken; they are determined to make war both upon West & East Florida. It is possible that my informant may have attached more importance and more prevalence to these sentiments, than sober observation and a more minute acquaintance with the characters of the men would warrant: but he represents them to me as being the sentiments both of the many and of the great. As to any co-operation which may in the event of an insurrection, be expected from this district, I have no doubt but that many are sufficiently disgusted with the issue of their late expedition, and none are now aggrieved by Spanish oppression: but a combination of leading men and public officers (who have probably flattering prospects of personal agrandizement) must have a formidable influence on such a population as ours, and I cannot but deem it highly expedient that every precautionary step should be taken by the national Executive which is suggested by the "act in addition to the act for the punishment of certain crimes against the U. S." or by any other law which is applicable to the occasion.

I do not look forward, however, without considerable anxiety to the conduct of the military department in this part of the national territory: I have seen too much of the imminent danger to which the public interests have been exposed, by the command being placed, (not in vitious but) in feeble hands, and I have flattered myself that the military power being now under the controul of the upright and intelligent mind of Col. Cushing, would no longer become subservient to the purposes of base intrigue, but be directed sole[l]y to the honour and interests of the nation.

I grieve, therefore, to hear, that there is a probability of his been [*sic*] compelled to appear at Washington on the Mississippi to answer, as it is suggested or supposed to some charge exhibited against him there by an inferior officer.[1] I speak, however, on little more than rumour, for I have expressed no wish for accurate information as to the cause of the order: but I tremble for the fate of this country, should a post so important be placed at a critical juncture, in the hands of a man incompetent either as to understanding or as to experience.

Our greatest security perhaps lies in the want of funds among those who may be disposed to interrupt the public peace, and to loosen the bands which unite together the American family.

But we cannot on the other hand be sure that funds may not find their way from distant countries, and the open anxiety which, it is said, is discovered on the Mississippi part of Florida, to exercise the attributes of sovreignty, (if it be really any thing more than the blustering talk of self conceited politicians) may derive its stimulus and its support from the promise of foreign aid. It may be French or British, or both, operating on different minds.

On Monday last I began to hold a court in this County. It should have set 12 days: but the clerk (a very drunken man lately appointed) had absented himself, & left no deputy, & had been seen sixty miles off on the road to Orleans the preceeding day.

I appointed one *pro tempero*, amidst much opposition, and loud charges from Major Buford a justice of the county court of tyranny & oppression, and of assuming by this act of appointing a clerk pro-temp the *legislative* functions. I persevered however, without remark on his observations, in doing what little business could be done, viz. receiving returns, swearing attornies, & adopting rules for the governt. of the new court, (for the absent clerk had all the papers) and then adjourned to the next term.

Bufford, Kennedy, M'Farland and others, leaders in the late expedition, as well as many of their adherents were armed with clubs, and several of them with dirks, and as soon as the court was adjourned, Kennedy stepped forward (the whole being in the open woods—for we have no Courthouse) & stated that he was upon his own dung hill and proclaimed Cap. E. P. Gaines a dam—d scoundrel & a coward &c. &c.—but after I came away, as I am told, observed that he now found him to be a gentleman, that tho' he (Ky) was on his own ground & could do what he pleased, & have Gaines assassinated in a moment if he thought proper, yet that no man should touch him, & upon this threw down his cudgel. From this & from the abusive language given to me by Buford, after I had mounted my horse; I am satisfied that the object was to raise a riot and to assassinate some of those who are dreaded by the violators of the law. I fear however that I am intruding too much upon you in detailing such disgraceful anecdotes: but possibly to some future American antiquary they would prove an interesting though mortifying memorial of the barbarism of the 19th. century. I have the honour to be dear sir very respectfully your most obedt sert

H. TOULMIN.

RC (PHi: Daniel Parker Papers).

1. On 18 Feb. 1811 Brig. Gen. Wade Hampton, believing that Col. Thomas Cushing had "failed in his duty, as an officer, in repeated instances," ordered him to Washington, Mississippi Territory, where, on his arrival, he was to consider himself under arrest. Cushing refused to obey on the grounds that it was impossible for him to travel to the place designated, whereupon Hampton, on 16 Mar. 1811, gave orders for his arrest at Fort Stoddert. The three charges Hampton made against Cushing—disobedience of orders, abuse of public trust and public property, and conduct unbecoming an officer and a gentleman—comprehended eigh-

teen specifications. These ranged from improper delay in obeying orders in a variety of contexts to adopting "an improper and unauthorized attitude" while in the command of his troops, including unduly alarming the officers of a foreign nation in amity with the U.S., and also accused the colonel of improperly opening and reading a letter addressed to Hampton from North Carolina congressman Nathaniel Macon. Cushing's trial was repeatedly delayed, largely because of the difficulties of assembling witnesses, and the court did not convene until 20 Mar. 1812. In May 1812 the court found Cushing guilty of the first and third charges and sentenced him to be reprimanded in General Orders (see Hampton to Eustis, 9 May 1811, and enclosures [DNA: RG 107, LRRS, H-346:5]; and copy of charges against Cushing [ibid., LRUS, H-1811]).

To John G. Jackson

MY DEAR SIR   WASHINGTON Mar. 7. 1811

I should feel my own reproach, in acknowledging at this date yours of Decr. 4. if I did not feel at the same time an apology, which I am sure your friendly candor will admit, in the peculiar pressure of public duties, during the interval. I have not however been unmindful of the object of your letter, and should have even have [sic] taken steps towards it, but for my ignorance of the standard by which you measure the cheapness & dearness of Merinoes, and for the consideration of the distance of the season when a ram could be employed, whilst in the mean time the risk & expence would both be avoided by delay. A further consideration was, that the continued importations, promised a reduction of prices, as well as a larger field of choice. I believe I may now say, that Rams may be had at about $200, and Ewes at about $100. If you chuse to make an experiment at these prices, and I can be useful in procuring the means, you well know how freely you may make use of me. I ought to observe at the same time, that as the Merino—I will not say mania, but ardor—is lower Southward, than Northward, it is probable that if you can avail yourself of a friend any where on James River, you may be supplied on better terms than at places within my sphere.

You will see the ground on which our affairs with F. & G. B. are placed by Congs.:[1] The ground taken by those powers will be made known, I presume, by communications from the former subsequent to Feby. 2. & from the latter subsequent to the change in the Executive Govt. which must have taken place in January.[2] After the multiplied proofs of wickedness, folly & instability which we have experienced, it would be weakness to flatter ourselves much; but I think the chances before us are less adverse than they have heretofore been, with the exception of Erskine's arrangement, which ought, on every reasonable calculation to have had a very different issue. For the news from our S. W. Quarter, I refer you to the inclosed Speech of Govr. Claiborne,[3] to which may be added the information direct from

Mobille, that altho' the Spaniards hold the fort, they maintain a friendly intercourse with the Amn. troops near it; the adjacent country, & the use of the River, being in the mean time, undisturbed. Whilst actual hostilities are foreborne on our part, the remnant of the Spanish authorities, will not be disposed to begin them. And there is ground for believing that the higher Authorities, at the Havanna at least are as much gratified with the respect mingled with our interposition of force, as they are offended with the latter.

Among the difficulties which crowd on us from abroad, and from the implacable spirit, which continues to sway the opposition party, are added others which flow from much nearer sources.[4] These I reserve for the disclosures of time, or of more leisure. Accept my affece. respects

JAMES MADISON

RC (InU: Jackson Collection). Enclosure not found.

1. The bill to supplement the provisions of Macon's Bill No. 2 by excluding British goods, vessels, and merchandise from American ports was reported back to the House on 6 Feb. 1811 (see John Wayles Eppes to JM, 31 Jan. 1811, and n. 1). It was amended repeatedly and debated at great length in the last week of February, during which time Federalist members continued to express doubts about whether France had actually repealed the Berlin and Milan decrees and whether JM's 2 Nov. 1810 proclamation rested on a sound legal basis. The measure passed the House on 27 Feb. and the Senate on 2 Mar. The final version of the bill contained three sections. The first exempted from seizure or forfeiture goods owned by Americans and imported from British ports in American vessels before 2 Feb. 1811. The second stipulated that in the event Great Britain ceased to violate American neutral rights the president was to declare the fact by proclamation and that the proclamation was to be considered sufficient evidence of the fact in any legal proceedings arising under section 4 of Macon's Bill No. 2. The third section imposed the penalties of nonintercourse against Great Britain and its dependent territories, with the exception of provisions for restoring any vessel or merchandise seized before it was known whether Great Britain had repealed its antineutral edicts before that date and for exempting American vessels that had sailed for the Cape of Good Hope before 10 Nov. 1810 (*Annals of Congress*, 11th Cong., 3d sess., 355, 356, 357, 358, 359, 360, 361, 909–32, 938–57, 989–91, 993–94, 998–1008, 1010–30, 1033–62, 1062–96; *U.S. Statutes at Large*, 2:651–52).

2. On 20 Feb. the State Department had received dispatches and newspapers from William Pinkney in London to the effect that the health of George III was *"not improving"* and that arrangements would shortly be made in Parliament to establish a regency council. In that event, Pinkney concluded, "our affairs will doubtless be placed upon a new and a better Footing," and he even speculated that the disgraced minister David Montague Erskine might be sent back to Washington with adequate powers to settle Anglo-American disputes. By mid-February several American newspapers were reporting that a regency had been established in Great Britain (Pinkney to Robert Smith, 19 Nov. 1810 [DNA: RG 59, DD, Great Britain]; *National Intelligencer*, 14 and 19 Feb. 1811).

3. JM probably enclosed a copy of William C. C. Claiborne's 29 Jan. 1811 address to the legislature of the Orleans Territory (see Rowland, *Claiborne Letter Books*, 5:121–26).

4. JM was very likely alluding to his difficulties with Secretary of State Robert Smith and the prospect of Gallatin's resignation.

From Joseph Anderson

DEAR SIR   WASHINGTON CITY March 7th 1811.

I do myself the honor to inclose you a letter which has been Signd by four of the delegation from Tennessee. In explanation of the introductory part of the letter, it may perhaps be necessary to inform you—that Under the two preceeding Administrations—I had Several Occasions in Conjunction with my Colleagues—to adress the Presidents, Under instructions, from the State Legislature of Tennessee, and in every instance—answers were given in Writeing, either by the Presidents themselves—or by One of the Departments, which Seemd to have the most immediate connection with the business, upon which the adress to the President was predicated. I therefore (for reasons Which will readily present themselves) have thought proper to explain the ground of the introductory part of the letter.

The answers which were recd. from the Presidents or the Departments, were regularly reported to the Legislature of our State. And upon the present Occasion It woud certainly be highly gratifying to the Undersignd— and not less Satisfactory to our State—to Observe that the adress presented in March last[1]—had recd. that mark'd attention from the Executive which our Legislature expect, and which its importance in our Judgment requires. Far be it from me, to presume to Suggest to you, the Course which it wou'd be proper to pursue. But impress'd as I am, with the deep interest all my fellow Citizens take in the Object to be Obtaind—I am Sure you will *duely appreciate* the *motives* that actuate me, in thus presumeing to adress you. Th⟨erefore⟩ permit me to assure you, of the most friendly Character—relying on your disposition to afford us, every benefit, which your Executive functions will authorise—I beg you to accept—assurance of my most Sincere Esteem and high respect—

JOS: ANDERSON

[Enclosure]

§ From Joseph Anderson and Others. *1 March 1811.* "The undersignd not haveing received any answer either from yourself, or from either of the departments, to the adress presented to you in the course of the last Session of Congress . . . feel themselves impell'd again to adress you." They will not make a detailed statement of the objects of that address but only note that "one of the difficulties . . . in relation to the communication by the way of Mobile, and which they had understood, had measureably impeded the other Objects, in relation to that communication, has been so far removed as to afford a free passage to our vessels."[2] They request that JM review the representation they had made in conformity with the instructions they had received from the state legislature, which they now enclose.[3] "You will please to Observe, that the Resolutions of our Legislature . . . have been passed Unanimously, and may be truely said, to be only a faithful expression of the Voice of the Whole people. We are unwilling to be thought importunate. But . . . we must be excused, for earnestly pressing the Several matters of our former adress upon your most Serious and deliberate consideration."[4] They request that JM communicate the results of his deliberations to the governor of Tennessee "in order that he may be enabled to lay before our Legislature, at their next meeting in September—the result of our application."

RC and enclosure (DNA: RG 107, LRRS, A-110:5). RC docketed by a War Department clerk as received on 9 Mar. 1811 and marked "file." Enclosure 3 pp.; signed by Anderson, John Rhea, Robert Weakley, and Jenkin Whiteside.

1. The March 1810 address to the president resulted from a resolution passed by the Tennessee General Assembly on 20 Oct. 1809, which noted the importance of the navigation of the Tombigbee River to Mobile for the citizens of the state and urged the U.S. government to facilitate access to the area by persuading the local Indians (mainly Cherokee and Chickasaw Indians) to exchange their title for lands farther west. The thirteen-page address, signed by the members of the Tennessee congressional delegation (PHi: Daniel Parker Papers), justified these requests at some length and argued that the extent of the lands within Tennessee that were claimed, but not actually occupied, by the Indians served to discourage migration to the state. Access to the waters of the Mobile, the delegation maintained, was necessary for trade with the Atlantic and to "enable our Citizens to carry their produce to Market, upon Such terms as wou'd afford them a reasonable profit upon their industry." If the administration was unable to comply with these requests to the fullest extent, the delegation sought at the least such an extension of the existing roads throughout the region "as will enable Settlements to be formd along those roads—for the convenience and accomodation of our Citizens, who may from time to time pass from the Waters of Tennessee to the Waters of the Mobile." They also suggested to the president that powers conferred on him by section 15 of the act of 26 Mar. 1804 were adequate for the accomplishment of these goals.

In addition to these matters the delegation desired the opening of a road from Tellico Blockhouse to Tellico Plains and "thence to the Cowee Towns, and thence to Petersburgh in Georgia" in order to shorten communications with that state. The delegation also pointed to defects in the existing treaties with the Indians with respect to the difficulties settlers experienced in obtaining the return of slaves "who have been carried into the Indian nations—by unprincipled Whitemen—and there sold to Indians—who after the purchase thus made refuse to give them up." The delegation suggested the establishment of a tribunal to which the Indians "wou'd be bound to Submit" in order to determine "the right of the property in Such cases." Finally, the delegation sought a road through Chickasaw territory from Clarksville "in Such direction as wou'd pass Tennessee River below the Mouth of Duck River to intersect the present Natchez Road at Some point in the Chickasaw Nation." Observing that the requests contained in the address would require a treaty, the delegation concluded by requesting that the president make the necessary arrangements as soon as possible and that the treaty commissioners be given instructions "commensurate to the Objects contemplated." The executive, they added, should "speak in a language that cannot be misunderstood by the Indians, as to the nature and extent of our *claim* and demand—and we pronounce that the Voice will be *heard*, and *regarded*" (printed in *Journal of the House of Representatives at the First Session of the Eighth General Assembly* [Knoxville, 1809; Shaw and Shoemaker 18739], pp. 98–100).

2. Anderson referred to JM's annexation of Spanish West Florida in October 1810.

3. The enclosed instructions have not been found, but filed with the delegation's letter are copies of the following documents: John Brown to Willie Blount, 4 Oct. 1809, requesting that the Tennessee General Assembly petition Congress to pass legislation enabling citizens to recover slaves who had been purchased by Indians from "a man who had no legal or lawful right to said Negroes" (2 pp.); a communication from Willie Blount to the Tennessee General Assembly, 11 Oct. 1809, suggesting that its members urge Congress to establish a tribunal to

deal with the grievance described by John Brown (2 pp.); and John Strother to Willie Blount, 15 Oct. 1809 (with a postscript dated 21 Oct.), discussing the extent of Cherokee and Chickasaw land holdings within and beyond Tennessee to which the Indian title had yet to be extinguished (3 pp.).

4. According to a circular letter written by Representative Pleasant M. Miller, a member of the Tennessee delegation, JM had already met with the delegation (probably sometime in April 1810) and informed them that while he accepted their claim that Americans had a right to navigate the Tombigbee River, he declined to act on their requests because of the complications that would ensue in U.S. relations with the Creeks and the Spaniards (*National Intelligencer*, 20 June 1810; see also Cherokee National Council to Return J. Meigs, 11 Apr. 1810, *PJM-PS*, 2:297–98 and n. 3; and Madison and the Collapse of the Spanish-American Empire: The West Florida Crisis of 1810, 20 Apr. 1810, *PJM-PS*, 2:308).

From Albert Gallatin

DEAR SIR   [ca. 7 March 1811]

I have long & seriously reflected on the present state of things, and on my personal situation. This has for some time been sufficiently unpleasant; and nothing but a sense of public duty and attachment to yourself could have induced me to retain it to this day. But I am convinced that in neither respect can I be any longer useful under existing circumstances.

In a government organised like that of the United States, a government not too strong for effecting its principal object—the protection of national rights against foreign aggressions; and particularly under circumstances as adverse and embarrassing as those under which the United States are now placed; it appears to me that not only capacity & talents in the administration, but also a perfect heart-felt cordiality amongst its members are essentially necessary to command the public confidence, & to produce the requisite union of views and action between the several branches of Government. In at least one of those points your present administration is defective; and the effects already sensibly felt become every day more extensive and fatal. New subdivisions, & personal factions equally hostile to yourself & to the general welfare daily acquire additional strength. Measures of vital importance have been and are defeated: every operation even of the most simple and ordinary nature is prevented or impeded: the embarrassments of Government, great as from foreign causes they already are, are unnecessarily encreased: public confidence in the public councils and in the executive is impaired; and every day seems to encrease every one of those evils. Such state of things cannot last: a radical & *speedy* remedy has become absolutely necessary. What that ought to be, what change would best promote the success of your administration and the welfare of the U. States, is not for me to say. I can only judge for myself; and I clearly perceive that my continuing a member of the present administration is no longer of any public utility, invigorates the opposition against yourself and must necessarily be attended with an increased loss of reputation to myself.[1] Under these impressions, not without reluctance and after having perhaps hesitated too long in hopes of a favorable change, I beg leave to tender you my resignation, to take place at such day, within a reasonable time, as you will think most consistent with the public service. I hope that I hardly need add any expressions of my respect and sincere personal attachment to you, of the regret I will feel on leaving you at this critical time, & of the grateful sense I ever will retain of your kindness to me;

Draft (NHi: Gallatin Papers). Incomplete and possibly not sent. Conjectural date assigned on the assumption that Gallatin probably did not compose this draft until he had received a letter from Joseph H. Nicholson, written on 6 Mar. 1811 (see n. 1). Draft later docketed in an unidentified hand: "Mr. Madison declined receiving Mr. G's resignation & Mr. Robert Smith Secy. of State was removed from office."

1. On 6 Mar. 1811 Joseph H. Nicholson forwarded to Gallatin a copy of that day's issue of the Baltimore *Whig* containing editorial comments, some of which had first appeared in William Duane's *Aurora General Advertiser*, attacking both Gallatin and JM. The burden of the attack on Gallatin was to insinuate that the treasury secretary, by virtue of his support for the Bank of the United States and some alleged connections with the Northwest Company, was an agent of British influence. These accusations, Duane observed, were "of serious import," and he added that the "secretary of the national treasury should be like Caesar's wife, not merely pure, but unsuspected." As for JM, the editor of the *Whig* dismissed him as "a worthy citizen, though destitute of that energy or 'decision of character,' *so requisite in an executive chief*"; and on those grounds he argued that George Clinton would be a better president (Nicholson to Gallatin, 6 Mar. 1811, *Papers of Gallatin* [microfilm ed.], reel 22).

On 1 and 2 Mar. 1811, as Duane and Irvine were printing their attacks on the administration, JM was visited by two deputations of congressional Republicans, including Henry Clay, William Harris Crawford, and Nathaniel Macon, who apparently urged the president to take action to counter the harmful effects of both the quarrel between Robert Smith and Gallatin and the differences between Smith and JM over foreign policy. Nicholson informed Gallatin that the visits from the deputations "have not had their due weight with Mr. M.," and he urged the treasury secretary to take further measures in response to the criticisms appearing in the *Aurora* and the *Whig*. In a postscript to his 6 Mar. letter Nicholson added: "You will also find in the Whig that the *Cabal* are beginning their Attack more openly on Mr. Madison, by holding up Clinton. I hope you will shew him the Paper" (Nicholson to Gallatin, 4, 5, and 6 Mar. 1811, ibid., reel 22; Brant, *Madison*, 5:278).

§ From John Morrow, Jr. 7 *March 1811*, *Pittsburgh*. "I am an unfortunate pilgrim hunted from one part of the U S to the other. . . . Every person appear[s] to know me, yet no person will confess it. . . . My nearest blood connections treat me as a slave, and . . . the[y] say I am disordered in my mind." This has been the case for more than four years. Has been told there is an "enormous sum of money" offered for him but cannot find out by whom. Was born in "this land of liberty" and trusts that freedom "the meanest citizen enjoys, will not be denied me." If his actions are ever considered disgraceful, he is "willing to go to any of the Territories, and live secluded," but hopes for mercy from the "first magistrate of a free and enlightened people."[1]

RC (DLC). 1 p.

1. Morrow wrote to JM again on 16 July 1811 (NN; 3 pp.), mentioning that he had been "grossly insulted" on 4 July. On this occasion, he claimed that "Mr. Jefferson was the first cause of my persecution" and that $1.5 million had been appropriated for that purpose. He further complained of being "calld a negroe wherever I go" and asserted that he should not be treated as a slave.

From Thomas Jefferson

DEAR SIR   MONTICELLO Mar. 8. 11.

On my return from a journey of 5 weeks to Bedford I found here the two letters now inclosed, which tho' directed to me, belong in their matter to you.[1] I never before heard of either writer and therefore leave them to stand on their own ground.

I congratulate you on the close of your campaign.[2] Altho it has not conquered your difficulties, it leaves you more at leisure to consider & provide against them. Our only chance as to England is the accession of the Prince of Wales to the throne. If only to the regency, himself and his ministers may be less bold and strong to make a thorough change of system. It will leave them too a pretext for doing less than right if so disposed. He has much more understanding, and good humor than principle or application. But it seems difficult to understand what Bonaparte means towards us. I have been in hopes the consultations with closed doors were for taking possession of E. Florida. It would give no more offence any where than taking the Western province, & I am much afraid the Percival ministry may have given orders for taking possession of it before they were put out of power.

We have had a wretched winter for the farmer. Great consumption of food by the cattle and little weather for preparing the ensuing crop. During my stay in Bedford we had seven snows. That of Feb. 22. which was of 15. I. about Richmond, was of 6. I here, and only 3½ in Bedford. Ever affectionately Yours

TH: JEFFERSON

RC (DLC); FC (DLC: Jefferson Papers). Misdated 8 Mar. 1812 in *Index to the James Madison Papers*.

1. One of the enclosed letters was C. L. Siegfried to Jefferson, 3 Sept. 1810, seeking a consular appointment in Königsberg, Prussia (DNA: RG 59, LAR, 1809–17; docketed by Jefferson as received 2 Mar. 1811).
2. Someone, probably an early editor, placed an asterisk here on the RC and wrote at the foot of the page, "*the session of Congress."

§ From William C. C. Claiborne. *8 March 1811, New Orleans.* Forwards a memorial from the Legislative Council and House of Representatives of the Orleans Territory.[1]

RC and enclosures (PHi: Daniel Parker Papers). RC 1 p. In a clerk's hand, signed by Claiborne. Printed in Rowland, *Claiborne Letter Books*, 5:173. For enclosures, see n. 1.

1. Claiborne enclosed a letter to him from Magloire Guichard, speaker of the Orleans Territory House of Representatives, and Jean Noël Destréhan, president of the Legislative Council, n.d. (1 p.), covering an undated memorial to JM (2 pp.; in French with translation), requesting that the president increase the number of U.S. troops stationed at New Orleans and throughout the Orleans Territory. In justification of the request the memorial alluded to the sparseness of the population of the territory, the defenseless situation of New Orleans, and the dangers from both external hostilities and internal insurrection. JM referred the memorial to the secretary of war who informed Claiborne that the request would "receive a due attention." In the interim, the secretary suggested that the governor implement a solution he had discussed with him sometime during the summer of 1810, namely that he embody a corps "from the Inhabitants of the city of New Orleans" that could serve under officers of the U.S. Army (Eustis to Claiborne, 25 Apr. 1811, Carter, *Territorial Papers, Orleans*, 9:931–32).

From Andrew Ellicott

DEAR SIR, LANCASTER March 9th. 1811.

If a messenger should be wanted to carry despatches to France, after my friend, and connexion Mr. Barlow goes to that country,[1] I take the liberty of offering myself for that service. I have several reasons, independent of mere curiosity for making this application.

On my return to this place,[2] I found a considerable degree of sensibility excited by the appointment of Mr. Barlow; nothing has been left undone on my part to shew that in the present situation of our affairs, it was the best thing that could be done. The federalists will be more easily reconciled to the measure than another section of our citizens, who are, perhaps from the want of proper information attached to an ambitious, and artful faction. If I should in a future communication be more lengthy, and explicit on the ambitious views of the party just mentioned, I wish you to attribute it to two motives, *first* friendship for yourself, and *secondly*, a desire to serve our common country which is the only ambition I have ever felt.

So long as I believe, as now do, that your views are patriotic, you will receive the feeble support of myself and pen, but affected patriotism has so often been used as the most certain road to power, that I am sometimes almost induced to suspect myself.

My best compliments to Mrs. Madison, and believe me to be with due regard, and esteem, Your sincere friend, and Hbl. servt.

ANDW. ELLICOTT.

RC (DLC).

1. JM nominated Joel Barlow to be minister to France on 26 Feb. 1811 and issued his commission the next day. The Senate confirmed the nomination on 28 Feb. by a 21 to 11 vote (JM to Barlow, 27 Feb. 1811 [DNA: RG 84, France, Despatches to the Department of State]; *Senate Exec. Proceedings*, 2:168, 172).

2. Ellicott had recently returned from Washington where, as he complained, he had been compelled to spend "a considerable portion" of the winter "on Wilkinson's business." For this he received "two dollars pr diem, when the best economist could not in that place exist upon less than three," and he thus considered himself "robbed of one dollar pr diem." While in the capital, Ellicott visited JM whom, he stated, "treated me with the greatest respect, and attention, and consulted me confidentially on some very important points." Ellicott was convinced that JM would have liked to help him with his difficulties in obtaining employment, but he suspected the president was deterred from doing so by "the fear of offending the present ruling power in this state, whose animosity appears to know no bounds" (see Mathews, *Andrew Ellicott*, p. 218).

From George W. Erving

DEAR SIR   NEWPORT March 10t 1811.

I arrived here on the evening of the 8t, & yesterday received from Mr Hamilton your letter of Feby 1st; to the five letters which it inclosed the most exact attention shall be paid.

If affairs in Florida have not progressed according to the reasonable views & expectations of government, this may be owing in part or principally to the encouragement which Folch has received to deviate from his first intentions, by the violent opposition which has been made to the act of the Executive, & by the grounds on which that opposition was maintained in congress; for on whatever motives his first project was founded, he undoubtedly meant to reserve to himself a complete justification before his own government & fellow-citizens, on pleas which the discussions referred to went to deprive him of: I say this however without any precise idea of what has passed, or of the order of occurrences in that quarter, for I have endeavoured in vain to collect it from the public papers: I know only that the spirit of opposition displaying itself with the utmost rancour on all great questions, where we come into contact with other governments, naturally enough begets an opinion, that we are really a "divided people"; and that this opinion prevails; its deleterious influence on our foreign concerns stands most completely exemplified in the conduct of England, because the government of that country is more fully possessed of this prejudice than any other; but I have had occasion to see also that even the old government of spain encouraged it, the new one, innoculated with english sentiments & feelings, cannot therefore be exempt from it.

Since the date of your letter, the expectation of a correct & consistent course on the part of France in the view to which you are pleased to refer, is as I presume from the documents which have been lately published, very much strengthened: I never did for one single moment beleive that the emperor was insincere in, or that he covered any of the designs with which he has been charged under the great measure in question; therefore coud not attribute whatever equivocal appearances presented themselves, but to doubts respecting the perseverance of the United States in the determination which they had avowed; doubts which perhaps naturally enough arose, & which due diligence & means were not employed to tranquillize by those whose business it shoud have been to have inspired confidence: Indeed without first supposing that the french government was buried in Œgyptian darkness as to any views of its true policy, as well as totally lost to all sense of honor & probity, it coud not be conceived that precisely at the moment when the course of event offerred to her the most eligible of all positions, she shoud not only let the occasion pass by, but so act as to terminate her friendly relations with this country, in the worst conceivable mode.

The "John Adams" has been ready for sea since the 7t inst; I wait in conformity to your order communicated by the secretary of state, to receive such instructions & communications as it may be thought proper to furnish me with subsequent to the 4t March:[1] I wrote from Boston to both Mr Hamilton & Mr Smith respecting the narrowness of the accommodations on board the vessel, & the number of passengers; I shoud not have taken the liberty of mentioning this subject to you, but that from Captn Dents[2] conversation I fear that some difficulties of a more serious nature may arise out of it: it seems that an extraordinary number of officers have been sent to join the vessel, this is I beleive an usual practice, at least it is beneficial to the service; but then the officers become very much crowded: two persons—viz a Mr Springer a german merchant, & a Captn Dickinson agent for an insurance company have permission from the secretary to go passengers, they are ordered into the ward room, I am told that the lieutenants refuse to receive them, & some threaten to resign: Mr Benson who had your permission to go whilst I was at Washington has brought his wife with him, there are not accommodations for her in the captains cabbin, unless I am turned out of my birth; the Captn is very much disgusted that no discretion upon the matter has been left to himself & hints at quitting the service on his return home; the order in favor of Mr & Mrs Benson is very positive & was given to Mr Benson open; it may be, presuming on that his manner & proceedings have not been calculated to reconcile the captain to subsisting difficulties; If finally in consequence of these, either the officers in the ward room shoud refuse to comply with the orders given in favor of the passengers, or any of them shoud resign, the embarrassment will be sufficiently distressing. With sentiments of the most respectfull attachment Dear Sir Your most obliged & obt St

GEORGE W ERVING

RC (MHi: Erving Papers). Docketed by JM.

1. On 23 Feb. 1811 JM had directed Erving to delay his departure for Europe so that he might take with him "the final result of the deliberations of Congress" (Robert Smith to Erving, 23 Feb. 1811 [DNA: RG 59, IM]).

2. John H. Dent had entered the U.S. Navy as a midshipman in 1798 and since 1804 had held the rank of commander (Callahan, *List of Officers of the Navy*, p. 159).

§ From James J. Voorhees.[1] *10 March 1811, Pittsburgh*. Considers himself "a persecuted Man," having had "futile, and vexatious Charges" brought against him in a court-martial at Pittsburgh. Claims that three members of the court were his "decided enemies" and had given testimony on the charges. Writes not to influence JM's judgment but in the hope that JM will review the testimony of the majority of the court and do justice to a man who has faithfully served his country.

RC (DNA: RG 107, LRRS, V-37:5). 2 pp. Docketed by a War Department clerk as received 10 Aug. 1811.

1. Voorhees (Vorhees) was from New Jersey and had been commissioned as a second lieutenant in the Sixth Infantry Regiment in 1808. He was dismissed from the service on 30 June 1811 (Heitman, *Historical Register*, 1:990).

To David Bailie Warden

SIR   WASHINGTON Mar. 11. 1811

Circumstances have occurred which make it proper that you should suspend your departure for France; till you receive further instructions on that point. Accept my respects.

J. MADISON

RC (MdHi: Warden Papers). Addressed by JM to Warden at Newport, Rhode Island, "care of G. W. Erving Minister to Denmark." Docketed by Warden.

From Benjamin Hawkins

CREEK AGENCY 11 March 1811.

General Mathews and the gentleman with him arrived here on the 9th. spent yesterday with me and set out this morning for Fort stoddert. They are in good health and well fixed for traveling. He revealed to me the object of his mission, and seems pretty confident of success. I told him to call on me, and all under my authority, to aid and assist him if necessary. He was sincerely impressed with the reception you gave him and the confidence you reposed in him as well as of all the heads of departments. In the course of the unreserved conversations we had together he told me he was apprehensive a party was forming against you; and that one of your Confidential officers was of it. R. S.[1] He had no authority for insinuating so much of his own knowledge or he would have mentioned it to you, but from others who mentioned it to him. We agreed if such was the fact and it should come to your knowledge that any of the heads of departments substituted their own Judgment to that of the President they should without reserve be dismissed. As the President was the man of the people and the secretaries the men of his choice. Of the great crould [sic] of visitors thro the agency I have never heared a single one express a sentiment unfavourable to your public standing.

Last year the General visited and remained some time with me on his first mission at a time unfavourable for traveling. He then seemed to think he would not on the score of his being called a Federalist receive the confidence of the Government which he was desirous of obtaining altho not desirous of obtaining an office. He was communicative and unreserved to me and in return as I always had an esteem for him, I was not reserved to him. I told him he was about as much a Federalist as we were, that all who knew him, knew he was a plain, blunt, honest man and at the time of our revolutionary contest had executed with zeal fidelity and consummate bravery the post assigned him. He certainly was a patriot from principle and having spent half a century in acts of usefulness if occasion should require, being healthy and of strong constitution, there was no doubt he would be called into service again, and perhaps his present mission would lead to it.

He told me you were healthy and seemed deeply impressd with the duties of your office, which I told him was to be expected, from the eventful period in which your lot was cast. Mrs. Hawkins who only knows you from your public life requests me to inform you her only son two years old in June is named James Madison that he is very healthy very active and promising and she hopes as he has the means he will one day have the opportunity by his acquirements and Patriotizm to render himself worthy of the name he bears. I am with unalterable attachment My dear friend your obedt servt

BENJAMIN HAWKINS

RC (DLC). Docketed by JM.

1. Hawkins referred to Robert Smith.

From the Inhabitants of New Haven

NEW HAVEN March 11 1811

The petition of the Inhabitants of the Town of New Haven in Connecticut, in legal Town meeting convened. Respectfully sheweth

That your petitioners are in general, either directly engaged in mercantile pursuits, or in the occupations connected with them; in those pursuits, they have embarked their fortunes, and from them, they have not only derived a subsistence for themselves, and their families, but have furnished employment, for great numbers of persons; to the mechanic, they have opened a market, for the productions of his labour and skill; to the Farmer for the products of his fields; and at the same time, they have essentially aided the public revenue, by duties paid on their importations.

The foreign commerce, in which your petitioners are engaged, is principally with the British West India islands. In conformity to the Laws of their Country, by which that trade was sanctioned, and without any suspicion, that it would suddenly be prohibited, they shipped, during the last summer and autumn, as they have always been accustomed to do, numerous Cargoes, which have been sold on credit in the Islands, on an engagement to receive payment in produce, when the Crops come in, which they usually do in the months of March & April. The property thus received, they have been, in consequence of the Non-importation Law, prevented from bringing home; and your petitioners have now, from this and other causes, a large amount of property, in the British West India Islands: which must remain there greatly to their loss and disadvantage, untill that Law is repealed; in the mean time their Vessels will be useless to them, their seamen unemployed, and a Commerce once profitable & flourishing abandoned.

Your petitioners while engaged in a lawful commerce, have thus suddenly, without time being allowed them to escape, been overtaken by these Calamities. Under such circumstances of suffering, they very naturally enquire, from whence they proceeded, and whether they were inflicted by a Constitutional authority. In making this enquiry they cannot forget, that one important grievance, Complained of in the declaration of Independance, was, "Cutting off our trade" and that to, "establish Commerce," was one of the great objects, proposed in that memorable instrument; nor can they bring themselves to beleive that in the National Compact, by the power "to regulate Commerce" the States intended to grant a power to destroy it.

Your petitioners, are far from imputing to the general Legislature, any but the most correct motives, in passing the non-importation Law: but the consequences of that law, are peculiarly destructive to their Interests: it places them in a state of uncommon embarrassment; it ruins their property;

it dries up the sources of their prosperity; and they perceive no relief except from its repeal.

If the operations of the Non-Importation Law, thus severe and oppressive, not only to your petitioners, but to all persons Concerned in Foreign Commerce; does not present one of those "extraordinary occasions" which authorize the President to convene Congress, your petitioners respectfully suggest that such "occasion" may be found in the change which has taken place in our Foreign relations. The presidents proclamation, and the Law in question, was founded on an engagement of the French Government, to revoke the Berlin & Milan Decrees. Those Decrees it now appears have in fact not been revoked—that Power has not ceased to violate our neutral rights, she sequesters our property in her ports; she burns & sinks our Vessels on the Ocean; and what is still more difficult to comprehend, after such acts, the authors of those injuries and insults receive by Law, a hospitable reception in our harbours.

Your petitioners therefore, respectfully, solicit the President of the United States, to convene Congress as speedily as his powers will constitutionally allow: in order to enable them, to take the subject of this petition into consideration and of granting to your petitioners such relief as the nature of the case requires. And your petitioners as in duty bound will ever pray

Sign'd by order and in behalf of the Town of New Haven

> James Hillhouse
> William W Woolsey
> Elias Shipman
> Noah Webster Jr:
> Isaac Mills
> Wm. Leffingwell
> Henry Daggett Junr.

RC (DLC).

From Richard Peters

Dear Sir   Belmont March 11. 1811.

Genl Armstrong, when in France, sent me over some Seeds; &, among them, about 2 Quarts of most remarkably fine *Rye*, of a Species entirely unknown here. With my usual Desire to disperse what I obtain in this Way, I distributed, in very small Portions, the whole of what I had, except about half a Pint. I planted my Modicum in single Grains, in Drills; &, after some

Growth, I found that each Grain produced 3 Plants; which I separated & transplanted. I never saw so strong & vigorous a Plant of the Kind. The Rye of this Part of the Country is very much deteriorated; & I am very anxious to obtain a Supply, so as to ensure & accelerate Abundance. I am advised by Genl Armstrong that I can do this in no Way, but by having a small Supply conveyed in some public Vessel; as he can not tell where it can be obtained, otherwise than thro' our Danl Parker, near Paris; at whose Farm he obtained the small Quantity he sent to me. I wrote to D. P. by the last publick Ship, which sailed from N. Port; but know not whether my Letter will arrive to his Hands; as no Person had the particular Charge of it. I have again written to him; & beg the Favour of you to have the enclosed sent. I am not acquainted with Mr Barlow, so as to justify my asking him to ⟨a⟩ssist in my Object. But, as I concieve the getting this Grain into the Country ⟨w⟩ill be a publick Benefit, I am induced to ask you to be so obliging as to ⟨me⟩ntion the Matter to him, so that if a Licence is necessary to warrant the Officer of the Ship to bring the little Parcell I expect, there may be no Difficulties on this Score.

I recommend your getting some into Virginia; as an Object well worthy Attention. Its Straw is solid & strong, so that it will not be likely to lay or lodge. I expect also, that it will resist the Fly. Its Meal is nearly as white as Wheat, & the Grain weighs 64 ℔ the Bushell. Genl A. could not tell me the botanical, or common Name, for this Grain; but said D. Parker knew *all about it.* With sincere Esteem I am truly yours,

RICHARD PETERS

RC (DLC). Damaged by removal of seal.

From Lafayette

MY DEAR SIR   LA GRANGE 12h March 1811

I Gratefully thank You for Your Letter Novr the 1st.,[1] and for the incessant Attention You are pleased to give, Amidst Your public Avocations, to My private Concerns. It is a Misfortune Attached to the Vicissitudes of My Life that the Munificence of Congress and the Exertions of My friends, intended to Make me Rich again, Must Be Employed to prevent My Being Utterly Ruined. But Here also I find as Great if not Greater a field for Respectful and Affectionate Aknowledgements.

Your kind informations Authorise me to Expect Every day the two Remaining patents to Complete the titles for Eleven thousand Acres in the Vicinity of pointe Coupee. It Seems that the Location Near the town Upon which Golden Expectations Had Been Raised is Now Become Very doubtful. M. duplantier writes, 12h July, that the Cession to the town Has Left much Less than 500 Acres, which, altho Under Water, may be Reckoned at drs. 20, or 25000. It is Still, Says He, the Best Spot to Be Had. But You know Better What it is proper to do, and as I am Sure You Will act for the Best, Every Circumstances Considered, permit me to Anticipate My fullest and Very thankful Assent to Any thing which Either in doing, or in for-bearing to do, You Will Have thought Most Adviseable. I Cannot Help Wishing, Since My Liberation Has Been So generously Undertaken, that it May Be Completed. The Remainder, if there Was Any Hereafter, Would Have Been divided Between my fourteen children and Grand children. But it Requires to liberate me, owing to the Uncommon Circumstances I Have Related, and to the Accumulation of interest and Expedients these ten Years, a Sum So Enormous, that to Effect it, is an act of Munificence and Kindness Beyond Which My Calculations ought not to proceed.

I Have Mentionned to You, 15h November, the proposal Made By Mr. david parish to part with a portion of the pointe Coupee Lands, and the Motives Which, Notwi[th]standing My Extreme Reluctance, obliged me to Y[i]eld to Necessity. 5000 acres, drawn By Lots, in presence of M. Russel, Have Been delivered to M. Alex. Baring who Undertaking to pay Himself for 300000 fr Leaving 20000 fr for future time, and to liquidate the claims of M. John parish for 47000 fr, and of my Brother in Law Grammont for 28000 Has Given Up His Mortgage on the totality of My property. This Measure Has Been Approved But Not imitated By Mm. parker and preble Who own two thirds of a Joint Mortgage With Mr. Ridgeway Amounting to 188500 fr. But as the Later is absent, and as it is inconvenient for the two others to take Land, it Has Been determined not to go farther in the Sale Which leaves me possessor of Six thousand Acres in the Vicinity of pointe Coupee.

While I Consider Your Letters 18. and 19 May[2] and that of M. duplantier 12h July I flatter myself that You Will not disapprove My Having Accepted the Cancelling of debts So Considerable and the Release of the Mortgage at the Rate of 75 francs about 15 dollars an Acre. But I am Sorry and Much Alarmed to See that not only at that price, But on Any Account Whatsoever No Loan Can Be Made, No Monney Can Be Had Connected With American Lands. It Had Been the Opinion of Mr. david parish Which I Have tried down to the Most trifling Sums. Several other Attempts Have Met the Same Repulse. The inexpressible But Not Unaccountable pressure and terror which Has Ruined or Stopped the General Course of Business ought to invite Capitals to the other Continent. It is far from Being the Case. The only Speculation Attended to, that Upon the discount of Bills to England or America, Engrosses what little Monney is not kept dormant, and on the European Continent, for now what passes Here, Good or Bad, Has that Extent, no offer Can Balance the advantages on change, or those of short Loans to threatened Merchants. I Have However Made a last and desperate Attempt in Holland. But I Have little Hopes, and do not know what then I shall do. Mr. parish, M. Le Ray, and others tell me the Monney Might Be obtained in America. Permit me, My dear friend, pressed as I am of a liberation, and much alarmed at My present danger, to Entreat Your kind Exertions in favor of that plan the only one, which Circumstanced as I am in Every Respect, Can Save me. And Since, owing to the Liberality of Congress and the Care of My friends there Will Exist a provision Equal to the purpose, it Would Be a pity Not to Avail Myself, to effect it, of the only Means to Which it Would Have Suited me to Be Under that obligation.

I Will not dwell on politics. Not only Because You Easily Anticipate Every thing I Might Say, Wish, or Even Hope, But also on Account of My Having not Had Lately Any Confidential Communications. This Letter goes With the dispatches of Mr. Russel who Can Give You Late intelligences. We Expect to Hear from You By Mr. Irwine who is said to Be Sent to danemark. Gnl Armstrong Will Have Mentionned and I Have Myself Expressed to You the good dispositions I found in the Actual prince of Sweden.[3] He was desirous of a Commercial, diplomatic, Confidential intercourse With the U. S., and whatever He is obliged to put forth, I am Convinced His inward Good will may Be turned to Some advantage.

Was I to Enter into Apologies With You, My dear Sir, I Would Have too Much to Say. I shall only Request My Best Compliments to our friends and offer You the Cordial tribute of My Gratitude, Respect and Most Affectionate friendship

LAFAYETTE

Permit me to inclose a letter to M. duplantier. Be pleased Also to forward that to our friend who, Since He is at Monticelo, Has Become a Very Bad Correspondent.[4]

RC (PHi). Docketed by JM.

1. *PJM-PS*, 2:609.
2. *PJM-PS*, 2:343, 346.
3. See Lafayette to JM, 20 and 26 Sept. 1810 (*PJM-PS*, 2:548, 549 n. 1, 560).
4. Lafayette enclosed his letter to Jefferson of 12 Mar. 1811 (DLC: Jefferson Papers; printed in Chinard, *Letters of Lafayette and Jefferson*, pp. 323–27).

§ From Bernard Smith. *12 March 1811, New Brunswick, New Jersey.* Transmits a paper containing an oration he delivered on 4 Mar.

RC (DLC). 1 p. Enclosure not found.

From Harry Toulmin

Dear Sir   Fort Stoddert, 14th March 1811

On monday last a report was brought to this place from Pensacola; that a fleet of 30 sail of British were off the Barancas, at the mouth of the bay. I felt extremely anxious to ascertain both the fact, and the sentiments with which such an event would be viewed by Govr. Folch: for altho' it might prima facie, be presumed that it would be very grateful to him as a Spaniard, yet without a minute knowledge of the state of Spanish parties and his relation to them, it could not be concluded with certainty but that he might still prefer an occupation of the country by the American government.

Col. Cushing, however, reasoning upon general principles as to the policy of the British administration gave no credit to the account.

Today I have seen a person who left Pensacola a few days since. He says that it was generally believed at Pensacola that a British fleet was at the Barancas, and that they were coming up to take possession of the town and to prevent the Americans from taking possession of Mobile. He moreover saw a very considerable quantity of balls of all sizes, landed from on board two small vessels, with a number of boxes *supposed* to contain musketts, all of which had been, ⟨as w⟩as said, taken from on board the vessels at the mouth of the bay, which could not then come up. Considerable firing was heard from the same quarter. This evening we have heard the report of several large guns, apparently in or near the bay of Mobile. I mention these things, without having any clear opinion upon the subject: under the impression that facts may be within your own knowledge which will enable you to appreciate these accounts more accurately than we can do it.

Capn. Gaines went yesterday to Mobile, in consequence of an application from Governor Claiborne to Genl Hampton, "to continue at or near the mouth of Dog river" (now included in the Parish of Pascagola) "as long as any opposition to the laws shd be manifested": but I suppose he will return, after having viewed the scite, as there are no people there, and the opposition which I suppose must have been alluded to, was on the Pascagola river 60 miles from that place. A predatory party it was said last week, was going thither from this county: but I have not heard that they have gone.

John Callier who had been on that river buying up land claims, it is rumoured, is taken prisoner, but by whom and on what account I cannot learn.

It is certain I believe that some other persons, connected with the conventional party had been taken by their opponents.

Col. Hawkins in a letter to me dated March 6th says "Col. M'Kee is at Fort Hawkins, & I expect he and Genl. Matthews will be soon your way." I have the honour to be very respectfully, dear Sir, your faithful & most obedt servt

H. Toulmin

RC (PHi: Daniel Parker Papers). Damaged by removal of seal.

To Richard Peters

Dear Sir   Washington Mar. 15. 1811

I have recd. your letter of the 12th.[1] and will not fail to put the one for Mr. Parker into the hands of Mr. Barlow who I am sure will take an interest in the object of it. I shall follow your good advice also, to engage his attention to the procuring a little outfit of the Rye for myself & my neighbors.

As you may not possess the variety of Maize from India, called Sackatosh, or sweet corn, I inclose you a few grains from a part of an Ear which has lately come into my hands. It is remarkable for its saccharine quality, which makes it peculiarly relishable in the soft state for the table; and I understand that throughout the winter, it becomes by boiling, very fit to be eaten in the same way. The grains sent are but one remove from the original seed from India.

I take this occasion to thank you for your instructive & entertaining little tract on the Tunisian Sheep.[2] I have had broad tails, 4 or 5 years on my farm, which agree in all the distinctive merits of yours, except that their wool is more coarse. I have lately recd. from Algiers several Rams of that breed, remarkable for the size of their tails; but with fleeces all coarse, tho' not equally so; but all useful for the loom. I have distributed them into different hands & situations, with a view to preserve the stock; as far [as] one sex only, with select mixtures can do it. I have found the mutton of the broad tails, superior by far to any I ever tasted of other sheep. Be pleased to accept my sincere esteem and most friendly wishes.

James Madison

RC (PHi). Docketed by Peters.

1. Peters's letter was dated 11 Mar. 1811.

2. In November 1810 Peters had forwarded JM a copy of "Communications on the Tunis Sheep. Extracted from volume II, Memoirs, Philadelphia Agricultural Society," pp. 211–60, inscribing it with the note: "Presented to Jas Maddison Esq⟨r.⟩ as a small Token of personal Esteem, by Richard Peters. Nov: 5. 1810." JM's copy is in the Special Collections Department, University of Virginia Library.

From Nathaniel Irwin

Bucks County near Newville Penna.

Sir   March 15th. 1811

Not having the honour of being known to Mr Granger, I have presumed to transmit the inclosed through your hands;[1] & to beg you will let him know how far the writer is entitled to credit. In such a case, I know, that simple justice is all that even a friend could expect of you. Happily, in the present instance, I have no occasion to draw on your friendship, having no more interest in the object, than another Citizen who sends & receives as much by Mail. With increasing respect, I have the honour to be, Sir, your quondam friend, & present hble servt

NATHL IRWIN[2]

P. S. A Bal[t]imore paper announces, that the president has been heard to say, that a summer session of Congress would be necessary, to commence about the 20th: May.[3] Should this be the case, & health permit, I will visit the City of Washington at that period, and (among other gratifications) will have the pleasure once more before I die, of seeing the man I once called my friend, supporting with dignity, the first Office in the U. States. If, Sir, your mind is nearly made up on the subject, perhaps it is not too much to expect a confidential line of information.

N. I.

RC (DLC). Enclosure not found, but see n. 1. On the RC, JM wrote at the foot of the page: "Mr. Irwin is a very respectable Clergyman; and throughout his active life has been a steady friend to the Independence & liberties of his Country. / J. M."

1. Irwin apparently enclosed a letter for the postmaster general, dated 14 Mar. 1811, complaining of irregularities in the delivery of the mail. Nine days later Granger returned Irwin's letter to JM, along with a copy of his response informing Irwin that the matter had been corrected. He disagreed, however, with Irwin's suggestion that the mail might be delivered better by sulky than by stagecoach (Granger to JM, 23 Mar. 1811 [NN; 1 p.], enclosing a copy of Granger to Irwin, 23 Mar. 1811 [DLC]).

2. Nathaniel Irwin (1746–1812) had made JM's acquaintance during their student days at the College of New Jersey at Princeton, and he corresponded occasionally with JM thereafter. Upon graduating in 1770, Irwin became a Presbyterian minister, and in 1772 he was called to the pulpit of the Neshaminy Church in Bucks County, Pennsylvania. His political career was limited to his service in the 1788 Pennsylvania ratifying convention, but throughout his life he played a prominent role in the affairs of the Presbyterian Church (Harrison, *Princetonians, 1769–1775*, pp. 88–92).

3. A report to this effect appeared in the Baltimore *American & Commercial Daily Advertiser* on 8 Mar. 1811. After mentioning that the state of "foreign relations" was the reason for the extra session, the editor expressed the hope that the Twelfth Congress would "retrieve that respect for the legislative character which the last two had forfeited by their imbecility. They must cease to legislate upon contingent circumstances, and attend more to principle, not in the *abstract*, but by an assertion of the national rights for the maintenance of which the physical resources of the nation are commensurate and pledged."

§ Presidential Proclamation. *16 March 1811.* Declares and makes known, in conformity with the provisions of section 12 of "An Act regulating the grants of land and providing for the disposal of the Lands of the United States, South of the State of Tennessee" (3 Mar. 1803),[1] of the act attaching lands ceded by the Choctaw Nation in 1805 to the land district east of the Pearl River (31 Mar. 1808),[2] and section 1 of "An Act concerning the Sale of the Lands of the United States and for other purposes,"[3] that "the sales for the disposal of all the public lands contained in the District East of Pearl River, not otherwise disposed of or excepted by law, and the survey whereof, shall have been completed and returned to the Register of the Land Office, prior to the first day of September 1811, shall be held at Fort St Stephens on the Mobile, Mississippi Territory, on the first Monday of September One thousand eight hundred and eleven."

Tr (DNA: RG 49, Proclamations of Public Land Sales). 2 pp. Printed in Carter, *Territorial Papers, Mississippi*, 6:182–83.

1. See *U.S. Statutes at Large*, 2:233–34.
2. See ibid., 2:479–81.
3. See ibid.

To Thomas Jefferson

DEAR SIR   WASHINGTON Mar. 18. 1811
   I have recd. yours inclosing two letters improperly addressed to you.
   A sketch in manuscript was brought by yesterday's Mail from N. York, saying that a vessel just arrived, stated that the Prince Regent had appointed his Cabinet; that Lord Holland[1] was prime Minister, Grenville Secretary of State, Moira[2] Commander in Chief &c. and that a new Parliament was to be called. Whether these details be correct or not, it is highly probable that some material change in the general policy of the Government, in relation to this Country as well as in other respects, will result from the change of the Men in power. Nor is it improbable that a repeal of the orders in Council, will be accompanied by a removal in some form or other, of the other condition required by the Act of May last. Still the attachment to maritime usurpations on public law, and the jealousy of our growing commerce, are sources from which serious difficulties must continue to flow, unless controuled by the distress of the Nation, or by a magnanimity not to be expected even from the personification of Fox in Lord Holland. Grenville is known to be very high in his notions of British rights on the Ocean; but he has never contended for more, on the subject of blockades, than that cruising squadrons, creating a manifest danger in entering particular ports, was equivalent to a stationary force, having the same effect. His principle however tho' construable into an important restriction of the modern practice, may be expanded so as to cover this abuse. It is, as you remark difficult to understand the meaning of Bonaparte towards us. There is little doubt, that his want of money, and his ignorance of commerce, have had a material influence. He has also distrusted the stability & efficacy of our pledge to renew the non-intercourse agst. G. B. and has wished to execute his in a manner that would keep pace only with the execution of ours; and at the same time leave no interval for the operation of the British or-

ders, without a counter operation in either his or our measures. In all this, his folly is obvious. Distrust on one side produces & authorizes it on the other; and must defeat every arrangement between parties at a distance from each other or which is to have a future or a continued execution. On the whole our prospects are far from being very flattering; yet a better chance seems to exist than, with the exception of the adjustment with Erskine, has presented itself, for closing the scene of rivalship in plundering & insulting us, & turning it into a competition for our commerce & friendship.

In the midst of other preplexities [*sic*], foreign & internal, a source has been opened very near me, and where co-operation agst. them was to have been rightfully expected, from personal obligations, as well as public duty. I find also that the appointment of Warden, is to draw forth the keenest resentments of Armstrong. I have no doubt however that the ground on which we stand is sufficiently firm to support us with the Nation, agst. individual efforts of any sort or from any quarter. Be assured always of my highest esteem and sincerest attachment

James Madison

RC (DLC). Docketed erroneously by Jefferson, "recd Mar. 2," but listed in Jefferson's Epistolary Record (DLC: Jefferson Papers) as received on 20 Mar.

1. Henry Richard Vassall Fox, third Baron Holland (1773–1840), was a nephew of Charles James Fox and a prominent Whig advocate of liberal causes. Together with Lord Auckland he had negotiated the Monroe-Pinkney treaty of 1806, an agreement rejected by Jefferson and JM on the grounds that it did not provide adequate guarantees against the Royal Navy's practice of impressing American seamen.

2. Francis Rawdon Hastings, first marquis of Hastings and second earl of Moira (1754–1826), was an army officer who had served in America during the War for Independence. As a prominent Irish peer, he was a leading advocate of Catholic emancipation. It was widely expected that as a close friend of the Prince of Wales he would be a member of any ministry formed by the Prince Regent.

From David Bailie Warden

Sir,   New york, 18 march, 1811.

I had the honor of receiving your letter, of the 11th Instant, the evening before the *John Adams* sailed from Newport: I have returned to this City to wait your instructions concerning my departure for France. I am, Sir, with great respect, your most obedient, and very humble Servt.

David Bailie Warden

RC (DLC); letterbook copy (MdHi: Warden Papers).

¶ From Robert Lewis Madison. Letter not found. *19 March 1811*. Described as a two-page letter in the lists probably made by Peter Force (DLC, series 7, container 2). Robert Lewis Madison (1794–1828) was JM's nephew, William Madison's son. JM may have been contributing money toward his education at this time (*WMQ*, 1st ser., 6 [1897–98]: 116; statement of the Reverend James Laurie, 29 Apr. 1846 [DLC: Dolley Madison Papers]).

To James Monroe

private & confidential

DEAR SIR   WASHINGTON Mar. 20. 1811

I may perhaps consult too much my own wishes public & personal, and too little a proper estimate of yours, in intimating the near approach of a vacancy in the Department of State,[1] which will present to your comparison, as far as lies with me, that sphere for your patriotic services, with the one in which they are now rendered.[2] Should such a transfer of them be inadmissible or ineligible, on whatever considerations, this communication, will I am sure be viewed in the light, to which its motives entitle it, and may rest in confidence between us.[3] In a contrary result, be so good as to let me have your agreeable determination as soon as possible. Permit me to add that even in this result, it will be best for reasons reserved for personal explanation, that the precise turn of the communication, may be confidential.

I am the more anxious to hear from you as soon as possible, since besides the more obvious calls for it, the business of that Dept. is rendered by the present conjuncture, peculiarly urgent as well as important. It would be of the greatest advantage, if it could be in the hands which are to dispose of it, in about two weeks from this date, and receive a close attention for a short period thence ensuing. It is probable that an interval of relaxation would thereby be rendered consistent with the public interest. Accept assurances of my great esteem and sincere friendship

JAMES MADISON

RC (DLC). Docketed by Monroe.

1. JM had requested the resignation of Robert Smith on 19 Mar. 1811 (see Memorandum on Robert Smith, ca. 11 Apr. 1811, and nn. 2, 3).

2. Monroe had been elected governor of Virginia on 16 Jan. 1811 (Ammon, *James Monroe*, p. 286).

3. Monroe had already been alerted to the possibility that he would be appointed secretary of state in a letter he had received from Senator Richard Brent of Virginia on 14 Mar. 1811. Although he had not been "expressly authorised" to offer Monroe the position, Brent mentioned that he had been consulted for his opinion as to whether Monroe would accept such an

offer. Brent further stated that he was sure Monroe would be offered the appointment after he had authorized Brent to say that he would accept. However, Monroe did not respond to Brent's letter of inquiry until 18 Mar., and Brent did not convey Monroe's response to Washington until 22 Mar. (Brent to Monroe, ca. 10 Mar. 1811 [DLC: Monroe Papers]; Monroe to Brent, 18 Mar. 1811, and Brent to Gallatin, 22 Mar. 1811, *Papers of Gallatin* [microfilm ed.], reel 22).

From Albert Gallatin

SIR,   TREASURY DEPARTMENT Mar. 22d. 1811.

The public business heretofore transacted by the Branch Bank at Washington will, at the end of this month be transferred to the Banks of Columbia and Washington. In order to have a general view of the subject, it is necessary to take into consideration not only the Treasury deposits, but also those made by those officers belonging to the War & Navy Departments who, by the 4th. sect. of the act of Mar. 3d. 1809 (9th. vol. page 265)[1] are directed to keep the public monies in their hands, in some incorporated bank, to be designated for the purpose, by the President of the U. States. And the following plan appearing to me to combine public convenience with that of the officers of government and of individuals, is respectfully submitted to your consideration. If, so far as relates to the officers abovementioned, it meets with the approbation of the Secretaries of the War and Navy Departments and your own, I beg leave to request that the approbation may be communicated to the officers concerned, and to myself, in the beginning of next week, in order that I may proceed with the arrangement and place the necessary funds in the two Banks.

1. The purser, navy-agent, superintendent of the navy-yard, paymaster of the marine corps, and generally the officers pertaining to the navy department, whose permanent residence is at the seat of government, to keep their public monies in the Bank of Washington.

2. The Pay Master of the Army to keep his, in the Bank of Columbia.

3. The accounts of dividends on the public debt payable at the seat of government, to be kept at the Bank of Columbia, from where they were taken when the Branch was established here, and who have agreed to keep an office for that purpose in or near the Treasury.

4. Payments by the Treasurer of all Warrants payable at the seat of government, and other than those drawn for the objects mentioned under the three preceding heads, to be made by drafts on either Bank, at the option of the person to whom the payment is made.

5. Payments by individuals into the Treasury to be made indiscriminately in either Bank, as may suit the convenience of such individuals.

The proportion of current business and of public deposits in each Bank, will therefore, be in a great degree, regulated by the convenience of the parties who have monies to pay in or to receive from the Treasury. I have the honor to be with the highest respect Sir, Your obedt. servant.

ALBERT GALLATIN

RC (DLC). In a clerk's hand, signed by Gallatin. Docketed by JM.

1. See *U.S. Statutes at Large*, 2:536.

From Mathew Arnold Hœvel

MAY IT PLEASE YOUR EXCELLENCY.   SANTIAGO March 22d. 1811.

By special request of the present board of Government in the Kingdom of Chile,[1] I have the honor to transmit to Your Excell & Government of the United States the enclosed Official letter, & am happy to add that the sentiments therein expressed are truly those which now in the highest degree animate this Board & the good people of Chile—and which sentiments I venture to assert will last with them towards the United States & its Citizens with preference to what any European Power may expect.

I beg leave to suggest to the Wisdom of Your Excellency, weither it would no⟨t be⟩ of moment to meet the wish of this Board in soon appointing an Agent here with ⟨whom⟩ they might treat on subjects highly interesting & advantageous to both nations.

The representatives of the people will meet in Congress next month for the first time, and a new Constitution is to be formed. I have the honor to remain with great regard Sir Your Excellencys most obedient & very hble Servt.

MATHW. ARND. HŒVEL
a Citizen of the U: S: of A. late of
New York now residing at Santiago.

[First Enclosure]

§ From Fernando Márquez de la Plata and Others.[2] *22 March 1811, Santiago.* Extends the hand of friendship from Chile to the people of the U.S. Encloses a "Declaration of Commerce" by which "the productions of our Soil and of our Industry will be common."[3] Adds that since "every description of Arms are to us objects of the most urgent necessity and especially Guns and Pistols, . . . the obligation would be immense if you would send us—as we earnestly beg of you to do, some artisans who know how to make them." Advises that "those of your fellow Citizens who navigate these Seas" have been asked to "permit the recent orders of this Govt. . . . to blot out from their Minds, the unfriendly ideas with which those who formerly governed here had doubtless inspired them."

RC and first enclosure, two copies (DNA: RG 59, NFL, Chile; and DNA: RG 59, ML); second enclosure (DNA: RG 59, NFL, Chile). First copy of RC damaged by removal of seal; second copy marked "Duplicate." First enclosure in Spanish; filed with the first copy are two translations, one in the hand of John Graham (4 pp.); a third translation is filed with the second copy. Graham's translation is printed in Manning, *Diplomatic Correspondence of the United States concerning the Independence of the Latin-American Nations*, 2:895–96. For second enclosure, see n. 3.

1. The *cabildo* of Santiago, in open session on 18 Sept. 1810, had established a junta to govern the kingdom of Chile during the captivity of Ferdinand VII. In January 1811 that body decided to open the ports of Chile to international trade (Simon Collier, *Ideas and Politics of Chilean Independence, 1808–1833* [Cambridge, Mass., 1977], pp. 44–93).

2. Fernando Márquez de la Plata y Orozco (1740–1818) was born in Seville, Spain, and after 1775 had served in minor positions in the viceroyalties of Peru and La Plata. Since 1803 he had been a member of the *audencia* of Santiago (Luis Galdames, *A History of Chile*, trans. Isaac J. Cox [Chapel Hill, N.C., 1941], p. 492).

3. The junta forwarded a copy of a decree, dated 21 Feb. 1811 (8 pp.; in Spanish, with a six-page translation), opening Chilean ports to the commerce of friendly nations. Filed with the duplicate copy of the RC (DNA: RG 59, ML) is a copy of a statement dated 22 Mar. 1811 (2 pp.), made by John MacKenna, governor at Valparaiso, confirming that the junta had ordered that "Anglo American Ships" be admitted to Chilean ports.

§ From John Laird.[1] *22 March 1811, Georgetown.* Encloses $220 at the direction of Robert Patton of Fredericksburg, to whom he asks JM to acknowledge receipt of the sum.

RC (DLC). 1 p.

1. John Laird was a Scottish businessman who had settled in Georgetown in 1800. In 1812 he was a trustee of the Georgetown Lancaster School Society (Bryan, *History of the National Capital*, 1:101–2, 484 n. 1).

From James Monroe

DEAR SIR   RICHMOND march 23. 1811

Your letter of the 20th. instant reached me yesterday morning. The subject which it presents to my view is highly interesting, and has received all the consideration which so short a time has enabled me to bestow on it. My wish to give you an early answer, in complyance with your request, has induc'd me to use all the dispatch which the delicacy & importance of the subject would permit.

The proof of your confidence which the proposition communicated by your letter affords, is very gratifying to me, and will always be remember'd with great satisfaction.

I have no hesitation in saying that I have every disposition to accept your invitation, to enter into the department of State. But in deciding this question, on your part as well as on mine, some considerations occur which claim attention from us both, & which candour requires to be brought into view, & weigh'd, at this time.

My views of policy towards the European powers are not unknown. They were adopted on great consideration, and are founded in the utmost devotion to the publick welfare. I was sincerely of opinion, after the failure of the negotiation with Spain, or rather France, that it was for the interest of our country, to make an accomodation with England, the great maritime power, even on moderate terms, rather than hazard war, or any other alternative. On that opinion I acted afterwards, while I remain'd in office, and I own that I have since seen no cause to doubt its soundness. Circumstances have in some respects changed, but still my general views of policy are the same.[1]

If I come into the government my object will be to render to my country & to you, all the service in my power, according to the light, such as it is, of my knowledge & experience, faithfully & without reserve. It would not become me to accept a station, & to act a part in it, which my judgment and conscience did not approve, and which I did not beleive would promote the publick welfare and happiness. I could not do this, nor would you wish me to do it.

If you are disposed to accept my services under these circumstances, and with this explanation, I shall be ready to render them, whenever it may suit you to require them. In that event, a circumstance of importance and delicacy will require attention from you as well as from me. It relates to the office which I now hold. I feel much difficulty in withdrawing from it, nor could I do so, but on considerations which it is fair to presume would be satisfactory to my constituents. I am persuaded that my fellow citizens would have no objection to my leaving this station, to go into the general government, at a crisis so important to the publick welfare, and to the republican cause, from an opinion, as the security of those great interests depends, in the present conjuncture, more on the councils and measures of the general than of the State government, that I might be able to render more service there than here. They would I am satisfied be reconciled to the act, if I received an invitation from you, suggesting a motive for it, arising out of the present state of publick affairs, which I might lay before the council when I communicated to it my acceptance of an appointment under the general government. I am dear Sir with great respect & esteem your friend & servant

JAS. MONROE

RC (DLC: Rives Collection, Madison Papers); FC (DLC: Monroe Papers).

1. On the FC, Monroe wrote here: "To my sentiments, on the points in which I differed from the administration I gave no eclat. I was restrained from it, by motives which need not be stated." He then crossed through these two sentences.

From David Ross

Sir   Davis's City of Washington March 23. 1811.

I arrived here last evening. The principal object which brought me to this City, is to attempt a settlement at the Treasury of the Accounts of George Webb decd who was the Agent in the State of Virginia and the Receiver of her Quota of Revenue for the General Goverment—altho not a nominal party I am deeply interested as the Creditor of Mr Webb, and his assignment upon Harvie[1] for the deposites in his hands when the Claims of the United States against him are satisfied, those deposites have been in the hands of Mr. Harvie & his family for twenty four years. I have addressed the Secretary of the Treasury upon the Subject who will no doubt do what is right & proper.

'Tis with Reluctance, and great diffidence that I have prevaild on my self to intrude upon your Excellencey a matter of considerable importance to my private Concerns.

The subject I alude to, is the Award made by your self Joseph Jones, and Henry Tazwell, at the City of Richmond 15th. June 1783.[2]

I took the liberty of mentioning this subject to you, the last time I had the honor of seeing you, at the department of State, some years ago, when you were pleased to observe, that if you could see the papers to refresh your memory, every thing on your part to promote Justice should chearfully be done.

I never mentioned the subject to either of the other arbitrators, as they soon afterwards became Judges in our Circuit Courts of law; Mr. Tazwell of his own accord mentioned to me the subject with very vivid sensations, and observed that the Award had given him vast uneasiness being Convinced upon mature Reflection that it was erroneous & might be the instrument of injustice, and he hoped and trusted the Courts would Correct it, as the Arbitrators had been misled by some case in the English books at that time, considered to be in point, but found afterwards not such authority as to be relyd upon, this conversation happened a short time before his death.

I was very little acquainted with the Law respecting awards, and felt confidence in the justice of the case, and sanguine that the finall decision would be favourable—indeed about this time the Venerable Mr Wythe the judge of our high Court of Chancery decreed a perpetual injunction against the Judgement at Law and published a short pamphlet on the subject, and an appeal was taken and since his death the decree has been Reversed, subjecting me to the payment of about twenty four thousand dollars & Costs.[3]

The Statement and Copy of the Court papers will Convey the necessary information. I could not procure the Original papers as the rule of the Court prohibits their being taken out of the Office.

The amount of the decree altho' sufficiently distressing, especially as no valuable consideration had been received—nevertheless 'tis rendered doubly distressing and vexatious from the following circumstance

I realy believe the plaintiff was so concious of the inquity [*sic*] of the decree that he was ashamed to demand payment in person and said nothing on the subject for twelve months, and then thro' his friends proposing a compromise and an adjustment of convenient payments, which I believe would have taken place in a short time, without farther trouble. About this time a cause which had been long depending was decided in our Court of Appeals by which I was entitled to a division of a Considerable estate in the upper Counties of Virginia two thirds of Considerable tracts of Land, about Twenty Slaves & Considerable sums of Money—the Administrator upon this estate hearing of this celebrated decree upon the Award, Contemplated a speculation on the decree & a fraudulent use of it, upon the estate and purchased it up privately at a low rate & four years Credit the decree, without any recourse on the plaintiff, he procured an Execo. & levied it upon the slaves and purchased them for a triffle as no other person could purchase with safety no one slave was sold but two thirds of each slave was sold, the other third vested in the Admr. and other Legatees. I have troubled you with this detail to shew how much the original injury has been aggrevated, tho tis believed that the sale will be sett aside.

I may reasonably imagine that at this point you are disposed to ask what can you do? what do I ask or expect? and must confess I'm at a loss for an answer; you'll readily imagine that under such Complicated & aggrevated injustice tis natural for me to seek for Legal relieff—that can only be found before a competent Court of Justice—'tis rather more than doubtfull if it can be again brot. forward, yet there are some circumstances which render it not altogether impracticable, especially if I can clearly shew that the Arbitrators were led into an error as to the law, by applying to this case some English Authorities which in fact was not sufficient legal authority. This brings me to the point, as to all I can ask, all that I can expect, and all I can hope for—which is simply this that your Excellencey would have the goodness to peruse the papers. This will convince you of the principles upon which you acted, & the other Arbitrators. You could not possibly found your Judgement upon the merits or the equity of the Case. I conceive the Arbitrators yielded up their own opinions, to what they conceived the imperious dictates of the Law; Now if the Arbitrators considered that to be Law, which was not, 'twas an unin[ten]tional and innocent mistake and an erroneous award or in other words not the real Judgement of the Arbitrators as to the merits of the case. But I believe no Court Can Compell Arbitrators to disclose the reasons and principles which governd them in making up their award. They may or may not disclose it at their own discretion.

Your superior Judgement will dictate whether you can do any thing in this case and what.

I can venture to say from what I have been informed that there is but one opinion prevails with the professional Genl: in Richmond that the Arbitrators were perfectly pure in their intentions altho' mistaken as to the law.

I am well aware that this address, would not only be considered exceptionable but offenceive to many respectable characters; who might think it a degradation to be thot. they had comitted an error however innocently done. Upon this occaision, altho' I not only feel serious regret, but also shame, at giving you so much trouble—I am under no apprehensions of giving offence, from a conviction, that such illiberal sentiments have no place in your mind. On the Contrary, that you would feel indignant, if your character was so much mistaken—as from motives of false delicacey you were deprived of the pleasure of being instrumental in facilitating Justice in any thing depending on your self.

If I do not find an appology in your goodness for this intrusion, I cannot expect to find it any where else. Be pleased to accept assurances of my sincere regard and esteem. Most Respectfully

DAVID ROSS

RC (DLC). Enclosures not found.

1. John Harvie (1742–1807), in addition to his service in the Virginia militia, the Continental Congress, and the Third Congress, was register of the Virginia Land Office, 1779–91 (*PJM*, 1:188–89 and nn. 1 and 2).

2. The details of this "Award" and JM's involvement in it are difficult to ascertain, the more so as JM on 15 June 1783 (a Sunday) was in Philadelphia, not Richmond. David Ross, Joseph Jones, and Henry Tazewell, however, were in Richmond in June 1783 as members of the Virginia House of Delegates, and both Jones and Tazewell were also concerned at that time with legislation for granting state revenue to the Continental Congress. Moreover, Jones, as a former delegate to Congress, had learned in April 1783 that he was responsible to Ross for some $7,700 in debts, a sum that had been incorrectly included in accounts of moneys owed by Virginia to Congress. Since JM in this period received bills drawn on Ross by the Virginia state treasurer, it is possible that his financial affairs, to some extent, were also intermingled with Ross's accounts in a manner that required settlement at a later time. As a member of the Virginia delegation in Congress in 1783, JM was regularly involved in decisions that either allocated congressional spending in Virginia or required adjustments in the sums the state owed to Congress. Many of these transactions necessarily passed through the hands of both Ross and George Webb, the Continental receiver general in Virginia (see Edmund Randolph to JM, 15 Jan. 1783, and Jones to JM, 28 June 1783, *PJM*, 6:45 n. 3, and 7:196–98 and n. 2; JM to Theodorick Bland, 6 May 1783, *PJM*, 7:16; see also the instructions to the Virginia delegates, 17 and 26 June 1783, *PJM*, 7:162 and n. 1, 192–93 and n. 4).

3. Ross, who had been appointed commercial agent for Virginia by Thomas Jefferson in 1781, appears to have been involved in several legal disputes, and it took many years to settle his financial affairs (see *PJM*, 3:60 n. 8). The details of two such cases, *Ross* v. *Pleasants, Shore, and Company, and William Anderson* and *Ross* v. *Pines*, bear some resemblance to the circum-

stances Ross described to JM, and these had been the subject of critical comment by George Wythe in his *Decisions of Cases in Virginia, by the High Court of Chancery, with Remarks upon Decrees by the Court of Appeals, Reversing Some of Those Decisions* (Richmond, 1795; Evans 29930), pp. 71–73, 147–65. No evidence has been found that JM was involved in these disputes.

From William Madison

Dr Brother   March 25th. 1811.

When I paid Gooch the $100. he said they exceeded the Sum he had written for, upward of twenty dollars. I saw him yesterday & he said that the sum mentioned in your letter[1] is still wanted for the purposes therein stated. I have drawn on Mr Patton for it on yr Acct. as I had directed him when I passed thro: Fredbg to send you $220. on my Acct which with the $100 pd. Gooch will make the amt you let me have. I wish to know if you have recd them. If you have not the order in favour of Gooch shall be placed to my Acct & the ballce immediately forwd to you. Doct Willis continues very low—but little hopes are entertained of his recovery. Yesterday was the first time that I ventured from home since my return from Washington—being confind by an indisposition produced by the excessive fatigue & exposure on the road from Alexandria to Fredbg. I was compelled to walk the greater part of the way thro. the mud & Snow. I am considerably reduced, but now hope I shall soon regain my usual plight. One of your Waggons is still engaged in carrying your wheat to market—price 10/2. Flour 52/. ℔ Bl. My Waggon is engaged in hauling the partnership flour. Gooch thinks there is no necessity to buy any more horses at this time. However if good bargains offer I will avail myself of them for you. Accept of my Affections

                                                                WM MADISON

RC (NjP).

1. Letter not found.

From David Ross

Sir   Washington 25 March 1811.

I am this moment favoured with your letter of this date,[1] relative to the Award of 1783. Your comunications upon the subject are in Unison with Mr. Tazwell's, as to the governing principles upon which the Arbitrators founded their award. I always considered the subject in the same view. You have given me all the information I could ask, or expect.

As the Law Statement & Reccord will be mere lumber in your office—I will withdraw them for the present, to save the trouble of copies.

I pray you to accept the sincere offerings of Gratefull thanks, for your condecension & trouble in this antient business. Most Respectfully

DAVID ROSS

RC (DLC).

1. Letter not found.

To James Monroe

private

DEAR SIR　　　　　　　　　　　　WASHINGTON March 26. 1811

I have recd. your letter of the 23d. and learn with much pleasure that you are not disinclined to the Station wch. the one answered by it, presented to your consideration. In discharging the duties of this Station, I am aware that the Functionary must carry into it, a just respect for his own principles, and above all for the dictates of his Conscience. But with the mutual knowledge of our respective views of the foreign as well as domestic interests of our Country, I see no serious obstacle on either side, to an association of our labors in promoting them. In the general policy of avoiding war, by a strict & fair neutrality towards the Belligerents, and of settling amicably, our differences with both; or with either, as leading to a settlement with the other; or that failing, as putting us on better ground against him, there is & has been an entire concurrence among the most enlightened who have shared in the public Councils since the year 1800. A like concurrence has prevailed in the opinion, that whilst on one hand, it is of great importance to the interests of the U. S. that peace should be preserved, and commerce obtained with the Continent of Europe, there are on the other hand, powerful reasons in favor of an adjustment with the great Maritime power, who, tho' liable to suffer much from our enmity, is capable also of doing us much harm or good, according to her disposition towards us. In favor of a cordial accomodation with G. Britain, there has certainly never ceased to be a prevailing disposition in the Executive Councils, since I became connected with them. In the terms of accomodation, with that as with other powers, differences of opinion must be looked for, even among those most agreed in the same general views. These differences however lie fairly within the compass of free consultation and mutual concession, as subordinate to the necessary Unity belonging to the Executive Dept. I will add that I perceive not, any commitments even in the case of the abortive adjustment with that power,[1] that could necessarily embarrass deliberations on a renewal of negociations; inasmuch as the variance of opinion turned not a little on different understandings of certain facts & constructive intentions, rather than on the merits of the questions decided; and as the questions more immediately interesting to the harmony of the two Countries, namely as to the Chesapeake, the orders in Council, and Blockades, are either of subsequent date, or left without any positive decision.

The strong ties which bind you to your present Station did not fail to occur, but having no doubt myself that the range & scope of the business in the Dept. of State, in times like the present at least, give to talents & services there, more importance than belongs to a local sphere, I readily concluded that the delicacy of the exchange proposed to you, was superseded not only by that consideration, but by the fair presumption, that it would equally accord with the patriotic views of your Constituents. I shall of course accompany the commission to be forwarded with a line referring to it. But it deserves our joint consideration whether remarks for a public use not usual, & connecting the magnitude of the Crisis, with a particular selection of services, might not afford to local or personal feelings elsewhere, an occasion for disadvantageous misconstructions or perversions. The Commission will bear date the 1st. of Apl. the date of the vacancy to be filled. Would it be possible for you to be here within a day or two after? You will find it convenient on every acct. to come in the first instance without your family; and there is important business that claims the earliest attention. Favor me with a line on the Subject, and be assured of my great esteem & sincere friendship.

JAMES MADISON

RC (DLC); draft (ibid.). RC docketed by Monroe.

1. JM referred to the Monroe-Pinkney treaty of 1806.

§ From M. Ruelle.[1] *26 March 1811, Rue d'Argenteüil, No. 38, Paris.* Observes that when he wrote on 18 Sept. 1810 [not found], it was not known in France that a party for the emancipation of Mexico had appeared, but his letter had predicted it. Regardless of the consequences of this endeavor, it will always be in the interest of the U.S. that Mexico and the other regions of Spanish America constitute themselves as republics and that the U.S. give them aid. It is no longer a matter of waiting for the outcome of the war in Spain that Great Britain wages against France, as it is clear that the king [of Spain] will never be restored to his throne and that the struggle can have no other outcome than the dismemberment of his dominions, the effect of which will be to place the colonies under a royalist yoke and the U.S. in an equally unsympathetic situation. Advises the U.S. to form a coalition with the Spanish colonies against the war France and Great Britain wage on their commerce. Such a coalition could not be withstood by any power and would secure the revolution in question. Declares that the salvation of the new world is in JM's hands. Mentions in a postscript an enclosed packet for Mr. Warden.

RC (DLC). 2 pp. In French.

1. Ruelle, who described himself as a former diplomatic agent, had been French chargé d'affaires in Holland during the rule of the Committee of Public Safety (Nasatir and Monell, *French Consuls*, p. 598).

§ From Alexander Hamilton.[1] *28 March 1811, New York.* "On the fourth of April, I expect to sail for Lisbon, from thence, I shall proceed to London & Paris. If you will introduce me, to some of your friends or my father's, you will much oblige me."

RC (ViU). 1 p.

1. Alexander Hamilton (b. 1786) was the second son of Alexander Hamilton (Syrett and Cooke, *Papers of Hamilton*, 3:667 n., 673 n.).

From James Monroe

Dear Sir   Richmond March 29. 1811.

I have received your letter of the 26th instant. Its contents are very satisfactory to me. The just principles on which you have invited me into the department of State, have removed every difficulty which had occurr'd to me, to the measure. They afford also a strong ground for hope, that the joint counsels & labours of those who are thus associated in the government, will promote the best interests of our country. To succeed in that most desirable object my utmost exertions will be made. I add with pleasure that I shall carry into the government, a sincere desire to harmonize in the measures necessary to that end, on the fair and liberal principles expressd in your letter.

I shall be prepard to set out for Washington on tuesday next, provided I receive your letter and the Commission which is to accompany it, on or before sunday. One days detention here after sunday, for the purpose of taking my leave of the council, in case these documents are previously received, is all that I shall require. Every preparatory arrangment of a publick and private nature, will be, by that time, compleated. I am with great respect and esteem yr friend & servant

JAS. MONROE

RC (DLC: Rives Collection, Madison Papers); FC (DLC: Monroe Papers). RC docketed by JM.

§ From Benjamin Rush. *30 March 1811, Philadelphia*. Introduces the bearers, Mr. Caldwell[1] and Major Plenderleath,[2] who were introduced to him as gentlemen of "uncommon worth" by his son-in-law in Quebec.[3] They hold, respectively, civil and military commissions under the British government. On their travels in the U.S. they wish "to do homage to the person and Character of the President of the United States."

RC (DLC). 1 p. Docketed by JM.

    1. James Caldwell (d. 1815) was a merchant, militia officer, and magistrate in Lower Canada (Frances G. Halpenny, ed., *Dictionary of Canadian Biography* [10 vols.; Toronto, 1966–91], 5:133–34).
    2. Charles Plenderleath was a major in the Forty-ninth Foot Regiment. He later fought with distinction against American forces in the War of 1812 (William Woods, ed., *Select British Documents of the Canadian War of 1812* [3 vols.; Toronto, 1920–28], 1:320).
    3. Rush's eldest daughter, Anne Emily Rush, had married Ross Cuthbert of Quebec in 1799 (Butterfield, *Letters of Benjamin Rush*, 2:783 n. 4).

To James Monroe

DEAR SIR   WASHINGTON Mar. 31. 1811

    I have the pleasure this moment of receiving yours of the 29th. inst: I am particularly glad to find that you will be able to set out at so early a day for Washington. To the advantage of preventing an inconvenient chasm in the public business, will be added the opportunity of a provident attention to the accomodations required by your establishment here. The House occupied by Mr. Smith is the best in the place, and I believe is not yet out of reach. He means also to dispose of certain portions of his furniture which might suit your purposes. These considerations taken together strongly recommend that you should not wait for the receipt of your Commission in Richmond, but consider what has passed between us sufficient ground for a communication to the Council. The actual receipt of the Commission cannot be a necessary preliminary. As well as I recollect, I did not receive mine as Secretary of State, till it was handed me on the spot, by Mr. Jefferson. In case of appointments at a great distance, it might be extremely inconvenient for any other course to be observed. It is the more desireable that you should not wait for your Commission, as I find that it will be tuesday morning before its date will be consistent with the understanding & arrangement here, & that your arrival would of consequence be thrown forward till the beginning of the next week. I might indeed, as the law authorizes, provide an Interim Functionary, for the current business requiring his signature, & not admitting delay; but, even for this limited purpose, there are objections to this resort where it can be avoided. I hope therefore you will find no difficulty in the mode of anticipation recommended, the more especially as your communication to the Council, may be delayed till tuesday morning, the time proposed for your setting out, and at which time your Commission will have been formally consummated & ready for delivery. Accept assurances of my sincere esteem & friendship

JAMES MADISON

RC (DLC: Monroe Papers); draft (DLC). RC docketed by Monroe.

To Thomas Jefferson

DEAR SIR   WASHINGTON Apl. 1. 1811

I intimated to you the offence taken by Armstrong at the re-enstatement of Warden. It is not improbable that it will be the ground of an open hostility. This will call into view his present denunciations of W. which are pointed agst. him as an Adventurer & Impostor from the commencement to the end of his career, in comparison with the patronage so long continued to him, and the sentiments heretofore expressed of him. Will you be so good as to send me the extract from A's letter written in the summer or Fall of 1808, which notifies the appt. of W. as Consul, and gives the favorable side of his character, as well as the objections to a confirmation of the appt. That letter was the only communication made on the subject.

You will have inferred the change which is taking place in the Dept. of State. Col. Monroe agrees to succeed Mr. Smith, who declines however the mission to Russia, at first not unfavorably looked at. I was willing, notwithstanding many trying circumstances, to have smoothed the transaction as much as possible, but it will be pretty sure to end in secret hostility, if not open warfare. On account of my great esteem & regard for common friends such a result is truly painful to me. For the rest, I feel myself on firm ground, as well in the public opinion, as in my own consciousness.

Wilkinson I find has lately recd. a letter from you, wch. he has shewn to his friends, with much apparent gratification. I understand at the same time, that the letter is cautious, and limited to the charge of privity with Burr. Did he disown to you the anonymous letter printed in Clark's Book,[1] or say any thing relative to that subject?

The latest information from Europe will be found in the inclosed papers. The indications from France are rather favorable. Should the Old King displace the Regent in England, little is to be hoped from that quarter; unless forced on the Cabinet by national distress.[2] In the last correspondence of Pinkney with Wellesley, the latter sufficiently shewed his teeth;

and recd. the severest scourging that was ever diplomatically inflicted.[3] Be assured always of my great esteem & affection

JAMES MADISON

RC (DLC). Docketed by Jefferson, "recd Apr. 3."

1. In his 1809 book attacking James Wilkinson for his involvement in the Burr conspiracy, Daniel Clark had included evidence to show that Wilkinson, in order to protect himself, had tried to implicate Clark in Burr's plans. One such document—said by Clark to be in Wilkinson's hand and which he described as being "highly characteristic of the man"—was an undated, unsigned letter, postmarked at New Orleans on 8 Jan. 1807 and addressed to D. W. Coxe, Clark's business partner in Philadelphia, which, Clark maintained, was really intended for him. Wilkinson's purpose in writing the letter, Clark believed, was "to create an obligation towards him for supporting my character, which he falsely insinuates was implicated, knowing the facts I possessed against him, fearful that I might discover that he had broken the engagement he had contracted at Loftus's Heights of quitting his Spanish connexion, and that I might feel myself at liberty to expose his guilt; and he therefore, while he acknowledges my innocence, wishes to make believe that he had been at some pains to support it." Clark then stated that he had communicated the letter to JM, "who appeared astonished at the duplicity and perfidy of the writer" (*Proofs of the Corruption of Gen. James Wilkinson, and of His Connexion with Aaron Burr* [Philadelphia, 1809; Shaw and Shoemaker 17221], pp. 110–11, 151).

2. JM probably enclosed information that appeared in the *National Intelligencer* on 28 Mar. and 2 Apr. 1811. Reports published in New York newspapers on 28 Mar. stated that three American vessels arriving at Bordeaux after 1 Nov. 1810 had all been admitted and that France would no longer require such vessels to carry licenses since these had become unnecessary after the repeal of the Berlin and Milan decrees. On this basis the *National Intelligencer* announced on 2 Apr. that "the French decrees were on the 3d February, as we have anticipated, formally abrogated, at least so far as concerns us." The news from Great Britain was that George III was recovering his health and that even if a regency bill should pass Parliament, "there would be no material change in the administration."

3. JM very likely referred to Pinkney's 10 Dec. 1810 letter to Lord Wellesley describing a meeting and a series of notes exchanged between 4 and 6 Dec. On those occasions, Wellesley had declined to give Pinkney any satisfactory information on either the appointment of a new British minister to the U.S. or the settlement of the *Chesapeake* affair. He had, furthermore, claimed that Pinkney had not given him any "authentic intelligence" of the repeal of the Berlin and Milan decrees. In response, Pinkney refuted Wellesley's arguments at length and closed his letter with an angry protest against "the pretension of the British Government to postpone the justice which it owes to my Government and country" (see *ASP, Foreign Relations*, 3:376–79). JM had already sent the correspondence to the House of Representatives on 19 Feb. 1811.

From Charles P. Howard

DR. SIR,   WOODLY. April 1 1811

Docr. Willis particularly requested that so soon as he was no more you should be informd of it. I have now to inform you that the melancholy event took place about noon this day. He was 36 years & about 6 Months

Old; as Docr. Willis was well known in your City & has many friends there, perhaps it may be well to have it announced in Gales, paper and as he was personally known to the Editor it may be sufficient to leave the form to him,[1] but of which you will be the best Judge yourself. All friends are well. With Esteem

C. P. HOWARD[2]

RC (DLC).

1. The *National Intelligencer*, on 6 Apr. 1811, reported the death of Dr. John Willis, husband of JM's niece and ward, Nelly Conway Madison Willis.
2. Charles Pitt Howard was a resident of Orange County, Virginia. He had married Jane Taylor, youngest daughter of Erasmus Taylor, in 1793 (Hayden, *Virginia Genealogies*, p. 674; *VMHB*, 26 [1918]: 401).

From John G. Jackson

MY DEAR SIR.   CLARKSBURG April 1st 1811

I often resist the desire to write you from a consciousness that the labors of your station make the task of reading letters irksome; & render any thing like a regular correspondence impossible. But as our meeting again is doubtful, or at best remote; I venture sometimes to obtrude myself upon you as the only mode in which I can have the pleasure of communing with you. A conjecture has reached me that Mr. Monroe was to fill the Office vacated by Mr. Smith & no doubt its truth or fallacy has been already established. As I heretofore conversed freely with you on that subject I think it not amiss to take the liberty of writing on it now. I am perfectly satisfied that his appointment *then* would have been beneficial at home & abroad. *Here*, because there are some who cling to him as a leader in opposition; whose insincerity would long since have been exposed. And elsewhere because the B Ministry consider him as feeling more cordiality towards their nation than you do because of the rejected Treaty and buoyed up by the supposed schisms amongst us imagine that Mr. M is an host in their favor. Perhaps I thought differently at your installation but of that I am not certain, as I was urged to mention the opinions of Others more than to suggest any of my own impressions.

Mrs. J as my letter to Mrs. M communicates[1] has presented me with a Daughter; they are like to do well.[2] So you see I am in better employment than quarrelling & fighting in Congress—Hercules threw by his club for the distaff—And well might I when it neither annoyed my enemies or benefitted my friends. I feel much doubt of the reelection of McKinley & so do our opponents it will be a drawn battle if such a result can be produced by a contest of almost equal strength. I salute you my Dr Sir With sincerest friendship your Mo Obt

J G JACKSON

RC (DLC). Docketed by JM.

1. Jackson's letter to Dolley Madison has not been found, but in her reply of 10 Apr. 1811 she sent her love and congratulations "on this pleasing adition." Dolley Madison also conveyed to Jackson several items of domestic and political news, principally that Monroe had become secretary of state and that "R. S. *does not go to Russia.* Just so. He has retired (the papers state) to what he was wont to be. Duane &c &c. take a *few liberties* with M on the subject tho they do not deny *his right* to make a secey to *suit him.*" On the subject of news from Europe, Dolley Madison mentioned reports that "our negociations are broken off at St. James's & that we have nothing to expect from them—that France has repealed her decrees &c &c & will do us all *favours.*" As it was "D. Room night," she concluded, "I write badly from haste as we have still, great croud's. The New french Minister is quite a polished modest man the Russians are all the rage & Moorea [Morier] in the background" (InU: Jackson Collection).

2. Since there is no record of her name or any further references to her, the child presumably did not live long (Dorothy Davis, *John George Jackson* [Parsons, W.Va., 1976], p. 373 n. 24).

§ From Robert Gilmor and Others. *1 April 1811, Baltimore.* "The Commerce of the United States with the River La Plata, has become very lucrative, and important, and the present ruling Power of that Country is well disposed to give greater Latitude and Freedom to it, if it should appear to be a desirable Event." The subscribers lament the "present calamitous Situation" with respect to the European belligerents and despair of the return of free navigation so long as the war continues. They believe it worthwhile for the U.S. to "improve the present auspicious Appearances in part of our own Hemisphere" and suggest that a consul or commercial agent residing at Buenos Aires or Montevideo would be of essential service. They recommend Luis Godefroy, a merchant of Montevideo, for the position. "He not only receives Him [the American] with Hospitality & Kindness, but is his Protector against the Rapacity of corrupt Officers. . . . He is now in this Country, and admires, and is attached to our Form of Government." The subscribers recommend him to the president and "solicit that He may be appointed Consul or Commercial Agent for Monte Video, Buenos Ayres, and other Ports in the River La Plata."[1]

RC (DNA: RG 59, LAR, 1809–17, filed under "Godefroy"). 4 pp. Signed by Gilmor and twenty-seven others, including Robert and John Oliver, and endorsed by Alexander McKim with a note to the effect that the subscribers were worthy of confidence. Addressee not indicated.

1. JM gave Godefroy an interim appointment as consul for Buenos Aires and all other ports below that place on the Río de la Plata on 30 Apr. 1811. At the same time he elevated Joel Roberts Poinsett to the position of consul general to the provinces of Buenos Aires, Chile, and Peru. On 13 Nov. 1811 JM sent Godefroy's name to the Senate for confirmation, only to see the Senate reject the appointment as "inexpedient" five days later (*Senate Exec. Proceedings*, 2:188, 190; William Spence Robertson, "Documents concerning the Consular Service of the United States in Latin America," *Mississippi Valley Historical Review*, 2 [1916]: 567). This rejection appears to have resulted from the efforts of David Curtis DeForest, a Connecticut merchant based in Buenos Aires, who arrived in Washington in early May 1811 to seek the

position that JM had just conferred on Godefroy. DeForest bitterly protested the appointment of the French-born Godefroy to both JM and Monroe; and after they declined to reconsider the matter, he succeeded, much to JM's annoyance, in persuading the U.S. senators from Connecticut, Samuel Dana and Chauncey Goodrich, to defeat the nomination (see DeForest to Monroe, 2 and 4 May, 8 June, and 12 July 1811, and DeForest to [Dana or Goodrich?], 22 Oct. 1811 [DNA: RG 59, LAR, 1809–17]; Benjamin Keen, *David Curtis DeForest and the Revolution of Buenos Aires* [New Haven, 1947], pp. 56, 57, 84, 85).

To James Monroe

DEAR SIR   WASHINGTON April 2, 1811

Altho' I have expressed a hope that you would leave Richmond before a Commission of Secretary of State, could reach it, yet as it may have happened otherwise, & as it may be agreeable to you to have it previously in your hands, I now inclose the document as just compleated.[1] There is the less objection to this step, as in case it should pass you on the road, another can readily be made out on your arrival here, preparatory to your taking the oath and commencing the functions of Office. Accept my affece. respects

JAMES MADISON

RC (MHi).

1. Monroe's commission for the office of secretary of state is signed by JM and dated 2 Apr. 1811 (NN: Monroe Papers). On the verso is a note by Buckner Thruston certifying that Monroe appeared before him in Washington to take the oath of office on 6 Apr. 1811.

§ From Clement Caines. *2 April 1811, St. Kitts.* Declares that JM's name has reached the West Indies and "is celebrated throughout the World." Conveys his "respect and high esteem" and encloses his "literary compositions."[1]

RC (DLC). 1 p. Enclosures not found.

1. Clement Caines was a prominent St. Kitts planter and opponent of the slave trade. His publications included pamphlets on the history and agriculture of the Leeward Islands and also the American Embargo of 1807–9 (Lowell J. Ragatz, ed., *A Guide for the Study of British Caribbean History, 1763–1834* [Washington, 1932], p. 283).

From John Drayton

SIR.   HOPELAND (SO: CAROLINA) April 3d: 1811.

I have the honor of addressing you, from my plantation; having been resident here, since the close of my late administration.

By information received from Charleston yesterday, from respectable

FROM WILLIAM O. ALLEN

Authority, I am informed Judge Bee's State of Health is extremely critical at this time; and it is proposed to me, to apply for the office, when the Vacancy takes place.[1] I have accordingly taken the same into consideration; and, more on account of my family than myself, have determined to apply to you for the same. What my pretensions to it may be, is with you to Judge. I have been regularly educated to the Law; & practised the same several years in this State: but since Marriage, I have relinquished it.

My reason for thus applying immediately to you sir, is this: should I be honored with the appointment, I will be satisfied you have done it more from your own good wishes & opinions, than from any impressions which you might have received from applications in my behalf. This, I hope sir, will excuse my thus intruding myself upon you: while I avail myself of the occasion to repeat to you my assurances of great consideration & respect, with which I have now the honor to subscribe myself sir Your most obedient Servant

JOHN DRAYTON

RC, three copies (DLC). Docketed by JM.

1. After Thomas Bee's death in February 1812, JM nominated Thomas Parker on 13 Mar. 1812 to be judge of the district court of South Carolina. Parker declined, and JM then nominated Drayton for the position on 5 May 1812 (*Senate Exec. Proceedings*, 2:235, 262).

From William O. Allen

DEAR SIR, SAINT LOUIS (Lous.) 4th Apl. 1811.
By the last mail, I received a letter, from H. Marshall Esqr. of Kentucky—The following is a Copy Vizt.

"FRANKFORD Feby 27th 1811."
"Sir Having heard that in consequence of your getting into your possession the papers of the late Mr *Lockasangne*[1] you are possessed of information important to me, as a party to a suit which Harry Innes has brought against me for alledging him to be a party in the old Spanish conspiracy I have taken the Liberty of addressing you, and most earnestly request you if you have any papers which throws light on that intrigue, and which in any way connects Innes with the parties concerned you would be so obliging as to state to[2] by mail, the amount of that information, should there be any letter from Innes, please to transmit the original, or a Copy, Further if you do know any thing be so good as to state to me the substance—should it not be evidence for me in the suit it may aid me in writing the history of Kentucky which I am engaged in and which will be imperfect without a developement of that intrigue.[3]

244

Pray let me hear from you even if you have no information to give; in as much as, untill I hear I shall not know but you might be the most material witness." Yours respectfully

"H. Marshall"

addressed—

"William O Allen Esquire
Cape Jerado
Postmarked Mississippi"
"Frankfort K paid 20
"March 2d" 12½
unpaid
"Cape Gerardeau
"the 22d March 1811
forwarded" The principal of those papers were delivered to Governor Howard, in compliance with a request contained in a letter, from the Secretary of War, to me of date, the 4th of May 1810.[4]

I wish Sir, to enquirer [sic], whither, I am *now* at liberty to state, that those documents are in the possession of Government?[5] Whether, it is compatible with your Views, that I should surrender, some few, that are yet in my possession, and that are immaterial as to Genl. Wilkinson, into the hands of Mr. Marshall? And, in fact, I very much desire to know the course, that may be pointed out by your Wisdom.[6]

In a government so *just*, and so much connected with the interest of *All*—I hold it, as an axiom, that the public good, should always, control the actions of every individual. But, beyond that consideration, there are other, powerful inducements, that tend to keep many of Mr M.'s political views at a distance—I know, that he is a federalist—That he was the apponant of the late, as I believe, he is of the present Administration. I am a Virginian, by burth a republican, and by education & conviction a friend to those, that he has been in the constant *habit* of opposing.

Governor Howard requested of me *secrecy—I have complied.*

If Sir, you should wish to know more of me than my name, I refer you to many papers now of file in the War Department—To 2 or 3 letters delivered in person to you, in the Winter 1806/7—To others transmitted since—To my former Townsman The Hble: B. Bassett—Mr. H. Clay, late of the Senate—Capt. I. A. Coles &c. &c. With profound respect & consideration, I tender my best wishes, and am Dr. Sir your Obedient Humble Servant

Wm. O Allen[7]

RC (PHi: Daniel Parker Papers). Docketed by a War Department clerk as received 15 May 1811.

1. Michel Lacassagne (d. 1797), a French merchant and business associate of James Wilkinson's, was a member of the Kentucky Convention of 1787 and first federal postmaster of Louisville. He was also an agent for Governor Carondelet and traveled to New Orleans in the 1790s to collect Wilkinson's pension from the Spanish government. During his court-martial in the fall of 1811 on charges of being a Spanish agent, Wilkinson succeeded in convincing the court that his dealings with Lacassagne were legitimate business matters (Jacobs, *Tarnished Warrior*, pp. 128, 134, 136, 152, 270–74).

2. Allen evidently omitted to write "me" here.

3. Humphrey Marshall, a Federalist and brother of Chief Justice John Marshall, had long been at odds with the Republican leadership of Kentucky over a variety of issues, both personal and political. In the first edition of *The History of Kentucky* (Frankfort, Ky., 1812), Marshall charged that the leaders of the movement to separate Kentucky from Virginia in the 1780s had intended to liberate the region not merely from its mother state but also from the Union at large in order to promote a connection with Spain. He depicted Wilkinson as the central figure in the "Spanish Conspiracy" but implicated other Kentucky leaders as well, including Harry Innes, who, he wrote, appeared to "discover a new moral excellence" in contemplating "treason" against the U.S. (see pp. 250, 300–304, 309, 315, 341–43, 349, 352–53). The libel suit of *Innes* v. *Marshall* dragged on for several years, and Marshall repeated his charges at greater length in the two-volume 1824 edition of his history, adding to them the corollary that the "Spanish Conspiracy" of the 1780s was the germ of Aaron Burr's schemes of 1805–6. In neither edition of *The History of Kentucky*, however, did Marshall employ material gained from the papers of Lacassagne that had been in Allen's possession.

4. In a 10 Jan. 1810 letter to Andrew Jackson, Allen had informed the Tennessee general that in the course of settling the estate of his brother-in-law, Robert K. Moore, he had uncovered Lacassagne's business papers, the contents of which proved the charges of treason and corruption made against Wilkinson by Daniel Clark. Jackson evidently informed the secretary of war, whom JM then instructed to write to Allen, requesting him to deliver the papers to territorial governor Benjamin Howard in order that copies might be made for the War Department (Allen to Jackson, 10 Jan. 1810, Sam B. Smith and Harriet C. Owsley, eds., *The Papers of Andrew Jackson* [3 vols. to date; Knoxville, Tenn., 1980—], 2:228–29; Eustis to Allen, 11 May 1810 [DNA: RG 107, LSMA]).

5. On 10 Apr. 1811 Eustis, at the direction of JM, laid copies of the documents referred to by Allen before Wilkinson. Three days later the general made a lengthy response, which began by questioning the value of fishing up "dubious" documents "from the depths of oblivion" at so late a date. He admitted that he had been aware of the papers for the past year but insinuated that they had been circulated by Lacassagne's "concubine" and several of his other enemies for the purpose of discrediting him. He then asserted that it was impossible for any one "to produce any authentic evidence of criminality, out of [his] long intimacy with Lacassagne." Warming to the subject, Wilkinson next declined to offer any explanation of the documents on the grounds that they were forgeries and that it was impossible for him either to recollect or to scrutinize many of the statements they contained because his own papers for the years 1796 to 1804 had been "destroyed by the mice" in Clement Biddle's garret in Philadelphia. He did, however, provide from memory an account of his business dealings with Lacassagne, during the course of which he questioned some of the details in the documents from the latter's papers. He concluded his remarks by denouncing "the vindictive spirit, envy, art and contrivances of [his] enemies" ("Observations of General Wilkinson upon certain documents recently received from the War Department, by order of the President of the United States," 13 Apr. 1811 [DNA: RG 107, LRUS, W-1809]).

6. In his acknowledgment of Allen's letter, Eustis returned the copies of "certain letters therein referred to" and declared that the "Originals are likewise at your disposal" (Eustis to Allen, 27 May 1811 [DNA: RG 107, LSMA]).

7. William Oliver Allen (d. 1820) was a Virginian who practiced law in St. Louis. In April 1812 JM commissioned him as a captain in the Twenty-fourth Infantry Regiment, and he served in the U.S. Army until 1818 (Smith and Owsley, *Papers of Jackson*, 2 : 229 n.; Heitman, *Historical Register*, 1 : 160).

From John G. Jackson

DR. SIR.   CLARKSBURG April 5th 1811
Judge Nelson has resigned his judicial office & the Executive of Virginia will soon appoint a successor.[1] The Law requires that he shall reside within the Circuit & the probability is that the preference will be given to a Candidate already here rather than incur the risque of offending by sending a stranger to us. My Friends have solicited my consent to be a Candidate & some of them have written to the Executive in my favor. If you can consistently with your judgment, & with perfect propriety (otherwise believe me I do not request it) it will afford me pleasure to be named by you to some friend at Richmond who would favor my views. Dr. Sir your Most Obt
                                                    J G JACKSON

RC (DLC). Docketed by JM.

1. Hugh Nelson resigned his position as judge of the eleventh judicial circuit of Virginia on 28 Mar. 1811 (Brown, *Voice of the New West*, pp. 101–2).

From Richard Peters

DEAR SIR   BELMONT April. 6. 1811.
I recieved your Letter & the Grains of sweet Corn; for which I return you Thanks. We have, here, that Species of Corn; but I always find that Change of Sied [*sic*] ameliorates. I am much obliged by your Attention to my Request as to the *Big-Rye*. I hope it will be successful; & that a most valuable Grain will be added to our Stock. I have hoed & cleaned my small Patch, planted last Autumn. I have never known any Plant exhibit such Appearances, in its early Stages, of Vigour & profitable Promise. I think I shall have more than a Bushell from my half Pint planted. I could encrease the Number of Plants by a Repitition of transplanting, by separating the Roots, but as I am now *well*, I do not care to venture being made *worse*, by an Attempt at being *better*. This is the Mistake of all Theorists.
Your Sheep I think must be the Barbary *Coast* Sheep. They are of the same Race, but not so good as the *Mountain* Sheep. I send to you a Speci-

men of the Wool of my Sheep; & a Sample of Home-spun Cloth, made from the original Ewe *Selima* & her Daughter, No. 2 in the Plate.[1] It might have been manufactured better at one of our Factories. But I chose the whole Operation should be domestic & *countryfied*. I therefore had it woven & dressed by a common good *Country* Weaver & Fuller. Being a good Republican, I have a Coat made for my own wearing. I could not get it dyed in the Wool, without more Trouble than I chose to take, or I would have had it *black*; & would have worn it for my *Costume*. It would have then been on a Par with my Office; which is happily situated—below Envy & above Contempt. You see I am *qualis* ⟨*eram?*⟩; neither ambitious nor vulgar.

I forgot to mention, in my Account of the Sheep, a curious Difference between the Structure of the Nostril of the Tunis, & that of any other Sheep. No Doubt all the broad tailed Race are similar; but this I do not know. The Tunis Sheep do not emit, from the Nostril, the Mucus in such Quantity, as to form a Nidus for the Progeny of the Sheep Bee, or Fly, which, in common Sheep (& in the Merino also) deposits its Nit, producing Worms in the Head of almost every other Sheep. The Interior of the Tunis Nostril is formed like that of the Camel; & calculated to exclude, at Pleasure, any Annoyances, or dangerous Air or Vapour, which in the sandy Deserts of African or Asiatick Climates, are frequently fatal to the human Race.

I have had, on the *Landsdown* Farm (adjacent to mine)[2] a full Proof of the Fact I mention—to wit—that the Tunis are exempt from the Diseases common to other Sheep; to which, of all others, the Merino is the most obnoxious. Mr C. Hare[3] caught the Merino-Mania; & purchased 80 Sheep—many Mongrels—but many true *Merinos*. He placed them on the Lansdown Farm for a few Weeks. I warned the Tenant against the Danger of infecting with their Diseases his fine Flock of Tunis Crosses, some high blooded Tunis & others English & Irish Sheep. But, like the Prophecies of Cassandra, my Prognosticks were disregarded. Yet Bones (the Tenant) took great Care to keep the Flocks apart. He, however, admitted a few Merinos into his Sheep House, for a few Nights. *Two Months* after the Departure of Hare's Sheep, & after several Frosts, he housed his Farm Flock. The Consequence was, that most of them caught the *Scab*, from the Infection left behind by the Merinos. The common Sheep were the worst, the English & Irish Breed (fine Sheep) a Grade better; but bad enough; the quarter blooded Tunis slightly affected; but the high blooded Sheep of this Race *not in the smallest Degree infected*. Even in the lowest blooded Tunis Sheep, there was no Excoriation; or Injury to the Fleece. But many of the Fleeces of the other Sheep became ragged; & of some, the greater Part of the Fleeces fell off. He has chiefly banished the Disease, by strong Infusions of Tobacco. All of the Tunis Blood recovered, by a few Washings. But the common Sheep are as bare in Spots, as is the Head of our national Eagle.

Some of them have lost their Forelocks; & imitate, too exactly, the Head of our national Emblem. This is well enough for a *sheepish* Exhibition of Humility. It is, however, *illiberal*, tho' not surprising, that our Eagle should be so continually pecked by the great Bullies of the Earth; when it remains always bareheaded & uncovered before them. Retournons a nos Moutons: I have had a Plan for importing some Sheep, from Tunis, in Contemplation for a long time past. I cannot obtain from Genl Eaton, the Information I have repeatedly required, of the exact Place from whence he procured my original Pair. He is un homme perdu; but I have taken Measures to get the necessary Information, & will prosecute my Plan. Mine must be a peculiar Species of the Breed. Yours very truly

RICHARD PETERS

RC (DLC). Docketed by JM.

1. Peters referred to a plate in the publication he had sent to JM (see JM to Peters, 15 Mar. 1811, and n. 2).

2. Lansdown was a property on the west bank of the Schuylkill River, about four miles outside of Philadelphia and to the south of Peters's estate, Belmont. In 1773 it had belonged to John Penn, and in 1797 it was purchased by William Bingham as a country seat. After Bingham's death in 1804, the property passed into the hands of the Baring family, who later leased it to, among others, ex-king of Spain Joseph Bonaparte during his years of exile (Margaret L. Brown, "Mr. and Mrs. William Bingham of Philadelphia: Rulers of the Republican Court," *Pa. Magazine of History and Biography*, 61 [1937]: 305–15).

3. Charles Willing Hare (1778–1827) was a prominent Philadelphia lawyer and professor of law at the University of Pennsylvania. He served for many years as Bingham's legal representative (*Pa. Magazine of History and Biography*, 26 [1902]: 476; ibid., 33 [1909]: 44).

From Thomas Jefferson

DEAR SIR   MONTICELLO Apr. 7. 11.
Your favors of Mar. 18. and Apr. 1. have been duly recieved. The extract from Armstrong's letter of July 28. 08. which you desire is in these words. 'My poor friend Warden writes to you, & asks from you the appointment of Consul for this place. I could not promise to do more than send his letter. He is an honest and amiable man, with as much Greek & Latin, & chemistry & theology, as would do for the whole corps of Consuls. But, after all, not well qualified for business. You have seen an order of Sçavans, really well informed, who, notwithstanding, scarcely knew how to escape from a shower of rain when it happened to beset them. He is of that family. No—the man for this place, ought to be a man of business, as well as a gentleman.' He then goes on to put Leavenworth's pretensions out of the way, should he have proposed himself.[1] The letter is headed 'private,' altho

relating as much to public as private transactions. What I saw of Warden, during the ten days or fortnight he staid here, satisfied me that he merited all the good which Armstrong says of him, & that he was by no means the helpless & ineffective man in business which he represents him to be. I knew, when I recieved the letter that Armstrong's fondness for point, and pith, rendered it unsafe to take what he said literally. He is cynical & irritable, & implacable. Whether his temper or his views induced his dismission of Warden, his persecution of him now, will render public benefit by the developement of his character. I have never heard a single person speak of Warden who did not rejoice in his appointment, and express disapprobation of Armstrong's conduct respecting him: and I am perfectly satisfied that, if the appointment is made to attract public attention, it will be approved. The other subject of uneasiness which you express must, I know, be afflicting. You will probably see it's effect in the secret workings of an insatiable family. They may sow discontent, but will neither benefit themselves nor injure you by it. The confidence of the public is too solid to be shaken by personal incidents. I do sincerely rejoice that Monroe is added to your councils. He will need only to percieve that you are without reserve towards him, to meet it with the cordiality of earlier times. He will feel himself to be again at home in our bosoms, and happy in a separation from those who led him astray. I learn that John Randolph is now open-mouthed against him & Hay. The letter which I wrote lately to Wilkinson was one of necessity written to thank him for his book which he sent me.[2] He says nothing in his letter of the anonymous letter in Clarke's book to which you allude. I have never seen Clarke's book, & know nothing of it's contents. The only part of my letter which regards Wilkinson himself is in these words, 'I look back with commiseration on those still buffeting the storm, & sincerely wish your Argosy may ride out, unhurt, that in which it is engaged. My belief is that it will; & I found that belief on my own knolege of Burr's transactions, on my view of your conduct in encountering them, and on the candour of your judges.' These are truths which I express without reserve, whenever any occasion calls for them. Whatever previous communications might have passed between Burr & Wilkinson on the subject of Mexico, I believe, that on the part of the latter it was on the hypothesis of the approbation of the government. I never believed W. would give up a dependance on the government under whom he was the first, to become a secondary & dependant on Burr. I inclose you a letter from Pere Gabriel.[3] In a Note of unfinished business which I left with you, you will see exactly how far he had a right to expect the government would go in aid of his establishment.[4] I fear the glimmering of hope that England might return to reason has past off with the return of her mad king to power. Present me affectionately to mrs. Madison, and be assured of my best wishes for your health & happiness, and that your labours for the public may be crowned with their love.

TH: JEFFERSON

RC (DLC: Rives Collection, Madison Papers); FC (MHi: Jefferson Papers). For enclosure, see n. 3.

1. Connecticut-born Mark Leavenworth was a merchant and speculator who had long been resident in Paris. He was a close friend of Joel Barlow's and in 1793 had been associated with Barlow in a scheme to form a company to seize Louisiana from Spain for France (Samuel Bernstein, *Joel Barlow: A Connecticut Yankee in an Age of Revolution* [Cliff Island, Maine, 1985], pp. 96–97; William Stinchcombe, *The XYZ Affair* [Greenwood, Conn., 1980], pp. 85–87).

2. On 10 Mar. 1811 Jefferson had written to Wilkinson to acknowledge receipt of the second volume of *Memoirs of General Wilkinson* (Washington, 1810; Shaw and Shoemaker 22056). The contents included a pamphlet entitled *Examination of General Wilkinson's Conduct in Relation to Burr's Conspiracy* (95 pp.), supplemented by an "Appendix to volume the Second" (136 pp.). Wilkinson had sent the volume to Jefferson on 21 Jan. 1811 for the purpose of refuting the calumnies made against him by his enemies, including "the profligate fictions & forgeries of Danl. Clark" (DLC: Jefferson Papers).

3. Jefferson enclosed a 9 Feb. 1811 letter he had received from Gabriel Richard on 17 Mar., relating to the Spring Hill Indian School at Detroit (printed in Carter, *Territorial Papers, Michigan*, 10:339–41).

4. See Memorandum from Jefferson, March 1809, *PJM-PS*, 1:1, 2 n. 4.

From Morgan Lewis

DEAR SIR   ALBANY 8th. April 1811

Accident has recently put me in possession of some facts which may possibly be interesting to you, and which I shall therefore in confidence communicate. A plan is formed, of which the outlines are, that at the ensuing Election George Clinton is to be your Opponent for the presidency and General Armstrong the Candidate for the vice presidency. An Appointment under the general government is to be procured, if possible, for Govr. Tompkins, for the purpose of enabling D. W. Clinton (should he succeed at the next Election, of which there is little prospect) to Administer the Government of the State. Genl. Armstrong has within a few days received a Letter from Washington, the writer of which informs him, that it is the Opinion of his friends there, which Mr. Secretary Smith assured him of and requested him to advertise the General of, that he should decline accepting any Office under your Administration, and that he should immediately acquire a residence in Pensylva.

General A——g immediately repaired to this place, where he has been a Week at the House of Judge Spencer,[1] with whom Mr. Clinton also lodges.

There, measures were taken to bring this State into the plan, which I trust will not be successful. This information may be relied on—I have it from a Source not to be questioned.

Mr. German the Senator from this State,[2] it is said, has already taken the field, and declares your Administration merits not the Confidence of the people.

Mr. W. P. Van Ness,[3] a Man of considerable intrigue, has lately attached himself to the Clinton party, and it is understood is to be rewarded with an Appointment under the general Government.

When I assure you sir there is not an Office in the Gift of any Government on Earth that I would accept, you will duly appreciate the motives of this Communication.

The Legislature of this State being on the Eve of Adjournment I am too much occupied to enlarge. I am sir your's respectfully

MORGAN LEWIS.[4]

RC (DLC: Rives Collection, Madison Papers). Docketed by JM.

1. Ambrose Spencer (1765–1848), a graduate of Yale and Harvard, had a lengthy career in law and politics in New York. A Federalist in his politics until 1798, he served at various times between 1793 and 1802 in the New York Assembly, in the state senate, and also on the Council of Appointment. From 1802 to 1804 he was state attorney general, and in the latter year he was appointed to the state supreme court where he remained until 1823, serving as chief justice after 1819. Both his second and third wives were sisters of DeWitt Clinton, with whom he was closely associated politically until they quarreled in 1811–12. Thereafter, his political efforts were devoted to advancing the career of his lifelong friend John Armstrong, who became JM's secretary of war in 1813. He was widely regarded as a dominant force in New York politics, at least until 1823 when his renomination to the state supreme court was rejected. He was elected to one term in the U.S. House of Representatives, 1829–31. His son, John Canfield Spencer, served in both the war and treasury departments during the administration of John Tyler.

2. Obadiah German (1766–1842), a Clintonian Republican, represented New York in the U.S. Senate, 1809–15.

3. William P. Van Ness (ca. 1778–1826), a New York lawyer, was Aaron Burr's second in the 1804 duel with Alexander Hamilton. In May 1812 JM nominated him to be a judge of the district court of New York (Kline, *Papers of Burr*, 1:584 n. 1; *Senate Exec. Proceedings*, 2:269).

4. Morgan Lewis (1754–1844) had met JM at the College of New Jersey in Princeton, from which he graduated in 1773. He served during the Revolution, mainly on the staff of Horatio Gates, and in 1779 married the sister of Robert R. Livingston. He entered politics in 1787 as a Federalist, but by the early 1790s he had joined the Clintonian Republicans and was appointed chief justice of New York in 1801. Between 1804 and 1807 he was governor of New York, during which time he broke irrevocably with both George and DeWitt Clinton. Throughout the summer of 1808 Lewis kept JM informed about the efforts of New York's Republicans to prevent JM's election to the presidency, and in 1811 he entered the New York state senate where he continued to oppose the politics of the Clintonians. In May 1812 JM commissioned Lewis as a brigadier general and quartermaster in the U.S. Army, but Lewis preferred a line appointment and was promoted to major general in February 1813. He led U.S. forces without distinction in the Canadian campaigns of 1813, and after the

fiasco at Chrysler's Farm in November, he was transferred to the command of the Third Military District where he remained until October 1814 (Harrison, *Princetonians, 1769–1775*, pp. 308–17).

§ From Jonathan Bull and Others. *9 April 1811, Hartford, Connecticut.* "The friends of the government have for some time past, contemplated with deep regret, the unhappy situation of the federal courts in this district"; they believe that some gentlemen, not friendly to the district attorney, have attempted a remedy by seeking his removal. Such a step would cause pain to the friends of Mr. Huntington, especially at a time when the reasons that are advanced for his removal are beyond his control. "We are however assured . . . that it is Mr. Huntingtons wish to retire from the turmoil in which he has long been unpleasantly involved, and that it is his determination to resign his office . . . as soon as he can do so, without its appearing to his enemies, to be the result of their intrigues." The signatories request JM to suspend any decision about Huntington's removal until such time as Huntington has an opportunity for "an honorable retreat" and JM can select a suitable successor.[1]

RC (DNA: RG 59, LAR, 1809–17, filed under "Huntington"). 1 p. Signed by Bull and six others.

1. Hezekiah Huntington, whom Jefferson had nominated as U.S. attorney for the district of Connecticut in December 1805, was still serving in office as late as 1825 (*Senate Exec. Proceedings*, 2:10, 3:253, 400).

§ From William Clark.[1] *10 April 1811, St. Louis.* Has frequently been asked by "small parties of Showonees resideing within this Territory" about assigning them a permanent tract of land where they might avoid disputes with their neighbors and "where the white people will not be permited to Sell them Spiritious Liquors." His efforts to prevent liquor sales have been "without complete effect . . . in a Country like this, where nine out of ten of the Indian Traders have no respect for our Laws." Part of the Shawnee and Delaware nations have a claim under the Spanish government to a large tract on the Mississippi, about halfway between St. Louis and the mouth of the Ohio. Several white families have "settled promiscuously on those lands, as the unappropriated land of the United States," which has caused discontent among the Indians who want either confirmation of their possession or the assignment of another tract "out Side of the Settlements." Encloses an address from a band of about forty Shawnee families residing near the Missouri on a branch of the Meramec River.[2] "They request a License of Three Miles Squar including their Towns, with promission to raise and Sell the Lead Ore." They are "a peaceable and well disposed people."

RC and enclosure (DNA: RG 75, LRIA). RC 2 pp. Docketed by a War Department clerk as received 25 May 1811. Printed in Carter, *Territorial Papers, Louisiana-Missouri*, 14:445–46. For enclosure, see n. 2.

1. Since his return from his voyages of exploration with Meriwether Lewis, William Clark (1770–1838) had been brigadier general of the territorial militia and superintendent of Indian affairs at St. Louis.

2. Clark enclosed an address to JM, dated 29 Mar. 1811 at Bourbos in Louisiana (2 pp.), from the Shawnee who had moved to the St. Louis region after their defeat by "that great Warriour [George Rogers] Clark." General Wilkinson had given them permission to occupy lands "about 120 Miles from St. Louis" where they would have been satisfied to remain, but after suffering raids from the Osage, they approached the territorial governor who told them to resettle nearer St. Louis. Declaring themselves to be "a Wandering people, not from inclination but from Necessity," and realizing the "Buffaloe & Elk is drove off to a great distance & Deer is getting scarce," they requested JM to grant them land where they could raise cows and hogs as well as sell lead ore. The address was signed by Onothe, or James Rogers, a chief of the band, and Noma, or Fish, a principal councilor. In acknowledging Clark's letter, the secretary of war granted the Shawnee their request, "subject to the will & pleasure of the President" and on the condition that whites be forbidden to intrude on the territory (Eustis to Clark, 31 May 1811, Carter, *Territorial Papers, Louisiana-Missouri*, 14:452).

§ From Albert Gallatin. *10 April 1811.* "Mr Gallatin will do himself the honor to dine with Mr Madison on Tuesday next [16 Apr. 1811]."

RC (NN: Gallatin Papers). 1 p.

§ From Pasquale Navarro. *10 April 1811, Naples.* Has produced a mathematical work that will astonish the geometers, as it deals with the resolution of the problem of the trisection of the angle, which has occupied the most renowned talents in the world for nearly twenty centuries. Sends JM a copy of his work so that it might be made public in the U.S., where science, letters, and the fine arts are cultivated.

RC (NHi: Gallatin Papers). 1 p. In Italian.

From James Maury

DEAR SIR   LIVERPOOL 11th. April 1811

With this is a Copy of the letter I had the honour to write to you on the 14th November, since which I have not received any instructions about your Tobacco ℔ Adeline. No part of it has been sold.

It now is more than twelve months since the commencement of the Unparalleled distresses to which the Trading Interest of this Country has been subjected. They still are so great that Government offer a Loan of Six millions to the sufferers; but, as the Act is but just passed and the Money not yet diffused, one cannot speak as to it's effects. It may produce relief, tho', probably, but temporary; because those distresses are more to be attributed to the difficulty of introducing goods from this Country into the ports of the Continent than to any other Cause.[1]

Under these circumstances foreign produce in general is greatly depressed and very unsaleable. The Stocks of Tobacco in this port and London only now are about 36.000 Hhds, of which 15.000 are here; about double the quantity at any past period. With great respect & esteem I have the honor to be your obliged friend and servant

JAMES MAURY

RC (DLC). Marked "Duplicate." In a clerk's hand, signed by Maury. Docketed by JM.

1. Beginning with banking failures in London in July 1810 and followed by company failures in Manchester the next month, the British economy experienced a sharp downturn, leading to a severe depression in 1811. Rising war expenditures had contributed to inflation, depreciation of the pound, and a drain on the gold reserves of the Bank of England. Napoleon's efforts to enforce the Continental System more stringently, especially in the Baltic region, resulted in a fall in British exports to Europe in 1811 to only 20 percent of the level attained in the previous year. At the same time, British exports to both the U.S. and Latin America declined to a comparable extent. Rather than reduce expenditures and return to the gold standard, however, Prime Minister Spencer Perceval responded by continuing to borrow money to carry on the war against France, and in March 1811 the ministry authorized the issue of £6 million in exchequer bills to assist business houses in distress (Watson, *The Reign of George III*, pp. 468–70; for a more extended discussion, see Crouzet, *L'economie britannique et le blocus continental*, 2:563–769).

Memorandum on Robert Smith

[ca. 11] April 1811

Having seen in the Aurora of the 5th. inst: & since copied into other Gazettes, an explanation which the Editor says he was authorized to make "of the rupture which has taken place between Mr. Madison, and Mr. R. Smith"[1] I have thought it proper, whilst the circumstances are fresh in remembrance, to preserve them in the following memorandum:

On the   [2] day of March Mr. S. called on me, as was common, on some point of official business. In the conversation, he alluded to the account in the newspapers, of the dismission of Mr. Pickering by Mr. Adams, as just published for the first time by the former.[3] Altho' the manner of Mr. S. did not denote any purpose beyond the ordinary conversation incident to such a topic, it happened to be the very day on which I meant to have sent for him in order to communicate the necessity of making a change in the head of the Department of State. Dropping therefore the case of Mr. Pickering, and breaking its apparent relation to his own, by the interposition of other subjects, I intimated that in coming over, he had anticipated my intention of sending for him, with a view to a conversation which would be as candid & explicit on my part, as it was in some respects delicate and disagreeable in itself. After remarking that I had delayed the execution of my purpose for some time after I had formed it, in order that my communication might have the character of being not the result of any sudden impulse, but of a deliberate regard to public considerations, and official duty, I proceeded to state to him, that it had long been felt, and had at length become notorious, that the Administration of the Executive Departmt. laboured under a want of the harmony & unity, which were equally essential to its energy and its success; that I did not refer to the evil as infecting our Cabinet consultations, where there had always been an apparent cordiality, and even a sufficient concurrence of opinion; but as shewing itself in language and conduct out of doors, counteracting what had been understood within to be the course of the Administration, and the interest of the Public; that truth obliged me to add, that this practice, as brought to my view, was exclusively chargeable on him; and that he had not only counteracted what had been the result of consultations apparently approved by himself, but had included myself in representations calculated to diminish confidence in the administration committed to me. He expressed surprize that I should have yielded to such impressions, declared that he had given no cause for them; observing that it was not to be conceived that a motive could be felt by him, to be otherwise than friendly personally, as well as to the credit of my administration. I told him that I had long resisted such impressions, well knowing that my conduct to him had merited a very different return. But that they were the result of facts and circumstances, brought to my knowledge, from so many sources and with so many corroborations, that it was impossible to shut my mind against them. I assured him that I had struggled agst. the belief as long as I could, that it was painful as well as difficult for me to suppose, that conscious as he must be of the friendship he had experienced in my nomination of him to the Department of State, and in the constant aids I had given him, in discharging its duties, he should privately set himself agst. me in any respect; but that what had harrassed my feelings in a degree equalled by no occurrence in a long political life, was the reflection that there were among those most nearly connected with him, a number of individuals whom I had always felt a gratification in classing among the best of my friends political & personal,[4] & for whom I felt the highest esteem & the sincerest affection; and that the idea of distressing them was most severely so to myself. He repeated his solemn denial of unfriendly conduct in any way towards me, or having done any thing tending to obstruct or embarrass the administration: that on the contrary he had been always personally my friend, and had contributed as far as he could to the credit & support of the administration: What motive could he have to be otherwise, being himself a member of it, and having neither pretensions nor expectations of any higher sort? What could have given rise to the unfavorable sentiments I had expressed, he was at a loss even to conjecture. I told him I was aware of the awkwardness of my situation, in being obliged to refer to information and evidence which had come to me in ways not permitting me to name to him the sources; but I could assure him that the sources were such as made it my duty not to disregard them;

and that unquestionably, he would himself, in my situation yield to the accumulated statements which had their effect on me. In what instances had
he set himself agst. me, or against measures espoused by the Administration? I reminded him of a conversation with Mr.   [5] reported by the latter, in which he had indulged himself in disparaging remarks on my official
character, & that of others in the Cabinet; on the general course of my
policy which he signified he disapproved; and in which he had communicated certain Cabinet proceedings, some of which were of so confidential
a nature that the gentleman did not consider himself at liberty to repeat
them. I had taken occasion before to drop him a hint that such a conversation had been given out; observing at the time, that I did it not because I
lent an ear to it; but that it might suggest circumspection. He slighted then
the report as proceeding from a source not likely to be listened to; and now
repeated the denial of the conversation, with an allusion to a report from
the same source, as to a conversation with another member of the Cabinet,
where it appeared, that no interview could have taken place. I admitted that
if this had been a solitary case, it would have been entirely dismissed from
my recollection; but this was far from being the fact; altho' I could not
equally enter into a specification of other cases. For examples in which he
had counteracted what he had not himself disapproved in the Cabinet, I
referred to the Bills called Macon's bills, and the non-intercourse bill; in
the consultations on which he appeared to concur in their expediency; that
he well knew the former, in its outline, at least, had originated in the difficulty of finding measures that would prevent what Congress had solemnly
protested agst., towit, a compleat submission to the Belligerent Edicts; that
the measure was considered as better than nothing, which seemed to be the
alternative, and as part only of whatever else might in the progress of the
business be found attainable; and that he neither objected to what was done
in the Cabinet, (the time & place for the purpose); nor offered any thing in
the place of it; yet it was well understood that his conversations & conduct
out of doors, had been entirely of a counteracting nature; that it was generally believed that he was in an unfriendly disposition personally and officially; and that altho' in conversations with different individuals, he might
not hold the same unfavorable language, yet with those of a certain temper,
it was no secret that he was very free in the use of it; and had gone so far as
to avow a disapprobation of the whole policy of commercial restrictions,
from the Embargo throughout. I intimated to him also that it was a complaint among our friends in Congs. that the Federalists frequently quoted
him for communications from our Ministers abroad, which was unknown
to others, the disclosures being sometimes such as to be deemed confidential, and to be turned agst. the administration.[6] I glanced also at the report
of his conversation with Mr. Morier, in which he (Mr. S) had expressed his
disapprobation of the whole course of policy observed by the U. States to-

wards G. B.[7] All these facts he repelled by a repetition of what he had before said. With respect to his motives for dissatisfaction, I acknowledged that I had been, for the reasons given by him, much puzzled to divine any natural ones, without looking deeper into human nature than I was willing to do: and it was on this account that I had so long resisted the impressions which had at length been made on me; that instead of having any just motives to become an adversary, I knew, and he must be conscious, that in my confidential intercourse with him, in my kindness in general; and above all in the labor I had taken upon myself in behalf of his official duties, and for his credit, as well as that of the administration, I ought to have found an opposite return. On this subject as well as every other, I told him, I meant as I ought to be entirely frank, and must therefore say, that it was an imperious consideration for a change in the Departmt. of State, that whatever talents he might possess, he did not as he must have found by experience, possess those adapted to his station; that this had thrown the business more into my hands than was proper, or consistent with my own duties; that as long as I considered him in the light I once did, I had cheerfully given him my aid, but that it was too much to be expected under actual circumstances, and that moreover, the increase of the public business had put it out of my power to do his share as well as my own; and that indeed throughout it was not done as well as might have been, by a mind appropriated thereto. I observed that I could appeal to himself for the fact that the business of the Dept. had not been conducted in the systematic and punctual manner, which was necessary, particularly in the foreign correspondence, and that I had become daily more dissatisfied with it. He did not admit that complaint was well founded; intimating that I had a particular way of thinking on this subject, and that his conduct of the business would fully justify itself on examination. I told him he could not but be in a great error; reminding him of the condition in which his correspondence, more particularly, was brought to me; which was almost always so crude & inadequate, that I was in the more important cases generally obliged to write them anew myself, under the disadvantage sometimes of retaining, thro' delicacy some mixture of his draft; that he must recollect that in the cases of Erskine & Jackson, the correspondence on his part had in a manner, fallen entirely on my hands.[8] I reminded him also of important failures to make seasonable communications to our foreign Agents; particularizing the case of neglecting, tho' repeatedly desired, to make known to our Minister at Paris, as was done to our Minister at London, that in case the Letter of the Duke de Cadore of Aug. 5. to Genl. Armstrong as reaching us through English newspapers, should it be officially confirmed, it would be the ground of a Proclamation as authorized by the Act of May; 1810. and the case of not keeping Mr. Shaler at the Havanna, duly informed of the state of our foreign relations, in consequence of which, as appeared by Mr. Shaler's letters he was unable to pursue the object of his mission with advantage.[9] I observed that if he had transmitted at once, in multiplied copies, & thro' different channels, the same information for the French Govt. as to the B. Govt. as to the light in which the letter of the D. de Cadore was viewed, it might, by removing uncertainty & distrust as to the course here, have prevented the delay & embarrasment resulting from the course there. The impression made by these remarks was shewn rather by his manner, than his comment which was limited to a general disclaimer of the justness of them; & to allusions to a report that he had expressed to Mr.   [10] Ingersoll, lately in Washington, a disapprobation of the Proclamation putting in force the non-importation act agst. G. B. which he denied to be fact, & said that he had sought out that Gentleman, and had obtained from him a satisfactory explanation. In this stage of the conversation, but in what particular connection is not recollected, it was noticed as a mark of his disinclination to co-operate in promoting measures for the better fulfilling the Executive trust, that altho' the Act of Congs. at the Session preceding that just closed, relating to our diplomatic establishment, & of course particularly affecting his dept. had been found so very inconvenient, and it had been so often suggested to him; as desireable that some active member of Congress, should be apprized of the expediency of amending or repealing the Act, yet no such hint had ever been given, till at length I had availed myself of an opportunity of explaining the matter to a member of the Senate, who readily introduced it to the Senate, but too late in the session, to receive an effectual attention.[11] He signified that he had not been in the habit of proceeding in such a way with business belonging to the Legislature: and seemed to disapprove or doubt the propriety of it. I remarked that where the intention was honest & the object useful, the conveniency of facilitating business in that way was so obvious that it had been practised under every past administration, & wd. be so under every future one; that Executive experience wd. frequently furnish hints & lights for the Legislature; that nothing was more common than for members of Congs. to apply for them; and that in fact, such communications, in cases not calling for formal messages, were indispensible to the advantageous conduct of the public business. A resort to formal messages on every occasion where executive information might be useful, was liable to obvious objections. He made no particular reply; but did not seem to acquiesce. Returning to the necessity of harmony & unity in the Executive Councils, in providing for which, I expressed a disposition to wound feelings any where as little as possible, he said he had himself regretted my situation, in reference to the want of cordiality among members of the Cabinet, declaring at the same time, that whilst he was aware of intrigues & hostilities carried on agst.

himself, he had abstained from every thing of that sort agst. others, disdaining at all times to stoop to such practices. I told him it was unnecessary to repeat observations which I had already made; that such was the state of things that a remedy had become essential in the view of the most considerate friends of the Administration, and that I wished for the reasons given, to make it as lenient as would answer the purpose. It had occurred to me that he might not be disinclined to serve his Country in a foreign mission; and that St. Petersburg, where there was a vacancy, might be an eligible as it certainly was an important situation. London more so, he remarked quickly. For London, I replied, another arrangement was thought of;[12] adding, with a view to repress miscalculations, that it was a place of discussions & negociations calling for appropriate talents & habits of business. He said he had for a considerable time entertained thoughts of retiring from the Department of State, and had looked towards a vacancy on the Bench of the supreme Court, likely to be produced ere long, by a death in Baltimore (alluding to Judge Chase).[13] I observed that in that event, it might be found most proper to seek a successor elsewhere, intimating also that he had been long out of the practice & study of the law, and that the Senate would probably be hard to please in such a case. He made light of that consideration; with an expression of confidence in his standing there, which led me to remark that he was not aware how much room there was for a different estimate, that he had assuredly lost ground extremely with the members of both Houses of Congress, insomuch that the prevailing sentiment, as brought to my knowledge in the most direct manner, and from some quarters not unfriendly to himself, called for some arrangement that would at least vary the composition of the Cabinet.[14] He ascribed unfavorable impressions agst. him as far as they might exist to intrigues & calumnies; signifying that there was however a body of firm friends personal & political, who would not desert him whatever course things might take. I did not admit that any considerable body of the Republicans, would in any event take side agst. the Administration; that on the contrary, many on whom he might perhaps count, had become dissatisfied with the course he had pursued; that it was not so much therefore the consideration alluded to by him, which weighed with me, tho' not without weight especially at the present crisis in Maryland (the approaching election of Senatorial Electors),[15] as the one I had before mentioned, namely the personal friends common to both of us, that made me desirous of smoothing the change become necessary, by proposing a mission to Russia, which I sincerely wished him to accept. I remarked that the services there tho' neither difficult nor laborious, might be important; that the station was respectable, and that it was desireable to find a minister whose political grade here had been such as would satisfy the expectations of the Emperor, and whose private resources would also aid his salary in bearing the expensiveness of that Metropolis & Court. He admitted an inclination towards a trip to Europe as more eligible than his situation here; and after a few uninteresting observations, concurred in the measure with a mutual understanding that the appointment would be postponed for some days, till he could wind up the business of his Department, and prepare for his departure from Washington. I observed that as the 1st. of April, closed a quarter it might be a convenient epoch, for the date of his Commission; in which he acquiesced. He said he supposed there would be no impropriety in letting it be known that the mission was on foot—None at all—After a short pause, May I say that the appointment is offerred to me. I have no objection, it being of course understood that it is to take place on the 1st. of April; and that you will let me be at liberty as many days previous as may be convenient, to take overt measures for supplying the vacancy; which he promised. The conversation closed with his proposal that it should be considered as entirely confidential, & my acquiescence in it.

From his conversations & conduct, for several days, in his office & elsewhere, it was not doubted that he persisted in his intention to accept the Mission, and was making preparations accordingly. Circumstances soon however began to denote & strengthen doubts, particularly his declining, after accepting my invitation to dine with a party including the Russian Legation, and as I did not hear from him as was expected and the 1st. of april approached, I sent for him.

On his arrival, I told him my object, and that I had, according to the understanding between us, caused a Commission to be made out for him. He said he was himself on the point of coming over to me,[16] with the view of returning into my hands, his Commission of Secretary of State, (handing it to me at the same time), and to inform me that he had determined to decline the other which had been proffered to him. However disposed he might have been to accept it under other circumstances, it was impossible he could do so under such as would give it the appearance of a mere expedient to get rid of him as Secretary of State. He had learned from Baltimore that a removal of him was believed to have been determined on, under the influence of intrigues agst. him, and that this intention was known even to federal members of Congress, as was evinced by their language on their return home; that the same impression existed elsewhere; that he had in fact, recd. letters from his friends not only in Baltimore, but in Penna. & N. York,[17] advising him by no means to make himself a party to the transaction, by accepting the Russian mission, which would be regarded as a mere cover for his removal. I told him I could not be answerable for the reports or assertions that might be propagated; that the course I had pursued was the one deemed proper in the circumstances which had resulted from that pursued by him; and had been as delicate and favorable to him, as could be reconciled with what I owed to the public & to myself; that in tendering him the Commission for Russia, I wished him to accept it for the reasons explained to him; that what the Federalists said on the occasion, must have grown out of the conversations which had, as was well known, been frequent & free among the friends of the Administration, on the necessity of a change in the Department of State. I availed myself of this turn of the conversation, to allude anew to the reports & complaints, that the Federalists were the first to get from him information of our foreign Affairs; and to its being understood that he had told Mr. Morier that the whole policy of the government towards G. B. had been contrary to his Opinion & advice. This he denied. I assured him there was full evidence that Morier had said so; that this was known to and believed by sundry members of Congs. and had contributed, with other causes, to strengthen the current running agst. him. I reminded him of the official letter from Mr. Morier to him complaining of the non-intercourse being enforced against G. B. during the actual conduct of France in which he (M) referred to a conversation in which he (S.) admitted that G. B. had a right to complain; I told him I had been surprized when he communicated the letter to me, to find no apparent intention of a formal disavowal of that circumstance; till I had pressed it on him as material to himself in case the correspondence should be brought before the public or Congress; and that I did not approve of the course, finally taken by him, of getting Morier to withdraw the letter and substitute another omitting the passage; a course less eligible than the one I had suggested, of a written disavowal, as Morier's communications to his Govt might correspond with his first letter, and might find their way to the public thro a Call for papers, by the British Parliament, in which case the statement would be without his contradiction.[18] These I observed were disagreeable topics, and I willingly turned from them, to repeat to him, that with a wish to consult the sensibility of common friends, I had been ready to give him in exchange for an office which he professed, no longer to relish, a foreign Mission which in itself did not appear to be unacceptable to him; and that it was still in his option, & would remain so for a short time longer, if he wished to deliberate further on the subject. He said he had made up his mind, & meant to be understood as having given his final answer to the proposal. He recurred to the aspect it wore of an indirect removal of him, from the department of State, and to the allegation of intrigues agst. him, which had been mistaken for a loss of Confidence with the public, & with Congs.; regretted the tendency of what was taking place to injure the Republican cause, observing again that he should be supported by a Body of friends, and that he knew he could stand on good ground in justifying himself to his Country. I assured him that neither my sentiments nor conduct in relation to him were in the least the effect of intrigues to which I should never listen, but of the facts & considerations I had unfolded to him; that I did not doubt the friendship for him of a number of respectable & weighty characters, but it was not less true, however disagreeable it might be to dwell on the circumstance, that with the public as well as among the members of Congs. in both House[s], the tide was setting strongly & extensively agst. him, that I regretted as much as himself a tendency in any occurrence to impair harmony among the Republicans, more especially at this time & in this State, but that I believed this was not likely to be much the case; conceiving that the administration rested on ground as solid as at any preceding period; & that for myself, I was entirely confident that what I had done in relation to him, could be justified not only to the public, if it should become there necessary, but even to the most partial of his personal friends; that I cd. have no personal objection therefore to any step he might take which would call the public attention to it. He said it was not his wish, however confident he might be of the ground on which he stood, to introduce any public discussion.[19] The conversation being at an end, he took his leave with a cold formality, and I did not see him afterwards.

On reading over the above, I recollect nothing worth mentioning which is omitted; unless it be thought an exception, that in some stage of the conversation, I alluded to the pretty general opposition made by his brother in the Senate to the measures proposed, or supposed to be approved, by the Executive, and its effect in strengthening the presumption with many, of a like spirit in the Secretary of State; explicitly declaring at the same time, that however I might be sometimes disappointed at the part taken by his brother, or regret it on account of his talents & his weight, I had always considered myself bound to suppose him actuated by a just respect for the independence of his station & his character; and that as he stood in no official connection with the Executive rendering him any wise responsible for his political conduct, I had never permitted myself to complain of it.

J. M.

Ms (DLC). In JM's hand. At a later time JM wrote on the cover: "(quere—if necesary to become public) / Memorandum as to R. Smith / Apl. 1811."

1. The 5 Apr. 1811 issue of the Philadelphia *Aurora General Advertiser* announced that the editor was "authorized" to state that the rupture between JM and Robert Smith arose from conflicts over four issues. The first was the two Macon bills and the Nonintercourse Act; the second was "certain nominations" JM had made to the Senate; the third was the practice of recommending measures "in secret, and individually, to members of congress, instead of the fair, unembarrassing, and open course of public recommendation"; and the fourth was the pecuniary transactions of "a certain public agent," which, the editor predicted, would probably come before the next session of Congress. Other grounds for the rupture included "Gallatin and his conduct with Erskine," which the *Aurora* had discussed in the past and, the editor

promised, would do so again in two pieces already prepared for the press. The editorial page also reported that Robert Smith had been offered "*banishment to Siberia*, but has declined."

2. Left blank by JM.

3. On 19 Mar. 1811 the *National Intelligencer* published five letters exchanged by John Adams and Timothy Pickering between 10 and 12 May 1800 relating to the dismissal of the latter as secretary of state. The next issue, on 21 Mar., announced that Robert Smith had been offered the mission to the court of St. Petersburg.

4. JM was probably alluding to the fact that the Smith family of Baltimore, on three occasions, had married into the Nicholas family of Virginia. George Nicholas married Mary Smith, sister of Robert and Samuel Smith; Philip Norborne Nicholas married Mary Spear, sister of the wife of Samuel Smith; and Wilson Cary Nicholas married Margaret Smith, another sister of Robert and Samuel Smith.

5. Left blank by JM.

6. See, for example, John Graham to JM, 1 Sept. 1809, and George W. Erving to JM, 28 Nov. 1809 (*PJM-PS*, 1:348–49 and n. 5, 2:88 and n. 5).

7. See John Wayles Eppes to JM, 31 Jan. 1811, and n. 3.

8. See Madison, Francis James Jackson, and Robert Smith, 9 Oct.-11 Nov. 1809, *PJM-PS*, 2:8–11.

9. In pursuing his instructions "to feel the pulse of Cuba as to an estimate of the inducements to an incorporation of that island with the United States," Shaler had held conversations with Cubans about the consequences for them of an Anglo-American war. The conversations, he reported, were "necessarily general" as he was "unable to give any specific information on the state of our foreign relations and the news lately from home being very uncertain" (Shaler to Robert Smith, 3 Feb. and 4 Mar. 1811 [DNA: RG 59, CD, Havana]; on Shaler's mission, see *PJM-PS*, 2:310–12).

10. Left blank by JM.

11. JM was referring to his disagreement with Smith over the bill to "fix the compensation of public ministers, and of Consuls residing on the coast of Barbary," passed by Congress on 1 May 1810 (see JM to the House of Representatives, 27 Apr. 1810, *PJM-PS*, 2:326 and n. 1).

12. In their reports to their governments that the "schism" in the cabinet between JM and Smith had broken out publicly, both Louis Sérurier and John Philip Morier mentioned that Secretary of War Eustis would replace William Pinkney in London (Sérurier to Cadore, 9 Apr. 1811 [AAE: Political Correspondence, U.S., vol. 65]; Morier to Wellesley, 26 Mar. 1811 [PRO: Foreign Office, ser. 5, vol. 74]). Rumors to this effect circulated for some time, and according to William Duane "both Mr. Madison and Mr Gallatin did endeavor to get rid of Dr Eustis by a proposition to send him ambassador to England." The proposition, Duane added, "was made in the Cabinet—that Mr Munroe moved to send an ambassador—and that Mr Gallatin said 'between the wind and water'—if one is to be sent, 'he should be from the Eastern states—a man of the highest standing—and in his opinion from Massachusetts.' It was not agreed to nor did the doctor take the hint" (Duane to Henry Dearborn, 9 Jan. 1812 [CSmH]).

13. Supreme Court Justice Samuel Chase died on 19 June 1811. JM replaced him with Gabriel Duvall of Maryland (*National Intelligencer*, 22 June 1811; *Senate Exec. Proceedings*, 2:189).

14. JM was probably alluding to the visits he received from deputations of congressional Republicans on 1 and 2 Mar. 1811 (see Gallatin to JM, ca. 7 Mar. 1811, n. 1).

15. JM referred to the elections for the Maryland state senate, to be held on 2 Sept. 1811 (*National Intelligencer*, 3, 5, and 7 Sept. 1811).

16. On 29 Mar. 1811 the Baltimore *Whig* printed a "rumor" that Smith would resign that day as secretary of state.

17. In his diary Joseph Gales, Jr., recorded that Smith declined the mission to Russia, "as it was rumored and believed, by the advice of General Armstrong" ("Recollections of the Civil History of the War of 1812," *Historical Magazine*, 3d ser., 3 [1874–75]: 161).

18. Morier's dispatches to Lord Wellesley contain no material that explicitly confirmed JM's fears on this score. However, the British chargé did report instances where Smith's conversations, if made public in the manner JM anticipated, had the potential to embarrass the administration (see Morier to Wellesley, 24 Jan. and 22 Feb. 1811 [PRO: Foreign Office, ser. 5, vol. 74]).

19. After leaving Washington on 6 Apr. 1811 Robert Smith returned to Baltimore, where he complained to one of his correspondents that "among the means employed to mislead the enfeeble⟨d⟩ mind of our panic-struck President he was told that Armstrong & I had at Washn. form⟨ed⟩ a plan to Oppose him at the ensuing Election!!" (Robert Smith to John Bullus, [8?] Apr. 1811 [MdHi]). He then spent the next few weeks compiling an attack on JM, which he seems to have completed by 7 June and published in Baltimore three weeks later in both newspaper and pamphlet form as *Robert Smith's Address to the People of the United States.*

To John G. Jackson

Dear Sir   Washington Apl. 12. 1811

I recd. at the same time your two letters of the 1st. & 5th. It was found that the appt. of a Judge to succeed Mr. Nelson, had taken place a week or two before. Your name had been brought into view under high auspices, but it does not appear that your willingness to accept the office (or the sufficiency perhaps of your health) was counted on. You say nothing on the subject of Merinoes; which was taken up in my late letter answering yours expressing a wish to acquire some of that breed of sheep. I can add nothing to the information therein submitted to you.[1] You will see that very late accts. have been recd. from Europe, particularly England. I inclose papers containing all the particulars which have appeared in reference to our Affairs.[2] The proper comments will occur to your own judgment. Accept my congratulations on the event which adds to your domestic happiness, with assurances of my esteem & friendship.

James Madison

RC (InU: Jackson Collection).

1. JM to Jackson, 7 Mar. 1811.

2. JM presumably enclosed some recent issues of the *National Intelligencer.* That published on 9 Apr. 1811 included some "very late & very important verbal news from England" to the effect that Pinkney's negotiations in Great Britain had completely broken down, that the minister was aboard the *Essex* en route to home, and that George III was recovering from his recent illness. The same issue also contained a lengthy editorial defining the U.S. position on neutral rights in order to distinguish them from the "maritime rights" of Great Britain. According to Sérurier, JM was the author of this editorial (Sérurier to Cadore, 10 Apr. 1811 [AAE: Political Correspondence, U.S., vol. 65]).

From Andrew Ellicott

DEAR SIR,   LANCASTER April 12th. 1811.

The zenith Sector which I used on the southern boundary of the United States, is principally owned by this commonwealth: the claim of the U. S. amounts to about 25 guineas. On my return home in the year 1800, I had it deposited in one of the public stores, but do not recollect which. Being lately appointed to determine the boundary between the States of Georgia, and N. Carolina,[1] on which the instrument before mentioned will be wanted, I must request the loan of it, so far as the U. S. are interested. I presume an order from you, or one of the departments will be necessary to enable me to obtain it from the person who has it in possession. As the instrument will probably want some repairing, the sooner I receive your answer the better.

My compliments to Mrs. Madison, and believe me to be with great esteem, Your sincere friend, and hbl. servt.

ANDW. ELLICOTT.

RC (DNA: RG 59, ML).

1. On 26 Apr. 1810 Representative William W. Bibb of Georgia had presented a petition from the state of Georgia to Congress on its boundary dispute with North Carolina. According to the terms of the 1802 act under which Georgia ceded its western lands to the U.S., the state "acquired a right to a certain tract of country, which was west of South Carolina, and separated from the States of North Carolina and Georgia." The tract in question lay south of the thirty-fifth degree of latitude, and the state of Georgia, after its surveyor general had run the line in order to "ascertain the extent and the quality of the Territory," extended "its law and Government over the people there resident." The state of North Carolina resisted the Georgia claim unless that state "would agree to sanction grants that had issued" from the former authority, and the North Carolinians also disputed that the surveyor general of Georgia had measured the boundary line accurately. After Congress failed to respond to Georgia's request for the U.S. to intervene by appointing "a proper person to run the dividing line between the two States," the Georgia authorities commissioned Ellicott in April 1811 to undertake the task. Ellicott completed the survey in May 1812, and his ruling, much to the displeasure of the Georgians, was that the boundary between the two states ran eighteen miles farther south than they had claimed (*Annals of Congress*, 11th Cong., 2d sess., 1987–88; *ASP, Miscellaneous*, 2:72–79; Mathews, *Andrew Ellicott*, pp. 219–26).

§ From Simon Snyder. *12 April 1811, Lancaster.* Transmits "an exemplified copy of an Act of the General Assembly of the Commonwealth of Pennsylvania, entitled, 'An Act to cede the occupancy and use of certain lands near Presque Isle, to the United States, for the purpose therein mentioned.'"[1]

RC (DNA: RG 26, Early Light House Correspondence, Misc. Letters Received). 1 p. In a clerk's hand, signed by Snyder.

1. The purpose of the legislation was to permit the construction of a lighthouse (see *Acts of the General Assembly of the Commonwealth of Pennsylvania* [Philadelphia, 1811; Shaw and Shoemaker 23652], pp. 221–22).

From Caspar Wistar, Jr.

DEAR SIR   PHILADA. Apl. 13. 1811

It is with great reluctance that I intrude upon your valuable time, but the occasion seems to demand it of me. The Patriotism of Mr. B. McClenachan during the revolution is I believe well known to you, & you are probably as well acquainted with his history since that period. He wishes me to state to you my opinion respecting his health, & capability of attention to the office which he solicits of you.[1] It is with great pleasure I say that the powers of his mind appear to me perfectly unimpaired by age, & his health is equal to the undertaking. He is some times afflicted with the Gout but is free from all other complaints & is very temperate.

The Ladies of this family join me in offering their best respects to Mrs. Maddison, who is I believe the only person connected with any of the Governments in the United States that enjoys the perfect approbation of all parties. With sincere respect I beg leave to subscribe Your friend & servant

                                                    CASPAR WISTAR JR.

RC (DLC). Docketed by JM.

1. Blair McClenachan (d. 1812), an Irish-born Philadelphia merchant and businessman, was an ardent Republican, prominent in the opposition to the Jay treaty, who served one term in the Fifth Congress (1797–99). After some business failures, he went to debtors' prison, and Alexander James Dallas recommended him to Gallatin for office as a Revolutionary "worthy" who, through no real fault of his own, was "old, infirm, and necessitous." "Misfortune and Poverty," Dallas added, had not "deprived him of his popularity," and he retained "the simplicity of a child, and the benevolence of an angel." JM gave him an interim appointment as commissioner of loans for Pennsylvania (Merrill Jensen and Robert A. Becker, eds., *The Documentary History of the First Federal Elections, 1788–1790* [4 vols. to date; Madison, Wisc., 1976—], 1:420–21; Alexander James Dallas to Gallatin, 24 Apr. 1811, *Papers of Gallatin* [microfilm ed.], reel 23; *Senate Exec. Proceedings*, 2:187).

§ From James G. Forbes. *13 April 1811, New York.* "As the annexation of the hanseatic towns to the French Empire may have given the finishing stroke to the official duties of my Brother John M. Forbes, the Consul at Hamburg during a period of nine fruitless Years of unprecedented interruption to neutral Commerce[1]—may I hope, that the President . . . will Consider my Brothers Conduct and afford him such continued marks of his approbation as he ever strived to merit."

RC (DNA: RG 59, ML). 1 p.

1. In order to improve the enforcement of the Continental System, Napoleon, in December 1810 and January 1811, had annexed and occupied the Hanseatic towns, the northern part of Hanover, and the duchies of Berg and Oldenburg (Lefebvre, *Napoleon: From Tilsit to Waterloo*, p. 235).

§ From Lemuel Sawyer. *15 April 1811, Jonesborough, North Carolina.* "My health is so precarious that it is with great difficulty I can continue in the land of the living, & that must be done by the greater part of my time travelling about in search of health, . . . & it takes more than the profits of my little estate to defray these expences." Seeks a post in the Mediterranean that would "barely afford a sustenance." Believes there is a vacancy in Tunis or, if there is one in Italy "where the emoluments would cover expences," he would happily accept it. If no vacancies exist, he would be glad to accept a post in Philadelphia or Baltimore. Addresses JM with "the frankness of a friend" and requests "a line in answer to this."

RC (DLC). 2 pp. Docketed by JM.

§ From Charles Hall. *16 April 1811, Long's Hotel, Washington.* "I have this moment arrived here and request the favor of an interview with you that I may communicate some matters of importance. I however particularly request the favor of its being in private with you only, and that you will not let any person know of this letter or of my being here, until you see me."

RC (NN). 1 p. Signed "Charles Hall / of the island of Barbados."

§ From Samuel Hanson of Samuel. *16 April 1811, Washington.* "The Memorial of S. Hanson of Saml, Purser, begs leave respectfully to represent That, for the last 7 years past, he has been uniformly oppressed by the official conduct of Thomas Turner, the Accountant of the Navy, . . . [who] has prevented the settlement of his Accounts to this moment." Finds himself constrained to trouble the president, since there is no other officer to whom the accountant is "legally amenable." Believes that the accountant is not under the control of the secretary of the navy and that "being appointed, not by the Secretary, but by the President, he was meant to be independent of, and, perhaps, a check upon, that Officer." Concedes that he can appeal the adjustment of his accounts from the accountant to the comptroller and he has done so, "but the Comptroller possesses no power to *enforce* the adjustment of my Accounts by the Accountant; nor procure my access to the documents and vouchers rendered by me to the Accountant in support of my claims." Is ready to prove "before any impartial tribunal, the truth of these Allegations" and asks the president to cause "an Examination into the conduct of the Accountant" to end his "persecution & oppression."

RC (DLC). 2 pp.

From Paul Hamilton

SIR   NAVY DEPARTT April 17th. 1811

The Accountant of the Navy has requested me to transmit to you the accompanying papers, which are intended to vindicate him from the Charges alledged against him in the Memorial of Mr. Hanson.[1] An actual inspection of the Documents in the Office of Mr. Turner, which I made immediately after you left the Memorial of Mr. Hanson with me, authorizes me to say that, the Memorialist is altogether in error. I have only to add that, if Mr. Hanson had pursued the proper course you would not have been troubled; and that his business could have been closed without the necessity of a Complaint. I have the honor to be, Sir, with great respect & attachment yrs.

PAUL HAMILTON

RC and enclosures (DLC). RC docketed by JM. For enclosures, see n. 1.

1. Hamilton enclosed Thomas Turner's "Remarks . . . in Reply to Mr. Hanson's Memorial to the President," 17 Apr. 1811 (6 pp.), in which the accountant stated that before receiving Hanson's 12 Apr. note he had no cause to suppose that Hanson was dissatisfied with the settlement of his accounts as purser between 1804 and 1809. Turner went on to describe the circumstances of two adjusted charges and enclosed copies of related correspondence: (1) Hanson to Turner, 12 Apr. 1811 (2 pp.); (2) Hanson to Gabriel Duvall, 12 Apr. 1811 (3 pp.); (3) Duvall to Turner, 3 Apr. 1811 (1 p.); (4) Turner to Duvall, 15 Apr. 1811 (3 pp.); (5) Turner to Thomas Tingey, 18 Mar. 1811 (1 p.); (6) Tingey to Turner, 25 Mar. 1811 (1 p.), enclosing (7) a copy of Tingey to Hanson, 26 Aug. 1808 (1 p.); (8) an account for hospital stores furnished by Hanson for the *John Adams*, 8 Aug. 1805, with Turner's objections to its irregularity and showing his deductions (3 pp.); and (9) Hanson to Turner, 10 Apr. 1811 (1 p.), enclosing (10) a copy of a voucher for $203.50 made out to Hanson by Andrew Balmain for pay and rations in 1809 and certified as a true copy by Lund Washington (1 p.).

From Michael Leib

SIR,   PHILADELPHIA April 18th. 1811

I just learned, that a vacancy has occurred in the office of Commissioner of loans, by the death of General Moylan,[1] and take the liberty to suggest to you, that the office would be acceptable to me.

My political pursuits, at the expence of my profession, as you will readily imagine, have not improved my fortune; and after a long time spent in the public service, I am compelled to look about me, to provide for an increasing family. The emoluments of this office are small; but to a man who can content himself with a sufficiency to render him comfortable, and whose ambition is limited to narrow bounds, they may afford him some solace for long and uninterrupted service.

Allow me to request that this letter may be considered as confidential. Accept, Sir, the assurance of my respect and regard

M LEIB

RC (DLC). Docketed by JM.

1. Stephen Moylan, tenant of Dolley Madison's Philadelphia house from 1796 to 1807, died on 13 Apr. 1811 (*PJM*, 16:353 n. 1; *National Intelligencer*, 20 Apr. 1811).

To Thomas Jefferson

DEAR SIR　　　　　　　　　　　　　　　　　　　　　　　W. Apl. 19. 1811

I have recd. your favor of 　　 [1] containing the requested extract from Armstrong's letter relating to Warden. A. has entangled himself in such gross inconsistencies, that he may perhaps not execute this threat to vindicate his removal of W. agst. my reinstatement of him. This consideration alone will restrain his enmity agst. both of us. You will see the conflict in which he is engaged with Fulton.[2] Pinkney is weekly expected by the return of the Essex. Previous to his taking leave of the Prince Regt. he ascertained by a correspondence with Wellesley, that his stay was wished for the mere purpose of delay and delusion. The mission of Foster,[3] like that of Rose, plays the same game.[4] The Convalescence of the King renders the Prince a Cypher; and his Cabinet is inflexible in its folly & depravity. The inclosed paper of Poulson, publishes from the "Courier" the Cabinet paper,[5] the doctrine which is to be maintained & modified for the purposes of plunder.[6] We have been long without official intelligence from France. The last was not unfavorable. Appearances & reports have of late engendered suspicions of foul play. The arrivals of two vessels from Bayonne, in the Delaware, with the notice of others to follow, indicate a renewal of trade. On the other hand extracts of letters seem to imply a continuance of the Iron policy in that quarter. The symptoms of approaching war between France & Russia seem to multiply.[7] I am sorry to trouble you with a recurrence to your dormant files, but as I know the facility afforded by the method of them, I will ask the favor of you [to] look under the "Anonymous" head for a long letter or letters, written from London, in the beginning of 1809; in a disguised hand, & signed "A Man." If recd. at all, it probably was forwarded by Lyman. Affectionately & respectfully

JAMES MADISON

RC (DLC). Docketed by Jefferson, "recd. Apr. 21."

1. JM left a blank space here; he referred to Jefferson's letter of 7 Apr. 1811.

2. JM may have detected the hand of Armstrong in a series of N.Y. *Evening Post* editorials opposing the appointment of Joel Barlow as minister to France. Those published on 21 and 22 Mar. 1811 attacked the minister-designate through his friendship with Robert Fulton and pointedly reminded readers that the two men had shared living accommodations in Paris as "the Nisus and Eurialus of modern times." These editorials also criticized Barlow and Fulton for their efforts to persuade the American, British, and French governments to finance Fulton's controversial experiments in torpedo warfare.

3. Augustus John Foster (1780–1848), son of an Irish M.P. and the duchess of Devonshire, had been appointed minister plenipotentiary to the U.S. in April 1811, and he served in that capacity until his departure from Washington after the American declaration of war against Great Britain in June 1812. He had previously resided in Washington as secretary to the British legation, 1804–8. His later diplomatic career until his retirement in 1840 was uneventful. He committed suicide in 1848 (Mayo, *Instructions to British Ministers*, p. 310).

4. In a dispatch written to Robert Smith on 12 Feb. 1811 shortly before he took his leave from the Prince Regent, Pinkney declared that "nothing is to be expected from this Government in the way of negotiation; and . . . our Rights must either be abandoned altogether or vigorously asserted." On 18 Feb. he further remarked that under such circumstances the recent selection of Augustus John Foster as minister to Washington "was nothing, or rather worse than nothing" (DNA: RG 59, DD, Great Britain; the dispatch of 12 Feb. bears a pencil notation by JM indicating that he had read the contents). Three days before JM wrote his 19 Apr. letter to Jefferson the *National Intelligencer* had published a lengthy editorial on "Our Relations with G. Britain," which according to Joseph Gales, Jr., was based on a conversation he had with JM on 13 Apr. The editorial stipulated three conditions for a settlement with Great Britain—that Great Britain must abandon the practice of impressment, modify its system of blockades, and repeal the orders in council—but also predicted that the diplomatic mission of Foster would not accomplish these goals. The editorial concluded that if the negotiations were unsuccessful, "it will be for the people of the United States, speaking thro' their delegates, to nerve the Executive arm, by rigorously enforcing the present nonimportation, or substituting for it some measure more consonant to the feelings of the nation" (*National Intelligencer*, 16 Apr. 1811; "Recollections of the Civil History of the War of 1812," *Historical Magazine*, 3d ser., 3 [1874–75]: 162–63).

5. Here JM originally wrote "P's Cabinet paper."

6. JM evidently enclosed a copy of the 17 Apr. issue of the Philadelphia *Poulson's American Daily Advertiser* which had reprinted a 31 Jan. 1811 editorial from the London *Courier* to the effect that a settlement of Great Britain's differences with the U.S. was neither to be expected nor even greatly to be desired. The editorial argued at length that the U.S. had sided with France in all matters relating to neutral rights and predicted that the Madison administration would demand for a settlement that Great Britain repeal not only the orders in council but also Fox's blockade of 1806, and thus accept, in effect, French definitions of the doctrine of blockade. In particular, the editorial rejected the claim made by several American newspapers (including the *National Intelligencer* on 15 Oct. 1810 [see *PJM-PS*, 2:586 n. 1]), that the limited British blockade of Guadeloupe and Martinique in 1804 could be adduced as evidence that the British government had accepted the position that specific ports had to be "actually invested" in order to maintain a legal blockade. To oppose this pretension, the *Courier* suggested that Great Britain explicitly adopt the position that it could control all the seas and that no nation or fleet could sail upon them without British permission. Neither should Great Britain, the editorial concluded, cease the practices of searching American vessels and impressing American seamen, nor should the ministry apologize for the *Chesapeake* affair. Excerpts from this editorial were reprinted in the *National Intelligencer* on 23 Apr. 1811.

7. JM had probably just read John Quincy Adams's December 1810 dispatch from Russia. The American minister stated that it was the "first principle of the present Russian policy . . . to keep upon good terms with France. This disposition is certainly not on the part of France reciprocal." Since Napoleon's marriage in April 1810, France's policy toward Russia had been increasingly hostile, to the point of demanding from the latter "measures ruinous to her own interests and derogatory to her independence." Russia had rejected the demands, but Adams believed it was "not probable that France will be satisfied with this," and he predicted that "relations between the two countries are approaching to a crisis on a point highly interesting to us." From every assurance he had received, Adams was certain "that the determination to

resist to the last has been deliberately taken here" (Adams to Robert Smith, 15/27 Dec. 1810, Ford, *Writings of J. Q. Adams*, 3:553–55).

From John Quincy Adams

Private   *April 19* [1811]

Since I had the honor of writing you last on the 8th February I have been informed that a commission has been sent to Count Pahlen for a temporary mission to the court of Brazil and that an optional authority is given him to go there immediately if he thinks proper. He is not however recalled from his mission to the United States and during his absence he is to leave Mr. Politico as chargé des affaires.[1]

The minister plenipotentiary from the Court of Brezil whose destination to this place was announced last October has not yet arrived but is expected as soon as the navigation will be free. In the mean time the Treaty between the two Governments rests suspended. I informed the Secretary of State of the arrangement which was concluded about this time last year and which was to continue in force untill the 11th: of March last.[2] The continuance of this arrangement for another year was agreed upon by Count Romanzoff with the Portugueze Chargé des Affairs—but is left unfinished owing to some recent incidents, untill the arrival of the Minister.[3]

These incidents probably arose from the situation of the relations between Russia and France which threaten an immediate war. The preparations for this event on the part of Russia have been great and incessant during the whole winter. I have not however until very recently expected that it would commence this spring nor do I yet consider it as inevitable but as at least extremely probable. There are per-haps secret negotiations already in train with England and the Spanish Cortes government have offered assistance in money to Russia to maintain the war. Should it break out Count Romanzoff will[4] *retire from the administration. The war will effect a great commercial revolution in the north of Europe. Of its prob-able issue it would not become me now to speak. At this moment Russia is undoubt-edly of the two parties the best prepared but the power of France and the manner in which the French emperor always makes war lead to the expectation that his movements will be rapid and his efforts powerful. The war may not be long.*

RC (DLC: John Quincy Adams Letters and Papers); letterbook copy (MHi: Adams Family Papers). RC unsigned. Docketed by JM, "April 19. 1811." Italicized passages are those en-coded by Adams and decoded here by the editors using a partial key (see Adams to JM, 7 Jan. 1811, n.). The coded passages were decoded by John Graham in a separate three-page tran-script, docketed by JM (DLC: John Quincy Adams Letters and Papers). Letterbook copy not encoded. Minor differences between the copies have not been noted.

1. Petr Ivanovich Poletika (1778–1849) was counselor of the Russian legation in Philadelphia, 1809–11. He later published a book on his experiences in the U.S. which was translated in Baltimore in 1826 as *A Sketch of the Internal Conditions of the United States and Their Political Relations with Europe. By a Russian* (see Bashkina et al., *The United States and Russia*, p. 1137; Nikolai N. Bolkhovitinov, *The Beginnings of Russian-American Relations, 1775–1815*, trans. Elana Levin [Cambridge, Mass., 1975], pp. 347–48).

2. See Adams to Robert Smith, 24 Mar. 1810 (Ford, *Writings of J. Q. Adams*, 3:407–10).

3. Russia was interested in developing direct trading links with the Latin American colonies of Portugal and Spain in order to alleviate the shortage of imports that had resulted from the adherence of Alexander I to the Continental System. Foreign minister Count Nikolai P. Rumiantsev had opened negotiations for this purpose in 1809 with the Portuguese chargé d'affaires, Rodrigo Navarro de Andrade (Russell H. Bartley, *Imperial Russia and the Struggle for Latin American Independence, 1808–1828* [Austin, Tex., 1978], pp. 42–49). Adams believed the issue was of interest to Americans since he suspected that the terms Rumiantsev negotiated with Portugal would set a precedent for the treaty of commerce that Russia was also seeking with the U.S. (see Adams to the secretary of state, 29 Apr. 1811, Ford, *Writings of J. Q. Adams*, 4:59–63).

4. Both John Graham's decoding and the letterbook copy have "immediately" here.

From Albert Gallatin

Sir   Treasury Department April 19th 1811

It appears doubtful whether the contemplated light house near Presquisile on Lake Erie can be erected under the act of cession of the State of Pennsylvania passed on 2d instt.[1] The act has an express provision that neither the jurisdiction or right of soil is ceded, but only the occupancy and use thereof for the purpose of erecting the light house.

The acts of Congress of March 2d 1795[2] & August 7th 1789[3] contemplate a cession of soil & jurisdiction in every case where a light house has been or may be fixed, and define the species of jurisdiction asked for by the United States. In point of fact, there is no instance within my Knowledge of the erection or support of a light house without having previously obtained such cession. No light house having heretofore been erected in the State of Pennsylvania, and the act of May 1. 1810[4] which authorises the erection of one at Presquisle having no special reference to that preliminary condition, it is possible that the Legislature of the State may not have attended to the general provisions above stated.

Under those circumstances, the question whether the erection of the light house shall immediate[ly] take place, or be suspended till the next session of Congress is respectfully submitted to the President. I have the honor to be with the highest respect Sir Your obedient Servant

Albert Gallatin

RC (DNA: RG 26, Early Light House Correspondence, Misc. Letters Received).

1. See Simon Snyder to JM, 12 Apr. 1811, and n, 1.
2. *U.S. Statutes at Large*, 1:426.
3. Ibid., 1:53–54.
4. Ibid., 2:611–12.

From John G. Jackson

MY DEAR SIR.   CLARKSBURG April 19th. 1811.

Your favor of the 12th. reached me on the 16th. The preceding day was that of our Election, on which the District turned & I am sorry to say the Federal Candidate obtained a majority of 102 votes—he is elected. Mr. McKinley never was here before & his coming ruined our hopes, as his manners &c are unpopular, & here the People vote for men more than principles. On the morning of the election I was taken up for the Assembly & voted in, which I truly regret as my old friend Prunty[1] was dropped, I can scarcely tell how it happened I was taken by surprise, yielding to the wishes of the People I forgot my condition & every thing that forbade my going to the Assembly. I was in hopes that the Office vacated by Mr. Nelson would have been tendered me And thereby I should have been extricated from the dilemma. Your letter disappoints that hope—it is all we have heard on the subject, & do not even conjecture who is sent from the land of Talents & illumination to enlighten us miserable backwoodsmen, who cannot furnish one Man to fill a local office amongst us. I care not who he is I will oppose his being confirmed by the Legislature, And if we are conquered—for in this at least we are united. We will make an effort to break the chains of servitude rivetted by the wise men of the East. Thank God they can not deprive me of popularity here and while my tongue & pen can urge any thing in the cause of our poor despised country, I will pourtray the condition we are reduced to: & risque every thing to vindicate our rights. Forgive me my friend for my warmth; it is monstrous injustice to reduce a district of 50,000 inhabitants abounding as all admit in eminent Lawyers: to the degradation of sending a Judge to us over our heads; of mediocre talents & totally ignorant of the great principles involved in our litigations: as much so, as to send a mere land Lawyer to plead Admiralty causes in the maritime districts. I write somewhat at hazard perhaps some one of our Lawyers is appointed; if so I acquiesce—we have several in whose judgment I can confide & I agree to the appointment of either. But if he is selected from abroad all I have written I persist in; and should it lead to an open rupture be it so, the Backwoodsmen are not in fault, they feel the wrongs heaped upon them & want only a rallying point to redress them.

The information you gave me concerning Merinos was satisfactory & I only forbore to write you because I would not presume to trouble you fur-

ther on that subject. I bid fair to succeed with my sheep beyond any calculation—upwards of 100 ewes have Lambs & the encrease of the old stock
is 33⅓ per cent—this autumn I shall procure a Merino Ram & enlarge the
stock several hundreds. Our Crops have a finer prospect than ever hitherto,
I am farming much more largely than heretofore having taken in five tene-
ments & discharged the tenants—rely on it your Eastern planters & farmers will find us entering your accustomed markets in competition with
you, & a new direction must be given to your industry. Were it not for
the vexation I indulge in concerning the neglect I complain of, you would
be pleased with the industry that surrounds me. I have four mills continually running & am building two others, beside mechanic shops, domestic
manufactures &c giving employment to a large number of persons. I am
vexed that I have a wish beyond it, but dame nature is to blame not I she
infused the fire &c &c & death alone can extinguish them. In whatever else
I may change my heart assures me I shall be stedfastly & unalterably your
friend. Dr. Sir your Mo Obt

J G JACKSON

RC (DLC). Docketed by JM.

1. John Prunty, a member of the Virginia state ratifying convention of 1788, represented
Harrison County in the Virginia General Assembly, 1785–90, 1798–1811, and 1814–15
(Swem and Williams, *Register*, p. 420).

From James Wilkinson

SIR   WASHINGTON April 20th. 1811
    The singular hardship of my situation, & the great Interests which I have
at Stake, will I flatter myself excuse this deviation from the regular course
of my communications to you, which considerations of delicacy towards
the Secretary of War imposes on me; for it would be as indecorous to
wound his feelings, as it would be unjust to myself, to leave you in the dark,
touching the result of the report of the Committee of the House of Representatives, appointed to examine into the causes of the mortality among
the Troops on the Mississippi;[1] with the professed object indeed to ascertain truths for the information of Government, but in Fact to criminate
me, which the whole Conduct of the two Committees & the Tenor of their
Reports make manifest.
    You have observed Sir that the proceedings of the Committee of 1809–
10 were published by order of the House;[2] and that the late Committee,
composed of the same chairman & several of the Members, true to their
purpose, after they had actually called for & examined my orderly Books,

& the testimony contained in the appendix to the 4th. Vol. of my Memoirs,[3] deemed it candid & wise to adopt the same Report, in the face of a Mass of Testimony which nought but the blindest prejudice could have resisted.

When the last Report was handed to the House, a motion was made to transmit the Documents to you which failed, because certain Members, friends to truth & Justice, had determined to call it up & stigmatise it; which the lateness of the Season & the pressure of more important business alone prevented; I hazard nothing sir in this observation, as a Majority of the Members of the House, personally acquited me of all blame in my Command on the Mis[sis]sippi, and with great frankness reprobated this report of the Committee.

But you will perceive under cover unquestionable testimony of this intention, in the Speech & Resolution of the Honble. Mr. Crawford of Pensylvania,[4] a Member of the Committee, which he committed to paper; and having made several fruitless attempts to command the attention of the House, He generously called on me after the adjournment, accompanied by Doctor Sage[5] & Mr. White Hill,[6] altho I had no acquaintance with Him, and furnished me his intended Speech & Resolution, with permission to publish them which I shall do: In the preliminary illustrations of the Testimony contained in the appendix, before referred to, which are nearly ready for the press. And in verification of these Facts, I take the Liberty to tresspass on your attention the original Letter of Doctr. Crawford on this Subject, which together with the Speech, I shall thank you to return after perusal.[7]

I trust Sir that in thus addressing you, I violate no essential Rule of propriety or expediency—if I do, I shall sincerely deplore it, and the best Apology I can offer in extenuation of the tresspass, will be the indulgence I have experienced on similar occasions from your Predecessors respectively; without pretending to your Confidence, I can say that I have endeavoured to deserve it; but I make strong claims to the Justice, of the Chief Magistrate of a Nation of Freemen, and am persuaded my expectations will not be disappointed.[8] With perfect respect, I have the Honor to be sir Your most Humble & obedient Servant

JA: WILKINSON

RC (DLC). Docketed by JM. For surviving enclosure, see n. 7.

1. *Report of the Committee Who Were Instructed . . . to Inquire into the Cause or Causes of the Great Mortality in That Detachment of the Army of the United States Ordered for the Defence of New Orleans* (Washington, 1810; Shaw and Shoemaker 21853) (printed in *ASP, Military Affairs,* 1:268–95). The report listed eight causes for the mortality of the troops, including the climate, the campsite, and the lack of adequate food and medical supplies, but the conclusion of the committee was that Wilkinson's decisions both to encamp and to detain the men at the Terre aux Boeufs site in 1809 were contrary to the orders he had received from the War Department. Because the report was not made to the House of Representatives until 27 Apr.

1810, it was too late for any action to be taken on it during the second session of the Eleventh Congress. Another House committee, again chaired by Thomas Newton, Jr., of Virginia, therefore reexamined the subject between 19 Dec. 1810 and 26 Feb. 1811, after which the chairman referred the House "to the opinion expressed in the report of last year, as unchanged by anything which has since appeared" (*Annals of Congress*, 11th Cong., 3d sess., 452, 1033).

2. See *Annals of Congress*, 11th Cong., 2d sess., 1997.

3. As Wilkinson indicated later in this letter to JM, the appendix to the fourth volume of his memoirs had not yet been published. According to an "advertisement" bearing the date 1 May 1811 that Wilkinson published in an 1811 edition of the second volume of his *Memoirs*, the contents of this appendix to "volume the fourth" provided "ample proofs to justify his command on the Mississippi in the year 1809, from whence he had been recalled under circumstances of disgrace, without a trial, or an opportunity to vindicate himself, although it was earnestly solicited, even before his recall" (see *Memoirs of General Wilkinson, Volume II* [Washington, 1811]; copy in DLC: Rare Book Division). A printed copy of the "Appendix to Volume the Fourth," followed by a postscript, is bound together with several other pieces of exculpatory material in a copy of the 1810 edition of the *Memoirs of General Wilkinson, Volume II* (DLC: Rare Book Division).

4. William Crawford (1760–1823), a graduate of the University of Edinburgh, resided near Gettysburg, Pennsylvania, and was a Republican member of the Pennsylvania delegation in the House of Representatives in the Eleventh through Fourteenth Congresses, 1809–17.

5. Ebenezer Sage (1755–1834) graduated from Yale College in 1778 and resided at Sag Harbor, New York. He was elected as a Republican to the Eleventh through Thirteenth Congresses, 1809–15.

6. Robert Whitehill (1738–1813) had a lengthy career in Pennsylvania state politics between 1776 and 1804 before he entered the House of Representatives in December 1805. He was reelected as a Republican to the Tenth through Thirteenth Congresses, 1807–13.

7. Crawford's "original Letter" to Wilkinson has not been found, but Wilkinson enclosed with it an address that Crawford had intended to deliver to the House of Representatives in his capacity as a member of the committee investigating the mortality of the troops at Terre aux Boeufs. Crawford dissented from the committee report, arguing that Wilkinson had not erred in his choice of the campsite outside New Orleans, that the diseases afflicting the troops there were endemic to the area and the climate in general rather than to the campsite in particular, and that the secretary of war's orders to remove the troops from Terre aux Boeufs caused greater mortality than the general's decision to encamp them there (ICHi: James Wilkinson Papers, vol. 3; 14 pp.).

8. After reviewing the findings of Newton's committee as well as the documentary evidence gathered by other committees sitting during the second and third sessions of the Eleventh Congress and charged with examining Wilkinson's dealings with Spain and his relationship with Aaron Burr, JM instructed the secretary of war on 1 June 1811 to inform Wilkinson that "the most full opportunity" to do justice to his honor and character "will be a reference of the whole to a military tribunal." The subsequent court-martial was held at Fredericktown, Maryland, between 4 Sept. and 25 Dec. 1811 (Eustis to Wilkinson, 1 June 1811 [DNA: RG 107, LSMA]).

§ From Charles Hall. *22 April 1811, Washington.* Encloses a printed copy of the treaty between Great Britain and Portugal "of which we were speaking this morning."[1] "This Copy contains the full Treaty, namely 34 Articles, which circumstance I mention because a spurious, or rather a mutilated, Copy was published in many papers containing only 19 Articles. . . . The 10th., 14th., 15th., 19th. & 28th. Articles deserve notice & shew that the Portuguese have been egregiously taken in."[2]

Also sends "a paper of Salt" made near Wilmington, North Carolina, "which is equal in quality to any Salt I have ever seen." Includes as well "a piece of Magnesia" which the seawater deposits in the salt vats; claims that this salt "must be more pure than Salt that is made from *boiling* because there is not any deposit, and this magnesia *is boiled up* with the Salt so made." The salt was made by a Mr. Garnier, who assured him that it "weighs over eighty pounds the Bushell, and that notwithstanding its good quality he cannot continue the competition with Foreign Salt unless a Duty is laid on that or a Bounty given to home made Salt."

RC (NN). 2 pp. Enclosure not found, but see n. 1.

1. Hall was evidently referring to the Treaty of Amity, Commerce, and Navigation between His Britannic Majesty and His Royal Highness the Prince Regent of Portugal, signed at Rio de Janeiro on 19 Feb. 1810 (see *Cobbett's Political Register*, 18 [1810]: 246–56, 318–20, 342–48).

2. Article 10 of the Anglo-Portuguese treaty granted British subjects trading in Portuguese dominions the privilege of naming special magistrates to act as judges conservator in tribunals to be established to hear all causes brought before them by such British subjects. Portuguese subjects trading in British dominions did not receive an equivalent concession. Article 14 stipulated that Great Britain and Portugal would not shelter criminals, traitors, and forgers in their respective dominions, particularly when the offenses involved desertion from the military and naval services of the two nations. Article 15 admitted all goods of British origin into Portuguese territories at a duty to be set at 15 percent of the prevailing local tariffs, the basis of which was to be "the sworn invoice cost of such goods." Article 19, by contrast, admitted Portuguese goods into British territories after payment of "the same duties that are paid on similar articles by the subjects of the most favored nation." Article 28 defined contraband and prohibited articles as those specified in "any former Treaties concluded by Great Britain or by Portugal with other powers" (ibid., 18 [1810]: 252, 255, 256, 320, 345–46).

From David Bailie Warden

SIR,   WASHINGTON, 23 April 1811.

My delicate situation renders it an incumbent duty to reply to all the insinuations made against me, which you are pleased to notice, otherwise, I would not dare to renew a subject, which has already, to my regret, occupied you too much.

It has been stated to you, Sir, that ten guineas will cover all expences in the prosecution, and defence of an american Prize case, before the Prize Court, at Paris.[1] It is surprizing, that any person, who is the least acquainted with this business, and who values truth, would venture to make this assertion. In some cases, the expences of printing memoirs alone will amount to that sum; and in all, not less is necessary for registering the papers at the Council of Prizes, copying extracts for a defence, and translating documents, to be filed, which, by a rule of the court, must be executed by one of its sworn translators. I never knew that any lawyer at Paris, took less than thirty Louis, for the defence of a Prize-case, and I have heard of some who received from one to two hundred as a recompense. It is an incontestible fact, that fifty, or sixty Louis is the sum usually paid. If the person, who levelled this report against me, ever resided at Paris, he must have known that the lawyers of that City do not give their labors for nothing. It will be sufficient to mention, that Mr. Russel, *chargé d'affaire*, at Paris, several months before his appointment, requested me to accompany him to his lawyer, to serve as interpreter, concerning a Prize case, of which he engaged him to prepare the defence, and he refused to take less than fifty Louis, for his labors and expences, altho' he would not consent to print his memoir in the case. Captain Prendergast, of the Ship Anne of new york, paid fifty Louis for the defence of that vessel—a fact well known to Mr. Mumford, Member of Congress.[2] Were it not tedious, I could adduce many other similar proofs. I had the honor of stating, in a former letter, that Mr. Pichon found that thirty Louis was too small a sum for the defence of a Prize Case; and he insisted on my demanding more from the Captains, or Agents, who had given me powers to superintend their business. This I refused, as it was contrary to our agreement, unless the property were restored. In that event, some recompence was promised him (as is stated on his receipts) which was to be left to the discretion of the Captain, or Agent. I have his letters on this subject. In a case of compromise, which gave him much trouble, he demanded, and received one hundred Louis, but with this I had nothing to do. But how can it be believed, that any American would offer more for the defence of his claim than was usual or just. The more rigid his economy was, the better was his prospect of recompence from the owners of the vessel and cargo. If there were blame, it must attach to the Agents, or to the lawyers, and not to me. The charge is the more unjust (I might with propriety say absurd) as I believe that I am the only Consul, or Commercial Agent, who, in all cases, had refused to accept a Commission. It is known to many persons, now in this Country, whom I could name, how much this subject was discussed, and how well it was understood. The annexed copy of a certificate, from those who employed me in a general, and special manner, in defence of their claims; many of whom visited my Bureau almost daily, who were acquainted with every circumstance concerning every case, and who knew me long and well, will be my defence against malicious insinuations, or false misrepresentations. It cannot be supposed, that it originated from political partiality, for two thirds of the subscribers are federalists, all are men of information and of business, of character and respectability. They were pleased with my labors—that I asked no commission, and that I saved them twenty, or thirty Louis in the prosecution of each case. Let my enemy, if he can, exhibit proofs of my having acted improperly, and, I will furnish a prompt, and I trust, a satisfactory reply. I do not find that I am arraigned by any Individual, who committed his business to my care—*nihil veri dicere, nihil falsi omittere*,³ seems to be the motto of the secret enemy who seeks my ruin. I feel secure in point of character. I am not at his mercy: I will meet him in any shape he pleases; I fear him not.

I thought it necessary to leave Mr. Pichon's certificates, and those of other lawyers, for the sums paid them for defending prize causes, with my agent, at Paris; but, I pledge myself, if required, to deliver them to Mr. Barlow, the American Minister, or to transmit them to the President, or to the Secretary of State of the United States. When I consider my zeal and industry in the prosecution of Prize Causes, my devotion to it during nine, or ten hours per day; the advantages which Americans enjoyed from the facility and privileges granted me by the Attorney General of that Court, and the numerous letters and memoirs which I wrote, I feel deeply injured by any imputation of blame. In some instances I may have been deceived by artful, and corrupt men: I may have erred from ignorance, or from mistake, but never from intention. I have ever felt an abhorrence of every thing mean, illegal, and dishonorable, & I could not willingly betray the trust reposed in me. If I could, for a bribe, have bartered my honesty, and the dignity of my office, there was a time, and opportunity, when I was supposed to have influence as the Secretary of the Minister—when I filled up the Bills, under the Louisiana Convention, and delivered them to the owners, who were ready to make sacrifices in the form of a Commission. Here, there was something worth buying if I had been mean enough to sell myself. The sanction which my conduct received by my appointment, induces me to believe that it is unnecessary to say more concerning the insinuation with regard to the vessel expedited by captain Haley. In a former communication it has, I think, been satisfactorily refuted. To corroborate my statement, I engage to procure certificates after my arrival at Paris. No article could have been shipped without Haleys' permission, and I challenge him, or any other Individual to prove any collusion on my part, or that I had any interest in the said vessel, or articles intended for embarkation. More than a year elapsed from the time of her departure from France till the annulment of my Consular powers, during which, my conduct was never questioned in relation to this affair, which circumstance, of itself, is a proof of my innocence, for all the particulars of the case were publickly known. If any charge could have been brought against me, the blackest art would not have been practised, and a purse offered, to induce a very promising young man, whom I occasionally employed in my bureau, and whose mother and sister whom he loves, are reduced from affluence to indigence, to perjure himself for the purpose of falsely criminating me. The youth spurned the offer, and preserved his Virtue. This I can prove. The circumstance occurred when I was no longer Consul.

It is not, Sir, to revive painful recollections, or to indulge invidious sentiments, or expressions that I beg leave to make the following observations. If General Armstrong had believed, or even suspected, that I had acted improperly as a man, or as a public officer, would he, after declaring that he had instructions to give the Consulship to mr. Russel, have employed much friendly argument to induce me to accept of the Consulship, of Nantes, or of Havre? Would he, thro Captain Haley, have offered me that of Bordeaux? and after my refusal of all these places, believing me unworthy of public trust, would he have invited me to accompany him home, and offered me his influence to procure from the Government a respectable employment in South America? After Mr. Russel refused to accept my place, do not his letters shew the condition, on which he proposed to continue me in it; and if these do not afford sufficient proof, mr. Devereux, of Baltimore, whom he employed as a mediator, and other individuals to whom I can appeal, will give testimony to this fact. If, in his opinion, I was unworthy of my public situation, of what use to him could have been the certificate, or declaration which he so artfully, and eagerly demanded? for if my conduct, or principles were bad, my written opinion of him would have been of no value? His open note to me, delivered by Mr. McCrae, of which I annex a copy, does not intimate any charge against me: as it states, for some reason, that the appointment was provisional, I adjoin a copy of another Note.

General La Fayette, who was grieved at my fate, wrote to him, at Bordeaux, that the object of my sudden departure for the United States was for the purpose of seeking employment from the government—after his return to this country, he knew that my friends were actively occupied to have me reappointed as Consul at Paris. He knew that for this purpose only I remained at Washington. He declared to Mr. Bullus, Navy Agent, at new york, to Mr. Duane, Mr. Irvine, and Mr Holmes, his relation, and to others, that he would not oppose me in any appointment which I had influence to procure, that he had no charges against me except that I "wanted nerve," of which I may have occasion to give an explanation. Mr. Duane, to whom I wrote on this subject, thus replies, in his letter of the 6th Instant.

"I never had any conversation with General Armstrong but in the presence of several other persons; once at a dinner given by Mr. Leiper, to many influential men here; and three, or four other interviews, at which there were no less than from three, to twelve persons: on those occasions our discourse concerning you was sometimes general, and sometimes apart to me, and, I declare, that I never heard him say a word to your prejudice, further than that you 'wanted nerve,' by which I understood, that your sensibility was constitutional, and that you were more liable to be affected by the collisions of the world, than political men usually are, or than they ought to be for their own comfort—a sentiment which I never thought disparaging to you; but, on the contrary, to be as likely to be the effect of a refined sense of honor, as of any other cause."

Mr Irvine, Editor of the Whig, at Baltimore, in his letter of the 14th Inst., in reply to mine on this subject, contains the following statement "In speaking of your dispute with General Armstrong, I mentioned to him some conversation I held with you also, that Mr. Duane informed me of his (A's) having assured him (Duane) that he had nothing to alledge against you, except a *want* of *nerve;* and he assured me from Washington that he neither had said, or should profer ought against you to balk your appointment."

I was recommended, in the warmest manner, to certain Senators by some of Genl. Armstrongs' acquaintances. If he had charges, or accusations against me, why did he not communicate them to these Gentlemen, or to the government? My public, and private conduct was exposed to public, and private scrutiny during Six months before my appointment. I presented letters of recommendation to Senators from some of the first men in almost every state in this Country. Members of the Philosophical, and literary Societies, of different Cities, employed an active interest in my favor.[4] The letters, which I brought to this Country, from Baron Humboldt, Bishop Gregoire,[5] Michaux,[6] Delile,[7] and twenty other gentlemen, friends to the United States, and distinguished by their scientific labors, and moral character, prove my standing at Paris. Need I mention, Sir, your nomination of me to the Senate, and the unanimous vote of that body in my favor, which was honorably noticed in newspapers of every description, all which are signal proofs of the confidence placed in my character—I might add another, the management of claims, at Paris, to an immence amount for which I have lately received instructions & procurations. Under such circumstances, I trust, Sir, that you will relieve me from suspence, and painful anxiety. Having full confidence in your justice, I know that you will not suffer my fortunes to be injured by vague insinuations which were perhaps intended, after my departure, to operate more against the government than against me. A sense of duty induced me to institute a prosecution for a libel which stated, that I was employed in vending french Licences. The Editors of the Evening Post, of new york, in which it appeared, refused to reveal the name of the author of this Calumny, but they have proclaimed my innocence, by publishing, in the same paper, of the 10th Inst, that the two charges of the libel, furnished by my secret enemy, were equally false. If General Armstrong had charges against me, it is to be presumed that he would have forwarded them when he remonstrated against my appointment.

My Counsellors and friends, at New york, write to me thus on this subject—"your fate depends on the government, and when we know the justice and Magnanimity which preside in that quarter, we are convinced, that if it be thought necessary, General Armstrong will be called upon to give proof of his accusations: if they be frivolous, of which we have no doubt, you will be forwarded on your mission without further delay. If he has insinuated charges, which are not substantiated, he is not entitled to credit."

It may not be improper, Sir, to seize this occasion to observe, that the expression, in my last letter to General armstrong, before he annulled my powers, which has attracted particular notice, was dictated with candor, & sensibility. I had often felt neglected, & wronged. Yet I declared, *"that unless he became my enemy, I could not be his"* that I was willing to forget the past, and that my friends, who interceded with him, for my continuance in office, would not be unmindful of the favor. I wrote what I felt at the moment—the plain and undisguised truth. I shunned artifice, which I might have employed, for I had then received, by the Hornet, communications from officers of the Government, and letters from Mr. Bullus, Dr Mitchill, and others assuring me, that I would be continued in office. Mr. Duane, gave the same information, in a letter, which was suppressed. Lieutenant Millar bearer of dispatches by the Hornet was addressed to me, in official capacity, from a supposition, that General Armstrong had left Paris. All this I concealed from a desire of shewing, what I more than once expressed, that he might exercise the same authority over me, as over other Consuls, and continue, or suspend my Consular functions. I have thus, Sir, given a statement of particular facts which will enable you to form a judgement concerning my conduct in those affairs, in which it has been secretly attacked. The injury to my character and fortunes which the insinuations against me were intended to operate, and the poignant feelings which they have naturally roused, will, I trust, serve as an apology for the length of this communication, and the self applause it contains, which, coming from me, in conjunction with almost any other subject, would be egotism itself. My plea is that of necessity. I am, Sir, with profound respect, your most obedient and very humble Servant

DAVID BAILIE WARDEN

RC and enclosures (DLC); partial letterbook copy (MdHi: Warden Papers). Minor differences between the copies have not been noted. Enclosures (3 pp.; in Warden's hand; docketed by JM) are copies of a testimonial on Warden's behalf signed by various American merchants and ships' captains and supercargoes at Paris, 10 Jan. 1810, with a covering letter from Richard Prendergast; a 9 Jan. 1810 testimonial from Edward Learned, supercargo of the *Harmony;* and a letter from John Armstrong, 13 Sept. 1810, notifying Warden that "Alexander McRae is appointed to the office provisionally held by you," to which Warden appended Armstrong's 24 Aug. 1808 letter informing him that "the President of the United States has been pleased to appoint you Consul and agent of Prize Causes, in the room of Mr. F. Skipwith." Also filed among Madison's papers (DLC) is another copy of the testimonials, with a copy of Jefferson to Warden, 11 Jan. 1811, written on the verso.

1. See Armstrong to JM, 3 Mar. 1811.
2. Gurdon Mumford (1764–1831) had served as Benjamin Franklin's secretary in Paris. After settling in New York, he was elected to the House of Representatives in the Ninth through Eleventh Congresses, 1805–11. As a presidential elector in 1812 he voted for DeWitt Clinton and Jared Ingersoll.
3. "Say nothing true and omit nothing false."
4. Partial letterbook copy ends here.
5. Henri Grégoire (1750–1831) had a lengthy ecclesiastical and political career during the French Revolutionary and Napoleonic eras. A member of the Convention of 1792–95 and a bishop in the Constitutional Church, the abbé Grégoire opposed Napoleon's concordat with Rome and his establishment of the empire. He also advocated the abolition of slavery (*Biographie universelle* [1843–65 ed.], 17:458–71).
6. François-André Michaux (1770–1855) was a botanist best known for his studies of American flora and his travel accounts of Kentucky and Ohio. JM may also have known of his involvement in the early 1790s in French-sponsored filibustering schemes against Spanish Louisiana (ibid., 28:221–22; *PJM*, 15:138 n. 2).
7. Warden was probably referring to Jacques Delille (1738–1813), professor of Latin poetry at the Collège de France (J. Balteau et al., eds., *Dictionnaire de biographie française* [17 vols. to date; Paris, 1933–], 10:836–37).

From Thomas Jefferson

DEAR SIR   MONTICELLO Apr. 24. 11.

Yours of the 19th. is recieved. I have carefully examined my letter files from July 1808. to this day, & find among them no such Anonymous letter as you mention. Indeed the strong impression on my memory is that I never recieved an Anonymous letter from England, or from any other country than our own.

Certain newspapers are taking a turn which gives me uneasiness. Before I was aware of it, I was led to an interference, which tho' from just motives, I should not, at a later moment, have shaped exactly as I did. I cannot therefore repress the desire to communicate it fully to you. On the 24th. of March I recieved a friendly letter from Duane, informing me of the distress into which he had been thrown by his former friends, Lieper & Clay, withdrawing their endorsements for him at the banks; the latter expressly for his attacks on John Randolph, the former without assigning any particular cause: & he concluded by asking whether, in Virginia, where he had been flattered by the support of his paper, 80. gentlemen could not be found, who would advance him their hundred Dollars apiece, to be repaid at short periods. I immediately engaged mr. Peter Carr here, & mr. Wirt in Richmond to set the experiment afoot, & one of these engaged a friend in Baltimore to do the same. But I mentioned to these gentlemen that, to apprise Duane of the grounds on which we interested ourselves for him, to wit, his past services to the cause of republicanism, & that he might not mistake it as an approbation of his late attacks on mr. Gallatin, of which we unequivocally disapproved, I would write him a letter. I accordingly wrote him the one now inclosed,[1] which I previously communicated to messrs. Carr & Wirt. It did not leave this till the 1st. of April. The thing was going on hopefully enough, when his papers of the 4th. & 8th. arrived here,[2] the latter written probably after he had recieved my letter. The effect at Baltimore I have not learned. But every person who had offered, here or at Richmond to join in aiding him, immediately withdrew, considering him as unequivocally joining the banners of the opposition, federal or factious. I have to give an account of this to Duane, but am waiting, in expectation of an answer to mine of March 26. In that I shall make one effort more to reclaim him from the dominion of his passions, but I expect it will be the last, and as unavailing as the former.

I could not be satisfied until I informed you of this transaction, and must even request you to communicate it to mr. Gallatin: for altho the just tribute rendered him in the letter was certainly never meant to meet his eye, yet as it is there, among other things, it must go to him. Ritchie has been under hesitation. His paper of the 16th. decides his course as to yourself.[3] And I propose to set him to rights, as to mr. Gallatin, through a letter to Wirt in which I shall expose the falsehood or futility of the facts they have harped upon. All this however is confidential to yourself & mr. Gallatin; because, while I wish to do justice to truth, I wish also to avoid newspaper observation.

With respect to the opposition threatened, altho it may give some pain, no injury of consequence is to be apprehended. Duane flying off from the government, may, for a little while, throw confusion into our ranks, as John Randolph did. But, after a moment of time to reflect & rally, & to see where he is, we shall stand our ground with firmness. A few malcontents will follow him, as they did John Randolph, & perhaps he may carry off some well meaning Anti-Snyderites of Pensylvania. The federalists will sing Hosannas, & the world will thus know of a truth what they are. This new minority will perhaps bring forward their new favorite, who seems already to have betrayed symptoms of consent.[4] They will blast him in the bud, which will be no misfortune. They will sound the tocsin against the antient dominion, and anti-dominionism may become their rallying point. And it is better that all this should happen two, than six years hence.

Disregarding all this, I am sure you will pursue steadily your own wise plans, that peace, with the great belligerents at least, will be preserved, until it becomes more losing than war, & that the total extinction of the national debt, & liberation of our revenues, for defence in war, and improvement in peace, will seal your retirement with the blessings of your country. For all this, & for your health & happiness I pray to god fervently.

Tн: Jefferson

P. S. Be so good as to return the inclosed as I have no other copy.

RC (DLC: Rives Collection, Madison Papers); FC (DLC: Jefferson Papers). For enclosure, see n. 1.

1. Jefferson enclosed a copy of his 28 Mar. 1811 letter to Duane (DLC: Jefferson Papers; printed in Ford, *Writings of Jefferson*, 9:310–14), written in response to Duane's 15 Mar. 1811 to him (DLC: Jefferson Papers). While indicating he did not doubt that Duane's attacks on Gallatin were grounded in the sincerity of his convictions, the former president defended the treasury secretary as a man of "pure integrity, and as zealously devoted to the liberties and interests of our country as it's most affectionate native citizen." Jefferson also discussed the possibilities, which, he stressed, were limited, of Duane's obtaining financial support for his newspaper from Virginia Republicans. He concluded by warning the editor of the dangers of his carrying his opposition to JM to extremes. "Leave the President free to chuse his own coadjutors, to pursue his own measures, & support him & them, even if we think we are wiser than they are, honester than they are, or possessing more enlarged information of the state of things. If we move in mass, be it ever so circuitously, we shall attain our object: but if we break into squads, every one pursuing the path he thinks most direct, we become an easy conquest to those who can now barely hold us in check."

2. The 4 Apr. 1811 issue of the Philadelphia *Aurora General Advertiser* reprinted from the Washington *Spirit of 'Seventy-Six* an ironic defense of Gallatin against the various charges of corruption, improper influence, and treason that Duane had made against him. Duane published the defense partly to point out that the *Spirit of 'Seventy-Six* (and by implication Gallatin as well) was under the influence of John Randolph of Roanoke, and partly because he regarded the irony of the defense as the equivalent of "a pretty *confession*" of Gallatin's guilt. In the issue of 8 Apr. 1811 Duane editorialized on the subject of "The Next President," claiming that Gallatin had usurped JM's functions and warning JM that if he expected to retain the presidency, he would have to arouse himself and take personal responsibility for the direction of public policy. Following the editorial Duane printed a letter from a "gentleman of high standing in New York" to his friend in Philadelphia. The letter declared that Gallatin had manipulated JM into a position of hostility toward the Clinton and Smith families, particularly after Vice President George Clinton had used his casting vote in the U.S. Senate to defeat the recharter of the Bank of the United States, and that Gallatin was now making an alliance with the Burrite faction in New York in order to seek the presidency for himself.

3. On the subject of the recent cabinet disputes, the Richmond *Enquirer* of 16 Apr. 1811 announced that Robert Smith ought to have been neither appointed secretary of state nor retained in that office and that JM, although he had made errors in some respects, was "guilty of no dereliction from republican *principles*." The same issue also contained a long editorial in support of the stand taken by JM in his negotiations with France and Great Britain. If France had repealed its edicts against neutral shipping and if Great Britain failed to do likewise, the editorial advised, the president should "*call congress* together and put it in their power to protect the rights of the nation."

4. Jefferson was referring to John Armstrong, and he was by no means alone in his suspicion that Armstrong might head an antiadministration party. Littleton Waller Tazewell issued a similar warning to Monroe in the belief that "at the head of this party you may expect to see General Armstrong. It will be supported by the Clintons, and a strong Republican phalanx in

New-York; by Leib Duane & Co. in Pennsylvania; and by the Smiths of Maryland. Its great object being to obtain the reins of government, and the means of achieving this end being derivable from the North and East only, you will of course expect that the motto of the party will be 'Free Trade' " (Tazewell to Monroe, 10 May 1811 [DLC: Monroe Papers]).

From Robert Brent

Sir   City of Washington April 25th 1811

I have ever been and am unwilling to trouble you in relation to any matters appertaining to my office, as paymaster, and the harmony of Intercourse that subsists between the head of the department, to which I belong, and myself has indeed rendered a recourse of this sort altogether unnecessary but on the present occasion, I trust that it will not be deem'd improper or indelicate by yourself or the Secretary of War that I should address myself immedeately to you.

I am desirous of having the liberty of depositing the public funds, which are placed in my hands, in the Bank of Washington, where they can be applied to the public purposes as conveniently and safely as in the Bank of Columbia in which last Bank I am advised that it is in contemplation of ordering them to be placed to the exclusion of the Bank of Washington and it is with a view to obtain this indulgence that I take the liberty of troubling you with this letter. I have the honor to be with sentiments of great respect Sir Your Obt Servnt

                                                    Robert Brent

RC (DLC). Docketed by JM.

From James Mease

Sir   Philadelphia April 25th. 1811.

I have not heard until to day that Mr Charles Swift late of this City, but now resident in Buck's County, is an applicant for the office of Commissioner of loans. Whoever has recommended him, will no doubt Say all that they think right with respect to his merits, political Services to the Country, and general pretensions to the office. I hope a few traits in his history, will not be deemed impertinent on my part. I shall Say no thing but what is well known.

Mr. Swift is the son of the late Mr J. Swift,[1] formerly a Merchant in this City; At the time that others were declining business, lending their money

287

to the U: States, and entering the army, Mr Swift retired to his estate in Buck's County, where he resided until his death about the year 1798. He was an avowed tory, and as Such was secluded from Society, in the patriotic district in which he lived. Charles remained with his father and Studied law. After the peace, he Settled as a lawyer in Philadelphia, but never appeared at the bar, except in one Cause, and that he lost, owing to want of talent. To oblige Mr Dallas, who had been extremely instrumental in procuring the election of Mr McKean, the latter appointed Mr Swift, register of Wills; Last year he had a stroke of apoplexy; He has never been conversant with Accounts, and if appointed must do his duty by means of another. I will venture to Say, that Mr Swift, has never written, or spoken one word in favour of republican or American principles in his life; influence in favour of them he could not exert, for he has never had the least of any kind in Society, and if he had, his proverbial indolence would have prevented him, even supposing that he was favourable to the Cause. Every one whose opinion I have heard, have expressed their astonishment at the presumption of the application, on his part, or in his favour. What talents he possesses are altogether Convivial.

I had determined to keep the application in favour of my father from him, or the public until the successor of Mr Moylan had been appointed. But one of the Gentlemen, to whom I did not mention my wishes on the subject, informed his friends of my application to him for his Certificate, and thus the affair became public. It has been highly gratifying to me, to find the Universal interest expressed with respect to the success of my father, by the few revolutionary characters remaining among us, and by numerous citizens of the first standing in Society. It is on such occasions that the advantages of a life of uniform integrity, and honorable political Career are seen and felt. With the highest respect—I remain your obd Servt

JAMES MEASE[2]

RC (DLC). Docketed by JM.

1. John Swift (b. 1720) was raised and educated in England, but after 1748 he played a prominent role in civic and social affairs in Philadelphia. He was instrumental in launching the annual balls known as the "Philadelphia Assemblies," and from 1762 to 1772 he was Crown collector for the port of Philadelphia. He also served as a Common Council member in the city, 1757–64. His son, Charles Swift (ca. 1755–1811), was admitted to the Philadelphia bar in 1779 and was one of the founders of the Pennsylvania Academy of the Fine Arts in 1805 (*Pa. Magazine of History and Biography*, 30 [1906]: 133–50; Van Horne, *Papers of Latrobe*, 2:15 n.).

2. James Mease (1771–1846) studied medicine under Benjamin Rush and graduated from the University of Pennsylvania in 1792. He was the author of a variety of works on agriculture, geology, and medicine and also of *The Picture of Philadelphia* (Philadelphia, 1811; Shaw and Shoemaker 23363) (Butterfield, *Letters of Benjamin Rush*, 2:652 n. 8).

§ From an Unidentified Correspondent. *25 April 1811*. "The Subject of this letter has given me much pain. It induces me to trespass on You for the 3d & last time. . . . No Benefit can result to me by this act; On the contrary I might draw upon myself, an host of Enemies, with the Secretary of War at their head. . . . The present letter is on the existing state of our Military Establishment & the arms & implements of War. . . . In adverting to our actual situation, the picture is gloomy."

Has some knowledge of the army and its officers, having lived two and a half years in a garrison where men did not know how to handle cannon and where the guns rusted. At Fort St. Charles at New Orleans the guns were only fired for salutes. "At fort St. Philip below New Orleans, . . . a work, now called complete, could not hold out 4 hours against six 20 Gun Ships, & a battery of 5 or 6 Eight Inch Howitzers, or Mortars, on the opposite side of the Missisippi." Fort Nelson in Norfolk harbor "is unworthy of the name of a fort." The works could be easily overrun, the guns have not been scaled in years, and the carriages are rotting. The guns at Fort Norfolk are better but also deteriorating. "There is said to be not even a Cannon Wad at either fort. . . . I would pledge my life that two Brittish 30-Gun Ships in open day would pass in silence both Forts." The caliber of the cannon varies greatly from twelve to thirty-two pounds. It is impossible to find shot to fit such a range; therefore accuracy in firing cannot be depended upon.

Army muskets are bad, especially the locks. Rifles are often damaged and the sights inaccurate, even those made at "the Harpers Ferry Manufacture, reputed the best in the Army." Has no knowledge of the pistols and sabers. Describes inspection methods for cannon and shot and refers JM to Toussard's *Artillery*,[1] volume 2, pages 551 through 566, for "the very critical inspections & proofs which cannon undergo in other Countries," and to volume 1, pages 352 through 356, for the "requisites & proofs of Shot." Other nations understand the importance of these matters. If the U.S. were at war with Great Britain and campaigning in Canada, and even if it were able to drive the enemy into its strongholds, many of the fieldpieces, muskets, and rifles would be unfit for further use. "We must either drag after us a large Quantity of spare arms at a great expence & inconvenience or numbers would be unarmed." If Great Britain were besieged in Quebec, for instance, heavy guns would be needed to batter the walls and to control the river. Quebec could not be taken, but Great Britain could raise the siege and drive the U.S. from Canada at immense cost and bloodshed, as was the case in 1777. Advocates therefore the thorough inspection of every implement of war, stressing that "in War, the best materials altho' at the most exorbitant prices are infinitely the Cheapest."

Deplores the want of a proper system and the low state of the "Science of Artillery." "But What can be expected when such men as B—— F—— McR—— S—— &c[2] are at the Head of that important branch of War. Not a solitary ray of *Military* Science ever illumined their Minds. Nor have they genius or Industry to become in their Stations even useful officers." Also criticizes the "Pitiful System of Artillery in the work laid before the Senate last winter."[3] His personal acquaintance with the officers in question, and their ignorance of a proper system, prompt him to make these observations. "Uniformity is the basis of War. It is also the Strictest Œconomy." Such a system was introduced in the French artillery by General Gribeauval under Louis XV which cost "immense difficulty"; however, "this System has triumphed over Europe." Describes at length Napoleon's use of artillery, especially in his Italian campaigns.

Offers eight regulations pertaining to ordnance that should "be framed by the Government," including: (1) designate the caliber for all fieldpieces; (2) establish specifications for their quality and construction; (3) establish specifications for quality and construction of gun carriages; (4) establish a "Standard Proof for all the Rifle musqet & Cannon Powder, according to which all cartridges shall be made"; (5) specify the dimensions for cannonballs and shells; (6) lay down the forms and dimensions for all caissons, ammunition wagons, and boxes; (7) determine the weight and length of all musket, rifle, and pistol barrels and establish the "qualities & proofs of all swords & other arms received into service"; and (8) organize an inspection system for all army equipment. Concedes this would require a general or inspector general of artillery of "great Talents, Industry & devotion to the Service," but such a man would save much money and preserve lives and even the honor of the country.

Begins a discussion of the army. The only regulations respecting a discipline were adopted in 1779 from Baron von Steuben's treatise, "a trifling & unworthy abridgement of the Prussian System which has lately sunk under more recent improvements." And Steuben dealt only with infantry, neglecting the artillery, cavalry, and riflemen, "such potent instruments in Modern War." Points out that French "conscripts are picked for these Corps before, draughted into the Infantry regiments." Makes several observations about the requirements of an army. First, it needs a "proper Organization & System of discipline & manœuvre" and a better staff system. "What is there called Staff is unworthy of the name." This is a fundamental organizational flaw, rooted in the defects of the laws which themselves must be corrected. Secondly, the army is dispersed over "an immense extent of Country in numerous detachments"; thus there are as many systems as there are detachments. If each detachment adhered to Steuben's system there would at least be "uniformity in ignorance" and there "would be no bad Habits to unlearn." Dispersal of the army also ensures that officers of inferior rank, captains and lieutenants, spend too many years in command at separate posts and "soon forget what they owe to their Superiors or Inferiors: They assume a certain license; become remiss in their duties & often degenerate into a State of Petty Tyranny." Thirdly, superior officers are "generally ignorant & conceited." Some have held office for a number of years; "others have seen a little Service, having held subordinate Stations in the Revolution"; and others have been elevated by "the blind Caprice of Fortune." The first two classes of officers believe there is no need for improvement and "are wise from absolute ignorance; . . . prejudice or want of talent." The third class is influenced by the example of the first two or is "restrained by their mean Jealousy," but from different causes they all reach "the same level of ignorance." Concedes, however, that some officers have the promise "to become ornaments to their profession & Country" and that many in the subordinate grades have the potential to become "highly useful." "But these want example . . . & a certain direction from their Superiors." Could verify these observations on the basis of his personal experience with those who composed the army at New Orleans in 1809, but "this is a subject too delicate for even an anonymous Guise & a certain conviction that this paper never meets eye, but yours." Begs JM to make inquiries about the military character of the officer corps; "make it of men who have some knowledge of *modern* military science" and who have "Honesty & Candor enough, to tell you the naked truth."

The need for "a *total* reform" of the military system is obvious. This is "the moment for Reform" and the moment to introduce a system based on the experience of modern warfare, "adapting it to our local situation & the Genius of our nation." Uniformity of system is essential for the efficiency of the military establishment. It is axiomatic that "all great changes should be effected in peace, & that they are absolutely dangerous in time of War." History proves that a superior enemy can only be combated by going beyond the state of improvement in the adversary for which he provides examples. Changes made in peace can also be tested by experiment and error would not prove fatal. Makes a few observations on reform, by which he means not a "partial or Pitiful Change such as was offered last winter under the name of an addition to the Baron de Steuben." Wants a "total & radical change," which will both perfect the armies of the nation and serve as a model to the militia. The secretary of war could make these changes, make a report, and the government would receive all the credit. And "certain ignorant men who now adhere to the army would be exposed & forced to quit it, ridding it of a load which Hangs heavy about its neck & which tends to suffocate every thing like improvement."

RC (NN). 31 pp. Signed "Republican." Docketed by JM.

1. Louis de Toussard, *The American Artillerist's Companion; or, Elements of Artillery* (2 vols.; Philadelphia, 1808; Shaw and Shoemaker 16337).

2. Henry Burbeck, Constant Freeman, William McRae, and Amos Stoddard were senior officers in the Regiment of Artillerists (Heitman, *Historical Register,* 1:51).

3. JM's correspondent was probably referring to "'A compendious exercise for garrison & field ordnance,' selected from the most approved authorities, by officers of experience," a paper sent to the Senate on 13 Dec. 1810 by the secretary of war in response to a Senate request for recommendations on how to improve the artillery and other branches of the state militias (see *ASP, Military Affairs,* 1:296).

From John G. Jackson

MY DEAR SIR.   CLARKSBURG April 26th 1811

Having commenced my sheep Shearing I cannot resist the desire to send you a sample of a singular fleece produced by a species of sheep purchased in this Country by me. The Animal is entirely covered with similar wool & has a curious appearance tho it differs from the ordinary sheep only in its wool. I presume it would be valuable in the manufacture of shawls &c. If you obtain any information of the use & value of such wool please advise me of it that I may encourage the growth of the sheep.

Your friends observe with concern the efforts of a faction, & of disappointed expectants to reduce you to their level. But they observe it undismayed as to its effects upon you, or upon the nation. The language of Parson Horne to Junius may with great truth be applied to them "You bite against a file cease Viper."[1] Such licentiousness & such collisions grow naturally out of our form of Government, their great corrective is public opinion, & the complete safeguard against them is conscious rectitude. You my dear Sir have both on your side. With affectionate regards to Mrs M yours truly

J G JACKSON

RC (DLC). Docketed by JM.

1. The quotation came not from one of the letters of the Reverend John Horne (later known as John Horne Tooke) to Junius but from William Draper's 27 Feb. 1769 letter to Junius. Draper had borrowed his reference from Aesop's fable 44 (John Cannon, ed., *The Letters of Junius* [Oxford, 1978], p. 50 and n. 1).

§ From William Barton. *26 April 1811, Lancaster, Pennsylvania.* "Having the honour of being known to You, and being altogether unacquainted with the Secretary of War (to whom, in ordinary cases, applications of this kind ought regularly to be made)," seeks a discharge for Jacob Hoff, who enlisted "about fifteen months since" in Captain Johnson's company of the Fifth U.S. Light Infantry Regiment. Hoff, who is a watchmaker and native of Lancaster, was induced to enlist by some "untoward circumstances in [his] affairs—altogether of a pecuniary nature." Before his enlistment he was a "reputable, intelligent and industrious man; and is said to be now wholly cured of a disposition to inebriety." Solicits JM's assistance at the request of Mrs. Hoff to obtain a discharge from the army for her husband, if possible before the regiment leaves Pittsburgh for New Orleans. Thanks JM for "the appointment you were pleased to confer on my son, Dr. Barton the younger, of a Surgeoncy in the Navy."

RC (DNA: RG 107, LRUS, B-1811). 4 pp. Docketed by a War Department clerk as received 30 Apr. 1811.

§ From Nathaniel Searle, Jr. *26 April 1811, Adjutant General's Office, Providence, Rhode Island.* Encloses a return of the state militia for 1810.

RC (PHi: Daniel Parker Papers). 1 p. Docketed by a War Department clerk as received 1 May 1811. Enclosure not found.

From Jesse Jones and Others

Sir April 27—1811

The Baptist Church on Neels Creek in Cumberland County in the State of North Carolina having Received intelligence Respecting the Affair of the

Baptist Church at Salem meeting house in the mississippi Territorry Considering the said affair as proceeding from Some of our Religious Connections and that the Same is not Consistent with the Spiritual Interest of Religion and that the tendency of Such a procedure if perpetuated would inevitably give to Religious Societies an undue weight and Corrupt influence in public affairs at large and diminish Religious enlargement impairing our Civil and Religious liberties and in fine Contaminate our national morals we therefore desire to assure you that we entertain a high Sense of and Confidence in Your Illustrious objection against the Bill[1] wherein we humbly conceive as eminent an Instance of patriotism have displayed as in any occurrence of the kind.
Signed by order and in behalf of Conference

JESSE JONES
[and five others]

The Baptist Church on Black Creek in Johnston County in the State of north Carolina having heard the above Read and approbated the Same. Signed by order and in behalf of Conference.
May the 4—1811

JAMES WHITENTON
[and five others]

RC (DLC). Postmarked Raleigh, North Carolina, 24 May 1811. Docketed by JM.

1. See JM to the House of Representatives, 28 Feb. 1811.

From Samuel Hanson of Samuel

29th April 1811.

S Hanson of Saml. respectfully begs leave of the President to acknowledge the receipt of a letter from the Secretary of the Navy, dated 27th. instant, "requesting him, by the direction of the President, to exhibit, specifically, the charges against the Accountant of the Navy, contained in his Memorial to the President, accompanied by documents to prove those charges."

He begs leave to refer the President to his *first* Memorial, in which he pledges himself "to prove the charges before any *impartial* Tribunal."[1] Such a tribunal he is sorry, yet, constrained, to say he should despair of finding in Mr. Hamilton. The evidences of Mr. Hamilton's prejudices against, and hostility to, S H of S, have been too many, and too *severe*, to afford any hope of an unbiassed decision. To omit others, of a more injurious kind, it is a fact that Mr. Hamilton has, himself, denied to S H. of Saml.

copies of official papers, to which he was as much entitled as to those refused by the Accountant—and that such refusal by the Accountant is one of the charges brought against him, on which the Tribunal will have to decide.

S H of S., therefore, respectfully submits to the consideration of the President the following tribunal:

Let the Accused, and the Accuser, each, appoint one Person. Let the two Persons, so appointed, agree upon a third, to be joined with them. Let them be required to give their opinions upon the truth or falsehood of the charges, and to transmit to the President those opinions, accompanied by the testimony which shall be adduced on both sides, subject, of course, to the ratification or rejection by the President.

The testimony to be offered by S H of S is chiefly documental—but some of it will be oral. Hence it will be necessary for the parties to attend the investigation, and mutually to confront each other.

Let the parties be furnished, if they shall require it, with copies of the decisions of the Referrees, together with transcripts of the testimony that may be adduced.

S H. of Saml. is induced to solicit this indulgence by the following consideration, viz. that, as the Tribunal, being *Human*, will, necessarily, be unendued with the attribute of Infallibility, the Accuser may be enabled, as far as the testimony may go, to counteract the imputation on his character involved in any decision by the tribunal, should such be given, stating any charges to be *"unfounded & malicious"*—as was the case in some of the decisions by the Court of Enquiry into the conduct of Captains Tingey and Cassin.

The President will excuse the Solicitude evinced on this head, when he is informed that his *character* is the only *External* comfort, under Heaven, of which S H of S has not been deprived by the malice & injustice of his Enemies.

He concludes by repeating to the President that, before a Tribunal, thus constituted, & thus instructed, he is ready to prove the charges preferred against the Accountant, and to prepare a specification of them.

S Hanson of Saml

RC (DLC). Docketed by JM.

1. See Hanson to JM, 16 Apr. 1811.

§ From Robert S. Marache. *29 April 1811, Philadelphia*. Has resided the last six years in Trinidad where he has a "respectable Commercial Establishment." As the commerce with the U.S. is "rapidly increasing," solicits position of commercial agent for the U.S. "should it appear to you expedient to have an agent there." Encloses a recommendation.

RC and enclosure (DNA: RG 59, LAR, 1809–17, filed under "Marache"). RC 1 p. Enclosure is a recommendation signed by William Jones and nine others (1 p.). RC and enclosure forwarded in a covering letter to James Monroe, 29 Apr. 1811 (ibid.).

§ From William Rogers. *30 April 1811, Harrisburg, Pennsylvania.* "Being in London in 1797 I entere'd into the Brittish Military Service in a Battalion of Infantry, and obtained some promotion therein during Ten Years Service. In 1807 I was induced to retire and come to my Friends at Philadelphia, and I now keep a Store in Harrisburgh, Pennsylvania." On the basis of his familiarity with military discipline "and the Regulations in Camps, Garrisons, and Quarters, also on board Ships," requests employment "in the Military Academy, Disciplining the Militia, or in the Military Establishment in any part." Wrote twice during the last session of Congress, giving Mr. Leib and Mr. Seybert as referees, but the letters were not answered, presumably because they were mistakenly addressed to Henry Dearborn.

RC (DNA: RG 94, Letters Received, filed under "Rogers"). 2 pp. Docketed as received 6 May 1811.

From William S. Dallam

KENTUCKEY May 1h. 1811.

William S. Dallam[1] altho an humble Citizen of Kentuckey *One* of the constituent members of the Great American Republic offers the incense of his most grateful Respects to President Madison for the appointment of Gove[r]nor Monroe as Secretary of State.

Will S. Dallam knew Gove[r]nor Monroe in Europe. His friendly attention and parental counsel to all Americans there, has created in him an attachment that will be measured by life and has occasioned him to observe with much interest his political life subsequently and altho he does not consider him possessing that comprehensive research in Political Philosophycal Theories with a Jefferson and a Hamilton yet he ranges him as a Practical and patriotic Statesman with a Washington. The Nobleness of feeling evidenced by President Madison in this appointment dignifies even the elevated situation in which his affectionate Countrymen have placed him, to select a Character held forth by Party as a Competitor at a moment supposed to be propitious to our Foreign Relations to participate in the fortunate event, announces unequivocally, "My Country is First."

Wm. Duane a Foreigner has censured *publicly* the appointment this has induced Will S. Dallam a native American to venture to express *privately* his approbation of it—no other subject that could have occupied the world could have forced William S. Dallam into the presence of the president of the United States. He loves Mr. Monroe because he is Good, Great, Affable and Kind.

Will S. Dallam has hitherto been content to paddle his Canoe and speak other Canoes, for the first time he has put out to sea and ventured to hail a Ship and altho it is not the polished *hail* of an experienced Mariner, as it will be the last, he hopes it will be passed over without remark. Will S Dallam wishes President Madison a pleasant and successfull Voyage and that the perpetual Cry of the Watch may be, "Alls well."

RC (DLC). Cover dated 12 Dec. at Frankfort, Kentucky. Docketed by JM.

1. William Smith Dallam, son of Richard Dallam of Maryland, settled with his father in Logan County, Kentucky. By 1805 he had moved to Lexington where he frequently entered into business arrangements with Henry Clay (Hopkins, *Papers of Henry Clay*, 1:176 n. 2).

To Thomas Jefferson

Dear Sir   W. May. 3. 1811

I have recd. yours of the 24 Apl. and return the letter inclosed in it; after having made the communication intended for Mr Gallatin. Your expostulations with Duane could not be improved; but he gives proofs of a want of candor, as well as of temperance, that will probably repel advice however rational or friendly. The great fulcrum of his attacks on Mr. Gallatin, is Erskine's statement of his favorable dispositions toward England; and these attacks he obstinately reiterates and amplifies, notwithstanding the public & solemn denial of Mr. G; whilst Mr. Smith & myself, tho' included in a like statement, under which we have both remained silent, have not been reproached on that account, and Mr. S. is become an object even of favor. A like want of candor is seen in the Comments of the Aurora, on the putative explanation of the rupture between Mr. S. & myself. Of the alledged points of difference, the main one, viz, the non-intercourse, it appears as his opinion on my side; yet he takes the other side generally without even alluding to the exception; and of late, restricts his comments to Macon's bills, or smothers the "non-intercourse" under an &c—or confounds the measure with the manner of its execution. Again, Whilst he admits, occasionally that the non-intercourse or rather non-importation now in force, is the best and the only adequate resort agst. the aggressions of G. B. he continues his abuse on the Government, for abandoning the interests & rights of the Nation. I have always regarded Duane, & still regard him as a sincere friend of liberty, and as ready to make every sacrifice to its cause, but that of his passions. Of these he appears to be compleatly a slave.

Our expected frigate is not yet arrived from Europe; nor is there any acct. of the departure either of Pinkney or Foster from G. B. The last acct. from P. was of Mar. 13. when he was packing up for his passage in the Frigate. Whether the delays, proceed from the approach of the Equinox, the posture of the Regency, or a wish to learn the result of things in Congress, or from some other cause, is unknown. From the jumble of accts. from France, it is probable, that the repeal of the Decrees is professedly adhered to; and that an exchange of the productions of U. S. & F. with an exception of certain articles, is permitted by the Municipal laws, under vexatious precautions agst. British forgeries & American collusions; and perhaps under some distrust of the views of this Government. Accept my high esteem & best affections

JAMES MADISON

RC (DLC). Docketed by Jefferson, "recd May 5."

From Paul Hamilton

DEAR SIR   May 3d. 1811.

Believing it to comport with the fidelity I owe you, I offer for your perusal the enclosed. Colo Butler[1] is a native of So. Carolina, served with credit many years in the legislature of that State, and was much respected in private life for his probity. He removed a few years since into Kentucky, and I have been informed by Gentlemen from that State, that he is there held in the highest estimation. I know him well. He is a most worthy man. I am respectfully & sincerely yrs.

PAUL HAMILTON

RC (DLC). Docketed by JM. Enclosure not found.

1. Anthony Butler (1774?–1849) served in the South Carolina House of Representatives, 1801 and 1802–4. He moved to Logan County, Kentucky, in 1807. In June 1813 JM appointed him lieutenant colonel in the Twenty-eighth U.S. Infantry (Edgar et al., *Biographical Directory of the South Carolina House of Representatives*, 4:87; *Senate Exec. Proceedings*, 2:368).

§ Presidential Proclamation. *3 May 1811*. Declares, under the terms of the 30 Apr. 1810 act providing for the sale of certain lands in the Indiana Territory,[1] that the tract of land to which the Indian title was extinguished under the 1809 Treaty of Fort Wayne and which adjoins the boundary line established by the Treaty of Greenville and was made part of the district of Cincinnati, "with the exception of such [lands] as are reserved by law," shall be sold at Cincinnati on the third Monday in October 1811.

Tr (DNA: RG 49, Proclamations of Public Land Sales). 1 p. Printed in Carter, *Territorial Papers, Indiana*, 8:119.

1. See *U.S. Statutes at Large*, 2:590–91.

From John Bullus

SIR   NEW YORK 4th. May 1811.
I have the honour of forwarding to you a Map of the western part of the State of New York, shewing the route of a proposed Canal from Lake Erie to Hudson's River—together, with the report of the Commissioners appointed to explore the route of an inland navigation from Hudson's River to Lake Ontario, and Lake Erie—which may not be altogether uninteresting.[1] With great consideration Your Most Ob: Serv:

JOHN BULLUS.[2]

RC (DLC). Docketed by JM. Enclosures not found, but see n. 1.

1. *Report of the Commissioners Appointed by Joint Resolutions of the Honorable Senate and Assembly of the State of New-York, the 13th & 15th March 1810, to Explore the Route of an Inland Navigation from Hudson's River to Lake Ontario and Lake Erie* (Albany, 1811; Shaw and Shoemaker 23551).

2. John Bullus, a partner in the New York firm of Bullus, Decatur, and Rucker, had been a naval surgeon during the Quasi-War and since 1807 had served as naval agent in the port of New York (William S. Dudley, ed., *The Naval War of 1812: A Documentary History* [2 vols. to date; Washington, 1985—], 1:547).

§ From Jorge Tadeo Lozano. *9 May 1811, Santa Fe de Bogotá.* Announces the repudiation of the Spanish government as a consequence of the French occupation of Spain and seizure of the person of the king. In order to preserve their independence and to provide for their security, the people have written a constitution of fundamental laws and created the state of Cundinamarca, of which he has the honor to be president. Requests independent governments to recognize its political existence and establish relations with appropriate firmness in order to influence the government of the colonial despot whose system they always renounce.[1]

RC (DNA: RG 59, ML). 1 p. In Spanish. In a clerk's hand, signed by Lozano. Docketed by a clerk as enclosing a copy of the constitution (not found).

1. Notwithstanding the lead that the junta of Santa Fe de Bogotá had taken in the efforts to establish a federal system of government in New Granada (see José Miguel Pey to JM, ca. 22 Dec. 1810, and n. 1), its members quarreled with the congress of provincial delegates on the grounds that the latter body was attempting to rule as a central, supreme government. The junta therefore decided to disregard the congress and in February 1811 organized another constituent body which established the province of Santa Fe as the independent state of Cundinamarca. The constitution of the new state, in addition to creating a representative

government with a separation of executive, legislative, and judicial powers, recognized the Roman Catholic religion as the only true faith and conferred upon Ferdinand VII the title of "King of the people of Cundinamarca." In the absence of the monarch, his powers were to be exercised by a president and his advisers and secretaries. Lozano was elected as first president and held office until he resigned after demonstrations against him on 19 Sept. 1811 (Henao and Arrubla, *History of Colombia*, pp. 211–16).

§ From Robert Patton. *9 May 1811, Philadelphia.* Has purchased the gray horse as JM requested "& will send him forward by Wm. D H Jones, Nephew to Mr. Chester Bailey of this City." The horse is "perfectly gentle, & well broke," and Mrs. Madison "may place great confidence in him." Encloses a receipt and advises JM that he can obtain a draft, when convenient, from either the Union Bank of Georgetown or the Washington bank on the Farmers and Mechanics' Bank in Philadelphia. Requests JM to pay $20 to the young man who will deliver the horse.

RC and enclosure (DLC). RC 1 p. Docketed by JM. Endorsed by William D. H. Jones, "recd. twenty dollars." Enclosure (1 p.) is a receipt, dated 4 May 1811, from Samuel Paul to Robert Patton for $130 "in full for a large Grey horse seven years old . . . & well boroke [*sic*] to harnass."

From Caesar A. Rodney

MY DEAR SIR,   WILMINGTON May 10th. 1811.
    The enclosed you will perceive embraces delicate subjects.[1] In the present posture of our affairs, it may be a question of some importance to decide whether, if indictments should be found, they should be prosecuted. The motives of those concerned in pressing them, are no doubt pure & laudable, but they may be too zealous. Any answer I can give, will be gratuitous & informal, as there exists no right to ask my opinion on the subject. I shall therefore decline a reply until I know whether your judgment coincides with mine.
    A cloud, I would fain hope, momentary again overcasts our prospects of reconciliation with France. The late intelligence ought not to be implicitly credited.[2] Very far from it. The news must be taken with many grains of allowance. The sources from which it flows are not of the purest kind. Your sea-faring men are prone to the marvellous, & often circulate unfounded reports. The merchants are interested in spreading such tales to sell a few pipes of brandy at an exorbitant price. The very arrival of a number of vessels with full & valuable cargoes in some measure contradicts the story. I saw, when lately in Philadelphia, an old client Mr. A. ⟨Reisch?⟩ who owns the two last vessels which arrived, & which I beleive he is about to send back to France, tho' he would not positively say so. I interrogated him closely on the subject of the various rumours afloat. The substance of his

reply was that the prospect was *rather unfavorable*. Tho' he is attached to the administration, he is still a merchant, & owns more tonnage than even Girard.

After all, this state of doubt & suspence is unpleasant & painful. The Essix will dispel all uncertainty. I really wish Mr. Barlow had sailed the moment he was appointed, but the importance of his immediate departure did not strike me so forcibly at that time.

There seems to be a decided opposition to us, forming, if it be not organised already, in Philada. But it will not affect the general sum of the state, which I now beleive will be more unanimous than on a former occasion. I also indulge hopes that the correct & upright course of the administration will remove the films from the eyes of those who are literally blind, or who see at least every thing inverted.

Amidst all our troubles how rapidly are we progressing as a nation. From the number of vessels passing daily in reveiw before me, on their way up the Delaware to Philada. a person would almost conclude our commerce was as free as the air.

I shall leave this for Washington as soon as I hear of the arrival of the Essix, or sooner if necessary. Yours Truly & Affectionatey.

C. A. RODNEY

RC (DLC). Docketed by JM.

1. The enclosure has not been found, but it may have related to a dispute between the U.S. marshal and the U.S. attorney for Delaware, on the one hand, and the collector for the port of Wilmington, on the other, over the seizure and sale of the property of John Bird in May 1810. The marshal, in selling the property to recover the value of a bond posted by Bird, had given the purchasers twelve months' credit in the expectation of obtaining a higher sum than could be then realized in a cash sale, but he later learned that he was likely to face a suit from the collector who was demanding the cash. The Treasury Department subsequently approved the marshal's conduct in the matter (see copies of James Brobson to Gabriel Duvall, 12 May 1811, and Duvall to Brobson, 24 May 1811 [DLC]).

2. Rodney probably referred to a report said to be from Nantes, dated 15 Mar. 1811 and published in the Boston *Columbian Centinel* and other papers, to the effect that France had reestablished the Berlin and Milan decrees and that American vessels had been prohibited from either entering or leaving French ports until further orders were issued. It was also reported that it was forbidden to speak to Napoleon on the subject of American affairs (*National Intelligencer*, 9 May 1811).

From Morgan Lewis

DEAR SIR,   NEW YORK 12th: May 1811

The most singular election we have ever had in this State is closed; and the result, though unknown, is, I fear, favorable to the views of Mr. Clinton; notwithstanding the large and unprecedented majority against him in the district where he resides.[1] This latter circumstance, though insufficient to prevent the attainment of his present Object, I consider as affording an assurance of future disappointment to him. It must convince the Inhabitants of the interior, that Mr. C. has really forfeited the confidence of those who have the best means of knowing his true character—a fact which no *assurances* could induce a belief of. The circumstance too, of his having received a powerful support from that section of federalists who, to use their own language, would support the Devil, were he hostile to your administration, must open the eyes of many; for the fact is too notorious to be concealed. It is admitted, and regreted by that portion, whose federalism has not taught them to forget that they are Americans.

There is very little diversity of Opinion as to Mr. C.'s ulterior Objects. The Office of Lieut. Governor is too insignificant to attract his Attention, but as a mean of placing him in the Government of the State, and thus assist his views toward that of the United States. To facilitate the accomplishment of these projects, it is believed Mr. Tompkins is prepared (if other provision can be made for himself) to cast the executive functions on Mr C. immediately, by a resignation.

Since I have been in this City, I have found among your friends here, considerable dissatisfaction at seeing, as they say, all the Offices of Government, with but one exception, in the Hands of Clintonians. The emoluments of whose appointments, they alledge, aid the elections against them. One of those Officers, the Marshall of this district,[2] it is asserted has committed repeated Acts of extortion and Oppression, which, if true, certainly ought not to pass unnoticed. In the post Office Department also, I have no doubt, though I cannot designate the Man, much improper Conduct has taken place. Previous to your Election, every News paper containing any thing friendly to it, and every Letter addressed to Individuals suspected of favoring it, were sure to be delayed, while those of a contrary description were regularly forwarded. The same game was played this Spring.

General A——g[3] is writing. I do not know the subject, though from an Observation which fell from his Copyist, I fear he is about to expose, what the Government has thought proper to conceal. Time will disclose. I am most truly Dr sir your friend & Servt.

Morgan Lewis.

RC (DLC). Docketed by JM.

1. In the election for lieutenant governor of New York, held in the first week of May, the returns for New York City revealed that the Federalist candidate, Nicholas Fish, had a majority of more than 1,450 votes over the combined vote of his two Republican opponents, DeWitt Clinton and Marinus Willett. Clinton, who was also serving as mayor of the city at the time, ultimately won the election (N.Y. *Evening Post*, 3 and 4 May 1811).

2. John Swartwout.
3. John Armstrong.

From Harry Toulmin

DEAR SIR   FORT STODDERT 14th. May 1811

The reports which I some time since communicated to you relative to the dispositions towards the government of the United States existing in a part of the country lately taken possession of, adjacent to the Mississippi, render it proper that I should state to you the impressions which have resulted from personal observation. I have lately been attending at Baton Rouge as a witness in the case of Col. Cushing: and as I travelled up the coast from New Orleans to that place, and returned eastwardly direct to Fort Stoddert, I endeavoured to ascertain the real feelings of the inhabitants. The result has been, that although I have no reason to doubt the accuracy of the statements made by my informant so far as they related to the temper of mind existing among the people residing near the Mouth of the Bayou Sara, yet that I do not believe that a similar state of mind exists in any part which I have visited, and that whatever degree of intemperate and unreasonable sentiments may have been entertaind in a particular settlement, there is no reason to fear that they have ever been so diffused thro' the country as to endanger the public tranquility. In those parts of the territory which I have visited, I think that there is an unfeigned satisfaction prevailing among a majority of the people in the general course pursued by the United States: and the very impolitic and unfriendly secret project of a junto in the late convention, of organizing thro' the agency of Reuben Kemper, a party in the Mississippi Territory who should make a common cause with the revolted subjects of the Spanish monarchy, seems to have met with universal reprobation in that part of West Florida which I have lately visited. The agent himself seems to be but little known and less respected.

The population of the country, encouraged by the prospect of the permanent establishment of the American government, seems to be rapidly increasing. As we passed thro' it on our way home, in places out of the usual channel of intercourse with the United States, much solicitude was discovered to know what congress had done for them or about them, what kind of government they were to be subjected to, what territory they were to make a part of, and, above all, how far the warrants of survey under the Spanish goverment, & permissions to settle, and the bare fact of settlement would become a foundation for estates in land under the new order of things. As to the large surveys, we saw none of the proprietors, and the mass of settlers certainly feel no interest in their establishment.

The progress of population is truly encouraging. There is now a path made by the footsteps of man all the way from Baton Rouge to Fort Stoddert, and thro' the whole way, consisting of 240 miles, there is no occasion to sleep out of a house more than one night. I am told that there are probably 100 families, all settled since I was last there, on the Pearl river and the main branch tributary to it, the Bogue Chitto, but the unsettled state of things and the want of a government properly organized, has exposed the people there as well as on the Pascagola, too much to impostors & pretenders to authority, mere disorganizers & plunderers, attached to no principles and to no nation. But little evil however has resulted to the People on Pearl, as they had the resolution to send the main man pretending to authority, a prisoner to N. Orleans:[1] but on the Pascagola, the want of any exhibition of the power of the United States thro' any civil or military officer, except a justice of the peace at the mouth of the river, has I am informed, created a doubt respecting the intentions of the United States to retain the possession of the country, and led to a scheme among a few, of tendering again their allegiance to the Spanish government.

I have written to them to assure them of the intention of the United States to provide for their protection and the maintenance of justice among them, and to warn them of the dangers and calamities which will be the consequence of their taking any steps which will produce in their country a new conflict of authorities. Though it is out of my province (if any thing indeed can be out of the province of a public officer when the vital interests of his country are so materially concerned) I shall, if necessary, go to the Pascagola settlement to strengthen the people in their allegiance. I hope however to see Govr. Claiborne here in a few days, as he assured me that he would speedily make a tour to a country so urgently demanding his presence. I took the liberty of suggesting to him the propriety of extending the jurisdiction of the territorial government and appointing the necessary officers, as far as the Perdido, leaving to Mobile (the only place occupied by a Spanish force) so much of the country only as that force may reasonably be supposed to be capable of controuling. Were this done, the east channel of the Mobile river, which is better than the west channel, & falls into the bay 7 miles from the town, might be navigated perfectly independent of Spanish jealousy, and if a few troops & a gun boat or two were stationed on the eastern bank, or at the mouth of Dog river, below Mobile (which latter would probably afford some protection to the people west of the river) no American vessel would feel itself obliged to pass Mobile, in acknowledgement of Spanish sovreignty. The governor acquiesced in the statement which I made to him, & requested a memorandm. of the proper lines, which I gave him, and which will probably include a tract of country of nearly 50 miles square, (poor indeed & very thinly settled) where we do not at present pretend to exercise any jurisdiction. I have the honour to be very respectfully, dear Sir, your most obedt. and most humb sert

HARRY TOULMIN

P. S. Nothing of importance has occurred either in Mobile or Pensacola. In our own settlement I believe that all ideas of new enterprizes have been abandoned.

Revenge on those who have frustrated former ones will be the only solace of disappointed ambition.

RC (DLC). Docketed by JM. On the verso of the postscript JM wrote in pencil, "for perusal."

1. For a description of this episode, see Cox, *The West Florida Controversy*, pp. 580–81.

To John Langdon

DEAR SIR: WASHINGTON, May 15, 1811.

Mr. Edward Coles, of my family, with an Elder brother proposing to visit Portsmouth, in a Northern ramble,[1] I take the liberty of asking in their behalf, the kind reception which you are always ready to give to those who are as worthy of it, as I know these young gentlemen to be.

I cannot lose this occasion of expressing the pleasure I have felt in learning that your country continues to be mindful of your long and distinguished services, and that your health enables your patriotism, to add new titles to their gratitude.[2] Be assured always of my highest esteem & most friendly wishes.

JAMES MADISON.

Printed copy (Alfred Langdon Elwyn, ed., *Letters by Washington, Adams, Jefferson, and Others, Written during and after the Revolution, to John Langdon, New Hampshire* [Philadelphia, 1880], pp. 51–52).

1. In January 1811 Edward Coles suggested to his brother that they go "as far North as my purse will admit, and if possible, to form a circle and take the falls of Niagara &c &c in our way" (Edward to John Coles, 28 Jan. 1811 [NjP: Edward Coles Papers]). On 15 May JM also wrote a similar letter of introduction for the Coles brothers to Elbridge Gerry in Boston (RC in the possession of the Cosmos Club, Washington, D.C., 1994).

2. Langdon, with some reluctance, had been reelected as governor of New Hampshire in 1811 (Lawrence Shaw Mayo, *John Langdon of New Hampshire* [Concord, N.H., 1937], p. 283).

From Hobohoilthle

I have received your talk[1] laid it before the Chiefs of my Nation and now give your their Answer. It is harmless. Your speach was delivered to Colo. Hawkins and he to us,[2] he is like an old Chief, and when things are rong he is to look into for both sides. You ask for a path and I say no, when the President sees my talk, he will Know I have Answered in full, I have examined it myself, my Chiefs and Warriors have examined it, they tell you I must not allow it and must say no. When the President sees my talk, he must know my people do not want to have such road. I am glad the President has Asked us without doing it first. He must know and I know we have some young people and they will mix to the disadvantage of each other. I have a little path here that the white people makes use of and my people are so mischievous that I have continued complaints of my people interrupting of them. You ask in addition a water path and road to the right of this. If we give it it will be much worse that way than this. I have a large family of people in the Country and cannot govern all so as to preserve a good understanding. What land we have left is but large enough to live and walk on. The Officers must not be going through our lands to hunt paths. I spoke last summer to you Colo. Hawkins and to the President about paths through our Country I told you no, and the President no, it would bring trouble on our Country. I am an old man and Speaker for our Warriors when we find a thing will not be good for us, we must say it will not do. I altho' an Indian have a little sense yet. The great god made us and the lands for us to walk on. I hope the great father our president will feel for us and pay attention, we hope he will pity us and not take from us our rights. When friends ask for property we must tell him straight words, if he Asks for the waters of Coosau or by land, my Chiefs and warriors now present never will say yes. I hope it will never be mentioned to us again. I am speaking to our great father the President of the United States. When he sees my talks in his great house of talks I hope he will take notice and give me an Answer. When his Answer returns to me if I am alive I shall See his Answer and be contented. I want to inform you of one of our own brothers the Choctaws. They sold you some land our property the land to the dividing ridge of Allabama & Tombigbee, they say they have not received any money for it and we have not yet settled it with them, as you have officers in that quarter, they ought to see to it. The Creeks are the oldest and the Choctaws the youngest brothers, it is the Creeks property, Coosau Micco Hummastaubeco, Pooor Mattauhau Aupuarumnubba,[3] they stole it from us. They stole our rights and Sold them to the United states. The lands sold were to the ridge but the whites come over and take other waters, and are settled on them. On a Creek above Cedar Creek called sil⟨ivan?⟩ both of which run into Allabamo there are settlements of White people. A path very large from the edge of the swamp on Tombigbee crosses these two Creeks. The path by James Cornells crosses allabamo about two miles below Cedar Creek above is Billosee. These lands were the hunting grounds of the Alabamo. Our own Colour are playing tricks with us about our lands and the white people encourage them is the reason why we say no about the path. The white people are as difficult to be restrained as the red, and are constant habitual intruders on indian lands. I shall look for an Answer to this Speach towards the fall. The two nations will meet put their heads together and settle about their property. And when we have settled About our Claims the President will know all about it.

After this notice if there should be any more encroachments on our lands I hope you will call on the officers and Soldiers to prevent it. This I suppose is the business of you Colo. Hawkins by order of the President. Cattle hogs and horses are put over & stray on our lands, some will be marking trees roads, paths my young people being about and seeing them will be killing and doing mischief and our young people will say our old people are crazy and do not look into our rights. The masters of the Stocks will be vexed with us. I hope you will see justice done to both sides that we may live in peace and be friendly. I have one article to mention to the President. The trading Store, you told us there would be a house & store on your land, that goods should be cheaper than any other merchants, that they should be exchanged for small furs and deer skins, we are distressed about the trade at our United states factory, want to know what is the reason at the factory there is no trade, my people trades at the Country stores. Lead and powder is very high, I understood by the treaties there was a house to keep goods for the trade, we are told that the goods were to come by way of savannah, and were to be reasonable but our people cannot get any, and we are really distressed, our poverty arises from a want of a Market for what we have we are a poor people in distress. I am ⁴ my father the President know the truth and hope he will pay attention to it.

his

Hoboheilthlee ⌒ Micco

mark

RC (DNA: RG 107, LRRS, H-347:5); Tr (DNA: RG 75, LRIA). RC in the hand of Christian Limbaugh, who certified it as a true copy from the original; witnessed by Limbaugh, Alexander Cornells, and Timothy Barnard. Enclosed in Benjamin Hawkins to William Eustis, 22 May 1811 (DNA: RG 107, LRRS, H-347:5); docketed as received 8 June 1811.

1. JM to the chiefs of the Creek Nation, 14 Jan. 1811.

2. After he delivered JM's address to the Creek, Hawkins reported that he had "added to the speech of the President whatever occured to me proper to remove such difficulties as from time to time had circulated among us, particularly that the right to use the rivers and roads

within the United states, belonged equally to the red and white man and was a right from Nature not to be violated by either." Hawkins further observed that "the sooner our Chiefs and warriors understood this the better. But all I could say was lost upon them for the present" (Hawkins to Eustis, 22 May 1811 [DNA: RG 107, LRRS, H-347:5]).

3. Hobohoilthle was probably referring to Hoomastubbee, Pushmataha (1764–1824), and Apukshunnubbee (d. 1824), who were the principal district chiefs of the Choctaw people. After 1805 all three received annuity payments from the U.S. under the terms of the Treaty of Mount Dexter, and during the War of 1812 Pushmataha and Apukshunnubbee were to be instrumental in persuading the Choctaw not to side with either Tecumseh or the Redstick Creek prophets against the U.S. Both these chiefs also participated in Andrew Jackson's 1814 campaigns against the latter (*ASP, Indian Affairs*, 1:749; Angie Debo, *The Rise and Fall of the Choctaw Republic* [2d ed.; Norman, Okla., 1961], pp. 22, 36, 40–41, 48–50, 52, 151; Frederick Webb Hodge, ed., *Handbook of American Indians North of Mexico* [2 vols.; Washington, 1907–10], 2:329–30).

4. Left blank in RC and Tr.

§ From Thomas A. Patteson.[1] *16 May 1811, Fort Hampton, North Carolina.* Informs JM of certain facts "relative to the situation of this place, and the consequent situation of its Commanding Officer." The fort is located on an island "within five hundred feet of the Sea shore" and is a popular resort, particularly during summer and early autumn. These facts "preclude the possibility of preserving the Dignity of ordinary hospitality or of a Commanding Officer with the rations Drawn by a Subaltern." In order to prevent "any material sacrifice, and for the preservation of a respectable Standing," requests an additional allowance for the commanding officer.

RC (DNA: RG 107, LRRS, P-257:5). 2 pp. Docketed by a War Department clerk as received 25 May 1811.

1. Thomas A. Patteson (d. 1814) of Virginia was a lieutenant in the Regiment of Riflemen (Heitman, *Historical Register*, 1:775).

From William Bentley

Sir,   Salem Mass. USA May. 17, 1811
    I have the great pleasure of assuring the President of the United States of America, that, in a great struggle, the friends of President Madison, & of their Country, in Salem have done their duty.[1] With the greatest respect, your devoted Servant,

                                              William Bentley.

RC (DLC). Docketed by JM.

1. In the elections held on 17 May 1811 for the Massachusetts General Court, Republicans won twelve of the fourteen seats from the town of Salem (Salem *Essex Register*, 22 May 1811).

From Albert Gallatin

Sir, TREASURY DEPMT. May 17th 1811

The Acts for adjusting claims to lands in the Territories of Orleans and Louisiana have, where the parties had not obtained complete titles, recognised only three species of claims as valid vizt. 1t. Orders of survey. 2d. permission to settle. 3d. possession for Ten consecutive years, prior to the 20th Decr. 1803.

1: Orders of survey must have been dated prior to the 1st. day of October 1800. the land must have been cultivated and inhabited and the parties residing in the province on that day: And the conditions attached to this concession must have been fulfilled.[1]

2: The permission to settle must have been granted prior to the 20th December 1803; and the land must have been cultivated and inhabited on that day. But a settlement commenced prior to the 1st. October 1800 & continued for three years is declared by the act to be sufficient proof of a permission. Only one tract & no tract greater than 640 acres to be allowed under this species of claim (with such farther quantity as by the Spanish usages was allowed to the wife and family of a settler) and only provided that no other tract is claimed in the territories under any french or spanish grant.[2]

3: The possession for ten years is in favor only of persons residing in the Territory on 20th. Decr. 1803 and cannot confer a right to more than 2000 acres.[3]

With the exception of the last species of claims, *Actual Settlement* on the 1st. October 1800 or on the 20th. Decr. 1803. is the essential requisite. If founded on an order of survey the quantity of land is not limited, but the conditions on which the completion of the grant might depend must have been fulfilled. If founded only on an actual or presumed permission to settle the quantity of land is limited to a quantity which it is understood could never exceed 960 arpens.

It will be perceived by the enclosed copy of the "general principles of decision" adopted by the board of Commissioners of Opelousas[4] that they have altogether set aside that essential principle. For they have not only admitted in addition to the Order of survey a new species of title, vizt. the requête or petition of the party signed by the Commandant which is nothing else than the permission to settle contemplated by the act: but they have in the face of the law declared that no fulfillment of conditions was necessary and expressly that no proof of settlement would in either case be required.

It is presumed that the Commissioners suppose that the 4th section of the Act of 3d. March 1807. has given them the right to make decisions on that principle. It is thereby enacted that the Commissioners shall have full powers to decide *according to the laws and established usages and customs of the*

French and Spanish Governments upon all claims to lands within their respective districts for tracts not exceeding one league square where the claim is by or for persons who were inhabitants of Louisiana on the 20th Decr. 1803; and that their decision when in favor of the claimants shall be final against the United States any act of Congress to the contrary notwithstanding. The last words apply only to the provisions by which it had been enacted that all the Commissioners decisions should be transmitted to Congress for approbation or rejection: and it is evident by the last mentioned act itself that the power to decide according to French & Spanish laws & usages was not intended to recognize new species of claims or to repeal the essential principles enacted by preceding acts. For the 1st. section actually repeals one of those principles, vizt. the rejection of orders of survey in favor of minors; and the 8th section provides that the Commissioners shall in their report of claims not confirmed by themselves make two classes of such as ought in their opinion to be confirmed, vizt. 1t. such as ought to be confirmed in conformity with the acts of Congress; by which are meant those of more than one league square. 2d. "such as though not embraced by the acts of Congress ought to be confirmed in conformity with the laws & usages of the Spanish Government"; which class could include no claims whatever, if according to the construction assumed by the Opelousas Commissioners, they had the power to confirm claims not embraced by the Acts of Congress when in their opinion they were in conformity with the laws & usages of the Spanish Government.

The provision which makes the decision of the Commissioners final, has however superceded that part of the 5th section of the Act of 21st April 1806 which had enjoined it on them to conform in their decisions to such instructions as the Secretary of the Treasury might with the approbation of the President transmit to them in relation thereto. When therefore the enclosed communication from the Opelousas Commissioners was received, nothing more could be done than to express my opinion of the impropriety of their principles of decision, and to refer them to those adopted by the Commissioners of New Orleans.[5] I had also understood that the danger of fraud was much less in that district than in upper Louisiana; and it is proper to add that, however injurious the proceedings of the Opelousas Commissioners may in that respect have been, it is believed that they have been actuated by the purest motives. The publication of their rules of decision has in the mean while created much dissatisfaction in the two other districts of New Orleans & St. Louis, and has particularly in the last increased the clamours against the Commissioners and placed them in a very disagreeable situation. The use which is made of this publication by disappointed land claimants and by those intruders whose object is to unite all classes against the operation of the land laws may be easily understood. And I have been informed by Governor Claiborne that even in the Opelousas District, there is great danger of numerous frauds being committed particularly in relation to réquêtes which may have been fabricated at pleasure and on which there was no other check but the obligation of an actual settlement.

Under these circumstances the question arises as to what ought to be done or can be done. The President may remove the Commissioners, which will effectually cure the evil; or a letter may be written in his name expressive of his disapprobation, which may perhaps produce some effect.[6] The propriety of adopting either of these, or some other measure in relation to this subject, is respectfully submitted. I have &c.

Letterbook copy (DNA: RG 49, Records of the General Land Office, Misc. Letter Book). Enclosure not found, but see n. 4.

1. Opposite this paragraph the clerk wrote in the margin: "Act of 2d. March 1805. 1t sect." (see *U.S. Statutes at Large,* 2:324–25).

2. Opposite this paragraph the clerk wrote in the margin: "2d. March 1805. 2d. sect. / 21 Apl. 1806 1 sect / 2d. March 1805. 2d. sect." (see ibid., 2:325–26, 391).

3. Opposite this paragraph the clerk wrote in the margin: "3d. March 1807. 2: S" (see ibid., 2:440).

4. These "principles of decision" had been forwarded to Gallatin on 16 Dec. 1810. In his letter of acknowledgment the treasury secretary observed that the board of commissioners had "adopted some rules not sufficiently strict, & calculated to confirm many unfounded claims" (Gallatin to the boards of commissioners at St. Louis, New Orleans, and Opelousas, 24 Apr. 1811, Carter, *Territorial Papers, Orleans,* 9:930–31).

5. These principles had been stated in Joshua Lewis and Thomas B. Robertson to Gallatin, 25 Jan. 1811 (ibid., 9:919–21).

6. JM evidently decided on a letter of "disapprobation," the contents of which repeated much of Gallatin's letter to him (see Gallatin to Levin Wailes, William Garrard, and Gideon Fitz, 24 May 1811, ibid., 9:934–36).

From Samuel Overton

Dr Sir   Nashvill Tennessee 18th of May. 1811

Shall I be permited to correspond with you as a man fair removed from my one native Country. What was the reson that the Minister from the Spanish Dominions in South America could not be duly received and accredited at the City of Washington. I do not now wright to you for an Office not being authorised to do so—th⟨o:⟩ as a ⟨former?⟩ Nieghbour you will not think me presuming & suffice it to say that you were first ellected to Congress from the District we were both born in and rased to what we *all is.*[1] You are presidant—and myself a priviate citizen let it be remember that this communication is not intended to Test for an office. With due respect I am your obedient St.

Samuel Overton

RC (DLC).

1. Members of the Overton family could be found in large numbers throughout Hanover, Louisa, and Orange Counties in Virginia. Samuel Overton was possibly one of the sons of Capt. James Overton and his wife, Elizabeth Garland Overton. Another of their sons, John Overton, migrated to Nashville, Tennessee, where he became the friend and business partner of Andrew Jackson (Malcolm H. Harris, *History of Louisa County, Virginia* [Richmond, 1936], pp. 397–99; William H. B. Thomas, *Patriots of the Upcountry: Orange County, Virginia, in the Revolution* [Orange, Va., 1976], p. 116).

¶ From Benjamin Henry Latrobe. Letter not found. *19 May 1811, Philadelphia.* Calendared by Latrobe in a list of "Letters written at Philadelphia May 1811" as forwarding a copy of his "⟨ann⟩iversary oration" (MdHi: Latrobe Letterbooks). Latrobe's *Anniversary Oration, Pronounced before the Society of Artists of the United States, . . . on the Eighth of May, 1811* (Philadelphia, 1811; Shaw and Shoemaker 23189) is reprinted in Van Horne, *Papers of Latrobe,* 3:67–84. It was also reprinted in the *National Intelligencer* on 20 July 1811, possibly from the copy Latrobe forwarded to JM.

From the Merchants of Hartford

HARTFORD, CONNECTICUT May 20. 1811.

The Memorial of the subscribers would respectfully represent, that,

They are deputed, in behalf of their fellow citizens, who are merchants in trade in the City of Hartford, and State of Connecticut, respectfully to present to the view of the President, the peculiar hardships, and embarrassments of their situation, arising from the severe operation of the "Non Intercourse Law" of March 2. 1811, in the hope that the Wisdom of the President, and his perfect knowledge of the relative situation of our country with foreign nations, may enable him to adopt such proper measures, as will, at least alleviate if not, remove the great hardships they suffer.

Your memorialists are engaged in commerce chiefly with, the islands of the West Indies, that part of the Continent which is adjacent, Great Britain, and such parts of Europe as are in alliance with Great Britain. They are, also, considerably engaged, in that important branch of manufactures, Ship-building, and thereby afford employment to the various mechanical arts connected therewith. Your memorialists would state, that, they have been educated to the occupations of commerce: that, their habits have become conformed to their employment: that, it is impossible for many of them, particularly those advanced in years, to change their profession, and become, suddenly, either manufacturers, or agriculturalists: that, hitherto they have been enabled to obtain a comfortable, and an honest, living, from their lawful occupations: that, any Law, preventing them from pursuing their accustomed commerce, takes from them their means of subsistence: That, the exports of their trade have consisted, almost entirely, of the produce, of their native soil, and the industry of its inhabitants: that, the imports have consisted of commodities, which, almost without exception, have been consumed in the country—thus, on the one hand, encouraging industry, by exporting it's surplus products, and, on the other, contributing to the expenses of their Government, a proportion of their earnings, in impost duties, which have been paid without drawback: that, by far the greater part of those ports in Europe, and the West Indies, to which they have been accustomed to trade, being in possession of the British, and the Non Intercourse Law allowing them to export a Cargo but not allowing them to bring one back, their trade, burthen'd as it is with double freight, and double insurance, and an exportation already overloaded, is really not worth pursuing: that, exportation is, therefore, gradually diminishing, in consequence of which many important products of the Country have greatly diminished in value, and now lie, unsaleable, on the hands of the farmer, who, on the other hand, is compell'd to pay a greatly increas'd price for most of those foreign commodities, which are imported chiefly for home consumption: that, such of their vessels as are commonly engaged in foreign trade, are, many of them, unemployed, and those which are not, are employed to great disadvantage, there being few ports, to which they can go, not in the occupation of the British, and these so overstocked that it is no longer advantageous to go there: that, they are compell'd, therefore, in order to find employment, to pursue a circuitous trade from one foreign port to another, and, in this way, their property is detained from their possession, as well as the seamen from their homes, much longer than is advantageous for either: that, the business of ship building is carried on, in the river Connecticut, to very considerable extent, a manufacture, highly advantageous, consuming chiefly a material which if not so consumed would be of little value to the country, and giving employment to great numbers of labourers and artisans: that, this manufacture, if the Non Intercourse Law continue in operation, must soon be suspended, as the demand for ships has, in a great measure, ceased, and they cannot now be sold, but with loss, whereby many industrious citizens will be, either, thrown out of employment, or compell'd to labour for the reduced compensation their employers can afford to pay them: that, some of your memorialists, who are engaged in trade to Great Britain, have, at this time, merchandize, to great amount lying in different ports of Great Britain, which the Non-Intercourse Law prohibits their bringing home: that, this merchandize is lying at the risque of the memorialists, incurring considerable expense, and depreciating in value in consequence of a loss of sale at the proper season: that, the capital of your memorialists is thus taken out of their hands, and transfer'd to a foreign country whence the Law makes it a crime in them to attempt to regain it: that, some of your memorialists have sustained great inconvenience and injury from having their vessels and property, coming from foreign ports, which sail'd from thence, not only long before the enacting of this Law could be known in foreign ports, but even before the existence of the law in their own Country: that, they have had their vessels libelled, the property seized, and detained from their possession, without a possibility of recovering it, but by incurring great trouble and expense, by submitting to the extortion of unreasonable fees, the demand of unreasonable bonds, and expensive litigation. These are the hardships and embarrassments, of which your memorialists complain, arising from the operation of the Non Intercourse Law, and affecting them personally. The destructive effects of this Law to the Country at large, though less within the actual knowledge of your memorialists, are not less real. Agriculture is impoverished, by the inability of the merchant to export to advantage the surplus produce of the Country. Our vessels come back empty from foreign ports, instead of returning laden with valuable cargoes, and paying, as formerly, rich tribute to the treasury of the United States. Numbers of our seamen have disappeared, either, having voluntarily entered into foreign service, or remaining abroad in the hope of employment. There is reason to fear, the difficulties and embarrassments attending the pursuit of the circumscribed commerce, yet lawful, may encourage a disposition, in all classes of citizens, to evade the laws, to defraud the revenue, to disregard the sanctity of oaths, to engage in practices of fraud and deception, or in open violence and resistance against the laws of the land: which evils are the more to be deprecated, as formerly, not a country on earth, we proudly believe, exhibited fewer instances of deception of this kind, than our own. And, finally, the neighbouring provinces of Great Britain will be made a common thorough-fare for the exportation and importation of all those commodities which our own Country either spares, or needs—thereby, transferring to our neighbours all the advantages arising from receiving, collecting, and transporting the former, and the profits attending the sale, and distribution of the latter. It is already seen, that our enterprizing merchants, and industrious mechanics quit their native homes, to seek security, and the means of subsistence undisturbed, in the provinces of Canada. It is also seen, that those provinces thrive, and fatten, on the commercial prosperity, we, unhappily, banish from our shores. And that the commerce, in the useful and necessary manufactures of Great Britain, has, in these provinces, increased in an unexampled degree; while it is notorious these commodities are distributed, at high prices, over the contiguous states, without paying to the Government of the United States, any part of that impost, which, heretofore, has been paid to the Government with ease, punctuality, and honour, by the merchants of the large commercial cities, on the seacoast. And the injury to the public revenue is infinitely less afflicting than the injury to the public morality, which thus yields to the temptation of fraudulent gain, with less reluctance, when necessity goads to desperate exertion.

Your memorialists think their prayer, for some mitigation of the evils they complain of, to be the more reasonable, from this fact. The Law of Non-Intercourse, the evil effects and embarrassments arising from which they so sensibly feel, was predicated on the belief that the Government of France had really repealed their decrees violating our neutral commerce. The fact is too notorious to require proof, that these decrees, so justly complained of, have, as yet, not been repealed in fact, even admitting they have been in name. This Law, operating so severely to their injury, has been enacted on a presumed fact, which, it is now apparent, did not exist. Common justice, therefore, they conceive, authorizes them to claim of their Government, if not to repair the injury consequent on such law, at least to replace the memorialists in the situation in which the law found them, by the repeal of the Act which occasions their embarrassment.

Your memorialists, therefore, with a deep sense, not only of their own sufferings but of those of their Country also, now apply to the President of the United States, under the conviction that he will hear their case with patience, and relieve them, if practicable, from the continuance of the evils they complain of; and if no other means present themselves to his view, they earnestly entreat him to consider the propriety of Convening Congress, at a much earlier period than usual, to take into consideration the necessity of removing from our commerce, all those unfortunate restraints, the operation of which, in aiming a blow at the interests of another nation, unhappily, has inflicted a severer wound on our own. And as in duty bound shall ever pray,

JOHN CALDWELL
[and thirteen others]

RC (DNA: RG 59, ML).

To Richard Cutts

DEAR SIR   W. May 23. 1811

I have recd. your favor of the 16th.[1] by the mail which brought the result of the Election at Salem. The general result I infer will fulfill your wishes. The atmosphere has for several days been filled with reports of an engagement between the Frigate commanded by Rogers and a British frigate.[2] You will estimate the testimony by the Contents of the inclosed papers. The occurrence is in itself so little probable that it will be doubted till regularly confirmed.

We are still looking out for the Essex; and may be disappointed when she arrives of any final decision of the prospects from France, as she cannot well bring dispatches from Russel subsequent to the knowledge of the Act putting the non-importation in force. The accts. hitherto recd. create perplexity rather than certainty with respect to the conduct of that Govt. Our Official intelligence does not justify the prevailing impression that no regard will be paid to the pledge given on the subject of the Decrees; but besides the ignorance & instability on the subject of commerce, it may happen, that on some pretext of inadequacy in the Act of Congs. new evasions or delays may be introduced. Certain it is that whilst the trade with this Country, is made subordinate to the grand object of destroying that of G. B. & apprehensions remain that the former will be a vehicle for the latter, obstructions & vexations will be more or less continued. And it seems extremely difficult to keep the public mind awake to the distinction between the Decrees relating to the trade of the U. S. with England, & those relating simply to the trade with F. herself. Of this confusion of ideas, England & her partizans take advantage, in order to divert attention from the British Orders, to French Municipal irregularities, and to turn the latter agst. the Govt. of the U. S. It seems also that this strategem is abetted by the inconveniences, particularly along the N. E. Coast, resulting from the clog put on the trade, particularly with the W. Indies. You will have noticed the renewal instituted at N. Haven, of addresses to the Ex. on this subject.[3] It is kept out of sight that with the exception perhaps of the W. Indies, there could be no inducement at present to continue the intercourse with the B. Dominions, this Country being sufficiently stocked with merchandize, & the British Market being glutted with our productions. The latest accts. from England are to be found in the Newspapers. It is doubted by many whether Foster's mission will not be suspended, notwithstanding the arrival of his baggage; and whether something like retaliation on the Act of Congs. may not be attempted. It would have been a provident security agst. such a project, if exports even in our vessels, had been prohibited to Nova Scotia, & E. Florida.

We are happy to hear that you all continue well, and offer affectionate remembrances. Yrs. Affecly.

J. MADISON

RC (MHi); Tr (NjP: Crane Collection).

1. Letter not found.

2. On 23 May 1811 the *National Intelligencer* published a series of letters from Norfolk, Virginia, reporting a clash on 16 May off Cape Henry between Commodore John Rodgers in the frigate *President* and an unnamed British vessel which was said to have been impressing American seamen. The commander of the British vessel, later identified as the sloop *Lille Belt* (or more commonly *Little Belt*), claimed that the *President* fired the first shot in an exchange during which the British incurred thirty-two casualties. A court of inquiry convened by Navy

Secretary Paul Hamilton on 30 Aug. 1811, however, concluded that the British commander had been responsible for both firing the first shot and commencing the general fire that ensued (Dudley, *Naval War of 1812*, 1:40–50; *ASP, Foreign Relations*, 3:471–99).

3. See the Inhabitants of New Haven to JM, 11 Mar. 1811.

To the Inhabitants of New Haven

WASHINGTON May 24th. 1811.

I have received, fellow Citizens, the petition which you have addressed to me,[1] representing the inconveniences experienced from the existing non-importation law, and soliciting that the National Legislature may be speedily convened.

It is known to all, that the Commerce of the United States has, for a considerable period, been greatly abridged and annoyed, by Edicts of the belligerent powers; each professing retaliation only on the other; but both violating the clearest rights of the United States as a neutral nation. In this extraordinary state of things, the Legislature, willing to avoid a resort to war, more especially during the concurrent aggressions of two great powers, themselves at war, the one with the other, and determined on the other hand against an unqualified acquiescence, have endeavored by successive and varied regulations affecting the commerce of the parties, to make it their interest to be just.

In the Act of Congress out of which the existing non-importation has grown, the state of commerce was no otherwise qualified than by a provision, that in case either of the belligerents should revoke its unlawful Edicts, and the other should fail to do the same, our ports should be shut to the vessels and merchandize of the latter. This provision which, like our previous offers, repelled the very pretext set up by each, that its Edicts against our trade with the other, was required by an acquiescence in like Edicts of the other, was equally presented to the attention of both. In consequence of the communication, the French Government declared that its Decrees were revoked. As the British Government had expressed reluctance in issuing its orders, and repeatedly signified a wish to find in the example of its adversary, an occasion for putting an end to them, the expectation was the more confident, that the occasion would be promptly embraced. This was not done; and the period allowed for the purpose having elapsed, our ports became shut to British ships and merchandize. Whether the conduct of the French Government has been, and will be such as to satisfy the authorized expectations of the United States; or whether the British Government may have opened, or will open the way, for the Executive removal of the restrictions on British commerce with the United

States, which it continues in its power to do, by revoking its own unlawful restrictions on our commerce, is to be ascertained by further information; which will be received and employed by the Executive, with that
strict impartiality, which has been invariably maintained towards the two
belligerents.

Whatever may be the inconveniences resulting in the mean time, from
the non-importation Act, it was not to have been supposed, that whilst it
falls within the necessary power and practice of regulating our commercial
intercourse with foreign Countries, according to circumstances, the Act
would be regarded as not warranted by the Constitution; or that whilst it
was a partial restriction only, and had for its object, an entire freedom of
our commerce, by a liberation of it from foreign restrictions unlawfully
imposed, it could be viewed as destroying commerce; and least of all, that a
likeness could be seen between a law enacted by the representatives of the
Country, with a view to the interest of the Country; and Acts of a Government in which the Country was not represented, framed with a view to the
interest of another Country, at the expence of this.

If appeals to the justice of the Belligerents, thro' their interests, involve
privations on our part also; it ought to be recollected, that this is an effect
inseparable from every resort, by which one nation can right itself against
the injustice of others.

If sacrifices made for the sake of the whole, result more to some than to
other districts or descriptions of Citizens, this also is an effect, which tho'
always to be regretted, can never be entirely avoided. Whether the appeal
be to the sword, or to interruptions or modifications of customary intercourse, an equal operation on every part of the community can never happen. Nor would an unqualified acquiescence in belligerent restrictions on
our commerce, if that could be reconciled with what the nation owes to
itself, be less unequal in its effect on different local situations and interests.

In estimating the particular measure which has been adopted by the National Councils, it may be reasonably expected therefore, from the candor
of enlightened Citizens, that with the peculiarity of the public situation,
they will be impressed also, with the difficulty of selecting the course most
satisfactory, and best suited to diminish its evils or shorten their duration;
that they will keep in mind, that a resort to war must involve necessary
restrictions on commerce; and that were no measure whatever opposed to
the belligerent acts against our commerce, it would not only remain under
the severe restrictions now imposed by foreign hands, but new motives
would be given, for prolonging and invigorating them.

These observations are not meant to anticipate the policy which the Legislature may henceforward find best adapted, to support the honor or promote the interest of the nation; or to prejudge questions relative to particular changes, which may be pointed out by experience, or be called for by

the state of our foreign relations. Neither do they imply any predetermination as to the measure of convening the Legislature, which it will be a duty to adopt or decline, as our national affairs may appear to require. The view of our situation presented to your patriotic reflections, has been suggested by that contained in your address; and it will have its desired effect, if it recalls your attention to the peculiar embarrassments with which the National Councils have had to contend; and enforces the importance of manifesting that union of all, in supporting the measures of the constituted authorities whilst actually in force, which is as necessary to their effect at home and abroad, as it is consistent with the right, and with the legitimate modes, of seeking a revisal of them. In the mode which the Town of New Haven has employed, I witness with satisfaction, that in exercising the right of freemen, the obligation of Citizens has not been forgotten; and that it affords a pledge and an example, which I am far from undervaluing. I tender you my respects and my friendly wishes.

JAMES MADISON

RC (CtY: Woolsey Family Papers); draft (DLC). RC in a clerk's hand, signed by JM.

  1. The Inhabitants of New Haven to JM, 11 Mar. 1811.

§ From George M. Troup. *24 May 1811, Savannah.* "A few weeks before the adjournment of Congress having been informed of a vacancy in the consulate of Antwerp I addressed a letter to Mr Smith nominating & soliciting the appointment of Emanuel Wambersie of Georgia to that office.[1] Will you do me the favor to sieze a leisure moment to turn to that letter & the recommendations which accompanied it." Encloses an old paper he accidentally found, believing it may be of use to the government. Does not doubt the accuracy of its contents at the time of its writing about thirty years ago; "allowing for shiftings of the Bar & destruction of land marks it may be considered correct now. Our People have so little intercourse with Pensacola by sea it may even at this day be a better description of the approaches to its harbor than our government is in possession of."

RC (DNA: RG 59, LAR, 1809–17, filed under "Wambersie"). 2 pp. Addressee not indicated. Enclosure not found.

  1. Troup to Robert Smith, 9 Feb. 1811 (ibid.).

From Hugh Chisholm

SIR   MONTPELIER May 26 1811
    Some time ago I give Mr James Leitch[1] a draft on you, for $200 without mentioning the thing to you, before, which I ought to have done, therefore

I will thank you to pay it when you find it convenient. We are at this time ingage on the other wing we got it to the Serface of the ground, and will use Every Exersion to finish it with Speed the other wing I will finish against you come hare, I am yours with Estteem

HUGH CHISHOLM

RC (DLC). Docketed by JM.

1. James Leitch (d. 1829?) was a merchant and storeowner in Charlottesville, Virginia, with whom Jefferson had business dealings over many years (Betts, *Jefferson's Garden Book*, pp. 460, 591; Woods, *Albemarle County in Virginia*, pp. 82, 139, 253).

From Thomas Jefferson

DEAR SIR   MONTICELLO May 26. 11.

As I sent you my first effort to keep Duane right, so I communicate the second,[1] which the failure of our measures to help him obliged me to write. It probably closes our correspondence as I have not heard a word from him on the subject. Ritchie is correct as to the administration generally. I have written to a friend there[2] what I am in hopes will put him right as to mr. Gallatin, altho, as my friend thinks, it is not certain.

⟨We have had much alarm as to the fly in our wheat. Some friendly rains however have enabled much of it to out-grow that danger. Good lands & husbandry have recieved little injury from it. But the indifferent present as yet rather a meagre appearance. You will be so good as to return me the inclosed after perusal & to accept the assurances of my constant affection.

TH: JEFFERSON⟩

RC (DLC); FC (DLC: Jefferson Papers). Second paragraph and signature, clipped from the RC, have been supplied within angle brackets from the FC.

1. Jefferson enclosed a copy of his 30 Apr. 1811 letter to Duane (DLC: Jefferson Papers; printed in Ford, *Writings of Jefferson*, 9:314–16), explaining that the attacks on JM and the administration printed in the *Aurora General Advertiser* in the first two weeks in April made it impossible to raise funds for the newspaper in Richmond. "The President's popularity," Jefferson wrote, "is high thro' this state," and he strongly hinted that once Duane learned of "such a mass of opinion variant from your own," he should reconsider the wisdom of his editorial policies. "The example of John Randolph," Jefferson added, "is a caution to all honest & prudent men, to sacrifice a little of self-confidence, & to go with their friends, altho' they may sometimes think they are going wrong."

2. Jefferson was probably alluding to his letters of 30 Mar. and 3 May 1811 to William Wirt (Ford, *Writings of Jefferson*, 9:316–19).

To John G. Jackson

Dear Sir   May 27. [1811]

I duly recd. yours inclosing a sample from your long fleeced Ewe. I have seen no ⟨way?⟩ particularly capable of deciding on its merits. I suspect the question of its value depends on the weight of the fleece, finding that wool nearly as long is not very rare in certain breeds, and that the coarseness of its staple brings it under the denomination of Combing wool. A chance only, of turning the specimen to acct. wd. justify attention to the means of p[r]eserving it. We are still under all the uncertainties relative to our affairs abroad, the Essex having not even arrived, & no authentic accts. having been recd. thro any other channels. You will see by the inclosed handbill what has passed between Rogers & a British Rover on our Coasts. Be assured always of my Affecte. respects

James Madison

RC (InU: Jackson Collection). Docketed by Jackson. Enclosure not found.

§ From Robert Patton. *27 May 1811, Philadelphia.* "I have received your favour [not found] enclosing a Draft on the Pennsa. Bank in my favour, for 130 Dollars which was paid on my presenting it. I am happy to find that the horse matches your old horse so well."

RC (DLC). 1 p.

§ To James Leander Cathcart. *28 May 1811, Washington.* Acknowledges receiving the several parcels of wine sent to him; has found them "very satisfactory." Those from the vault of Mr. Carvalhal seem to be "unusually fine & well flavored," and "a couple of pipes more . . . would be extremely acceptable." Also requests three pipes of the St. Roque to be forwarded. Mr. Monroe requests two pipes of the St. Roque, and Mrs. Lucy[1] would like one as well—"the 8 pipes to be consigned to Alexandria; or if no early conveyance be found for that port, Norfolk or Baltimore."

RC (MH: Dearborn Papers); draft (DLC). RC 2 pp.

1. "Mrs. Lucy Washington" in draft.

From James Barbour

Sir   Orange May 29th. 1811

The inconvenience of my situation as connected with the post office is such as induces me to make an effort to remedy it. Not having the pleasure of an acquaintance with the head of the post office department I have taken the liberty to present the subject to your consideration. The most convenient post office in the County is Orange Court House. The road leading to Charlottesville by my house is the most convenient and the nearest way but notwithstanding this circumstance there is a Stage mail and also a horse mail on the town road. I feel no disposition to change that arrangement yet I think but Just that we should have at least a horse mail once a week. The population on this road is very numerous and respectable and from the remoteness of the post office it is to us almost useless. A post office established at a Public house on my land (called Barboursville) fourteen miles from the Ct House under the direction of John Bradley would produce a convenience to a multitude of People who with myself are anxious for such an establishment. If this subject is within your controul and you can spare time enough from business of more importance to attend to this, the favor will be duly appreciated by very many respectful Friends. I am with Sentiments of the highest esteem yr Obd Sert.

Js: BARBOUR[1]

RC (DLC). Docketed by JM.

1. James Barbour (1775–1842) was a resident of Barboursville, Virginia, and a near neighbor of JM's. He entered the Virginia House of Delegates in 1798 supporting JM's Virginia Resolutions, and he remained a member of that body almost continuously until 1812. He served as governor of Virginia during the War of 1812 and thereafter as U.S. senator for Virginia, 1815–25, secretary of war, 1825–28, and briefly, until 1829, as U.S. minister to Great Britain. Throughout his career Barbour's political views and actions were usually in close harmony with those of JM. When JM died in 1836 Barbour served as a pallbearer at his funeral and then delivered the eulogy at the memorial service held at Orange Court House (Charles D. Lowery, *James Barbour, a Jeffersonian Republican* [University, Ala., 1984], pp. 18, 19, 61, 81, 151, 184, 234).

¶ From Richard Cutts. Letter not found. *29 May 1811*. Mentioned in JM to Cutts, 16 June 1811, as transmitting the news of the Republican ascendancy in the Massachusetts legislature.

From Charles P. Howard

DEAR SIR   MOWBRAY May 30th. 1811

Having been choosen One of the Directors for carrying into effect the Turnpike authorized between Fredericksburg & Swift R Gap and it being contemplated to proceed immediately with the Work, we think it necessary before the next meeting of the board for each individual of it to obtain all the information in their power. As there is great deficiency of talent in this Country on subjects of this kind we hope our friends abroad will aid us by giving such information as may be wanted. As Stone & Gravel will be inconvenient to a considerable part of the Road between this and Frederg wood has been named as a Substitute; but I suppose myself that it has not had a trial sufficient to justify a dependance on it. I think it probable that it will be used unless good reasons are assign'd to the contrary on which subject as well as others that may be connected with it shall thank you for your Opinion.

It has been said that as much produce has gone to Fredg this year as has gone to Baltimore by Land & there can be no doubt but the increase hereafter will be in favr. of the former and as the Law directs that 8 ⅌ Ct. may be demanded on the Money expended on the first 20 Miles which is to commence at Fredg and that the Old Road shall be closed, I think are inducements for all that want good interest and good security to adventure in the Stock 5$ on each Share will be demanded on subscribing and the balance to be paid by instalments as it may be wanted. Do you think any of your Citizens would take any? About ⅓ of the Stock has already been taken.

The Crop of Wheat appears to be much injured, tho the alarm I think is greater than the case warrants. With Esteem

C. P. HOWARD

RC (DLC).

§ From Herman Vosburgh. *31 May 1811, New York.* "I have been engaged for the last three years in establishing an Extensive Manufactory on the Bronx River about Twelve miles from this City for the purpose of making paint articles from metallick substances of the growth and produce of the United States." Has obtained a charter from the state legislature to incorporate a company for twenty years with stock of $100,000. Among his stockholders are mercantile houses that have annually imported articles such as red lead, litharge, and patent yellow and white lead from Great Britain, all of which he expects to have ready by 10 June. Has encountered both "external and local prejudices" against American manufactures. "The cold apathy of some the scornful sneers of the ignorant and the wilful misrepresentations of others probably self-interested are in my view a great cause why American Manufactures have languished so long." Looks to JM as "the Executive head and father of the American People" for some "sentiments . . . of favourable import respecting the Manufactures of this Country." Eight million people "must and ought to be stimulated by every possible encouragement emanating from the highest authority." Has waited for some years for Congress to recommend those branches of the arts and manufactures that might be carried on in the different states where raw materials are available.

His company sent an agent to the Louisiana country to see "at what price we could obtain metallic lead at the mines, we calculating to consume at our establishment from four to five hundred Tons annually." The supply is available, but he has been hampered in obtaining it by the lack of a nationally circulating currency and the difficulties of transporting large sums of specie. Believes that the U.S. holds large tracts of mineral lands and supposes that the government "might be induced to sell in small tracts and to encourage settlers, agree to take Metallick Land in payment thereby not only furnishing *our* annual supply but also the whole Market of the Atlantic States." Requests JM's impressions on the subject and, if permitted, wishes to show them to the directors of the company.

Is an American by birth and has for a number of years "persued the manufacturing of the finer Sorts of Copal Japan and Enamel Varnishes and of sundry paints." Believes he can best serve his country by establishing a permanent manufactory in this line of business. Is confident of success and wishes to forward JM some samples shortly. "I fervently Trust that every means will be made use of that can diffuse the arts of peace throughout our common Country which alone are able to preserve the patriots last best hope and shed . . . blessings *inestimable* and Honours less transient than the blood staind fields of Desolated Europe can bequeath to the rising generations of our fellow man. . . . May you long enjoy the Exalted Station you fill with great happiness to yourself and preeminent usefulness to our common dear Country."

RC (DLC). 4 pp. Docketed by JM.

§ From Robert Wickliffe.¹ *2 June 1811, Lexington, Kentucky.* States that the present marshal for Kentucky has decided to resign. Recommends as his successor the marshal's son, Robert Crockett, who "is in the prime of life and possesses fine talents." The younger Crockett served as a deputy under his father and is familiar with the laws of the state. His appointment would be widely approved.²

RC (DNA: RG 59, LAR, 1809–17, filed under "Crockett"). 1 p.

1. Robert Wickliffe (1775–1859) was a prominent Kentucky lawyer. He occasionally represented Fayette County in the Kentucky House of Representatives (Lewis Collins, *Collins' Historical Sketches of Kentucky: History of Kentucky . . .* [rev. ed.; 2 vols.; Covington, Ky., 1878], 2:200–201).

2. JM gave Robert Crockett an interim appointment as U.S. marshal for Kentucky and sent his nomination to the Senate for confirmation on 13 Nov. 1811 (*Senate Exec. Proceedings,* 2:187).

To Jesse Jones and Others

June 3. 1811

I have recd. fellow Citizens your address,¹ approving my Objection to the Bill contain[in]g a grant of public land, to the Baptist Church at Salem Meeting House Missippi Terry. Having always regarded the practical distinction between Religion & Civil Govt as essential to the purity of both, and as guaranteed by the Constn: of the U. S. I could not have otherwise discharged my duty on the occasion which presented itself. Among the various religious Societies in our Country, none have been more vigilant or constant in maintain[in]g that distinction, than the Society of which you make a part, and it is an honourable proof of your sincerity & integrity, that you are as ready to do so, in a case favoring the interest of your brethren, as in other cases. It is but just, at the same time, to the Baptist Church at Salem Meeting House, to remark that their application to the Natl. Legislature does not appear to have contemplated a grant of the Land in question, but on terms that might be equitable to the public as well as to themselves. Accept my friendly respects

Draft (DLC). Addressed by JM "To the Baptist Churches on Neals' Creek & on Black Creek, N. Carla."

1. Jesse Jones and others to JM, 27 Apr. 1811.

From John Quincy Adams

(Private.)

SIR   ST: PETERSBURG 3. June 1811.

I received on the 29th: of last Month, together with some other despatches from the Secretary of State, one, enclosing a Commission to me, as an associate Justice of the Supreme Court of the United States; a new letter of leave to His Majesty the Emperor of Russia; a blank Commission for a Secretary of Legation, or Chargé d'Affaires, and an Instruction, in consequence of this new appointment to return to the United States, as soon as the public interest and my own convenience will admit.[1]

The new mark of confidence which you have been pleased to shew me, in the nomination to an Office so highly honourable, and so far as could relate to my own personal interest and concerns so acceptable, has made on my mind an impression which no time can obliterate, and which leaves me the more earnestly to regret my incapacity to meet it with a return the most agreeable to you—by assuming and discharging its duties in a manner to justify that Confidence and do honour to your appointment.

In the letters which I had the honour of writing you on the 7th: of Jany: & 8th: of Feby last, I intimated to you that the peculiar Circumstances of my family would probably make it impracticable for me to embark with them for the United States, during the present year, and in the former I informed you that under those Circumstances, if you should judge that the termination of my mission here had become expedient, I should remain here as a private individual untill the next Summer. This obstacle to my departure remains, as when those letters were written; and should my Successor at this Court arrive during the present Season, I shall find myself under the necessity of obtaining the Emperor's permission to reside here, probably untill this time next year, but at least untill I can commence my homeward voyage, without exposing to extraordinary and unnecessary dangers, lives which ought to be dearer to me than my own.

There are contingencies which might enable me at a very late period of this Season to embark, but I have little hope to reckon upon some of them, and still less inclination to anticipate the rest. My expectation is to be detained here the next Winter, by ties which the affections of a husband and a parent can neither dissolve nor sever.

I cannot expect, nor however it might suit my convenience can I permit myself to desire, that you should keep an office of such importance vacant a full year longer to await my return, and this consideration is decisive to induce me to decline the appointment. It might also relieve me from the necessity of expressing to you other motives operating upon my disposition to produce the same result, some of which are of peculiar delicacy, and for the avowal of which I must in a special manner solicit your candour and indulgence.

My Education to the Law was regular, and during several short periods in the course of my life, I have been in professional practice at the Bar: But its studies were never among those most congenial to my temper, and the great proportion of my time has been employed in occupations so different from those of the Judicial tribunals, that I have long entertained a deep and serious distrust of my qualifications for a seat on the Bench. This Sentiment was so strong, that it induced me soon after my return from Europe in 1801 to decline the proposal of being a candidate for a vacancy in the Supreme Court of my native State, at a time when I was in private life, and when that situation would have been altogether suitable to my own convenience. It has long been known to my most intimate friends, and would have been communicated to you, had the prospect of such a nomination ever presented itself to me, as sufficiently probable to warrant my interference to prevent it. In the present instance the reluctance would be much increased, by a conviction as clear to my understanding, as it is impressive upon my feelings, that there is another person, a friend whom I most highly value, in every respect better qualified than myself, for that particular Office, and whom my warm wishes, perhaps more than the rigour of principle, have considered as having pretensions to it, at least far superior to mine.

I speak of Mr: Davis, the present District Judge for Massachusetts,[2] a man of whom an intimate acquaintance of many years entitles me to say that he is equally estimable by the purity of his heart, the firmness of his temper, and the solidity of his judgment—Whose education and professional practice have been with little if any interruption devoted to the Law; and who by an experience of ten years in his present Station has been peculiarly prepared for the duties of an Office so exactly analogous to it.

I am aware of all the considerations, which may perhaps concur in giving you other views connected with this subject, and which may lead your ultimate determination to another person. Mr: Davis's political opinions and more especially those of his social connections may render it necessary to contemplate the possible operation of his appointment to this place upon the public Sentiment. The extent and influence of this reflection it would not become me were it even within my competence to discuss; but you will, I am persuaded permit me the recollection that Mr: Davis on one signal, and not untrying occasion, manifested at once the steadiness of his mind, his inflexible adherence to the Law, his independence of party prejudices and controul, and his determination to support at the Post allotted to him the Administration of Government in all Constitutional Measures.[3] I may perhaps estimate too highly the qualities of which in that instance he gave such decisive proof, and you may not have been made acquainted with the power of that influence to which he then proved himself inaccessible. I need not enlarge upon it, and can apologize to you for having said so much, only as it will explain to you the motives upon which I should have such serious disinclination to occupy a place, which my heart and my reason would so perfectly concur in assigning by preference to another.

I must then intreat you, Sir, to confer upon some other person the Office as a Judge of the Supreme Court to which you have had the goodness to appoint me. The impossibility of my return to the United States in due time to assume its duties, must of itself forbid my acceptance of it. The other reasons which would in any case impel me to decline it I should have suppressed but for the high sense of my personal obligation to you for the nomination, and the wish to be justified in your opinion for renouncing the Post for which you have judged me suitably qualified.

I shall therefore wait for your further Instructions respecting my continuance at this Court. It may be proper for me however to add that the public expectation in the United States, and that of the Emperor and his Government here being now fully prepared for my removal, I earnestly solicit that the motive of my personal convenience may be set aside whenever you shall think my recall expedient on public considerations. If the condition of my family should delay my return home, when the want of my Services here has ceased, I had much rather bear the charge and inconvenience to which it might subject me than remain an unnecessary incumbrance upon the public.

I shall at all Events remain here a time sufficient to receive your ultimate determination not only upon my letters of 7. Jany: and 8. Feby. but also upon this one, and I beg you to be assured that on my return to the United States, whenever you shall deem it proper, and I shall find it practicable, whether in public Office of any kind or in retirement, the grateful sense of your kindness, and the most fervent wishes for the prosperity of your public administration, and the promotion of your personal happiness, will be among the sentiments nearest to my heart. I am with perfect respect and attachment, Sir, your very humble and obedt Servt:

JOHN QUINCY ADAMS.

RC (NN: Lee Kohns Memorial Collection); letterbook copy (MHi: Adams Family Papers). RC docketed by JM.

1. See Robert Smith to Adams, 26 Feb. 1811 (DNA: RG 59, IM).

2. John Davis had been nominated judge of the district of Massachusetts by President John Adams on 18 Feb. 1801 (*Senate Exec. Proceedings*, 1:381).

3. Adams was probably referring to Davis's 1808 decision to uphold the constitutionality of the Embargo in the case *United States* v. *The William* (see Douglas Lamar Jones, "'The Caprice of Juries': The Enforcement of the Jeffersonian Embargo in Massachusetts," *American Journal of Legal History*, 24 [1980]: 320, 323–24).

From Asher Robbins

NEWPORT R. ISLAND, 3d June 1811.

I hope, Sir, the occasion of my addressing you personally will be received, as a sufficient apology for the liberty, which I have taken. I have recently been informed, from a source entitled to respect, that whilst you were deliberating upon the selection of a Successor to Judge Cushing, you received a letter from, this State, denouncing me as a monarchist in principle; and that the standing of the writer was such, as to give it effect.[1] I owe it to myself to declare to you Sir, that the representation is a calumny, fabricated without the least regard to truth, and for which I defy the writer to give even a specious excuse, from any thing I ever did or wrote or said. No. Sir. Always ardent and undisguized in my Sentiment of zeal for the Union of these states—of devotion to the Constitution as the means of perpetuating that Union, and thereby making our republican institutions immortal—and of gratitude to those, whose labors like yours have eminently contributed to this national establishment so full of present good, and of future promise, it is impossible for this Calumniator, to give even a specious coloring to his charge. Such Communications, I presume are deemed confidential, and that it would be improper therefore to request to you to expose the one to which I allude. In this situation I can only appeal to you sir, for protection; and must pray you to do me the justice, to beleive, that, the injurious charge, was a calumny, without excuse, or palliation. With sentiments of the highest esteem & attachment I am Sir Your devoted frd & Servt

ASHER ROBBINS.

RC (DLC). Docketed by JM.

1. David Howell to JM, 26 Nov. 1810.

From Gideon Granger

June 5. 1811

G Granger presents his compliments to the President—returns Mr. Barbour's letter,[1] and informs the President that he has established an office at Barboursville, and directed the horse mail to be delivered there weekly. He has also directed the contractor to furnish the President, while at his Seat, with Intelligence & lines of Correspondence on the arrangement of last Summer.

RC (DLC). Docketed by JM.

1. James Barbour to JM, 29 May 1811.

§ **From Clement Biddle.** *6 June 1811, Philadelphia.* "I find that Mr. Carrington is returned from Canton & as he may not probably go back a Vacancy in the Consulship may take place." Requests the place for his son, George W. Biddle, who has resided there for several years and is "much respected and esteemed particularly by the Gentlemen of the British factory." Has written to Monroe on this subject.

RC (DNA: RG 59, LAR, 1809–17, filed under "Biddle"). 2 pp. Addressee not indicated.

§ **From John Millar.** *6 June 1811, Darien, Georgia.* Gives an account of his life and his efforts to study and become a physician. "I was advis'd by a gentleman to complete my studies in the southern climate, as . . . the manner of treatment was different to what it is in the Northern States & in all probability would be a better place for one of that profession." Moved to Georgia from Kentucky in October 1810 to continue his studies, but his funds have proved to be insufficient. Requests the sum of $500 to defray his expenses including the cost of purchasing instruments and medicine to begin his practice "in a place that really wants a physician."

RC (DLC). 2 pp. Docketed by JM.

§ **From Cornelio de Saavedra and Others.**[1] *6 June 1811, Buenos Aires.* The signatories state that their government, desiring to secure the fullest safety from attacks from abroad by peoples who either are its enemies or assault its liberty, seeks arms from the U.S.—a generous nation which appreciates in the most noble manner the just liberty of men. This task is entrusted to Diego de Saavedra and Juan Pedro de Aguirre, for whom the assistance and protection of the U.S. government is requested. In order to ensure the success of their mission, which depends on the greatest and most solemn secrecy, they will travel with passports under the names of Pedro Lopez and Jose Cabrera, which will also avoid compromising the U.S. in any way in the eyes of England or any other nation that might needlessly take offense. This measure is undertaken to communicate with the U.S. government through the medium of JM and to recommend these commissioners to his protection.

RC (DNA: RG 59, NFL, Argentina). 2 pp. In Spanish. Signed by Saavedra and fifteen others. Translation printed in Manning, *Diplomatic Correspondence of the United States concerning the Independence of the Latin-American Nations*, 1:321.

1. Cornelio de Saavedra (1760–1828) first rose to prominence in Buenos Aires during the resistance to the British assaults on the city in 1806–7. He was subsequently elected first president of the popular junta established in Buenos Aires on 25 May 1810 (see Junta of the Provinces of the Río de la Plata to JM, 11 Feb. 1811, and n. 1). Joel Roberts Poinsett did not rate Saavedra's abilities very highly, describing him as "an intriguing ambitious Man, but without talents to conceive an extensive design or to see beyond the consequence that may immediately result from it." Saavedra's presidency did not survive the difficulties arising from the efforts of the Buenos Aires junta to extend its authority over the other provinces of the La Plata region, and he was ousted from power on 26 Aug. 1811 after forces loyal to the Supreme Central Government Junta in Spain defeated an army sent from Buenos Aires at Huaqui on 20 June 1811. Saavedra went into exile in Chile and did not return to Buenos Aires until 1818 (Poinsett to Robert Smith, 11 Apr. 1811 [PHi: Poinsett Papers]; Levene, *A History of Argentina*, pp. 191–202, 240–70).

To Thomas Jefferson

DEAR SIR   WASHINGTON June 7. 1811

I return the letter from you to D.[1] on the subject of Mr. G.[2] He seems to be incorrigible. If I am not misinformed, his eyes are opening to the conduct & character of Mr. S, with respect to both of which he has suffered himself to be misled partly by his own passions, partly by those who took advantage of them. You see the new shapes our foreign relations are taking. The occurrence between Rogers & the British ship of war, not unlikely to bring on repetitions, will probably end in an open rupture, or a better understanding as the calculations of the B. Govt. may prompt or dissuade from war. Among the items in these will be the temper here, as reported by its partizans. The state of parties in Massts. is in this view important, especially as it will attract particular notice by its effect in degrading Pickering who has made himself so conspicuous in the British service. On the other hand much impatience is shewing itself in the Eastn: States, under the nonimportation. The little embarrassment which occurs in procuring returns for the apples[3] & onions sent from Connecticut to the W. Indies, is generating remonstrances as in the case of the Embargo. I have been obliged to answer one from N. Haven headed by Hillhouse, which they have not yet published.[4] The protracted delay of the Essex still leaves us a prey to the ignorance & interested falsehoods which fill our newspapers. It would seem that G. B. is determined agst. repealing her orders, and that Bonaparte is equally so agst[5] the destruction of her commerce, to which he readily sacrifices his own commerce with the U. S. As to the blockade of England (the decree to which alone the Act of Congs. & the Proclamation have reference), there is no evidence of its being continued in force. All the Official evidence is on the other side. And yet by a confusion of ideas or artifice of language, the appearance is kept up that the ground of the non-importation has failed, and that it is consequently a wrong to G. B. After all, we must remain somewhat in the dark till we hear more on the subject; probably till the return of the vessel that carried to France, the Act of Congs. putting in force the non-importation, for wch. Bonapt. seems to be waiting. After a severe drought, we have had a copious rain. I hope you have shared ⟨in⟩ it & that it will have aided the wheatfeilds in their conflict with the Hessian fly. Be assured of my constant & truest affection

JAMES MADISON

RC (DLC). Docketed by Jefferson, "recd June 9."

    1. At a later time JM interlined the remaining letters of "Duane."

    2. At a later time JM interlined the remaining letters of "Gallatin."

    3. At a later time someone, possibly JM, interlined "articles" here.

    4. Both the 11 Mar. petition from the New Haven town meeting and JM's 24 May response were published in the *National Intelligencer* on 20 June 1811.

    5. At a later time someone, possibly JM, crossed through "agst" and interlined "on."

From James Jay

DEAR SIR,   NEW YORK June 7. 1811

When the just measures of Government meet with so much opposition as they do at present, it becomes the duty of every friend to his Country to support them. With this view I acquaint you that there are persons in this City and other parts of the State, who are taking measures, on a large Scale, to introduce British goods from Canada into the adjacent States. One part of the Scheme is to fix Agents for the purpose in Montreal and other convenient places. This hint I hope may enable you to defeat or at least diminish the impending Evil. It would be best not to mention my name on the occasion; and this I suggest, not from any personal consideration, for I care not if this Letter should be published, but lest it may prevent me from getting further information on the subject.

I hope you enjoy good health, and should you continue to possess that blessing, I have no doubt but our Country will triumph over her foreign and domestic Enemies. With great regard, I remain Dear Sir Your Very humble Servt.

JAMES JAY [1]

RC (DLC). Docketed by JM.

    1. James Jay (1732–1815) was the older brother of former chief justice John Jay.

§ Account with St. Mary's College. *7 June 1811*. Lists charges to JM for John Payne Todd between 11 Dec. 1810 and 7 June 1811, including two quarters' tuition, books, and extra money advanced, amounting to $63.08½.

Ms (MdBS: Day Book, 1810–13). 1 p.

§ From George Joy. *9 June 1811, Copenhagen.* Reports arrival on 30 May of Erving who gave him JM's letter of 28 Jan.[1] The documents he sent to JM and the secretary of state will show how he protracted the most important cases until Erving's arrival, and he has no doubt decisions can be delayed "till Mr: Erving has had sufficient opportunity to confer with Count Rozenkrantz." His own conversation with the latter and the cabinet secretary suggest outcomes favorable to the objects of Erving's mission. Is willing to offer his services but perceives no disposition in Erving to accept them,[2] and he will therefore have no further communication with the minister of foreign affairs. Has endeavored to inform Erving of the "diversity of Character" between government officials, on the one hand, and the prize courts, on the other; has also warned him of the king's desire to exercise whatever power he can.

Hopes Erving's reluctance to accept his services will not work against Erving's goals. Fears Erving "may have paid some attention to the miserable trash that has been circulated about me" in the newspapers, where an author writing as "Jay" called him an "old Tory and a London Broker." Denies charges that he has justified British policies toward America and refers JM to the publications he sent him under the signature of "Conciliator,"[3] and the copies of suggestions under his own name written to members of Parliament. Any man in London will attest to the truth of this, but if JM is affected by any of these insinuations, he will "certainly be at the pains of collecting the most ample Evidence to refute them."

Asserts that he always considered American resistance to British oppression legitimate and justified. Until the time he met JM he had never been more than sixteen months in England, though JM will never "get over the Idea of 'the English Relations in which I stand.'" Had intended, after arriving in Virginia, to end his days in the U.S. Has been much in England since then, but he has also been in France, Holland, and Germany.

When he thought ten years ago of seeking public employment JM mentioned the pretensions of "persons *at home.*" He had responded that George Erving, Jr., with no more pretensions than himself, had just been sent to the consulate in London. "Now comes the same Mr George Erving, no longer junr., his father having since died in London, with a letter from you speaking of 'the English relations in which I stand.'" Protests the injustice of this, mentioning that Erving's father was "'an *old Tory*' of such notoriety as to be nominated a Mandamus Counsellor" and that Erving himself had been educated in England and had not spent five years of his life in America. Joy's father was a Tory whose five sons all opposed his politics, although "it might be erroneous, to derive any inference from this, unfavorable to the Americanism of Mr. Erving" given his relationship with his father. "If any inference is to be drawn I do think it more unfavorable to him than to me." Has three brothers in America and one in England. Of the patriotism of the former, nothing need be said; of the latter, refers JM to Dr. Eustis, his classmate at Cambridge, and to former president Adams. Does not believe that this connection should "angli-

cize" him and repeats that his purpose was to promote American interests by sham-
ing the British government into abandoning their "unjust and impolitic measures."

"Perhaps you will say the objection lies only against an Employment in a Department of france," but he has already stated that he would serve even at the Tuil-
eries in a just cause. Refers JM to his correspondence with Smith in July[4] and with
JM himself on 2 Sept.[5] Asks to be given the consulate at Copenhagen and, assuming
that Erving will not remain long, to combine it with the position of chargé d'affaires. The king will have no objections and high officials have hinted they "would
even like it." "It is known that I have cleared every ship that her Officers have
thought fit to place in my hands." His meetings with officials also suggest their
willingness to diminish American causes of complaint. Does not believe that "anything pernicious can be inferred" from this intimation, "but I rather perceive in it
an indication of the mutual benefit to be derived from that sort of intercourse upon
which I have before observed as recommended by you to General Armstrong."

Discusses at length the details of one case as yet undecided and about which he
wrote to Smith in December.[6] Apologizes, as always, for the length of his letters;
promises to make his next letter shorter.

RC (DLC: Rives Collection, Madison Papers). 22 pp. For probable enclosures, see n. 2.

1. Letter not found. In a forty-seven-page letter written to John Quincy Adams on 8 May
1812, a copy of which he later forwarded to JM (DLC), Joy described in detail the circumstances under which Erving delivered JM's letter to him. Joy provided Adams with little information as to the contents of JM's letter beyond mentioning that it was evidence of his "un-
abated friendship" with the president and that JM had described Erving as "a person of talents
and experience," a claim that Joy disputed in every way he possibly could.

2. In order to demonstrate his willingness to assist Erving, Joy evidently enclosed copies
of the following letters: Joy to John Quincy Adams, 27 Apr. 1811 (DLC: Rives Collection,
Madison Papers; 6 pp.); Joy to Erving, 11 May 1811 (DLC; 3 pp.); Joy to Erving, 25 May 1811
(DLC; 1 p.); Joy to Erving, 2 June 1811 (DLC; 2 pp.); Erving to Joy, 2 June 1811 (DLC; 1 p.);
Joy to Erving, 5 June 1811 (DLC; 1 p.); Erving to Joy, 5 June 1811 (DLC; 1 p.).

3. See "Extracts from Notes on the Report from the Committee of the House of Commons on the Commercial State of the West India Colonies, . . . appending thereto with a short
notice of the Pamphlet entitled Concessions to America the Bane of Britain by Conciliator,"
enclosed in Joy to JM, 5 Oct. 1807 (DLC). In his his 11 Oct. 1807 letter to JM, Joy enclosed
"Further Extracts from Notes on the Report from the West India Committee" by "Conciliator" (DLC).

4. See Joy to Robert Smith, 10 July 1810, with postscripts dated 13 and 20 July (DNA: RG
59, CD, Copenhagen).

5. See *PJM-PS*, 2:521.

6. See Joy to JM, 19 Dec. 1810, and n. 5.

From Jonathan Russell

SIR   PARIS 10th June 1811.

I have learnt with much pain that Mr Pinkney, the American Minister at
London, has publicly censured, with great asperity, my conduct, as it relates

to him, since I have been entrusted with this legation. The only charge however which he has preferred against me, with any precision, is that my correspondance with him has been incorrect, inasmuch as I did not communicate to him the seizure of the New-orleans-Packet & that while I was remonstrating here against this seizure I was endeavouring to prove to him that the decrees under which it was made had ceased to operate.[1]

In making this charge he warms himself, I understand, into all his eloquence & sparing neither my head or my heart, he endeavours to prove at once my imbecillity & perversity. Nor is he fastidious in selecting the tribunal before which he arraigns me—and friends & foes—foreigners and fellow citizens have alike to listen to his accusations. Samuel Williams Esquire of London, who is probably not unknown to you as the nephew & correspondent of Mr. Pickering has written to an American Gentleman here that Mr. Pinkney has declared to him that "my conduct had been so incorrect that he should open no more of my letters & that I must be recalled."

It is thus I am brought to trial before an agent of the adversaries of the administration—for an offence which I am not conscious of having committed—& for which I am to be condemned, unheard, to suffer the double punishment of indignity & disgrace.

Before such a tribunal I cannot consent to plead, but before you, Sir, I appear and I doubt not I shall be judged with liberality & justice. In doing this I am actuated by a solicitude only to vindicate myself in your opinion, for, situated as I am, the punishment threatened by Mr Pinkney has no terrors for me. His contumely with whatever indecency accompanied I can regard with indifference & I shall be out of office long before the displeasure of my government, however it may be urged by his spleen, can overtake me.

The great end which I have proposed to myself in all my proceedings since I have been here has been to promote the glory of your administration by preserving if possible the honour & peace of my country. I found our relations both with this country & with England in a very critical state—it was uncertain in what manner the revocation of the Berlin & Milan decrees would be executed or whether this revocation would produce the repeal of the British orders. The entire extinction of all these offending edicts was however required by our rights and our interests. All my feeble efforts were therefore anxiously directed to the accomplishment of this object & while I excited the good faith of this government for the performance of its engagements I endeavoured to represent its conduct, through Mr. Pinkney, to its enemies as sufficient to exact from them the abolition of a system which had hitherto professedly rested on the sole basis of retaliation. Solicitous as I was however to take from the British cabinet this pretext for perseverance in its injustice I stated no fact to Mr. Pinkney which the truth did not warrant & I concealed none from him, of a decided character & which of course it would have been useful for him to know. The inclosed file (No. 1) contains every word on this subject which I have written to him.[2] If the course which I have pursued was not obviously pointed out by true policy still I should have been strongly persuaded to adopt it at the suggestion of Mr. Pinkney himself. In his first letter addressed to me (No. 2) he asks for evidence *confirmatory* only of the revocation of the French edicts & of the effect of that revocation.[3] This request of his appears alone sufficient to justify me for not attempting to prove to him that those decrees were still in force. Such proof, unless of a character to settle conclusively the fact—and in this case I should not have withheld it—would have served only to have embarrassed Mr Pinkney & to have clogged his negociations. I did not therefore communicate to him my apprehensions or those equivocal occurrences which occasionally alarmed me. Among the latter was the seizure of the New-Orleans-Packet. I felt it my duty to remonstrate against this transaction to the Government here[4]—and to communicate my remonstrance, like every other of my official acts, immediately to my own government. Before however I addressed to Mr. Pinkney an account of this event I conceived it became me to ascertain its real character. If it should prove to be the mere unauthorized act of a subordinate officer, the premature knowledge of it would have been to him a source of perplexity only. Had he indeed possessed this knowledge he probably would have concealed it from the British government, for the proceedure of the officer at Bordeaux, in this stage of it, proved nothing either for or against the revocation of the decrees—and this is the construction which Congress appears to have put upon it in passing the supplementary law. Such a concealment might have been regarded by the British ministry as unfair & uncandid & have subjected him to unpleasant reproof, when detected. I can but think it very unreasonable therefore in Mr. Pinkney to comment in so harsh & undignified a manner on an omission which has saved him from the dilemma of disclosing a fact that might have suspended his negociations or of concealing it to the injury of his standing with the court near which he resided.

In fine I cannot beleive that Mr. Pinkney, is well founded in his complaints, that I wrote the note of the 10th of December to the Duke of Cadore—that I transmitted a copy of this note to my government & that I did not communicate to him the fact to which it related.

If the *publication* of this note has been attended with disagreeable consequences to Mr. Pinkney I certainly am not responsible. I wrote that note for the government here that it might arrest the proceedings of one of its officers before they should become a violation of its engagements. I rendered a prompt account, as was my duty, of what I had done to the government I served, but the publication of this account was not an act of mine nor can I beleive myself answerable to Mr. Pinkney for any chagrin it might have occasioned him. Indeed I must take the liberty to declare to you most sincerely that the publication of my note in question was entirely unexpected to me & that I learnt it with much regret. It came however to the British ministry when the real character of their policy was ascertained— after they had determined to persist in their orders altho' they knew of no fact here inconsistent with the revocation of the decrees or which could longer bear them out on the principle of retaliation. They may indeed still cavil but surely they can deceive no one—and in my estimation it is no imperfect justification of the omission of which Mr. Pinkney complains that it has furnished this test of their system.

I hope that what I have said will be sufficient to persuade you of the correctness—if not of my deeds—at least of my intentions & that—if I have not done right I sincerely meant to do so. I must hope also that the accusations of Mr. Pinkney—for I doubt not he will prefer them to you— will be examined with candour & fairly weighed against the reasons I have assigned for my conduct.

It is indeed to be lamented that any controversy should arise between the mandatories of our government abroad, & still more to be lamented that these should declaim against each other before foreign nations whose obvious interest it is to encourage dissention. This mode of indulging a wounded temper cannot promote their own reputation—the interests of their country or the dignity of the government which they serve. If influenced by these considerations I be silent before the public & therefore condemned—I shall feel proudly indemnified for this injustice if to the acquital of my own conscience I can add your approbation.

I have sent by this opportunity to the secretary of State a concise history of the case of the New-Orleans-Packet.[5] I persuade myself that the facts there set forth will fully vindicate the course of proceedings which I adopted in relation to her. If it should be thought proper to communicate this statement to the public I should hope that many strange comments made on my conduct—& which I cannot consent to notice in any other way—might be corrected.

With regard to the *tone* of my letter to the Duke of Cadore on this subject, which appears to have alarmed the very sensitive friends of this Government, I must avail myself of this occasion to say that no offence was given by it—but on the other hand it arrested the proceedings against the New-Orleans-Packet & gave me a personal standing here with the minister which I had not before. To this tone indeed I may fairly ascribe much of the consideration & civility which I have since enjoyed. I beg you to be assured of the very great respect with which I am Sir Your faithful & Obedient Servant

JONA RUSSELL

RC and enclosures (DLC: Rives Collection, Madison Papers); FC (RPB-JH: Russell Papers). RC docketed by JM; also docketed by Monroe. For enclosures, see nn. 2 and 3. Minor differences between the RC and the FC have not been noted.

1. Although JM, in his acknowledgment of Russell's letter, wrote that the information concerning Pinkney's charges was "not confirmed by any thing heretofore known to me," the minister, in his 13 Mar. 1811 dispatch to the State Department, did complain about Russell's handling of the *New Orleans Packet* case. The publication in Great Britain of Russell's 11 Dec. 1810 letter to Robert Smith reporting the seizure of the vessel in Bordeaux under the Berlin and Milan decrees, Pinkney declared, would have the "worst possible effect" had the ministry been seriously contemplating issuing fresh instructions on colonial importations. Pinkney further complained that none of Russell's letters to him in December 1810 made any mention of the *New Orleans Packet*, nor did they inform him of any development that might adversely affect the American interpretation of the Cadore letter (JM to Russell, 15 Nov. 1811 [DNA: RG 59, DD, France]; Pinkney to Robert Smith, 13 Mar. 1811 [DNA: RG 59, DD, Great Britain]; Russell to Robert Smith, 11 Dec. 1810, printed in *ASP, Foreign Relations*, 3:390–91).

2. Russell enclosed copies of his letters to Pinkney under the dates of 26 Sept. and 1, 11, 13, 27, 29, and 30 Dec. 1810 (10 pp.). In his letter of 27 Dec. 1810 he mentioned that he had *"learnt the Seizure & capture of two or three American vessels"* but that it was "unnecessary to enter into a particular detail of the circumstances which attended these cases" since the French government had already instructed the Council of Prizes to suspend them and not judge them under the principles of the Berlin and Milan decrees. Russell conceded that although the conduct of the French government "may not be entirely satisfactory," it would "at least be sufficient to procure from the British Government a repeal of the orders in Council."

3. Russell enclosed a one-page extract from a 7 Oct. 1810 letter from Pinkney stating that it would be "obviously prudent, even if it be not *absolutely necessary*, to furnish me with all such further evidence, as can conveniently be gained, *confirmatory* of our expectation that the French repeal of the Berlin and Milan Decrees will take effect on the 1st of november." Specifically, Pinkney requested *"after the 1st of november the most decisive proof* in your power that the repeal *has taken effect*—at least an official letter from you to me stating that fact."

4. In his 11 Dec. 1810 dispatch to the State Department, Russell had included a copy of his letter of the previous day to the duc de Cadore, protesting the seizure of the *New Orleans Packet* (see *ASP, Foreign Relations*, 3:391).

5. Russell to Monroe, 9 June 1811 (printed ibid., 3:502–3).

§ To Asher Robbins. *10 June 1811, Washington.* Acknowledges receipt of a letter from Robbins.[1] "Its declaration of your principles & sentiments on certain subjects will have the attention which is due to the frankness and explicitness with which it is made." Does not authorize "any inference from this assurance, that might prejudice any individual whatever in your estimation."

Printed summary (*The Collector*, No. 801 [1967], item A-98).

1. Robbins to JM, 3 June 1811.

§ From William Lambert. *10 June 1811, Washington.* Encloses for JM's "inspection and transmission, a communication to bishop Madison, relating to the longitude of William and Mary College from Greenwich, by computation from the end of the Solar eclipse of June 16th. 1806."

RC (DLC). 2 pp. Enclosure not found.

§ Edward Coles to Dolley Madison. *10 June 1811, New York*. Observes that it is impossible to comply with his promise to write on everything that interests him. "As you expressed some curiosity to know how the Smiths &c would treat me, I requested Payne, who told me he was about to write, to inform you that I was treated quite civilly by them all, but that their displeasure with the President and yourself was very apparent."[1] Mentions having "waited on Mr. & Mrs. R. Smith" who "received us very civilly." "After conversing some short time we rose to take leave, when Mrs. Smith asked me if I had been to see Gen. Smiths family, on my answering in the negative, she said she would go with me to shew me the way. We met with the same kind of reception at Gen. Smith. Our visits were the next day returned. We dined & were twice invited to take tea at Gen. Smiths. None of them made any enquiries after you, or the President, except Mrs. Gen. S., who ask[ed] after *your* health. I was quite diverted at the caution & sameness of the enquiries of Gen., and Mr. & Mrs. R. Smith. 'I hope you left our friends well in Washington' said they. The Smiths are said not directly to vent their spleen, but to spur on their relations & friends, many of whom are extremely abusive of the President & Col. Monroe. As a proof of which, it is only necessary to tell the President that those abusive & scurrilous pieces signed Timolean, that made their appearance some time since in the Whig,[2] are now publicly known (indeed he boasts of being the author), to be from the pen of George Stevenson, the son-in-Law of P. Carr, & the nephew of the Smiths who lives in the counting room of Gen. Smith. I believe I have said too much about this little clan, whose vanity or weakness is such, as to make them believe that they can make & unmak⟨e⟩ any administration; but you will excuse me for having written so much when I tell you that *you* are somewhat a *favourite* with them, for on meeting in the St. Dr. Leib, who is one of their leaders in Phia., he made no other enquiry but after *your* health."

Congratulates her on the safe arrival of her brother, John. In a postscript mentions that while he was in Philadelphia some friends of B. C. Wilcocks requested that he recommend Wilcocks as consul for Canton.[3] "I promised to name him to the President as a person anxious to obtain the above appointment. I have no doubt but what he has furnished letters of recommendation,[4] but in order to comply with my promise, I wish you to name this to the President."

RC (NN). 4 pp.

1. In acknowledging Coles's letter on 15 June 1811, Dolley Madison wrote that "Payne gave me the *little* account you directed, & I exult in my heart at the full indemnification we have for all their Malice, in Colo. Monroe's talents & virtue" (owned by Mr. and Mrs. George B. Cutts, Brookline, Mass., 1958).

2. Essays under the pseudonym of Timoleon, the fourth century B.C. liberator of Greek Sicily from Carthage, appeared occasionally throughout 1810 and 1811 in the Baltimore *Whig*. The most recent of these had been published on 9 Apr. 1811 in the form of some remarks on the "late change in the department of state." By way of introduction, Timoleon described how JM, as secretary of state, had written diplomatic instructions for James Monroe during the latter's tenure as American minister in London in order to advance President Jefferson's goal of negotiating an Anglo-American convention to "secure our neutral rights." Monroe had violated those instructions by making "*forbidden* concessions" to Great Britain, yet, Timoleon complained, he was now restored to the good graces of the administration "without having atoned for a single error."

This development led Timoleon into reflections on the baneful influence of Gallatin over administration policy in general and Maryland state politics in particular. Treasury tactics, as revealed in the attack on the house of Smith and Buchanan after the failure of Degen and Purviance in Leghorn and also in the more recent attacks on the Clintonians by the "Martling Men" in New York City, were then denounced by Timoleon for their tendency to divide the Republican party and thus facilitate the return of the Federalists to power. Further to this purpose, Timoleon claimed that after September 1810 Gallatin had embarked on schemes to "brighten the tarnished reputation of Mr. Monroe," and that in February 1811 he had communicated to several members of Congress his intention to see Robert Smith ousted from the cabinet. Even Timoleon himself had learned of the plot, but "never having been personally intimate with either of the Smiths, [he] did not apprize them of it." He did, however, criticize JM for having "neither firmness nor ingenuousness . . . to acquaint Mr. Smith with his intentions directly" in seeking to replace him in the State Department.

 3. JM nominated Benjamin Chew Wilcocks to be consul at Canton on 31 Dec. 1812 (*Senate Exec. Proceedings*, 2:313).

 4. See Jared Ingersoll to JM, 4 June 1811; William Jones to [JM?], 4 June 1811; Benjamin C. Wilcocks to JM, 5 June 1811; Benjamin Rush to James Monroe, 5 June 1811 (DNA: RG 59, LAR, 1809–17, filed under "Wilcocks").

¶ To James Jay. Letter not found. *10 June 1811.* Acknowledged in Jay to JM, 1 July 1811. Discusses the smuggling of British goods from Canada into the U.S.

From Alexander Wolcott

Sir,   Middletown Ct. 11 June 1811

I received a letter a short time since from a Mr. Jacob Ogden Jr., a native of this State, now residing at Havana, informing me that he contemplated establishing himself in business, either at Buenos Ayres or at Monte Video and expressing a wish to be appointed consul at one of those places. With regard to the expediency of such an appointment I have formed no opinion. I have had very little personal knowledge of Mr. Ogden since he was 21 years old, (he is now about thirty) but have frequently heard of his progress in the world, and of his reputation. Owing to the failure of his father in business he started in the world pennyless, but he is now, not only flourishing as respects property, but has established a character for more than common industry, intelligence and integrity, and if it should be thought expedient to appoint a commercial agent of any sort, at either of the places mentioned, I have no doubt that Mr Ogden is perfectly well qualified for the place.

May I be permitted, Sir, to avail myself of the present occasion, tho late, to say a word respecting your nomination of me as a Judge of the Supreme court of the United States. You have given me, Sir, an indubitable proof of high confidence in me; of this I am proud, for this I am grateful; as these are the only sentiments, of any force that the whole of the transaction has at any time excited, so these, I beg leave to assure you, will be durable. As to the result, or the causes that produced the result, in the Senate, so far as respects myself I think not of them; indeed my knowledge of the characters of men had prepared me for something like it. I regret only, that, whatever may be your opinion of those causes, the affair must have occasioned you a degree of mortificatn. For myself, it is no boast to say that calumnies old or new affect me not. I have, long since, been compelled to learn what malice can do and to place myself out of its reach by contemning its efforts. I beg you Sir to accept assurances of my unfeigned gratitude and perfect respect.

ALEX. WOLCOTT

RC (DLC). Docketed by JM.

From Alexander Hamilton

DEAR SIR,   LISBON June 12th 1811

If I have not already, too much trespassed upon your attention, permit me to observe, that the commercial Interests of the United States, are now unrepresented in Portugal. The consulate office, in consequence of the absence of Mr Jarvis, has become vacant.[1] If it comports with your feelings & does not interfer, with the arrangements of Government, I should be happy, through your personal influence, to obtain this station. From the natural indolence & love of ease, that pervades this country, this will always be an important mart, for American productions. As the true policy of our country is to secure, an honorable tranquility, we should avoid exotic transactions as productive of vexatious changes & confirm those arrangements, founded in mutual interests. These degenerate people, are so excessively ignorant, that an attempt to reformation by revolution, would be productive of the most sanguinary consequences & from the nature of such ingredients, would terminate in a more extreme slavery. The laws of this nation I understand, are excellent, they are however a dead letter.[2] The influence of our commercial rival, has already evidenced its invidious effects, by the adoption of a system of exclusion, that prohibits the admission of all liquors, from the United States, that may arrive here, after the *10th May past.* Should security & tranquility be restored, the ascendancy of Great Britain, will be more dependent upon personal influence, than national power. The councils of Portugal, will represent the prejudices of individuals, themselves dependent upon commercial calculations & private affections.

Should you have time, to reply to my request a letter addressed, to the care of Mess: Le Roy Bayard & McEvers New York will be carefully trans-

339

mitted to Mess Baring Brothers & Co London my commercial correspondents. My intention is to be in England, about the last of August.

The combined forces, in Spain & Portugal have dearly purchased their late victories & from present appearances, there is every expectation, of a decisive battle, on the plains of Merida. Marshalls Soult & Victor have about 50.000 Men. Lord Welington 60.000. The[y] have advanced from Seville to the relief of Badajos.[3] The issue will decide, the fate of th⟨ree⟩ nations. Accept the respects of Your Obedt Hum: Servt.

A HAMILTON

RC (DLC). Postmarked New York, 1 Aug.

1. After returning to the U.S. in November 1810, William Jarvis resigned the Lisbon consulate in February 1811. JM nominated George Jefferson as his replacement on 1 Mar. 1811, but Jefferson did not take up his duties in Lisbon until February 1812 (Jarvis to Robert Smith, 6 Feb. 1811; George Jefferson to Monroe, 8 Feb. 1812 [DNA: RG 59, CD, Lisbon]; *Senate Exec. Proceedings*, 2:173).

2. Hamilton was alluding to the situation produced by the exile of the Portuguese court in Brazil and the fact that after 1809 the Portuguese army was under the command of the British major general William Beresford.

3. Badajoz, a fortress guarding the southernmost invasion route from Spain toward Lisbon, had been captured by French forces under Marshal Nicholas-Jean de Dieu Soult in March 1811. British efforts to retake the position over the summer of 1811 were unsuccessful (Sir John W. Fortescue, *A History of the British Army* [13 vols.; London, 1899–1930], 8:120–250).

§ Account with Joel Barlow. *12 June 1811*. Lists items "Bot. of Joel Barlow," including seventy-three bottles of burgundy "called Clos de vegiot" at $1.50 per bottle; twenty-one dozen of porter and ale at $2.25 per dozen; eight bottles of "Old Chateaux Margaux this is the same wine as is usually sent to the President from Bordeaux with the difference that this has been in bottle 5 years," at $1 per bottle; "2 Cases Barsac" for $117; twelve bottles of white Jurançon for $12; twenty-four bottles of champagne for $48; and six bottles of "Langon 25 or 30 years in bottle, when drank it ought to be decanted in the Cellar," for $6. Payment of $356.75 received for Barlow by William Lee.

Ms (DLC). 1 p. In an unidentified hand, signed by William Lee. Docketed by JM.

From the Tammany Society of Chillicothe

SIR,   CHILLICOTHE (O) 14th. June 1811

The Tammany Society, Or Columbian Order of Wigwam No. 1, whence the other four branches in the state of Ohio have originated, Unanimously requests leave to address you, at the present momentous Crisis of our public affairs.

They have not been indifferent spectators of the trying and difficult scenes, which you have had to pass through, as Executive of the National Government. The unjust and destructive Edicts passed by the two great belligerent powers of Europe, against our Neutral Commerce and Rights; the repeated, insulting aggressions committed on our own coasts, and even in our own waters; the diplomatic finess practised by accredited Ministers; and the apologists for such outrages in our own country, have all tended to make your situation peculiarly embarrassing. But this numerous society of Democratic Republicans, have viewed with the sincerest pleasure, the promptness with which you have met pacific overtures, the firmness with which you have contended for the rights of your countrymen, and the forbearance which the spirit and genius of our government dictated. And Judging from the past they are impelled to express their entire confidence in, and reliance upon your Wisdom, firmness, and patriotism as Executive of the United States, in this trying season. And they are firmly determined to support with their lives and fortunes such necessary measures as the Government of our Country may adopt, for the preservation of our Rights and Liberties; And the promotion of the National Welfare.

Signed in behalf of the Society

EDWARD TIFFIN
Grand Sachem
SAML. WILLIAMS secretary

RC (DLC); FC (OHi: Tammany Society, Chillicothe Wigwam Records). RC docketed by JM.

§ From David Meade Randolph.[1] *14 June 1811, London.* Asks that JM consider this letter "with mingled feelings of justice and friendship"; however, if his official conduct has been weighed and found unworthy, asks that JM "treat this essay with silent contempt." The reasons for his departure were known to few, but "the interruptions of commerce" have disappointed his hopes, and he is now engaged in enterprises requiring "privations, patience and infinite persevereance" in order to be able to support his "unfortunate family" in the future. These reflections have led him to seek the consulate in Lisbon or that in London "shoud the present Incumbent here, by a seriously apprehended dissolution, vacate his Office."[2]

RC (DLC). 4 pp. Docketed by JM.

1. David Meade Randolph (1760–1830), a brother-in-law of Jefferson's son-in-law Thomas Mann Randolph, had served as U.S. marshal for the eastern district of Virginia from 1791 to 1801, when Jefferson removed him on the grounds that he had packed juries. Both his government accounts and his personal finances were in considerable disarray, and in 1808 he left for England "upon a scheme so little likely to succeed, that nothing but despair could have suggested it" (*PJM-SS,* 1:120–21 n. 5, 236, 237 n. 1; Martha Jefferson Randolph to Dolley Madison, 15 Jan. 1808 [owned by Mr. and Mrs. George B. Cutts, Brookline, Mass., 1958]).

2. William Lyman, U.S. consul in London since 1804, died on 22 Sept. 1811. Chargé

d'affaires John Spear Smith appointed Reuben G. Beasley consul ad interim in his place (N.Y. *Commercial Advertiser*, 12 Nov. 1811; Beasley to Monroe, 27 Sept. 1811 [DNA: RG 59, CD, London]).

§ Resolution of the Court of the District of Columbia. *15 June 1811.* "The Grand Jury state to the Court that they have received representations on the oaths of credible persons that Nancy Gerry a free mulatto girl about Eight years old, was during the month of May last Sold as a slave by Samuel Askum, to ¹ Oliphant of Georgia, to which state she is presumed to have been carried, said Oliphant being an Inhabitant of Georgia. The Jury request the Court to Communicate this statement to the president of the United States in order that fit measures may be pursued for the reclamation of the said Nancy Gerry."

Ms (DLC). 1 p. Signed by Samuel Harrison Smith, foreman, with a certification by William Brent, clerk, that "the above copy . . . is, by Order of Court, forwarded to the President." Docketed by JM.

1. Left blank in Ms.

To Richard Cutts

DEAR SIR   W. June 16. 1811

If I mistake not I have already acknowledged your favor of May 29. which brought the first information of the republican ascendancy in your Legislature. It was little to have been supposed that at this date I should be obliged to repeat that we remain without authentic information of a decisive character from both F. & G. B. This is the fact nevertheless; and it is very questionable whether the Essex when she comes, will not leave us dependent on the arrival of the John Adams, for the course finally adopted by France. You will observe by the Norfolk paper that a polite salutation has been exchanged between Decatur, & the Commander of a B. frigate. It seems the latter first announced his own Ship, and then inquired what Decatur's was, and that at the moment of the mutual civility, one of Decaturs Guns went off by real accident. The explanation was readily given, and as readily accepted.¹ In a late Boston Patriot, notice was taken, in the ship news, of a vessel spoken on the 24 May, bound to N. Y. from Sicily, & that Mr. Payne the American Consul for Tripoly was on board. This was followed by a report from N. Y. that he had landed with his *lady*, on the Sound; which has been since followed by information that he had landed near Cape Henry. On the latter supposition some acct. might have reached us from himself; yet no mention is made of such an incident even in the Norfolk papers which would be very apt to have adverted to it, under the head of marine intelligence. It is said that the vessel from Sicily has approached

N. Y. & that her owner is now in Washington seeking interposition in her behalf. I have had no communication with him however, nor any sufficient oppy. of learning what he may know with respect to our Brother. We are endeavoring to be ready to set out for Montpelier on the 5 or 6th. of July, but not without apprehensions that the delay of the expected Ships, may interfere with our purpose.

With affectionate remembrances, including our itinerant Cousins if with you, be assured of my esteem & best wishes.

JAMES MADISON

RC (MHi); Tr (NjP: Crane Collection). Cover of RC bears the notation in JM's hand: "Mrs. M. writes by this mail, to Mr. E. Coles *at Boston.*" Docketed by Cutts.

1. The 18 June 1811 issue of the *National Intelligencer* reported under a 12 June dateline from Norfolk, Virginia, that on the evening of 16 June the frigate *United States* fell in with the British frigate *Euridice* and the sloop of war *Atalanta*. On hailing the frigate, one of Decatur's guns "unluckily went off," but the British commander received the explanation with "great politeness" and "civilities were exchanged." "The accidental going off of the cannon," the report concluded, "is not to be wondered at when it is recollected that the frigate's guns are discharged with locks and not with matches."

¶ From John C. Payne. Letter not found. *Ca. 18 June 1811.* Mentioned in Dolley Madison to Anna Payne Cutts, 20 June 1811 (MHi): "This Morng. Mr. M has a short letter from John at Drummond Town near the Capes of Virga. He has been unwell there, but promises to 'be with us in a few days, when he will explain the causes of his sudden return &. &.' "

From William B. Wood

DEAR SIR   NASHVILLE TENNESSEE 19th. June 1811

I have taken the liberty of informing You of our safe arrival in this coun-try on the 22d of May—it being past the season for making a crop an object I thought it best to hire out our negroes and rent a House in this place which I have succeeded in beyond my utmost expectation, in consequence of this arrangement I have had an opportunity of seeing many parts of this state also the County of Madison (Missippia Territory) which I give a most decided preference to any part of this Country—from its great advantage as a Cotton Country and its advantagee's in many other Respects, I am very much disposed to make a small purchase there, but in consequence of all the Valuable lands being allready entered and the price being considerably advanced, say from four to Eight Dollars I find my funds are insufficient to comply with my wishes, without making sale of a part [of] my negroes which are all Young and increasing in Value daily. In preference to doing this I have taken the liberty of making application to you for the loane of eight hundred or a thusand Dollars, which if not too great an inconvenience to you, will be a considerable accommodation to me, assuring you at the same[1] that I will use my greatest deligence in returning it. I was compell'd to leave in Virginia one fourth of the sales of my land as an indemnity to Mr. Dawney as Executor to meat the payment of the claim of securityship pending between B. Winslow[2] and my father's estate which has been a considerable draw back on my funds in the mean time I remain Dear Sir Yr Mo Obt & H St

WILLIAM B. WOOD[3]

RC (DLC).

1. Wood evidently omitted to write "time" here.

2. Benjamin Winslow (ca. 1737–1826) was a resident and sometime tax collector in Orange County, Virginia (*PJM*, 8:55 n. 2).

3. William B. Wood, the son of Joseph and Margaret Wood, was related to JM by virtue of his aunt having married JM's brother Francis Madison, and Wood himself had married one of Francis Madison's daughters, Elinor Madison, in 1804. The Wood family had owned a property north of Orange, Virginia, and had been customers of the Madison family ironworks (Madison County, Virginia, Marriage Register, 1:254; Thomas, *Patriots of the Upcountry*, pp. 123, 133).

§ From Joshua Gilpin.[1] *19 June 1811, Philadelphia.* Wrote to Barlow some weeks ago soliciting through him "the appointment to a Consular Office, Agency, or some similar object in England."[2] Has been informed by Barlow that JM expressed himself "in terms which command the utmost respect and gratitude which I can feel." Hesitates to trouble JM again, but is on the eve of departing for abroad. "It was my intention at the time I wrote to Mr Barlow, to remain in this country probably some time, and to wait here the chance of any object which might occurr." But his concern for the welfare of his family on the voyage has convinced him "to embark with them in a few days." Believes that the imminent return of Pinkney and the expected arrival of Foster might create an opportunity for an appointment. Defends his motives for seeking a position and admits that the emolument is a concern "in a country where the expences of life are beyond those here and where public duties of any kind still increase that expence." As a merchant, has experienced losses during the last four years, but maintains it is the duty of everyone "to submit to those measures which the public interests require."

RC (DNA: RG 59, LAR, 1809–17, filed under "Gilpin"). 3 pp.

1. Joshua Gilpin (1765–1841) belonged to a prominent Philadelphia family of merchants, manufacturers, and land developers. He had traveled in Europe between 1794 and 1801, during which time he married Mary Dilworth, the daughter of a Lancashire banker. His son Henry Dilworth Gilpin, attorney general in the administration of Martin Van Buren, oversaw the final editing and publication of the first edition of JM's writings, *The Papers of James Madison . . . Being His Correspondence and Reports of Debates during the Congress of the Confederation and His Reports of Debates in the Federal Convention* (3 vols.; Washington, 1840) (see Jo-

seph E. Walker, ed., *Pleasure and Business in Western Pennsylvania: The Journal of Joshua Gilpin, 1809* [Harrisburg, Pa., 1975], pp. iii-v; *PJM*, 1:xviii).

2. Gilpin to Joel Barlow, 16 May 1811 (DNA: RG 59, LAR, 1809–17).

To Elbridge Gerry

private

DEAR SIR   WASHINGTON June 21. 1811

I thank you for your polite communication of the Speech to your Legislature.[1] The solid & seasonable truths so emphatically inculcated in it, can not fail to do much good. The noise & anger which it is exciting, prove that the faction is deeply stung by the exposure of its guilt, and will increase the public indignation, by rousing a more diffusive attention to the subject. The delay of Mr. Pinkney & Mr. Foster continue to exercise our patience. From the arrival of the former, little not already known can be expected, as it appears that the latest communications from Paris did not reach England in time for him. The return of the John Adams which may now be shortly looked for, will supply that failure. With respect to Mr. F. there are obvious considerations forbidding much reliance on the purport of his mission. On the other hand, some hope is awakened by the reports that it proceeds from the decision of the Prince Regent, agst. the will of the Cabinet, and is meant to keep the path open for amicable arrangements. If this be really the case, it is possible that Mr. F. may have authority to do something on the more critical points depending, altho' the mode will be awkward, and the result diletory. Be pleased to accept my great esteem & friendly respects.

JAMES MADISON

RC (owned by Mr. and Mrs. Philip D. Sang, Chicago, Ill., 1958).

1. No letter from Gerry to JM communicating his 7 June address to the Massachusetts legislature has been found, but the *National Intelligencer* published the address on 15 June 1811. Its contents were almost wholly devoted to criticisms of the Federalists for their organization of petitions and public "assemblages" to oppose administration policies, most notably JM's proclamation of 2 Nov. 1810 and the Nonintercourse Act of 2 Mar. 1811. In particular, Gerry took exception to Federalist arguments that justified forcible resistance and disunion as legitimate means of political opposition.

From Captain Armstrong

FATHER AND BROTHERS   21 June 1811

We your brothers and children Send this letter by our grandson and relation, having first talked with him and one of our White brothers, and now

345

desire that you would listen, and accept the good wishes of myself and My chiefs, and of all your children at Green Town.[1]

FATHER & BROTHERS

You have often Wished me and my Chiefs to come and See you, as I have been told by my White brothers; We have now thought of doing So, and are ready, and on that account am glad that my grandson and relation has called on me, on his way to See you; and I take this opportunity to Write to you. Now my father and brother We have determined to come and See you With my chiefs and captains, and wish you to send me an answer by my Grandson and relation and hope that you, our father and brother Will provide for us what may be necessary; as we wish to meet with no hindrance on the way, as our White brothers, near me, Say that you will do it; and we would have come and seen you before but did not know how to proceed untill now; and we hope you will send a letter to us by our Grandson and relation that we may know your Mind.[2]

THOMAS LYONS
WOLF
CAPT PIPE
ABRAHAM WILLIAMS

RC (DNA: RG 107, LRUS, A-1811). Headed "Capt Armstrong chief of the Delawares at Green Town to our great father and brother the president of the U. States." Cover marked "favd by James Logan"; docketed by a War Department clerk as received 12 July 1811.

1. The letter was probably written from Greenfield, a town in Indiana Territory between the east and the west forks of the White River, where the main body of Delaware Indians had settled after the Revolution (*Handbook of North American Indians: Northeast*, vol. 15 of *Handbook of North American Indians*, ed. William C. Sturtevant [9 vols. to date; Washington, 1984—], p. 223).

2. JM did not encourage his correspondents. Writing to the Indian agent John Johnston on 21 Sept. 1811, Eustis noted that several Indians from the western regions had wished to visit Washington, but he added that "the general answer has been . . . that during the winter and while congress is in session, the concerns of the nation will so occupy the mind of the President, that he will not have time to attend to those of the Indians: th⟨e⟩ agent[s] have, therefore, been instructed to postpone the intended visits until the spring of the year or until further advised" (DNA: RG 75, LSIA).

From the Inhabitants of New Bedford, Massachusetts

NEW BEDFORD (MASSACHUSETTS), June 22d. 1811.

The Inhabitants of New Bedford, legally convened in Town Meeting, Respectfully represent:

That an active Commerce is highly conducive to individual prosperity, and the most productive source of national wealth and improvement. The well founded expectation, that a prosperous commerce would be a primary object of the political cares of the national administration, to whatever hands it might be confided, was a powerful inducement to the original adoption of the Federal Constitution, by the Citizens of the Maritime States, and the subsequent successes which attended their commercial enterprizes, justified their confidence, and invigorated their attachment to the Union. The wisdom and energy which characterized the Federal administration, immediately after the organization of the Government, changed the aspect of our National affairs from despondency to hope, and from hope to the actual fruition of commercial advantages, surpassing even the expectations of the most sanguine. The substantial benefits of this extended commerce, were not confined to the Merchants alone. By the revenues derived from it, it enriched the National treasury, without oppressing the people by direct taxation; it revived publick credit, enhanced the value of every species of property, augmented the quantity, and accelerated the circulation of the precious metals, and enabled the laborious husbandman, the active mechanic, the industrious manufacturer, and every order of Society, to reap an increased reward of their toils. It vivified and invigorated all the channels of industry, made them flow with greater activity and copiousness, and exhibited experimental proof that the interests of all classes of the community are intimately and inseparably interwoven. Commercial connections & habits were established, and a spring was given to successful enterprize, the elasticity of which has not been destroyed by all the late embarrasments and restrictions, both foreign and domestic, with which it has been encumbered.

When revolutionary France set at naught all those obligations of international, as well as of municipal law, which had been respected for ages; and involved Europe in warfare and confusion; it was to be rationally expected that, during this awful conflict, the fury of which does not yet subside, the neutral commerce of the United States would sometimes suffer from the concussions of the belligerent nations; that many inconveniences would be experienced from the rapacity of lawless power, and many from the unavoidable interference of neutral and belligerent claims. But it was not expected, that the constituted authorities of our own country, would conceive it to be their duty, instead of alleviating, to increase the difficulties, by permanent restrictions, more injurious to the vital interests of American Commerce, than all the Imperial decrees and Royal orders of foreign powers. Of these decrees and orders, when known, the prudent and intelligent Merchant could see and avoid the danger. He could direct his capital to flow in a different channel: But our municipal restrictions paralysed every effort, and cut off every prospect of succesful enterprize.

A short Embargo, or a temporary Non-intercourse, to prevent the mercantile capital of the nation from falling unguardedly a prey to the ravages of an enemy, may be justified by the actual commencement of war, or the well grounded apprehension of immediate hostility. The right to enforce these measures is incident to such a state of things. It appears to be an attribute, not of the power of regulating commerce, but of prosecuting War. We can discover, upon a fair construction of the Constitution, no delegated authority to arrest, for an indefinite period, in a time of peace, the whole active commerce of the United States, to circumscribe the sphere of its action, to prescribe for it a particular destination, or to prevent the mercantile class of citizens from pursuing their own interests in such channels as appear to them to offer the fairest prospect of success.

Admitting, however, the constitutional right to adopt and pursue that system of restrictions under which our Commerce has long been languishing, admitting also the purity of the motives, and the plausible expectations of a succesful issue, with which that system was originally commenced, still the important question of the expediency of continuing, for an indefinite period, the operations of that system, remains. The experience of several years appears to have fully evinced, that in all its variety of forms, it is inadequate to the accomplishment of its object; that as a measure of coercion upon foreign powers, it is totally ineffectual, and, as a permanent or durable system of municipal law, pregnant with disastrous consequences to ourselves; that, however plausible it may be in theory, it is, in practise, hostile to the best interests of our country. Under this system, business of every kind stagnates, failures multiply, property of every description depreciates, the national revenues diminish to an alarming degree, and a well founded apprehension exists, that the glow of patriotic attachment to the Union, which was enkindled by a grateful sense of the benefits derived from it, will cool in the hearts of the citizens, in proportion as those benefits cease to flow.

Although the present domestic restrictions of American commerce are nominally but partial, interdicting merely the importations of British Merchandize, Yet when it is considered that the trade of the United States with Great Britain, her colonies and dependencies, was of great extent and importance, and, in fact, constituted almost the only branch of active commerce which could be pursued with profit, or even with safety; and when it is further considered, that exportations must cease of course, when importations are prohibited, it will be perceived, that this interdiction, though partial in its name, is almost total in its nature. All the consequences, therefore, which would flow from a total interdiction of commerce, will flow, in an almost equal degree, from the system now in operation.

But these consequences are not the only evils to be apprehended, under existing circumstances, from a perseverance in our present course. The interdiction of importations from the territories of one belligerent, while they are freely admitted from those of the other, may, with some plausibility, be considered by the former, as a departure from that strict line of neutrality, which we have hitherto professed inviolably to maintain. She may conclude that we are embarked in the cause of her enemy, and thus we may be unexpectedly involved in a war with England, and (what if possible is still more to be deprecated,) an alliance with France, the duration and calamities of which are incalculable. It is therefore, to be hoped, that some measures, consistent with our national safety and honour, may be speedily devised and adopted, to ward off these impending disasters, and to restore to the United States a neutral commerce, unembarrassed by domestic regulations.

Against such measures, France can have no just cause of complaint. The non-importation act of March last, was founded upon an assumed state of things, which is discovered not to exist in fact. Notwithstanding the solemn declaration of the Government of France, that the decrees of Berlin and Milan were revoked, all the information upon the subject, whether official or unofficial, which has since been made public, enforces the conviction, that the declaration is fallacious; that those decrees are still considered as fundamental laws of the empire; that they have not yet ceased to have their effect of violating our neutral commerce, or at least, as well since that pretended revocation, as for a series of years before, that seizure, conflagration, or confiscation, under some pretext, awaits every American vessel which, (unless sailing from a favoured port, and protected by a special license from the Emperor,) arrives within the controul of France or her cruizers. These injuries are further aggravated by the consideration, that, during this series of aggression, the vessels of France, and even those cruizers which are preying upon our innocent commerce, have uniformly received, and still enjoy in the ports of the United States, all the courtesies of hospitality and friendship.

The correctness or incorrectness of the conviction above stated, does not, however, essentially vary the question of our right to liberate our commerce from the existing restrictions. The act of Congress, out of which the present state of things has unexpectedly grown, "had for its object, not merely the recognition of a speculative legitimate principle, but the enjoyment of a Substantial benefit."[1] The proclamation declaring the revocation of the edicts of France, was issued, and the non-importation act enforced, upon the express presumption, not only that the abrogation of those edicts "would leave the ports of France as free for the introduction of the produce of the United States, as they were previously to the promulgation of those decrees,"[2] but also that "satisfactory provision for restoring the property surprized and seized by the order, or at the instance of the French Government, must be combined with a repeal of the French edicts; such a provision being an indispensable evidence of the just purpose of France towards the United States."[3] This express requisition not having been satisfied, either by a "preliminary restoration of the property," or even by an assurance, "that it will become immediately," or at any period, "the subject of discussion, with a reasonable prospect of justice to our injured citizens,"[4] but on the contrary, a system of interdictions having been substituted for those decrees which were declared to have been revoked, "producing the same commercial effects,"[5] it cannot surely be urged, with the least colour of truth or plausibility, that the faith of the United States is pledged to France, for a further perseverance in their present system. In every point of view in which the subject is presented to consideration, it is accompanied by the unwavering conviction, that the United States are absolved, by the conduct of France, from every supposed obligation to adhere to a continued execution of the existing non-importation acts, and perfectly free to adopt any measures, which may appear to them to be dictated by the interests of the country.

The habits and occupations of the Inhabitants of New Bedford, are commercial, or intimately connected with, and dependent upon, commerce. A great proportion of their capital, in consequence of the present obstructions of commerce, is lying inactive and unproductive, either in England or in the United States. They therefore feel, not only in common with their fellow citizens at large, but with peculiar force, the pressure of the times. Deeply impressed with the truth and importance of the sentiments which they have here expressed, and of the reality of those impending dangers which they have partially and briefly enumerated, they are prompted, as well by their patriotism, as by their interests, to represent to their Rulers, the accumulating difficulties and apprehensions, under which they are labouring; in the anxious hope that an alleviation may be obtained. For this purpose, they respectfully pray, that Congress may be speedily convened to take the subject into their consideration, and that, in the mean time, such other measures may be adopted for the public relief, as may be constitutionally confided to the discretion of the Executive. Signed by order, and on behalf of the Inhabitants of said Town;

ALDEN SPOONER		
ROGER HASKELL	}	Selectmen.
JOSEPH CHURCH		being all the
Attest. JOHN PROUD Town Clerk.		selectmen of
		the Town.

RC (DNA: RG 59, ML).

1. The petitioners quoted from Robert Smith to Louis-Marie Turreau, 18 Dec. 1810 (see *ASP, Foreign Relations*, 3:402).

2. Ibid., 3:402.

3. See Robert Smith to John Armstrong, 5 July 1810 (ibid., 3:385–86). JM had drafted these instructions for Robert Smith in his own hand (see *PJM-PS*, 2:402–4 and n.).

4. See Robert Smith to John Armstrong, 5 June 1810 (*ASP, Foreign Relations*, 3:385).

5. See Robert Smith's letter cited in n. 1, above.

§ Presidential Proclamation. *22 June 1811.* Declares and makes known under the acts of Congress for the sale and disposal of public lands south of the state of Tennessee that the public lands west of the Pearl River in Mississippi Territory, to which the Indian title has been extinguished and which have not been exposed to public sale under the terms of the presidential proclamation of 22 Oct. 1808, shall be for public sale at Washington, Mississippi Territory, on the second Tuesday in November 1811.

Tr (DNA: RG 49, Proclamations of Public Land Sales). 2 pp. Printed in Carter, *Territorial Papers, Mississippi*, 6:200–201.

To Richard Cutts

Dear Sir   W. June 23. 1811

I congratulate you & Mrs. Cutts on the event which has relieved your anxieties; the more so as it gratifies your joint desire of introducing a female series into your Nursery.[1] We learn that our brother John landed on the Eastern shore South of the boundary between Va. & Maryland, & that he has been detained by sickness from which however he was recovering, with the expectation of setting out hither about this date. Our patience is Still exercised by the delay of the Essex, and also of Foster.[2] You will have noticed the paragraphs saying that the dispatches from France arrived in England too late for the Essex.[3] We shall probably therefore be kept in suspence as to that quarter till the arrival of the Jno. Adams, of which nothing more is known than that she arrived at L'Orient about the middle of april. What Foster will have in his pocket can not even be conjectured. The only favorable circumstance is a report taken from private letters which you have doubtless seen in print, that his mission has been decided on by the P. Regent, in spite of the repugnance of his Cabinet. Adieu with best wishes for yourself & Mrs. Cutts &c &c &c.

JAMES MADISON

RC (NjP: Crane Collection); partial Tr (ibid.). RC docketed by Cutts.

1. JM was referring to the birth of Dolley Payne Madison Cutts (d. 1838), who was to become one of Dolley Madison's favorite nieces (Ethel Stephens Arnett, *Mrs. James Madison: The Incomparable Dolley* [Greensboro, N.C., 1972], pp. 265, 271–77, 338).

2. In conveying the same news about Foster and Pinkney in a letter to her sister Anna Payne Cutts, Dolley Madison added: "We expect too Mr S—— 's [Smith's] *book, opening the eyes of the world on all our sins* &. &." (Dolley Madison to Anna Payne Cutts, 20 June 1811 [MHi]).

3. On 20 June 1811 the *National Intelligencer*, under the heading of "Latest from England," reported that John Spear Smith had arrived at Dover from France on 6 May but had failed to meet with Pinkney, who had already sailed on the *Essex* for the U.S.

To the Grand Sachem of the Tammany Society of Chillicothe

Sɪʀ   Wᴀsʜɪɴɢᴛᴏɴ June 23. 1811

I have received the letter of the 14th. instant which you have addressed to me, in the name of the Tammany Society of Wigwam No. 1. in the State of Ohio.

The circumstances in our national situation, to which you refer, could not but render it peculiarly embarrassing to those entrusted with the national rights & interests. Whilst Justice, however, continues to be the basis of our policy, and the great body of our fellow Citizens remain firm, in sentiments & determinations, such as are expressed by the Society of which you are the organ, our Country will be found adequate to every trial to which it may be exposed. The approbation which the Society bestows on the share I have had in the public transactions, and its confidence in my further efforts for the public good, are entitled to my thankful acknowledgments; to which I add a tender of my respects and my friendly wishes.

Jᴀᴍᴇs Mᴀᴅɪsᴏɴ

RC (OHi: Tammany Society, Chillicothe Wigwam Records); draft (DLC). JM's reply was also printed in the *National Intelligencer*, 25 July 1811.

From George W. Erving

Private

Dᴇᴀʀ Sɪʀ   Cᴏᴘᴇɴʜᴀɢᴇɴ June 23. 1811

Soon after my arrival here (viz on the 1st. inst) I saw Mr Joy, & delivered to him the letter which you was pleased to put under my care. I find that this gentleman has done very considerable service to several cases wherein he has been employed, & has obtained the liberation of property which stood in very perilous predicaments, yet it is the general opinion amongst the americans here, by all of whom (even those who have employed him) he is disliked, that he has done considerable mischeif also: & I can readily beleive this, as to the case in general; for as he has not engaged in any case without making a condition with the claimant to receive large commissions, (never less than 2½ per cent on the value of the property in question) & his efforts have been applied exclusively in favor of those who have so employed him; & as he was admitted to a species of official consideration by the members of this government in general; it was concluded that he had no good opinion of the cases in which he did not interfere, & they were so far supposed to be abandoned by our government; some say that to promote his views in particular cases he suggested as much, but I do not beleive that he can have been guilty of a proceeding so iniquitous; yet in one of his letters to Mr Gessen (or Jessen)[1] the kings private secretary, which has been seen by respectable gentlemen here, he did say, speaking of a certain captain, that he had now applied *to him*, & tho his application had been so tardy, *nevertheless* he really beleived that he was an american: be the fact as it may, the prevailing opinion that he was pursuing such a course operated in terrorem, & induced several to employ him, who otherwise woud not have employed him; a great majority however, not chusing, or not being authorized to give him the commissions which he demanded (in the convoy cases he required 8 per cent, alledging that a part was to be employed in bribery) & some actuated by more general, & by liberal motives, refused to have any thing to do with him; he has obtained however enough of this business, to have produced a very large sum of profit to himself: they say that he has made use of bribery; I have no reason to beleive this (his proposal in the convoy cases apart) but in his having gratuitously assured me, & calling heaven to witness, that he had not: but independent of such means (if they have been used) he has obtained all his consideration here by shewing your letters to the foreign ministers, the ministers of state, & indeed to every body; I am well assured that he even gave them to Mr Gessen to be shewn to his majesty. Mr Joy on my first arrival repeatedly offerred his services, & from his style of writing I conclude that he supposed they woud be very important to me; but not forseeing that my business coud be promoted by any such aids, & having previously formed the very worst opinion of, & feeling the most complete antipathy to him, I have kept myself in entire reserve. Mr Gessen above mentioned is supposed to have more influence with the king than any other person, thro' his means Mr Joy has done his business, & thro' him sometime since procured ten licences, to be used for vessels then laying in Norway to secure them a free passage into the Baltic; he carried these licences to Gottenburg, & offerred them for sale to all the american captains there (for they were made in blank) at some enormous percentage on the value of their cargoes; the captains to a man rejected them & he returned back without being able to sell one licence; in the mean time some of those captains wrote to Mr Saabye stating Mr Joy's offers, & seeing that the king was disposed to grant licences, they presumed that they were granted gratis & begged him to procure them: an application was made to Mr Gessen either by Mr Saabye or by some agents of the captains; the answer given was that no licences woud be granted but to Mr Joy: these facts which are well known have injured Mr Gessen as well as Mr Joy in the opinion of the american supercargoes & masters now here, amongst whom there are several very respectable men. I have thought it my duty Sir to make you acquainted with these transactions of Mr Joy.

In my official letters I have spoken very respectfully of the character of M. de Rosenkrantz, but not in stronger terms than it is intitled to;[2] he is not supposed however to have as much influence with the king as Mr Gessen has.

Tho' I have said that our commerce has not been so entirely sacrifised as was imagined in the U. States, yet certainly the mischeif has been very considerable: You will see sir I am sure with very great satisfaction the immediate alteration which took place on my arrival here, the good effects already produced, & the prospect of a more favorable termination of this mission than was expected. In my first interview with Mr de Rosenkrantz, which I made a very long one, I endeavoured to form an opinion as to the general character of this government, & of its particular feeling as to our claims: it presented itself to me like a virtuous man, who under the pressure of misfortunes was delivering himself over to irregular habits, a numbness, a total insensibility of the nerves seemed to be taking place, it required to be roused by some strong stimulus; the almost suffocated principle of its virtue might be excited & reestablished by bitter reproaches, but woud die away under a soothing & emolient treatment: I coud anticipate nothing but disappointment, or procrastination, equivalent in the actual state of things to disappointment, by appearing in forma pauperis, or by any procedure from which a hope might be derived of putting aside our claims: under these impressions I wrote my first note to Mr de Rosenkrantz,[3] & in all our conversations have evinced a strong sense of the injuries received: whether the course taken has been upon the whole the best, perhaps can only be determined by the final result, but I had also in view an immediate advantage, which I think has been attained, & which I hope will be preserved: I reached Copenhagen at a very critical moment, precisely at the time when our vessels began to arrive, the only two which had arrived had been captured & condemned, (their appeals are now pending) about the 9t or 10t of June the great body of them appeared, but none of these have been brought regularly into the courts, some few only have been slightly examined, the great majority of them have passed without any kind of interruption.

No mention has been made in my instructions of the convoy question, nor was I previously aware that there were any vessels coming under it; in a conversation however which I had the honor of having with you on the 7t Jany you supposed the probability of such cases existing, & treated the subject in its connection with the belligerent pretension to search: I noted down at the time the distinctions which you directed to be observed on this delicate point, but on my arrival here finding that the kings instructions to his cruisers had expressly declared neutral bottoms to make free cargoes (contraband of war excepted) & learning that the 8 vessels of the convoy cases which had been finally condemned had been all under such circumstances as not to require any kind of interference in their favor; finding that the search for contraband had not in any case been the pretext for capture, but a new law subjecting to confiscation all vessels which have made use of convoy; so it appeared to me that I ought to confine myself to contesting with this new doctrine.

As to the vessels which have been finally condemned I have thought it best to avoid entering upon that part of my business, till the pending cases shoud be favorably disposed of, that the first attention was due to the claimants who stood in momentary danger of losing their property; & if the course determined on with respect to these, shoud be not to take them out of the jurisdiction of the courts, but to direct its decision on them, which I think will be the course, then I calculated upon strengthening by these very decisions the argument against those which have already been passed.

I took the liberty of writing to Mrs Madison from Newport respecting her protegé Mr Tayloe;[4] further to apologize to her for the manner in which I thought it necessary to mention that young gentleman & his father, I pray you Sir to have the goodness to let her know, what I will take the liberty of here stating: there is a regulation in france that all letters arriving from abroad shall be delivered to the police, therefore previous to going ashore from the "John Adams" I recommended Captn Dent to have all the sealed letters which might be on board the ship put into the letter bag; the officers were therefore summoned to deliver up those in their possession, & with the same view I directed Mr Tayloe who was considered as one of my family, to deliver up such as he might have, he gave me some which on my repeatedly asking him he repeatedly declared to be all he had, & which together with those delivered to me by Messrs Lewis & Winthrop also of my family, I put into the bag; I now learn that Mr Tayloe (it might have been that he did not fully understand me) reserved some letters delivered to him by his friends in Baltimore (by General Smith I think) but with them a parcel from Miss Paterson to the king of Westphalia, which had it been found on him in Paris, or had he delivered, woud have exposed him to a prison; perhaps for life; & me to a great deal of embarrassment; fortunately for himself he is an heedless young man & left the parcel in question on board the vessel. I trust in your goodness to excuse my troubling you with these particulars in consideration of their being intended for Mr[s] Madison.

In Paris I received all the assistance from Mr Russell which he coud afford me; but I have not received the hoped for communication from thence, & conclude that the business has gone to rest: it is however of very little importance even on the certificate of origin question, & on all others I trust that I shall be able to get on without it. Mr Russell appears to be a worthy man of a shrewd sensible mind, he is rather vain & one Easily sees that he is particularly so of his style in writing: his celebrated letter which has been so much, & as I told him so justly censured, was partly the child of that vanity; his indiscretion was the want of tact in his metier, & his promptness in entering into difficulty, a mixture of honest ardor with the desire of recommending himself at home, directed by that strong preoccupation against those with whom he was engaged, which seems to prevail in the mind of every american there: for the rest I beleive him to be a sound republican & an honest man; nor is he awkward as has been described; he presents himself as well as most men & the want of that courtly ease which is acquired by habit, is well supplied in him, by a manly self-possession which seems to be the offspring of a truly republican & independent mind. With the most sincere & respectful attachment Dear Sir Your very obt St

GEORGE W ERVING

RC (MHi: Erving Papers).

1. Peter Carl Jessen (1772–1830) was cabinet secretary in Denmark from 1808 until his death (C. F. Bricka, ed., *Dansk biografisk lexikon* [19 vols.; Copenhagen, 1887–1905], 8:483).

2. In his dispatch no. 2, written to Robert Smith from Copenhagen on 23 June 1811 on the subject of his first two meetings with Count Rosenkrantz, Erving described how the minister had objected to Erving's use of the term "spoliations" to describe the condemnation of American vessels by Danish tribunals. Rosenkrantz urged Erving to soften his language, hinting that otherwise he might not be able to present either the American diplomat or his notes to the king. Not wishing to jeopardize his mission at so early a date, Erving reluctantly did so and agreed to provide the count with a French translation of his note in which the phrase "injustice which has prevailed" was replaced by "injury produced." Reflecting on the episode, Erving concluded that Rosenkrantz was a man of "the most favorable character; his manner is every thing which can be desired, and his dispositions . . . are sincerely friendly as well as just" (DNA: RG 59, DD, Denmark).

3. Erving to Rosenkrantz, 6 June 1811 (printed in *ASP, Foreign Relations*, 3:522–23).

4. John Tayloe had entered the navy as a midshipman in November 1809 and was serving on the *John Adams*. His father was introduced to Erving by Paul Hamilton, who told the diplomat that "the son was intended to be the bearer of dispatches from Paris to London, & as he was young, inexperienced, & did not understand a word of the french language, it was desired that [Erving] shoud take him under [his] care to Paris," a request apparently endorsed by Dolley Madison. Erving consented at first, but then had second thoughts after speaking with Senator Richard Brent of Virginia who agreed that "it was very improper that such a young man, & particularly the son of one so notoriously an enemy to the President, shoud be made a bearer of dispatches." Tayloe's father subsequently wrote to Erving asking that his son continue with him *"during* [his] *residence in Europe,* under [his] *special direction & controul."* Erving finally decided that he would take Tayloe no farther than Paris, explaining to Dolley Madison that he felt the expectations of Tayloe's father were "not very reasonable" (Callahan, *List of Officers of the Navy,* p. 535; Erving to Dolley Madison, 14 Mar. 1811 [MHi: Erving Papers]).

From Henry Lee

DEAR SIR   ALEXA. June 24h. 1811.

Having omitted to mention one or two circumstances to you in the case of my neighbor Mr Yeaton[1] who has lately presented to govt. a petition from the commercial part of this town, praying the remission of his fine, I am compelled reluctantly to occupy yr. time by letter.

This gentleman & Rob. Young[2] were partners during the period, when the transaction took place, which in the sequel has been to him so afflicting. What is strange [is] that while Yeaton has been disgraced & amerced Young has been rewarded, having been promoted to the command of a regt. of militia. Their ship the Hero took to amsterdam a cargo of tobacco to pay the govt. debt due in holland so far as its proceeds went. The Secretary of the treasury gave to this ship a special passport, which in[duced?][3] Yeaton to risk his ship. She is still detained there going on now in the second year. Here this man suffers considerably.

As soon as the Judgement of the court below was confirmed above, Mr Y retired from business in a great degree, nor will he ever resume it, until his mercantile character is releived, to be done only by the supreme authoritys annulment of the sentence.

His petition has been confined to a particular class of his fellow citizens, as he deemed it improper to refer to others, which if he had done, I am persuaded not ten men in the town would have with-held their Signatures.

Indeed I do beleive that the gentleman never intended to violate our laws, for he is a fair dealer & a zealous advocate for Mr Jeffersons restrictive system.

Governor Langdon who is his personal friend selected this gentleman from his knowledge of him for the exportation of flower from this port, when special licences were necessary during the embargo.

This affords testimony in his favor worthy of respect.

Upon the whole I beleive you will do an acceptable act to the community by remission & what is more momentous, you will undo an incorrect Judgement. I have the honor to be with the deepest respect Yr. Sincere friend & hum: sert.

                                                      HENRY LEE

RC (DLC).

1. Lee probably referred to William Yeaton, who had been a merchant in Alexandria as early as 1802. Although Lee mentioned that Yeaton had "retired from business in a great degree," Alexandria newspapers in 1811 occasionally carried advertisements from the firm of Yeaton and Conway (see T. Michael Miller, comp., *Artisans and Merchants of Alexandria, Virginia, 1784–1820* [1 vol. to date; Bowie, Md., 1991—], 1:80, 90, 265, 267; *Alexandria Daily Gazette*, 11 July 1811).

2. Robert Young served on several occasions as a justice of the peace and also on the Or-

phans Court in the District of Columbia. In 1805 JM had offered him a consular appointment in Havana, which he declined (*Records of the Columbia Historical Society*, 5 [1905]: 282; ibid., 24 [1922]: 68; JM to Robert Young, 22 Jan. 1805 [DNA: RG 59, DL]).

3. Lee wrote "in-" at the bottom of the first page but neglected to complete the word on the second page.

§ From Ludwell Lee.[1] *24 June 1811, Belmont.* "A relation & friend of mine, Mr. Mordecai Booth of Winchester, wishing to get a place now vacant in the department of war; in the disposal, as he says, of Mr. Simmons; has requested of me to mention his wishes to you.... I hope I do not presume, too much on our acquaintanceship, to ask this favor of you." Adds that Booth is qualified for the position.

RC (DNA: RG 59, LAR, 1809–17, filed under "Booth"). 1 p. Addressee not indicated.

1. Ludwell Lee (1760–1836) was a son of Richard Henry Lee. He studied law at the College of William and Mary, served with Lafayette during the Revolution, and represented Prince William County in the Virginia General Assembly. A Federalist in his politics, he retired from public life after 1800, moved to Loudoun County, and near Leesburg built the house he named Belmont (Lee, *Lee Chronicle*, pp. 280–81).

To Joseph Gales

[25 June 1811]

J. M. with his thanks to Mr. Gales returns the newspaper sent him—with an anticipated paragraph of the Mercantile Advertiser.

RC (owned by Gallery of History, Las Vegas, Nev., 1994). Date supplied from docket. Signed on verso by Thomas Gales, Jr.

From George Keyser

SIR.   BALTIMORE June 25th. 1811.

You will please to pardon the Liberty, I have taken, by forwarding you a Copie of An address, to the people of the United States, Under the Signature, of Robt. Smith Esq. late Secretary of State.[1] I May appear to you to be Officious, but Sir, to adopt a Sentiment of Mr Smith to Mr Jefferson, I never did abandon a freind, so long as he was worthy of Confidence.[2]

I pray you Sir to Accept My hearts Best wishes for your Health and Happiness. I remain Sir, your Most Obt. and Verry humble Sevt.

GEO KEYSER[3]

RC (DLC).

1. Keyser no doubt forwarded a copy of *Robert Smith's Address to the People of the United States,* which appeared both in pamphlet form and in installments in the Baltimore *Whig* on 24, 25, 26, and 27 June 1811. In the 24 June issue, the editor of the *Whig* anticipated that the publication of Smith's pamphlet would "make a deep impression on the mind of every honest man" as well as bring about *"a correction of the abuses which have crept into executive practice."* Among the latter, the *Whig* specifically criticized JM for holding cabinet meetings on the grounds that the Constitution "recognizes no *presidential cabinet.* It invests the president with certain powers, and makes *him* responsible for their exercise." The editorial conceded that the president could require *written* opinions from departmental heads but maintained that the formation of an executive cabinet was an abuse of the second section of article 2 of the Constitution insofar as it could lead to "contemning useful advice, and making disagreement in opinion a ground for censure."

2. Keyser alluded to the appendix of the *Address* where Smith had published a series of letters exchanged with Jefferson to show "how *unfounded* are the tales with respect to Mr. Jefferson, to which certain underlings of Mr. Madison, for the purpose of sustaining him, have found it expedient to resort." In a [5] May 1811 letter to Jefferson, Smith had concluded by thanking the former president for his conduct toward him, adding "that however disposed I may be to forgive an enemy, I never did abandon a friend."

3. George Keyser was the owner of a china store on the corner of North Liberty and Baltimore Streets (*The Baltimore Directory for 1810* [Baltimore, 1810; Shaw and Shoemaker 19415], p. 108).

§ To Napoleon. *25 June 1811.* Addresses to him a letter of credence appointing Joel Barlow as minister plenipotentiary to France.

Tr (DNA: RG 84, France, Despatches to the Department of State). 1 p.

§ From Charles N. Baldwin. *26 June 1811, New York.* "Having issued from the press the first number of a periodical work;[1] the only one of this nature in this city; I have ventured to send the first number for your inspection, not doubting your liberality, and desire to encourage literature and S[c]ience in this country." Solicits JM's assistance and adds in a postscript, "If you feel inclined to patronise the work you will please to let me know, . . . and I will transmit the next number to you by the next mail."

RC (DLC). 2 pp. Docketed by JM.

1. Baldwin very likely forwarded the first issue of *The Literary Miscellany; or, Monthly Review,* a short-lived journal he published in New York in 1811.

§ From Cornelio de Saavedra. *26 June 1811, Buenos Aires.* "My Son Don Diego de Saavedra will have the honour of placing in Your Excellency's hands this Letter." He is accompanied by Juan Pedro de Aguirre, and JM will perceive their purposes from the credentials.[1] Their mission is "to procure the necessary aid of arms against every European, who is opposed to the cause of that Liberty which the People of America have recovered." Refers JM to their instructions[2] and stresses the importance of the envoys' concealing their true names from the public, the former being a captain of dragoons and the latter the present secretary of the cabildo. Assures JM his government will take "particular pleasure in establishing with their Fellow Countrymen of N. America, all kinds of mercantile relations," and will also preserve "the Strictest friendship" toward JM.

Translation of RC (DNA: RG 59, NFL, Argentina). 1 p. In the hand of Richard Forrest. RC (ibid.) in Spanish. Translation printed in Manning, *Diplomatic Correspondence of the United States concerning the Independence of the Latin-American Nations*, 1:322.

1. After arriving in the U.S. the envoys requested an interview with Monroe on 25 Oct. (Jose Cabrera and Pedro Lopez to Monroe, 25 Oct. 1811 [DNA: RG 59, NFL, Argentina]).
2. See Cornelio de Saavedra and others to JM, 6 June 1811.

§ From George Thompson.[1] *26 June 1811, Shawanee Springs, Kentucky.* Has seen the late act of Congress laying off districts in Orleans Territory, in each of which a land office is to be opened.[2] Recommends Abraham J. McDowell as register for one of those offices. "He is a native Kentuckian; a fine person, his manners very interesting, his politicks truly republican." Adds in a postscript, "In the foregoing letter [I] addressed you in your Public Character, I now feel a wish to speak to you as an old acquaintance & friend, whom I have not seen for many years. I am confident you will be pleased to hear that I am happily settled in this country and doing well. I hear from you almost every week, and to know that your countrymen respect you in Public and private life is extremely grateful to yr. old friend."

RC (DNA: RG 59, LAR, 1809–17, filed under "McDowell"). 2 pp.

1. George Thompson had represented Fluvanna County on several occasions in the Virginia House of Delegates between 1779 and 1791 (*PJM*, 11:409 n. 3).
2. "An Act providing for the final adjustment of claims to lands, and for the sale of public lands in the territories of Orleans and Louisiana" (*U.S. Statutes at Large*, 2:617–21).

From Benjamin Henry Latrobe

Sir,   Washington, June 28h. 1811.

The considerations which arise out of my engagement with the public in the direction of the public buildings are so interesting to me, and involve so entirely my future residence and the means of supporting my family, that unwilling to occupy more of your time that [*sic*] I can help, in listening to what I have to suggest on the subject, I take the liberty of submitting to you a wish, that a meeting with the Secretary of the Navy, in whose department the principal part of my services have been lately rendered and yourself may be allowed me, when the whole merits of my case may at once be laid before you & the Secretary, and an ultimate decision had. I will speak to the Secretary on the subject and await the arrangement you may be pleased to make respecting such an interview.[1] On the statements I shall then be able to lay before you, you will, I doubt not, be able to form a correct judgement as to what will be due in justice to me, as well as to the public, and it will give me an opportunity of removing such impressions respecting my case, as may have been injurious or explaining circumstances that may have been doubtful. I am with high respect Yrs. &c

B H LATROBE

RC (DLC); FC (MdHi: Latrobe Letterbooks). RC docketed by JM.

   1. Latrobe sought an interview with JM and Hamilton to discuss the financial problems he was experiencing after Congress had adjourned in March 1811 without making any appropriation to continue work on the Capitol. His salary was at least nine months in arrears, the total amount for labor and other materials owed him exceeded $5,000, and he was relying on work at the Navy Department to tide him over until the next session of Congress. In April 1811 Latrobe sent the navy secretary an account of $2,764.58 for some castings required to build a steam engine in the Washington Navy Yard, but by mid-June he had still not learned whether the account would be paid. Moreover, the architect was troubled by rumors circulating in Washington that he had executed the plan for the Capitol in ways that had displeased Jefferson, and he believed his fears on this score had been confirmed during some of his conversations with JM. At the subsequent interview it was agreed, according to Latrobe's recollection nine months later, that his annual salary as surveyor of the public buildings would be reduced to $1,500 because of the payments he would receive from the Navy Department and that it would then cease altogether after 1 July 1811 (see Van Horne, *Papers of Latrobe*, 3:36–37 n. 5, 40, 52–53; Latrobe to Hamilton, 17 June 1811, *Papers of Benjamin Henry Latrobe* [microfiche ed.], fiche 85; Latrobe to JM, 30 Mar. 1812 [DLC]).

§ From Edmund M. Blunt. *28 June 1811, New York.* "Permit my enclosing for your inspection a copy of the Nautical Almanac which I assure your Excellency is correct.[1] I was this day informed at the Navy Office the Officers of the Navy were using the Edition published by Mr John Garnett.[2] Mr Garnett's Almanac for 1811 contains Nine Errors! that for 1812 Thirteen Errors!!! . . . No work should have national encouragement which is not entitled to private patronage." Requests a reply.

RC (DLC). 2 pp. Docketed by JM.

   1. *The Nautical Almanac and Astronomical Ephemeris for the Year 1812* (New York, 1811; Shaw and Shoemaker 23485). This was apparently Blunt's adaptation of a British work with the same title.
   2. Garnett's edition of *The Nautical Almanac and Astronomical Ephemeris*, printed in New Brunswick, New Jersey, had gone through seven American impressions since 1804 (Shaw and Shoemaker 6854, 8960, 10940, 13171, 15694, 18166, 20830).

§ From James H. Blake. *29 June 1811, Washington.* "It is rumoured that a new Appointment of Register for the County of Washington, is about to take place; should that be a fact, I beg leave to solicit of you that Appointment." The demands of his "numerous family" are as great as "those of any other individual can well be." Does not want this request to be understood as a wish for the present occupant to be removed.[1]

RC (DNA: RG 59, LAR, 1809–17, filed under "Blake"). 1 p.

1. On Blake's quest for office and JM's responses, see Blake to JM, 6 Jan. 1810 (*PJM-PS*, 2:163 and n. 1).

§ Presidential Proclamation. *29 June 1811*. Under the act of Congress, passed on 25 Feb. 1811,[1] authorizing the president of the U.S. to remove the land office established for the sale of lands ceded by the Cherokee and Chickasaw in the Mississippi Territory from Nashville to any place he judges most proper within the district for which it was established, he directs that the said land office be removed to "Huntsville otherwise called Twickenham, in Madison County," to be opened on or before 7 Aug. 1811.

Tr (DNA: RG 49, Proclamations of Public Land Sales). 1 p. Printed in Carter, *Territorial Papers, Mississippi*, 6:203.

1. See *U.S. Statutes at Large*, 2:649–50.

§ From James Leander Cathcart. *30 June 1811, Madeira*. Has heard that Jarvis has resigned the Lisbon consulate and wishes to be considered for the post in the event of a vacancy. "The Consulate at Madeira is a paltry situation the emoluments trifling, not near sufficient to maintain my family." All trade is engrossed by a few houses, there is no commission business, and he has been vegetating "in the same dull annual routine" with no prospects for betterment. "You know Sir, when I return'd from the Mediterranean that I return'd *poor*, . . . & I know that you were among those who most promoted the idea that Cathcart ought to be provided for; but in two years no vacancy occur'd but the Consulate of Madeira which I was induced to accept from want as I justly consider'd that half a loaf was better than no bread." Laments that his circumstances obliged him "to publish the barreness of my purse." Hopes his friends and JM will bear him in mind and, if the vacancy at Lisbon is already filled,[1] requests that he be considered for the consulate at Liverpool if it becomes vacant. Refers to Jefferson's 10 Feb. 1802 note to the Senate[2] as proof of the regard in which he is held; seeks promotion to "insure the prospect of competency & the liberal education of my Children."

RC and duplicate (DNA: RG 59, LAR, 1809–17, filed under "Cathcart"). 4 pp. Docketed by Monroe.

1. On 2 July 1811 Cathcart wrote again to JM (ibid.; 3 pp.; duplicate, DLC), mentioning he had heard that George Jefferson had been appointed to Lisbon but that he might not accept owing to his health, "which is very delicate." Cathcart suggested that Madeira was a better place than Lisbon for the restoration of Jefferson's health as the Portuguese capital was in danger of being seized by the French, contained nearly one-eighth of the total population of the nation, and was never very healthy. "Mr Jefferson is in quest of health as I am of emolument," Cathcart pointed out. "Should he be disposed to exchange situations we may both be suited to our satisfaction." If Jefferson agreed to this proposal, Cathcart requested that JM not disapprove of the exchange.

2. On 1 Feb. 1802 Jefferson had nominated Cathcart as consul at Tripoli (*Senate Exec. Proceedings*, 1:406–7).

From Jacob Barker

RESPECTED FRIEND   NEW YORK 7th Mo 1. 1811.

The duties imposed on Cotton imported into England from the United States in American Vessels were so much greater than on Cotton imported in English Vessels that when our ports were open to English Vessels it was very difficult to procure freights at low rates for American Ships while English Ships came here and procured good freights without delay, and it is now understood that the British Government have or are about to increase the duties so considerably on American Cotton and other articles when imported in American Vessels that if the present restrictions imposed by our laws should be removed and those duties continue our vessels will not be able to find employ on any terms as the difference will be much more than the whole freights now charged in American Vessels which I beg leave to suggest for thy consideration as I am deeply interested in navigation. With esteem I am thy assured friend

                                                        JACOB BARKER[1]

RC (DLC).

1. Jacob Barker (1779–1871) was born to a Quaker family in Nantucket and entered the commission business in New York where he subsequently became a prominent merchant. In his politics he was a Republican, and he had recently visited Washington as an opponent of the recharter of the Bank of the United States. Although he appears to have had misgivings about the wisdom of the War of 1812, he continued to support JM's administration and was actively engaged throughout 1813 and 1814 in efforts to raise war loans for the Treasury Department. He also assisted Dolley Madison in evacuating Washington during the British invasion of August 1814 (see Barker, *Incidents in the Life of Jacob Barker of New Orleans, Louisiana; with Historical Facts, His Financial Transactions with the Government, and His Course on Important Political Questions* [Washington, 1855], pp. 5–6, 30–32, 37, 39–109).

From James Jay

DEAR SIR   NEW YORK July 1st. 1811

The many failures that have happened in this City, have produced much distress among its inhabitants. I have not escaped unhurt. An anxiety to assist two persons who are dear to me, but who ultimately proved unfortunate, hath occasioned me to lose many thousand dollars more than I can afford. When friendship and affection have long held possession of a warm breast, prudential considerations yield to their influence. The Loss I have sustained, obliges me to make an effort to reestablish my fortune, which was but moderate before. With this view I wish to revisit Europe. To go from hence to England, and from thence to the Continent, might, I apprehend, excite suspicion of a person's being a partisan or even a secret Agent of the British Government, subject one to some disagreeable circumstances, and be detrimental to one's pursuits. And to go from hence in a merchant ship directly to France, should the vessel be taken and carried into England, a person, besides losing much time, would at least be subjected to much trouble & useless expence. For my own part, I should expect no favor from that Government. Some of its members were not pleased with certain measures I openly took in London, in regard to American Affairs, after the Ministry had refused me a passage to America; and they all may have heard, from what transpired during my late applications to Congress, that both before the war, and during the two first years of it, in which I was detained in England, I uniformly made the British Post Office the means by which I speedily transmitted to our friends in France & America, early information of the Plans & Designs, political & military, of the British Government against our Country: a maneuvre in politics, rather too mortifying to the adverse party to be easily forgiven.[1] For these reasons I take the Liberty to ask you, whether myself & Son could not be accommodated with a passage to France, in the frigate which is to take out Mr. Barlow. I beg you will favor me with a speedy answer, and if it should be in the affirmative, I should be glad to know on what terms or at what expence, the passage could be had.

Your Letter of the 10th. Ult. I received in course. It might not perhaps be amiss if some person living at the intended Scene of action were to be engaged to transmit information of what passes on the subject, to an authorised Officer as near as possible to the place in question, who could take his measures accordingly to punish the Offence. Health and happiness attend you.

JAMES JAY

RC (DLC).

1. James Jay's somewhat eccentric activities in Great Britain and France during the peace negotiations of 1782–83 accomplished no result other than the embarrassment of his brother, John. James Jay had also lodged over the years a series of claims on Congress for depreciation on money and other properties advanced in the cause of the Revolution, including the use by the Continental Congress of an invisible ink he had invented. As secretary of state JM had reported favorably on the latter claim in 1807, but the matter was not settled until 1813 (Richard B. Morris et al., eds., *John Jay: The Winning of the Peace; Unpublished Papers, 1780–1784*, vol. 2 of *John Jay* [2 vols. to date; New York, 1975—], pp. 250–53, 265, 498–99; JM to the House of Representatives, 26 Jan. 1807 [DNA: RG 59, DL]; *ASP, Claims*, p. 421).

From George Luckey

The love of country is strong in most nations; and one might expect would be so powerful in a free State that it would lead forth every citizen to strive by all means to promote the public interest. In this every one has it in his power to do something by Word or deed. We know that it is peculiarly difficult at this period for the constituted authorities to direct the Vessel of State amidst the convulsions that are in the World; through the open Violence of envious contending rivals, their artifices & entreagues; the prepostrous conduct of selfish & undiscerning men. These things are against us; but we hope & trust that the disposer of all events, who in times past has saved; & granted us surprizing & unexpected deliverance will ever espouse & Vindicate our righteous cause & direct those in authority to suitable measures & crown their labours for the public Welfare With success. An individual cannot Judge of the measures of Government nor say what ought to be done, nay the united Wisdom of our nation may think it difficult in what manner to proceed for the best. If covetousness would permit us one would suppose it might be best for us for a season to confine our trade entirely within the limites of the United States & their Jurisdiction; we have here the best productions of every clime & this could be transported with safety according of the exigence of the differsent states from one to another & this might tend to promote the most cordial affection among the differsent parts of the union. In the present condition of the World instead of making gain we loose every way by our intercourse With foreign nations. May You dear sir be ever assisted & directed in a Work too arduuous [*sic*] for most of mortals, & enjoy all those comforts present & future which religion alone has afforded in times of need & christianity directly tends to inspire, is the earnest prayer of yours

Geo. Luckey

RC (DLC).

§ From an Unidentified Correspondent. *1 July 1811, Maryland.* "I advise you as a Friend to arouse from your Lethargy. Look at the Nation. The People are all but ready to Burst into a Flame. A Flame of Discord. This is the Hour Of Trial—it is more Dangerous than the Time that tried Men's Soul's. . . . Do not slumber at the Helm in the Storm lest Our ship may Broach too & founder. May God be your Comfort and give you Consolation in the Hour of Trial for you need it."

RC (NN). 1 p. Signed "A Friend." Docketed by JM.

From Thomas Jefferson

DEAR SIR   MONTICELLO July 3. 11.

I have seen with very great concern the late Address of mr. Smith to the public. He has been very ill advised both personally and publicly. As far as I can judge from what I hear, the impression made is entirely unfavorable to him. Every man's own understanding readily answers all the facts and insinuations, one only excepted, and for that they look for explanations without any doubt that they will be satisfactory. That is Erving's case.[1] I have answered the enquiries of several on this head, telling them at the same time, what was really the truth, that the failure of my memory enabled me to give them rather conjectures than recollections. For in truth I have but indistinct recollections of the case. I know that what was done was on a joint consultation between us, and I have no fear that what we did will not have been correct & cautious. What I retain of the case, on being reminded of some particulars, will re-instate the whole firmly in my remembrance, and enable me to state them to enquirers with correctness, which is the more important from the part I bore in them. I must therefore ask the favor of you to give me a short outline of the facts which may correct as well as supply my own recollections. But who is to give an explanation to the public? Not yourself certainly. The chief magistrate cannot enter the Arena of the newspapers. At least the occasion should be of a much higher order. I imagine there is some pen at Washington competent to it. Perhaps the best form would be that of some one personating the friend of Erving, some one apparently from the North.[2] Nothing laboured is requisite. A short & simple statement of the case, will, I am sure, satisfy the public. We are in the midst of a so so harvest; probably one third short of the last. We had a very fine rain on Saturday last. Ever affectionately Yours

                                                          TH: JEFFERSON

RC (DLC: Rives Collection, Madison Papers); FC (DLC: Jefferson Papers).

1. Among the matters raised by Robert Smith in his *Address* was the discovery he made in December 1809 that George W. Erving, while serving in London between 1801 and 1805 as consul and claims agent under article 7 of the Jay treaty, had been allowed a commission of 2½ percent on the money paid by the British government to settle American claims, a sum amounting to $22,392. Smith declared that Erving's compensation was improper and that when he sought an explanation, JM remarked that "he had no knowledge or recollection of any of the circumstances of this affair" and "took occasion abruptly to call [Smith's] attention to some other subject." Smith then wrote to Erving on 19 Dec. 1809 requesting an explanation, and Erving, after his return from Cadiz in 1810, gave Smith a letter from JM, dated 3 Nov. 1804, authorizing him to retain the money in question. There was, Smith added, no trace of this transaction in the State Department records, apparently because the letter was a *private* one and not an *official* one.

Smith waxed eloquent and at great length on the impropriety of JM's actions in allowing

Erving to receive compensation far in excess of his salary of $2,000, but JM told him to give Erving's claim "the sanction of the state department" and, moreover, "to consider and put on *file*, as a *public* letter, the *private* letter of Nov. 3 1804." When Smith stated in response to a Senate request for information that "duty would constrain [him] to set forth all the circumstances of this transaction," JM "manifested great perturbation and fretfully said, that the call of the Senate was evidently made with a view to injure him. In connexion with this unprecedented observation," Smith concluded, "I perceived unequivocal indications of dissatisfaction with respect to myself" (*National Intelligencer*, 2 July 1811; see also Gallatin to JM, 8 Feb. 1811, and nn.).

2. *A Review of Robert Smith's Address to the People of the United States* appeared in installments in the *National Intelligencer* on 4, 6, 9, and 11 July 1811 and was also reprinted in pamphlet form (Philadelphia, 1811; Shaw and Shoemaker 23808). The author was Joel Barlow, who had acted as Erving's attorney while he was settling his accounts with the State Department (see treasury receipt, 13 Mar. 1811, signed by Thomas Tudor Tucker [DNA: RG 217, First Auditor's Accounts, no. 23,872]). William Lee, however, claimed that the *Review* was his work, "corrected by Barlow," adding that it gave him "a great standing with the President" (Lee to Susan Palfrey Lee, 9 Sept. 1811, quoted in Mann, *A Yankee Jeffersonian*, p. 140).

§ From Daniel Buck. *4 July 1811, Chelsea.* Presumes on JM's "known goodness" to make "a few quiries, and suggestions." Asks if there is reason to suppose that any nation endowed with superior resources and imbued with the rights of man can remain in colonial subordination "and suffer her resources to be drawn from her by a remote power." Is it possible that Spain's American provinces might return to a dependency on "that old, decrepid, and desolated kingdom"? The state of Europe will ensure that the spirit of revolution and innovation will spread throughout the American continent "so far as civilization extends." The balance of power among European nations will no longer be contended for, the practice of colonizing will be exploded, and all American nations will seek "a close and friendly league." A new balance of power between Europe and America will be created, one "more congenial with the nature of things . . . and more propitious to general commerce." The "never ending contest, to hold the balance of power in Europe" has led to the oppressed state of the world and it will only end by giving one belligerent "absolute dominion" over the other.

Self-interest and self-preservation require the U.S. "to attempt a new order of things." It is said that the mouths of the St. Lawrence, Hudson, and Mississippi Rivers can be united for less than the cost of a single campaign during the Revolutionary War. A canal from Lake Champlain could establish communication between the St. Lawrence and the Hudson, and the western lakes could be similarly united with the Mississippi. This is no "chimerical expedient"; the expense would be next to nothing and the U.S. could certainly generate the commerce to sustain it as well as the naval force to protect it. This would "in some measure" substitute for foreign commerce and "enable us abundantly to supply our brethren at the south, while they continued their struggle for independence." Precious metals from Mexico and Peru would also replenish the treasury and compensate for the present loss of revenue.

Argues that England is unlikely to repeal the orders in council and make foreign commerce free, that "universal dominion" is the real aim of Bonaparte, and that the "total distruction of Great Britain, is but a minor object, though considered absolutely necessary to the accomplishment of his great design." Napoleon is unlikely to relax his Continental System to restore neutral rights unless he could make the system "operate with still greater force and effect upon great Britain." Likewise, Great Britain has pursued the goal of complete maritime supremacy for nearly two centuries and "for more than half a century, been in the actual possession of that ascendancy." Great Britain is "contending for existence," and restrictions on neutral commerce are necessary for it to maintain the contest. Even if this is not strictly true, it is impossible for Great Britain to support a marine force on the basis of its legitimate sources of revenue; therefore its plea of necessity still stands. Otherwise, it would soon "dwindle into that state of insignificance, which nature, unaided by art, and the lawless ambition of man, has marked out for an insignificant Island."

Points out that instructions to the American minister in London reveal that "the genius of our free government" is in collision with the "fundamental maxims" of the British constitution. Neither side can prevail without admitting the superiority of the other. Great Britain is inflexible and no concessions can be expected from it. "If she should grant what we justly require, it would, at once, diminish that superiority [and] give a complete triumph to her determined enemy."

Many might think that this situation entails Britain's destruction. It might also be thought that East and West Florida will soon be incorporated into the U.S., "that upon the fall of the parent state, the British provinces in America will find their interest to be identified with ours; and that by natural causes, now obviously in operation, . . . there shall be no balance of power, known in the world, but that between the two continents, and no interest, but that of perfect freedom of commerce, and the cultivation of the arts of peace." All this can be achieved without any "violent effort" on the part of the U.S. Asks if anything might retard the onset of this state of affairs, which leads him to inquire about the object of the present embassy to the U.S. It cannot be to atone for the attack on the *Chesapeake*, renounce the right of impressment, repeal the orders in council, or abolish paper blockades. Assumes Great Britain either is seeking the repeal of the Nonintercourse Act to strengthen its commerce and eventually "establish her tyranny" or is attempting to dissolve the Union. Fears a "sort of Copenhagen negociation."

Complains about those Americans who defend Great Britain as the world's "last, and only hope" against ruin and despotic slavery. Suspects a concert might be formed "to draw off the northern and eastern states, with the British provinces to take shelter under the British navy, to withstand the mighty, and lawless power of Bonaparte." Concedes there might be no immediate danger of this, but it could be attempted over time, and the U.S. could become the scene of war and "the battles of France and England would, for a series of years, be faught [*sic*] here as they now are in Spain and Portugal."

Since writing the above, has learned of the congressional actions on East Florida. Supposes the province has been obtained and that all is quiet there now. If so, asks if war, "with a view to exclude all foreign Jurisdictions from this northern section of the Continent," is necessary. Letters of marque and reprisal and privateering will be sufficient to prevent a concert with Great Britain to endanger the nation. And if a project for internal commerce is developed and the Canadians invited to participate, it would "conciliate their friendship, and soon induce them to follow the example of the Floridas."

Assumes that JM has considered and weighed all these matters. Has only offered his thoughts as further weight in the scale and to confirm that such opinions are shared "even in the deepest recesses of obscurity" and by one who has always opposed "restrictive energies" to coerce an enemy unless they are accompanied by "vigourous and energetic measures of external force."

RC (DLC). 8 pp.

§ From James Chamberlain. *4 July 1811, Mount Locust, Jefferson County, Mississippi Territory*. "This strange app⟨licatio⟩n will I have no doubt surprize you—but dire necessity compels me to it." Relies on JM's "known philanthropy" to save him and his three children. Explains that he was ruined by the Embargo, although he approved of the measure. Shortly before it went into effect, he purchased property to be paid for by cotton sales, but cotton prices fell by almost two-thirds from the usual price. He also lost two slaves purchased at the same time from men who opposed the system and who now "laugh at my admiration of the measure." Has tried to pay his creditors, but in addition to the low price of cotton, "an uncommon drought last summer" left him with only half a crop of cotton and a third of corn. His mercantile house stopped payment, too. He must pay $1,156 by the third Monday in September or the rest of his property will be forfeited and he risks going to prison. Requests $600 to save some of his property and his family and promises to repay the whole in person in two years. "I know you woud not hesitate to releive me, for in all events whats Six Hundred dollars—or Six thousand to Your Excellency's Goodness and services—but a drop."

"A Republican *indeed* can do no wilful wrong—therefore on you I trust my hopes." Has no one else to assist him as his relatives were ruined at the time of the Revolution. His father, about seventy years old, lives in Kentucky in "low Circumstances." Mentions that he was born 9 Aug. 1778 in Loudoun County, Virginia. His father immigrated to Kentucky about fifteen years ago, and he moved to this territory in 1800, where he has lived comfortably. In a postscript lists his property: five "valuable *field negroes*"; his livestock; three tracts of land in West Florida and the Mississippi Territory, all of which are "in a state of nature" and can be converted to cash; and his three sons, named Louis Washington, Ferdinand Lee, and Jefferson Madison, to whom he wishes to give "a Liberal Education."

RC (DLC). 5 pp.

§ From Pierre Samuel DuPont de Nemours. *4 July 1811, Paris*. Sends two manuscripts that will prove his attachment to the country which has become that of his children and where he hopes to finish his days. One manuscript is a much corrected edition of his work on American finance that was sent to Jefferson last year.[1] The other manuscript is the second, equally corrected, edition of his plan for American national education.[2] Cannot recall whether he acquainted JM with this last work, but in any case it will be useful to reintroduce it to him. It is said that Barlow treated the same subject not long ago with great success.[3] If he agrees with Barlow on several points it will prove their reasonableness; if he differs on others, it will be good for JM to judge and add his own insights.

Encloses a packet for his children. Also encloses four copies of the last volume of Turgot's works[4]—one for JM, one for Jefferson, one for the American Philosophical Society, and one for his children. Requests the favor of his children being allowed to respond under the cover of the secretary of state. Requests the even greater favor of permitting his children to use the Treasury Department to send money to him in Europe. Thanks JM again for granting him permission to travel on a U.S. vessel.

RC (DLC). 3 pp. In French. Docketed by JM.

1. For DuPont's correspondence with Jefferson on American finance and political economy between 7 Sept. 1810 and 17 May 1812, see Chinard, *Correspondence of Jefferson and Du Pont de Nemours*, pp. 158–99. Jefferson had already passed on to JM, in his letter of 8 Dec. 1810, the copy he had received of the treatise on finance.

2. See *PJM-PS*, 2:5 and n. 1, 7, 104, 197–99.

3. See *PJM-PS*, 1:176–78 and n. 3.

4. See *PJM-PS*, 2:5 and n. 2.

§ From Bossange & Masson. *5 July 1811, Paris.* Acknowledges JM's letter of 7 Jan. 1811 mentioning receipt of their edition of Homer's *Iliad.* "The favourable admission you have given it by granting a place in your Library cause us to beg the same honour for the Second work of the Illustrious translator, La Jerusalem Délivrée."[1]

RC (DLC). 1 p.

1. *Jérusalem délivrée; poëme traduit de l'italien,* trans. C. F. Le Brun (Paris, 1811), was a translation of Torquato Tasso's epic of the First Crusade, *Gerusalemme Liberata.*

¶ To James Jay. Letter not found. *5 July 1811.* Mentioned in Jay to JM, 11 July 1811. States that it would be agreeable to him if Jay's request for permission to travel to Europe in a U.S. vessel could be granted but the secretary of the navy has made arrangements that will not allow private passengers.

From James Taylor

DEAR SIR   BELLE VUE KENTUCKY July 7th. 1811.

Inclosed I send you a letter I lately recieved from my friend Judge Coburn.[1]

It was intended for my sight alone;[2] but as it explains the cause why he did not attend his Court in Louisiana last Spring, I had a wish that you should see it from under his own hand.

This letter contains some expressions which so well comports with my own sentiments & feelings, as to our political & foreign relations, and beleiving that they are not at varience with your own, that I have ventured to inclose it to you without his knowledge or consent. By this letter you will see his sentiments on those subjects undisguised.

There may be some clamors against the Judge on the score that he has not his family in the Territory, but I am sure there cannot be another Objection made, and I am induced to think there may be urged some good reasons urged [*sic*], why a Judge who is not on the spot to enter into the party fealings of the two opposite interests, which have uniformly divided more or less all the different Territorial Goverments, is better able in many *grand* questions to decide correctly.

In the event of our Govt. having to contend with either of the two belligerents I am confident you will find no section of the Union more disposed to support the rights & dignity of the Nation than this part of the Western Country.

I lately spent several days among our friends in the neighbourhood of Louisville in the state they were generally well, except the old Commodore, he has been a long time confined with his thigh, and he was very anxious to have his leg amputated. I was present at a Consaltation of Surgeons, they decided against it for the present, he is geting better slowly.

I hope this may find your self & Lady in good health. I have the honor to be with great friendship & esteem Dr. sir Your friend & Servt.

JAMES TAYLOR

RC and enclosure (DNA: RG 59, ML). For enclosure, see n. 1.

1. Taylor enclosed an 18 June 1811 letter he had received from Coburn (3 pp.; printed in Carter, *Territorial Papers, Louisiana-Missouri*, 14:461–62). The judge explained that illness had prevented him from attending his court in the spring. The remainder of the letter discussed politics. Coburn mentioned that "our Senator" (John Pope) had been "handled roughly by his constituents," leading the judge to conclude that "plain simple, and honest republicanism; has an easy task to perform, compared to time-serving & duplicity" of "equivocal men." Convinced that "prattling Lawyers, were not the best statesmen," Coburn further remarked that "young, inexperienced politicians . . . are not the best men for the management of the great concerns of a Nation." He was gratified to see "our old and faithful servant Monroe" back in office, having feared that "Randolph and his party had seduced him." He suspected that "the good old Thomas Jefferson has smoothed the way to Mo[n]roe's return to our councils. The faithless British pirates have recd a check, which wd. seem to promise some good. May it serve to deter them from future aggressions."

2. Taylor was Coburn's brother-in-law (see Taylor to JM, 8 Feb. 1807, printed ibid., 14:91).

To Thomas Cooper

DEAR SIR   WASHINGTON July 8th 1811

By the return of the Frigate Essex, I have received from Mr. McRae on whom the Consulate at Paris provisionally devolved, an answer to my letter addressed to Mr. Warden on the subject of the Chemical books you wished to procure.[1] I subjoin the requisite extract "A stranger & almost entirely ignorant of the language even of the Country, I have been obliged to avail myself of the aid of Doctr. Patterson a young American patriot of distinguished merit, (son of the Director of the Mint at Philada.) to procure a partial supply, the best we could obtain, of such books as Judge Cooper's letter described, which are forwarded to L'Orient for the purpose of being conveyed by the Essex to Mr. John Vaughan whom the Judge has named as his friend. These books were purchased at so cheap a rate, as to render it entirely unnecessary that I should trouble you with the draft which your friendship for Judge Cooper had invited. I regret very much that it is not in our power at this moment to procure the Abbe Haüy's Porcelain illustrations of Chrystallography; but hope we shall be able to forward them by the next suitable conveyance. As to a new Edition of Loysel sur l'art de la Verrerie, Dr. Patterson assures me that the Judge is misinformed. He says that after strict enquiry, he has ascertained that there is only a single Edition of that work."

Draft (DLC).

1. See Alexander McRae to JM, 26 Jan. 1811, and n. 2.

To the Heads of Departments

July 8. 1811.

J. Madison requests the favor of a consultation with the heads of Departments tomorrow (tuesday) at 12 oClock and that they remain to dinner with him.

RC (NHi: Gallatin Papers). Addressed to the secretary of the treasury. In a clerk's hand. Another copy (NjP: Crane Collection) is addressed to the attorney general.

To Thomas Jefferson

DEAR SIR   WASHINGTON July 8. 1811[1]

Your favor of the 3d. came duly to hand. You will have noticed in the Nat: Intelligencer that the wicked publication of Mr Smith is not to escape with impunity. It is impossible however that the whole turpitude of his conduct can be understood without disclosures to be made by myself alone, and of course, as he knows, not to be made at all. Without these his infamy is daily fastening itself upon him; leaving no other consolation than the malignant hope of revenging his own ingratitude and guilt on others. The case of Erving, will probably be better explained in the Newspaper,[2] than I can here do it. The general facts of it I believe are, that the three offices at London were centered in him, with one of the salaries only; it being understood at the time that he would be made Assessor to the Board under Jay's Treaty, in which case he would be well recompenced. The Board declined to appoint him, giving preference to Cabot. Still however a certain portion of the business passed thro' his hands. On this he charged, the usual commission of 2½ per Ct. accruing from the individuals, and not from a public fund. Having paid over the whole of the money of individuals in his hands, to the public, instead of retaining his Commission, a resort to Congs. became necessary. Whilst the subject was before them, doubts were excited as to the merits of the case, and a call made on Mr. Gallatin for information. His report put an end to the difficulty. The appropriation was immediately made, and but for the perverted view of the matter now before the public, would never more [have] been thought of. The Treasury officers, tho' politically adverse to Mr. E. do him much justice on the occasion, declaring that his official transactions throug[h]out as presented in his accts. are models of clearness and exactness, that he appears to have saved or gained to the public by his vigilance & assiduity 60, or 70,000 dolrs. that there remains a surplus of unclaimed monies, to a considerable amount, the greater part of which will probably never be claimed, & finally that the only error committed by Mr. E. was his not avoiding the necessity of asking Congs. to give back the amount of his Commission, by deducting it himself from the sums paid into the public coffers.

It has been thought best, whilst Mr. Monroe is in communications with the B. & F. Ministers here, to be silent on the subject. As the latest information from Russel, is prior to the arrival of the non-importation Act, the state of our affairs at Paris may be conjectured. Pinkney brings, of course, nothing; Foster being the channel of English news.[3] I do not know that he has yet opened himself compleatly to Mr. Monroe; but from the conciliatory disposition of the Prince Regent, and the contrary one of his Cabinet, still deriving an ascendency from the convalescence of the King, you will be very able to dive into the character of the mission. You will perceive in the printed paper inclosed, a step by the British Minister, which, very unseasonably it would seem, denotes an increasing rigor towards this Country.[4] According to a preceding interposition with the Court of Admiralty, cases under the orders in Council, had been suspended.

I had promised myself a release from this position immediately after the 4th. July. It will be some days yet before I shall be able to set out. Considering the excessive heat for some days past, no time has yet been lost. The weather has been as dry as hot. In general the drought has been so severe as to ruin almost the oats & flax. The crop of wheat, tho' shortened, will be tolerable, in tolerable land, where the Hessians have not committed their ravages. Be assured of my most affectionate esteem.

JAMES MADISON

RC (DLC). Docketed by Jefferson, "recd July 10."

1. Under the dateline someone, possibly an early editor, has interlined: "quere—as to omitting in this other preceding letters what relates to Mr Smith."

2. The matter of Erving's accounts was discussed in the fourth installment of the *Review of Robert Smith's Address* in the *National Intelligencer*, 11 July 1811, and again with some additional information in the issues of 13 July and 1 Aug. The reply generally followed the outline JM gave to Jefferson in his letter, while stressing that JM had merely confirmed Jefferson's 1804 decision to allow Erving "just and reasonable compensation" for his expenses. The *Review* also chided Robert Smith for placing a sinister emphasis on the private nature of JM's November 1804 letter to Erving when its contents could only take effect "as a public voucher." And if Erving's compensation had been as improper as Robert Smith had alleged, the *Review* asked, how could it be explained that only a few months earlier his accounts had been approved not only by Smith himself but also by the Treasury Department, the comptroller, the auditor, the president, and the Senate. Since Erving was abroad again and unable to defend himself, the *Review* reasoned that Smith could have had no other motive in reviving the matter in his "silly memoirs" than to defame JM. The *Review* concluded its discussion by publishing Gallatin's 8 Feb. 1811 letter to JM reporting on Erving's accounts, which JM three days later had sent to the Senate.

3. Augustus John Foster had arrived in Washington on 30 June 1811. He presented his credentials to JM on 2 July (*National Intelligencer*, 2 and 4 July 1811).

4. The enclosed paper has not been identified.

From Henry Dearborn

DEAR SIR,   BOSTON July 8th. 1811

I take the liberty of presenting you a copy of an Oration pronounced on the 4th inst. by my Son,[1] as to its merit, I can only say, that I hope the imperfections & defects may be in some measure ballanced by the honest zeal of the author. The two Mrs. Coles[2] were with us at our festival. They set out this morning for the District of Maine. Please to ask Mrs. Madison to accept the tender of my best respects, and to ac[c]ept for yourself assurence of respectful regards.

H. DEARBORN

P. S. We have had five unusually hot days. The Thermometer each day up to 98 or 99.

RC (DLC).

1. Henry Alexander Scammel Dearborn, *An Oration, Pronounced at Boston, on the Fourth Day of July, 1811; before the Supreme Executive and in the Presence of the Bunker-Hill Association* (Boston, 1811; Shaw and Shoemaker 22672).

2. Dearborn was referring to Edward and John Coles.

§ From Jonas Humbert.[1] *8 July 1811, New York.* Apologizes for writing a long letter, but as one who supported the Jefferson administration, JM's nomination, and the Embargo, he was "*marked* two years ago as a *victim*, and lately *sacrificed* to *gratify the Clinton faction* in this City." Has been prevented from acting in his job as an inspector of flour and meal, which has deprived him of the means to support his family. At the time of JM's nomination to the presidency, there were few in the city who supported their country. Their timidity arose from fear of displeasing the Clinton family—especially DeWitt Clinton—and James Cheetham, whose press was wholly devoted to the views of the latter. The friends of Clinton were, and still are, as hostile to the Jefferson administration as any Federalists in the state. "The partizans of Mr De Witt Clinton were determined, if possible, to blast the unsullied fame of president Jefferson, prevent your election, in order to raise De Witt Clinton on the ruin of both." The city was in consternation, arising from the assiduity of Gurdon S. Mumford in propagating the notion of "Virginia influence," but Dr. Samuel L. Mitchill, on his return from Washington, "gave me full satisfaction, that the Nomination was fairly made." Discussed with Frank and White, the editors of the N.Y. *Public Advertiser*, the "unhallowed attacks . . . against Mr Jeffersons policy, and base obloqui uttered against Mr Madison" in Cheetham's *American Citizen*. These young men were unable to counter the "gigantic pen" of Cheetham, who had also engaged the "formidable genious" of Tunis Wortman, whose own mind had been poisoned by Mumford, "one of the most virulent enemies of Mr Jefferson as well as of your Self."

He informed the editors he would furnish them with a "Systematic exposure of the views of oppositionists" and thus expose Clinton's schemes in the *Public Advertiser*. He wrote five essays under the pseudonym of "Diodorus Siculus,"[2] six as "Zenophon,"[3] and some other pieces as well. "These effusions annoyed the Clintonians." To his satisfaction, some were reprinted in the *Aurora*, "at that time correct in politics." Has never regretted the course he pursued even though it cost him his position. Offers to name men appointed by Jefferson in New York who oppose the administration and who "are, now, every day, exulting in the attack of Robert Smith, on Mr Madison—declaring that De Witt Clinton is the man that ought to be president."

The business he previously pursued proved "injurious" to his health, and he needs a situation where he can support his family. Is acquainted with Governor Tompkins, Henry Rutgers, William Few, Nathan Sanford, and Samuel L. Mitchill. The last two "wrote in my favour, but to no purpose, to the Council of Appointment."

RC (DLC). 4 pp.

1. Jonas Humbert was the secretary of the New York Tammany Society (N.Y. *Public Advertiser*, 20 Apr. 1808).

2. The first five essays under the pseudonym of "Diodorus Siculus," addressed to the "virtuous and independent republicans" of New York, appeared in the N.Y. *Public Advertiser* be-

tween 12 and 21 May 1808. The nineteenth and final essay in the series was printed on 13 July 1808. Humbert took the pseudonym from the Sicilian-born historian Diodorus Siculus, a contemporary of Julius and Augustus Caesar and author of histories of the world and Caesar's Gallic wars.

3. The six "Zenophon" essays, addressed to the "friends of our republican form of government and American independence," appeared in the N.Y. *Public Advertiser* between 22 July and 28 Sept. 1808.

§ From William Lambert. *8 July 1811, Washington.* "A letter lately received from bishop Madison, inclosing a statement to him from Mr. Blackburn, professor of mathematics at William and Mary College, relative to a supposed error in the calculation of the longitude of that college, transmitted by you some weeks ago,[1] has made it necessary for me to explain the objectionable part of the computation, by demonstrating to the bishop, a misapplication of the rule referred to by Mr. Blackburn. The inclosed will, it is hoped, remove any remaining doubt on the subject.

"As Dr. Maskelyne[2] and M. de la Lande,[3] have proposed different rules to ascertain the Moon's parallax in latitude, which do not give the same result, it is essential in practical astronomy, that both and each of those rules should be investigated; for upon the correct determination of that element, the longitude of a place, especially one far distant from another meridian, will materially depend."

RC (DLC). 1 p. Docketed by JM. Enclosure not found.

1. See Lambert to JM, 10 June 1811.
2. Nevil Maskelyne (1732–1811) was astronomer royal from 1765 until his death.
3. Joseph-Jérôme Le Français de Lalande (1732–1807), as well known for his atheism as his scientific achievements, was professor of astronomy at the Collège de France.

From Edmund Randolph

Lexington Virginia July 9. 1811.

Without one feeling, left of the character of a partizan, but still living to friendship, a man, whose hand is known to Mr. Madison, asks him, whether he recollects, or ever heard, that after Colo. Hamilton, had been severely pressed for a supposed misappropriation of the money, devoted by law to special purposes,[1] he, Colo H, produced a letter, authorizing it, signed by President Washington, while on his tour to South Carolina:[2] that the President at first denied its existence in positive and vehement terms, *not having preserved a copy of it;* but that it was afterwards acknowledged by him, and registered in the treasury department, ut valeret, quantum valere potuit?[3]

RC (DLC). Unsigned; in the hand of Edmund Randolph. JM's docket, "July 9 1811 and Aug 8 1811," is obscured by a sheet attached to the verso.

1. Randolph referred to the resolutions introduced by William Branch Giles in the House of Representatives in February 1793, and supported by JM, condemning Alexander Hamilton's conduct as secretary of the treasury. The resolutions, in essence, charged that Hamilton

had misapplied appropriations intended to repay the foreign debt to repayment of the domestic debt, much of which was held by the Bank of the United States (see *PJM*, 14:450, 455–69; for Hamilton's responses, see Syrett and Cooke, *Papers of Hamilton*, 13:523–79, 14:2–6, 17–67).

2. Randolph probably had in mind Washington's 7 May 1791 letter to Hamilton (Syrett and Cooke, *Papers of Hamilton*, 8:330).

3. "That it may fare as well as it could."

§ From David Meade Randolph. *9 July 1811, London*. Offers JM some "political remarks—emanating from some interesting communications with several distinguished characters" on both the ministerial and opposition sides of the policy questions agitating Great Britain. Makes some comparisons of "National Greatness"; finds that in Great Britain it is measured by "Wealth and power" and in the U.S. by *"National equality of Rights & community of happiness!"* Regrets that "garbeled extracts" of the most violent American party prints have persuaded John Bull and the ministers of America's "deadly hostility" but believes that the people of Great Britain "possess similar doctrines of Liberty and religious tolleration" to those held in the U.S. Has obtained information from "certain distinguished characters" in Ireland that has persuaded him *"their* feelings, policy, *ultimate views*, and the unceasing leaven forming the basis of the Irish character, are not only congenial, but aspire to be identified with our more fortunate Countrymen; whose hopes are kept down by contemplating the vast difference of space across the *Irish Channel*, and the Atlantic!" These remarks are prefatory to enclosing a communication from Sir Jonah Barrington,[1] "which has resulted from personal interviews I had been honored with, by the celebrated Mr. Grattan[2] and others."

RC and enclosure (DNA: RG 59, ML). RC 6 pp. For enclosure, see n. 1.

1. Randolph enclosed a 6 July 1811 letter he had received from Jonah Barrington, formerly an Irish member of Parliament and at that time an admiralty court judge in Dublin (7 pp.). The judge expressed his wish that American concerns in Ireland, particularly in Dublin, be better regulated, and he claimed that many "Embarrassments" resulted from the want of "an *efficient* consul in Dublin." Specifically, he believed that trade in Ireland was suffering from the "misconduct" of American ship captains, most notably their failure to observe their articles of agreement with their crews, and he even cited cases where American captains had procured press gangs "to impress their *own American* sailors to avoid the payment of their wages." Barrington doubted whether his admiralty jurisdiction extended to these problems, lamented the lack of consular appointments throughout Ireland generally, and declared that both he and his friend Grattan agreed that these issues could not be managed under the articles of union between Great Britain and Ireland. Barrington further mentioned that he had forwarded a recommendation to the president "last year" (not found) for a consul in Dublin because communication with such an official was essential for him on many occasions.

2. Henry Grattan (1746–1820), member of Parliament for Dublin, was well known for his sympathy to American independence, parliamentary reform, Catholic emancipation, and opposition to the union of Great Britain and Ireland.

§ From James T. Austin. *11 July 1811, Boston*. Asks if JM can spare the time to read the enclosed pamphlet, written by "a zealous admirer of his administration."[1]

RC (DLC). 1 p.

1. Austin very likely enclosed a copy of his pamphlet, written under the pseudonym of "Leolin" and published on 30 June 1811, *Resistance to the Laws of the United States; Considered in Four Letters to the Honorable Harrison Gray Otis* (Boston, 1811; Shaw and Shoemaker 22216). The first three "Leolin" letters had been written in April 1811 during the Massachusetts state elections, and they critically explored the violent and disunionist implications of the call made by Harrison Gray Otis for resistance to the 2 Mar. 1811 Nonintercourse Act. The fourth letter, dated 19 June 1811, was a further attack on Otis for his criticisms of Gov. Elbridge Gerry's 7 June 1811 address to the Massachusetts legislature, which had also deplored Federalist methods of opposing the policies of JM's administration (see JM to Gerry, 21 June 1811, and n. 1).

§ From Richard Brent. *11 July 1811*. "Mr Alexander Scott of George Town has by letter informed me that he is an applicant to Government for a Consulate to Tunis." Scott has asked him to give JM his opinion on the application, and he willingly complies. Scott is a "steadfast Republican" and is not only fit "for a Consulate to Tunis but perfectly qualefied to discharge the duties of a much higher diplomatic Station."

RC (DNA: RG 59, LAR, 1809–17, filed under "Scott"). 2 pp. Docketed by Monroe.

§ From James Jay. *11 July 1811, New York*. Expresses his disappointment at receiving JM's letter of 5 July. Explains his circumstances and background for the benefit of the secretary of the navy, who "may probably be ignorant of my history." Gives an account of his life, beginning with the collection he made in Great Britain for Columbia College before the Revolution and his decision to support the cause in America, thereby sacrificing "the prospect of succeeding to a large fortune in England." Alludes to his having advanced money in the common cause, to the services he rendered General Washington, "from whence, by his own acknowledgment, he derived great advantage in his military operations," and to the suffering and distress he endured. Recalls that Lord North had once wished to get him a passage to America but was unable to grant it. "The President of the United States tells me it would be agreeable to him if my request could be gratified, but informs me, that the Secretary of the Navy has made Arrangements which will not admit of private passengers! . . . Don't you think if the President had expressed to the Secretary his inclination that my request might be gratified, but that the Secretary would have accomplished it? What a strange fellow was Jefferson! he invited Tom Paine, & offered him a passage in a frigate, without, as it seems, consulting the Secretary of the Navy about it."

"It occurs to me, that Mr. Hamilton was apprehensive that if he should accommodate me with a passage, other persons might apply for the same. The features of my Character & Conduct in regard to our Country prior to & during the Revolution, are so strongly & singularly marked, that I am inclined to think that no person could complain had a Case thus circumstanced been made an exception in a general rule against private passengers. But to say no more on this subject, had I applied to Mr. Hamilton instead of writing to yourself, I should have acquainted him, that in crossing the Atlantic several years ago, some new thoughts in Naval Science occurred to me; that a subsequent voyage threw farther light on the ideas that had presented themselves to my consideration; and that I should be happy to have so good an opportunity, as sailing in a frigate would afford, of prosecuting a subject which promises to be of considerable importance." Will now sail to France alone as his son declines to go. Supposes "some fair one has sequesterd his heart."

RC (DLC). 3 pp.

§ From Isaac Cox Barnet. *12 July 1811, Paris.* "For nearly fourteen years I held the appointment of Consul for the United States in this Country." Believes his impartiality and integrity in the discharge of his duties are beyond suspicion. Encloses a letter exhibiting the sentiments of those who can judge his conduct. Also appeals to the testimony of "Mr. Monroe and Mr. Bowdoin late Ministers plenipotentiary to France and Spain," as well as that of Mr. Mercer, his former colleague on the American commission in Paris.[1] Concludes that his removal was the result of "malevolence and the confirmation of it from misrepresentation."[2] Requests to be reinstated, "or if there exists doubts on either of these points . . . I ask to be heard." Mentions that he has a wife and children dependent on him for support but addresses himself to JM's "justice and not [his] Sympathies."

RC and enclosures (DNA: RG 59, CD, Paris); Tr (DNA: RG 84, France, Misc. Correspondence Received). RC 2 pp. Enclosures are a petition dated 4 July 1811 (2 pp.), recommending Barnet as a man of integrity and as being capable of serving as American consul general in Paris. The petition bears sixteen signatures, including those of Peter Whiteside, Robert Crane, and Jonathan Vanderlyn. The second enclosure is a one-page letter addressed to JM by Pierre Samuel DuPont de Nemours, dated 1811 (in French). DuPont declined to sign the petition on the grounds that he was not an American citizen but stated that he shared the esteem in which the petitioners held Barnet. RC and enclosures were forwarded in the 12 July postscript to Barnet's letter to Monroe, 8 July 1811 (DNA: RG 59, CD, Paris).

1. Under article 6 of a convention signed in Paris on 30 Apr. 1803 to pay the sums owed by France to American citizens, Robert R. Livingston and James Monroe, as U.S. ministers to France, were authorized to establish a commission of three to examine documents relating to those claims that the French government declared had already been liquidated. John Mercer and William Maclure of Virginia, along with Isaac Cox Barnet, were appointed to the commission (Miller, *Treaties*, 1:519–20; Dangerfield, *Chancellor Robert R. Livingston*, p. 381).
2. Minister John Armstrong had suspended Barnet from his functions as consul at Le Havre in June 1809 (Skeen, *John Armstrong*, p. 114).

§ From Charles Livingstone. *12 July 1811, Boston.* "We deem it a duty, as good subjects, to make such private Communications as may tend to avert the evils which may arise from Mr Smiths late unwarantable attack on your Character." Much has been said by the two parties at Boston on the measures of government, and "so much will be expected to be said by way of Calumny . . . that little solid advantage can be derived from any publications from these sources." Another plan must therefore be pursued. Recommends Dr. Rufus L. Barrus of Boston as "a gentleman of uncommon influence and extensive acquaintance, . . . Strongly attached to the present administration, [who] moreover has never distinguished himself publickly by a shew of party Zeal so as to loose [*sic*] the Confidence of the Federal Citizens." Barrus has done much private communication "through the medium of apparent standing betwixt the two parties," and his candor, uprightness, and "exclusive knowledge" make him "the fittest person and the best auxiliary at the present Crisis." He is a gentleman in whom JM may place "the utmost Confidence" and is worthy of esteem and encouragement. If JM has any doubts as to "the utility of this measure," a private letter to the gentleman himself will remove them.

RC (DLC). 1 p. Signed by Livingstone as "Chairman of the present private Committee." Docketed by JM, "Recd Novr. 4. 1811."

§ From John Stark. *13 July 1811, Derryfield.* Introduces the bearer, Benjamin Franklin Stickney, whom he mentioned last fall.[1] "He is about five feet nine inches high; has blue eyes, light brown hair, and is a little marked with the small pox." As Stickney has tendered his services to the public, he does not think it proper to engage in any business that may prevent his immediate attention to any directions JM may give him. "From an opinion that he cannot imploy his leisure of suspence better than in travelling—he is about to undertake a tour into the Southern States, and will call on you in his way at Washington."

RC (DLC). 1 p.

1. See Stark to JM, 12 Oct. 1810 (*PJM-PS*, 2:578).

To Lafayette

MY DEAR SIR   WASHINGTON July 15. 1811

Your favor of Mar. 15. by the Essex came safely to hand.[1] I can not disapprove the disposition you have made of a portion of your land on the Mississippi. And it will be extremely grateful to me, if the residue should prove as good a fund as has been estimated by the most sanguine of your friends. I can add nothing on this subject to what I have heretofore said, having received no information from Mr. Duplantier or others in that quarter, since my last. I have forwarded to him the letter inclosed in yours to me; and presume it will lead to further accounts from him, either thro' me, or directly from N. Orleans, in case the commercial channel should be left sufficiently open by the policy of one and the power of the other Governments which have latterly united their respective efforts in destroying the intercourse of nations. I have paid due attention to that part of your letter which states the difficulty of arranging loans in Europe, and suggests the substitution of experiments here. I regret that I am not justified in encouraging a reliance on the latter recourse; the less so, as I find by consulting with Mr. Gallatin on the subject, that his better judgment confirms mine, that the Market of this Country will not avail you. Notwithstanding the increase of capital, and the diversion of part of it from foreign Commerce, turnpikes, canals, manufacturing establishments, with the Banks & public Stock, absorb the whole, & are all preferred to loans to individuals, even with the best securities. I wish fervently that it were otherwise, as far as your accomodation would require. But the wish proves only what is I am sure already known, the cordial interest I take in whatever concerns your comfort & welfare; & of which I pray you to accept this renewal of my assurances.

JAMES MADISON

RC (NIC: Dean Collection).

1. No letter of this date has been found. JM was probably referring to Lafayette's letter of 12 Mar. 1811.

From Morgan Lewis

DEAR SIR,   STAATSBERG 15th. July 1811.

I take the Liberty to enclose you an Account of a celebration of the fourth of July,[1] to shew you the Temper which endeavours are making to excite in this quarter. The Toasts, considered in connection with those given by the Baltimore party at Jones',[2] shew decidedly a concert between the malcontents there and here; and that the present vice president is on the List of *those to be abandoned.* I am happy to inform you, that Genl. A. was the only one of nine of my family connections, who reside within ten miles of the place of celebration, who attended the fête, the rest declined an Invitation sent with great formality. Chanr. Livingston is your friend, and I presume will so continue. Whether the Clinton Party, as the followers of D. W. C. & Judge Spencer are denominated here, will unite in the Opposition is yet to be decided. Spencer, pronounces Genl. A, on all Occasions the greatest man America ever produced; but a warm personal friend of D. W. C, observed on the Chairman's Toast, that the old Gentleman was too early in the field.[3]

The neglect manifested towards Govr. Tompkins is not easily accounted for. They know him to be firmly devoted to the Clinton Interest, and that your friends support him from prudential motives solely, without a particle of confidence in his independence; of which truly he has not a particle. Were I to conjecture, it would be, that their Object is to identify him with your friends, in the Hope that he may by them be supported for the vice presidency; a thing believed to be in contemplation with your friends at Washington. In such an Event they would get rid of him, at an easy rate, and should he be successful, will have a devoted friend at the head of an important Branch of the Government. Time will unfold. With sincerity your friend & hume Servt.

MORGAN LEWIS.

RC and enclosure (DLC: Rives Collection, Madison Papers). RC docketed by JM. For enclosure, see n. 1.

1. Lewis enclosed a newspaper clipping (probably from the Newburgh *Political Index*) reporting the events of a dinner held at Loop's Hotel in Red Hook, New York, on 4 July 1811. The first volunteer toast after the dinner was to Robert Smith, "the late secretary of state; he deserves well of his country." Other toasts were offered to the defense of American rights at home and abroad and to John Armstrong, which drew cheers from the assembled guests. The Swedish consul in Baltimore, Mr. Aguiton, proposed a toast to the president of the U.S., which, apparently, was not greeted with the cheers normally given on such occasions.

2. Lewis referred to the Independence Day celebrations held at the tavern of Benjamin Jones as described in the 5 July 1811 issue of the Baltimore *Whig*. Among the seventeen toasts proposed on the occasion was one to JM in his capacity as president, but some of the other toasts, such as those drunk to the congressional Republicans who had ensured the defeat of the bill to recharter the Bank of the United States, were tinged with antiadministration politics. Lewis was undoubtedly most concerned about the toast to John Armstrong—"he deserves well of his country; he is no sheep-shearing sycophant"—and that to Robert Smith— "he has honestly exposed delinquency; let the people make proper use of it."

3. The publication of Robert Smith's *Address*, in addition to the controversy it provoked in the nation's newspapers over the charges that Smith had raised, was also the occasion for some discussion of the next presidential election. The general sense of the prospects canvassed during the summer of 1811 were best summarized in a piece of doggerel, published under the headline of "THE NEXT PRESIDENT" in the *Alexandria Daily Gazette, Commercial & Political* on 10 July 1811:

> "Who will be the next President causes great doubt,
> As all parties agree that whiffling Jemmy goes out;
> Those who thought of George Clinton their hopes must forgo,
> And Armstrong is likely to rival Monroe;
> But our *late* honest minister, true, faithful Bob,
> Is determin'd that he'll have a hand in the job;
> And he is the fittest we all must suppose,
> For we're sure he can never be lead by the *nose!*"

§ Dolley Madison to Anna Payne Cutts. *15 July 1811*. Discusses the financial difficulties of her brother, John, after his return from Tripoli and announces that he will not accompany Barlow to France. "You ask me if we laughed over the Smith Pamphlet. Mr. M did, but I did not. It was too impertinent to ex[c]ite any other feeling in me, than anger. He will be sick of his attempt when he reads all that will be replyed to it." Mentions that "Eustis declared against Smiths Pamphlet, as soon as he saw the Book. Hamilton is enraged, & writes, or intends it on the subject. You may guess how the other Secys feel & speak. In short, the Smiths are down whatever harm they may have done to M." Has seen little of Foster and cannot discuss the state of the negotiation with him.

RC (owned by Mr. and Mrs. George B. Cutts, Brookline, Mass., 1958); partial Tr (ibid). RC 3 pp.

From John Langdon

DEAR SR.   PORTSMOUTH July 16th. 1811

I had the honor of receiveing, few days since your letter by Mr. Edwd. Coles and Brother,[1] who very politely called upon me, and with whom I was much pleased. I feel myself much gratified, in thus hearing from you, as it brought to my recollection the many years we have walked together thro' the land of tribulation, and the many pleasant, as well as anxious, hours we have spent together.

I pray you Sr. to accept of my grateful acknowledgements for the interest you take in my welfare and happiness, which I most sincerely reciprocate. Mrs. Langdon Joins me in our best respects to yourself and Lady. The best of Heavens blessings attend you.

JOHN LANGDON

RC (DLC). Docketed by JM.

1. JM to Langdon, 15 May 1811.

§ To David Gelston. *16 July 1811, Washington.* "The smallness of the sum, and the probability that it might be augmented by some further advances, have occasioned a delay in remitting $11.81. due to you, as intimated in your letter of Octobr. 5. last."[1] Encloses a draft for the sum on the Manhattan Bank.

RC (NNMus). 1 p. Docketed by Gelston.

1. See *PJM-PS*, 2:572.

From George Joy

DEAR SIR,   HELSINBORG 18th July 1811

Having a Copy of the Letter from the Danish Chancery to the Admiralty enclosed in my Letter to you of the 1st Inst:[1] and hearing very suddenly of an Estafette bound to Gottenborg whence a schooner is about sailing to the U. S. I beg leave to hand you the said Copy annexed and am always very respectfully, Dear sir, Yr. friend & Servt.

GEO: JOY

RC and enclosure (DLC: Rives Collection, Madison Papers). Postmarked and forwarded at Baltimore on 10 Sept. For enclosure, see n. 1.

1. Joy's letter to JM of 1 July has not been found, but evidently Joy had forwarded another copy of the document he now enclosed from the Danish Chancery, dated 28 June 1811 (2 pp.), and written in response to a memorial from "Consul Joy" requesting information on whether the Danish crown had instructed an admiralty court to condemn six American vessels. The Department of Foreign Affairs had replied that the crown had given no such instruction, nor did it believe that another royal instruction suspending such cases until the arrival of an American minister was applicable in the circumstances. The six vessels in question had been taken while making use of an English convoy and the Danish crown had already stated that petitions on behalf of such cases "must be pointedly rejected."

¶ To Benjamin Hawkins. Letter not found. *18 July 1811*. Acknowledged in Hawkins to JM, 13 Oct. 1811. Discusses political matters and his difficulties with Robert Smith.

From Benjamin Henry Latrobe

SIR, WASHINGTON July 19h. 1811.

My duty, as Chairman of the Commissioners of the Columbia turnpike roads obliged me to spend the whole of this morning upon the line leading towards Monty. C. House, and I transmit to you the annexed accts., not so early as I could have wished, but still I hope in time to meet your object in calling for them.[1]

The whole of the Sheet iron required by the letter of your superintendent at Montpelier was sent to you, but only part of the Glass, as we had not a sufficient quantity of cut Tables to meet the whole. The price charged for the Iron is the exact cost to the public including the expense of cutting & packing for *you*. That of the Glass is the charge settled by our Glazier Mr. Walter Clarke. In respect to Harvie's account, it was thought just at the time that he should pay for refitting your Coachee here.[2] But he has resisted every idea of such an allowance, and I do not think it could be maintained under all circumstances excepting as an *equitable* one. He says that he can prove by many witnesses that Jacob was drunk when he took away the carriage, & a man wholly unfit to take charge of it; that he cannot be called upon to pay for damages incurred after delivery to your coachman, that to raise the carriage after such a journey was an expence always necessary, & requiring to be repeated from time to time, that the alteration of the front, was not communicated to him before it was made, or he might have done it himself, & much more of the kind. The rejected fronts were allowed for at 10$ as stated.

He has further charged for Lamps & Cypher omitted in his bill. It will be necessary to examine his bill to see whether this is actually so. I have stated his account as under these circumstances it would stand, & have drawn out an acct. also, between yourself and me, in which I have assumed the debt of Harvie, & charged the Iron & glass as well as the money paid by myself (as ℔ Vouchers) so as to bring all the transactions into one view & to close them with the most convenience to yourself. Any monies paid by you for small articles of Household expense, might be charged against the balance of 73$.55, and I shall be credited in the furniture fund when I receive the Vouchers or it may stand over for future adjustment. For the Materials sold, I account to Mr. Munroe in the general account under the head.

I sincerely hope that your temporary retirement from the fatigue of attendance at the seat of government will be cheered by the health of yourself & Mrs. Madison,[3] & by events favorable to the prosperity of our country. I am with high respect Yr. faithful

B H LATROBE

RC and enclosures (DLC); FC and copies of two enclosures (MdHi: Latrobe Letterbooks). RC docketed by JM. For enclosures, see n. 1.

1. Latrobe enclosed three accounts. One shows a charge to JM of $138.09 for sheet iron and crown glass taken from "Materials from the Capitol not applicable to public use," which was certified by Latrobe as received in full on 19 July 1811 for Thomas Munroe (1 p.). The second account, between Latrobe and Peter Harvie, a coachmaker, dated 20 July 1811, shows charges to Harvie of $840.57 paid to him by Latrobe and $88 for the lining of a chariot, against which is credited $798.78 for "his account rendered" and $30 for lamps and a cipher on the coachee made for JM, leaving a balance of $99.79 due to Latrobe (1 p.). In the third account, between JM and Latrobe, 20 July 1811, JM is charged for the materials from the Capitol as well as freight costs and $32.12½ for repairs to the coachee—a total of $173.34— and credited for the amount of $99.79 due from Peter Harvie, leaving a balance of $73.55 due to Latrobe from JM (1 p.).

2. This coachee was evidently the one that Latrobe had purchased for Dolley Madison in March 1809 (see *PJM-PS*, 1:73–74).

3. The next day Latrobe wrote to Dolley Madison to decline the "kind invitation" she and JM had extended to Latrobe and his wife to visit Montpelier over the summer. The "favorable opinion" the Madisons had of his character, Latrobe added, "overbalances far the vexations which have pursued me during my whole connexion with the general government, and render the wish, I have often entertained to put an end to it, vain" (Latrobe to Dolley Madison, 20 July 1811 [NN]).

From Henry Lee

DEAR SIR   ALEXA. July 19h. 11.

The day after I had the honor of seeing you, I visited my young friend. His sentiments respecting the late pamphlet accord entirely with my own as does his respect for you. From his pen may be expected an answer which if executed with his usual ability will I think be found complete.

I do not fully take yr. distinction (a material one) as to the probable govermental conduct, had it been called to accept restoration of our neutral rights unaccompanyed with compensation for spoliation. I ask therefore for it on a scrap of paper to be enclosed in yr. answer which to the following subject I very much wish.

Gen Wilkinson & myself have grown up thro war & peace in the nearest intimacy until the late accusations agst his honor & his allegiance were announced. The spanish business I ever beleived would turn out merely commercial, mingled with schemes & professions to endear him for the moment to the royal agents uncontaminated with vice private or public, & pointed only to secure his preference in the mart of new orleans. I consequently disregarded it. But the presumed association with Burr I confess struck me as probable & drew me from my old friend. Since my perusal of his vindication[1] & of the documents supposed to substantiate the charge, I could not for a moment hesitate in pronouncing my conviction of his innocence, which was followed by my declaration of the fact on the first fit opportunity.

This has introduced me into an acquaintance with his manifold & oppressive injurys & as my cast of mind brings me closer & closer to a friend in adversity, I cannot forbear to struggle for the much injured & greatly distressed general.

When I last saw him he put into my hands many additional letters from cool & reflecting men, all uniting in the opinion that he must avoid Frederic town. These opinion[s] confirm his own Jealousy & render him wretched in the extreme.

I never could see any objection to the gratification of misfortune in every minor request. The change of place is among the least accompaniments of the generals trial & why he cannot be gratifyed when so seriously alarmed I confess excites my wonder. Especially when govt. refrain not from expressing always their sense of his merit in crushing a menacing conspiracy, as well as their hope that he may establish his innocence.

Vast is the difference between the accused & the accuser & when the nation accuses, the defendant ought to be encouraged, not discouraged.

You suggested that alexandria the place preferred originally by the secretary of War, may become sickly in the autumn. This is possible, but very improbable, & the court might be instructed in such event to adjourn to a more salubrious spot, which would satisfy every member.

The favor the general prays sir, is really so small in itself, as it concerns the prosecution, so great in its presumed effect on himself, as without its grant he is persuaded he cannot have a fair trial, that I must be permitted to say in my Judgement, goodness & greatness alike command his gratification.

I pray you to be assured that I interfere with extreme reluctance, but I cannot do otherwise, when I see adversity full & bitter in its force agst an unhelped individual. I have the honor to be dear sir truely & affectionately yr. friend & ob: h: sert

HENRY LEE

RC (DLC). Docketed by JM.

1. Lee was probably referring to Wilkinson's pamphlet *Burr's Conspiracy Exposed: And General Wilkinson Vindicated against the Slanders of His Enemies on That Important Occasion* (Washington, 1811; Shaw and Shoemaker 24447).

§ From Alexander I. *20 July 1811, St. Petersburg.* Announces that he wishes to employ his envoy Count Pahlen elsewhere and assures JM of his goodwill toward both the U.S. and its president.

RC (DLC). 2 pp. In French.

§ From Samuel Hanson of Samuel. *20 July 1811.* Submits to JM "the enclosed literal copy of the original" on the assumption that "it is impossible that the President could have sanctioned, by his approbation, any official communication so palpably defective in *form*, so, it is possible that he may not have been apprised of the *substance*."[1] Appeals to JM's sense of justice to say whether it is his impression that Hanson is "chargeable 'with numerous previous instances of disrespect towards the President'" and, if so, to point out "in any mode not incompatible with the established official Etiquette, the instances of disrespect alluded to by the Secretary of the Navy." Declares that he is "unconscious of any instances of intentional disrespect towards the President, and anxious to preserve the only advantage *now* left him, his *character*, trusts that the President will not deem the present appeal either unjust or unreasonable."

RC and enclosure (DLC). RC 1 p. Docketed by JM.

1. Hanson enclosed a copy of a 16 July 1811 letter he had received from Paul Hamilton (1 p.) revoking his appointment as a purser in the navy. Hamilton justified his action on the grounds that Hanson had failed to obey orders to submit his books to the accountant of the navy and that by virtue of his conduct in his dispute with the accountant he was both in disregard of his oath of office and guilty of numerous instances of disrespect toward the president.

From Benjamin Henry Latrobe

SIR,   [ca. 22 July 1811]

Mr. Barry has expressed to me Your wish that your Glass should be sent by your Waggon. I will send tomorrow morning the *Glass*, the Box of Locks &c, the Keg of White lead to the President's house that these things made [*sic*] be ready. Mr. Deblois informs me, that the boat to Fredericksburg will not sail for 10 days to come. He is now making an intermediate trip.

In Mr Dinsmore's letter he states that it is unnecessary to send on the Sheet copper. It is however here but if you think it will be useless to you, it may be retained for the use of the public, sheet copper being in frequent demand, & should we ventilate the Hall of Representatives in the Manner I suppose the only effectual one we shall want *that* & much more.

I never received from you any drawing of ornamental Moulding to be made of composition by Geo: Andrews,[1] & I believe that were I acquainted with the purpose for which you want it I should be tempted to dissuade you from its use *in the country.*

Next week the Water closets, & the leaky Gutters of the roof will be throroughly [*sic*] repaired at the President's house.[2] Mr. King the Master smith at the Navy Yard is absent which has occasioned delay for a fortnight. With high respect I am Yrs.

B H Latrobe

RC (DLC). Undated; dated ca. February 1811 in the *Index to the James Madison Papers.* Date here assigned on the assumption that Latrobe wrote this letter after his 19 July 1811 letter to JM but before his 6 Sept. 1811 letter to JM (see also n. 2). The letter very probably was written shortly before JM's departure from Washington for Montpelier on 25 July 1811.

1. This may have been the "egg & Dart Moulding" JM had received a drawing of in the fall of 1809 (see James Dinsmore to JM, 29 Oct. 1809, *PJM-PS*, 2:44).

2. In his 28 Mar. 1812 letter to JM, Latrobe recalled a conversation with JM on "about the 1st of July last" in which he reported on the state of the roof of the President's House. The "platforms covering the Gutters," Latrobe added, "were rotten, and must be replaced" (Van Horne, *Papers of Latrobe*, 3:272–73).

§ From James Leander Cathcart. *22 July 1811, Madeira.* Acknowledges receipt of the duplicate of JM's letter of 28 May. "I feel great satisfaction that the wines I sent to your address are approved & will endeavor to execute your present commission similar to the last by the first good conveyance."

RC (DLC). 1 p.

To Richard Cutts

Dear Sir   Washington July 23. 1811

We are at length about to exchange Washington for Montpelier.[1] The morning after tomorrow is fixt for our departure. The state of our affairs with France may be collected from the printed accts. Some obscurities hang over them as they respect the degree of our commerce with them.[2] The Decrees seem not to be in operation in any sense giving pretext for the refusal of G. B. to revoke her orders in Council. Foster stroaks with one paw and scratches with the other. The Blockade of May is put on a manageable footing, contrary to the partizans of G. B. who had chosen that for the difficulty. The ground she has taken for herself, is that the evidence of the repeal of the F. decrees, is not satisfactory; and that the repeal must comprehend the *whole* of the decrees, as they relate to British commerce as well as to neutral rights. It is held out also that the non-intercourse, whilst such a repeal is witheld by France is a ground for retaliation by G. B.[3] Congs. will be convened about the first of Novr. Barlow will sail in a few days. These hints are for yourself, till you can refer to another source for the information. I hope you will recollect our wishes that you & Mrs. Cutts may find it practicable to see us in Orange before we leave it in October. With affece. remembrance to her, and the little cherubs around, accept assurances of my esteem and friendship.

JAMES MADISON

Photocopy of RC (ViU: Cabell Gwathmey Collection). RC offered for sale in Sotheby's catalogue no. 6251, *The Paul Perlin Collection of Presidential Campaign Memorabilia*, 12 Dec. 1991.

1. JM and his family left Washington on 25 July. The next day they stopped at Fredericksburg, Virginia, where JM was persuaded to attend a public dinner given in his honor (*National Intelligencer*, 27 and 30 July 1811).

2. The *National Intelligencer*, on 23 July under the headline of "Very Late From France," published news from Bordeaux, dated 17 June, to the effect that American vessels detained in France since 2 Nov. 1810 had been released on the condition that they take away the proceeds of their cargoes in silk, brandy, and wine. It was also reported that duties on all American produce imported into France, except tobacco, might be reduced by one-half.

On 24 July 1811 Sérurier called on JM to pay his respects before the president departed for Montpelier. He recorded that JM had received the recent news from France with pleasure but without surprise. The minister mentioned, however, that JM regretted that American vessels detained under the Berlin and Milan decrees had yet to be released and that he had also complained that French duties on American imports were excessive and onerous. Sérurier disputed these matters at some length, but he was unable to remove the "coldness" he detected in the president's manner. After JM had terminated the conversation with the observations that he desired a "good settlement" with France and that he had instructed Joel Barlow to request that Franco-American relations be placed on a firm, unvarying, and liberal basis, Sérurier concluded that the revocation of the Berlin and Milan decrees had become a "personal" matter for the president and that it would be a subject of much debate in the coming months. The next day, the administration newspaper announced that "it may be inferred from the official and other information, that the Berlin and Milan decrees as they violate our neutral rights are not in operation, and that some relaxations are taking place in the commercial intercourse with France, though by no means as yet in the extent desired. With respect to the other objects of complaint and demand by the United States no change has taken place" (Sérurier to Cadore, 24 July 1811 [AAE: Political Correspondence, U.S., vol. 65]; *National Intelligencer*, 25 July 1811).

3. In his 14 July 1811 letter to Monroe, Foster had stated that since the U.S. persisted in its "injurious measures" against British commerce, "His Royal Highness has in consequence been obliged to look to means of retaliation against those measures" (*ASP, Foreign Relations*, 3:438).

To Henry Dearborn

DEAR SIR   [ca. 23 July 1811]

I had the pleasure of duly receiving yours of the 8th. inclosing a Copy of your son's oration. In the hurry of the period, I have been able to give it a flying perusal only. But I do not accede to your limitation of its merits so much to an honest zeal. It has claims to a much higher character, with the addition of this laudable feature.

I am just on the point of leaving Washington where I have been detained by the diplomatic operations between Mr. Foster & Mr. Monroe, and subjects connected with our foreign relations. The state of them with France may be collected from the printed informations. The arrival of Mr. Foster, has yielded nothing that promises an amendment of things with G. B. Altho' it would seem that the case of the Blockade of May 1806. is put on a manageable footing, contrary to the calculations of those who took that ground for G. B. and agst. the administration; yet another ground, disowned by them, but apprehended by us, is taken by the B. Govt. on which it is impossible to meet her. It is required, as a condition of the repeal of the orders in Council that the F. Decrees shall be repealed not only as they relate to the U. S. but as they relate to G. B; not only that we shall trade with G. B. but that the ports of her Enemy shall be opened to her trade: and the idea is held out of retaliating on our non-importation act, if it be not fort[h]with rescinded. Our present conclusion is that Congs. shall be convened on the last of Ocr. or first of Novr. which will be as early as will be convenient,[1] and will at the same time afford a chance of having a return from Europe to be laid before them. Accept my high esteem & friendly regards.

JAMES MADISON

It will be proper to be reserved on this communication, till something in the newspaper may appear that will furnish a fitter source to be referred to.

RC (PHC). Headed *"No. 41."* Undated; date here assigned by comparison with JM to Richard Cutts, 23 July 1811. Docketed by Dearborn.

1. In reporting this news to Lord Wellesley, Foster mentioned that Monroe "seemed to apologize for an earlier period not being named, as was generally expected, on account of the Unhealthiness of this City during the Autumn and the Desire of the President to receive further Intelligence from France and England . . . by the Return of the Frigate that had taken Mr. Barlow to France" (Foster to Wellesley, 5 Aug. 1811 [PRO: Foreign Office, ser. 5, vol. 76]).

§ From Ebenezer H. Cummins.[1] *23 July 1811.* Has just heard that "the consulship at Tripoli is without an officer, in consequence of Mr. Payne's determination not to return again." If so, he offers his services. Has been disappointed and deceived in his expectations of military life where his present rank is "discouraging." Would prefer an active life. Refers JM to Dolley Madison and Monroe "who have had some better opportunities of knowing me and my pretensions."

RC (DNA: RG 59, LAR, 1809–17, filed under "Cummins"). 4 pp. Marked "private."

1. Ebenezer Harlow Cummins (1774–1848) first wrote to JM on 31 July 1808 seeking a clerkship in the State Department (DNA: RG 59, LAR, 1801–9). He evidently settled in the District of Columbia, where in May 1813 he became publisher of the Georgetown *Spirit of 'Seventy-Six*, a position from which he was ousted by November of that year when he announced that he would establish the *Senator*, a journal to be devoted to publishing the proceedings of that body. After 1815 he appears to have resided in Philadelphia where he became the editor of the *Evangelical Repository*. He published several works, including a *Biographical Memoir of Aaron Burr, D.D., Senior* (1816), *A Summary Geography of Alabama* (1819), and with JM's approval in 1820, a critical edition of a British account of the War of 1812, *Baine's History of the Late War* (Brigham, *History and Bibliography of American Newspapers*, 1:94; Cummins to JM, 13 Dec. 1820, JM to Cummins, 26 Dec. 1820 [DLC]).

To Jonathan Russell

SIR   WASHINGTON July 24. 1811
  I have recd. your letter of Jany. 2. with the sketch of a convention arranged between you & the Marquis of Almanara. The purity of your views is attested by the guarded manner of your proceeding, as well as by the explanations in your letter. But it is proper that you should be apprized, that such a transaction would be deemed inadmissible on different grounds; were it without the feature given to it by the individual agenc[i]es and interests, so justly denounced by you. For information on other subjects, which it may be interesting to you to receive, I refer to the communications of the Secretary of State.[1] Accept Sir my respects & friendly wishes
                                         JAMES MADISON

RC (RPB-JH: Russell Papers); FC (DLC).

1. On 27 July Monroe informed Russell that JM approved of the manner in which he had discharged his duties in Paris and that he now wished to appoint him chargé d'affaires in London in the place of John Spear Smith. Russell was to remain in London until "a Minister shall be appointed, which will be done as soon as the Congress convenes." It was to be hoped, Monroe added, that "the British Government will proceed to revoke its orders in Council and thus restore in all respects, the friendly relation which would be so advantag⟨eous⟩ to both Countries" (DNA: RG 59, IM).

From Paul Hamilton

SIR,   NAVY DEPARTMENT 24 July 1811
  I have the honor of submitting to your consideration the paper herewith marked A—which exhibits a view of the navy appropriations up to the 23rd ins. inclusively.[1]

By this paper it will appear that the aggregate balance of the appropriations unexpended, is $1,316,577:61; but that two of the appropriations viz for "Repairs of vessels," & for "Qrmaster & Barrack master's Dept of the Marine corps" are exhausted.

Upon the appropriation for repair's there is an apparent balance of $698:10 unexpended; but there are drafts upon that appropriation, at this time unpaid, to the amount of $21,008:27—leaving on this day a real deficit exceeding 20,000$.

To meet these drafts, & to provide for current expenses, I respectfully recommend a transfer of One hundred thousand dollars, to be made in equal proportions from the appropriations for "Pay of the Navy" & for "Provisions."

Upon the appropriation for "Qr master & Barrack Master's Dept of the Marine Corps" there are at this time drafts unpaid, amounting to $552:70. To meet these drafts & to provide for current expenses, I respectfully recommend a transfer of 6000$ from the appropriation for "Pay &c of the Marine Corps.["]² I have the honor to be with great respect sir, Yr mo obt &c.

PAUL HAMILTON

RC and enclosure (DLC); letterbook copy and copy of enclosure (DNA: RG 45, LSP). RC in Goldsborough's hand, signed by Hamilton. RC and enclosure docketed by JM. For enclosure, see n. 1.

1. Hamilton enclosed a "Statement of Navy Appropriations 23rd July 1811" (1 p.) showing undrawn balances in the Treasury Department totaling $1,274,060.78 for all branches of naval expenditure except "Repairs of Vessels," "Q. Masters Dept.," and "Salt petre." The balances in the hands of the treasurer amounted to $42,516.83.

2. Filed with the letterbook copy is a copy of an authorization Hamilton apparently enclosed for JM's signature (1 p.), directing the transfer of two sums of $50,000, one from the pay and subsistence fund and the other from the provisions fund, both to be applied to the repair of vessels fund. The sum of $6,000 was to be transferred from the pay fund of the Marine Corps to the Quartermaster's Department of the same service.

Presidential Proclamation

[24 July 1811]

BY THE PRESIDENT OF THE UNITED STATES, OF AMERICA

A PROCLAMATION.

WHEREAS great and weighty matters claiming the consideration of the Congress of the United States form an extraordinary occasion for convening them, I do by these presents appoint Monday the fourth day of November next for their meeting at the city of Washington; hereby requiring the respective Senators and Representatives then and there to assemble in

Congress in order to receive such communications as may then be made to them, and to consult and determine on such measures as in their wisdom may be deemed meet for the welfare of the United States.

In testimony whereof, I have caused the seal of the United States to be hereunto affixed, and signed the same with my hand.

Done at the city of Washington, the twenty-fourth day of July, in the year of our Lord one thousand eight hundred and eleven; and of the independence of the United States the thirty-sixth.

JAMES MADISON.
By the President,
JAMES MONROE
Secretary of State

Printed copy (*National Intelligencer*, 25 July 1811).

§ From William Esenbeck.[1] *24 July 1811, Washington.* Proposes to convince JM that the president has the power "to settle as Arbitrator the difference between the Belligerents by Telegraph."

RC (NN). 1 p.

1. William Esenbeck was a messenger in the Treasury Department (*Records of the Columbia Historical Society*, 9 [1906]: 228).

§ From John Mason. *24 July 1811, Indian Office.* Informs JM that Samuel Tupper, factor in the trading house at Sandusky, has asked permission to resign and suggests that Jacob B. Varnum of Massachusetts be appointed in his place.[1]

RC (DNA: RG 75, Letters Received by Superintendent of Indian Trade); letterbook copy (DNA: RG 75, Letters Sent by Superintendent of Indian Trade). RC 1 p.; with JM's notation, "Approved."

1. Jacob B. Varnum was the son of the Speaker of the House of Representatives, Joseph B. Varnum.

§ From Charles Holmes. *27 July 1811, Charleston.* Lays before JM "some (of the many) circumstances, relative to the revenue Department of Charleston District." Explains that he was a revenue inspector for nearly five years, during which time no complaints were made about him, but he believes the collector has unjustly censured his conduct. Has believed for some time that the revenue laws were being evaded, but no efforts were made to stop this until the surveyor, at his suggestion, directed him to detect as many cases as he could. He found many instances of smuggling, which were concealed for months, and made several seizures, but in one case where he took two bags of coffee he was reprimanded by the deputy surveyor and had to return the coffee to the owner. On the night of 20 Apr. 1811 he caught two men smuggling oranges into the house of Joseph Sibley. On searching the house he found the oranges had been removed, but he seized eight turtles shipped from Nassau, contrary to the Nonimportation Act. The collector, Simeon Theus, was not satisfied they had been smuggled and kept them for several days before selling them as perishable articles. As no one came forward to claim the turtles the collector then instructed him to institute legal proceedings against Sibley, who was held to bail for $400. Seven or eight weeks later he obtained an affidavit against the master of the sloop importing the turtles from Nassau, Joseph Clerck, which he took to the district attorney, who then held Clerck to bail for $400. The collector released Clerck from his bail, "contrary to all rule and Law," and Sibley has now also applied to be rid of his bail. Does not know whether the suit against Sibley has been withdrawn, but he [Holmes] has been reprimanded and dismissed for being vigilant in enforcing the law. Other men, "notorious for being Drunkards, and Others incapable of doing their duty," have been retained in office.

Since Theus came into office, "there [h]as been but one Officer sworn into Office, agreable to law (Sec 20th) and that by the Officers own request to this day!!!" Cannot explain why the law is not being observed, but he deduces the following from the above circumstances. First, while things remain in their present situation, "Your Honrable Executives time and tallents in recommending any perticular Law (be they ever so good and wise) is totally lost, and that of Congress equelly disapears, in making them Laws of the land, while ever these Laws are not carried into effect, by the proper Officers appointed for that pu⟨rpose.⟩" Second, the collector who dismisses his officers "for strictly doing their duty, makes a breach i⟨n the⟩ Laws of the United states, and throws an Opening, (even to inviting) to smugling, without Molestation." And third, when the laws are set aside by those charged with enforcement, "it will not be wondered at, to see those (and there is not a few) who only seeks for an Oppertunity to break them." Hopes he has not incurred JM's displeasure by addressing him.

RC (DLC). 3 pp. Docketed by JM, "Recd. April 7. 1813 [*sic*]." Filed with the RC is a three-line permit, dated 23 May 1809, with Holmes's note: "A Specimen of Carolina Permits (Q. is it agreeable to Law[ )]."

§ From Timothy T. Edwards. *29 July 1811*. States in a memorial that he sailed from New York on 14 June 1807 as master of the *Brutus* bound for the Coromandel Coast, that he arrived there in mid-November, and that he set out for New York with "a valuable cargo" the following May. On 6 Sept. the *Brutus* was captured by a French privateer commanded by Alexis Grassin, taken to Cayenne, and "condemned stock & fluke as then alledged under the Milan decree in the Court of Admiralty for that Colony." Declares that his cargo did not include contraband of war and that when the decree was issued on 17 Dec. 1807, the *Brutus* was anchored in the roads of Madras. Grassin, his vessel with the name changed to the *Diligente*, and also the vessel's owner, Jean Baptiste Goyan, are now in Philadelphia. Edwards went to Philadelphia to see them but was advised that no U.S. court would take cognizance of a suit and that although the *Brutus* "had been condemned in a Court of Admiralty very oppressively," the matter was between the U.S. and France. Estimates his losses at $10,000. As the *Brutus* was wrongly condemned, he asks that Grassin and Goyan not be permitted to depart until full restitution is made for the "robbery committed."[1]

RC and enclosure (DNA: RG 76, France, French Spoliation Claims). RC 2 pp. In a clerk's hand, signed by Edwards. Enclosure is an affidavit dated 29 July 1811 (1 p.), signed by Theodore Sedgwick of the Massachusetts Supreme Court, to the effect that Edwards stated the facts of his memorial under oath.

1. The case of the *Diligente* had already come to the notice of the administration and occupied much of its attention during the summer of 1811. The privateer entered Philadelphia on 30 Apr. 1811 as a vessel in distress, after having first thrown overboard most of its cannon and then taken on several gun carriages from a British prize. Aggrieved American ship captains evidently recognized both the vessel and its captain, Grassin, who was the object of popular displeasure as he walked through the streets of Philadelphia. On 18 May 1811 the French minister therefore demanded that the authorities protect French nationals and their property from disorder, and Monroe, on 4 June, instructed the governor of Pennsylvania to comply with this demand. After receiving further information that Grassin intended to arm and equip his vessel while it was in port, however, Monroe ordered the collector at Philadelphia to take steps to prevent this violation of American neutrality. The collector duly reported that while no guns had been added to the *Diligente*, the captain had adapted the captured gun carriages to the gun ports of the vessel. The collector then turned the matter over to the district attorney, who had Grassin arrested and tried for breaching the Neutrality Act of 1794 (Sérurier to Monroe, 12 May 1811 [DNA: RG 59, NFL, France]; Monroe to Simon Snyder, 4 June 1811, Monroe to John Steele, 18 July 1811 [DNA: RG 59, DL]; Steele to Monroe, 27 July 1811, Alexander James Dallas to Monroe, 27 July 1811 [DNA: RG 59, ML]).

§ From David Holmes. *29 July 1811, Washington, Mississippi Territory.* "I left Virginia within so short a period after my appointment to the Government of this Territory, that I had no opportunity of adjusting my private concerns, and was consequently unable to bring with me the residue of a small patrimony." This has inconvenienced him, but until now "considerations of public duty" have prevented him from seeking permission to return. Is confident Mr. Daingerfield can administer the territory in his absence; wishes, therefore, to return to Virginia in the fall, provided JM believes "no event will occur during the winter which may require the attention of both Mr. Daingerfield and myself to the Public business." Plans to depart in early October but will remain if the public interest would be promoted thereby.[1]

RC (DNA: RG 59, TP, Mississippi). 3 pp. Docketed with the notation "granted 31 Augt." Printed in Carter, *Territorial Papers, Mississippi*, 6:214–15.

1. In conveying JM's permission to Holmes, Monroe remarked that the "accommodation" was "justly due to your long absence, and the promptitude with which you undertook the trust confided to you by the Government" (Monroe to Holmes, 31 Aug. 1811, Carter, *Territorial Papers, Mississippi*, 6:219).

From the Right Reverend James Madison

MY DEAR SIR,   WILLIAMSBURG July 30. 1811
    Your Kindness in transmitting Mr. Lambert's Calculations &c. has induced me to take the Liberty of forwarding the enclosed to you. I hope we shall not expose you to a similar Interruption.

I cannot refrain expressing my Astonishment at the late Publication of R. S.[1] I beleive there is not an honest American who does not view it with Detestation; &, that instead of injuring the present Administration, it will serve only to heighten the Estimation in which it is held by good Men. It is lamentable, indeed, that he should have been so forgetful of the Kind of House in which he himself lived; it looks as if he would not have a single Pane left. Certain it is, that his own Publication affords abundant justificatory Reasons for his Dismissal. I am, with sincerest Respect & Esteem Dr Sir, Yr Friend

J MADISON

RC (DLC). Enclosure not found.

1. Someone, possibly JM at a later date, interlined the remaining letters of "Rt. S*mith*."

From John Graham

DEAR SIR   DEPT OF STATE 31st July 1811.

The Packet for the Secretary ⟨o⟩f State containing the Letters which I supposed you would wish to read, is left open—and put under Cover to you. I have supposed that this would be the most convenient arrangment. Should you prefer any other you will be pleased to let me know.

Mr Barlow left us yesterday intending to Lodge at Marlbro: and to get to Annapolis early today. We have furnished him with a Copy of Mr Fosters last Letter[1] and of the Communications from Mr Dallas in relation to the arrest of the Captain of the French Privatier the Diligent.[2]

The inclosed was received under Cover from Mr Adams[3]—with it came three Letters from him to this Dept—there [*sic*] are down to the 11th March and ⟨seem to contain⟩ nothing very new or important. So much of them however is in Cypher, that we have not been able to get thro: them in time for this Mail. They will be forwarded by the next Mail.

I hope that you & Mrs Madison had a pleasant Journey and arrived safely at Montpelier. With Sentiments of the most Respectful attachment I am Dear Sir Your Mo: Obt Sert

JOHN GRAHAM

RC (DLC). Docketed by JM.

1. Foster to Monroe, 26 July 1811 (printed in *ASP, Foreign Relations*, 3:443–45).
2. See Timothy Edwards to JM, 29 July 1811, and n. 1.
3. Graham may have enclosed John Quincy Adams to JM, 8 Feb. 1811. Of the three letters to the State Department "down to the 11th Mar." Graham mentioned as having received from Adams, two, dated 12 and 19 Feb. 1811, were docketed as received on 31 July (DNA: RG 59, DD, Russia).

From the Inhabitants of Knox County, Indiana Territory

SR.   [ca. 31 July 1811]

In obedience to the wishes of a numerous meeting of our fellow Citizens assembled for the purpose of taking into Consideration the state of this Country in relation to Indian affairs, We have the Honor to address you. In approaching the chief Magistrate of our Country, who is so deservedly Celebrated for the talents, which distinguish the Statesman, and the virtues which adorn the man—We should not do Justice to our own feelings, and the feelings of those whom we represent if we neglected to express our confidence in his administration and our sincere respect and esteem for his person.

In fulfilling the duty which has been assigned to us Sir, it is scarcely necessary that we should do more than to referr you to the Resolutions which are enclosed, they contain a true Statement of facts and a true picture of the feelings of the Citizens of this part of the Country. It is impossible to doubt but that the combination which has been formed on the Wabash is a British Scheme, and it is equally certain that this banditti is now prepared to be let loose upon us and that nothing but vigorous measures will prevent it. In this part of the Country we have not as yet lost any of our fellow Citizens by the Indians but depredations upon the property of those who live upon the frontiers & insults to the families that are left unprotected almost daily occur.

The impunity with which these savages have been so long Suffered to commit crimes has raised their insolence to a pitch that is no longer Supportable. We are not Sir, advocates for unnecessary rigor towards our Indian neighbors. The Character which some of us Sustain as minister⟨s⟩ of the Gospel of Christ will Shield us from the supposition that we wish to plunge our Country in an unnecessary war. Our object is peace but we are fully pursuaded that, that blessing can now only be secured to us by the exertion of some vigor.

Let the savages be made sensible that every aggression from them will meet with a correspondant punishment and Indian depredations will seldom be heard of. Since the adoption of the Resolutions under which we act, we have listened to the speech delivered by the Brother of the prophet to Gov. Harrison and if a doubt remained upon our minds as to the designs of the Confederacy he has formed It has been Completely removed.[1] Shall we then quietly wait the stroke when we see the weapon is Suspended over us; we hope and trust that this will not be expected and that the general Government will take effectual measures to avert the danger, What these measures Shall be we will not presume to dictate, but We beg leave most respectfully to observe that we conceive that the Country will forever be exposed to those alarms which are at once so injurious to its Settlement & the Interest of the U. S. as long as the Banditti under the Prophet are Suffered to remain where they now are. The people have become highly irritated and alarmed and if the Government will not direct their energies, we fear that the Innocent will feel the effects of their resentment and a general war be the Consequence. The Western Country Sr. is indebted to your Predecessor for an undeviating attention to its prosperity and the gratitude and attachment which they feel towards that distinguished patriot can never be effaced—with equal confidence they look up to his Successor who persuing the same course of politics with regard to the European powers is to them Sufficient proof of coincidence of Sentiment in that which relates to the Continent.[2]

That you may be the means under providence of establishing the affairs of your Country and settling its interest in every quarter of the Globe upon a Secure and lasting foundation and that you may long live to enjoy the Blessing of your countrymen for the happiness you procure for them is the sincere prayer of your Fellow Citizens

SAML. T. SCOTT
[and six others]

[Enclosure]

At a meeting of a very Considerable number of the Citizens of the County of Knox at the Seminary in Vincennes, on Wednesday the 31st of July 1811.

When, Colo. Ephm. Jordan was appointed President and Capt. James Smith Secretary. Thereupon Gen W. Johnston addressed the meeting in which he informed them of the present Situation of the Inhabitants of not only the Town but Country, in regard to the Shawnes Prophet, his Brother Tecumseh and their confederacy of Indians, and advised, that, for the safety of the Citizens some resolution should be fallen into, & therefore Adjt: Daniel Sullivan introduced the following Resolutions, which were read and Explained in an audable voice both in the English and French Languages, were unanimously adopted, as follows Viz.

1st. Resolved that it is the opinion of this meeting that the safety of the persons and property of this frontier, can never be effectually secured, but by the breaking up of the Combination formed by the Shawanoe prophet on the Wabash.

2nd. Resolved that we consider it highly impolitic and Injurious as well to the inhabitants of the United States as that of the Territory to permit a formidable Banditty, which is constantly increasing in number, to occupy a situation which enables them to Strike our Settlements without the least warning.

3rd. Resolved that we are fully convinced that the formation of the Combination headed by the Shawanoe Prophet, is a British Scheme and that the agents of that power are constantly exciting the Indians to hostility against the United States.

4th. Resolved that the Assemblege of Indians at this place, at this time, and under the circumstances which attended it; was calculated to excite the most serious alarm and but for the energetic measures, which have been adopted by our executive, it is highly probable that the threatened destruction of this place, and the massecre of the inhabitants, would have been the Consequence.

5th. Resolved that a temporising policy is not calculated to answer any beneficial purpose with Savages, who are only to be controlled by prompt and decisive measures.

6th. Resolved that a committee to consist of the Revd. Samuel T. Scott, the Revd. Alexander Devin, Colo. Luke Decker, Colo. E. Jordan, Daniel Mc.Clure, Walter Wilson Esquire & Colo. Francois Vigo or a majority of them be and they are hereby appointed to prepare and forward to the Executive of the United States a respectful address on the behalf of this meeting, assuring him of our attachmt. to his person and administration and requesting him to take Such measures, as his wisdom may dictate, to free the Territories in this quarter from future apprehensions from the prophet and his party—and that he be also requested to insist upon the surrender, by the Indian Tribes, of those who have murdered our fellow Citizens and provide compensation for such as have lost their property.

7th Resolved that we approve highly of the prompt and decisive measures adopted and pursued by the governor of the Territory. We are convinced, that the Situation in which we stand with the prophet and his adherents rendered them Necessary for our Safety and from them we confidently expect such a termination of the presumptious pretentions of this daring chief as must be pleasing to every patriot and honorable to himself.

Resolved that these resolutions be printed in the Western Sun and also the address which may be prepared and forwarded to the President in pursuance of them.

P. S. The printer will please to insert the 7th Resolution before the 6th and let, the 7th Stand 6th & 6th the 7th in print.

JAMES SMITH Secretary   EPHM. JORDAN
                                                          president

---

RC (DNA: RG 107, LRUS, W-1811); enclosure (ibid., R-1811); Tr and Tr of enclosure (DNA: RG 46, TP, Indiana). RC undated; date provided on the basis of the date on the enclosed resolutions. Tr incomplete. RC and enclosure printed in *National Intelligencer*, 5 Sept. 1811.

1. Following some angry exchanges with Tecumseh over the surveying of lands ceded by the 1809 Treaty of Fort Wayne, over the seizure by the Prophet of the 1811 salt annuities that

William Henry Harrison had shipped to several of the Northwestern Indian tribes, and over the allegation that supporters of the Shawnee brothers had been responsible for the murder of settlers on the Illinois River, William Henry Harrison concluded that the Indians gathered at Prophetstown might attack Vincennes. On 24 June 1811 he therefore informed Tecumseh that the matter of the lands ceded in 1809 was "in the hands of the President" and warned him that if he wished to come to Vincennes, he must do so not with a large force but only with "a few of your young men." Tecumseh responded by arriving in the territorial capital on 27 July with a party Harrison estimated to be "about three hundred persons," most of whom were armed warriors. During the discussions held on 30 July, Tecumseh addressed the American settlers' fears in a speech Harrison described as "long and somewhat artful," but, the governor believed, "his designs were more completely developed by it than anything that I have yet heard from him." According to Harrison, Tecumseh claimed that "he had at length brought all the northern Tribes to unite and place themselves under his direction" and that the U.S. "had set him the example of forming a strict union amongst all the fires that compose their confederacy." After the meeting at Vincennes was over, Tecumseh "was to set out on a visit to the Southern Tribes to get them to unite with those of the North." In the interim, he hoped that there would be no further settlement of the lands ceded in 1809 and mentioned that on his return "he would then go and see the President and settle everything with him" (Harrison to Tecumseh, 24 June 1811, Harrison to Eustis, 6 Aug. 1811, Esarey, *Letters of Harrison*, 1:522–24, 542–46).

2. On 17 July 1811, in response to earlier letters about the prospect of Indian hostilities, Eustis reported he had already ordered the Fourth Infantry Regiment from Pittsburgh to Newport, Kentucky, adding that "if the prophet should commence, or seriously threaten, hostilities he ought to be attacked." Three days later, Eustis supplemented these orders by stating that he had "been particularly instructed by the President, to communicate . . . his earnest desire that peace may, if possible, be preserved with the Indians." Only if "absolutely necessary" was the Prophet to be attacked, since "circumstances conspire at this particular juncture to render it peculiarly desirable that hostilities (of any kind or to any degree not indispensable [*sic*] required) should be avoided" (Eustis to Harrison, 17 and 20 July 1811, Esarey, *Letters of Harrison*, 1:535–37).

¶ From John Jacob Astor. Letter not found. *August 1811*. Mentioned in Astor to Jefferson, 14 Mar. 1812 (DLC: Jefferson Papers) as an application to the president for permission to import from St. Joseph's goods purchased for the Indian trade which were being excluded from the U.S. by the Nonintercourse Act. JM apparently replied that Congress had left no power with the executive to grant permission.

§ From John Bishop. *1 August 1811, Glasgow*. Has read that there are 33,000 weavers in New York. Information from his son in Philadelphia indicates that "Manufactury in said Country is but in its Infancy." Wishes to inform JM of the steps taken by Great Britain to improve the weaving business in Scotland. A board of trade was created "for fisheres Manufactures and Improvements in Scotland," with trustees, which had little effect at the time. The board then procured two men from Holland "and set them up in the Manufacturing of Holands, every Encouragement was given to these men, and to the Weavers to incite them to make progress." Scotland can now make both plain and fancy goods. Tells a similar story with respect to muslin manufacturing in Ireland. The Scotland Board of Trade also "has given ample countinance to every Inventer of Machinery," as in the case of the inventor of a reed-making machine who was rewarded with £100 sterling. Believes the weaving business in New York could provide the basis for muslin manufacturing in America, but reed-making machinery is necessary. Offers to come to the U.S. with his three sons "all Bred to the Reed-making upon Machinery of the best Construction in Britain." However, all machinery is forbidden to leave the country and can be confiscated and the individual imprisoned for life. The man who made his reed-making machinery is familiar with machines for cotton mills and could be of essential service to America; "he would have no Objections to come over," but they lack money. "It would be absolutely Necessary, that you should bestow a sum of Money to us at our arrival, of no less than from one to two Thousand pound Sterling." Requests JM to reply to him, "Reed-maker N 447 Gallowgate Glasgow North Britain." Lists in a postscript "the Number of persons we have which we will bring along with us," including his wife, three sons, one daughter, a fourth son, already in Philadelphia, who has a wife and son, and the machinist with his wife and two children.

RC (NHi: Gallatin Papers). 3 pp. Addressed to the "Right Honourable Lord Precident and Congress of the United States of America." Postmarked 12 Oct. at Philadelphia.

To James Monroe

DEAR SIR   MONTPELIER July [August] 2. 1811

I just find by the letters from W. that you had at length been liberated from your detention there. Mr. Graham having left the packet for you unsealed, I have glanced over the papers relating to Grassin & the letters of Foster.[1] I am glad to find that the *Owner* of the Privateer, domicil[i]ated here, is taken in hand. There can be no legal difficulty I presume in dealing with him. Foster seems more disposed to play the diplomatist, than the conciliatory negociator. His letter though not very skilfully made up, is evidently calculated for the public here, as well as for his own Govt: In this view his evasion & sophistical efforts may deserve attention. Accept my cordial respects

JAMES MADISON

RC (DLC: Monroe Papers). Misdated by JM. Date corrected on the basis that JM was not at Montpelier on 2 July.

1. See John Graham to JM, 31 July 1811, and nn. 1 and 2.

From William Thornton

DR. SIR   WASHINGTON CITY 3d. Augt. 1811

I lie still so very sick in bed I am obliged to get Mr. Lyon to write a few lines for me, we were exceedingly obliged by the kind attention of your amiable Lady and self, at the time of your departure, and if your good wishes could have reinstated me I should not be now lieing in the low situation I am in. Since I had the pleasure of seeing you Major White was here, who has trained some of my Horses & informed me if the Colt of King Hirem[1] which is four years Old, at your house could be got up he would send a rider expressly for him, and would train him for me on very easy terms. The Sire of that Colt has been in Georgia for five years & I never have received for his services one Dol., but if one of his Colts was tried and could run it perhaps might bring the Horse into vogue. I am willing to take the Horse at his valuation, or if you prefer keeping him yourself it will be perfectly agreeable to me, and the same justice shall be done to him that would be done if he was my property. Mr. Whites boy will be the bearer of a copy of this, I know the Horse is of more value in consequence of his being a year Older, and if you should not be inclined to keep him, I must pay the more for him or take a two year Old Filly valued at three to make up the difference. I wish this to be perfectly obtional [*sic*] with yourself as it will make no difference whether you or I have the Colt. I am so fatigued by only dictating these few lines that I must bid you an affectionate and sincere adieu—

WILLIAM THORNTON.

RC (DLC). Signed by Thornton. Docketed by JM.

1. King Hiram was a British racehorse imported by Thornton, probably in 1800. He let the horse in 1807 and it was kept at the property of David Martin in Saundersville, Georgia, until 1816 (Harrison, *Early American Turf Stock, 1730–1830*, 2:378–80).

From James Monroe

DEAR SIR   ALBEMARLE Augt 5. 1811

I arrived here late yesterday eving. having taken Richmond in my route. I had the great satisfaction to find Mrs. Monroe & our youngest daughter in better health than I had anticipated, as I had to find Mr Hay & our eldest. The early hour at which the post rider has called renders it impossible for me to say any thing on publick affrs. by this opportunity. I shall immediately turn my attention to them, & not permit another to pass by without availing myself of it. Be so good as to present Mrs. Monroe's & my best respects to Mrs. Madison & believe me sincerely & respectfully yours

JAS MONROE

RC (DLC: Rives Collection, Madison Papers).

From Edmund Randolph

CHARLESTOWN, JEFFERSON COUNTY VIRGINIA
August 8. 1811.

Having removed hither to pass the fall and winter under the roof of my daughter Taylor, I did not receive your late letter until yesterday.[1]

If the analogy between the case at Philadelphia, and the more recent one at Washington, be strong enough to merit the application of it, with the following clue, a second search at the Treasury may perhaps succeed. Giles's resolutions had been defeated, before Colo. H. suggested thro' one of his indirect conduits to the ear of the President, that during his tour in the south, he had sanctioned by two letters the measure, which was so severely criminated.[2] He mentioned the circumstance to me, with surprize and passion, declaring in the most excluding terms, that he never did write or cause to be written, letters to that purport. Some days afterwards, Colo. H. put them into the President's hands, and by him they were communicated to me with an instruction to write to Colo. H. avowing them. This I did, and it would seem impossible that upon a subject, on which his sensibility was so much kindled, that a document of justification should have been laid aside, as a private paper. These facts are most distinctly recollected.

On my journey through Staunton, where various people were assembled at the court of chancery, the topic, to which the above relates seemed to be given up on all sides, after the review in the National Intelligencer had explained it:[3] and I suspect, that the only remaining difficulties in the public mind are the article concerning Serrurier's information, and the abandonment of the Condition, which Armstrong was charged to annex to the enforcing of the nonimportation, or nonintercourse law against Great Britain.[4] These things are not perfectly understood. Adieu my ancient friend, from whom neither time nor circumstances shall sever me.

RC (DLC). Unsigned; in the hand of Edmund Randolph. Docketed by JM, with his notation, "Giles Resolutions on the transfer of money by Sey. of the Treasury / see July 9. 1811." Below the docket JM wrote in pencil: "Randolph's acct. of the sanction of Gen. Washington to Hamilton's irregular proceeding / to be looked over."

1. JM's letter has not been found, but in the "Detatched Memoranda" written during his retirement JM recorded that Randolph's 8 Aug. letter was written "in consequence of an intimation, that from an enquiry at the Treasury Department it did not appear that any such paper as that described had been deposited there" (see Randolph to JM, 9 July 1811). After reflecting further on the episode, JM concluded that the document Randolph was seeking had been treated by both Hamilton and Washington as a routine transaction and that the former "forbore to avail himself of the document he possessed, or to involve the President in the responsibility he was willing to take on himself." "It is proper to remark," JM continued, "that Mr. Randolph's statement came from a dismissed officer, and that it was subsequent to a para-

lytic stroke which ended in greatly enfeebling his mind. But there is reason to confide in his declaration that he retained no feeling of a partizan; and that the tenor of his letters indicates no incompetency to the task assumed in them. The explanatory facts stated carry indeed the greatest probability on the face of them." JM therefore assumed that the evidence that Washington had endorsed Hamilton's actions, unless it had been mislaid or destroyed, "must be among the papers of Col: Hamilton." As for Randolph's motive in contacting him on the matter, JM ascribed it "to the friendly feeling in the writer to J.M. who had taken an active part in the discussions produced by Mr. Giles's Resolutions" (Elizabeth Fleet, ed., "Madison's 'Detached Memoranda,'" *WMQ*, 3d ser., 3 [1946]: 545–48).

2. Randolph was probably alluding to George Washington's letters to Alexander Hamilton of 7 May and 29 July 1791 (Syrett and Cooke, *Papers of Hamilton*, 8:330, 588).

3. Randolph was referring to the *Review of Robert Smith's Address to the People of the United States*.

4. In his *Address to the People of the United States*, Robert Smith had argued that neither the French revocation of the Berlin and Milan decrees nor the Nonintercourse Act of 2 Mar. 1811 complied with the conditions JM had previously stipulated for the lifting of trade restrictions with France, namely that the repeal of the decrees should be coupled with the restoration of all previously seized American property in order to justify the imposition of nonintercourse against Great Britain. Smith had also pointed out that on 20 Feb. 1811, before the passage of the Nonintercourse Act on 2 Mar., Sérurier had officially communicated the "fixed determination" of the French government *"not to restore the property so seized"* (*National Intelligencer*, 2 July 1811).

From Baptist Irvine

Sɪʀ,   [9 August 1811]
    The servility, the scurrilous style, and scandalous matter, of those who would be thought your friends, defenders, and guardians, leave no other resource to one who would correct their fals[e]hoods, than to address yourself. With *them*, no man, who values incorruptibility, can farther correspond or communicate.

    When your revered predecessor, the illustrious Jefferson, stood at the helm of government, we had no *open* violations of trust or truth, by little pensioners [of] the public, clerks in the departments: but, since your election, the public spirit has been broken by submission-bills, and all confidence shaken by underhand hints instead of direct recommendations to congress.

    "So doth the greater glory dim the less."[1]

    Jefferson's acts were visible, palpable, they stood justified by their merit; and he left them to the criticism of a discerning people. You may be assured, sir, that the public *compare* men with men, and measures with measures—And Wonder already stares, that oblique, side-way methods should be necessary for *your* vindication, if you had nerve and honesty to resort to acts that would by their own worth and weight withstand the public scrutiny.

It "seems," that you did not assume the exercise of all the powers for which you were responsible, *immediately* on coming to the presidency—you erected or continued a "cabinet" contrary to the spirit and letter of that constitution you had sworn to support. You consulted the men who composed it, not about the business of their respective departments, but promiscuously on every thing! What was the consequence? *You* meant to divide *your responsibility*, and *they* resolved (as was natural) to share *your power*. Their assumption was the effect of your timidity.

Differing in opinion with Robert Smith, a separation ensued. Your hirelings attacked him, leaving neither his talents nor integrity without a blow or a slander: if they have not wounded him it is not their fault. As if afraid to meet the real charge in Mr. Smith's "Address" that of your *inefficiency* (or too much pusillanimity) to execute the presidential duties, your Janissaries (or those subsidized by your pretended friends, but real enemies) affect to extract from Smith's pamphlet, *what it does not contain*, the accusation of peculiar devotion to France. Here where there is no enemy, the "Hessians" are brave; where there are no witnesses, except "the British party in America," whom no man credits, the same "Hessians" demonstrate, that the sun shines, that "French influence" is a chimera; and it is most true. But, Mr. Smith, in defending his own opinions, (and I do not agree with him in *all*) only shows that you seemed willing to make concessions *both* to *England* and *France*. *Pusillanimity* is one thing, *disaffection* is another. We all acquit you of the latter—from my soul, *I* do. I will no[t] stop here, to apostrophize the fools, who are so officious as to tender you disservice by their service; who seem ready to forget British impressment, plunder and insult, nay, to forget the treasonable conduct of the "British party" when in power, all forsake of displaying their loyalty, by detesting "French influence," which nobody believes, or sees—except in reverie or vision; and "vision (we are told) is the art of seeing things invisible!"[2]

It was to put an end to this confusion and perversion, that the writer of this penned a letter to a reported hireling of yours in a subordinate station at Washington;[3] who being unprincipled (he possessing bad principles) was said to have been employed to write *against the democratic party*, in this state by way of forcing them to support you, for fear of their own overthrow. I knew how vulnerable this wretch was; and, for the purpose of giving the public mind time to cool, I reminded him of the danger to which he would expose himself and others, if he stirred up the embers any more. My letter contained a reference to his own diabolical conversations respecting you, *et cetera*, which would have caused an honest man, with any sensibility, to run and throw himself at your feet, and entreat your mercy. Instead of this, he calculates on the delicacy of those whom he abuses, (and whose well intended letters he publishes *in part*,) to conceal his crimes as being *too gross to be named.*[4]

He, sir, is supposed to be your vassal; call on him, make him produce the *vital part*, or the WHOLE of my letter, to you in private: You will then see how anxious *I* was to save your feelings, and the honour of the wretch, if he had any. Call upon him to exhibit my letter: then, call upon me to substantiate the charge—☞ *Next*, ask yourself, whether if you admit his testimony in one case, you must not recognize it throughout?[5] and oh! at what expense!

With my warning before his eyes, his appearance (two days after!) in the National Intelligencer, with a mass of fals[e]hood, induces the belief that he was *forced* or *bribed* to the measure, and that *he had no alternative between sacrificing truth and honour,* or, *forfeiting his office.*

Much false insinuation is foisted into certain publications about R. Smith's Influence over this paper and its editor. Yet, the world could not persuade us to swerve from the cause of truth—We never consulted R. Smith, never received a communication or a hint from him, and even said to the little vassal, as we have to others, "that, for R Smith, bating where he was connected with the democratic party, or was made the victim of foul treatment and base denunciation, we cared no more than we did for Timothy Pickering, for, we made it our study to avoid obligations to *all public men.*" This was during a conversation in which he observed, "that if Mr. Madison was a dupe, (though honestly inclined) he was more dangerous than a knave." His *Saturday's* story, however, to us, was at complete variance with his remarks on *Monday!* He best knows *the reason.* He saw R. Smith on Sunday. On *Saturday*, the vassal said (to the writer) that, certainly, R. Smith had been "very badly treated," on *Monday*, several parts of his "Address" were "d——d disingenuous."[6]

[Since the vassal's exposure of *his own perfidy* in the government paper, a friend of R. Smith, in conversation, related the following: The vassal called at R. Smith's on Sunday morning; introduced the subject of his difficult situation; he was in danger of being sacrificed, where he was, and could he obtain support for Mrs. ——[7] for a year or two, ☞ *et cetera*, he would attempt to get into the practice of the law. This he must do, or worse: ☞ *Dick Forrest* had on such a day stepped into his room, and declared (as if in your behalf I suppose) that "this was no time for splitting hairs—every man must now take a part for or against the government!" Meaning, that Mr. *Madison* was *the government*—and every man who did not take side with *him* in opposition to R. Smith, must be considered as an enemy to the government. Are we, sir, come to this? Have we a government of *men*, and not of *Ideas*, measures, principles? I must suppose this officious *federalist* (Richard Forrest) abuses his commission. The master of the ceremonies may fancy himself prime minister. But, why mention, (as the vassal did) the menace held out? his pecuniary embarrassments? the necessity for *his* taking sides?—(a clerk take sides!) Mr. Smith saw the creature wanted *a bid;* and, on his part an end was *instantly* put to the dialogue in contemptuous silence. I need not paint the mortification of the vassal; which is doubtless since removed, by going to a better market—I must add, that R. Smith disclaims having known the character of the vassal—hence the offers of library, instruction, &c. and hence his requital![8]

The generosity of Mr. Smith's offer to the vassal, in the letter of July 1, is accounted for by the deceitful professions of the latter: When the rupture took place, he said, in substance, to Mr. S. "Now, I am undone; Gallatin's influence will deprive me of my office, since you are no longer in the Department." Poh! replied Mr. S. you have nothing to fear, if you conduct yourself discreetly: Mr. Monroe is a mild man; and, beside, you and Mrs. —— are very intimate at Mr. Madison's, &c.[9] The vassal persisted in speaking of his ruin; he must prepare to practise law, if he could get admission, &c. And so on this occasion Mr. S promised any assistance in his reach. Who ought to have expected *a bribe*, from such discourse?

Look at the infamy of the vassal: Ere the time he addresses Mr. S. with crocodile concern, he boasted that his place or a better was secure; that he had laid an anchor to windward, &c. And, report says, that he, like Dick Forrest, (a ranting federalist,) has been flattered with the hope of a consul's appointment—but this I do not believe. However, as it is evident that Mr. S. never can descend to the level of the vassal, I thought this digression the more necessary.][10]

In Maryland, sir, the attempts to agitate us by hired mercenaries leagued with federalists, is unavailing—We do not forget the measures of '98; we do not forget the tyranny of the feds. in the state and general governments; but this is a *state election*, and we will no more regard the rupture between you and Mr. S. than the song of a Zany. When the *presidential election* comes on, however, we may turn to it. I know, your underlings can enlist partizans: the misrepresentation and scurrility lately shed in showers, prove the omnipotence of your subordinate officers over certain presses—What did this seem to say on your part? "Were Smith but out of Venice, *I* could make what merchandize I would."[11] It may not so fall out—We still remember Gallatin's proposals to Erskine, we remember, you did not relish Smith's *disavowal* of such offers being authorised. We recollect Gallatin's interference in the Bank question, on behalf of the federalists and British agents—and, if you couple yourself with him, you cannot hope for a re-election. Apropos—the little vassal told me, that as *your Virginia friends had given Mr. Gallatin up, you* WAITED *for an opportunity to* dismiss him without injury to the party. *What party?* Surely, Mr. Gallatin aids none but the federal party. And; if nothing impels you, but the *trade Winds of Virginia*, you must steer a strange course.* But take what course you may, recent experience convinces me, that you can draw a host of "parasites" around you,

---

*The patriotism and superior talent of that state, I acknowledge and revere. I only mean to say, that a president of the *United States* ought not to be guided by a particular state.

whether they are hired by the postmaster general, or not. I suppose, they act on their old maxim, as described by a noted author: "It is safer for a man's *interest*, to blaspheme God, than to be of a party out of power, or to be thought so." Even the little vassal boasts of directing a press at Richmond; (how many elsewhere I know not,) and another at the same place has manifested a contempt of truth and candour worthy of a loyal pensioner.†

Detesting the hidden machinery employed to blast suffering persecuted worth and reputation; fearing lest the poisoned chalice should be returned to your lips, I, from the best motives, gave a caution to your vassal which has been disregarded. Let him produce the letter *to you*, or any friend *you* may commission. *I pledge my honour* to substantiate his calumny in due season. I cannot mention the vassal's name on the same page with my own; nor is it necessary. He is now so branded that all can recognize him. The public know how to estimate the testimony of a being who cannot open his lips, until he has first violated faith or oath: Let him to the letter, and defend himself. If you and he dread it, we may at next session of congress let you know a little of it. If he fancies he can render federalism triumphant in Maryland, he is deceived. We care neither for *his silence* nor his disclosures—though we are ashamed of the baseness which intimidates, or pensions, or encourages, a miscreant, to invent falsehoods or conceal truth for the purposes of deception.

On this topic, Sir, I need not trouble you or the public again, if your instrument exhibit my letter to you *entire*. *If he dare not*, you ought to suspect the reason. I have thus, Sir, performed the irksome duty of exposing turpitude.

B. IRVINE.

☞ It is expected that every unbought *independent* press will republish the preceding; that truth and reputation may be vindicated, flagitious vice exposed, and harmony restored among political brethren.

---

†A gentleman of this city informed its editor of the little perjurer's character last winter; yet, Mr. Ritchie affected lately to treat his testimony with respect![12]

Printed copy (Baltimore *Whig*, 9 Aug. 1811).

1. Shakespeare, *Merchant of Venice*, 5.1.93.
2. Jonathan Swift, "Thoughts on Various Subjects," Herbert Davis, ed., *The Prose Writings of Jonathan Swift* (6 vols.; Oxford, 1951–68), 4:252.
3. Irvine referred to the State Department clerk John B. Colvin.
4. On 8 Aug. 1811 the *National Intelligencer* had published several letters exchanged between Baptist Irvine and Colvin, on the one hand, and Colvin and Robert Smith, on the other, describing events following the publication of Robert Smith's *Address*. This correspondence was accompanied by lengthy comments and explanations from Colvin himself. The letter referred to here by Irvine was one he had written to Colvin on 17 July 1811, recalling some

discussions they had held about the rupture between JM and Robert Smith and including a reference to a report Irvine had received from a gentleman to the effect that Colvin intended to come out in favor of the president. If Colvin did so, Irvine's source warned, he would be "vulnerable." By way of explaining this remark, Irvine mentioned that his source had claimed that "on ⟨a⟩ certain occasion you had spoken in the most ⟨c⟩ontemptuous style of Madison" and that the State Department clerk had known that "certain measures ⟨w⟩ere in operation for procuring [JM's] nomination ⟨and⟩ election." At this point in Irvine's letter the editors of the *National Intelligencer* inserted the comment: *"This part of the letter contains an ⟨a⟩llusion too execrable for insertion: the allusion ⟨was?⟩ no doubt made to prevent the publication of the letter—⟨t⟩he whole story is an invention."*

5. Irvine was repeating here a remark made to him by his informant about Colvin's conduct that "if Madison resorts to Colvin's testimony in one case, let him be prepared for recognizing it throughout" (ibid., 8 Aug. 1811). This was a reference to a letter written by Colvin on 22 July 1811, and published in the *National Intelligencer* the next day, in which Colvin attempted to discredit Robert Smith by announcing that the former secretary of state had *not* been responsible for drafting some of the diplomatic communications that in his *Address* he claimed JM had lacked the nerve to approve. Colvin specifically mentioned the first drafts of the 5 July 1810 letter to John Armstrong (see *PJM-PS*, 2:366–67) and the 18 Dec. 1810 letter to Louis-Marie Turreau, both of which he said he had written himself. Smith's claim to their authorship, Colvin added, "involved considerations of a personal nature, hostile to Mr. Madison and his administration, more than they embraced any views of public good."

6. Monday was the day of the week on which Colvin's 22 July 1811 letter to the editors of the *National Intelligencer* was written. On that occasion the State Department clerk did not use the expression "d——d disingenuous" to describe the claims made by Robert Smith in his *Address*, but he did affirm that the "facts and the inferences" in that pamphlet were "fabricated, misrepresented, or strained." On that basis Colvin concluded "from Mr. Smith's own declarations, that with respect to the alleged existence of French influence in the cabinet, Mr. Smith does not himself seriously believe what he insinuates" (ibid., 23 July 1811).

7. This was probably a reference to Colvin's wife, since Colvin mentioned in a 5 July 1811 letter to Robert Smith that he was "destitute . . . of property, and of the means of current support for Mrs. Colvin" (ibid., 8 Aug. 1811).

8. After Robert Smith had published his *Address* in late June 1811, Colvin confessed that he became anxious about his own prospects for continued employment at the State Department. He accordingly resolved to go to Baltimore "to speak to the republican editors of newspapers there . . . to induce them if possible to relinquish their defence of [Smith's] pamphlet." Shortly before his departure, however, Colvin received a letter, dated 1 July 1811, from Robert Smith, suggesting that he establish a law practice in Baltimore and offering him the services of his advice and law library in the event of his deciding to leave Washington. Colvin declined this offer, explaining at length in his 8 Aug. letter to the editors of the *National Intelligencer* why he had done so and why he regarded the letter communicating that offer as "marked with Mr. Smith's habitual cunning." One month after these transactions occurred, Colvin placed a notice in the *National Intelligencer* announcing that he had entered the practice of law and could be consulted at his room in the boardinghouse run by Mrs. Eliza Doyne on Pennsylvania Avenue (ibid., 3 Aug. 1811).

9. Colvin's version of this conversation was: "On going out of office" Robert Smith said: "'Mr. Colvin, I give you my honor that they will turn you out of place: they will invent against you some scandalous story, and make it a pretext for your expulsion: I therefore advise you immediately to ask leave of absence, go off to New York, and set up a paper. The public will think you can say a great deal about the president, and every body will take your paper.'" Colvin declared that it was the "cruel" intent of this "cunning" and "insidious counsel" that finally destroyed his belief in the integrity of Robert Smith (ibid., 8 Aug. 1811).

10. Irvine's brackets.

11. Irvine paraphrased Shylock's remark to Tubal: "I will have the heart of him [Antonio] if he forfeit, for were he out of Venice I can make what merchandise I will" (Shakespeare, *Merchant of Venice*, 3.1.116–18).

12. In the next day's issue of the *Whig*, Irvine added a further note here: "The explanation to the editor of the *Enquirer*, we learn, was made in the spring of 1809."

To Albert Gallatin

DEAR SIR   MONTPELIER Aug. 10. 1811

I have recd. safe the manuscript of Dupont, and the pamphlet sent with it.[1] The letter from Foster to you,[2] I have handed on to the Secretary of State. The exemption of Articles for the use of pub. Ministers, from the impost, was founded in courtesy, & has been continued from respect to a course of precedents. The plea that it was required by the L. of N. cannot be sustained: Still less could this plea be applied to such a case as that presented by Mr. F. and as the case is without the plea of usage or even precedent, the L. of N. as construed by ourselves, could alone justify the exception to the general rule established by the Act of Congs. It is not improbable that if the case had occurred, at the passage of the Act, it might have been provided for, like that of vessels bringing despatches for Pub: Ms. But even this is doubtful. Mr. F. ought however to have an answer, that he may take his measures with a knowledge of the reception his supplies will find at the Custom houses, and it may be proper to hear from the Secretary of State, before the answer be decided on. If in the mean time the articles expected should arrive, and a forfeiture be incurred, it will be for consideration how far the remitting power, may properly be applied; either absolutely, or provisionally with a reference to the final decision of Congress.

You have taken a proper step in your suggestion to Govr. Holmes, with respect to the trespasses on the pub: lands.[3] I am not sure that the intrusion law would not reach the case; but as it is a law departing from common right, the construction of it ought to be rather strict than free; and as Congs. will soon have an opportunity of providing a remedy, it seems best to trust for the present to the remedy you have pointed out, which may perhaps be seconded by an apprehension of removal under the intrusion law if found necessary.

I hear nothing as to foreign intelligence more than is seen in the Newspapers. I have not yet seen the Secretary of State nor heard more from him, than that he had reached home.

From the information recd from Washington, this will probably find you at N. Y. on your way to Boston. I hope you will find the ramble advantageous to your health, as well as otherwise agreeable. Mrs. M. joins in best respects to Mrs. Gallatin. Accept my esteem & affectionate wishes.

JAMES MADISON

Our Crops of Wheat were pinched by a drought, and suffered from the Hessian fly. They are suffering also in the small Cocks in which they remain for the most part in the fields, exposed to the present spell of rainy weather. The Crops of Indian Corn will be unusually great. This result is secured by the rains which are damaging the Wheat.

RC (NHi: Gallatin Papers).

1. See Pierre Samuel DuPont de Nemours to JM, 4 July 1811.

2. On 4 Aug. 1811 Augustus John Foster had written to Gallatin, informing him that he was expecting the delivery of some boxes of preserved fruits and liqueurs from the West Indies at Norfolk, Virginia, and directing him to instruct the collector there to allow for their free importation as a matter of diplomatic privilege (see DNA: RG 59, NFL, Great Britain, with Gallatin's deleted note "Give usual instruction to Collector of Norfolk. A. G.").

3. JM had evidently seen a 9 July 1811 letter from deputy surveyor Thomas Freeman in the Mississippi Territory to Gallatin reporting his disagreement with Governor Holmes over whether to remove intruders who were cutting cypress timber on the public lands. Gallatin docketed the letter, adding a note to the effect that "the intrusion law authorises the removal of persons who shall take possession of the public lands or attempt to make a settlement thereon. The question arises," he continued, "whether persons committing the trespass & depredations herein stated can be considered as having taken possession & subject to removal under the statute. If determined in affirmative, the instructions to the Governor should go from the Department of State." Beneath this observation, Gallatin addressed the following note to JM: "I have in the meanwhile written to Govr Holmes suggesting the propriety of instituting suits at common law for trespass & also applying to court for injunctions or such other writs as may be efficient in stopping waste. A. G." Following Gallatin's comment, JM wrote in pencil: "Better to trust to this till Congs meet, than to seek remedy in a doubtful construction of the Intrusion law" (DNA: RG 59, TP, Mississippi; printed in Carter, *Territorial Papers, Mississippi*, 6:205–7).

From James Monroe

DEAR SIR   ALBEMARLE Augt. 11. 1811

The incapacity for business produc'd by so long an application to it at Washington, has been increasd since my return home by a fall from my horse, being taken off by a limb of a tree under which he passed. My head, & left shoulder were bruis'd, & my leg cut a little by the stirrup, but I have almost recover'd from these injuries. I have walk'd about to day, & expect to be able to ride tomorrow.

I inclose you recommendations in favor of two persons to succeed Mr Freneau in the office of Commissr. of loans in So Carolina.[1]

Mr Gales has written to enquire whether the Statment in the Aurora of rudeness being offerd to me personally by Mr Foster is correct.[2] It certainly is not so. But whether, since the proceeding & judgment in the admy. in the case of the Fox & other vessels, the statment ought to be contradicted or even noticd, as not heard of, is doubtful at least at this time.[3] I have intimated to Mr Graham that I will answer Mr Gales (thro Mr G), in my next on the subject, suggesting a doubt as to noticing it for the reason herin stated. I shall be glad of a line from you on it in the inter[i]m. Respectfully your friend & servt

JAS MONROE

RC (DLC: Rives Collection, Madison Papers). Docketed by JM. Enclosures not found.

1. JM nominated Morton A. Waring to be commissioner of loans for South Carolina on 3 Dec. 1811 (*Senate Exec. Proceedings*, 2:194).

2. On 5 Aug. 1811, William Duane, who had repeatedly declared that Foster's mission was "only a business of *amusement and procrastination*," editorialized in the Philadelphia *Aurora General Advertiser* that the British minister had "fallen nothing short of the insolence of one of his predecessors, in the style and part which he has assumed, and he has exceeded him in personal indecorum and even personal rudeness." Duane further charged that Foster had resorted to "menaces" in his talks with Monroe over the Nonintercourse Act of 1811 and that the secretary of state, although responding with "dignity and temper," had been obliged to delay his departure for Virginia by three days as a consequence.

3. The Philadelphia *Aurora General Advertiser* also reported on 5 Aug. 1811 recent news from Great Britain to the effect that on 18 June Sir William Scott had condemned the *Fox* and fifty-four other American vessels under the orders in council. The *Fox* had sailed from Boston for Cherbourg and was captured on 15 Nov. 1810. In response to defense claims that the Berlin and Milan decrees had been repealed, Scott had ruled that there was no evidence that this was the case and that Great Britain could not accept French conditions for the repeal of the orders in council without loss of its "rights sanctioned by the acquiescence and general custom of Europe." In communicating the news of the decision to Monroe on 7 Aug., John Graham remarked: "This looks inauspiciously, particularly when connected with the Reports that the Indians are making war on our Western Frontier, that the British are sending reinforcements to Canada, and are endeavouring to get possession of the Island of Cuba" (DLC: Monroe Papers).

To James Monroe

DEAR SIR   MTPELIER Aug. 11. 1811

I snatch the opportunity by the bearer of yours of this date, to send to the Ct. House for the next rider who does not call here, the line you request in answer. As the report alluded to is erroneous as I supposed it to have been, a contradiction seemed to be due to the manner in which it was given to the public. Mr. Gales you will see has undertaken one which will probably be sufficient.¹ Notwithstanding the late unseasonable as well as unwarrantable condemnations, it is best to pursue a steady course of fairness & truth towards that Govt. A more delicate question is whether, the same considerations both foreign & domestic, do not require the statement made by Mr. Gales as to the blockade of May 1806. to be now adapted to the disavowal of Mr. Foster, of the construction put on his communication on that subject.² I regret much the injurious accident to your health. It is fortunate that its consequences are passing off. Yrs

JAMES MADISON

RC (DLC: Monroe Papers).

1. The editor of the *National Intelligencer*, in noting the claims made in the Philadelphia *Aurora General Advertiser* on 5 Aug. and also reporting that they had been repeated in the Baltimore *Whig*, stated that while he could not say that the charges of Foster's insulting behavior were "contrary to fact," he was sure that he would have heard of them had they been true. It was his belief, he wrote, that the interviews between Foster and Monroe had been "conducted in a perfectly decorous and friendly manner" (*National Intelligencer*, 8 Aug. 1811).

2. On 25 July 1811 the editor of the *National Intelligencer*, in summarizing the month's negotiations between Foster and Monroe, declared that "with respect to [the blockade of May 1806], it is understood to be placed under a construction and on a footing to render it no longer an insuperable difficulty." This statement embodied a conclusion that Monroe had incorporated into his 23 July 1811 letter to Foster: that the president "has received with great satisfaction the communication, that, should the orders in council of 1807 be revoked, the blockade of May of the preceding year would cease with them, and that any blockade which should be afterwards instituted should be duly notified and maintained by an adequate force." In his reply of 26 July Foster wrote that he was at a loss to understand how JM could have drawn from his letter "the *unqualified* inference, that should the orders in council of 1807 be revoked, the blockade of May, 1806, would cease with them." Disavowing this interpretation, the British minister declared that "the blockade . . . will not continue after the repeal of the orders in council, unless His Majesty's Government shall think fit to sustain it by the special application of a sufficient naval force; and the fact of its being so continued or not will be notified at the time" (see *ASP, Foreign Relations*, 3:442, 443).

From William Thornton

DR. SIR   WASHINGTON Augt. 12th. 1811

The boy that Mr. White meant to have sent down has met with a dreadful accident, been severely bit by a Horse that he was training, I must endeavour therefore to look out for an other if I can meet with one in time. I still remain sick in bed, of what the Doctors call a Rheumatick favour [*sic*] which must wear itself out, but I think is wearing me out very fast, we have had very severe rains here lately almost every day and the people hereabouts & about Prince Georges Coy., Maryland, think they shall make double crops of Corn. I am sorry to hear that in Jefferson County & over the Mountain the corn is taselling 3 feet high not having rain for near two Months. I feel still so sick that I am obliged to finish after presenting my best respects to your lady & family & am Dr. sir with the highest respect your sincere friend

WILLIAM THORNTON.

RC (DLC). Docketed by JM.

§ Account with Robert Patton. *12 August 1811.* States JM's account with Patton between 26 July 1810 and 12 Aug. 1811, listing debits for various plantation supplies—osnaburgs, bar iron, "blister'd steel," curry combs, butter, nails, molasses, cotton, sugar, coffee, and "mill saw files"—and cash paid to JM, Gen. William Madison, and others. The account includes credits to JM of £486 for 180 barrels of flour and £173 2s. 4d. for 346¹⁴⁄₆₀ bushels of wheat and shows a balance due to JM of £491 4s. 11d.

Ms (DLC). 1 p. Signed by Francis J. Wiatt for Robert Patton.

From William Eustis

DEAR SIR,   WASHINGTON August 13th. 1811.

Your favor of the 10th. enclosing a Letter from Lt. Voorhis was received this morning.¹ That officer was with me yesterday—he appears to be a good man and bears his sentence like a good christian: he has merit and in case of war may still be useful.

At the time of leaving the city for Harper's ferry the business & state of the office did not admit of my absence for so long a time as a visit to Montpelier implied: it was therefore concluded to return to the city and to embrace a more favorable opportunity, which we are awaiting. The armoury does equal credit to the govt. and to the conductors. The work is good, and is still improving. With the new arsenal which has been erected they are enabled to store all the arms which are on hand & probably will be those manufactured for another year. After this time a new arrangement will be required. It was contemplated (and had I not inspected the site it would have been done) to erect a third arsenal on the square which encloses the other two: but the ground is not sufficiently extensive: they are too nearly neighboured by private lots which when built upon (as they must be at no distant day) will increase the danger from fire. We must either build on the hill at a distance of half a mile, or (which appears preferable) commence in another year the delivery to the states of manufactured arms (contract) under the Law for arming the militia and thereby make room in the stores both at H. Ferry and at Springfield for those manufactured at each of those places. Fifty thousand stands is perhaps as large a number as ought to be deposited in any one place. The city continues healthy, and is not altogether desolate. In a short conversation with Mr F. the evening before he left us, I thought he discovered some solicitude and did not appear to be perfectly satisfied with the state of the relations between our country & G. B.

The works in the harbour of N. York will be completed in the beginning of October & from what has been done and is still doing in other ports we shall not be altogether defenceless.

Genl. W (as I hear) has said that he will have the court Martial in Frederick town. Dr. Thornton continues low—but not dangerous as we are informed. In the hope of coming to your peaceful mansion, we are with our best respects to Mrs M. Dr Sir, yr obedt. servt.

W EUSTI⟨s⟩

Mr Payne disappointed us very much in not taking a seat with us according to appointment: & the more so as we spent a very agreeable day with Mrs. Washington.

Letters from P. Chouteau, Agent for the Osages state a request that some of their chiefs may come on a visit to the seat of Govt.—they are dissatisfied at the delay in satisfying their treaty & will probably refuse the annuity.[2]

A similar request is made by the Choctaws whose agent states one object of their visit to be to meet the Osage chiefs before their common father & to agree on a permanent peace.[3] Letters are prepared assenting to the proposals & will be sent out unless instructions interdictory shall be received in the course of a week.[4]

RC (DLC). Docketed by JM.

1. JM's letter of 10 Aug. has not been found, but he evidently enclosed James J. Voorhees's letter to him of 10 Mar. 1811.

2. See Pierre Chouteau to Eustis, undated, but docketed as received 7 Aug. 1811 (Carter, *Territorial Papers, Louisiana-Missouri*, 14:464–68).

3. See Silas Dinsmoor to Eustis, 17 July 1811 (DNA: RG 107, LRRS, D-138:5; docketed as received 2 Aug.).

4. See Eustis to Silas Dinsmoor, 20 Aug. 1811, and Eustis to Pierre Chouteau, 30 Aug. 1811 (DNA: RG 75, LSIA). In the first of these letters Eustis conveyed JM's permission for a visit from the Choctaw chiefs. He stipulated, however, that the visit be postponed until the following spring as it would be inconvenient to receive the chiefs during the coming session of Congress. In the second letter Eustis announced that the Osage Indians could visit Washington subject to the time being arranged by Indian agent William Clark.

§ From Aaron Vail[1] and Strobal Vail. *13 August 1811.* "Stephen Vail of Butler County purchased of the united states some years ago 380⁰⁰/₁₀₀ acres of Land and made full payment for the same the 11th. August 1806 as per receipt on which land he had layed out a small town sold the Lotts and gave his Obligations to make deeds in a Certain time." Since Stephen Vail's decease it has been impossible to make out deeds for purchasers of the lots, who are now prosecuting and causing the estate great inconvenience and expense. "We have frequently made Application at Cincinnati for the patten but are always put of[f]. . . . The necessity of our haveing a right for the land in a short time Compel us to wright these few lines to you." A receipt from the Cincinnati land office for $233.88 paid by Stephen Vail on 11 Aug. 1806 is transcribed in a postscript.

RC (DNA: RG 49, Records of the General Land Office). 1 p. Forwarded by JM to Gallatin from Orange County, Virginia, on 12 Sept. 1811.

1. Aaron Vail had been commercial agent at Lorient between 1803 and 1808 (*PJM-SS*, 2:238 n. 1).

From John Graham

DEAR SIR   DEPT OF STATE 14th Augt 1811

The Letter which you did me the Honor to write to me on the 10th Inst.[1] I received yesterday, together with those which it covered. I have now the pleasure to return Mr. Adams's (Letter) de cyphered:[2] with the other I can as yet do nothing. I will make an effort before the departure of your next Mail to find out generally its objects; but I am by no means confident that I shall be able to do even this, for my knowledge of the Language in which it is written is very imperfect and of course not such as is best calculated to encounter such a production.[3]

We have had a great deal of Rain here since your departure, more particularly within the last 8 or 10 days. It is apprehended that we shall, in consequence, have a sickly Season. Fortunately the weather has c⟨l⟩ear⟨ed⟩ away cool and windy, and as yet the City is I beleive very healthy. With Sentiments of the Most Respectful Attachment I have the Honor to be, Sir Your Mo Obt Sert

JOHN GRAHAM

RC (DLC). Docketed by JM.

1. Letter not found.

2. Graham was probably referring to one of John Quincy Adams's two dispatches to the State Department written under the dates of 12 and 19 Feb. 1811 (see Graham to JM, 31 July 1811, and n. 3). For a deciphered version of their contents, see Ford, *Writings of J. Q. Adams*, 4:12–18.

3. Letter not identified, but it was evidently written in Portuguese (see Graham to JM, 16 Aug. 1811).

To James Monroe

Dear Sir   Aug. 15. 1811

Among the papers herewith inclosed are letters from the Govt. at Santa fee,[1] and among these one to the French Minister at Washington inclosing another to the Minister of Foreign relations at Paris. In opening the general packet addressed to the Executive, that for Serrurier was so involved as to be opened unintenti[on]ally at the same time. The more important one for Paris escaped this accident. I send the whole to you, with a request that you will desire Mr. Graham to have the proper portions handed to Mr. Serrurier with the requisite apology & explanation. I do not recollect John Mary de Bordes, who applies for a passport, & a letter of introduction at the Havanna. Mr. Graham, in forwarding the former, may intimate that it is contrary to usage to grant the latter. Accept my best respects & wishes

                                                        JAMES MADISON

RC (KB). Addressee not indicated, but identified as Monroe on the basis of internal evidence and the contents of Monroe to JM, 16 Aug. 1811.

1. JM probably enclosed the ca. 22 Dec. 1810 and 9 May 1811 letters he had received from José Miguel Pey and Jorge Tadeo Lozano, respectively.

From George Joy

My Dear Sir,   Elsinure 15th. August 1811

I have just crossed the Sound in much better Health than when I left this place.

You will perceive, in the concluding Paragraph of my letter to my Brother of the 21st. ultimo,[1] that it was not my intention to cross the Atlantic very soon. Some Murmurs that have reached me have induced serious thoughts however of making the Voyage from this place; and further consideration, to take England in my way.

I have not seen Mr Smith's Pamphlet; but I have seen several comments upon it; & tho' God knows how little I can expect to affect, in stemming the Current that it appears to have produced, that little is most devoutly at your Service.

If indeed I had no other Expectation than from my own abstract Efforts, a double Voyage across the Atlantic would be too ridiculous, but as the public Evidences of impartiality on the side of the Gouvernment (tho' they appear to me demonstrable enough) are suspected of insincerity, and in the letters that I have from you in England, there is an artless Exposure of feelings on the occasion, that cannot fail to do honour to your heart, and, according to my Judgement, ought to convince the most obstinate of the sincerity of your professions in that respect; I conceive it will be better to take them with me, as well as the Evidence of their effect upon certain Members of the last administration, than to trust to my Memory, which tho' *passablement au fait* may have less Credit with the public than with you.

I hope I shall not be drawn from the path of still life that I have chosen to a public Justification of the measures I have been pursuing without a public Commission, or a public Salary; tho' I am advised by my friends to invoke the Press and have just received, among other incentives, a scrap from the national Intelligencer, containing an extract of a Letter from London, whose wise Author *knows* it to be false that I was appointed by Mr Pinkney. As the national Intelligencer is supposed to have all reasonable information from the Govt. on simple requisition, and Mr Pinkney's Instructions must be registered in the office of State; I don't think it is quite ⟨just?⟩ to treat an absent Man this way. It is chiefly objectionable as having the appearance of your Indulgence—an event that I must acknowledge would shake my Philosophy, indifferent as I certainly am to the trash itself.

I hope, my dear Sir, the day is far distant when such appearances will become realities; but should the miserable testimonials, which can alone be produced, succeed in perverting the Evidences of my Efforts in your Mind; should that difference take place which the consciousness of rectitude in my own, could not fail, in that Case to produce; I shall still owe it to the public, (in comparison of whom any possible differences between you and me must be the mere dust of the Balance,) to produce those Evidences which strike me as of weight, if not indeed conclusive of the question of truth and fidelity on your Part. For myself I only desire that the facts relating to my Agency in Denmark may be exhibited to the Gouvernment as they are, and in their turn, and this, as matter of simple Justice, I confidently trust will be matter of Course. I rest always very sincerely Dear Sir Your friend & servt.

Geo: Joy

RC (DLC: Rives Collection, Madison Papers). Marked "Duplicate." In a clerk's hand, corrected and signed by Joy, and bearing his notation, "broken open after sealing by mistake."

1. Letter not found.

§ From George C. Allen.[1] *15 August 1811, Cantonment Washington, Mississippi Territory.* "I was ordered to Fort Pickering by Genl. Hampton and took command of that Post on the 1st. August 1810. and remained in comd. until the 1st. July 1811 When I was ordered to this place by Colo. Purdy. The paymaster has refused me double rations which has been alowed to every other officer who commanded there before me." Asks JM to consider the situation of the post and the "grate number of Millitia men and others who daily called on me Which I had to entertain." His expenses greatly exceeded his pay. Has written twice to the secretary of war but has received no reply.

RC (DNA: RG 107, LRRS, A-160:5). 2 pp. Docketed by a War Department clerk as received 16 Sept. 1811.

1. George C. Allen of Tennessee was a lieutenant in the Seventh Infantry Regiment (Heitman, *Historical Register*, 1:158).

§ From John Leonard. *15 August 1811, Barcelona.* "When I had the honor to receive the appointmt. of Consul of the UStates at Barna no doubt I was consider'd properly qualified, and I have the satisfaction to enclose a document in confirmation thereof." Does so because he has seen a duplicate of a letter in the hands of Mr. Thorndike, signed by Robert Smith and dated 27 Feb. 1811, revoking his consular commission and directing him to turn over the consular papers to John Carroll. Has never seen the signature of Smith and doubts the authenticity of the document.[1] Complains that to divest a person of office in this manner amounts to declaring him guilty of a misdemeanor; and as consuls are generally merchants who depend on honor and credit, the proceeding amounts to "Capital punishmt." without cause or trial. States that an investigation should be made and a consul notified of charges in order to justify himself; "99 in a hundred of these Kind of charges are ficticious & malicious." Further argues that hasty measures are unnecessary as Barcelona is blockaded by sea and without communication by land; there is no "pressing demand" for consular functions. With one exception there has been no call for him to perform any services, and it is three years since an American vessel entered Barcelona. Declares that he has done his duty to his nation with credit and therefore the letter is "ficticious or produced from wrong impressions." Requests that justice be done to him and concludes by noting that he has never received an acknowledgment of the letters he has written to the State Department during his eight years as consul at Barcelona.

RC and enclosure (DNA: RG 59, LAR, 1809–17, filed under "Leonard"). RC 4 pp. Enclosure 3 pp.; partly in Spanish.

1. The document was authentic. On 27 Feb. 1811 Robert Smith did write to Leonard to inform him that the president was revoking his commission and directing him to turn over the papers of his office to John Carroll (DNA: RG 59, IC).

From John Graham

DEAR SIR   DEPT OF STATE 16th Augt 1811.

Not being able to hear of any one here who understood the Portuguese Language—I have endeavoured myself to find out what was the object of the writer of the Letter you sent me. It seems to be to induce you to enter into an alliance with England against France: and to propose to all the Nations "of Asia, Africa, Europe and America" to make common cause against her—to forbid all commerce or communication with her, and to destroy her armies whereever they were to be found. Under this state of things the writer seems to suppose that the Commerce of the World might be freed from all kinds of restrictions or Duties and that the Paper Money of Great Britain and of the United States would pass every where as current as Gold & Silver now do. He says too that this Country and the Brasils might have a Navy in common. For myself, I am strongly tempted to think the writer is deranged; but if you are disposed more accurately to ascertain what are the contents of his Letter I can send it to Phia where I presume some one can be found who will be able to read the greater part of it. With the Highest Respect I have the Honor to be, Sir, Your Most Obt Sert.

JOHN GRAHAM

Mr Monroe having desired me to send him translations of the Letters received from Chile[1] & Buenos Ayres[2]—I have thought that you might possibly want to take a look at them on their way to him and have therefore put them under an open Cover which will go inclosed to you.

RC (DLC). Docketed by JM.

1. Mathew Arnold Hœvel to JM, 22 Mar. 1811, and enclosures.
2. Junta of the Provinces of the Río de la Plata to JM, 11 and 13 Feb. 1811.

From James Monroe

DEAR SIR   ALBEMARLE Augt. 16. 1811

Mr Gales's notice of the publication in the Aurora relative to Mr Foster was precisely what it ought to have been.[1] It was undoubtedly proper to prevent such a statment going to the nation as a fact, & the mode of contradicting, being without a compromitment of the govt., the true one.

I will endeavor to be with you in the course of the ensuing week. I expect to be able to wear my boot in that time, and as soon as I can I will be down.

I have directed the explanation to be made to Mr Sirrurier, by Mr Graham. Very respectfully & truly Yrs

JAS MONROE

RC (DLC: Rives Collection, Madison Papers).

1. See JM to Monroe, 11 Aug. 1811, and n. 1.

§ From Hay Battaile.[1] *16 August 1811, White Sulphur Springs.* "On my way to this place, I call'd on Mr Gooch . . . to get a pair or a Ram of your broad Tail Sheep; understanding that he had the disposal of them, he inform'd me that he could part with none without your orders, but that he had no doubt, but you would spare me one or both as you were geting a stock of two other breeds, that you liked much better; that he would speak to you and write me what was your determination; having not heard from him; I fear he has forgot to speak to you." Takes the liberty of addressing JM on the subject and would appreciate a line "directed to me at this place."

RC (DLC). 1 p.

1. Hay Battaile was a distant kinsman of JM's, having married a daughter of Col. Lewis Willis in 1793 (James Madison, Sr., to Joseph Chew, 19 Feb. 1793 [ViW]).

From John Quincy Adams

(Private.)
SIR.   ST: PETERSBURG 17. August 1811.

The Event, anticipated in the letters which I had the honour of writing you on the 7. Jany: 8. Feby: and 3d: June, has happened at the time when it was expected. On Monday Evening last the 12th. instt: I had a daughter born, the first example I believe of an American, a native of Russia.[1] As it would have been impossible for me to have accomplished since the Commencement of this year's navigable season, a Voyage to the United States, before this occurrence, so it leaves my family in a Condition equally disqualified for that undertaking, untill the present Season will be past. My determination to pass the ensuing Winter here remains therefore as at the date of my former letters.

That the private concerns and situation of my family, should in any manner affect the arrangements of your public administration has been and still is to me a source of some uneasiness. Aware that my particular convenience and accommodation, was the only motive to the permission in the first instance granted me last October to return to the United States, and an essential one to the subsequent appointment to which you had the goodness to nominate me, I have sincerely regretted, that I could not avail myself of these facilities for going home, or manifest to you my sense of your kindness, by pursuing precisely that course, which from the combined effect of considerations both of a public and private nature you had deemed most advisable.

With regard to the Seat on the Bench of the Supreme Court of the United States, you will have perceived that my incapacity to return in due time to undertake the discharge of its duties, was not the only circumstance that swayed my mind to decline it. I submitted other objections, to the consideration of your candour and indulgence; though I presumed and yet hope, that it was itself sufficient to induce an appointment of another person to the Office.

A variety of reports have reached this Country, some of them through the medium of newspaper Publications, and others by the channel of letters, respecting the appointment of a successor to the mission at this Court. During part of the Summer I was in expectation of his arrival from day to day. Untill you had received my letter of 7. January, you could not have been informed of the Cause which must personally detain me, and in the full expectation of my return, the immediate appointment of a person to take my place might naturally have been thought expedient.

It has scarcely been possible for me not sometimes to surmise, that among the arrangements which have taken place in the public administration at home, there might be objects of convenience or of facility to yourself or to the public service, which might be promoted by the substitution of another Minister at this Court, and by my recall. Were this clearly ascertained to me, I should still more strongly regret that my detention here has been the occasion of protracting the accomplishment of such an object. If when you receive this letter a new appointment shall not have been made, I can but repeat the assurance in my former letters, that any dispositions of this place, which you shall think promotive of the public interest, however they may affect my personal situation and concerns, shall have my cordial and cheerful acquiescence. I am with perfect respect, Sir, your very humble and obedt: Servt

JOHN QUINCY ADAMS.

RC (CSmH); letterbook copy (MHi: Adams Family Papers). RC docketed by JM.

1. The child, Louisa Catherine Adams, died on 15 Sept. 1812 (Paul C. Nagel, *The Adams Women: Abigail and Louisa Adams, Their Sisters and Daughters* [New York, 1987], pp. 187–88).

§ From Oliver Fitts. *18 August 1811, Warrenton, North Carolina.* Understands that Moses Mordecai of Raleigh will accept the judgeship in the Mississippi Territory. "I have been intimately acquainted with him from his infancy and do not hesitate to say he is a man of unblemished moral Character."[1]

RC (DNA: RG 59, LAR, 1809–17, filed under "Mordecai"). 2 pp.

1. After receiving an appointment as a Mississippi territorial judge from JM in April 1810, Fitts resigned the post within the year because of family difficulties arising from the death of his wife (see James Turner to JM, 20 Mar. 1810, *PJM-PS*, 2:279; Turner to JM, 22 Feb. 1813, Carter, *Territorial Papers, Mississippi*, 6:357).

From Henry Lee

DEAR SIR   ALEXA. Aug 19th. 11

   I received the other day a letter from my long loved friend Mr Stoddert
requesting my correction of the statement of a conversation, wherever he
may have misconceived my meaning. In this letter he expresses a high respect for yr. personal character, an admiration of yr. private virtues & an
anxious wish to beleive that you was actuated by a sincere desire to close
our affairs with G B: as I had asserted. He recapitulates a conversation you
held with a gentleman in fredericksburgh when lately in that town according throughout with my report of what had passed between us, but going
farther in manifestation of yr. wish to return to amity, with G B. than had
been represented by me. In conclusion, I am requested to say, whether the
statement referred to me is correct. To this letter which I intended to have
transmitted to you, but which is mislaid I sent the enclosed reply.[1] You will
I trust excuse the trouble I unexpectedly give, when I tell you that I am led
to it by my knowledge of the gross misrepresentations which prevail of
every incident connected with you, of my fixed contempt for the despicable
practice & my immutable aversion to be considered capable of participation in the vulgar vice. Mr Stodderts letter affords additional evidence to
the catalogue which exists of the conviction of a large & respectable class
of the nation, that you never can depart so widely from the system of policy
adopted by yr. predecessor as to take G B cordially by the hand. Thus persuaded, nothing short of an actual settlement of past differences with the
British govt. will ever convince this portion of the community, that your
professions are sincere. They will not detract from yr. personal purity, as
they will consider you sincere in yr. opinion of the fact, but so completely
bewildered by long cherished prejudices as to be incapable of self knowledge in this particular. In this way, will be explained & reconciled their
esteem & veneration for yr. moral character with their persuation that yr.
declarations of solicitude to settle our dispute with G. B are destitute of
sincerity. I anxiously wish & hope that a few months will prove their error
not only because I should be gratified in seeing yr. measures approved &
supported by this intelligent & respectable portion of our fellow citizens,
but from my unceasing desire to see united in the bonds of amity two
nations so exactly calculated to promote each others good, & between
whom the torch of discord should never be lighted. The only two nations
of the many in the world who understand the meaning of liberty, which
best political blessing of God to man will flourish so long as its two potent
votarys continue to cherish good will & friendship, & will become endan-
gered whenever they imbrue their hands in each others blood.

   God forbid that this latter alternative should ever occur, but occur it
must & will, unless this state of semi-warfare is exchanged shortly for the

solid enjoyments sure to follow the return of amity peace & good will. At this moment we are liable to events which may hurry the two nations into war, in contravention to the will of the two governments. If this be correct & a recollection of the affair of the little Belt affirms it to be so, are we not hourly exposed to its repititions & can these take place without plunging the two nations into blood & slaughter. Why then shall we delay the propitious epoch of restoration to our mutual concord & permanent peace. If obstacles not to be surmounted do interpose they ought to be made known to the nation & we ought to be prepared for war. A continuance in the present state of half war, is of all others the most debasing to the national character & nearly as injurious as war itself to individual prosperity. Take us out of the odious condition by restoration of amity, or by drawing the sword.

It is better to fight our way to future peace, than to drag on in this state of disputation & irritation, which must lead to war & perhaps at a period not so favorable to us as the present moment.

In expressing to you these sentiments I am sure you will derive new proofs of my solicitude for yr. magistratical honor & for our countrys good. I have been brought into this exposition of my opinions from the fulness of zeal which overpowers my mind whenever it is turned to the degrading & deteriorating condition of our country & fellow citizens, which never fails to urge me to contribute my mite to their releif.

Long as this letter is already I cannot refrain from rehearsing two matters current in this city, as they strike me to be of that sort proper for you to know, whether false or true.

Shortly after yr. departure a Mr Davis (brother to a Doctor Davis who once edited a paper in New-york under the auspices of Col. Burr)[2] came to the city & there gave out that he had been sent by General Armstrong to you for the purpose of announcing his contritition [sic] in having heretofore opposed yr. administration, & of assuring you of his future cordial co-alition & support. In furtherance of this change in his conduct, Davis asserted that he was particularly charged by Armstrong to inform you that he had been urged by R Smith & General W while in this city last winter to establish a gazette in New York for the purpose of driving you from yr. station.

Mr Davis affected great mortification in finding that you had left Washington & expressed occasionally a determination to wait upon you in yr. retirement.

What this man could have in view by his visit is as inexplicable to me as are the tales which he circulated false.

I have seen a letter from Genl. Armstrong written about the time that Davis left N York speaking of the man with abhorrence & contempt &

warning his friend against countenancing the individual or accrediting his fabrications.

General Wilkinson with whom I conversed on the subject, seemed very uneasy lest the reports might reach you & might induce you to beleive him as intriguing with Smith & others. He wrote instantly to Armstrong communicating Davis[']s tales & requiring an explanation so far as he was concerned.

Armstrong's answer had not arrived two days ago, but Wilkinson assures me that he never heard Smith or armstrong or any other person propose the measure alluded to, unless indeed a conversation with Colvil the clerk[3] last winter may be construed into such a proposition. This reptile suggested the wisdom of such a step & if I did not misconceive Wilkinson, went so far as to say he had serious thoughts of executing some such plan for the purpose of assailing you with all his might. I am persuaded poor Wilkinson is entirely innocent & I trust you will so consider him.

The other affair concerns Colvil principally; it is generally said, if not universally, that when the Secretary of State saw Colvill's reply to Smiths pamphlet, that he became extremely offended at the clerks breach of official trust & that he determined to cleanse his department by immediate dismissal of the culprit. Monroe called at the Govermt. house in the evening & communicated to you his intention. You instantly left the room when yr. lady whom Monroe found sitting with you interceded in Colvils behalf & prevailed on the secretary to recede from his determination. This tale is bottomed on Mr Dawsons authority and it excites real distress among yr. real friends, in as much as it seems to confirm previous reports respecting Colvil, which had become obsolete in a degree but are now revived.

I give to you these incidents as I heard them related, you will give to them the attention they may merit. I early did myself the honor to tell you that the union of the name of Colvill to yr. name would be received with horror by all who truely love you, this I have seen already completely verified. He may be the vile wretch he is represented to be, whether or not, he certainly is a very tattling impertinent & meddling gentleman, ready to talk write or act as his interest may dictate, in the habit of pretending to much secret intercourse with yr. family & of communicating the interchange of such intercourse whenever & wherever he can promote his views. I am my dear sir always Yr. faithful friend & most ob: h: sert.

HENRY LEE

RC and enclosure (DLC). RC docketed by JM. For enclosure, see n. 1.

1. Lee enclosed a copy of a 14 Aug. letter he had sent to Benjamin Stoddert (2 pp.), in response to a 7 Aug. letter he had received from the latter. Lee recalled having said that JM "was disposed to go as far on closing our difficulties With Great Britain, as any Sensible Fed-

eralist would go, who preferred the permanent interest & honour of his Country to all Other Considerations." Lee also recalled discussing Foster's mission on two occasions with Monroe and lamenting that the negotiations seemed to have been suspended. Monroe had responded that his conferences with Foster continued "as usual, that some delay had become Un-avoid[a]ble, the Cause of which he trusted Would be removed, as soon as Mr. Foster heard from his Court & that no reasons had occurred to induce him to despair of a happy termina-tion to our differences in the Course of a few Months." Lee further reported Monroe as saying that "the President would go all lengths to accomplish it, Consistent With the honour & Interest of the Nation." On the basis of these exchanges Lee concluded that "Concord & Amity" would be restored with Great Britain, though he observed that Stoddert had appar-ently attributed all the conversations he had reported to JM alone. JM, Lee wrote, had con-fined himself "entirely to his own Opin⟨ion⟩ & Wishes, saying nothing about Mr. Foster or the negotiation." All the conversation on the latter subject "was derived from the Secretary of State only."

2. Matthew Livingston Davis (1773–1850), the New York newspaper editor and associate of Aaron Burr, was not a physician, but his younger brother, George Davis (ca. 1778–1818), was. He was a graduate of Columbia College and had been commissioned as a naval surgeon in 1799 (Kline, *Papers of Burr*, 1:525 and n. 2).

3. Lee was referring to the State Department clerk John B. Colvin.

§ From Aaron Fontaine.[1] *19 August 1811, Louisville, Kentucky.* On the basis of "our former acquaintance," introduces his son, Maury Fontaine, who is about to take up his appointment as a midshipman in the navy.

RC (NN). 1 p.

1. Aaron Fontaine (1753–1823) had resided in Louisa County, Virginia, prior to his re-moval to Kentucky sometime before 1802. His son, Maury, resigned his midshipman's ap-pointment in November 1811 (*PJM*, 15:479 n. 1; Callahan, *List of Officers of the Navy*, p. 199).

From William Eustis

Dr. Sir,   Washington August 21. 1811.

The enclosed Letters from Governor Harrison create a strong presump-tion that hostilities will not be commenced by the Indians.[1] The movement with a respectable force up the Wabash proposed by the Governor appears from the light in which things are placed, to be adviseable: and in prefer-ence to militia it appears to me that Boyd's Regt. (who are distant from Newport where they are now halted to Louisville 150 miles & from thence by Land to Vincennes 120 miles) ought to be taken. This force with two companies of regulars from Vincennes & two troops of cavalry or mounted rifle men will I presume secure a peaceable march to the extremity of the new purchase. To receive a seasonable notice of your approbation previ-ous to issuing the order would be highly gratifying: but as time is all important in order to enable Boyd's command to reascend the waters before the winter sets in I am in doubt whether it is necessary to await an answer.

In answering the Agents on the subject of a visit from the several Indian chiefs I have stated that as the season is already far advanced, and the engagements of the President during the session of Congress may prevent due attention to the Chiefs, it is desireable that their intended visit should be postponed untill the spring of the year.

The two Mr Coles leave the city this day and will probably be at Montpelier in the course of the week.

Pressed by the departure of the mail I have time only to ask a return of the Ltres from Govr. Harrison. With the greatest respect

W. EUSTIS

RC (DLC). Docketed by JM.

1. Eustis probably enclosed two letters he had received from William Henry Harrison under the dates of 6 and 7 Aug. 1811. In the second letter Harrison reported that Tecumseh had left Vincennes in order "to excite the Southern Indians to war against us" but added that "I do not think that there is any danger of any further hostility until he returns." Harrison announced his own plans in the interim to take advantage of Tecumseh's absence and seize "a most favorable opportunity for breaking up his Confederacy" (Esarey, *Letters of Harrison*, 1:542–51; listed as received 20 Aug. 1811 [DNA: RG 107, Register of Letters Received]).

¶ To Anthony Charles Cazenove. Letter not found. *22 August 1811*. Acknowledged in Cazenove to JM, 6 Sept. 1811. Places an order for Madeira wine from Messrs. Murdoch.

To James Monroe

DEAR SIR   MONTPELIER Friday 23d. Aug. [1811]

I ascribe to the heat of the weather my not having yet had the pleasure of your promised visit. We hope when the obstacle is removed that we shall have the gratification increased by the company of Mrs. Monroe. Among the papers now forwarded is another note from Mr. F.[1] His late ones breathe a spirit which it is difficult to account for without the painful supposition that he believes it not uncongenial with the sentiments of the P. Regt. as well as of the Cabinet. At his age & with his prospects, he would scarcely pay court to the latter, in opposition to the views of the former; especially in a stile beyond the mere policy of decent respect for the views of the Cabinet. Are you aware that the Extra rider deposits his return Mail at Fredericksbg where it passes into the general Mail for Washington. Your communications to the Dept. of State ought therefore to be sealed &

franked as in other cases. I happened to observe that those of the last week, were deficient in both respects; & of course applied a remedy. Accept my best regards.

JAMES MADISON

RC (DLC: Monroe Papers).

1. JM was very likely referring to Foster's 16 Aug. 1811 letter to Monroe, written from Philadelphia and calling the attention of the secretary of state to an earlier letter he had written on 23 July to protest the large number of "suspicious" vessels fitting out in American ports. Foster repeated his protest, claiming that these "suspicious" vessels were fitted out "nominally as Merchant ships, which have afterwards become Cruizers against the British trade." The minister added that he had been specially instructed by the Prince Regent to complain of these practices as a breach of American neutrality (DNA: RG 59, NFL, Great Britain).

§ From James Cooper, Jr. *23 August 1811, Philadelphia.* Offers himself as a candidate for the position of consul at Santiago de Cuba, recently vacated by the death of Maurice Rogers. "Having a perfect knowledge of the place from a long Residence, & being particularly intimate with its local Mercantile Usages, many Merchants of this Port, have intimated a wish that I had the Appointment, & would transact their business."

RC (DNA: RG 59, LAR, 1809–17, filed under "Cooper"). 2 pp. Endorsed with the signatures of twenty-two Philadelphia merchants. Enclosed in Cooper to Monroe, 3 Sept. 1811 (ibid.).

To Richard Cutts

DEAR SIR   MONTPELIER Aug. 24. 1811
    I have recd. your favor of the   instant.[1] I hope you will never withold a line to me when convenient to yourself, from an apprehension that it would not be so to me. The only regret I could ever feel would be, that my returns might so little repay you. To supply the deficiency, I again inclose some of the S. Newspapers, in wch. you may possibly find things worth reading, and not republished in papers nearer to you. The hostile effusions from Baltimore, having a source not to be mistaken, seem for the present to be relaxed. That they will be renewed in every shape that deadly hatred can prompt, is to be looked for. The entire failure or rather recoil of the attempts hitherto made, will be far from assuaging the vindictive sensation. We begin to wonder at the delay of the Jno. Adam[s], as we did at that of the Essex. From the last information, she must be either waiting in France or must experience a tedious passage. The state of our affairs with England,

speaks to you thro' the circumstances which have been mentioned in the Gazettes. We have had good crops of Wheat; and are promised most exuberant ones of Indian Corn; the weather at the critical period having been first wet, & then very hot. My Thermometer however since my return hither, has never quite reached 88°. At present the weather is delightfully cool. I wish our enjoyment of it could be made compleat by the association of your hous[e]hold. Remember me affectionately to Mrs. C. & the little ones; and accept my esteem & best regards

JAMES MADISON

RC (MHi); Tr (NjP: Crane Collection). RC docketed by Cutts.

1. Left blank by JM. No letter from Cutts to JM in August 1811 has been found.

To William Eustis

DEAR SIR   MONTPELIER Aug 24. 1811

I have recd. yours of the 21. with the letters from Govr. Harrison, and herewith return the latter. As the exhibition properly managed, of an imposing force on the Northern frontier beyond the Ohio, may in several views, be of critical importance at the present juncture, I concur in your opinion of the measure and of the expediency of applying Boyd's Regiment in aid of it. The late caution to Govr. Harrison, agst. needless hostilities, will conspire with his own reflections, in making the occasion subservient rather to preventing them, hereafter, than to bringg. them on at present. That immediate commencement of them, is not meditated by the Prophets party seems to be fairly inferrable from the communications recd. by you. If the visit from the Southern Indians can be conveniently parried till the Spring, it will be then preferable for the reasons which you intimate.

We have at length an exchange of a hot spell of weather for an opposite extreme. We hope it will have its effect in reconciling Mrs. E. & yourself, to the journey in which we are interested. Accept my esteem & best regards

JAMES MADISON

P. S. I add to the inclosures an address in support of Govr. H's proceedings,[1] & a letter from J. Green. The latter you will please, after perusal to send to the Treasury Dept.

RC (MHi: Eustis Papers). For surviving enclosure, see n. 1.

1. Inhabitants of Knox County, Indiana Territory, to JM, ca. 31 July 1811.

From Caesar A. Rodney

My Dear Sir,   Wilmington August 24th. 1811.

The enclosed letter is from Mr. Kintzing of Philada. of the house of Pratt & Kintzing.[1] With Mr. Hogan I am personally unacquainted, but I rely with much confidence on the character given him by Mr. Kintzing whom I have long known. In my professional line I have in one case, where Mr. Hogan was a witness, observed with pleasure his integrity & his candor. Mr. Kintzing is well disposed towards the administration, & is as much of a republican as the zeal of his partner will admit.

In this part of the country there is but one sentiment, on the subject of Mr Smith's publications, among the friends of goverment; and the federalists appear to be perfectly silent—His writings have proved ruinous to his own cause. Well might Job exclaim "Oh that mine enemy had written a book."[2] There is a great deal of sound sense & justness in this passage. Mr. Smith's book has been highly benificial to the administration. It has drawn forth conclusive testimony in their favor, from the most authoritative source, if any evidence were required, to refute a groundless calumny, which they who circulate, do not beleive.

It is reported that a British sloop of war is within our capes & has captured a ship bound to Lisbon. But the report wants confirmation. A French privateer is at anchor off New Castle & there is another in the Bay. Perhaps the British are on the "look out" for them. Present my best respects to Mrs. Madison & beleive me Dr Sir Yours Truly & Affectionately

C. A Rodney

RC (DLC). For enclosure, see n. 1.

1. Rodney enclosed a 20 Aug. 1811 letter he had received from Abraham Kintzing (DNA: RG 59, LAR, 1809–17; 1 p.) mentioning that Patrick Hogan was about to take up residence at Santiago de Cuba and suggesting that he be appointed consul there to replace the deceased Maurice Rogers. Hogan had apparently served for several years as an agent and supercargo for Kintzing.

2. Rodney paraphrased Job 31:35, "Oh that one would hear me! behold, my desire *is, that* the Almighty would answer me, and *that* mine adversary had written a book."

§ From Aaron H. Palmer. *24 August 1811, New York.* Solicits JM's patronage of an office he has established in New York for the translation of "all kinds of Papers and Documents relating to Commercial, Maritime, and Judicial Proceedings," in French, Italian, Spanish, Portuguese, Dutch, German, Swedish, and Danish.

RC (DLC: Madison Collection, Rare Book Division). Printed broadside; signed, dated, and addressed by Palmer.

From Paul Hamilton

DEAR SIR   CITY OF WASHINGTON August 25th. 1811

The subject of the enclosed letter as connected with our naval establishment being important, before replying to the suggestions of the Governor,
I beg leave to refer it to your consideration and to receive your instructions.[1] Should you rather make it ground for a communication to Congress,
on the letter being returned, I will lay it up specially for the purpose.

We have no news here. Of late we have had unusually heavy rains, insomuch as that, a great part of Pennsylvania Avenue has been twice over-
flowed, and I have seen some of the good people, in the small houses along
it, standing knee deep in water, on the first floor—since which, the heat for
days successively has been intense, the Mercury rising on an average to 92.
Notwithstanding the City continues to be healthy, though if the hot
weather lasts a little longer, I cannot doubt that the coming will prove to
be a second edition of the last September. Dr. Thornton who has been for
some weeks confined by a severe illness to his bed, is now so far convales-
cent as to be able to ride out.

I earnestly hope that you and Mrs. Madison are in the possession of perfect health; and that you will return to this place renovated for future
duties.

I present to you both the united best wishes of my family and self, and
avail myself of this occasion to renew to you the assurance of the sincere respect and cordial attachment with which I have the honor to be,
Dr. Sir, yrs.

PAUL HAMILTON

P. S. In a late excursion to the mountains in company with Mr. & Mrs.
Eustis and Mrs. Hamilton, I had the pleasure of spending part of a day and
a night at Mrs. Washington's. She was very hearty, and spoke of taking a
journey into Pennsylvania, for the purpose of placing her Son at College.
A misfortune which befell Dr. Eustis and rendered traveling painful to him,
prevented our extending our journey farther, otherwise, I believe we would
have paid our respects to you. The expedition however is again a subject of
consultation in the same party at my house today at dinner.

P. H.

RC (DLC). Docketed by JM. For the enclosure (2 pp.), see n. 1.

1. On 21 Aug. 1811 Hamilton acknowledged the receipt of two letters, dated 2 and 6 July,
from Orleans territorial governor W. C. C. Claiborne; and he promised that he would transmit the latter letter, which he described as being of importance and relating to the naval
establishment, to the president (DNA: RG 45, Misc. Letters Sent). The 6 July letter reported
that Claiborne was about to meet at Pascagoula with Col. Francisco Maximilian de St. Maxent,
the acting Spanish governor at Pensacola, to discuss the demand Claiborne had made on

29 June of the commander of the Spanish garrison at Mobile that he allow unrestricted passage on the Mobile River to U.S. vessels carrying supplies to Fort Stoddert. Although Claiborne could not say "what may be the issue of the Contemplated Conference," he had previously assumed that the Spanish authorities would reject his demand, in which event he had already instructed the commander of the U.S. naval vessels that would convoy the supply ships to "oppose force to force," should any attempt be made to detain them. The news Claiborne conveyed to Hamilton that Spain had appointed the duke del Infantado to be captain general of Cuba, however, led the governor to surmise that in expectation of the duke's early arrival, "the Spanish Agents are greatly desirous, that things at Mobile, should for the present, remain in Statu quo."

"As regards Cuba," Claiborne continued, "permit me to observe, that its dependence on a foreign Power, is seen by me, with sincere regret; The destiny of that Island, is highly interesting to the United States; It is in truth the Mouth of the Mississippi, and the Nation possessing it, may Controul the Western Commerce. Next to acquiring the sovereignty of Cuba, it is most important to my Country, that it be placed in the situation, *Malta formerly was;* erected into an Independent State, and its Sovereignty guaranteed by the United States and other Nations. Unless ⟨an⟩ Act of that kind takes place, the possession of the Island of Cuba, will sooner or later be cause of War; and may tend to destroy the good understanding, which might otherwise exist, between the United States, and the *Countr⟨y⟩ now termed Spanish America;* A *Country* that cannot from the nature of things long remain, in *its* present Collonial Condition." In a postscript Claiborne added that he had no doubt the Spanish commander at Mobile had been ordered "to oppose the passage of our vessels" and that he had received news that a battery had been recently erected in front of the fort for that purpose (DNA: RG 45, Misc. Letters Received; see also Claiborne to Commodore John Shaw, 10 June 1811, Claiborne to Governor Folch "or the Officer Commanding the Fort at Mobile," 29 June 1811, Rowland, *Claiborne Letter Books,* 5:270–71, 281–82).

From John K. Smith

S ı R,   NEW ORLEANS August 25th 1811.
     I have now the honor to enclose you the two remaining plats of Land located for Genr. La Fayette.
     Mr. Duplantier who has been very much indisposed for many months past & who besides has been Occupied in settling his late merchantile Concerns* (having failed) promises to afford a particular statement of the situation Value &c. of the lands which have been located for your information. I have the honor to be with great respect Sir yr Ob St.

                                                                          J K SMITH

*Mr D. will be possessed of a Competent fortune after settling his Concerns.

RC (DNA: RG 49, Special Acts, Lafayette Grant, La.). Docketed by Gallatin, "Smith enclosing La Fayette's two Surveys." Below the docket is a note in Gallatin's hand dated 18 Mar. 1813: "Congress has not acted on the rejected claim of Cooley. The issuing of patents to La Fayette was from delicacy (Mr Madison being his agent) suspended to give time to any such act on the part of Congress. Sufficient time having elapsed, & La Fayette having sold the land,

the patents are now requested. No legal objection appears on the papers and the Commissioner of the General land office is requested, if he discovers none, to have the patents issued and deliver⟨ed⟩ for Gen. La Fayette's use to Mr Madison. His obedt. Servt. Albert Gallatin."
Enclosures not found.

From James Monroe

DEAR SIR   [ca. 26 August 1811]

Some very interesting domestick concerns which could not well be postponed, seconded by the state of the wound on my leg, prevented my having the pleasure of waiting on you in the last week, but I shall be with you to morrow if no accident presents an obstacle to it. I shall bring all the papers with me which it will be necessary to submit to your view at this time. Indeed many things have been postponed, to afford me an opportunity before I took any step in them, of se[e]ing & consulting you. I do not know however that any injury has occurr'd as yet by the delay in any case. I am dear Sir very sincerely your friend & servant

JAS MONROE

RC (DLC: Rives Collection, Madison Papers). Dated ca. August 1811 in *Index to the James Madison Papers*. Conjectural date assigned here on the assumption that Monroe wrote in response to JM to Monroe, 23 Aug. 1811. Docketed by JM.

From William Eaton

(Confidential)   NEW YORK 29th. of August 1811.

Your Excellency will please excuse the freedom I take, (being as I presume intirely unknown to you) but Conceiving it the duty and priviledge of every republican to impart their Ideas to Each other, in a decent plain and familiar way—and having a great anxiety to avert the impending Storms—Which I think—more than commonly threaten at this time, inspires me with confidence and impels me to write. I wish Sir I could make you acquainted with my sincere motives, and Particular attachment, to your Person, Administration, and our Countrys welfare, without giving you all the trouble I shall now do. My Countrys future greatness, Prosperity and happiness, has from my youth been the great Solicitude of my heart—Perhap[s] too much so, for my private interest—and this also adds to prompt this address. Be pleased Sir, here to permit me to Express to you—the pleasure I have derived from Every Executive act of ⟨your⟩ Administration (except in the one only instance of the appointment of Mr Smith as Secretary of State). I did not then think him fit for the Station, and I now think he has Shamefully abused the confidence placed in him and forfeited all right to the confidence of the republican Citizens of the United States. The importance of Unanimity of Sentiment at the present (I think awful) Scituation of the times, and the Choice of our next President are the Stimulants to this Communication. We are I think you will admit Sir, on the very brink of a war, with England. There is not, I think Sir—a person in the Union— who wishes more than I do—to punish her for her Insolence, injustice and Encroachments on our rights and her barbarity and inhumanity to the Seaman of the world, and her utmost defiance of the God of nations who has made the seas for the free high road for all to traverse. But Sir, I fear, really fear, if we at this Perilous time are compelled to go to war with her—we as a nation Shall be ruined. Then Sir—Can we not avert it for a time? Say till after the next Presidential Election? Shall we not in attempting to Scourge her as she really merits more than Equally Scourge ourselves? Shall we not Sir, considering the many Timothy Pickerings we have among us and the wealth they have—be unable to designate the Enimy from the friend? and would not Sir their resources be a great aid and Stimulant, with the ungovernable man—to throw us in to Confusion? Could we Sir banish from among us so great a Portion of our Citizen? But Sir what is best to be done I do not pretend to Say. God only knows—and may he alone direct the movements of our Government—that they may redound to the Glory and good of all. I have lately, been admitted to private Conferences (not having declared my Political Sentiment there) of some influential Federalists and find it Sir to be a determination among them, in case of war with England, to aid her, and oppose the measures of our government all in their power— and Sir I really believe they wish, and Stir England to make war at this time. Now Sir—if this is the Case, any reasonable man must foresee that the above must throw us into Confusion. The Choice of the next President Engages my thought, now Sir—because—I think an Early nomination by the great Leading Republicans and a tender of your Services another term of 4 years would, if Shortly done, be a means of preventing a greater division in that great body of the People than is already made. You no doubt have been apprized Sir, that a very Large, influential, and Powerful party who now call themselves Republicans in this State and making arrangements in the other States to carry the Election of President to their own likings and who if not Counteracted or united will sap the very foundation of Republicanism. They have Engaged and are Engaging Printers and Presses to Send to almost Every State—(this I know from a Brother of mine who is a Printer[1] and who has been applied to, to go to the Southward for this purpose). And here Sir I beg Leave to anxiously intreat you to offer again and in Season for the great Station you now fill with so much honour, that the People may form a decisive mind at once—and may that God who orders all things, so in Mercy order, that you may be retained in office to

434

the great blessing of us all. I hope Sir you will have the goodness to Consider this Letter only as the pure motives of Friendship and disinterestedness and that I do not wish to assume the ability to give advice, but convey to you the thoughts of a Simple individual actuated by a pure desire for his Countrys welfare. You perhaps Sir, may wish to know who the person is who is giving this trouble to one who is now over Loaded with cares for his Countrys welfare. I beg to be permitted to trouble you to notice my Political history, that it may in Some measure give a first proof of my attachment and desire to be useful. I am a native of the State of Massachusetts born in 1772 brought up in the neighbourhood and acquaintance of our much Lamented Col John Whiting who died at Washington Last Autumn[2]—and also Timothy Whiting Esqr his Brother—untill 21 years of age. In 1797 began to display my Republican Sentiments in Bridge Port Connecticut where I commenced mercantile Pursuits—and here I first reaped the fruits of political persecution. In 1799—I removed to Philada. where under the notice of Doctor Leib, I became an Influential advocate for and Supporter of Mr Jefferson A[d]ministration untill the autum of 1803. From the fall of 1803 to some time 1804 at the request of Republican friends (not to be named) I travelled in the New England states princippally to aid the Republican cause—attended the trial of Col Gardner in Boston in June that year[3]—found this to aid me astonishingly in the cause I Embarked—from Autum 1804 to the 1st of May the present year I have resided in New Bern (N. C.) and under the Eye of Mr Blackledge—by Extensive businiss became Influential throughout his Exlection district and also many places in the back counties of that State—and there I Continued to Exert my feeble abilities in aid of the great Republican cause. In August at the Congressional Election in 1807 in New Bern before a very large assemblage of voters—(Each party nearly Equal) (having previously imbibed very Exalted Ideas of your ability and attachment to our Countrys welfare)—I there proposed 9 Cheers to be given for you as a candidate for the then next President. This was received and Echoed by the Republicans with such unbounded approbation—I ever after was persecuted there by the federalist. The 2d of October same year we had a Son born and Mrs E. being a true Democratic Republican, we took the liberty to Call him Charles, James, Madison, he is now an uncommon promising child. The 1 of may the present year my mercantile pursuits (owing to the Embarrassed Scituation of the times) having failed—I removed to this city, with the intention to make this State my residence. I have Expended I presume 2000 Dollars in the cause of Republicanism and hope I may yet be placed in a Scituation to aid it as much more.[4] My oldest Son William S. 15 years of age is a true genuine republican, and bids fair to make my place good. I am Sensible Sir were you to notice and answer all such communications, you could not render your Country that Service it demanded or you have so beneficially bestowed. I shall therefore Expect you to make this Confidential—and shall not Expect a reply, Unless you might wish to Command my Services, in which Case I shall be happy Sir and able to present you with unquestionable, Credentials of my attachment, fidelity, activity, and honour. I have the honour to be Sir, very Respectfully, your Excellencys most obedt Servt

WILLIAM EATON

RC (DLC).

1. Eaton could have been referring to either of the printers Ebenezer or Theophilus Eaton. The former had published newspapers in Rome, Geneva, and Scipio, New York, around the turn of the century, and in 1807 he established the *North Star* in Danville, Vermont. The latter had published in 1808 *The President* in Oxford, New York (Brigham, *History and Bibliography of American Newspapers*, 1:717, 2:1082, 1407).

2. See John Graham to JM, 5 Sept. 1810, *PJM-PS*, 2:528.

3. On 20 June 1804 Lt. Col. Robert Gardner and three other officers of the First Division of the Legionary Brigade were court-martialed on three charges—unmilitary conduct, neglect of duty, and disobedience of orders—preferred by their commanding officer, Brig. Gen. John Winslow. The trial excited "much public interest," and after Gardner was found guilty of two of the three charges against him, he was dismissed and forbidden to hold any military commission for the remainder of his life (Boston *Columbian Centinel & Massachusetts Federalist*, 23 and 27 June and 1 Aug. 1804).

4. At this point Eaton wrote and then crossed through: "I Expect shortly to be free from Embarrassments within this State Sir."

§ From the Seventy-Six Association of South Carolina. *29 August 1811, Charleston.* Transmits according to resolution a copy of an oration delivered on 4 July by member Benjamin A. Markley.[1]

RC (DLC). 1 p. Signed by Joseph Johnson and four others.

1. *An Oration, Delivered on 4th July, 1811* (Charleston, 1811; Shaw and Shoemaker 23284).

§ From Josef Yznardy. *29 August 1811, Rota.* Reports developments since leaving Cadiz in February 1810 when the French closed the port. Has been refused access to the city, but has been able to communicate with Hackley. Describes the efforts he and his son have made to rescue American property and repatriate seamen when eight vessels were stranded in the Bay of Cadiz in March 1810. Met with little success. His son was detained by a British naval officer; a vessel he had hired was sold by the Spanish, and its owner is now demanding to be repaid. Mentions that French corsairs have seized several American vessels and brought them into Cadiz, Seville, and Sanlucar de Barrameda. His protests have not been answered satisfactorily, and in April and May 1811 he sent copies of these protests to Hackley and Meade in Cadiz so that they might inform JM. Discusses the personal and financial hardships he has endured in the course of doing his consular duty and suggests that the U.S. should now pay what it owes him on the accounts he has remitted to the secretary of state. These circumstances explain what has happened to the consulate at Cadiz. Fears that the region, and Andalusia as well, will suffer famine as a result of military occupation and poor harvests.

RC (DNA: RG 59, CD, Cadiz); duplicate (DLC). Each RC 3 pp.; in Spanish; in a clerk's hand, signed by Yznardy.

§ From Daniel Lescallier. *30 August 1811, Norfolk, Virginia.* "I have the honor to inform you of my arrival in the United States, and at Norfolk, in the capacity of Consul general of france by the Emperor's Decree of Octr. 7th. 1810. My residence is to be at N. York."[1] Regrets that JM will not be in Washington when he passes through the city in a few days.

RC (NN). 1 p.

1. JM issued a proclamation on 25 Sept. 1811 recognizing Lescallier in his capacity as consul general for France (*National Intelligencer,* 15 Oct. 1811).

¶ To John Graham. Letter not found. *31 August 1811.* Acknowledged in Graham to JM, 3 Sept. 1811. Transmits a memorandum of purchases to be made and forwarded by Mr. Barry.

§ Account with St. Mary's College. *1 September 1811.* Lists charges to JM amounting to $16.50 for one quarter's tuition "ending this day" and school supplies for John Payne Todd.

Ms (MdBS: Day Book, 1810–13). 1 p.

From John Armstrong

Dear Sir,   Rhinebeck 2d. September 1811.
The enclosed paragraph, coming from the quarter it does, would not have made any declaration from me either proper or necessary,[1] (any more than that in the National Intelligencer, by which it was followed),[2] had not a common friend, for whose opinions I have much respect, hinted to me the propriety of Stating, either privately to you, or publicly in a Newspaper, what was the fact. In choosing between these two modes I could not hesitate & hence it is that I now offer to you the assurance, that the first mentioned paragraph is substantially false, attributing to me conversations I never held. Indeed the anachronisms in the story will entirely destroy its credit with those who give themselves the trouble of enquiring into dates, as I did not arrive in Washington, untill after M. Erwing's appointment had been confirmed by the Senate.[3] I beg you to beleive that I am, with the highest respect and consideration, Your most Obedient & very humble Servant

                                        John Armstrong.

437

RC and enclosure (DLC). RC addressed by Armstrong to JM in Orange County, Virginia. Docketed by JM. Enclosure dated March 1812 in the *Index to the James Madison Papers* (see n. 1).

1. Armstrong enclosed a newspaper reprint of an article that had first appeared in the Baltimore *Federal Republican* to the effect that the former minister to France, after leaving Washington the winter before, had stopped in Baltimore where he was "generally communicative and unreserved on the subject of public men and measures." The report alleged that Armstrong had "indulged a propensity to sarcasm" on the matter of "foreign appointments," especially those of James Bowdoin and George Erving. Armstrong was further said to have been most critical of the latter, both for his being the son of a Loyalist and for his conduct throughout the crisis occasioned by the electoral tie between Burr and Jefferson in 1800. Erving's subsequent career in Europe had been characterized by "follies and indiscretions" to the extent that JM had seen fit to reprove him on the basis of a letter he had received from Armstrong, and it was also claimed that JM had told Armstrong that he would never again nominate Erving to office. Erving, however, paid a visit to Monticello, and after he returned to Washington bearing a letter from Jefferson, JM nominated him to the court of Denmark, a decision which Armstrong disapproved and which JM reportedly told Armstrong he had made *"in opposition to his own judgment,"* adding that *"the appointment rested with the Senate, and . . . he should be pleased with a rejection."* The report repeated the allegation, made by Robert Smith, that Erving had fraudulently pocketed $22,392 of public money and concluded with the verdict that JM was "a mere tool of Jefferson, and wanting in integrity and intellect to fit him for the station he holds."

2. The *National Intelligencer*, on 13 Aug. 1811, in noting the *Federal Republican* account of Armstrong's actions in Baltimore, declared that there could be "no doubt that ⟨th⟩is gentleman will seize the first opportunity of authorising a contradiction ⟨of⟩ a report calculated and no doubt in⟨te⟩nded to weaken the confidence repos⟨ed⟩ in him by republicans as a sound politician."

3. Erving's nomination as special minister to Denmark was confirmed by the Senate on 20 Dec. 1810, the same day on which Armstrong arrived in Washington after returning from France (*Senate Exec. Proceedings*, 2:158; Armstrong to JM, 11 Dec. 1810, n. 1). In his private correspondence Armstrong had certainly expressed himself sarcastically about Erving's mission to Denmark. Writing to Jonathan Russell on 19 Jan. 1811, he had expressed surprise at Erving's selection "(after so distinguished An anti-gallican Career in Spain) to be Minister of the U. S. at a Court so notoriously under french influence as that of Denmark," and he added that "this consideration, with others, would have defeated the nomination, had it been decided on by the Senate one day later than it was. Even the Presdt. was heard to say, that he wished the nomination to fail" (RPB-JH: Russell Papers).

From William Eustis

DEAR SIR,   WASHINGTON Septr 2. 1811.

Since the receipt of your Letter of the 24th of August enclosing the papers from Govr. Harrison &c nothing very remarkable has occurred. The alternation of alarm and of quiescence observable in the public papers, particularly in those of New York, is the natural consequence of the variegated intelligence from Europe and of the movements of the British Marine on the coast. By a letter from Baltimore I am informed that a vessel arrived at that port passed a squadron of three ships of the line in the gulph stream in the night conjectured to be the fleet under Sir J. Yorke.[1] In case the aggressions shall be multiplied and come nearer I fear we shall be obliged to adjourn the court martial. The absence of so many field officers, and more particularly those of the artillery, from the posts on the sea board, is sensibly felt: and but for the confidence that no act of hostility will be authorised by the B. Government previous to the receipt of Mr Fosters despatches, I should think that Colo. Burbeck & Major Stoddard should be remanded to N. York & Major Porter to R. Island. At the former place I am assured the works will be completed in all the present month, and that on an emergency the guns may be all mounted within that time. R. Island is still vulnerable. With the highest respect

W. EUSTIS

RC (DLC). Docketed by JM.

1. Ever since Foster had raised in mid-July the prospect of British retaliation against JM's policy of nonintercourse, speculation was rife as to what this might involve. The *National Intelligencer*, on several occasions, alluded to the matter and had discussed whether it would take the form of commercial restrictions or "maritime war," including the possibility of a blockade of the American coast. On 29 Aug. the administration newspaper reported news from London, under 1 and 5 July datelines, that Rear Admiral Sir Joseph Yorke had sailed for America with a "small squadron" of five vessels, said to be "large enough to blow the whole American navy out of the water." The conduct of the squadron, however, was said to be contingent upon how the U.S. settled the dispute over the incident between the *Lille Belt* and the *President* (see JM to Richard Cutts, 23 July 1811, and n. 3; *National Intelligencer*, 25 July and 20, 29, and 31 Aug. 1811).

§ From Chauncy Hall. *2 September 1811, Meriden, Connecticut.* Describes a diving outfit he invented in October 1810. Presents six propositions so that "a man may Live and Work in the Diveing Dress under Water," including the capability of raising or moving ships. Recalls putting his thoughts on paper in Washington and receiving letters patent for this invention by JM's direction in December 1810.

RC (DLC). 3 pp. Cover marked by Hall, "In Confidence."

§ From the Tammany Society of Newport. *2 September 1811, Newport, Rhode Island.* The members express their indignation at the insults inflicted on the nation by the European belligerents, but they are satisfied that administration overtures "to the two great contending powers, have produced on the part of one, a manifestation of a more just and liberal policy." They regret that truth, reasoning, and argument have failed to remove the orders in council and the "long catalogue of aggressions of the other." While they would be the last to advocate war, if it should prove necessary they will contribute their best efforts to attain their rights, convinced as they are of "the uprightness of your conduct throughout the whole course of your public life, and the perfect justice of our countrys cause." They invoke the "great Spirit, who presides over the destinies of all" to direct the national councils and take JM "under his peculiar care."

RC (DNA: RG 59, ML). 1 p. Signed by Nicholas Easton, grand sachem, and witnessed by Bernard Hill, Jr., secretary. Cover marked "Private." Docketed by JM.

From John Graham

DEAR SIR   DEPT OF STATE [3 September 1811]

Mr Hamilton arrived last Night with the Despatches by the "John Adams." By the advice of his Father I have decided that he should go on with them to you—thinking it probable that you might wish to make some enquiries of him on subjects not touched on in the Letters.

It was my intention not to have opened any of the Despatches but I thought it right to inform the Heads of Departments who were here that I was ready to do so if they wished it and Mr Hamilton signifying a desire to know the contents of Mr Russells Letters they were opened accordingly and submitted to him & the Secy of War.

There are some Letters from Mr Adams of later date than those heretofore received, say to the 19th May—much of them being in Cypher they are detained to be decyphered. He had not received intelligence of the change of situation intended for him.

I had the Honor to receive your Letter of the 31st. Augt this Morng. and have seen Mr Barry and given him the Memo it contained. He promises to purchase the things immediately and send them on as you direct. I wish they were now ready as in that case Mr Hamn. could take them with him.

For the first time since I was a Child I have had a severe bilious fever. Since thursday week I have been confined to my Room. The arrival of the Despatches brought me to the Office today but I yet feel almost too feeble & weak for Business. With Sentiments of the most affectionate attachment I am Dear Sir Your Mo: Obt Sert

JOHN GRAHAM

The Letters inclosed in yours have been sent as directed. The Prospect of the Maryland Election is much against us.[1]

RC (DLC). Dated ca. September 1811 in *Index to the James Madison Papers*. Date assigned here on the basis that Paul Hamilton, Jr., arrived in Washington on 2 Sept. 1811 (*National Intelligencer*, 3 Sept. 1811). Cover marked by Graham, "Mr Hamilton."

1. Graham's alarm about the prospects in the coming contest for electors of the Maryland Senate may have been heightened by two essays signed "A Democrat," appearing in the *National Intelligencer*, 29 and 31 Aug. 1811, and written in response to a series of attacks on the administration by "A Sincere Republican," printed in the Baltimore *Federal Republican*.

From Paul Hamilton

Dear Sir   Washington Septr. 3d. 1811

The John Adams arrived at Boston on the 28th. ult., and my Son reached this place with his dispatches on yesterday; and as I do not consider him as having entirely fulfilled his duty untill he shall have delivered them to you, I have desired him to proceed with them by this days Mail. The informality of his not carrying them to Mr. Monroe, in the first instance, will be accounted for and excused by the circumstance of his residing beyond you— he will be at your command, to convey the papers to Mr. Monroe, after you have seen them, if you think proper so to employ him—and I will not conceal that I shall be much gratified, if by doing so, you afford him an opportunity of paying his respects not only to Mr. Monroe, but to Mr. Jefferson also, for both of whom I have taken care to inspire him with great veneration.

Mr. Graham has afforded me the perusal of the letters from Messrs. Smith & Russell—those from the first being of old date, and considering the late decisions by Sir William Scott afford no interest.[1] Mr. Russell's to the Departt of State, and the copy of one from him to Mr. Smith remove every doubt as to a revocation of the french Decrees;[2] and I think it would be a happy circumstance if they could speedily be communicated to the public, provided you think it consistent with propriety.

My Son having great anxiety to set off I shall, at presents [*sic*], only add my best wishes and affectionate regard for you and Mrs. Madison in which my family join me. I am Dr. Sir truly yrs.

                                                                PAUL HAMILTON

RC (DLC). Docketed by JM.

1. Hamilton had evidently been reading a series of dispatches and other material sent by John Spear Smith to Monroe between 5 and 27 June 1811. Letters under the dates of 5, 6, 8, and 16 June dealt with seizures under the orders in council and the reluctance of the British ministry to consider the repeal of those orders. Letters dated 19, 26, and 27 June were concerned with Sir William Scott's condemnation of the *Fox* and other vessels (DNA: RG 59, DD, Great Britain; extracts printed in *ASP, Foreign Relations*, 3:420–21).

2. Hamilton referred to Jonathan Russell to Monroe, 15 July 1811, enclosing copies of Russell to John Spear Smith, 5 and 14 July 1811. The first of these enclosures informed Smith that to the best of Russell's knowledge the Berlin and Milan decrees had not been executed against American property since 1 Nov. 1810. The second discussed the matter in greater detail, pointing out that legal complexities relating to particular cases should not be construed as evidence that the French decrees were still in force, although Russell conceded at the same time that it would probably be French policy to employ "municipal" regulations to exclude British produce from Europe. This last matter, Russell observed, was of no concern to the U.S.; it was sufficient that the Berlin and Milan decrees had ceased to operate on the high seas. Great Britain, he concluded, could therefore no longer justify the orders in council on any principle of the law of retaliation.

Russell's 15 July covering letter also enclosed his correspondence with French officials on these subjects and reported the release of many previously detained vessels. In response to

441

Russell's request for a clear statement to be sent back on the *John Adams* of the French regulations that would govern trade with the U.S., the duc de Bassano replied that "no such communication would be made here, but that M. Serrurier would be fully instructed on this head." Otherwise, Russell announced that American produce (except sugar) would be admitted to France without special licenses, that coffee, sugar, and colonial produce would be admitted with licenses, and that everything arriving from Great Britain or places under its control would be prohibited (DNA: RG 59, DD, France; extracts printed in *ASP, Foreign Relations,* 3:447, 504–8).

From Levett Harris

SIR,   ST PETERSBURG 3 September 1811.

Mr. Swinguin,[1] who will have the honor to deliver this letter to Your Excellency, is a young Gentleman of rank & family: he goes to America attached to Mr. Kosloff the new Consul Gl. Successor to mr. Daschkoff; but principally with a view to see the United states & to Study our manners & customs.

The Count Romanzoff has particularly recommended him to me, and as Mr. Swinguin has cultivated the fine Arts with Success the Chancellor seems to take a lively interest in his visit.

Permit me therefore Sir, to second the anxious desire of Mr. Swinguin in procuring him by means of this introduction the honor of Your Excellency's Acquaintance. I have the honor to be, with the highest consideration, Sir, Your most Obedient humble Servant

LEVETT HARRIS.

RC (NN). Docketed by JM.

1. Harris was referring to Pavel P. Svin'in, secretary-designate to the new Russian consul general Nikolai Kozlov. Kozlov was appointed to Philadelphia after Andrei Dashkov had been promoted to replace Fedor Pahlen as minister to the U.S. on 9 Aug. 1811 (Bashkina et al., *The United States and Russia,* pp. 534 n. 9, 774 and n. 3).

From Paul Hamilton

DEAR SIR.   CITY OF WASHINGTON September 4th. 1811

The enclosed I have just now received, and altho' it contains nothing specifically important, yet having connection with our foreign relations I think it not amiss to forward it to you. I think that, combining this arrival with the certainty of the departure of Sir Joseph Yorke with his squadron from England, something interesting must very soon be developed.

I have the satisfaction to inform you that the admission here among the knowing ones is, that the elections in the State of Maryland for Electors of a state senate, which took place on Monday last, have resulted favorably to our cause. In Baltimore (City) the republican Majority in favor of Edward Johnson was above 900. In Frederick, Nelson & Cockey had a majority of more than 400.[1] As these are places where uncommon exertions were made by the Federalists, I mention them as striking instances of our success, particularly the latter which heretofore has been against us, and where a certain pamphlet, in an improved shape, was circulated with unceasing industry and activity.[2] This thing was actually reprinted, and seasoned with federal additions annotations &c carried in loads into that County as I have been well informed. However, these good people, for this time, in their ardor have "leaped over the horse instead of jumping into the saddle." With the usual respects to Mrs. Madison I remain my dear Sir yrs. truly

PAUL HAMILTON

RC (DLC). Docketed by JM. Enclosure not found.

1. The returns for electors of the Maryland Senate were printed in the *National Intelligencer*, 5, 7, and 12 Sept. 1811.

2. Hamilton was presumably referring to Robert Smith's *Address to the People of the United States.*

To James Monroe

DEAR SIR   MONTPELIER Friday [6 September 1811][1]

Mr. Hamilton from the John Adams reached me yesterday. He reposes to day, and will be with you tomorrow. I send by the bearer, the dispatches opened at the Dept. of State &c. The packets of less importance Mr. H. will take with him tomorrow. The Secy of the Navy you will observe suggests the disclosure of the intelligence recd. from Mr Russel.[2] An abstract of the matter in the letter to Mr. Smith at London, for Mr. Gales wd. be eno'.[3] Yrs.

J. M.

RC (DLC: Monroe Papers).

1. Date assigned on the basis that 6 Sept. was the first Friday after the arrival of the dispatches by the *John Adams* in Washington on 2 Sept. (see Paul Hamilton to JM, 3 Sept. 1811).

2. See ibid. and n. 2.

3. In response to Monroe's subsequent instructions (see Monroe to JM, 7 Sept. 1811), the

editor of the *National Intelligencer*, on 14 Sept. 1811, published a summary of Russell's letters to John Spear Smith to the effect that ongoing proceedings against American vessels in France should not be construed as evidence that the Berlin and Milan decrees were still in force, as French judges had ruled that the decrees had been abrogated on 1 Nov. 1810.

From Anthony Charles Cazenove

SIR   ALEXANDRIA Septr. 6th. 1811
I have been honoured with your letter of 22d. Ulto. containing an order for a pipe of Messrs Murdoch's L. P. Madeira Wine which went forward per brig Louisa McNamara & expect the wine will come out in her. There is no doubt but these gentlemen's wine improved by one or two years of our climate will prove of a very superior quality, & I hope merit your attention.

I beg leave to express my hope that the report in the papers of your having broken your leg by a fall from your horse is without foundation,[1] & am with high regard very respectfully Sir Your most obedt. Servt.

ANT CHS. CAZENOVE

RC (DLC).

1. The Virginia *Alexandria Daily Gazette* on 6 Sept. 1811 carried an erroneous report, taken from a Richmond newspaper three days earlier, that JM had fallen from his horse and broken his leg.

From Pierre Samuel DuPont de Nemours

MONSIEUR LE PRÉSIDENT,   6 Septembre 1811.
J'ai l'honneur d'envoyer à Votre Excellence des *Mémoires Sur la vie* d'un Grand Homme, dont je vous ai déja fait passer *les Oeuvres,*[1] où vous aurez vu combien votre République naissante lui donnait d'esperance et lui inspirait d'attachement. Ces Mémoires complettent l'Edition.

Ils vous Seront portés par une branche de ma Famille qui me précede dans mon retour aux Etats-Unis. Elle est composée de Madame de Pusy[2] ma Belle-Fille qui m'avait accompagné dans mon premier Voyage; et de Ses deux Enfans, une demoiselle de dix Sept ans, un Garçon de douze, qui avaient aussi êté de mon voyage, quoiqu'alors dans une bien tendre enfance.

Ces enfans ont perdu leur Pere, Mr de Pusy, qui a fait par ordre de votre Gouvernement le Projet de fortification et de défense de la Baie de New-York, de maniere à empêcher tout Bâtiment ennemi d'approcher de la Ville, de la bombarder, de pénêtrer dans la Riviere d'Hudson, de la remonter jusqu'à West-Point, d'en ravager les bords. Ce Projet qui couvrirait aussi une partie du New-Jersey, les trois petites villes d'Amboy, Newark, Elyzabeth-Town, et que les Ouvrages de Governor's Island ne peuvent Suppléer, aurait il est vrai couté trois millions de dollars. Il est vraisemblable qu'il Sera exécuté quand l'état de vos Finances le permettra. On avait pensé que la moitié de la dépense en pourrait être faite par la Confédération générale; un quart aux frais de l'Etat de New-York, et le dernier quart à ceux de la Ville. Mais à quelque époque que l'exécution en soit retardée, les Enfans de l'habile Ingénieur qui l'a imaginé et qui en a fait tous les détails, tous les devis que votre Excellence a Sous les yeux, ne peuvent pas être regardés comme étrangers à votre République.

Je vous demande pour eux, Monsieur le Président, votre bienveillance; et vos bontés, Si elles peuvent leur devenir nécessaires ou utiles.

Je sais que vous les accordez déja à mes Enfans, qui, par les Succès de la Manufacture de Poudre à feu que le plus jeune d'entre eux a établie, contribuent aussi à la défense des Etats-Unis.

Leur Sang, ni le mien, ni celui de mes petits Enfans, n'y seraient point ménagés, Si ce dernier azyle de la liberté du monde pouvait être attaqué.

J'éspere que Votre Excellence a reçu mes idées Sur les changemens que le dérangement de votre commerce maritime peut nécessiter dans le système de vos Finances; et la Seconde Edition de celles qui concernent l'Education publique américaine, dont Vous avez eu une premiere connaissance avant mon départ.

Vous voyez que moi et les miens voulons payer les dettes de notre reconnaissance pour l'hospitalité de votre bonne Nation, et que nous tâchons de le pouvoir.

Je vous Supplie, Monsieur le Président, de continuer d'ordonner à vos Capitaines de me recevoir à bord, quand je me Serai acquitté du travail que je dois encore à mon Pays natal.

Permettez moi d'esperer que ⟨Votre⟩ Excellence voudra bien agréer toujours mon zêle, et mon très respectueux attachement.

DUPONT (DE NEMOURS)

CONDENSED TRANSLATION

Sends the memoirs of the life of a great man, whose works he has already sent JM. They will be presented by members of his family returning to the U.S., including his stepdaughter, Madame de Pusy, and her two children. The children have lost their father, M. de Pusy, who designed the plan for defensive works for the bay of New York and the adjacent areas. Discusses the cost and financing of the plan. Asks JM's kindness for his family and hopes JM has received his writings on American finances and education. Also requests that JM continue to instruct American ship captains to receive him on board when he has finished his work in his native country.

RC (DeGE); draft (ibid.). RC docketed by JM. Minor variations between the RC and the draft have not been noted.

1. DuPont referred to his *Mémoires sur la vie, l'administration, et les ouvrages de Turgot*, which he included in the second edition of his works of Turgot (see *PJM-PS*, 2:5 and n. 2).

2. Jean-Xavier Bureaux de Pusy (1750–1806), formerly Lafayette's captain of engineers, secretary of the National Assembly, and a Napoleonic prefect, had married Julienne Poivre, daughter of DuPont's second wife, Marie-Françoise-Robin Poivre (J. Balteau et al., *Diction-naire de biographie française*, 7:690; *PJM-SS*, 2:305 n. 3).

From the Inhabitants of St. Clair County, Illinois Territory

SIR—   Septr. 6th. 1811.

In approaching the chief Magistrate of our country, we should not do Justice to our feelings, were we to neglect expressing our confidence in his administration, and our sincere respect and esteem for his person. And, although we are situated far from the seat of our National government; and not possessed of the best means of information respecting our National concerns—we humbly conceive, that, at the present crisis when our dearest interests demand such an agreement in political opinion as may ensure weight and efficacy to the general government—silence on the situation of our public affairs might be considered Treason against our individual happiness and the general prosperity of our common country. At a time when unwarrantable aggressions and unprecedented depredations are repeatedly made on our neutral rights, in sequestrations and impressments by the powerful belligerent Nations; and when their emmisaries are taking every advantage of the disaffected part of our community, to sever the union, and to cause the fair fabric of United Columbia to totter and tumble into ruin: It is the interest, and it becomes the duty of every patriotic citizen, of United America, to rally round their Standard pledging their lives and property in support of our Constitution, the delegated authority, and that administration that conducts our National affairs (as we conceive) for the best in this portentous dilemma now before us.

Yet we view with gratitude an allwise providence, presiding over our American affairs, ruling and directing those at the helm of government: So that, notwithstanding that dreadful Vortex of war and devastation into which the nations of Europe are hurled, and which is spreading ruin and blood-shed through all their borders: we have hitherto escaped the dreadful calamity. We therefore assure you, Sir, that we are happy that you, together [with] the united wisdom of the general government, have been enabled to steer clear of any alliance with either of the belligerent powers of the Old World. But at the same time we assure You of our firm support should you be obliged to seek by open war, the just and equal rights of a long injured Nation, who have borne innumerable injuries and insults, from those governments from whom we have not deserved them: And we assure you, Sir, that should a Just war with any Nation, be absolutely necessary, we are willing to support it with our lives and property. And prefering war to an inglorious peace, we stand ready for either event, praying that, that God who overrules all events will still smile on you, and the Nation over whom you preside, and have us all under his holy care and protection. While Addressing you in general terms, we wish to remind you of the precarious situation in which we are placed at this time, by the hostile movements of our Indian neighbors. They having murdered two young men in this neighborhood this season, and dangerou[s]ly wounded two other men, took a young woman prisoner, and plundered a considerable property in horses and household goods. The young woman was afterward, fortunately rescued from her captors by a party of men who pursued, and overtook them before they reached their Village. It appears from the best information we can get, that they do not intend to make any reperation. All which probably, has been communicated from other sources; It is very certain that British emmissaries who are trading within our limits, are instigating the Indians to war with the United States.

We beg leave, Sir, to mention an other local grievance under which we labor, in order that through you, as through a powerful and happy medium we may reach our National legislature. We humbly conceive, sir, that were the public lands given to actual Settlers at a reduced price, and moderately taxed thereafter for a term of time, the industrious poor would have it in their power to become owners of freeholds, and thereby escape a state of Vassalage: and likewise be enabled to raise their families respectably; from which would arise useful citizens. But numbers of us, who now address you (short of some propitious turn of fortune) cannot entertain the pleasing hope of becoming owners of a competent portion of the soil for the ra[i]sing of our families; if the present price is still required in Cash, whilst there is such a scarcity of the circulating medium, which, at present cannot be procured for the produce of this Country. We therefore earnestly wish that some means could be devised without eventually curtailing our National revenue, whereby the poor of this country could be poss[ess]ed (in fee simple) of a small portion of lands. We conclude Sir, with our best wishes for your health and your present and future prosperity. Signed by order of the convention

Robt. McMahan Chairman
J. Messigner Secy.

RC (DNA: RG 107, LRRS, M-42:6). Addressed to JM "from a convention of 170 Members." Docketed by a War Department clerk as received 16 Dec. 1811.

From Benjamin Henry Latrobe

Sɪʀ, WASHINGTON Septr. 6h. 1811

It was my intention to have undertaken the survey of the line of the Western Navigation of the State of New York, and I had already accepted the Office of Engineer offered to me by the Commissioners of that State, when you left the city. But on reconsidering the duty I have to perform for the Navy department here, & the injury which so long an absence might occasion to my other concerns I resolved to give up the task at least for this season, & did not therefore go to the Northward as I proposed.

Immediately after your departure, I had a compleat examination of the roof of the President's house and as soon as the weather would permit the Plumbers of the Navy Yard repaired the Lead & provided & laid down a new Sheet in the place of that which had been blown off by the Storm, as well as of another which was very faulty. The Wind Vane has also required and received the repair.

The Platforms over the Gutters were entirely rotten, & have been removed as they stopped up the Waterway. Mr Lenox has undertaken to replace them & Mr Combes to furnish the timber on the faith of the public. Without them the house will not be habitable next winter; because the steepness of the roof, and the action of the Sun upon the Iron occasions the Snow immediately after it has fallen in any Mass to descend into the Gutters, unless prevented by their being covered.

The Stables are also now putting into the order your [*sic*] desire by Mr Lenox.

We have not yet begun to paint the Roof an operation as essential to its preservation as any other, but Mr. Barry has promised to set about it as soon as the weather, which after a very uncommon spell of rain, promises to be fair, will permit him.

Mr. Munroe suggests that if you would permit it, the bills for these works of absolute necessity might be paid out of the balance remaining of the Hotel appropriation as a loan.[1] This balance is about 2000$. The condition of the West side of the Capitol, so often represented to Congress occasions great injury to the finished part of the building. It is impossible to remedy this entirely but I shall at my own expense prevent any injury to the Senate Chamber.

If it is possible so to arrange my affairs as to spare a fortnight during the present month I propose taking a short journey into Virginia & shall endeavor to show to you my respect by calling upon you at Montpellier. I am with great truth Your faithful hble Servt

B H LATROBE

RC (DLC); FC (MdHi: Latrobe Letterbooks). RC docketed by JM.

1. Latrobe referred to the appropriation for Blodget's Hotel (see Robert S. Bickley to JM, 8 and 18 May 1810, *PJM-PS*, 2:336–37 and n. 2, 344 n. 2).

From an Unidentified Correspondent

Sep. 6. 1811.

"Illustrious" Madison! *canting "Fellow Citizen"!!!*

☞ ☞ ☞ I hope you and all your infernal Set, are now *in the Suds:* if you are not yet, a post or two, will convince you.

War, *has* taken place, between Britain, and the United States; you may recollect this, & credit anonymous' account, *in future.*

All, that I have predicted, & warned you of, will come to pass. *A commence,* you will hear of, ere this reaches you.

I have little to say, on the subject, you must go to Giles, the arch-demagogue, to comfort you! Jefferson is off, for hell.

G–d send *the people* a good deliverance: the infernal Scoundrels at the head, must, & will fall.

Remember that,

HONESTUS.

I pity *the Woman!*—but you, yourself, have let the Blood hounds loose. While naked as a child, you have insulted a man in iron armor. Are we to lie down, & suffer for your destructive insanity!!!?

☞ I am as confident, as that I now exist, that you have sold your Country— that you have entered into a treaty with—🖑 🖑 🖑

☞ the infernal Spirit of Hell!

which all your art, and all the art of your abetters, will be exercised—*to conceal!*—and get your detested necks, *out* of the Halter!—but, you will soon find *the flood come down upon you,* & call upon the mountains, *in vain,* to cover you: the honest spirit of the misled multitude, will rouse—you & those demagogues will be like dust & chaff in that burning fiery hour. *All will foresake you, & call aloud for vengeance!* There never was known, since the foundation of the World, such a scene of Folly, of infatuated & infuriated madness, in a Government, as our's, owing to your own infatuation, in believing, like an ideot, that the people mt. be lead like lambs to the slaughter. No, the people *are honest,* & *mean well,* but they have been most shockingly deceived in chusing *you!*

The poor hoodwinked mob & rabble cry—*"there will be no war"!!!* It is *gone out of your hands. I say, there will be a War, of the most determind kind;* but what care you?—while Carter's mountain has room for the immortal hero!—& his lick spittle! But mountains won't cover you. Eternal Justice

449

must *& will* overtake both the poor shivering wretches; an indignant people will drag you forth! *You* can see the clouds gathering, but defy the storm.

This is written with Spirit, but every word of it is founded, and the predictions will prove

True.

☞ Look at the genius of *our* duels, one or both always killed! Behold the spirit of *our* Suicides, wife, children, & self, all go together.

Offer 50 cents Reward, to find the author of this; I will claim it, & surrender directly; but I will publish a copy of it, & all preceding communications to you. I'll suffer cheerfully for my Country's good. No, no, you canting Scab, this country does not belong to Americans, it belongs to Napoleon Boneparte, it is sold to him. It was bought *of you* by him; it once belonged to the gallant Sons of Columbia, but it no longer belongs to them. Jefferson commenced the Sale, *you, by his Orders,* knocked it down! We live under his nod, or the same thing, under his lick spittle's fiat!!!!!!

I tell you, Smith has done your business; he has let the Cat out of the bag. *His word with the party is as good as yours.* They believe him, & they plainly say, that you are an infamous rascal, & a public thief. O! what vengeance awaits you! I think I hear you cry, with horror:

O save me, save me, ere the thunders roll
and hell's black Cavern swallows up my Soul.
I am in Earnest—as you will most assuredly find—*too late!*

RC (NN). RC includes several unrecognizable characters and symbols.

¶ From Benjamin Rush. Letter not found. *6 September 1811.* Acknowledged in JM to Rush, 20 Sept. 1811. Forwards a copy of a pamphlet received from the earl of Buchan.

From James Monroe

Dear Sir   Albemarle Sepr. 7. 1811

The dispatches from France & England have kept me constantly occupied since their receit yesterday. A note to Gales shall be sent by the next mail.

I now send a project of an answer to Mr Serrurier's former letter, which you will dispose of as you find proper.[1] I shall send one by the next mail, on the subject of his last letter, relating to the late proceeding in Phila.[2] I have just recd. a statment from Mr Dallas of the conduct of the French consul in that affair.

I enclosed to you on monday last by the mail directed to Orange Ct. house, my answer to Mr Foster, the substance of which was shewn to you when at your house.[3] I fear it was not left there, as I have not heard from you on the subject. It may possibly have been forwarded to Washington by the inattention of the post master at Milton.

Mr Hamilton has just arrived here. Your friend & servt

JAS MONROE

Mr Robertson comn. is sent for your signature.[4]

RC (DLC: Rives Collection, Madison Papers).

1. The enclosed "project" has not been found, but it may have related to the contents of a note Sérurier had sent to Monroe on 3 Sept. complaining of the action of the marshal of Pennsylvania in detaining a French dispatch vessel, the *Balaou* (also referred to as vessel no. 5), bound for Batavia. The vessel, after entering the Delaware River in distress on 23 July 1811, was recognized as an American ship that had been confiscated by French authorities eighteen months earlier, whereupon the former owners brought suit for restitution in U.S. district court. Sérurier protested the proceedings as an illegal insult to French sovereignty and demanded that Monroe instruct the court about the limits of its jurisdiction. Monroe responded on 14 Sept. 1811 with a note to the effect that American courts were independent of government control, but he added that the president had directed him to inform the U.S. district attorney of the administration's views on the matter. The secretary of state restated these assurances to the French minister when the administration returned to Washington in October. The matter then seemed to be settled when the U.S. district court ordered the release of the vessel, but in November 1811 the case was appealed to the U.S. circuit court, which reversed the previous decision and sent the case back for trial (Sérurier to Monroe, 3 Sept. 1811 [DNA: RG 59, NFL, France]; Sérurier to Bassano, 9 Oct. and 8 Nov. 1811, the latter enclosing copies of Monroe to Sérurier, 14 Sept. and 12 Nov. 1811, and Sérurier to Monroe, 3 Nov. 1811 [AAE: Political Correspondence, U.S., vol. 66]).

2. Monroe was probably referring to Sérurier's 3 Sept. 1811 letter reminding him that he had written to the secretary of state a month earlier seeking a decision from the U.S. government on the case of Captain Grassin and his vessel in Philadelphia (DNA: RG 59, NFL, France).

3. No communication from Monroe to JM under the date of 2 Sept. 1811 has been found. The "answer to Mr Foster" may have been a response to the British minister's note of 16 Aug. 1811 (see JM to Monroe, 23 Aug. 1811, and n. 1). That Foster did not receive any answer from Monroe at this time is confirmed by the fact that the minister wrote to Monroe again on 21 Sept., pointing out that his notes of 23 July, 16 Aug., and 1 Sept. on the subject of "suspicious vessels" had yet to be acknowledged (DNA: RG 59, NFL, Great Britain).

4. The commission was for Thomas B. Robertson, secretary of the Orleans Territory, whose term of office was due to expire on 18 Nov. Robertson received a temporary commission from Monroe on 20 Sept. 1811, and on 3 Dec. 1811 JM nominated him for a further four-year term (Carter, *Territorial Papers, Orleans,* 9:958–59; *Senate Exec. Proceedings,* 2:194).

§ From James V. S. Ryley.[1] *7 September 1811, Schenectady.* Has been informed by "A Gentleman Just arrived from Detroit," that his son, John, is bound for Washington with a deputation of Ottawa chiefs "on subjects of National Concern."[2] In the present crisis of foreign relations "it behoves every real American . . . to exert himself for the public good"; suggests that the chiefs be sent via Schenectady on their return home, as he knows that nation well and can talk to them in their own language. Wishes to do good for his country and to see his child. In a postscript requests an acknowledgment of his letter and to be informed of the destination of the deputation.

RC (DNA: RG 107, LRRS, R-157:5). 1 p. Docketed by a War Department clerk as received 24 Sept. 1811.

1. James Ryley (Riley) was originally from Schenectady, New York, where he had married a Mohawk woman and may have been a deputy postmaster. Both he and his son, John, were Indian interpreters in the employ of Gabriel Godfroy, the Indian agent at Detroit (*Michigan Pioneer and Historical Collections*, 13 [1888]: 337; Carter, *Territorial Papers, Michigan*, 10:477).
2. In seeking permission to travel to Boston and other places on the East Coast in the fall of 1811, Michigan territorial governor William Hull had suggested that he bring with him some of the sons of the "most influential Chiefs, of the Ottawa, Chippewa, Pottawattamie, Shawnese and Wyandot Nations, who are destined to be Chiefs themselves" (Hull to Eustis, 6 Apr. 1811, Carter, *Territorial Papers, Michigan*, 10:348).

To William Eustis

DEAR SIR   MONTPELIER Sepr. 8. 1811
Your favor of the 2d. was duly recd. The course which the B. Govt. pursues, particularly in sending a Squadron to our Coasts, with such menacing indications, calls for our vigilance in every respect; and incidents may ensue, which would make a stronger claim on the services of the Members of the Ct. Mart: at Frederick town, than is made by the Object of that Court. It is so desirable nevertheless that this object should be fulfilled, that I think we ought not to be too hasty, in interfering with it; I am the less willing to presume a sudden & perfidious blow agst. our forts or towns, as the most recent articles of information from Europe do not favor temerity in the existing Cabinet of G. B. and as Mr. Foster's communication to Mr. Monroe, founded on the arrival of the special Messenger, and relating to the encounter between a frigate & the British Ship, simply demands in the usual form, a disavowal & reparation on the part of this Govt., *modestly* referring to the example given by G. B. in the case of the Chesapeake.[1] Perhaps it might not be amiss, to signify to the officers at Fredk. Town, the expediency of holding themselves in momentary readiness to repair to their military posts. It might be well also for you & Mr. Hamilton to consult on the Mutual arrangements and orders, which might most contribute to the security, of the ports & places requiring the most prompt attention. N. York, of course, will not escape it.
I enclose a letter from Mr. Strode in behalf of a Mr. Morrison, whose case is better known to you, than to me. I signified this to Mr. M. and

remarked that you would doubtless make the proper decision on it.[2] As it is not a time for diminishing the chances of multiplying arms, it is the more natural to lean to the indulgent side, as far as necessary rules will permit, and future confidence may be secured. Accept my respects and best wishes

JAMES MADISON

RC (PHi: Daniel Parker Papers). Docketed by a War Department clerk as received 10 Sept. 1811 and enclosing "a letter from John Strode—and a petition from A. King." Enclosures not found.

1. In a 4 Sept. 1811 letter to Monroe, Foster, in response to instructions sent to him on 4 July 1811, sought a disavowal and reparations for the incident involving the *Lille Belt* and the *President*. This "expectation," the minister added, "was the more natural, from the example afforded by His Majesty's Government in the case of the Chesapeake" (Foster to Monroe, 4 Sept. 1811, *ASP, Foreign Relations*, 3:472–73; Wellesley to Foster, 4 July 1811, Mayo, *Instructions to British Ministers*, p. 326).

2. No communication from JM to a Mr. Morrison has been found, but its contents probably related to a suit pending against the firm of Whelen and Morrison for nonfulfillment of an arms contract with the U.S. On the day he received JM's letter, Eustis authorized the purveyor of public supplies to suspend the suit provided he was satisfied that the firm could supply the contract in reasonable time (see Eustis to Tench Coxe, 10 Sept. 1811 [DNA: RG 107, LSMA]).

From Paul Hamilton

DEAR SIR   CITY OF WASHINGTON Septr 9th. 1811

Sickness in my family which has occupied much of my time for some days past has prevented my forwarding, at an earlier moment, the enclosed copy of a letter from Capt. Porter for your information.[1] As Capt Porter's operations are sanctioned by the orders which, some months since, in obedience to your instructions I issued to the Commanders of our Vessels of war, I shall inform him that his conduct is approv'd. I regret that the sitting of the court on the case of Commodore Rodgers deprives us, at present, of the services of two of our 44s, but I hope that in a few days the proceedings will terminate, and those ships will go to Sea; and that their appearance on the coast will have a salutary effect in restraining the insolence offered to our ports by anything under ships of the line. You have no doubt noticed well the accounts of the destination of a british squadron to the American Coast under Admiral Yorke. What may be [the] extent of their intentions can only be conjectured, but I think that we may assure ourselves that, at least, they will bear heavily on our trade, and occasionally manifest their contempt for our laws by putting into our ports under mere pretences of distress &c: indeed, I shall not be surprized if even in squadron, they make at times a display in Hampton Road. If you think these things probable, and that it is proper to prepare for service on the Chesapeake some of our Gunboats, I shall be glad to have your instructions on that, or any other point which may be suggested to you as entitled to attention. To see our little navy, if called to the defence of our country, requite by it's services the expence which is bestowed on it is amongst the most ardent desires of my heart; and I request you to believe that nothing that may conduce to render it as effective as possible shall be omitted.

I trust that my Son has reached you in safety with his dispatches with which he left this on tuesday last.

Mrs. Hamilton is now confined to her bed with a fever of some days duration, the daily exacerbations of which are preceded by most distressing Agues. My son Edward also has not been clear of fever for 6 days past. Capitol Hill is at this moment as much infested with ague & fever as I have ever known the rice country of So. Carolina to be—other parts of the City are very healthy. I fear that the canal will prove to be a very great injury to the health of this part of the City.[2]

May health & happiness constantly attend you and Mrs. Madison. I remain, Dear Sir, with sincere respect and attachment yrs.

PAUL HAMILTON

RC and enclosure (DLC); letterbook copy (DNA: RG 45, LSP). RC docketed by JM. For enclosure, see n. 1.

   1. Hamilton enclosed a copy of a 31 Aug. 1811 letter he had received from David Porter of the *Essex* (2 pp.), stating that he had heard the British frigate *Tartarus* had entered Hampton Roads in violation of the Nonintercourse Act. Porter sailed to Hampton Roads, intending to expel the British vessel with the aid of gunboats. On his arrival, he learned that the *Tartarus*, "in consequence of a letter received by her commander from Norfolk [had] cut her cable and gone to sea in the night."

   2. Hamilton referred to the canal then being constructed by Benjamin Henry Latrobe for the Washington Canal Company and the city government (see Van Horne, *Papers of Latrobe*, 3:100–102, 108–9).

From William Eustis

SIR,   WAR DEPT. Septr. 11. 1811.

I have the honor to enclose for your consideration a Letter from W. Jones Esqr Judge Advocate requesting instructions relative to the proceeding of the General Court Martial in the case therein mentioned.[1] If the court shall determine that they will not take cognizance of any charges implying offences of more than two years standing, those laid in the five first charges, together with all the specifications of the eighth charge, excepting the last, will, it is presumed, be omitted or not tried, as will appear by reference to a copy of the charges which is also herewith enclosed. I am however strongly impressed with an opinion that the Court will take cognizance of all the charges. With the highest respect your obedt. servt.

W. EUSTIS

RC (DLC); enclosures (DLC: Rives Collection, Madison Papers). For first enclosure, see n. 1. Second enclosure is a copy of the charges against James Wilkinson and a list of witnesses for the prosecution (11 pp.).

1. Walter Jones was participating in the court-martial of James Wilkinson in Fredericktown, Maryland, which had opened on 4 Sept. On 9 Sept. 1811 Jones sent Eustis a progress report (2 pp.; docketed by JM), mentioning that the first two days of the trial had been taken up with accommodation problems. Wilkinson's opening statement consumed more than two days, during which time he succeeded in having three of his judges set aside. "The next question that was stirred," Jones continued, was "the jurisdiction of the Court to take cognizence of those charges, which bring forward offences of more than two years standing. Genl W. strongly insists upon the Court's entertaining jurisd⟨ict⟩ion, and so far from availing himself of the limitation exp⟨ress⟩ly waves it, and professes to demand a trial as an act of justice to himself. This may probably prevail with the court to proceed, otherwise it is probable all those charges affected by the limitation would be dismissed. The court has consented to hear Genl W——n's counsel argue the point in question this morning." In case the court decided to dismiss the charges affected by the limitation, Jones sought advice on whether the court should proceed on the other charges or be dissolved.

From Paul Hamilton

DEAR SIR   CITY OF WASHINGTON Septemr. 11th. 1811

The enclosed was presented me this morning by Mr. Smith, the gentleman in whose behalf it was written. He stated that he had been waiting here for three weeks expecting your arrival, on which, he intended to deliver it, but as he was informed that the period of it was uncertain he had been advised by his friends to offer it to me. He stated to me, most positively, that he knew the contents and that they had now relation only to an application which he made for a Chaplaincy in the Navy, and to no other subject; intimated that delay was inconvenient to him (in a pecuniary way I believe), and with much earnestness requested me to open it. I hesitated—on which he produced me other papers calculated to shew that he was entitled to credence and urged his request that I would open the letter. I felt a confidence in him, and knowing that if the letter proved to be such as he described it to be, in the event of it's being first opened by you, conformably to that confidence with which you have hitherto honored me, you would return it to me to be acted on, I ventured to open it: and altho' I have not been deceived in the contents as described by Mr. Smith, a little reflection subsequently has shewn to me, most feelingly, that I have erred in violating, under any assurance the seal of a letter directed to you, accompanied by any representation howsoever plausible. I have sought consolation in the candor which excites this letter. This will serve me to a certain but a very limited extent, for, even if you are so indulgent to me as to excuse the act, I shall ever feel self-reproach for it, while the compunction which I feel causes a determination that, under no circumstances, it shall be repeated.

I have assured Mr. Smith of the success of his application,[1] for, he appears to be an interesting man, and we need men of his description as Chaplains in our Navy, of which grade of officers, we now have only three.

I am happy to inform you that Mrs. Hamilton is now mending, altho much reduced. Our hopes of partaking of your hospitality at Montpeleir, this season, are at an end. If we live to see the next, we trust that we shall not be disappointed in complying with the repeated invitations of yourself and Mrs. Madison, of which we shall ever retain a grateful remembrance.

All our united best respects and most friendly wishes are offered to you and Mrs. Madison; and with great sincerity and truth I conclude yrs.

PAUL HAMILTON

RC (DLC). Docketed by JM. Enclosure not found.

1. Smith's application evidently did not succeed. In February 1812 the navy still had only three chaplains, none of whom was named Smith (*ASP, Naval Affairs,* 1:257).

James Robertson to Willie Blount

NASHVILLE, septr: 11. 1811.

"There is in this place a very noted Chief of the Chickesaws, a man of truth, who wishes the President should be informed, that there is a combination of the Northern Indians, promoted by the English, to unite in falling on the frontier settlements, and are inviting the Southern tribes to join them."[1]

Tr (DNA: RG 59, ML).

1. This paragraph was extracted from a 9 Sept. 1811 letter from Chickasaw agent James Robertson to Tennessee governor Willie Blount. Robertson mentioned that the Chickasaw chief who wished to convey the information to JM was John Brown. Blount forwarded the letter to the War Department to be used "for the interest of the United States" (Blount to Eustis, 16 Sept. 1811 [DNA: RG 107, LRRS, B-521:5; docketed as received on 24 Sept. 1811]).

§ From James Leander Cathcart. *12 September 1811, Madeira.* Advises that the wines JM ordered are cased and awaiting a vessel for Alexandria or Baltimore. Both JM's and Monroe's wines will be forwarded as soon as a ship is available. "I have taken the liberty to include the Pipe of wine for Mrs. Lucy Washington in the bill I have drawn upon you this day in favor of Matthew Cobb Esqr. of Portland for £378. Stg." Wishes to be able to serve JM in the future. Adds in a postscript an account for five pipes of wine at £60 per pipe, five cases at £3 per case, and one pipe cased for Mrs. Washington at £63.

RC (DLC). 2 pp.

To John Armstrong

DEAR SIR   MONTPELIER Sepr. 13. 1811
Your favor of the 2d. instant, inclosing a newspaper statement of a conversation imputed to you, has been recd. with the respect due to the motives for the communication.

I need scarcely say that evidence of that sort could have no weight with me, when opposed by so much improbability, and by the predispositions which it could not fail to find in me. I might add that the disproof furnished by the contradiction of dates, did not escape notice. Accept my respects and good wishes

J. M.

Draft (NjP: Crane Collection).

From John Graham

DEAR SIR   WASHINGTON 13th Sepr 1811
I should have answered by the last Mail, the Letter you did me the Honor to write me, expressing a hope that my Health was returning;[1] had I not been so sick on the day of its departure that I could not sit up. In consequence of a powerful dose of medicine, I am some what better, and have begun again to take Bark tho: I very much doubt whether my Stomach is properly prepared for it.

The City is I think more sickly than I ever knew it to be, tho the fevers are said to be of a cast that yields to the power of Medicine. By this Mail you will receive many Letters from Mr Smith,[2] Mr Erving[3] and Mr Adams.[4] I opened such of them as I thought might probably be in Cypher. With Sentiments of the most Respectful attachment I have the Honor to be your Most Hble Sert

JOHN GRAHAM

457

Be pleased to let Mrs Madison know that I have sent her Letters to Mrs Crawford & Mrs Knapp[5] and that I beg to be most respectfully presented to her.

As it is possible that they may not be able to get thro the deciphering of Mr Adams Letters, at the office today, in time for the Mail—I will mention that it appears from a p⟨ar⟩t of one of them which I read, that he declines the appointment of Judge and intends to remain a little longer in Russia.[6]

RC (DLC).

1. Letter not found.
2. Graham was probably referring to the newspapers and other documents John Spear Smith had enclosed in his dispatches to Monroe between 3 and 22 July 1811 (DNA: RG 59, DD, Great Britain). Much of this material dealt with the departure of Sir Joseph Yorke's squadron for the American coast and British reaction to the incident between the *Lille Belt* and the *President*.
3. Probably the dispatches Erving sent to Monroe between 23 June and 15 July 1811 (*ASP, Foreign Relations*, 3:521–36).
4. Probably dispatches from John Quincy Adams written between 2 and 29 June 1811 (Ford, *Writings of J. Q. Adams*, 4:89–122).
5. Mary Phille Knapp was the wife of John Knapp, who had moved from Philadelphia to Washington to establish a lumber business. A friend of William and Anna Thornton, he was also employed as a clerk in the Treasury Department (*PJM*, 17:55 and n. 1; *PJM-SS*, 1:57 and n. 4).
6. See John Quincy Adams to JM, 3 June 1811.

From James Monroe

Dear Sir　　　　　　　　　　　　　Albemarle Sepr. 13. 1811

Permit me to submit to your consideration a subject of peculiar delicacy. It is to suggest a doubt of the propriety of your making a visit at this time to this neighbourhood.[1] You will be satisfied that I do suggest it from an attachment to your fame & that of your administration.

If you come up, it being just before the meeting of Congress, it will be concluded, & probably so represented in the gazettes, that all the measures of the govt., at this important crisis, are adjusted at the interview. It will not be material that the idea is erroneous & false. The impression will be the same as if the fact was true.

By declining to come up our friend will not suppose that the omission proceeds from a want of regard. He will not even suspect it. But if he knew the real motive, he could not but approve it. There is no necessity however for his ever knowing it. The necessity of preparation for hasty departure for Washington, compy., interruption &ca, are a sufficient & just excuse.

You may be satisfied that every step you take at this time is watched & criticised with severity, & that light things may do harm. Some friends have been cooled, others made enemies; whom the constant & unshaken course of the distinguished personage on whom they have principally relied, cannot restore to their former state.

It is not without concern that I make this suggestion, but I feel that I should fail in the just claim you have on me if I did not. It is in the most perfect confidence, that I submit the subject to your consideration. Should you determine to come up, & drop me a line, I will have the pleasure to meet you there. I am very sincerely your friend

JAS MONROE

RC (DLC: Rives Collection, Madison Papers).

1. Monroe was suggesting that JM cancel his pending visit to Jefferson at Monticello.

To James Monroe

DEAR SIR   Friday evening. [13 September 1811]

I have just recd. your favor of this date. I need not express the perfect confidence I feel in the friendly & considerate inducements to your suggestion. But having made definitive preparation for the intended visit; having in no instance omitted it for many years, & the motive being strengthened by the late one recd. by myself, I think the omission, if tested by prudential calculations of a political nature, would be more liable to objection, than conformity to the usual course; whilst every other consideration is in favor of this conformity. I shall therefore yield to the feelings of personal esteem & friendship; and abide whatever may ensue. These feelings will be the more gratified by the pleasure which the trip promises of an opportunity of seeing you. Accept assurances of my great esteem & cordial regard.

JAMES MADISON

We propose to set out tomorrow morning & to be at Monticello in the Evening.

RC (DLC: Monroe Papers). Undated. Date supplied by comparison with Monroe to JM, 13 Sept. 1811.

§ From John R. Phillips. *13 September 1811, Newport, Delaware.* Admits to some embarrassment in approaching JM, but the village of Newport wishes this autumn to erect and finish by subscription "a neat but plain building as a house for public worship (with a burying ground attachd. to it)." The principles of the plan are that "it will be free to all but belonging to none under the Care of a Committee appointed Yearly from among the citizens of the Village & its neighbourhood." The committee will form a constitution and raise the sum necessary to pay for the building. Asks JM whether, if they are short of funds, they might look to him to make up the deficiency.

RC (DNA: RG 59, ML). 2 pp.

To Albert Gallatin

Dear Sir   Montpelier Sepr. 14. 1811.

The inclosed Letter was brought to me by the young gentleman in whose behalf it was written. He had other respectable recommendations addressed to you, which he has doubtless forwarded: His personal appearance does not make against him. He therefore stands in fair comparison with the other candidates to be taken into view, and who are better known to you than to me.

The accounts by the Jno. Adams fortify the ground on which we stand as to the cessation of the F. Decrees:[1] but are liable to unfavorable remarks in several points of view. It is evident however, that there is an increasing desire in the French Govt. to be thought well disposed towards us; the policy of which particularly at the present moment explains itself. Mr. Foster in pursuance of instructions by the special messenger, has put in a formal demand of disavowal & reparation of the affair of the little Belt;[2] accompanying it with a copy of the instructions under which Bingham cruised.[3] The answer of Mr. Monroe refers to & repeats the explanation given at Washington; adhering to the ground on which no notice of the case, beyond a disavowal of hostile orders, could be taken without the obvious preliminary on the part of the B. Govt.[4] The tenor of the instructions to Bingham, and the manner of their communication, afforded an apt occasion, for expressing the disposition here to meet every proof of an amicable one on the other side, in the way most suited to a favorable & general adjustment of differences. Late communications from Mr. Erving shew that the Danish depredations have ceased & that the loss on the whole will be so reduced as to form no essential proportion to what was threatened.[5] The cases on which the D. Govt. was most inflexible were those in which our Vessels had availed themselves of B. Convoy. Most of them appeared to be desperate.

We are just setting out on a visit for 2 or 3 days to Monticello. Mr. Jefferson was with us a week or two ago; and seemed to enjoy good health, with the exception of a troublesome rheumatic affection near the hip.

Mrs. Madison offers Mrs. Gallatin her Affectionate respects. Be pleased to add mine, & to accept them for yourself.

James Madison

RC (NHi: Gallatin Papers). Cover marked *"private"* by JM. Enclosure not found.

1. See Paul Hamilton to JM, 3 Sept. 1811, and n. 2.

2. See JM to William Eustis, 8 Sept. 1811, and n. 1.

3. The instructions of Rear Admiral Herbert Sawyer to Capt. Arthur Batt Bingham of the *Lille Belt* on 19 Apr. 1811 directed him to deliver a packet to the British vessel *Guerriere*, either off Charleston or the Virginia capes or off New York. Failing that, Bingham was to cruise for as long as his supplies lasted before heading back to Halifax. While cruising, he was to pay due regard to protecting British trade and to the destruction of enemy vessels. He was to be "particularly careful not to give any just cause of offence to the Government or subjects of the United States of America, and to give very particular orders to this effect to the officers you may have occasion to send on board ships under the American flag." Nor was he to "anchor in any of the American ports but in case of absolute necessity" (enclosed in Foster to Monroe, 4 Sept. 1811, *ASP, Foreign Relations*, 3:475).

4. In responding to Foster's demand on 14 Sept., Monroe reminded the British minister that on two earlier occasions, on 2 and 16 July 1811, he had already stated that Commodore Rodgers had not been sailing under orders to reclaim impressed American seamen from British vessels and that he had made these statements "in order to obviate misapprehensions which might obstruct any conciliatory and satisfactory propositions with which you might be charged." Monroe added that the circumstances of the encounter between the *Lille Belt* and the *President*, as the administration understood them, might equally well entitle the U.S. to demand redress from the British government, and he further noted that five years had now elapsed without the U.S. receiving the reparations owed to it in the case of the *Chesapeake*. With regard to Captain Bingham's situation, Monroe concluded by reporting that JM saw in Sawyer's instructions "a token of amity and conciliation which, if pursued in the extent corresponding with that in which these sentiments are entertained by the United States, must hasten a termination of every controversy which has so long subsisted between the two countries" (ibid., 3:476).

5. See John Graham to JM, 13 Sept. 1811, and n. 3.

From William Eustis

Dear Sir,   Washington Septr 14th 1811.

It is with reluctance that I am obliged again to trouble you on the subject of the court martial, the details of which it was hoped might have been arranged by the department. Since my last it appears that it has been determined to take congnizance of all the charges. A new demand, as will be explained by the enclosed copy of a Letter from the Judge Advocate, is now made by the General thro the court for Colo. Cushing & several other officers from the Mississippi.[1] When the request for Colo. Cushing was made by the General to the Dept he was answered that the Colo. was in the hands of a court martial—had pleaded to the charges—that the court at his instance had been adjourned to the first of December to give him an opportunity to procure testimony, and in case of his being ordered to Maryland that he could not return by the time assigned for the meeting of the court in December.[2] The General was then refer'd to Mr Jones for the purpose of making an arrangement by which the deposition of the Colo might be taken. When the motion was made to the court for the order lately given Mr Jones offered as I am informed to admit the declaration of the General to any point wch. was to be sustained by the evidence of Colo. Cushing.

When Colo. Pike was applied for at a late period it was answered to the General that had the application been made in season an arrangement might have been adopted for the purpose: but so many field and other officers had already been ordered from that command, & two of the former grade being in arrest, the public service did not admit of a compliance. Colo. Covington being added to the list brings to recollection a letter which is herewith enclosed which was put into my hands by Mr. Munroe on the evening previous to his leaving the city, apparently in the hand writing of the General;[3] this with other circumstances discovers a disposition to bring together by some means or other the personal friends of the General. The other officers named, if they had been material witnesses should have been ordered on the intimation of the General at an earlier day. From information which I have received, it is probable that a personal accommodation to themselves has been the ground work of the application with an ultimate view to increase the number of friends. To be compelled to know & to state the indirect means which are practising is truely painful. To be convinced of their existence and at the same time to be forbidden to act upon them is embarrassing. After the General had moulded the court to his liking and gained a controul over it wch as I am well informed has been evident in every instance hitherto & of which there can be no higher proof than their order enclosed which was issued under a knowlege of all the circumstances; it was to have been expected that he would have been satisfied and have suffered the trial to proceed.

In the case of Colo. Cushing, practice & general principles sanction the releasing an officer from arrest as well as a private from a guard house for the purpose of giving testimony before a court martial—whether an application of the principle under the peculiar circumstances of the Colo. is admissible I must confess I have doubts. Genl. Hampton in a Letter written a short time previous to his visit to the seat of Govt. begs that his resignation may be cotemporaneous with any order which takes Colo. C from the arrest in which he has placed him. If he should adhere to this determination (which has not hitherto been communicated to you Sir, because it was deemed hasty & which is now made known from a sense of duty) after he shall see that it is at the instance of the Court: two great objects will be effected by Genl. W. Cushing will probably never be brot to trial. It will be hors de combat. With respect to Covington Pike & the other officers who (in case an order is given) cannot be expected to arrive in less than three months unless there arise some unforeseen occurrence I perceive no other derangement of service than the passing of their commands to other officers some of whom will be of inferior grades. The question arises shall the request be granted in toto—shall it be declined in toto—or shall it be granted with the exception of Colo. Cushing. A denial is a disrespect to the court (which whether they have or have not merited I presume not to determine) and this will be added in high colours to the alledged system of persecution. In my life I do not recollect an instance of greater embarrassment. Confidentially I have consulted Mr Hamilton who sees the stratagem but is of opinion that the safest course is to comply.

In forming a judgment it is impossible to exclude from consideration the high presumption (founded on the disposition already manifested by the court) of a complete and (I should not be surprized to see attached the word) *honorable* acquital of every charge and specification.

In this dilemma, inclining to an opinion that the request of the Court cannot be altogether disregarded unless circumstances affecting the public safety should be deemed such as to justify it, I beg leave to solicit your advice & direction, so far as you may judge proper to afford the one or the other. To render justice to the General & to the country in a manner correspondent with your views & directions, is the highest ambition (in the care) of Dr Sir, your faithful & respectful

W. EUSTIS

The request of the President of the court as expressed in his Letter[4] will be complied with as soon as a suitable person can be found to assist Mr Jones, who was informed by me a day or two previous to his leaving the city that he would require an asst. and who was requested to cast about in his own mind for a proper character.

It was stated to the court by the Judge Advocate that ordering Colo. C. to this court w'd discharge him from his arrest—& as he had pleaded to the charges would release him from any obligation to the court before which he was bound to appear—& it does not appear that *this* court have given an opinion to the contrary.

RC and two enclosures (DLC). RC docketed by JM. For surviving enclosures, see nn. 1 and 4.

1. Eustis enclosed a copy of an 11 Sept. 1811 letter he had received from Walter Jones (3 pp.), transmitting a court order requiring the attendance of certain witnesses on Wilkinson's behalf, namely Colonels Leonard Covington and Thomas Cushing, Lt. Col. Zebulon Pike,

Capt. Benjamin Wallace, and Lieutenants Thomas Jessup and Timothy Spann. Jones mentioned that Wilkinson had already applied to the War Department for these witnesses and had been refused. It was common knowledge that Cushing was under arrest pending his own court-martial, but Jones wished to have War Department advice and orders on the prospect of his attendance anyway. Wilkinson, Jones added, did not wish to delay the court for want of witnesses, but "so tired out is he [Wilkinson] with the persecutions under which he has laboured for so many years, that no matter with what consequences to himself, he shall submit his cause to the court upon the evidence as soon as even that which may be ready is gone through." Jones doubted that the court would sit long enough to wait for further witnesses, assuming that it could even get to the evidence already available, "which has even 'til now been postponed for preliminary questions." After two days of deciding procedural questions— the limitation arising under the eighty-eighth article of war and the propriety of the court interfering on the subject of witnesses—Jones hoped that the court could go ahead "in an uninterupted course upon the main business."

2. See Toulmin to JM, 6 Mar. 1811, and n. 1.

3. This enclosure has not been identified.

4. Eustis enclosed a copy of an 11 Sept. 1811 letter he had received from Brig. Gen. Peter Gansevoort, who was presiding over Wilkinson's court-martial (2 pp.). He suggested the expediency of naming supernumerary officers to attend the trial, which "bids fair to be long & tedious," in case vacancies should occur. Colonels Backus, Burbeck, and Freeman had already been removed and replaced by the only available supernumeraries, Majors Armistead, Stoddart, and Swift. The judge advocate, moreover, was in poor health, and the court had been compelled to adjourn that day for this reason. Gansevoort therefore suggested that an assistant judge advocate be named. So far, he continued, the trial had advanced only to the reading of the charges and to some preliminary questions. If an assistant were hired, Gansevoort recommended "his allowance be liberal, and adequate to so tedious and generally an unthankful business."

From James Taylor

MY DEAR SIR   NEW PORT KENTUCKY Sept 14th. 1811.

I am informed that application will be made to you in favor of a Mr. [1] Sloo for an appointment as Indian Agent.[2] He informs me that he was in the revolutionary army from nearly the beginning to the close in the quarter Master department, & that his father was an officer during I think the whole War. I have known Mr. Sloo for a number of years slightly but not well enough to speak of my own Knowledge as to his merit. He informs me Mr. Morrow, Doct Campbell & Mr Worthington[3] will advocate his pretentions & some others. I am of opinion his capacity is good, for he appears to be a Man of business and I have understood he is so. I know it is unpleasant to have so many applications for office & I endeavor to get clear of it as much as possible, I must therefore refer you to the Gent before mentiond for a better account of his pretentions to office.

I Presume you are informed that some examination has been caused by the Secy of the Treasury into the official conduct of Genl. Jas. Findlay receiver of Public Monies for the district of Cincinnati.[4] I think the report by

Mr McLean (the agent)[5] will be highly honorable to the Genl. It has been delayed owing to the absence of some of the Witnesses. I was one who was examined by the directions of the Secy.

I have this day done my self the honor to write to Mrs. M. which I have taken the liberty of enclosing. With the greatest respect & esteem I have the honor to be Dr sir Your friend & servt

JAMES TAYLOR

RC (DNA: RG 107, LRRS, T-180:5). Readdressed by JM to the secretary of war at Washington. Docketed by a War Department clerk as received 1 Oct. 1811.

1. Left blank by Taylor.

2. No such application has been found, but on 16 Apr. 1812 JM appointed Thomas Sloo as a commissioner to examine land claims in the Kaskaskia district. In 1814 he appointed him as register of the land office at Shawneetown in the Illinois Territory (Gallatin to Sloo, 16 Apr. 1812, Carter, *Territorial Papers, Illinois*, 16:211; *Senate Exec. Proceedings*, 2:531).

3. Jeremiah Morrow, Alexander Campbell, and Thomas Worthington made up the Ohio delegation in the Twelfth Congress.

4. Gallatin had ordered an examination of the books of the Cincinnati receiver's office on 10 May 1811. Not only had the public moneys in the hands of previous receivers been defective for reasons of robbery and defalcation, but Gallatin also knew that Findlay had obtained temporary loans in order to meet his payments to the treasury and then had repaid the lenders from public funds. He was unable to account for this situation other than by supposing that the receiver was in the habit of making loans to his friends (Gallatin to James Findlay, 10 May 1811, and Gallatin to John McLean, 10 May 1811, *Papers of Gallatin* [microfilm ed.], reel 23).

5. New Jersey–born John McLean (1785–1861) in 1811 was a lawyer and newspaper editor residing near Cincinnati. He was subsequently elected as a Republican to the Thirteenth and Fourteenth Congresses (1813–16) and later served as postmaster general in the administrations of both James Monroe and John Quincy Adams (1823–29). From 1829 until his death he was an associate justice of the Supreme Court.

§ From the Officers of the Second Brigade and Second Division of the Ohio State Militia. *14 September 1811, Chillicothe.* At a time when the nation's peace and prosperity are threatened by the European belligerents and "the menaces of cruel savage hordes" on the western frontier, it is the duty of every American soldier to avow his confidence in the administration. The committee formed by the officers therefore addresses JM as the chief magistrate of "a *free, independent people.*" They have long witnessed JM's forbearance and perseverance in trying to obtain respect for neutral rights while also preserving the blessings of liberty and peace. "The prospect of our national affairs, at present, seems gloomy," though there is hope that one of the belligerents will cease its aggressions. "Should we however be again deluded with the idle tale of *negotiation,* and the thunder of war be heard on our shores, we pledge ourselves . . . to unsheath the sword and . . . meet the *dread appeals to arms!*" They anticipate the coming session of Congress with "mingled sensations of pleasure and concern" and await "the alternative of *peace,* or *war.*" In the negotiations with Great Britain, the just cause "*must* come to issue." "Posterity will judge of the conflict. It will redound to the American name, that we sought not the quarrel; it was the choice of *our* enemy. Let *her* atone for the transgression."

RC (DNA: RG 59, ML). 3 pp. Signed by Duncan McArthur, chairman, and James Denny, secretary. Docketed by JM.

To William Eustis

DEAR SIR   Sepr. 15. 1811

I have recd. yours of the 11th. inclosing a letter from Mr. Jones acting as Judge Advocate at Frederick Town. As the case of Genl. Wilkinson is in possession of the Court Martial, who will judge of the extent of their own jurisdiction, as well as decide on the merits of the questions within it, no instructions seem to be requisite, in the present stage of the proceeding; unless it be in reference to the event of refusing cognizance of a part of the charges; and in that event, I see no sufficient ground on which the residue of the charges could be withdrawn. If those, not transferred by the H. of R. to the Ex. had been witheld, that distinction might have accounted for such a course; but it cannot well be applied to the withdrawal of the charges. When the result of the trial presents itself, we must take up whatever questions may grow out of it, and fall within Executive competency.

I return the letter of Sibley,[1] and the proposal in favor of Dr. Thos. J. C. Monroe,[2] with the usual note of approbation. Accept my esteem & best wishes

JAMES MADISON

RC (PHi: Daniel Parker Papers).

1. JM had evidently read a 17 July 1811 letter from John Sibley, the Indian agent at Natchitoches, to Eustis, describing the organization of armed bands in the so-called neutral ground between the Río Honda and the Sabine following an incident in which some American "brigands" had robbed a party of Spaniards. Sibley's concern, however, was that the ultimate purpose of the armed parties was to intervene in the Mexican revolution. He also reported "another Collection of Bad men & some Women," whom he described as escapees from American jails, who had established a settlement at Pacan Point on the Red River, much to the annoyance of the Caddo Indians. The Indians were demanding the removal of the community, but this, Sibley predicted, would be difficult as it was growing rapidly in size, in part because its members were enticing slaves to abandon their masters (DNA: RG 107, LRRS, S-436:5; docketed as received on 11 Sept. 1811 and bearing Eustis's notation to the effect that the contents had been confirmed by the commanding officer at Natchitoches and that reinforcements had been sent there).

2. On 20 Nov. 1811 JM nominated Thomas J. C. Monroe of Ohio as a surgeon's mate in the Sixth Infantry Regiment (*Senate Exec. Proceedings*, 2:191).

¶ To John Graham. Letter not found. *16 September 1811*. Acknowledged in Graham to JM, 18 Sept. 1811. Forwards a check for $1,200 and requests Graham to send him the same amount in Virginia banknotes.

From Paul Hamilton

DEAR SIR   CITY OF WASHINGTON Septemr. 17th. 1811

I have the honor of now transmitting to you the proceedings of the Court of Enquiry in the case of Commodore Rodgers, the result of which abundantly justifies the confidence you have been pleased to repose in the correctness of the Commodore's statement of facts.[1] You will observe that amongst the many officers who gave testimony before the Court, the Surgeons and Purser were not included, for the substantial reason assigned by Commodore Decatur in his enclosed letter.[2] The exclusion of these officers was not only judicious, but may be made useful in invalidating the testimony of Binghams officers of the same grades, whose depositions have been lately laid before you.[3] In reviewing the attitude in which this affair is now placed I think it may safely be asserted that, the respectability of each Member of the Court, of the witnesses also, their number and concurrences of testimony, all combine in forming a Mass of Evidence not to be resisted, and which places the Commodore above the reach of censure or even of suspicion. I have given Mr. Gales a small intimation for his paper of today,[4] and when you return me the proceedings, if you approve it, I will deliver them to him for publication in detail, which is rendered perhaps more necessary by the manner in which certain prints are now handling the subject.

Conformably to your wishes repeated consultations have [taken place][5] between the Secretary of War and myself, relative to the defence of our Ports and the result as relating to my Department is, that 20 Gunboats have been ordered to be immedeately equipped at New York, 10 at Norfolk and 3 at Wilmington N. C. These are, for the present, to be half manned (12 men each) and in case of emergency will, it is hoped, be able to procure volunteers enough to make up a complement without delay or difficulty. There having been no appropriation made for the purpose, you will perceive that this augmentation of our force is affected by the scantiness of our funds, but if you think it would be best to extend still more our armament, regardless of that circumstance, relying on any expence being provided for by Congress your directions shall promptly be complied with. Our Frigates and other cruising vessels that are at this time fit for service, are disposed of in such a manner as is best calculated to prevent insult in our ports and on our coast—cruising near home, and frequently putting into our Harbors. There having[6] three british Cruisers on the coast of New York beseting for some time past, our commerce, Commodore Rodgers, conformably to orders, has put to sea before this with his and Com. Decaturs Ships and the Sloop of War Wasp; and as he will, no doubt, meet with the british squadron it will be ascertained, probably, whether their views are hostile or not. The Commodore writes me that he is "still on the right side and intends to continue so" I am therefore perfectly satisfied that he will be too discreet to commit, in any way, the neutrality of his Country.

Mr. Eustis of course will communicate with you on the affairs of his Departt. I have therefore only to add that with undiminished respect and attachment I am yrs.

PAUL HAMILTON

RC (DLC); letterbook copy (DNA: RG 45, LSP). RC docketed by JM. Enclosures not found, but see n. 1.

1. The court of inquiry on the encounter between the *Lille Belt* and the *President*, established by Hamilton on 24 July 1811 and convened under the authority of Commodore Stephen Decatur on 30 Aug. 1811, completed its proceedings on 13 Sept. 1811. It issued its findings under eighteen heads and concluded that the letter sent by Commodore Rodgers to the secretary of the navy on 23 May 1811 was "a correct and true statement of the occurrences which took place between the United States' frigate the President and His Majesty's ship the Little Belt." For the proceedings and the findings, see *ASP, Foreign Relations*, 3:477–99.

2. Decatur may have excluded the testimony of the surgeons and the purser on grounds that men of these ranks could not have been in a position to have observed which of the two vessels in the engagement had actually fired the first shot (see n. 3).

3. Accounts from British witnesses of the *Lille Belt–President* episode had been enclosed in Foster's 4 Sept. 1811 letter of protest to Monroe. Both the surgeon and the purser on the British vessel stated that Captain Bingham, on two occasions, twice hailed the *President* "very loudly," that he received no response, that the *President* had opened fire first, and that the exchange of fire lasted from forty-five minutes to one hour (see *ASP, Foreign Relations*, 3:474). The *National Intelligencer*, on 17 Sept., dismissed these accounts on the grounds that they were not made under oath, that witnesses such as a surgeon, a purser, and three others were "all the men on board" who could be got to testify to Bingham's version of events, and that such witnesses not only had no command but were required by duty to remain below deck and "must have had less opportunity than almost any other of deciding on a fact which occurred above."

4. The 17 Sept. issue of the *National Intelligencer* announced the conclusion of the court of inquiry and observed that the testimony of all fifty-one witnesses summoned corroborated Commodore Rodgers's version of events. The newspaper also discounted British accounts of the episode.

5. Words in brackets were omitted in the RC and have been supplied from the letterbook copy.

6. Hamilton appears to have omitted a word here.

From John Graham

DEAR SIR   DEPARTMENT OF STATE 18th Sepr 1811

Finding myself better today than I have been since I was last taken sick I rode to the Office this Morning and found on my Desk the Letter you did me the Honor to write to me on the 16th. I immediately sent to the Bank and have been enabled to get Virginia Notes for the amount of the Check excepting $100 which is sent in a note of the Bank of Columbia. I was some what at a loss whether you intended that I should send one half the amount of your Check by this Mail and the residue by the next or whether I should send one half of the notes by this Mail and the other half by the next. I have taken a sort of middle course calculated to lessen the risque of sending a large sum by the Mail and to prevent you from being disappointed should you want part of the Money before the arrival of the next Mail—that is, I now send $200 and one half of nine Notes (amounting to $800) and by the next Mail I shall send $200 more and the other half of the above mentioned Nine Notes. With Sentiments of the most Sincere & Respectful attachment I am Dear Sir your Mo: Hble Sert

JOHN GRAHAM

RC (DLC).

§ From James Leander Cathcart. *18 September 1811, Madeira.* Encloses an invoice and bill of lading for the six pipes of wine JM ordered on 28 May—five pipes for JM and one for Mrs. Lucy Washington. Pipes no. 1 and 2 are from the vault of John de Carvalhal, the remainder from the private stock of Henry Correa. Assures JM of the purity of the wine, mentioning that "the vintages of the four last years have been remarkably bad & new wines are now sold at double the price that the[y] were formerly." Has consigned the wine to Colonel Stricker, the navy agent at Baltimore, who will forward it where JM wishes. Reminds JM of his earlier request to be considered for the consulate at Lisbon in the event [George] Jefferson declines it. "I repeat the request as this Consulate does not furnish the means of maintaining so numerous a family as mine." Should his application succeed, JM will "make a family happy who have long been the sport of Fortune & whose prayers have long been offer'd up at the throne of grace for your temporal & eternal happiness."

RC and enclosures, two copies (DLC). RC 2 pp. Docketed by JM, with a pencil notation below the docket: "Ready for files." Enclosures are an invoice for £378 (1 p.) and a bill of lading (1 p.). Duplicate copy of RC bears a postscript, dated 27 Sept. 1811, to the effect that Cathcart was sending the letter via Philadelphia while the wine had been shipped on 21 Sept. directly to Baltimore on the *Dumfries.*

To Benjamin Rush

DEAR SIR   MONTPELIER Sepr. 20. 1811

I have recd. your favor of the 6th. inclosing the Pamphlet from the Earl of Buchan.[1] Could a portion only of his liberality & philanthropy, be substituted for the narrow Councils and national prejudices, which direct the course of his Government, towards the U. States, the clouds which have so long hung over the relations of two Countries, mutually interested in cultivating friendship, would quickly disappear.

Will you permit me to trouble you with the inclosed volume from Mr. Dupont de Nemours; to be disposed of according to its address.[2] Accept Dear Sir my high esteem and affectionate respects

JAMES MADISON

RC (DLC: Rush Papers).

1. In March 1811 David Steuart Erskine, eleventh earl of Buchan (1742–1829), had sent Rush several copies of *The Earl of Buchan's Address to the Americans at Edinburgh, on Washington's Birthday, February 22, 1811*, in which Buchan had described the U.S. as a nation where "the perfection of society" had been nearly attained (Butterfield, *Letters of Benjamin Rush*, 2:1089).

2. JM evidently forwarded a copy of the last volume of Turgot's works which DuPont had sent him on 4 July for the American Philosophical Society.

From John Graham

DEAR SIR   DEPT OF STATE 20th Sepr 1811

I had the Honor by the last Mail to acknowledge the receipt of your Letter of the 16th Inst. covering a Check for $1200—and requesting that I would remit you the amount in Virginia Notes one half by the last Mail and one half by this.

In compliance with this request I had the Honor to send you by the last Mail (18th Inst) $200 in notes of the B of Virginia that were not cut, and the one half of nine notes which were cut, (amounting to $800). I have now the Honor to inclose you the other half of these Notes—and also $200 in notes that are not cut. Making in the whole $1200 the amount of the check. I hope that this Money will reach you and that the plan I have adopted for sending it safely will in no way prove inconvenient to you. Our City yet continues sickly. For myself, I think I am getting well, tho: I have as yet very little appetite.

I beg to be presented to Mrs Madison and to renew the assurances of the great & Respectful Esteem with which I have the Honor to be, Sir, Your Most Hble Sert

JOHN GRAHAM

RC (DLC). Docketed by JM. Filed with the letter is a note in Graham's hand: "Covering $200—and the one half of seven Notes of $100 each and also the one half of 2 Notes of 50 Dol: each."

¶ To William Eustis. Letter not found. *21 September 1811*. Acknowledged in Eustis to JM, 25 Sept. 1811. Gives instructions relating to the attendance of officers at the court-martial of James Wilkinson.

From William Eustis

DR SIR, WASHINGTON Septr 25th: 1811.

Your Letter of the 21st instant was received yesterday. By the mail of the same day an order issued to General Hampton directing the attendance of all the officers named in the request of the Court Martial.[1] A duplicate of the order was also confided to Lt Colo. Backus, a member of the court objected to by Genl. Wilkinson and discharged, who is ordered to the Southward to supply the place of one of the field officers ordered from that station, with directions to deliver it to General Hampton in order that the earliest notice may be given to the concerned.

The proceedings of the court martial in the case of Surgeon's Mate Huston,[2] as also the Letter from Jeffersonville Ky recommending Mr Wood for a commission in the army is received by the mail of this morning.

The West end of the city continues healthy—Capitol hill less so. Looking with impatience for your return which will relieve us from the quasi exile of the last two months, we are with our best respects to Mrs Madison, Dr Sir, your respectful

W EUSTIS

RC (DLC). Docketed by JM.

1. On 24 Sept. 1811 Eustis ordered Hampton to arrange for the attendance of those officers Wilkinson had requested as witnesses at his court-martial (see Eustis to JM, 14 Sept. 1811, and n. 1). Eustis added that "the limits assigned to Col Cushing under his arrest, will be enlarged to admit of his attendance. The court for his trial, which was adjourned to the first of December, will be adjourned to a more distant period" (DNA: RG 107, LSMA).

2. Eustis had forwarded the proceedings in the court-martial of Robert Huston to JM on 18 Sept. 1811. JM approved the findings of the court but remitted the sentence (Eustis to JM, 18 Sept. 1811 [PHi: Daniel Parker Papers; 1 p.]; Eustis to Leonard Covington, 25 Sept. 1811 [DNA: RG 107, LSMA]).

From David Meade Randolph

DEAR SIR, LONDON 26th September 1811

The event which my letter of the 14th June last was designed to anticipate, you will have communicated from the proper source:[1] Whilst my additional appeal to your *private* or *Official* character, as your regard to a due consistencey of conduct shall determine, is, for the sole purpose of referring you to my friend John Marshall of Richmond, and such other persons as may be deemed equal to any degree of responsibility, which you shall find requisite, and his confidence in my integrity and honor, can supply. And, whatever shall be your pleasure, I shall regard with personal respect, and as proof of your public dignity. Having the honor to be your faithful Countryman &cc &cc

D M RANDOLPH

RC and duplicate (DLC). RC docketed by JM.

1. Randolph referred to the death of London consul William Lyman (see Randolph to JM, 14 June 1811, and n. 2).

§ From John Rennolds. *26 September 1811, London.* Observes that the death of General Lyman on 22 Sept. has created a vacancy in the London consulate. Offers himself as a candidate for the position. Although "not authorised from a personal acquaintance" to solicit JM's friendship, he feels sure the "late Ministers at this Court," with whom he is well acquainted, will vouch for his character. Describes himself as a Virginia merchant who has resided in London for some time but who retains a "natural attachment" for his native soil.

RC (DNA: RG 59, LAR, 1809–17, filed under "Rennolds"). 2 pp.

§ John Martin Baker to Collector at Port of Discharge. *28 September 1811, Palma, Majorca.* Requests the collector at the port of discharge to receive articles from Jesse Y. Hinks, captain of the schooner *Ruthy* of Boston, for delivery to JM. Lists the articles in a postscript: "One Qr. Cask 7. Years old Granache White Wine / One Bag Soft Shelled Almonds. / Three Boxes Capers. / Three Boxes Olives."

RC (DLC). 2 pp. Docketed by JM.

§ Account with Dinsmore and Neilson. *28 September 1811.* Lists charges for enlarging and furnishing at Montpelier the drawing room, passage, dining room, large bedroom, kitchen, and "S. W. Wing."[1] Also included are charges for the construction of the temple and labor for the period 30 Sept. 1810 to 28 Sept. 1811. The total amount of the charges is £1,088 8s. 7½d., with a balance due of £378 10s. 7½d. as of 28 Sept.

Ms (ViU: Cocke Papers). Two large ledger sheets. At the foot of the account, JM wrote in pencil: "Sepr 30—$300 as pr. receipt." For a discussion of the construction at Montpelier in the summer of 1811, including a reproduction of some of the accounts rendered at this date, see Hunt-Jones, *Dolley and the "Great Little Madison,"* pp. 66–72 (with this account reproduced at p. 68).

1. Since the southwest wing had been completed the previous year, Dinsmore should have written "N. W. Wing" (see Hunt-Jones, *Dolley and the "Great Little Madison,"* p. 71).

To Richard Cutts

DEAR SIR,   MONTPELIER, Sepr. 30. 1811

I have received your favor of   [1] with the pleasure I could not but feel in learning that the accident to your shoulder was so far advanced towards a cure. It is with a very different feeling I am given to understand that any doubt exists as to your coming to Washington this winter, where besides considerations of a public nature, the social ones would be so interesting to us. I shall not give up the hope that you will not yield to obstacles which may not be absolutely unsurmountable and that we may even have you and your family with us at an earlier day than that to which you have limited the chance of the gratification.[2]

Nothing has occurred latterly to vary the complexion of our foreign prospects, beyond what you will have gathered from the printed accounts. If a change takes place in the British Cabinet or France should disappoint the calculations somewhat encouraged by recent appearances, Congress will probably have occasion for all their wisdom and patriotic energy. From the accounts of latest date, it would seem that the *insane* sovereign of Great Britain cannot long be in the way, of better councils, in case his successor should be disposed to adopt them toward this country.[3]

We are in the moment of setting out for Washington,[4] and in the hurry incident to it. We are all well except J. Payne, whose indisposition has settled into an ague and fever. This is his well day and I hope his sick one tomorrow may not disqualify for a short ride from my brother's to Dr. Winston's.

Accept for Mrs. Cutts and yourself our affectionate regards and wishes.

JAMES MADISON.

Tr (NjP: Crane Collection).

1. Left blank in Tr. No communication from Cutts to JM in this period has been found.

2. Cutts had been elected to represent a Maine district in the Twelfth Congress, but he was to be absent for much of the first session. He had severely fractured his shoulder after slipping on some ice as he was leaving the wharf in Boston. He was also reluctant however, apparently for business reasons, to support the preparations for war that dominated congressional proceedings between November 1811 and June 1812 (postscript by Mary Cutts to a copy of Dolley Madison to Anna Cutts, May 1812 [owned by Mr. and Mrs. George B. Cutts, Brookline, Mass., 1958]; Roger H. Brown, *The Republic in Peril: 1812* [New York, 1964], pp. 138–39, 156, 223 n. 11).

3. Throughout September accounts printed from British newspapers reported that George III had suffered a "dangerous relapse" in his illness, and his death was said to be "not very remote." The death of the monarch would have entailed the dissolution of Parliament and a general election (see *National Intelligencer*, 14, 17, and 24 Sept. 1811).

4. JM returned to Washington on 3 Oct. (ibid., 5 Oct. 1811).

From Thomas Cooper

DEAR SIR   NORTHUMBERLAND October 4. 1811

About two years ago, I requested you to procure for me, by means of Gen. Armstrong, or Mr Warden, some books on Chemistry and Mineralogy, which the irregularity of intercourse between this Country and France, prevented me from obtaining.[1] You were so kind as to write on the subject to Paris and directed the amount of what the books might cost, to be paid by one or other of those Gentlemen on your credit.

From Gen. Armstrong or Mr Warden, I have never received one line of communication. About two months ago, I heard accidentally that Mr Duane Editor of the Aurora, had received from France some books corresponding to the List I took the Liberty of sending to you. I stated the case (your kind interference, and the titles of the Books I had sent for) in a note to my friend Dr. Armstrong,[2] with a request he would transmit it to his brother the General. He did so. But hitherto neither he or I, have received a line in answer.

Under these circumstances, I have taken the Liberty of writing to you, lest the books may have been mistakenly sent to a wrong destination, and you charged with their Amount. That Duane has received some such books, I know, because he sent *Loysel sur L'Art de la Verrerie* to my son in Law in the City for me to translate if I thought fit; I had already translated it; but my proposed publication has been neglected in consequence of my continual expectation of the books I looked for. Soon after the last April Session, the Legislature of Pennsylvania addressed the Governor to remove me from my situation as Judge, which I had held 8 years, *as I thought* reputably to myself and usefully to the Country.[3] An account of the proceedings in my case,[4] I shall take the liberty of sending by young Mr Nourse who is on a visit in this Town. I do not expect that you should peruse it, for you have occupations for your valuable time far more important. But I have a right to say that I have lost no friend on the bench or at the Bar; and the encreased and flattering attentions of the late Governor McKean and Mr Dallas, both known to you, assure me, that my offence must have been in reality of a nature purely political, and I am conscious of none.

In June, the Trustees of Carlisle College (Dickinson College) made me the *voluntary* offer of the Chemical Chair in that Institution, which I accepted. I am here (Northumberland) on a visit only to my friend Mr Priestley during the Vacation: so that if you should find occasion to say any thing on the subject of this letter, be good enough to direct to me as Chemical Professor at Dickinson College, Carlisle. I remain with true respect Dear Sir Your obliged friend and Servant

                                                    THOMAS COOPER

RC (DLC).

1. See Cooper to JM, 19 Aug. 1810 (*PJM-PS*, 2:495–96).

2. James Armstrong (1749–1828), elder brother of John Armstrong of New York, had graduated with a medical degree from the College of Philadelphia in 1769. He resided near Carlisle, Pennsylvania, served in the House of Representatives during the Third Congress (1793–95), and was a lifelong trustee of Dickinson College (Skeen, *John Armstrong*, pp. 1, 2, 35, 41, 49, 222).

3. Cooper was removed as a presiding district judge, a position he had held since 1804, after an address from the two houses of the Pennsylvania Assembly to the governor. Fifty-three charges were levied against him, including wanton and cruel tyranny in sentencing, abuse of suitors and their counsel from the bench, contempt for the acts of the legislature, setting aside jury verdicts, use of office for personal advantage, ridiculing the doctrines of various religious denominations, intemperance, and immorality. Eight of the charges were upheld to justify his removal (Malone, *Public Life of Thomas Cooper*, pp. 198–210).

4. *Narrative of the Proceedings against Thomas Cooper, Esquire, President of the Eighth Judiciary District of Pennsylvania, on a Charge of Official Misconduct* (Lancaster, Pa., 1811; Shaw and Shoemaker 23479).

§ From the Cambridge Light Dragoons. *5 October 1811, Cambridge, South Carolina.* The subscribers, citizens of Cambridge and vicinity, "have long since associated ourselves . . . under the name of the Cambridge Light Dragoons" in order to "aid in protecting, the Honor, independence, and safety of these United States from foreign invasion or internal commotion." They have been watching "with vigilance, and attention the situation of our foreign Relations with France and Great Britain" and fear that "an awful Crisis is at hand" with the latter. "If the Goddess of peace must be assailed in her last Sanctuary, the Nation should be prepared to meet the daring Assailant with a terrible Vengeance. We therefore . . . beg leave to tender to the constituted Authorities our best services in case of Emerg[e]ncy. Our swords shall be drawn at the first summons, and when drawn our Motto shall be an *honorable Peace* or *interminable War*, for we would sooner be buried in the Ruins of our Country, than survive to witness her disgrace."[1]

RC (DNA: RG 107, LRRS, B-61:6). 2 pp. Signed by James Bullock, captain, and thirty-six others. Docketed by a War Department clerk as received 16 Dec. 1811.

1. In acknowledging the address on 24 Dec. 1811, Eustis reported that the president had read it with the satisfaction "which results from the knowledge that the sentiments of our enlightened fellow Citizens so well accords with his own." The president appreciated their motives, Eustis continued, and should it be necessary to call on their services, "he will rely with Confidence on your carrying your laudable professions into practice" (DNA: RG 107, LSMA).

To Richard Cutts

DEAR SIR   WASHINGTON Sunday Sepr. [October] 6. 1811

A letter just recd. by Mr[s.] M. from Mrs. C. informs us that you had set out on a trip for Boston. This will probably find you returned, and I hope without any such accident as befel your former one. Mr. J. Q. Adams declines his Judiciary appt. Another is of course to be made as soon as the Senate are in session. Be so good as to give me without delay, information of the state of Mr. Lincoln's eyes, and his probable disposition on the subject. You will oblige me also by any other information which may aid me in a fit choice.

We continue well except J. Payne who is not yet free from his intermittent. He joined us here the day before yesterday; and is in the hands of Dr Elzey,¹ who is famou⟨s⟩ as a bilious Physician.

We remain without important news from Europe farther than the Newspapers give it. With affece. respects to Mrs. C. Adieu

JAMES MADISON

RC (MdHi). Misdated by JM. October date assigned on the basis that JM was not in Washington on 6 Sept. 1811 and that 6 Oct. was the first Sunday falling after JM's return to that city. Docketed by Cutts.

1. [William?] Ellzey was a physician who resided at Eighteenth and G Streets in Washington. His wife was a member of a circle that regularly played cards with Dolley Madison (*Records of the Columbia Historical Society,* 5 [1902]: 94; Van Horne, *Papers of Latrobe,* 3:376 and n. 3).

From Albert Gallatin

(CIRCULAR.)

SIR,   TREASURY DEPARTMENT, October 7th, 1811.

IT has been suggested that the provisions of the non-intercourse Act which forbid the importation of articles of British growth, produce or manufacture are violated by certain coasting vessels, in the following manner. Masters of vessels bound from a port of the United States, to another port of the United States enter on their manifest, certified by the Collector of the port of departure, a quantity of Plaister of Paris or other foreign articles not actually shipped at the time. They afterwards receive, either at Passamaquoddy, at some port of a foreign Colony adjacent to the United States, or at sea from another vessel, prohibited articles answering the description in the manifest, and then proceed to the port of destination, where the fraud is covered by the entry on the manifest.

Although the existing provisions of the Coasting Act may not in every respect, be sufficiently strict or precise to enable the Officers to prevent altogether those fraudulent attempts, they may with due vigilance and attention be generally detected. The Collectors of the ports of departure should, in all cases where foreign goods, particularly of British growth or manufacture, are entered in the manifest, require specific instead of vague entries, and as far as practicable ascertain whether the articles thus entered are actually on board. Thus such entries as "a quantity of Plaister" or "twenty bales merchandize" are altogether inadmissable. The entry should specify the number of tons of plaister, the precise quantity of any other specific article, the marks of the bales, the nature, quantity, and estimated value of merchandize contained in each. Except in the last case, that of merchandize in bales, or other packages, there is no difficulty in ascertaining whether the quantity entered is actually on board; and even in the case of dry goods, there should be no hesitation, when necessary, to send an Inspector on board and to examine, as in the case of dry goods transported with benefit of drawback, whether they are actually shipped. This should be done in every instance where the goods entered are of great value, where the supposed shipment is out of the ordinary course of business, or where the character of the vessel, master or shippers, or any other circumstance induces a suspicion that a fraud is intended.[1]

Coasting vessels ought also on their arrival in any port to be watched with great vigilance, and the quantity and nature of the foreign articles on board be immediately ascertained and compared with that entered on the manifest. Greater precaution will be necessary with respect to vessels coming from, or arriving in Maine, Massachusetts or Georgia, and generally with such as have performed voyages which have admitted of their touching at a foreign port, or of meeting by appointment other vessels at sea. Those from Passamaquoddy (which includes Eastport) and all those laden in whole or in part with Plaister of Paris are at present particularly liable to suspicion;[2] as it is ascertained that almost the whole of what had been legally imported into that District has long ago been exported coastwise, and that a considerable quantity of that article now in the United States, has been illegally imported in the manner above stated.

I must also call your attention to the importations of articles of British (principally colonial) produce, made in vessels coming from St. Bartholomew or from Spanish or other permitted ports, and accompanied with papers intended to prove that such articles are the produce of a Spanish, Swedish or other permitted port. Although there may be some articles the origin of which cannot by inspection be easily ascertained, yet I am informed that most of them may always be distinguished by grocers or other dealers in such articles; that the sugar and rum of the British Colonies never can be mistaken for similar articles of the Spanish or other Colonies. It appears therefore necessary that such articles should on their arrival be examined by the Inspectors or other proper Judges; and whenever they shall from inspection appear to be of British growth or manufacture, they must be seized and libelled, any certificates or other documents of exportation or origin notwithstanding. It is indispensable to assert and enforce the principle that such papers either forged or fraudulently obtained in a foreign

477

port, shall not supercede the evidence arising from the examination of the article itself. The restrictive and even ordinary Revenue Laws of the United States would otherwise be altogether defeated. If Jamaica Spirits can, with the help of an Havanna certificate, be forced upon us as Spanish Rum, there is nothing to prevent the importation of Irish linens or British cloth, under the name of German or Danish manufactures, or even that of Madeira wine, under the designation of Teneriffe.[3]

Other plans, not known at the Treasury, have probably been devised for the purpose of introducing British goods into the United States; and I have to request that whenever any new information is obtained on that subject, it be communicated without delay to the Collectors to whom it may be useful, and also to this Office. I am, very respectfully, Sir, Your obedient servant,

ALBERT GALLATIN
Secretary of the Treasury.

RC (DLC). A printed broadside, addressed to "The Collector of the Customs," and signed by Gallatin. Marked by Gallatin, *"For information,"* and bearing his marginal notations (see nn. 1 and 3). Docketed by JM.

1. In the margin opposite the first two paragraphs, Gallatin wrote: "The defects alluded to are 1. that no vessel bound to a port in same or adjacent state is obliged except in some cases to clear or enter—2. that no inspection of merchandize on board coasting vessels is directed by law except in cases of goods claiming drawback."

2. For a discussion of the trade in plaster of paris as a medium for smuggling, see Gerald S. Graham, "The Gypsum Trade of the Maritime Provinces: Its Relation to American Diplomacy and Agriculture in the Early Nineteenth Century," *Agricultural History*, 12 (1938): 212–18.

3. In the margin opposite this paragraph Gallatin wrote: "The substance of this paragraph had already been written on several occasions to many collectors. It was thought eligible to make the instructions general."

From William C. C. Claiborne

DEAR SIR,   NEAR NEW-ORLEANS October 8h 1811

As my Commission as Governor of Orleans, will expire on the 17th. of January next, I take the liberty to request you to consider me a Candidate for honor of a reappointment. I am very grateful for the many proofs of Confidence you have already given me, and If I know myself, the favorite wish of my heart has always been, to merit by a faithful discharge of my duties, a Continuance of your good opinion.

As the Ordinance for the Government of this Territory, makes no provision for the exercise of the powers of Governor, in case of Vacancy, except when arising from death, removal, or resignation, or in case of necessary Absence, it has heretofore been customary to make the Nomination, some time *previous to the term of service expiring*.[1] If this Rule should be observed on the present occasion, it would relieve me from some embarrassment, and prevent the public service from sustaining Inconvenience. Among the Measures, I contemplate directing, in the event of my continuance in office, is an early Session of the Territorial Legislature: & which will become the more necessary, should the Convention, which is to Assemble in November, deem it expedient to form a Constitution, since it is probable, that some Legislative pro[v]isions Adapted to the contemplated change, will be indispensible.

On the question as to a State Authority, there is some division of sentiment; But a majority of the Citizens seem favorable to the Change, and my impression is, that the Convention will readily acceede to the *terms* proposed by Congress.[2] I presume however, it will not be possible to make such arrangements as to bring the State Officers into Power, at an earlier period, than one year from this date; And in the mean time, it will be essential to the preservation of good Order, & the public surety, that the Territorial Authorities should be operative and in ful[l] force.

I learn with sincere regret, (thro' the medium of the News-papers) that your exertions to secure for the U. States, the great Blessing of Peace are not likely to be successful. The pulse of the English Government seems high for War, and instead of receiving reparations for the Many Wrongs offered our Country, we hear daily of further Aggressions. An honorable Peace is certainly the wish of every faithful Citizen; that it is the wish also of our Rulers, I do not believe, a man in America (whatever some party Writers may state) doubts; But I fear Sir, a Crisis will soon arrive, when we must make War, or abandon our Rights as a Nation. At such a Crisis, our Nation will *unquestionably be united*, & the Government firmly & bravely supported.

The City of New-Orleans is again visited by that dreadful Scourge, the Yellow Fever, and many Good Citizens have fallen Victims. The Mortality is greatest among Strangers; but the old Settlers are not exempt.

The Members of the Convention are to assemble by Law, at New-Orleans on the first Monday in November; But I suspect many of them will be so apprehensive of the Fever, that a quorum will not be found until about the last of that Month.

I ask the favour of you to present my most respectful and friendly Wishes to Mrs. Madison, and to permit me to Subscribe myself Your faithful friend and Most Obt servt

WILLIAM C. C. CLAIBORNE

RC (DLC). Docketed by JM.

1. On 25 Nov. 1811 JM nominated Claiborne for another three-year term as territorial governor. He also sent him at that time his commission (*Senate Exec. Proceedings*, 2:192; Carter, *Territorial Papers, Orleans*, 9:981).

2. In March 1810 the territorial legislature had petitioned Congress for the admission of Orleans to the Union, particularly requesting as it did so that the territory be exempt from the requirement of having a population of 60,000. The matter was not decided during the second session of the Eleventh Congress and, accordingly, was taken up again after December 1810 when it was complicated by a debate over whether the territorial boundaries should be defined to include those portions of West Florida annexed under the provisions of JM's 27 Oct. 1810 proclamation. After deciding to make separate provision for the West Florida region, Congress passed on 13 Feb. 1811 an enabling bill permitting the free white male American citizens of the territory to elect a constitutional convention in September 1811. The convention was to meet in November and frame a constitution subject to the following terms: that the constitution be republican in form and consistent with the U.S. Constitution; that the constitution secure "the fundamental principles of civil and religious liberty"; that the laws and legal proceedings of the new state be recorded in English; that the state forego any claims to own or to tax "waste or unappropriated lands" within Orleans Territory which were to be at the sole disposition of the U.S.; and that the state renounce any claim to impose tolls or taxes on the Mississippi and other waterways leading to the Gulf of Mexico. JM signed the bill into law on 22 Feb. 1811 (Carter, *Territorial Papers, Orleans*, 9:873–77; *Annals of Congress*, 11th Cong., 3d sess., 25, 37–43, 43–64, 65–66, 67, 83, 103, 121, 126, 413, 466, 514, 516, 518–42, 555–79, 993, 1030, 1096, 1102, 1103; *U.S. Statutes at Large*, 2:641–43).

From the New York State Canal Commissioners

SIR   NEW YORK October 8th 1811.

The enclosed Exemplification of a Statute passed the eighth of last april will shew that we are empowered to make application, on behalf of the State of New York, to the Congress of the United States, on the subject of a Canal betwe[e]n the Great Lakes and Hudson's River.[1]

An object of such general concern seems to be within the scope of that information which is to be communicated to the National Legislature by the President of the United States, and therefore, we deem it our duty to place it in your hands.

We do not assign reasons in it's support because they will not escape your penetration; neither do we solicit your patronage because we rely on your patriotism. It is submitted to your consideration in the most simple form and we have charged two of our Members Gouverneur Morris and Dewit Clinton to give you Sir, in presenting this Letter, the personal assurance of that respect with which We have the Honor to be Your most obedient servants

GOUVR MORRIS
[and six others]

RC (NHi). Signed by Morris, DeWitt Clinton, Simeon DeWitt, William North, Thomas Eddy, Robert R. Livingston, and Robert Fulton. Docketed by JM. Enclosure not found, but see n. 1.

1. In April 1811 the New York State Legislature had created the New York State Canal Commission with an appropriation of $15,000 in order to advance the project of constructing a canal between the Hudson River and Lake Erie. The commission had seven members—all of whom signed the above letter to JM—and its purposes were to seek aid, both from other states and from Congress, to receive land grants and loans, and to negotiate the purchase of the assets of the failing Western Inland Lock Navigation Company, which had been incorporated in 1792 to open a waterway from Albany to Lakes Seneca and Ontario. Two of the commissioners, Gouverneur Morris and DeWitt Clinton, visited Washington in December 1811 where they lobbied both JM and Congress for support, but without success (Ronald E. Shaw, *Erie Water West: A History of the Erie Canal, 1792–1854* [Lexington, Ky., 1966], pp. 45–47).

§ From John Hawker. *8 October 1811, Plymouth.* Encloses a memorial for JM's consideration. Mentions that the orders in council are still in force and that "Vessels and Goods belonging to Citizens of the United States; comeing from or bound to France are often sent in here & are Condemned."

RC and enclosure, two copies (DNA: RG 59, LAR, 1809–17, filed under "Hawker"). RC 1 p. Enclosure (6 pp.) is a memorial by Hawker describing his service in various vice-consular positions in England since 1791 and requesting that he be appointed consul at Plymouth.

From James Wilkinson

SIR   FREDERICK TOWN MARYLAND October ⟨9⟩th. 1811

When I agreed to waive all exception to the Jurisdiction of a Military Tribunal, and submit to a rigorous Scrutiny of my Conduct for more than twenty years past, I did hope, & I am sure it was your intention, Sir, that the proceedings against me should not only be free & unbiased, but that there should not be even cause for Suspicion, that the Government felt any Interest whatever in depriving me of the benefit, of a fair & impartial decision of the Court to whom my case had been referred.

This impression, combined to my sense of the Justice & Integrity of your Character, has encouraged me respectfully to represent to you, Sir, that the Conduct of the Accountant of the War Department, (who has been attending here as it would seem, from his own declarations, in the Double Capacity of a Witness for the prosecution & paymaster to the officers of the Court) has been all along designed to excite & to rivet the most injurious prejudices against me, with a view if possible to influence the impending trial.

Not satisfied with reviling me in the Taverns & on the streets of this Town in malignant & approbitious terms, Mr. Simmons had the presumption last Evening to make use of the high authority of your name in a manner calculated to impress a beleif, that his own unworthy & improper interference, is sanctioned by the predetermination of the President in my Case.

Convinced as I am that this course of proceedings on his part, is entirely without your Knowledge or approbation, and conceiving it to be no less indecent than it is unfair: The respect which I owe to you, as well as a sense of Justice to myself, seem to render it a Duty, that I should address you personally & directly on the subject; and that you may be particularly apprized of the Kind of language in which Mr. simmons indulges Himself, I beg permission to submit to your consideration the enclosed Statement of Lt. Leroy Opee an officer of Character & a Man of unblemished reputation.[1]

You will I trust, sir, have the goodness to pardon me for suggesting to your reflection, that if Mr. simmons' Deportment & conversations, would be highly improper & unbecoming in any private Individual, when appearing in the Capacity of a Witness, even in an Ordinary Criminal prosecution, this impropriety is extremely aggravated, by the remark which will naturally be made, that Mr. simmons is a public Officer of no inconsiderable responsibility, seeking to exert whatever Official influence he may Himself be supposed to possess, and pretending to call to his Aid the Authority of his Superiors, for the purpose of affecting the result of an Enquiry, in which my Life & Honor and every Interest & feeling dear to the Heart of Man are all staked upon the Issue. With perfect respect, I have the Honor to be sir Your very Humble & obedient Servant

Ja: Wilkinson

RC and enclosures (DLC). Date of RC obscured by blot. Docketed by JM as dated 8 Oct. but acknowledged by him as 9 Oct. (see JM to Wilkinson, 12 Oct. 1811). For enclosures, see n. 1.

1. Wilkinson enclosed a copy of a letter he received from Lt. LeRoy Opie of the Fifth Infantry, dated 9 Oct. 1811 (1 p.), covering a copy of a "statement of a conversation" Opie had held with William Simmons on 7 Oct. (1 p.). Opie mentioned to Simmons that he had read a newspaper report that Dr. Samuel Latham Mitchill was to become secretary of war, to which Simmons replied that "he had heard nothing of it, that Doctor Eustis did not intend to resign, unless Wilkinson was to resume the command of the Army." Opie surmised that Wilkinson might be acquitted, to which Simmons was said to have replied that "the court could not, or if they did the President could not confirm the sentence, and that General Wilkinson would never command the army again." In justice to Simmons, Opie wrote to Wilkinson, he assumed that Simmons's "observations were not conveyed from his own knowledge of the decision of the Secretary or President, but I suppose from his own opinion." Wilkinson later reprinted Opie's statement of this conversation in his memoirs but omitted Opie's qualifying remark that Simmons had no firsthand knowledge of the opinions of JM and Eustis (James Wilkinson, *Memoirs of My Own Times* [3 vols.; Philadelphia, 1816], 2:461–62).

From Thomas Jefferson

DEAR SIR   MONTICELLO Oct. 10. 11.

Mrs. Lewis, the widow of Colo. Nich Lewis,[1] has requested me to mention to yourself the name of a mr. Wood, an applicant for a commission in the army. On recieving the request I rode to her house to ask something about him, observing to her that something more than his name would be necessary. She candidly told me at once that he was a very capable young man, connected with her only as being a brother to one of her sons in law, that he had married a respectable girl in Louisa, but became so dissipated and disorderly in his conduct that his father in law drove him off and procured an act of divorce from his wife, who is now married to another husband. This affected him so that he went off to the Western country, and, as she has been informed, became quite a new man: but had no knolege of it herself. She was inclined to suppose it true as her son Nicholas had written to her pressingly on his behalf and had particularly urged her to get me to mention him to you. To this neighbor I can refuse nothing, and I therefore comply with her request, stating the grounds on which we are both put into motion, and adding some information which perhaps may not be conveyed by others. The old king dies hard; but he will die. I wish we were as sure that his successor would give us justice and peace. I think it a little more than barely possible, relying on his former habits of connection, not on his principles, for he has none worthy of reliance. Ever affectionately your's

TH: JEFFERSON

RC (DLC); FC (DLC: Jefferson Papers).

1. Nicholas Lewis (1734–1808) was a neighbor of Jefferson's and had managed Jefferson's business affairs while he was in France. He had married Mary Walker, daughter of Dr. Thomas Walker (Betts, *Jefferson's Garden Book*, p. 19 n. 16).

To James Wilkinson

SIR   WASHINGTON Octr. 12. 1811

I have received your letter of the 9th inst: inclosing a statement of a private conversation between Lt. Opie, and Mr. Simmons Acct. of the War Department, made by the former.

The considerations out of which the Court Martial in your case grew, would attach particular regret to any circumstance affecting, even in appearance or opinion, the justice and fairness of the proceedings, as they relate to yourself, as well as to the public. And you very justly take for granted that the Executive would be incapable of any other views or sentiments. Accept my respects

JAMES MADISON

RC (ICU); FC (DLC).

From David Howell

SIR,   PROVIDENCE October 12, 1811.

My only Son[1] will have the Honor to deliver this Letter. I have endeavoured to impress his mind with Just views of your personal character & political measures, &, I am authorised to assure you of his Support.

He is a young man of regular habits, united with much benevolence & a laudable zeal in the *Republican* cause, which received his first political attachments.

Whatever patronage it may fall in your way to afford him, during his Term of Service in the Senate of the United States, will be rendred to a young man of the highest Sensibility; and, you may be assured, will be reciprocated, to the utmost of their means, both by the Father & Son. With the greatest consideration, I have the Honor to be, Sir,

RC (DLC). Signature clipped. At a later date, someone, probably JM, supplied the name of David Howell.

1. Jeremiah Brown Howell.

§ Executive Pardon. *12 October 1811, Washington.* JM remits the sentence of death imposed 12 Aug. 1811 by a court-martial at Baton Rouge on Sgt. Peter B. Conger of the Consolidated Infantry Regiment for the offense of desertion. Leaves standing that part of the sentence reducing Conger to the ranks.

Tr (DNA: RG 107, LSMA). 1 p.

From Benjamin Hawkins

CREEK AGENCY 13th. Octer. 1811

I have had the pleasure my Dear friend to receive your favour of the 18th July. To a man of my standing with you there was no need of the frank declaration you have made to ensure a continuance of my confidence in your political conduct and to convince me that you are invulnerable in that

484

part where you have been so violently assailed. I had known but little of the character of Mr. Smith and that little much in his favour. As soon as I red his publication I was disgusted with the man, and with his production; It appeared to me a weak wicked and illjudged thing engendered in the basest passions and would recoil on and punish its author.

I this summer was visited by a man of genteel appearance, infirm health, without a letter of introduction who called himself Felix O'Hanlon an Irishman by birth, who had been a colonel in the spanish service afterwards a Major in that of the British which he left on the score of his religion and now one of the Commissaries for the supply of fresh provisions to the army and Navy in the West indies and southwardly on the spanish coast. He spent some weeks with me, is a man of information and of much anecdote. On leaving me for Charleston he commenced a correspondence with me on political subjects, the successor of Madison &ca. which is now carried on, a part of which is as follows. In my reply of 26 august to a letter of his of 3 or 4 pages of the 18th. July. "You say Madison aught and might be saved by genius, his very difficulties would he be advised would turn out to his honour and interest. On this subject I have to remark I think him not in the least danger. The great body who support him are the landholders, they are Republican and they will support him. The Conduct of the Exsecretary has recoiled on himself and he is fallen! fallen! fallen! into the abyss of contempt in a national point of view. However the Republicans may jar among themselves they will be in unison on great fundimental points. There is not a man in America I know better or esteem more than Mr. Madison he will act from advise and be grateful for it if his judgment is convinced not otherwise. The happiest part of my life was that in which I was associated with him under the Confederation as well as constitution of the U:S. We both well know what it is to be in the minority, as well as the respect due to the majority. We conformed to the Laws, resisted only during their passage. In the senate particularly such was my political situation that most of the great constitutional questions were settled by the Vote of Mr. Adams our President. I lived then with my political opponents on terms of friendship always believing Mr Adams an honest man and could altho opposed to him tolerate the reasons he assigned for all his Votes one excepted relative to the ratio of Representation which was negatived by General Washington.[1]

["]There was no such thing as men in office calumniating their own government and being apologists for the injuries done us by foreign Governments. We were then National men driving to a desirable end by different ways. We had had our Arnold brave as Cæsar as long as he remained in service and a traytor only when he deserted us. We have lately seen men holding public offices traytors to their Country and claiming the thanks or future confidence of their country for being so. I have ever been a firm admirer of our present constitution. I voted for its adoption in my native state and was five years in the senate of the United states. I think it the perfection of human wisdom, that it will last with time itself if administerd on liberal republican principles. As to Mobile I think Governor Claiborne has possession of the whole of the Country we claim, except the fort of Mobile only. If you could in this or any other line render your adopted country any service It would be well received and if you think proper to confide any thing to me on this subject or thro' me to the Government you can do it in perfect safety."

In his reply of the 21st septr. which embraces several topics "as to Mobile there are a variety of reasons why it aught to be saught possession of all I wish to say, on that subject is I would from my local knowledge of the spanish character and a perfect one of their language and having been in their service, More my near relative Cornet ORiley holding at this moment high situation at Havanah [have] an opportunity of settling the surrender or surprise of the fort as would cause no noise nor arouse any serious un- kind feeling towards the administration. To this I would pledge myself no purchase no pay, except bare expences. You are if you think with me at liberty to communicate this to the President.

["]In case of a War with Great Britain I have arranged a plan which would raise this Country to a height that would command the respect of the Belligerents and astonish the world to each of these statements I pledge myself in the fullest manner nor would I ought solicit that results would not justify. You know so do I, that it is not wisdom for a person who has capacity to plan or genius to direct in issue schemes of such extent and magnitude without having the advantage in some degree arising from it."

Mr. Hambleton one of the men captured by the spaniards near Mobile where Majr. Hargrave was taken, has with three others been liberated.[2] He left the Havanah 21 days past and came by the way of pensacola. The Capn. of the Vessel told him there were two spanish gentlemen on bord going to adjust the surrender of Mobile to the americans. The gentlemen landed at pensacola.

The Convention with the Indians sent on to the Department of War will shew you how happily we have succeeded in the road business and for a mere trifle, considering the extent of territory thro which they are to pass and the wildness of our people.[3] With sincere wishes for your health & happiness I am my Dear friend Your obedient servant

BENJAMIN HAWKINS

RC (DLC). Docketed by JM.

1. Hawkins referred to Washington's veto of the first apportionment bill on 5 Apr. 1792 (see *PJM*, 14:261–62).

2. Hargrave and Hambleton had been members of the filibustering party captured by

Folch at Saw Mill Creek on 10 Dec. 1810. If Hambleton and three others were released at this time, the remaining prisoners were not. Claiborne was still interceding with the authorities in Havana for their release as late as the summer of 1813 (Toulmin to JM, 12 Dec. 1810, and n. 1; Claiborne to Vincent Gray, 14 July 1813, Rowland, *Claiborne Letter Books*, 6:239–40).

3. On 26 Sept. 1811 Hawkins persuaded a reluctant council of the Creek Indians at Too-kaubatche to accept demands for the opening of a road through their territory which they had earlier rejected in May 1811 (see Hobohoilthle to JM, 14 May 1811). Hawkins informed the council that JM had considered their May decision to be "unreasonable and not satisfactory," adding that JM regarded "red and white people within the United States as one people, with respect to the use of water courses and roads." Reminding them that the U.S. had incurred some expense to secure Indian land rights in Tennessee and Georgia, Hawkins continued: "The President has given full time to the Indian Chiefs to understand these truths, and to explain them to their young people, . . . [but] the period has now arrived when the white people must have roads to market and for traveling wherever they choose to go through the United States. The people of Tennessee must have a road to Mobile, and the post paths must become a road for travellers and both of these roads will be used by the troops of the United States in marching from post to post as the public good may require." In return for opening the road, the Creek Indians were to receive between 1812 and 1814 one thousand spinning wheels, one thousand pairs of cotton cards, and a quantity of iron, at a cost Hawkins estimated to be $4,350.62 (Hawkins to Eustis, 3 Oct. 1811, Grant, *Letters of Benjamin Hawkins*, 2:592–94).

From Henry A. S. Dearborn

HOND. SIR, BOSTON. Octo. 14. 1811

At the request of my friend N. Bowditch Esqr.[1] I have enclosed you one of his papers containing the result of his calculations on the Elements of the Orbit of the Comet which for some weeks has appeared in the northern regions of the heavens.[2] I have known him for some years & have no doubt but he is the ablest astronomical mathematitian in this country & equal to any in Europe. He is a self educated man. If there is any one in Washington, or in the vicinity of your estate in Virginia, who can furnish him with answers to the questions contained in a note at the bottom of the paper,[3] you will confer a great favor on him, by causing them to be forwarded to him at Salem. I have the honor to remain your Obt. Servt.

H. A. S. DEARBORN[4]

RC (DLC); enclosure (DLC: Madison Collection, Rare Book Division). RC docketed by JM. For enclosure, see n. 2.

1. Nathaniel Bowditch (1773–1838) was the son of a cooper in Salem, Massachusetts, and he was apprenticed in a ship chandlery. He supplemented his self-education with observations made in the course of his voyages after 1795 and in 1799 prepared *The New American Practical Navigator*, a work which was to go through ten editions during his lifetime and several more thereafter. Between 1804 and 1823 he was president of the Essex Fire and Marine Insurance Company, and he published many papers in the *Memoirs of the American Academy of Arts and*

Sciences. He also translated and published the works of the French mathematician and astronomer Pierre-Simon Laplace (Robert E. Berry, *Yankee Stargazer: The Life of Nathaniel Bowditch* [New York, 1941], pp. 6, 20–21, 111–22, 143, 180–81, 210–11, 221–22).

2. Dearborn enclosed a printed circular entitled "The Comet," a series of calculations of the "geocentric longitudes and latitudes of the Comet," based on observations taken at Cambridge and Nantucket, Massachusetts (1 p.).

3. In a postscript to his circular Bowditch stated that he wished to make "a complete collection of the observations of the Eclipse" and requested that information on such observations, including the latitudes and longitudes where they were recorded, be sent to him.

4. Henry Alexander Scammel Dearborn (1783–1851), the son of JM's former cabinet colleague Henry Dearborn, had attended Williams College and the College of William and Mary. When Henry Dearborn took up his position of major general in the U.S. Army in 1812, JM appointed his son to be collector for the district of Boston and Charlestown, a position he held until 1829 (*Senate Exec. Proceedings,* 2:278).

From Ninian Edwards

ELVIRADE RANDOLPH COUNTY ILLINOIS TERRITORY

SIR   Octr 16. 1811

I have the honor to enclose you the proceedings of a meeting of the citizens of St Clair county and their address to you. All of which I am convinced is the result of apprehensions of danger, entertained not merely by timid minds but by men well acquainted with the geographical situation habits and disposition of the Indians alluded to—Experienced in Indian warfare and as much distinguished by their valour as any other citizens in the Western country.[1]

The principle facts stated in the address I have already had the honor to communicate to the war department.[2]

The Indians residing about Lake Michigan and on the Illinois river and its waters are those who have committed the depredations which have so much alarmed and agitated this territory, the Northwestern parts of which are very much exposed to their attacks. Whether those Indians visit our frontiers by land or water they pass thro Peoria or its immediate vicinity both in coming and returning. A garrison therefore at that place would in my opinion hold in check all those from whom we have most danger to apprehend and in several respects be attended with very benificial consequences.

Believing the proposed measures to be expedient and necessary to the safety of the territory I have thought it my duty thus far to support the prayer of the enclosed petition, but I had no knowledge that any such was even contemplated till I received the enclosed papers. I have the honor to be With the highest respect Sr Yr Mo Obdt St

NINIAN EDWARDS.

RC and enclosures (DNA: RG 107, LRRS, E-3:6). Docketed by a War Department clerk as received 12 Nov. 1811. For enclosures, see n. 1.

1. Edwards enclosed the proceedings of a meeting of the militia officers and other inhabitants of St. Clair County, Illinois Territory (2 pp.), requesting Edwards to forward a memorial addressed to the president (5 pp.). The memorial complained of Indian attacks in the area of the Illinois River over a period of five or six years; mentioned that the settlers had restrained their desire to retaliate for fear of punishing the innocent "for the transgressions of the Guilty"; but also complained of horse thefts and murders during the previous spring. The settlers declared they were "no intruders but living on their own farms" on the frontier, and they beseeched JM to establish a garrison at the village of Opea on the Illinois River and another on the eastern bank of the Mississippi, six or eight miles below the mouth of the Illinois River. The memorial concluded by referring JM to the governor for a statement of the urgency of the matter (printed in Ninian Edwards, *History of Illinois, from 1778–1833: And Life and Times of Ninian Edwards* [Springfield, Ill., 1870], pp. 288–91). Edwards was to forward another copy of the RC and enclosures in his 15 Feb. 1812 letter to William Eustis (DNA: RG 107, LRRS, E-37:6; docketed as received 10 Mar. 1812).

2. Edwards had repeatedly complained to the War Department about Indian hostilities on the frontier; see his letters to Eustis of 7, 20, and 22 June 1811 (Edwards, *History of Illinois*, pp. 285–87).

From Paul Hamilton

Nav: Dep'mt 16. Octo: 1811.

I have the honor to submit to Your consideration the paper herewith marked A. which is a statement of navy appropriations up to the 15. instant inclusively.

By this paper, You will perceive, Sir, that the aggregate unexpended balance on that day, was $785.491.13.: but that of the appropriation for "repairs of vessels" there was only, on hand $1532..8.—& only $508.36. of the Appropriation for "quarter Masters department of the Marine corps." These balances indeed, are merely nominal; for on the appropriation for "Repairs of vessels" there are at this time requisitions unpaid, to the Amount of nearly $30.000. vizt

Requisition by Navy agents at Cha'ston $7.600
Do   Do   Nfolk   5.000
Do   Do   NYork   6 000.
Do by the purser Do this place   6 394.25
$28.175.32[1]

and on the appropriation for Qrmasters Department Marine Corps, the inevitable demands for fuel not yet provided & other Articles, will really exceed the apparant balance on hand.

Under these circumstances Sir, I take the liberty of submitting to You, the propriety of a transfer of funds, in aid of these appropriations, from other appropriations which I beleive can spare the transfer & should You approve such transfer, I have to request Your Signature to the enclosed paper. With the highest respect I have the honor to be Yr: Mo. ob.

P. HAMILTON

Letterbook copy and copy of enclosure A (DNA: RG 45, LSP). Enclosure A is a "Statement of appropriations Treasury 15. Octo 1811" (1 p.). Second enclosure not found.

1. Arithmetic error in letterbook copy.

§ From George Luckey. *17 October 1811.* Acknowledges receipt of JM's letter [not found] and is glad he is in good health. Concedes that the people suffer hardships because of the injustice and cruelty of men filled with envy, but they have it better than many others and enjoy liberty when many men are not pleased with liberty. Deplores those who wish to be masters of the world and denounces them as madmen. When he wrote to JM,[1] it seemed best to some to restrict U.S. trade to this country, but every day the state of affairs changes and at this juncture who can say what is best? Suggests allowing merchantmen to arm and defend themselves on the high seas and give the captors by law half the booty captured. Profit was made in this way during the American war and people are eager for wealth. Also suggests negotiating with Europeans to defend both them and the U.S. against the despot of the sea, who will never be fair unless compelled. Excessive forbearance will break the spirit of the citizens and be the cause of much evil. Long ago God gave Americans liberty, peace, and safety, and He still defends these things. The U.S. cause is best, for it is the cause of justice and truth. Americans can fight to the end to defend the country, but they see the enemy striving to divide and weaken them. Exhorts the nation's leaders to be of good spirit. They have the wishes and prayers of all good men; and just as the Israelites fought, so too Americans are fighting bravely against enemies who are the enemies of justice and truth, as well as of much else. Advocates reliance on God who will be with Americans and make them successful.

RC (DLC). 2 pp. In Latin; signed "Georgius Luckey." Docketed by JM.

1. Luckey to JM, 1 July 1811.

From George Joy

DEAR SIR,   LONDON 18th Octer: 1811

The Constitution is now daily expected at Cowes; and by her I hope to embark for the U.S. I am just now advised of a Bag at the N. York Coffee House for Letters to be sent by a fast sailing ship from Liverpool, and send this in the presumption that it may arrive before the Constitution.

I am advised of the Condemnation of the Julian, Hercules, Catharine & Atlantic, (carried into Dantzic in May last,) by the Council of Prizes in

Paris, without further appeal, on Bond to produce further Proof, as in former Cases. I am also advised by a Gentleman who left Copenhagen the 22nd Ult: that two of our ships, on leaving Elsinore, homeward bound, were pursued by a french privateer, taken, out of Danish Jurisdiction, & carried back; and I have this day a Letter from Copenhagen of the 26th informing me that a Revision of all the Papers in the Case of certain Property in the charge of a Mr: Fisher, of Philadelphia, (and which I presume relates to five Vessells & valuable Cargoes detained since last Year at Kiel,) has been granted by the King, on a requisition from the Captors.

In hopes of the pleasure of seeing you, soon after, if not before you receive this, I rest very respectfully & sincerely, Dear sir, Your friend & servt:

GEO: JOY.

If this should arrive before me, or other Letters from me on the subject, I hope there will be no urgent necessity for filling up the Consulship, vacant by the Death of Genl. Lyman.

RC and enclosure, two copies (DLC: Rives Collection, Madison Papers). First RC postmarked at Boston on 26 Dec. Second RC marked "Copy"; in a clerk's hand, signed by Joy. Enclosure is a copy of Joy to Joel Barlow, 15 Sept. 1811 (2 pp.), written at Gothenburg, informing Barlow of his departure from Copenhagen and claiming success for his mission in Denmark.

§ From William Picket. *18 October 1811, Charlestown, Massachusetts.* "My Son Capt Wm S Picket has just Arrived into Boston from Naples in the Brig Alexander and had the Inclosed Packet committed to his Charge but on his Voyage home was boarded and had his Papers examined and his Letters broke open by the Cruisers of one of [the] Belligerents." Hopes JM will accept this apology for the packet being opened. Mentions in a postscript that he is acquainted with Richard Cutts.

RC (DLC). 1 p.

From Richard Cutts

DEAR SIR   SACO October 19th. 1811

On my return from Boston I found your favr. of the 30th Ulto. from Montpelier, Yours of the 6th Inst. came to hand several days past, on receipt of it, I wrote immediately to Judge Lincoln requesting an explination of the conversation that took place between us last May. I have waited several days for his answer—as soon as it arrives I will forward it to you—if he does not incline to accept the appointment, I most sincerely hope he will point out some of the most prominent Lawyers in the district from whom you may make a fortunate selection.

If Judge Lincoln declines, as I fear he will, Joseph Story of Salem the present speaker of our House of Representatives,[1] & the Honble. Ezekiel Bacon appear almost the only Candidates in this State, they are both young & yazooists. As you are personally acquainted with both of them, I am convinced you can form a better opinion of their Merit & qualifications than myself. Since writing another person has occured to my Mind, likewise known to you, I mean Mr. Plummer of New Hampshire, formerly a Federal Senator in the UStates Senate since a Republican, & now the Republican Candidate to Succeed Govr. Langdon. I mention him only for your consideration.

I regret to state that my late trip to Boston has caused my shoulder to continue very weak & some times painful. I cannot use it but very little, without the assistance of my other hand, being my right arm increases the misfortune, if the disability had been in the left arm I believe we should have surmounted all other obstacles & set our faces towards Washington, we cannot reconcile ourselves to the loss we are about to suffer, without the most painful sensations—if my shoulder should get better soon, we may even at the eleventh hour attempt the journey, if deprived of the happiness of seeing you this winter, we can only say that our constant prayers will be for your health & happiness, & that of Mrs. M—not forgetting Mrs. W. and our other friends. We hope your next will announce the better health of John Payne. I am with the highest respect & esteem yr St

RICHARD CUTTS

RC (NN). Docketed by JM.

1. JM nominated Joseph Story to be an associate justice of the Supreme Court on 15 Nov. 1811. The Senate confirmed the appointment three days later (*Senate Exec. Proceedings*, 2:189, 190).

From Christopher Ellery

PROVIDENCE Octr. 21. 1811.

Believing it proper to make a communication to the President of the United States, in its nature partaking of importance, I have adopted the mode best calculated, as it seemed to me, for the purpose, by inclosing the copy of a letter which I have written to several members of the United States' Senate, of the republican party. The views inducing me to this act will be readily conceived from the contents of the letter: it is, therefore, further necessary only to tender assurances of profound respect, and, if permitted, sincere esteem and personal attachment

CHRIST. ELLERY

[Enclosure]

DEAR SIR   PROVIDENCE, R. I. Octr. 21st. 1811.

In addressing you at this time I am actuated by a principle of duty: If personal considerations influence me in any, the least, degree, they are so intermingled with what, to me, seems to be patriotic feeling, that not only is my conscience wholly at ease while contemplating the possible results from this communication, but my sense of honor irresistably urges me to the act. As it is not my wish to court difficulties or embarrassments of any kind, labouring already under cares and troubles more and greater than my feeble powers can effectually struggle against; as it is far from me to invite distinction among my fellow citizens, contenting myself with the reputation I now enjoy; my request is that you will have the goodness to receive this letter as intended, confidentially. My motives & views being pure, assurances of perfect respect are tendered in lieu of apology: and, with permission; I proceed to my subject.

It were desirable that you should have a more particular acquaintance with the political state of things in Rhode Island than your important engagements will probably allow you opportunity to acquire—the knowledge, therefore of our public concerns which you possess must suffice—at least going upon the belief that your information relative to us is sufficiently accurate for forming correct opinions upon the collateral matter connected with that which I have the honor now to present you, it becomes useless to trouble you with circumstances engendered in political iniquity and whose fruit is temporary, if not lasting, disgrace to the democracy which ought to prevail and flourish here, where, truly, the soil is favorable to the plant. I shall, then, merely observe, in one sentence, that the ascendancy of federalism, so called, in this state, has grown out of the practices of men who, collectively, may, very appositely, in my judgment, be denominated the Fenner-faction. Of this faction Jeremiah B. Howel, who will shortly claim a seat in the Senate of the Union, is an humble instrument—a tool simply, because his qualities fit him only to be made use of—and but a poor tool will he prove to be *in whatever hands he shall be managed.* This man has a few days since, resigned a post in the customs held by him several years. He acted as inspector (tidewaiter) previous to his election as Senator U. S.—at the time of his election—and continued to act (serve) until the fifth day of this month. By the inclosed certificate,[1] granted at my request, this statement is confirmed. When speaking of his *election,* it is in reserve that he was ineligible. Whatever may be the opinion of another on the propriety or impropriety of selecting a tidewaiter, wholly undistinguished by talents, for the honorable body to which you belong, to my mind it assumed somewhat of the character of making a consul of a horse, or sending boots as representatives to an august assembly. Such however was not the intention. The person, I am persuaded, was destined to be locum tenens

493

for his father, who was to have been created senator in season to prevent the resignation of the son in the revenue department; but unluckily for the contrivers of the scheme, the current of events has run counter to their designs, and the son is under the necessity of quitting a certainty at home for an uncertainty at the seat of government. Whether these or other more vile expectations existed, or not, is in a measure, immaterial; though if the motives for the extraordinary appointment could be clearly ascertained rather than drawn from circumstances, which might prove deceptive, it were well that it should be done. Enough for the present purpose is it to state the naked fact, viz, that he, thus elected to the senate, held an office under the United States *before—at the time of his election—*and *has continued to hold it many months,* nearly twelve, *after his election;* although, in his capacity of inspecto⟨r,⟩ under oath to support the constitution, which declares that no person so holding an office shall be a member of either house during his continuance in office. Howel was chosen, if in reality chosen at all, to serve in Congress for six years from the fourth day of March last. The Constitution, its spirit, its powers, its constructions are, however, well known to you, and it might be impertinent in me, even if qualified for the discussion, to attempt the constitutional question arising out of the case before us. It is for the senate to decide whether Howel was ineligible; whether his continuance in the place of inspector after the 4th of March last; whether these or other legal bars will prevent his entrance into the legislature of the Union, or not; but permit me to believe, that, provided a tidewaiter, not remarkable for wonderful abilities, could be, constitutionally precluded from a seat in senate, it would comport with their dignity to shut doors against him; especially if disgraceful means had produced the exaltation of the tidewaiter in preference to gentlemen distinguished for love of their country and its republican institutions. If this revenue-officer does present himself to perform the duties of Senator, and if he is legally forbidden to discharge those duties, then, considering that the introduction of the matter, herein communicated, to the senate, must depend on a knowledge of facts, which, in all probability, would remain hidden from them, without the voluntary disclosure of some individual, it is pardonable, assuredly, in one who has had the honor of sitting in senate, and whose respect for that house is unbounded, to invite the attention of members, personally known to him, to the subject—so deeply interesting, in his estimation, to every member, honorable men as they all unquestionably are.

It is possible that our General Assembly (to convene the last monday of October instant) may, conceiving a vacancy to have happened, elect anew; yet it is possible that they may not; for divers reasons; one, that in case the Senate U. S. first declare the vacancy, the path of the General Assembly would, thereby, become smooth & easy; another, that J. B. Howel, but of late in the ranks, or even profession, of republicanism, might, his character being by them accurately weighed, be agreeable to them, for a while at least, equally with another; which other they might, if the constitution is as in this letter understood, send forward, making their own choice of the time when, after the Senate, opposed to them in politics, should have been, according to their conception, degraded by association with a person contemptible on the score of meanness, evinced by service in an inferior grade while claiming to be elected to an elevated station, if not for poverty of intellect.

Moreover, classing Howel as senator, he was the constitutional adviser of the President on the question of appointment of the Collector of the Customs, whilst serving too under the collector in a capacity but little at variance, in many of its features, from menial. How could the Collector, though so disposed to do, displace the Senator-inspector? Perhaps he would thus have done if his inspector had not been (as he must have apprehended) a senator; and for the very reason, a very good one, that his inspector was a senator. Thus, may it not be fairly inferred? has the influence of the supposititious member secured in office the inspector—not indeed through want of energy, virtue or dignity in the collector, but rather because of the mingled contempt & pity with which he must be imagined to have contemplated, daily, the compound creature exposed to his observation, the monster in office—both his master and his man!

Does not the constitution reach a case like this? May not any member of senate demand a decision upon it? And is it not the duty of a Citizen, to whose eye the object is exhibited in lively colours, to bestow his endeavours in attracting towards it the notice due to its merits.

The collector's certificate I have judged to be a sufficient paper whereon to originate any motion or proceeding; confirmatory evidence may be obtained at the Treasury, where returns will be found shewing the holding of the inspector's place by J. B. Howel as before mentioned.

I will detain you no longer, Sir, than is necessary to assure you, that, whether erroneous or correct in the ideas I have advanced, or in the mode of expressing them, they are the offspring of an honest heart, animated with sentiments of the highest respect and esteem for yourself

CHRIST. ELLERY

RC and enclosures (DLC). First enclosure marked "Copy." For second enclosure, see n. 1.

1. Ellery enclosed an affidavit (1 p.) certifying that Jeremiah Brown Howell resigned his office as inspector at Providence on 5 Oct. and surrendered the commission granted him on 25 May 1801 to the collector, Thomas Coles.

§ From the Tammany Society of Brookhaven, Long Island. *21 October 1811*. The society's members have deemed it expedient to address JM "at the present very critical time & posture" of public affairs and to express their confidence in his talents and patriotism. "We are not unmindful of [the] enviableness of our condition. . . . Nor have we been idle Spectators of those events w⟨hich⟩ threaten our peace & hazzard our rights as an independent nation." They express indignation at the repeated insults the country has sustained from the European belligerents and resolve "to stand by & defend the measures of our Goverment in a redress of wrongs, a reperation [*sic*] for the past & a security for the future." They are pleased to note "some symtoms of returning justice on the part of *France* instanced in the repeal of her unjust & iniquitous Decrees against Neutral Commerce" but regret "the want of a similar disposition on the part of Great *Britain*—Who from the infamous & unprovoked murder of Pierce[1] to the present time have been guilty of repeated outrage." The ocean "has been constantly infested by her piratical forces, in violation of every principle of national Law. By them our people have been murdered—our property seized & condemned, our Seamen impressed & enslaved, our sovereignty invaded & our Government openly vilified & insulted—Justice has in reality been stricken from the Catalogue of their virtues."

JM's constant exertions to make an "honorable accommodation" are proof of his sincere regard for the best interests of the country. They regret "the disposition, which has for a length of time been manifested by a portion of our fellow Citizens [who are] endeavoring to counteract & render abortive, the wisest & most salutary measures of Goverment. These attempts it is our imperious duty to oppose so far as they tend to tarnish our reputation or hazzard our peace & national *Independence*."

"While we reflect upon . . . the prospect which exists of being compelled ultimately to engage in the 'unprofitable contest' as the only alternative by which redress can be obtained, we embrace this opportunity of assuring you & our fellow Citizens generally of our sincere approbation of the measures of your administration—our attachment to the invaluable principles of our Goverment & our fixed resolution to exert every faculty of our nature, in vindication & support of all such measures as shall be judged expedient for the attainment of ample & complete atonement for the accumulated wrongs which our Country has sustained."

RC (DNA: RG 59, ML). 3 pp. Signed by Charles H. Havens, grand sachem, and John M. Williamson, secretary.

1. John Pierce was an American seaman killed by a shot from HMS *Leander* in American territorial waters in April 1806, after his vessel had neglected to come to. His funeral in New York City provoked episodes of mob violence against British nationals (Perkins, *Prologue to War*, pp. 106–8).

§ From Oliver Whipple. *22 October 1811, Georgetown.* Has been unable to call on JM in person and, fearing that his prospects for either a consular appointment at Glasgow or an Indian agency are vanishing, seeks the position of sergeant at arms in the U.S. Senate, recently vacated by the death of Mr. Mathers.[1] "Your Excellency has it in your Power, to do me essential Service, thro' the medium & Friendship of the honble. Mr. [Richard] Cutts of the House, he is personally acquainted with the members of the Senate; your Intimations to him, backed with your good wishes to oblige me, would induce him to use his influence with the Senate." A similar suggestion to Mr. Varnum would also be gratefully acknowledged. Had intended to leave for New England this fall, but now that this vacancy has occurred, he will try his fortune with the Senate. "I have this Satisfaction That I have of late rendered your Excellency Services (tho' unknown to You) and it is in my Power further to do so, on many Occasions." Has sent a circular to all members of the Senate on the advice of friends, "on the Tenor of the one inclosed." Sends a copy to JM to show the grounds for his actions.[2]

RC (DLC); enclosure (DLC: Madison Collection, Rare Book Division). RC 2 pp. Docketed by JM. For enclosure, see n. 2.

1. James Mathers died on 2 Sept. 1811. Mountjoy Bailey of Maryland was elected as his successor on 6 Nov. 1811.

2. Whipple enclosed a printed circular letter, dated 22 Oct. 1811 (1 p.), describing his background in New Hampshire and Maine and seeking the position of sergeant at arms on the grounds that he intended to reside in the capital and practice law in Georgetown while also fulfilling the duties of the Senate post. This appointment would allow him to bring his family to Washington and he would be "enabled with economy to live in a decent manner, and not unmindful of benefactors."

From John Pitman, Jr.

HOND. SIR,   PROVIDENCE (R. I.) October 24th 1811.

You will pardon this intrusion of a stranger whose motive is the public good and the support of the administration. A schism (as you have no doubt ere this learned) has again appeared in the Republican party of this State. To this I must principally attribute the recommendation of David L. Barnes Esqr. the present judge of this District, by some leading republicans of this State, to fill the vacancy occasioned by the death of Judge Cushing. He was recommended I believe rather to defeat the appointment of Mr. Robins, for reasons too long here to detail, than from any hope that he might be appointed.

I was informed by David Howell Esqr. that recommendations would go on for Judge Barnes, and, in case of his appointment, for himself as District Judge, and for myself as District Attorney. This was told to me as a secret. It was one that I very unwillingly kept, for I did not feel disposed to mount this ladder of promotion, and was more than half resolved to write you then as I now have. Supposing however that there was no probability that Judge Barnes would be nominated to the Senate, I concluded there was no necessity for adding to your troubles.

Finding however that considerable difficulty occurred in filling this vacancy, and understanding that Mr. Adams declines the office, I have felt it my duty to endeavor to prevent an appointment, which might possibly happen, and which, should it happen, would tend to bring the administration and the Court into contempt.

Judge Barnes is a man of moderate capacity—what he possesses is not of that kind required for a Judicial station—he is generally considered as unfit for the Office which he now holds. He is a federalist in heart, though formerly, he seemed to affect moderation. He is a sycophant of the Merchants of this town, who, almost to a man, are the bitterest opposers of government. They have lately made him a President of one of the Insurance Office[s], where he does daily drudgery, and sucks in the sweet refection of Anglo-federalism for $500 a year. His appointment to his present office by Mr. Jefferson was one of those unaccountable things which sometimes happen. It was perhaps amidst the wreck of judges that at that time prevailed that his low cunning and hypocrysy enabled him to seize upon the plank which slipped from one of his brethren. You probably will not consider this letter as entitled to your consideration, without some knowledge of its author. Upon this point I will refer you to Richard M. Johnson from Kentucky, and Mr. Howell one of our present Senators. I beg however that the contents of this letter may not be communicated, particularly to the latter Gentleman, for reasons sufficiently obvious. He is the son of the present District Atty, and may be disposed, though I do not know that he is, to further the views of his father. I hope that you may not be reduced to the necessity of choosing between Mr. Robins and Judge Barnes. Mr. Robins is a man of talents, but his integrity is doubted, and his politics have not as yet gained him the confidence of the republicans of this State. However I should prefer him to Judge Barnes. I am with sentiments of respectful consideration Your Obedt. Servt.

JOHN PITMAN JUNR.

RC (DLC). Docketed by JM.

From Two Chiefs of the Wyandot Nation

FATHER   SANDUSKY 24th October 1811

In behalf of ourselves & a number of our people We wish to Say a few words. Father we live on The United States Land at Lower Sandusky. Some of our own people have taken up the Tomahawk against us, & are murdering us day by day. Several of our people have been Killed & many more are threatened with Death, how many we do not Know. Father we beg you would interpose your Athority & Influence, Correct those who are murdering us & Stop the further progress of Destruction among us. Father we beg you to Correct the Crane,[1] it is his party who are Cutting us off. Father We beg that you will not delay but hasten to Relieve us. We request that this Letter may be Kept Secret for if it Should be Known our lives would be taken immediately.

Father Perhaps this may be the last time that we Shall have an Opportunity to express our Affection & Confidence for you but we trust in God for Protection & Pray that your Safety & happiness may be objects of his Care.

Bowl his ╍╂╍ Mark

Wasp his ╾╊ Mark

Two of the Chiefs of the
Wyandot Nation

RC (DNA: RG 107, LRRS, W-23:6). Witnessed by Samuel Tupper, Indian agent. Docketed by a War Department clerk as received 13 Dec. 1811.

1. Tarhe, the Crane (1742–1818), was a Wyandot of the Porcupine clan. After the Battle of Fallen Timbers in 1794 he was instrumental in persuading the Wyandot in the Ohio country to accept the 1795 Treaty of Greenville, and he adhered to the terms of the agreement, despite growing opposition from those among his people who came to support Tecumseh and the Prophet. He later accompanied William Henry Harrison and the Northwest Army in the campaign of 1813 that climaxed at the Battle of the Thames (Hodge, *Handbook of American Indians North of Mexico*, 2:694).

From William Eaton

SIR,   NEW YORK 25th of October 1811

I took the Liberty to address your Excellency Some time ago.[1] The magnitude of the subject is so weighty on my mind—I Cannot refrain from troubling you again—at this very important time. I will not again Sir in So Short a time harrass your mind—with Such Communications. Next monday week Sir—a Speech from you will be Expected by Congress—and as I think much of their Conduct will be governed by What you may be pleased to recommend to them—and Eventually terminate to be of the utmost Consequence to the United States—I Earnestly intreat you Sir, not to advise war Measures, or the Establishment of a Large Naval or land force— by land force I mean a Larger Standing army. The Militia ought to be the Safe guard of a Republican Government, and Can by its aid, with other Laws, placed under Such regulations—as to make the Government Respectable. Your Enimies, wish to distroy the Popularity of the Administration, and they know, if they can bring about Either of these measures they will Effe[c]t it. The Enimies of the Country also know it—and are instruementa⟨l to⟩ bring it about—for the ruin of both Gover⟨nment and⟩ Country. Any reasonable person Sir must know we Cannot have a Navy to Cope with Englands without involving us in Such a debt as Shall bring on a revolution of Government Eventually—of course then any Larger Navy than Just to protect our Seaports at home, must be money thrown away—as they would imediately Copenhagen them—and help instead of hurt our Enimies. A Large Standing army Sir will also involve us in debt breed discontent among our Citizens, make them become very vicious and much less vertuous—check Agriculture, Population, and domestick manufactures and internal improvements—open a door to the many aspireing to office to take advantage of it—Change our form of Goverment place themselves in power—and distroy our Liberty and happiness. In fact Sir—by Either War, Navy, or Army—we have Every thing to loose, and as Sure as we are alive, nothing to Gain. Would it not Sir be adviseable for the Goverment to Say to the merchants we cannot Considering the Embarrassment of the times, protect your property abroad—we will do all in our power to protect and aid you at home—if you will Ship abroad you must do it at your own risk and peril—lay Such heavy duties, as to make it Equal to prohibition of importation of foreign Goods. This would Encourage our own Manufactures and Embarrass theirs, and be the means of bringing us more [. . .] Surplus provisions—by these means the [. . .] Mechanics and Merchants would thrive instead of becoming, bankrupts, and our internal happiness and peace Secured. But Sir if this Cannot be done—another Embargo, will by ¾ths of The real Serious thinking American Citizens be by far preffered to War, Navy, or Army. The Society of friends and all other Religious Societies are opposed to War—the farmer also—and these added together make the Great mass of our Stable Citizens. I know Sir there is a Considerable large party for war but these Sir are Generally a restless ungoverned Set of office hunters and men aspiring to power—and who are doing Every thing in their power to insure the Popularity of the Administration and place themselves in office. Witness the powerfull party in this State Called Clintonians. I hope Sir you will be pleased to give these Ideas a Consideration—and pardon me for the trouble I have given you—and Consider them actuated by a Sincere desire for your own and our Countrys Glory. And I pray God he will be pleased to aid you in your address to Such a degree that the world may be astonished at your wisdom and that it may redound to Convince that we are determined to be a Just and Virtuous people. I am Dear Sir very Respectfully your Excellencys Most Obedient Servant

WILLIAM EATO⟨N⟩

RC (DLC). Pages damaged at lower edges.

1. Eaton to JM, 29 Aug. 1811.

To Tobias Lear

The notice that the departure of the Store vessel is taking place,[1] being sudden, I cannot specify the several letters for which I am indebted. I believe from successive references recollected by me, that none have miscarried. I must particularly thank you for the Sheep & Wheat accompanied by one of them.[2] The Wheat was sown partly by myself, and partly by several friends among whom it was distributed in order to multiply experiments, and secure its propagation. In every instance however it was put so late into the earth, that another year will be necessary to test its merits. It was remarked that it did not escape the aggressions of the Hessian fly, more than other Wheats in the vicinity. This circumstance attracted notice, because it decides a late Theory, which maintains that the Egg of that insect is deposited in the *grain*, and may be destroyed by steeps; unless indeed the insect be known in Barbary, which I presume not to be the case. The Sheep arrived all safe; one of them proving however to be a wedder, not a ram. The others, were disposed of, 1 to Mr. Jefferson 1. to Capt: Coles, 1 to Govr. Claiborne, and one to a friend in this neighborhood. For myself, I retained the ram with 4 horns, The oldest Broad tail, and the lamb of that breed; hoping in that way to prolong my possession of an imported breeder. The Lamb however was killed by accident before he reached my farm; and the 4 horned ram died soon after. Retaining therefore, the old ram only, and finding the mutton of the broad tails,[3] of which I have for some years had a mixture of blood in my flocks, I am induced to ask the favor of you to procure me a pair, or if readily to be done, more than one pair of those animals. The only objection to the breed is the coarseness, and almost hairiness of the wool. It is desireable therefore, that, as differences were noticed in the fleeces, the selection be made of the individuals least objectionable on that score. Perhaps there may be broad-tailed families in Algiers, cloathed with fine fleeces; finer even than those of our ordinary sheep. It is certain than [*sic*] in Tunis, towards the Mountains at least, there are broad-tailed sheep, with fleeces considerably finer than our common wool. I have seen samples of them, from a flock of Judge Peters, who sent them to me, with a sample of Cloth made of the material, & with an Eulogium on the longevity, the mutton, & other merits of the Sheep.[4] I understand also that, Southward of Tripoli, there is a broad-tail sheep, equally remarkable for the succulence of the meat, & a fineness of wool, almost rivalling that of the Merino.

I should not take the liberty of asking this favor from you, after receiving that for which I am making acknowledgment; but that I make it a condition, that [you] throw all the trouble on an agent, and all the expence on me; and that you point out the mode in which it will be most agreeably repaid. As another store vessel will soon follow, you will have two opportunities, of sending the sheep. The present, if equally convenient, will be the most eligible.

For intelligence I refer you to communications from the Dept. of State, and to the Newspapers, which will accompany them. From the latter you will gather the gen[e]ral state of our relations with Europe, the progress of things in Spanish America; and the temper of this Country as to both. The general state of things at home will also be disclosed thro' the same channel. With the exception of our embarrassed commerce, the prosperity was never greater. As the basis of it we have more universally redundant crops of every kind, than we remembered. Accept my respects and friendly wishes

JAMES MADISON

It occurs that a wine made in Algiers is spoken of as of good quality. As a rarity at least, a cask of it will be acceptable, if the price be not disproportionate to the quality, and either of the vessels can be engaged to bring it.

RC (owned by Stephen Decatur, Garden City, N.Y., 1961). Docketed by Lear, "recd. Decr. 18. 1811."

1. On 26 Oct. 1811 JM issued a proclamation announcing that the brigantine *Paul Hamilton* was bound for Algiers with a cargo of naval stores and other articles in fulfillment of the treaties between the U.S. and that regency (DNA: RG 59, DL).

2. See Lear to JM, 12 July 1810, and Richard Forrest to JM, 12 Sept. 1810 (*PJM-PS*, 2:412–13, 538).

3. JM presumably meant to write that he found the mutton of the broadtails superior.

4. See JM to Richard Peters, 15 Mar. 1811, and n. 2.

§ From Henry Aborn and Others. *Ca. 28 October 1811, Washington.* The memorialists have learned that "in the allotments of the military Divisions of Washington City," they have been assigned to the command of Joseph Wheaton. They point out that "efficient organization" requires that "those who are appointed to places of Command, should enjoy the respect and esteem of those who by law are bound to obey," and that "without this co-operation in a certain degree, experience has uniformly shewn that all laws are unavailing." They therefore protest against the command of Joseph Wheaton and request the revocation of his commission, submitting the following facts.

"That the said Joseph Wheaton, did some time since in the Book store of William Duane, and at a time when he was Sergeant at arms of the House of Representatives, declare in the presence of General Jackson, the father of John G. Jackson, Esqr. and P. Bishop Esqr. then members of Congress,[1] that he had while acting in the capacity of Sergeant at Arms, destroyed many hundreds of the democratic newspapers, intended for the members of congress. When asked that if in doing so, he was doing his duty? He replied he was doing a duty to society in stopping the progress of such vile Stuff. He was ask'd if he had destroyed any of the news-papers of Cobbet?[2] He replied that, Cobbet, was not so bad as the democratic printers, that he would not only burn the news-papers, but the Editors of them also, and the first should be the Editor of the infamous Boston Chronicle,[3] and next the Editor of the infamous Aurora, at the head of whom he would burn alive, and more, were he president of the U. States, he would send every D——d democrat out of the Country, that they were destitute of principle. He was told that this was the language of Genl. Dayton,[4] he replied they were also the sentiments of his heart. A deposition relative to the above facts is sworn to before Samuel Smallwood Esqr. one of the magistrates of this City, by William Kane, now resident here & formerly agent of William Duane. That the said Joseph Wheaton, at the time when Aron Burr, was arrested, said that Mr. Jefferson, on that occasion had exceeded the powers delegated to him, adding with a sarcastic smile, 'when Colo. Burr, was fighting the battles of his Country, where was Jefferson? skulking into a cave at Carters Mountain![']

"That Joseph Wheaton, some time since, when acting as Sergeant at Arms to the House of representatives, the members of which was then in session with closed doors, being ask'd at the door by a citizen of the District, what Congress were about? He replied, no good Sir! they are merely obeying the mandates of Bonaparte! For this conduct he afterwards appologized to congress.[5]

"That the said Joseph Wheaton, did make a declaration before William Brent, Esqr. clerk of the Court, and others, speaking of his business with the Genl. Post Office department, and of the refusal of the Post master General, to admit his claim against the public, 'By G–d I will take a pistol and some day or other, go up to Mr. Grangers Coach and blow his brains out!' and this because the Post master General, will not permit him to defraud the public.[6] That the said Joseph Wheaton, is notoriously the friend of the Traitor Burr, and a man whose character is so well known, that he is universally despised by the well meaning and virtuous part of the Citizens of this District."

RC (DNA: RG 107, LRRS, P-315:5). 4 pp. Signed by Aborn and ten others. Undated, but docketed by a War Department clerk as received 28 Oct. 1811.

1. George Jackson of Virginia and Phanuel Bishop of Massachusetts had served together in the Sixth Congress, 1799–1801.

2. British-born editor William Cobbett had published *Porcupine's Gazette*, a strongly pro-Federalist and anti-French newspaper, in Philadelphia between 1797 and 1799.

3. In 1799 the Boston *Independent Chronicle* was published by Thomas Adams and his brother, Abijah. They were twice indicted for seditious libel, first under the Sedition Act of 1798 and then under a common-law indictment brought by the state of Massachusetts (James Morton Smith, *Freedom's Fetters: The Alien and Sedition Laws and American Civil Liberties* [Ithaca, N.Y., 1956], pp. 247–57).

4. Jonathan Dayton of New Jersey, while serving as Speaker of the House of Representatives during the Fifth Congress (1797–99), had barred Benjamin Franklin Bache of the Philadelphia *Aurora General Advertiser* from the floor of the House in order to prevent him from reporting the debates (ibid., p. 190).

5. Wheaton held the position of sergeant at arms of the House from 1789 until his failure to be reelected at the commencement of the first session of the Tenth Congress in October 1807. The reasons for this failure are unclear, but a petition that he sent to the House on 22 May 1809 praying for reinstatement in the office "from which he had been ejected" was unsuccessful (*Annals of Congress*, 11th Cong., 1st sess., 57).

6. During the first session of the Twelfth Congress, Wheaton unsuccessfully presented

petitions seeking payment of an award made in his favor "under a rule of the circuit court for the District of Columbia, in suits brought against him by the Postmaster General, on behalf of the United States, for alleged defalcations in carrying the mails of the United States between the city of Washington and New-Orleans" (*Journal of the House of Representatives,* 12th Cong., 1st sess., 1:79–80, 181, 326, 2:869).

§ From John Tyler. *28 October 1811, Greenway, Virginia.*[1] "Great delay and inconvenience attended the last court at Norfolk, owing to there not being an Advocate on the spot where most of the admiralty business is done." Vessels are seized and injustices occur when owners are not informed of specific charges because the district attorney resides at Richmond. Officers make seizures without adequate legal advice, and witnesses, being "generally sea-faring men, [are] here to day and there to morrow." Nor can depositions be taken until the court has jurisdiction, except by consent, and "in the mean time the witnesses are heard of no more." Suggests the advisability of having an advocate in Norfolk, with power to call on the attorney for assistance in cases of great consequence. Also suggests that the marshal be empowered, whenever he serves a citation, to recognize witnesses to appear at the next court.

"The Judge out of Term, has in some cases suffer'd the vessels under siezure to proceed on thier voyages, the Owners or Masters giving bond and security . . . to abide the decision of the court—thence the necessity of appointing persons to appraise the same. This step, the Court has by law the power to take, but not the Judge at his chambers, but which seems inherent in the Admiralty Jurisdiction." Believes it would be wise to define specifically the powers of public functionaries, leaving nothing to discretion regarding public or private rights. Has discussed the matter with Mr. Newton; "he will aid in this business, and also suggest other amendments necessary in the Admiralty Department."

"The Courts in Norfolk are held in June and December; not the most pleasant Seasons in the Year for business. The last mention'd period calls the Judge from home in the Christmas holy-days, a time, which most old fashion'd people prefer to be with their families. This affords great delight to me who have many children and grand-children scatter'd about the world, but who gather together at that Season. If the time for holding the court at Norfolk could be chang'd to the first of May and November, there would be full time enough to attend in Richmond."

RC (DLC). 2 pp. In an unidentified hand. Postmarked Richmond, 4 Nov.

1. Greenway was Tyler's estate in Charles City County (*WMQ,* 1st ser., 1 [1892–93]: 172–73).

From William Lambert

Sir,   City of Washington, October 29th. 1811.

Permit me to submit the inclosed to your perusal, as the copy of a communication to several members of Congress, on their arrival in this city;[1]

and at the same to assure you, that while this mark of confidence and respect is offered, it is not expected or wished, that you should take any step in my favor incompatible with the strictest propriety. I have the honor to be, with great respect, Sir, Your most obedient servant,

WILLIAM LAMBERT.

RC (DLC). Docketed by JM.

1. Lambert apparently enclosed some extracts (DLC; 3 pp.) from the "collection of precedents" he had been authorized to compile under the terms of resolutions approved by the House of Representatives on 26 Apr. 1810 and 16 Feb. 1811 (see *Annals of Congress*, 11th Cong., 2d sess., 1987; ibid., 3d sess., 973). These, in turn, were part of a larger work published by Lambert as *A Collection of Precedents, Consisting of Proceedings and Decisions on Questions of Order and Appeals, in the House of Representatives . . . from the First Session of the First Congress, to the End of the Third Session of the Eleventh Congress* (Washington, 1811; Shaw and Shoemaker 23174). Lambert suggested changes to the record of the House journal on some points of order that had occurred during the third session of the Eleventh Congress. He concluded that the cases he had listed "ought . . . to be stated on the journal in a different manner than they have been. It is not pretended, that the substitutes I have offered, are the best that could have been proposed; but it is believed, that the sense of the House would be *as well expressed* by them, as in the entries which now make part of their record."

§ From Matthew Cobb. *29 October 1811, Portland.* Encloses a bill of exchange dated at Madeira, 12 Sept. 1811, and drawn by James Leander Cathcart on JM for £378 sterling. "You will oblige me, by paying this sum into the State treasury, receive from the Secrey. thereof, a draft or Check on the Maine Bank in this place, which your Excellency will please to forward to your Hble Servt."

RC and enclosure (DLC). RC 1 p. Docketed by JM, "Recd. Novr. 5. 1811." Enclosure (1 p.) is a bill of exchange signed by Cathcart (see Cathcart to JM, 12 Sept. 1811).

From Jeremy Bentham

SIR, LONDON 30th Octr. 1811.

The offer which it is the ambition of this Address to submit to the consideration of the President of the United States is addressed (you will see immediately) not to the person, but to the Office. By an explanation thus early made some reading will be saved to you. The respect, of which the offer itself is its own best testimonial needs not, I presume, any more words for the expression of it.

To come to the point at once—Give me, Sir, the necessary encouragement, I mean, a Letter importing *approbation* of this my humble proposal,[1] and, as far as depends upon you yourself—*Acceptance* I will forthwith set about drawing up, for the use of the United States, or such of them, if any, as may see reason to give their acceptance to it, a *complete body* of proposed law, in the form of Statute law, say in one word a *Pannomion*²—a body of Statute law, including a succedaneum to that mass of foreign law, the yoke of which in the *wordless*, as well as boundless, and shapeless shape of *common*, alias *Unwritten* law, remains still about your necks—a *complete* body or such parts of it as the life and health of a man, whose age wants little of four and sixty, may allow of.

This letter Sir, I mean the letter above stipulated for, when once I have it in hand, I have my *reward*. I have my *employment:* and the honor inseparable from the employment is the only retribution, that *can* be *accepted* for the labor of it. I say *accepted*, Sir, not *required* or *expected* but *accepted:* for from this word corollaries will be deduced, the utility of which, with reference to the proposed Service, will, I flatter myself, when brought to view, as they will be presently, not appear exposed to doubt.

The *plan* of the proposed work, and therein the supposed *advantageous results*, the prospect of which forms what the proposal has to depend upon for its acceptance, the circumstances of *advantage* attached to the nature of the *terms* on which the work would be executed, the declared *objections* which it ought to be prepared for together with the *answers* which those objections seem to admit of, the latent, but not the less powerful, *obstacles* which it may have to contend with, the sort of personal *assistance* in the way of information, which should it be thought serviceable I should be ready and willing to receive for the purpose of it, the *advances* already made towards the execution of it, on all these several topics some sort of explanation may naturally be looked for: on all of them something in the way of explanation shall accordingly be attempted, though in that state of extreme and proportionably disadvantageous compression, without which no reasonable hope could be entertained of that promptitude of return which may be requisite to success.

Before I come to particulars respecting the proposed *plan* with its supposed *advantages*, it will be necessary for me to make reference once for all, to a view of it which is already in print. I mean the Work in 3 Vols. 8vo. which, under the title of *Traités de Législation Civile et Pénale . . . par M. Jeremie Bentham &c.* was in the year 1802 published at Paris by my Genevan friend M Dumont.³

One Copy of it was, upon its publication, sent, I understand by the Editor to his Countryman Mr Gallatin, Secretary of the Treasury to the United States: whether, in your part of America, any other Copies of it have ever been in existence, it has not fallen in my way to know.

Far as those papers were from being considered by the Author as having attained a state approaching to that of a finished work, yet of the plan which, on any such occasion as that in question, was then, and still would be, proposed to be pursued, a conception sufficient for the purpose here in question, may, if I do not deceive myself, be obtained from them. Of the *details*, even of the proposed *text*, they exhibit samples more than one, nor those of small account. So much of the plan being already *there*, it might seem that nothing, in explanation of it, could be necessary in this place. But, without some preconceptions, how slight and general soever, of some of its most striking peculiarities, what it will immediately be necessary to say of it in the gross might scarce be found intelligible.

[§]1. Nature and supposed advantages of the proposed *form*.
Matter and *Form*—to one or other of these two heads, whatsoever features whether of excellence or imperfection, may be distinguishable in a plan, framed for any such purpose, will, it is believed, be found referable.

1. As to *matter*, in the character of a *test* of, and *security* for, the fitness of the work in this respect, of one constituent portion pervading the whole mass—the rationale it may be termed such will at first glance be seen to be the efficiency, that of this alone a slight mention may, to the present purpose, be sufficient.

By the rationale I mean (for a sample See 'Traités &c.') a mass of *reasons* accompanying in the shape of a perpetual commentary, the whole mass of imperative or regulative matter, to which alone any body of law as yet extant has ever yet been found to give admission.

Not a single point of any importance settled, but that in the *rationale*, the considerations by which the provision made in relation to it was determined, will be to be found: and by the connection which, through the medium of the *all governing principle*, viz the principle of *utility*, these reasons have with one another, and the repeated application made of the *same* reason to different parts of the text, the quantity of space, occupied by matter of this description, will be found much less than could readily have been imagined.

This *constituent part* or *appendage*, call it which you please, this *perpetual commentary* of *reasons*, is what I will venture to propose as a test, and the only test, by which either of the *absolute* fitness or unfitness of any one proposed body of laws taken by itself, or of the *comparative* fitness of each one of any number of bodi[e]s of law standing in competition with each other, and proposed as capable of serving for the same division in the field of legislation, any satisfactory indication can be afforded: a test to which accordingly, by a predetermined and preannounced resolution, every such composition ought to be subjected.

Without this appendage, to draw up laws is of all literary tasks the easiest: power and will, wherever it happens to them to meet, suffice for it, of intellect there is no need. On the other hand, if, *with* this addition, the task is of all tasks the most difficult, it is at the same time *that*, in the execution of which whatsoever trouble may be found necessary to the surmounting it will find itself most worthily and richly paid for, by real and important use.

2. As to form—here again by one word *cognoscibility*, every sort and degree of excellence which, under *this* head, can be given to a body of law, will be found expressible. On the fact of its being *present* to the mind of him on whose part, to the effect indicated, *action* or *forbearance*, is on each occasion, called for, *present*—that is to say in the degree of *correctness* and *compleatness* necessary to the accomplishment of the legislators purposes depends, on each occasion, whatsoever good effect the law can be, or can have been designed to be, productive of. But on the *form* thus given to the *matter*, will depend the degree of excellence in which the property of *cognoscibility*, as thus explained has been given to it: on the *form* therefore will, in a proportionable degree, depend the practical good effect of whatsoever degree may have been given to the matter of the law.

Taking *cognoscibility* then for the *end*, the following may serve as a sample of the *means* or *securities* that in the plan in question, have been devised and provided for the attainment of it.

1. Division of the whole *Pannomion* into two separate parts, the *General Code*, and the System of *particular* Codes.

In the General Code are comprised all such matters, of which it concerns persons in general to be apprised: in the System of particular Codes, each particular Code contains such matters only, with which some *one* Class or denomination of persons only have concern: some *one* class or denomination, or in case of correlative classes of persons, running together in pairs, such as *husband* and *wife*, *Master* and *Servant*, and so forth, some two or other such small number of classes or denominations, whose legal concerns are thus inseparably intermingled.

Merely for illustration sake, number of particular Codes, as above, say 200: average length of each 5 pages. Consequent advantage, burthen of legal matter to be borne in mind by each person reduced from 1000 pages to 5 pages. Such, in respect of *cognoscibility*, is the advantage which this single arrangement suffices to produce. To more such classes, it is true, than one, will one and the same individual person be commonly found aggregates: I mean of those Classes which as above, would have, each of them its separate Code. From the sort of saving in question, a correspondent deduction would accordingly be to be made: but for illustration thus much without going any farther into calculation may, it is supposed suffice:

From *General Code* to *Particular Codes*, and *vice versâ*, frequent references will of course be necessary: nor, in the working up of the one can the texture of the other consistently with clearness and mutual consistency pass unheeded. But all this is a matter of detail for which no room can be found here.

2. In each Code, as well *particular* as *General*, an ulterior distinction noted and acted upon, is the distinction between matter of *constant* concernment, and matter of *occasional* concernment. To produce the effect aimed at in the

making of a law, to produce the effect of *guidance*, that which is matter of *constant* concernment must in all its magnitude, in all its detail, be borne in mind at all times: while, in the case of that which is but matter of *occasional* concernment, the bare *knowledge* or *suspicion* of its existence will in general be sufficient, matters being so circumstanced, that before the time for action comes, sufficient time for *reference* to the text of the law, and for perusal of its contents, may on all occasions be found.

3. In each Code in which it is found requisite, and in particular in the *penal* branch of the *General* Code, in which it will *throughout* be found requisite, another distinction and division made is that between *Main text*, and *Expository matter* or *Exposition*.

The *Expository* matter consists of explanations given of or on the occasion of, this or that particular word in the *Main Text*. In the *Main text* each word so explained is distinguished by a particular *type*, accompanied by a letter or figure of *reference*, by which means the fact of its having received explanation is rendered manifest to every eye.

In the course of the Pannomion, should this or that same word be employed in ever so many hundred *places*, one and the same explanation serves for all of them, and by the appropriation of the particular type to the expression of these leading terms, of which an explanation is thus given, notice of the existence of such explanation is in every place presented to the eye: care being taken all along to apply the explanation to every such passage, to the end that it may be found conformable to the sense, intended in each such passage to be conveyed.

So moderate will the number of these *essential* terms, these expounded words be found, that the labour necessary to the giving correctness and consistency, to the part of the language, the import of which is thus fixed, fixed by authority of law, needs the less be grudged.

4. To the *Penal* Code belongs an ulterior distinction peculiar to itself: matter descriptive of the offence in its ordinary state, and matter indicative of the several causes of *justification*,[1] *aggravation*[2] and *extenuation*[3] with the grounds of *exemption*[4] from punishment, which apply to it.

From beginning to end, one object kept in view and aimed at is— that, the whole field of legislation being surveyed, surveyed and travelled through over and over again in all directions, no case that can present itself shall find itself unnoticed or unprovided for. Of this object the compleat attainment may be too much for human weakness: but by every approach made towards it, the science is advanced, and, in all shapes, the security of the people against suffering, sudden and unlooked for suffering, is encreased.

Note. Examples (1) *Consent. Self-defence.* Lawful exercise of *Public power.* Lawful exercise of *domestic power* &c. (2) *Premeditation. Confederacy* &c. (3) *Unintentionality Provocation* (contemporaneous or recent) &c (4) *Insanity. Infancy* &c.

5. *Promulgation-paper:* for formularies of all sorts, *Conveyances* and *Agreements*, as well as instruments of judicial *procedure, paper,* of a particular size and form and appearance in other respects, provided, with a margin of Letter-press, in and by which, in the instance of each such species of instrument, intimation is given of the whole text of the law relative to the species of transaction therein in question: intimation, Vizt. according to the quantity of room occupied by it, given, either *in terminis,* or in the way of *abstract* with indication of, and with reference to, any such portion, as is found to occupy too much room to be given *in terminis.*

In particular, to the whole business of *Conveyances* and *Agreements* would thus be given a degree of simplicity, certainty, and security, of which, even after the many improvements which, I am certain must have been made in all the United States upon the original chaos, no adequate conception would, I believe, be readily formed, antecedently to experience.

In and by this method, one useful result is looked for and I hope provided for, vizt. that, to such persons by whom in respect of its *matter,* the work may in this or that part of its extent be disapproved, in respect of its *form,* it may still be found of use. Seeing the *reasons,* in which the proposed provision has found its support and final cause, each such disapprover will thereby have before him such a view as, I hope, will not be an indistinct one, of the force which in the shape of reason and argument he has to combat. On the one side (he may see cause to say) this or that reason seems defective; and taken all together, the whole mass of reasons appear insufficient and inconclusive: or, on the other side the nature of the case affords such or such a reason, no mention of which is, in this work, to be found.

Thus it is, that, even where the reasoning may appear erroneous or inconclusive, and the proposed provision improper or inadequate—even in these places, if the matter be stated with that *clearness,* which it has been the object of the workman to give to every thing that ever came from his pen, and which, on the occasion in question, would, in a more particular manner, be the object of his endeavour and his hope, even his *errors* may, by serving or helping to bring to view the opposite truths, be found not altogether devoid of use.

In this way it is that both in point of *matter* and in point of *form,* his endeavour would be to give to the work such a character and complexion, as shall be found correspondent to the progress, made, in these our times, in every other line of useful science: to the end that, neither in the whole nor in any part, in matters of law any more than in matters dependant on mechanical or chemical science, shall the lot of the present inhabitants of your part of the globe, be determined by the unexperienced and ill considered imaginations of primæval barbarism.

As matters of law stand at present, Sir, in *your* Country (not to speak of *ours*) on what sort of basis is it that every man's dearest and most important interests stand or rather fluctuate? On some random decision, or string of frequently contradictory decisions, pronounced in this or that barbarous age, almost always without any intelligible reason, under the impulse of some private and sinister interest, perceptible or not perceptible, without thought, or possibility of thought, of any such circumstances or exigencies, as those of the people, by whom the country here in question is inhabited at the present time: pronounced by men, who, if disposition and inclination depend in any degree on private interest, were as far from being *willing*, as from being in respect of *intelligence able* to render their decisions conform- able to the interests, even of the people by whose disputes those decisions were called for, and whose situation alone it was possible that in the fram- ing of those decisions, they should have in view.

Since the year in which the Work, edited by Mr Dumont, was published in French at Paris, vizt. in the year 1802, that same language has given birth to two authoritative codes, the one already a *Pannomion*, or at least designed to become such, published by authority of the French Emperor,[4] the other, confined as yet to the *penal* branch, published by authority of the King of Bavaria.[5] In both instances, the compositors have done me the honor to take into consideration and make mention of that work of mine. On the proposed occasion in question, I should not fail to make correspondent return, and make my best profit of their labours.

The examination of them is what I have as yet postponed, waiting for some particular occasion by which such examination might be applied to some particular use. But to warrant a man in pronouncing, and with confi- dence, that, in and by each of those Works, a prodigious benefit has been conferred on their subjects, by the respective Sovereigns, it is not necessary to have read so much as a single page. Executed as well as the nature of men and things admits of its being executed, no other literary work can vie with it in usefulness—executed in the very worst manner in which in the present state of society it is at all likely to be executed, it can scarcely when com- pared with the chaos to which it comes to be substituted, fail to be produc- tive of clear profit in the account of use.

*   Of some of the leading features by which the Work here proposed would be distinguished from both these—a work composed for the use of men who are in use not only to think, but to speak and print what they think, from works composed for the use of men who scarce dare speak what they think, and to whom it has been rendered impracticable to print what they think, a slight sketch, Sir, has just been laid before you.

For securing the aptitude of it in point of *matter*, in the *proposed English* work, the *rationale* above described: in neither of those French works, any security at all in this shape or any other.

---

*Note What is here enclosed in a bracket Mr President will be pleased to make public with the rest, or suppress, as in his judgment may be most fitting.

For securing the aptitude of the work in point of *form*, for securing to it the maximum of *cognoscibility*—and thereby the advantage of producing to the greatest extent possible, in respect of number of *observances* compared with number of *non-observances*, whatever effect it purposes to itself to produce, in the proposed English work, 1. Division into General Code and System of particular Codes: 2 Division of the tenor of the law throughout into *Main text* and *Expository* matter: 3 In the Penal Code, not to insist on any such division as the usual and already familiar one into *General titles* (titles of general application) and Particular titles (each applying exclusively to a particular species or tribe of offences) division of *Main text* and *Expository matter* together, into *definitional* matter descriptive of the main body of each offence, and matter indicative of the several causes of *justification, aggravation, extenuation* and *exemption*, which apply to it.

For securing, on every imaginable occasion, perfect *notoriety*, to each new set of *rights* acquired and correspondent obligations contracted, vizt. by whatsoever *instruments* of conveyance or agreement contracted, and that not only as soon as contracted, but also before contracted, and thence before the time when repentance would come too late, in the proposed English work, the already described *Promulgation paper*.

In neither of those French works for the necessary cognoscibility above described is any security at all in any of the just above mentioned or in any other shape declared or discernible.

Here, Sir, you see a *memento* given—it was not put to use here—was even a *gauntlet* thrown down, it was not taken up. Circumstanced as those respectable and truly useful servants of the public were, causes for such abstention might, without much difficulty, perhaps be found; causes, however, which it would be more easy to imagine than useful to express.

That in the United States any similar or any other causes should be found, not only operating, but operating with effect, to the neglect of all those securities for the adaptation of law to the only useful ends of law, is a result, the bare possibility of which cannot, by a feeling mind, be regarded with indifference.

The encouragement not only stipulated for, as above, but demanded in advance, is a gem of too high a price, to be cast, either *into* the Sea, or *across* the Sea, without thought, or without such prospect of a suitable return as the nature of the case admits of.

Of the presumable fitness of any person for the execution of a literary work proposed by him, no evidence so apposite can, I suppose, be looked for, as that which is presented by a work or works, where any such happen to be in existence, taking for their subject the subject itself which is proposed to be taken in hand, or any part or parts of it.

An assortment, as nearly complete as could be formed, of such of my printed Works as have taken for their subject any part or parts of the field

of legislation, accompanies this letter, and solicits the honor of your acceptance. They are the fruit of above 45 years devoted to the study of the
science, and, for little less than the whole of that time, without a view to
any thing but the improvement of it.

If to a discerning mind, such as that to which this offer considers itself as
addressed, any such *loose presumptions* as are capable of being afforded, by
tokens of attention and approbation given by foreign authorities, can be of
any use, it can only be by *contributing* to produce, should such be the result,
a recurrence to the only *direct* and *proper* evidence.

Citizenship of France, decreed by one of the National Assemblies, on the
same occasion on which the like mark of approbation was bestowed on
Joseph Priestly and *Thomas Payne*.[6] In one of the legislative Assemblies held
during the Consulate of the present Emperor, elogium pronounced by one
of the Members on the above mentioned Work and printed in the official
paper.[7] Nomination [(]though by subsequent incidents rendered fruitless)
to the then existing Institute of France. Translation of that same Work
made by Order of the Russian Government and published in the Russian
language, besides another published in the same language without authority. Translation of another Work on the mode of providing for the *Poor*,[8]
made and published during the Consulate by the municipality of Paris, and
(if I have not been misinformed) *since* put, in some shape and degree or
other to public use—these tokens, together with the notices taken as above
in the French and Bavarian Codes, may, it is hoped, have the additional good
effect, of rendering it pretty apparent, that Governments of the most opposite forms and characters, have found something to approve, nothing considerable to disapprove, and nothing at all to be apprehensive of, in the views
and dispositions with which the task here proposed would be taken in hand.

In a man's writings, the character of the *moral* part is not so clearly delin-
eated as that of the *intellectual* part of his frame.

Artifice, in pursuit of some private end, might give birth to an offer such
as the present, unaccompanied with any such intention as that of giving
effect to the engagement sought: levity though pure from original insincerity, might intervene at any time and be productive of the same failure.

On the question concerning *intellectual* aptitude, the evidence lying before you, the judgment, Sir, will be your own. As to what regards *moral*
promise, the nature of the Case refers you in course to the gentleman, be
he who he may, who, in this Country stands charged with the Affairs of
your State. Transmitted to him, your Letter, I mean the necessary letter of
authorization above stipulated for, may, according to the result of his enquiries, be delivered or kept back.

§2. As to the *Advantages* that promise to result from the *gratuitousness* of
the proposed service, though there is not one of them, that seems much in

danger of escaping the observation of the distinguished person to whom the proposal is addressed, yet as it will naturally have to pass through a variety of hands, in all of which it cannot promise itself exactly the same degree of attention, it may not be amiss that these features of recommendation should in this place be distinctly brought to view.

1. In the first place, no *pecuniary* charge whatever being to be imposed on the public or any part of it, the great and prominent objection which public works in general have to encounter, has here no place: and be the chance for useful service rated ever so low, still, should any the smallest portion be reaped, it will be all clear gain.

2. By supervening imbecillity, by death, or even the levity and caprice on the part of the proposed Workman, should the work be left in a state ever so far from compleatness, still, to the public there would be no positive loss: the situation in which in this respect it would find itself, would, at the worst, be but what it is at present, be but what it would have been, had no such proposal been made.

3. On these terms the situation of the Workman stands altogether out of the influence of any sinister motive, from which either an undue *protraction* of the business, or an undue *acceleration* of it might be apprehended: *protraction*, as if a salary were given, to be received during the continuance of it: *acceleration*, as if it were a sum of money to be once paid, or a life annuity to commence at the completion of it.

4. In respect of the *commencement*, and so far in respect of the *completion*, of the work, it admits of a degree of promptitude, the want of which might otherwise be fatal to the whole design. If money were necessary, consents— I need not set myself to think or to enquire in what number—would be requisite to be obtained: obtained, not only for the fixation of the sum, but for the origination of the measure, and therefore if not for the giving of *any* answer, at any rate for the giving any definitive and sufficient answer to this address. As it *is*, a single fiat, a letter how short soever from the authority to which this address is made, suffices for giving commencement to the work: and whatever subsidiary matters may hereinafter come to be suggested, may without inconvenience wait, in that case, all proper and accustomed delays.

5. It must I think be acknowledged to be a feature of advantage in any proposal, if it be such as to clear from all possible suspicion of sinister interest, all such persons to whom it may happen to take a part in the giving introduction or support to it.

To this sort of advantage, if there be any imaginable proposal that can lay claim, this I think cannot easily avoid being recognized to be thus happily circumstanced.

With or without any particular individual in the character of proposed workman in his eye, suppose the pre:eminent person to whom this proposal

514

is submitted—suppose him bringing forward a plan, tending to the accomplishment of the proposed work, but accompanied with a plan of *remuneration* in the ordinary shape and mode. What would be, be he who he may, the *motives* to which the proposal would be referred?—referred, by adversaries at least, not to speak of friends?—they are by much too obvious to need mentioning.

Supposing it the good fortune of this proposal to obtain the sort of approbation which it aspires to, I have set myself to consider, by what public tokens it may be natural and proper for that approbation to declare itself. The inability I have found myself under, of obtaining the documents necessary to secure me against falling into misconception respecting such of the functions of your high Office, Sir, as may be found to have application to the present case, will, I hope, in case of mis-supposal, obtain for me the benefit of your indulgence.

The steps, to any or all of which it may happen to be taken in this view, present themselves to my imagination as follows.

1. To lay the proposal before Congress at its meeting, with a *recommendation* to take it into consideration, stating or not stating the provisional authorization given or intended to be given to the author.

2. To cause a *Minute* to be made in the books of the Presidents' Office, stating a resolution on the part of the *President* for *the time being* to lay before Congress any such part of the Work as may come to have been transmitted during his continuance in Office, together with a recommendation of the like operation, in the like event, to *future* Presidents.

3. To transmit a Copy of this proposal, accompanied with the like recommendation to the legislative bodies of each of the several particular States.

4. To cause it, on public account, to be printed and published by authority, as other public documents are in use to be.

For affording to me the necessary encouragement, any one of the above testimonies of approbation would, if notified to me by the President, be sufficient: but the greater the number of them that may come united, the greater of course, and the more operative would be the encouragement.

Two things require to this purpose to be distinguished—1. the *design* itself.—2 any work that may come to be presented by me in execution of it.

If, by any approbation bestowed upon the *design* itself, you were to be pledged for the like or any other tokens of approbation to be bestowed on any *work* done in execution of this same design, this would be an objection against the bestowing any such provisional approbation on the design itself. When it comes, the work might appear ill adapted to its purpose, and, on that or any other account, not likely to be approved by the respective constituted authorities, on which the adoption of it would have to depend.

With submission, it appears to me Sir, that, on the supposition that the design itself has met your approbation, it would not be a committal of yourself, were you to undertake for the forwarding either to Congress, or to the several Legislatures, for their consideration, any work that shall have been transmitted by me, in execution of the design so approved. For, contrary to expectation, when produced suppose the work to prove, in your judgment, to ever so great a degree absurd and even ridiculous, nothing will there be to hinder you from saying so: wherever it goes there it will lie: nor will it impose, on any person, any such trouble as that of taking it into consideration, unless some person or other should happen to be to such a degree impressed with the contrary notion, as to make the proper motion for causing it to be taken into consideration, as in the case of any particular law proposed in ordinary course.

As to *the expense of printing*—to any such extent as in the different cases may appear requisite, an expense so moderate would hardly, I should suppose, be grudged, by those to whom it belongs to judge: if it should, it would not be grudged by *me*.

§3. Against an enterprize of the sort in question, an host of jealousies and fears will naturally be springing up and arming themselves with objections. To such as appear best grounded or most plausible, I proceed to submit such answers as the nature of the case presents to me.

Objection the 1st. *"Disturbance to property and other existing rights."* "What?" (cries the man of law) "remove our land marks?" "revolutionize our property?" throw every thing into confusion? "Is this what you would be at?" "and is this to be the practical fruit of these fine theories of yours?"

Such, Sir, if not where *you* are—such at any rate would be sure to be his language *here*.

My answer is—so far as the objection confines itself to the law of private rights, when these and any other number of declamatory generalities in the same strain have been expended, the only real mischief which they hold up to view, is that which is reducible to this one expression—to *existing expectations disappointment, productive of the painful sense of loss.*

What then is this mischief, by the apprehension of which this proposed Pannomion is thus to be put aside?

It is the very mischief, under which it is impossible that, for want of a written, and visible, and intelligible, and cognoscible rule of action, in a word for want of a *Pannomion*, the people in your country should not be at present labouring: the very grievance from which it is the object of this my humble proposal to be admitted to afford them my best assistance towards working out their deliverance: the principal grievance which it would not only be the object, but to a considerable degree the sure effect of a Pannomion to remove.

Throughout the whole extent of the territory of the United States (new acquired dependencies excepted, in which matters cannot but be still worse) what is it that at this moment forms the basis of the rule of action? What but an ideal and shapeless mass of merely conjectural, and essentially uncognoscible matter; matter without mind, work without an author, occupying, through the oscitancy of the legislature a place that ought to be filled, and exercising in it the authority that ought to be exercised by law?

Nullis lex verbis, a nullo, nullibi, nunquam
Law, in no *words*, by no *man*, *never*, made:

Law which, having for its authors—not the people themselves, nor any persons chosen by the people but the creatures, the ever removable and compleatly and perpetually dependent Creatures of the King alone,[*] had of course for its main object—not the good of the people, but as far as the blindness or patience of the people would permit the sinister & confederated interests of the creator, under whose influence, and the creatures by whose hands it was spun out:

Law, blundered out by a set of men, who in their course of operation not being at their own command, but at the command of the plaintiffs in the several causes, were all along as completely destitute of the *power*, as, under the influence of sinister interest, they could not but be of the *inclination*, to operate in pursuit of any clear and enlarged views of utility, public or private, or so much as upon any comprehensive and consistent plan, good or bad, in the delineation of the rights they were conferring and the obligations they were imposing: and which accordingly never has been, nor, to any purpose, good or bad, ever could have been, nor ever can be, the result of antecedent reflection, grounded on a general view of the nature of each case, of the exigencies belonging to it, or the analogous cases connected with it: nor in a word any thing better than a shapeless heap of odds and ends, the pattern of which has, in each instance been necessarily determined, by the nature of the demand, put in by the plaintiff, as above:

Law which being, in so far as it could be said to be *made*, made at a multitude of successive periods, and for the use and governance of so many different generations of men, imbued with notions, habituated to modes of life, differing more or less widely from each other, as well as from those which have place at present, would, even had it been well adapted to the circumstances and exigencies of the times, in which its parts respectively came into existence, have, to a considerable extent, been thereby rendered not the better adapted, but by so much the worse adapted, to the notions and manners now prevalent, to the state of things at present in existence:

Law, which, by its essential *form* and character, as above indicated, is, so long as it retains that form, altogether disabled from either giving to itself,

---

(*) Till the revolution this was compleatly true, and even since it has not wanted much of being so.

or receiving from any other quarter, improvement or correction, upon a scale of any considerable extent: which, even upon the minutest scale, can not give to itself any improvement in the way of *particular utility*, but at the expense of *general certainty:* nor even at that price, but by a course of successive acts of arbitrary power, productive in the first place of a correspondent succession of particular disappointments, followed, each of them in proportion as it comes to be known, by those more extensively spreading apprehensions of insecurity, which are among the inseparable concomitants and consequences, of that ever deplorable, howsoever originally necessary and unavoidable, taint of iniquity, inherent in the very essence of *ex-post-facto* law.

Of *ex-post-facto* law did I say? Yes: for that which by common sense, speaking by the mouth of *Cicero,*[9] has been spoken of as the most mischievous and intolerable abuse, of which, in the form in which it is called *Written* or *Statute* law, the rule of action is susceptible, is an abomination interwoven in the very essence of that spurious and impostrous substitute, which, to its makers and their dupes, is an object of such prostrate admiration, and such indefatigable eulogy, under the name of *Common* or *Unwritten Law.*

Of *unwritten,* or rather of *uncomposed* and *unenacted* law (for of *writing* there is beyond comparison more belonging to this spurious than to the genuine sort) of this impostrous law the fruits, the perpetual fruits, are in the *civil* or *non-penal* branch, as above, *uncertainty, uncognoscibility, particular disappointments* without end, *general sense of insecurity* against similar disappointment and loss: in the *penal* branch, *uncertainty* and *uncognoscibility,* as before, and, instead of compliance and obedience, the evil of transgression mixed with the evil of punishment: in both branches, in the breast and in the hands of the Judge, power every where arbitrary, with the semblance of a set of rules to serve as a screen to it.

Such are the fruits of this species of mock law, even in the Country which gave it birth: how much more pregnant with insecurity—with unexpected and useless hardship as well in the shape of *civil law,* as in the shape of *penal infliction* and non-prevention of crimes, must it not necessarily be in a country, into which the matter of it is continually *imported:* imported from a foreign country, whose yoke the American nation, has, to all other purposes so happily for both nations, shaken off.

Not that I am by any means unaware of the prodigious mass of rubbish, of which on the importation of English Common Law into America part was, on the change of place naturally, or even necessarily, left behind, other parts since the original importation, at different times so wisely and happily cast out of it: religiously-persecuting laws, manorial rights, tithes, ecclesiastical courts, distinctions between law and equity in several of the States at least, secret Rome-bred mode of extracting tithe money I believe every where, and so forth. Not that I am by any means insensible to the prodigious alleviation, which from the removal of so large a portion of it, the burthen can not but have experienced.

But though, of the whole mass already imported, as well as of each successive mass, as they come respectively to be imported, there is, and will be, so much the less that needs to be *attended* to, yet, from the respective magnitudes of those several masses, no defalcation ever has been made, or can be made. The consequence is—that what alleviation so ever the burthen of the law has ever received, or can ever receive as above, vizt. by successive patches of *Statute* law, applied to the immense and continually growing body of *unwritten* alias *common* law, is confined to the *matter*, leaving the *form* of it as immense, as incomprehensible, and consequently as adverse to *certainty* and *cognoscibility* as ever.

Yes Sir, so long as there remains any the smallest scrap of unwritten law unextirpated, it suffices to taint with its own corruption—its own inbred and incurable corruption, whatsoever portion of *statute* law has ever been or can be applied to it.

So far then as disturbance to existing rights is the disorder in question, the proposed operation so far from producing, or aggravating such the disorder, presents not only the sure, but the only possible remedy. Disturbance?—a state of disturbance—of perpetual and universally extending disturbance is the very state in which they have hitherto existed: have existed, and, until fixed and secured by the application of this sole remedy, are condemned to remain till the end of time.

All this while, incapable as it is of serving in any tolerable degree, in its present state, in the character of a rule of action and guide to human conduct, nothing could be much further from the truth, than if, in speaking of the matter of which English Common law *is* composed, a man were to represent it as being of no use. Confused, indeterminate, inadequate, ill-adapted, and inconsistent as, to a vast extent, the provision or the non provision would be found to be, that has been made for the various cases that have happened to present themselves for decision, yet in the character of a repository for such cases it affords, for the manufactory of law, a stock of materials which is beyond all price. Traverse the whole continent of Europe, ransack all the libraries belonging to the jurisprudential systems of the several political states, add the contents all together, you would not be able to compose a collection of cases equal in variety, in amplitude, in clearness of statement—in a word, all points taken together, in instructiveness—to that which may be seen to be afforded by the collection of English Reports of adjudged cases, on adding to them the abridgements and treatises, by which a sort of order, such as it is, has been given to their contents.

Of these necessary materials, the stock already in hand is not only rich, but one may venture to say, sufficient: nor, to the composition of a *compleat* body of law, in which, saving the requisite allowance to be made for human weakness, every imaginable case shall be provided for, and provided for in the best manner, is any thing at present wanting but a duly arranging hand.

Objection 2. *Foreign Yoke.* It was to free ourselves from the yoke of foreign law that we took up arms against the Monarch of England, and shall an obscure subject of the same nation fasten another such yoke upon our necks?

It may perhaps appear an idle precaution to bring to view in the character of an objection capable of being urged, an observation so palpably void of substance. But it is not always by the most rational argument that the strongest impression is made. At any rate the answer will, I flatter myself, be found sufficient.

1. The yoke, the foreign yoke, is already about your necks: you were born with it about your necks.

What your proposed Scribe does, if he does any thing, is to facilitate to you the means of relieving yourselves from it.

2. Year by year, or rather *term* by *term*, that is *quarter* by *quarter*, the mass and burthen of it receives, at present, its encrease. What he does, if he does any thing, will be to help, relieve you from such encrease.

3. By him, let him do what he may, no yoke will be imposed: nothing like the imposition of a yoke either done, or so much as attempted. By him, let him do what he may, no act of power will be performed, not any the minutest particle of power exercised. The honour for which he is suing is that of being admitted to work in the character of a Servant. Labor alone will be his part: acceptance, rejection, alteration, decision, choice, with as much, or as little labor, as it may be your pleasure to bestow upon it, will be yours.

Yes, if, to have part in the governance and plunder of you for seven years, he were to be occupied in cringing to you, and in flattering you, for as many days or weeks, then indeed there *might* be power for him to exercise, then indeed there might be a yoke for you to take upon you, and him to impose: but any such authority is not more completely out of his reach, than it is and ever would be out of his wish.

4. In suing to be thus employed himself, it is no less opposite to his wish, than above his power, to exclude from the same employment any of yourselves. But of this a little further on.

Heavy or light, by your own hands, if by any, will the burthen if any, be imposed.

5. Innumerable are the yokes, the additions to the existing foreign yoke, by which, until you take this only method of securing yourselves against all such nuisances, the burthen you now labour under will continue to be *encreased.*

Not a year, not a quarter of a year, but, here in this Country fresh loads are produced, of the excrementitious matter of which this burthen is composed. Of this matter, this or that portion, will it, or will it not, by such or such a time, have in your Country begun to swell the load? Upon arrivals or non-arrivals—upon winds and waves—upon good or ill humour between the two nations, will even *possibility* depend in the first place.

Let *possibility* be now converted into fact. The produce of the last twelve month, or of the last quarter, or such other portion as accident may have determined, is now arrived: Upon whom on the occasion of each cause will the acceptance or rejection of it, and of each particular portion of it, depend? Upon yourselves all together? Upon your appointed legislators? upon the aggregate of all your legislative bodies? or upon any one of them? No: but on each particular occasion, upon the will of some one or other such small number of yourselves, acting as Judge or Judges.

Take for example any one such Judge, upon this or that case that chance has brought before him, this or that English decision, (let it be supposed) bears: will it, or will it *not*, be taken by him for his guide? On contingency upon contingency depends the answer. The last cargo, has it, in the whole or any part of it, come into his hands or under his cognizance? if not the whole, but a part only, *what* part? The case produced to him, will he, or will he not pay regard to it? Yes or no depends (for I see not how it should fail of depending) altogether upon his good pleasure. If it be such as suits his views he makes use of it: if it be such as does not suit his views, he turns aside from it.

6. Innumerable, and many of them still more obscure than your proffered servant, are the workmen who at present, bear, each of them a part, in the fashioning of these successive accretions to this your foreign yoke.

At present—under the existing system of blind and sheepish acquiescence, who are they who thus, in conjunction in each instance with this or that Judge—become respectively the arbiters of your fate? Speaking of individuals to say who, is, in any instance impossible: speaking generally, a Judge or bench of Judges, nominees of a foreign monarch—or to speak more correctly, as well as particularly a mixt yet uncommunicating multitude, composed of Judges, Advocates, self appointed Note-takers, Law Report writers, Law treatise makers, Law abridgment makers, and publishing law booksellers.

Suppose on the other hand the proposed work executed, the proposed Pannomion compleated; in what state would the rule of action be among you in that case? Comprized it would be the whole of it, in a small number of Volumes; the part necessary to each man in some *one* small Volume: the whole heap of foreign lumber, existing and future contingent, as compleatly superseded, rendered as completely useless, as an equal quantity of *School Divinity*, or Rome-bred *Canon Law*.

Wide in this respect, is the difference, between a situation in which not a particle of labour has place without a correspondent particle of power attached to it, and a task which would have to consist purely of labour without any the least particle of power attached to it.

But, though thus bare of power would be the Service in question if rendered by an obscure and unknown foreigner, the case not only might be, but naturally would be, very different, if a service of the self same nature were to find the performance of it lodged in the hands of a native. In *that* case, whatever *reputation* and consequent influence it might happen to a man to obtain by the execution of it, would, in his situation, and for his benefit, convert itself into so much *power*. In power in short, not only would the performance of the Service *terminate*, but it is in power that the choice of the person for the performance of it would have *originated*. If therefore the business finds itself in the hands of a foreigner, there will be at least *this* advantage that the judgment to be pronounced upon it will stand so much the clearer of the influence of local, as well as personal, enmities and partialities, and the work stand so much the better chance of being judged and decided upon, on the ground of its own intrinsic merits, its own fitness for the intended purpose.

Discussions of this sort do not, it must be confessed, shed any very brilliant lustre upon human nature; but so it is that we are constituted: and being thus constituted it is impossible for Us to act either prudently or beneficially, any further than as we know ourselves for what we are.

As to local jealousies, to my eyes dissention, be the seat of it where it may, is never a pleasing object. But though in some measure it depends on a man's choice what objects he shall fix his eyes upon, it depends not altogether upon his will what objects shall pass before them.

By the words *northern* and *southern*, if my eyes or my memory do not deceive me, one cause of division more or less active has been indicated as having place, and more or less frequently manifesting its influence in your confederacy. Supposing this to be so, what is then the consequence? For public Service in this or any other line, if a member of the southern division presents himself or is held up to view, jealousy and opposition gather in the northern regions, and so *vice versâ*.

Another source of division, though to my unpractised eyes not so clear and intelligible a one as the foregoing, is that which is brought to view by the words *democrats* and *federalist*.

Under these circumstances, be the nature of the work ever so uninviting, if a hand were to be offered for it, from one of the sides distinguished as above, in the natural course of things it would find on the other side hands drawn up in array, and prepared if possible to repel it. Such at least would be the case *here*. Such in a word would be the case (for such has ever hitherto been the case) wherever there have been parties—wherever there has been either liberty or the appearance of it. If to this rule the land of the United States afford an exception, it is a land—not of men, but angels.

Such then are the perils which, a work of the sort in question would have to encounter, if proposed for a native workman: perils which in proportion to the utility of the work, would, it is apprehended be more likely to receive encrease than diminution: from these perils, at least, it would be saved by acceptance given to a remote and foreign hand.

Objection 3. *Foreigner's necessary ignorance.*

A foreigner by whom the territory has not, any part of it, ever been, or will be visited, who with the population, with the territory or its local peculiarities, never has had, nor proposes ever to have any the least personal acquaintance—a person so circumstanced a person thus ignorant—unavoidably and incurably ignorant—of so many necessary points of knowledge—is he a person who, with any propriety, can be looked to for any such service?

1. To this question one answer may be given by another question. The legislators, such as they are, to whose combined exertions the loads of *writing*, of which our and your *unwritten* law is composed, owe their existence, have already been laid before you and brought under review: Our Advocates, our Judges, our Note-takers, our Report makers, our Treatise and Abridgment makers, our publishing Law booksellers. By how many of all these functionaries, has the legislative System of the United States been ever studied—been ever so much as thought of, or the Country visited?

2. Another answer is—that, upon a closer scrutiny, the points, which present a demand for local knowledge; would not, it is supposed be found to cover, in the field of law, so great an extent, nor yet to be so difficult to discriminate beforehand, as upon a transient glance, general notions might lead any person to imagine.

3. Nor, if I may venture to say as much, would it be easy to find any person, more compleatly aware of the demand, presented by the nature of the case, for attention to those local exigencies, nor more completely in the habit of looking over the field of law in this particular view.

Of this disposition, and this habit, exemplifications of considerable amplitude may be seen in the already mentioned work, which for these nine years has been under the public eye: and by that work Sir, I am saved from the need of attempting on the present occasion to give you any farther trouble on this head.

Thus in the case of penal Law. Of the *genera* of Offences, as distinguished or distinguishable by their *generic* names—Murder. Defamation. Theft. Robbery and so forth—definitions for the most part the same all the world over. But for particular species, occasion may be afforded, by particular local circumstances: and so in regard to causes of aggravation, extenuation, justification, or exemption, with demand for corresponding varieties in respect of *satisfaction* or punishment. And so in regard to *contracts*.

Accordingly, in any draught which I should draw, care would be taken, not only to keep the distinction all along in mind, but to keep pointed towards it the attention of all those to whom in dernier resort it belonged to judge.

4. I say *to those to whom it belonged to judge:* for as it never would be by myself, neither by any one else, let it be forgotten; that of any body of proposed laws to which it may happen to have been drawn up by the proposed draughtsman, there is not any part, of which the legislative bodies in the several United States will not take, each of them according to its competence, perfect and effectual cognizance: cognizance no less perfect and effectual than what has been taken of any other portion of the matter of law to which their sanction has respectively been given or refused.

Whatsoever therefore may, in relation to the local points in question, be the ignorance of the proposed and supposed foreign draughtsman, and, in his draught whatsoever may have been the errors produced by these ignorances, all such errors will, for their correction, have the same instruments and opportunities, as any other errors that ever have been, or may ever come to be made and corrected.

5. Not but that, on this as on most other occasions, it is more to be desired, that errors, of whatever kind, should, particularly in such a work, have never been made, than that, having been made, they should be corrected: and, by original exclusion, not only the time and labour necessary to correction would be saved but the danger of non correction avoided.

And here perhaps, Sir, may accordingly be seen one use in the sort of assistance, the idea of which will come to be submitted to your consideration, a little further on.

Objection 4. *Shame of being beholden to a foreigner.*

But a foreigner—How necessary soever the work itself may be would it not to American Citizens be matter of just shame, to see a foreign hand entrusted with, or so much as employed in the execution of it? America—the whole population of United America—the 8 or 9 millions or whatever may be the amount of it—among such multitudes of hands, constantly occupied in the business of legislation, does it not contain so much as a single one, competent to such a task?

A question this, which will be apt to appear, much more within my competence to put, than to find an answer for. I shall venture however to submit answers more than one.

1. In the first place what I beleive is certain is—that whatsoever number of persons thus qualified, may, at this time, be in existence, no one such person has as yet at any time made himself known as such, or been recognized as such.

2. In the next place, be the number of persons, in an equal, or by any amount superior, degree, competent to the task in question, ever so great, of the offer here submitted it is no part, either of the design, or tendency, to deprive the United States of the Services of any one. On the contrary, among its tendencies is that of calling forth into action, to this very purpose, and on this very occasion, whatsoever qualifications or capabilities, of the kind in question, may happen to be in existence.

3. Of this sort of national jealousy, if the effect be to call forth into existence any competitors who would not otherwise exist, so far at least, if the work itself supposing it well executed, be deemed a useful one, in such case, as well the utility of this offer, as the propriety of giving acceptance to it, will be out of dispute: and, in such a competition, the danger that the work of a perfect stranger should, to the prejudice of local interests and influences, obtain an undue preference, will hardly appear very formidable.

4. If on the other hand, it should happen to it, either to be the only work produced, or, finding rival works to contend with, to be really, in the judgment of the competent judges, thought better adapted than any other to the intended purpose, any such supposition as that, on the occasion of such a work, these same judges would see their Country less well served, or not served at all, rather than see it served by a foreign hand, and that accordingly, they would put it in the power of any foreigner, to preclude them from the benefit of a good body of law, or so much as a single good clause in a law, merely by being the first to propose it, is that sort of supposition which, if seriously made, would not, I imagine, be very generally well received.

5. Whatsoever disposition toward jealousy it might happen to an offer of this sort to have to encounter, a man, of whom it was perfectly known, that in person he could never be present, to give to any one the sort of offence which such a disposition supposes, should naturally, on this supposition, present such a ground for acceptance as should give him on this one score at least, the advantage over a native. On affections of this kind distance in respect of place, especially when the continuance of it is certain, produces an effect intimately analogous to, and little different from that of time. In the present case, were the proposed Workman already numbered among the dead, he could not be more effectually placed out of the sight of the people, and in particular of the constituted authorities, in whose Service it is his ambition thus to place himself, than to the day of his death, he would find it necessary to remain, if this his offer found acceptance.

6. So far from operating as an objection, at least in the mind of any Gentleman, who fills the high station to which this offer is addressed, what I should expect is—to find this very circumstance of foreignership placed, and on this very score, to the account of advantage.

There are certain situations, and those highly important ones, for the filling of which, it has been a known maxim among republican States, to resort to foreigners in preference to Natives.

Among the Italian Republics, this sort of policy was applied sometimes by usage, sometimes by positive law—not only to the subordinate situation designated among us by the title of *Judge* but to that of *Podesta:* a sort of supreme Monarchical Magistrate to whose power, while it lasted, it seems not very easy to assign any very distinct limits. My books are not at present within my reach but, in the case of the Podesta, instances more than one will be found in Sismondi's lately published history of the Italian Republics; [10] and, in the case of Judge, I have read laws to that effect in the Codes of Italian States, more than one: and if I do not mis-recollect, these instances or some of them are mentioned in the *Defence of the Constitution of the United States* by Mr Adams.[11]

Of this preference the cause, the *efficient* cause seems manifest enough. For any of those great and enviable situations, seldom could a man, whose character was such as to afford him any chance of finding acceptance, offer himself, without raising up against himself, besides a band of rivals, a much larger host of adversaries.

Nor was the justificative cause, the reason, much less clear or impressive. In any such powerful situation no native could seat himself, without bringing into it, in his bosom, a swarm of sinister interests, partialities and prejudices.

§4. On the subject of *alienage.* I gave intimation of an expedient, which I will now venture upon the liberty of suggesting, and on which, it being to myself, personally speaking, a matter of indifference, you will be pleased, Sir, to bestow what regard it may seem to merit.

If at any time, supposing me occupied in the work in question, it were thought worth while, by your Government, to Commission any Citizen of the United States, residing for any purpose of his own, or sent hither for that particular purpose, to take a part in it, and give me the benefit of his information and assistance in the execution of it, whatsoever instruction I may be thought capable of affording, on the subject of legislation, should be always at his command: and whatsoever information, not possessed by him, I am myself master of, it should be my study to make him master of as fully and as expeditiously as possible: always understood that the same considerations, which forbid the receipt of the fruits of public munificence, would oppose the same inexorable bar to the acceptance of the individual's mite.

The probability, of my living long enough to put the last hand to such a work, being of course altogether precarious, my endeavours would be, as speedily as possible, to put him in a way of filling up whatever deficiency it might be my lot to leave.

The Gentleman so commissioned would I suppose be a person distinct from him who stood charged with the Affairs of the United States at this Court or in this Country in any diplomatic character, principal or subordinate, and that for more reasons than one.

1. His whole time would not be too much for such an employment.

2. In his instance, a more intimate acquaintance with the general state of the law in the United States might, perhaps, be thought requisite, than for any such diplomatic character would be thought altogether necessary.

3. In the event of a rupture between the two Governments, (a contingency, the calamitousness of which affords no reason why on this any more than on any other occasion, it should be left unprovided for) the general liberality of the times (and I hope this Country will not to this purpose be considered as affording an exception) leaves me little apprehension, that a person whose commission were known, and declared to be confined to this one object, would not be allowed to continue in this country, for that particular purpose, notwithstanding any interruption of diplomatic intercourse.[a]

§5. The degree of advance already made by my labours in the field of legislation and the order of priority in which, if undertaken, the several distinguishable parts of the Pannomion would be proposed to be executed— these seem to be of the number of the topics, on which something will on such an occasion be expected, and on which accordingly it will not be allowable for me to be altogether silent.

On these topics on the other hand, any considerable details would, if comprised within the compass of this paper, swell it to such a bulk, as to subject to too great a degree of uncertainty its prospect of finding a reader, in the exalted and busy station to which it is addressed.

The point for your consideration, Sir, supposing the Work itself a desirable one, will, unless I misconceive the matter be found to be—whether if this proposal should be passed by without acceptance the rejection will leave an adequate probability of seeing the work executed, at any future period, and under other circumstances, to equal advantage? and in particular, whether there be any such probability, that any other person will arise, who, having, without receipt or prospect of pecuniary retribution, made equal advances in the prosecution of such a design, shall, upon the same desirable terms, be ready to undertake to do what depends upon him towards the completion of it?

(a) Note desired to be kept private.

A Gentleman with whom I am well acquainted, a Russian born, who at the time of the rupture between Russia and this Country had for many years been Chaplain to the Russian Embassy, and whom I have seen doing business at our Secretary of States' and Admiralty Offices, has all along continued here; having done so even in the time of the Mad Emperor Paul.

To enable you to afford to yourself a proper answer to these questions, the following statements, compressed as they are, and consequently, in a proportionable degree, deficient in point of specific information, may yet perhaps be found to suffice.

1. In regard to the *Penal* Code the work is already in a state of considerable forwardness. That it was so, so long ago as the year 1802, not to speak of a much earlier period, may be seen from the work edited in that year in the French language by Mr Dumont. What may be seen upon the face of that work is indeed a sample but it is no more than a sample: a great deal more had even then been executed than is there exhibited; perhaps the greatest part of the whole: a few months, indeed a very few, would, if I do not much miscalculate suffice for the completion of it—I mean *in terminis*.

2. As to the *Civil* Code, in the adjustment of the *terms* of it, but little advance has been made: but, in respect of *leading principles*, of which in regard to *form* as well as matter, a pretty ample view may in that same work be seen, they have long ago been settled.

3. Of the subject of the Judicial Establishment (the *Judiciary* is I think the more concise denomination it goes by with you) a pretty full view may be seen in the printed, but never yet published papers drawn up about the year 1790 on the occasion of the French Revolution:[12] Copy herewith sent, as per list. To adapt it to the purpose of the United States, if the System actually in force there should be regarded as susceptible of improvement, would of course require considerable modifications.

4. As to *procedure, judicial procedure* in the adjustment of the principles of that branch of the law, considerable progress was necessarily made, of which the result was brought to view, and may be seen in the course of the enquiry made into the subject of the correspondent part of the Official Establishment as above.

Since that time farther advances were made and presented to view in the work intituled Scotch Reform & published Ao. 1806 Copy herewith sent.[13]

In addition to this, a work compleat or nearly so on the subject of *Forthcomingness*—Vizt. on the most effectual and in other respects most proper, means to be employed for ordering matters in such sort that, whether for the purpose (as they say in French) of *justiciability*, I mean being placed at the disposal of the judicial authorities, or for the purpose of *evidence* (I mean being made to furnish evidence) as well all *things* as all *persons* requisite shall, on each occasion, be *forthcoming*, lies by me in manuscript.

5 The subject of evidence has been examined in its whole extent and sifted to the bottom. A work of mine on this subject under the title of *The Rationale of Evidence* enough to occupy two moderate sized quarto volumes, has been for some time in the hands of another friend of mine,[14] and will be in the Printers' hands in the course of about two months.

For drawing up a Code *in terminis*, grounded on the principles there laid down, very little time would suffice. Of the customary *exclusionary rules*— rules which are not in the law of any Country either consistent with one another, or adhered to with any tolerable degree of constancy—the place would be mostly occupied by a set of correspondent *Instructions:* Instructions from the Legislator to the Judge, pointing out, *inter alia*, as causes of *suspicion*, those circumstances which in general are employed in the character of causes of absolute and inexorable *rejection*.

On several subjects not included, as well as those which are included, under the above heads, disquisitions may be seen in the subjoined list of printed Works. But, to the present purpose, no separate mention of them seems requisite.

The printed but never published fragment on the subject of the *Art of Tactics* as applied to *Political Assemblies*,[15] is but one Essay, out of some *thirty* or *forty*, which were at that time written and which, taken together, did not want much of having gone through the subject in its whole extent.

But this is a subject, I should scarcely myself propose to include in the *Pannomion*. It is a subject on which each political body will naturally feel itself disposed to legislate, or at least act, according to its own views of its own exigencies, meaning exigencies considered with a view to the public good, the good of that part of the public Service—not to speak of particular interests and prejudices.

As to *constitutional law*, I mean that branch which regards the mode of appointing the several public functionaries, with their respective powers and obligations—with you I believe the appellation has a sense somewhat more extensive—As to *Constitutional law* thus explained, I mention it for no other purpose than to show that it has not been overlooked. In respect of the *matter* no demand for alteration has presented itself to my view nor should I myself be disposed to look out for any. In respect of the *form* something might possibly be found needful to adapt it to the other parts.

But though it were to be transcribed without the alteration of an iota, still, for symmetry and compactness, it might be necessary it should go through the hands, by which the other parts were drawn up.

As to the order of operation—I mean as between the different parts of the proposed Pannomion—the *penal* Code is that which I imagine has already presented itself to your thoughts as the part which claims the first place. In respect of the *matter* of it, it is that in which the demand for variation presented by local circumstances will naturally be least extensive: and the comparative progress already made in it, would, in default of material reason to the contrary, be of itself sufficient to determine the preference.

I know not whether the legal circumstances of your recent territorial acquisitions will be thought to add any thing to the reasons for acceptance.[16] In the character either of subjects or fellow citizens, you have to make provision for the legal exigencies of a new mass of population, differing from you not less in laws and customs than in language. In the state of these their laws, alteration in many points must already have been necessitated, alteration in many others must be continually in contemplation. Besides the advantage of having the work done, whatsoever there may be of it to be done, upon an already considered and comprehensive plan—might it not, to the new citizens in question, be in some degree a matter of satisfaction, to learn that the preparation of the business was consigned to hands, for whose impartiality there would be such a security as could scarce have been in contemplation otherwise?

To contemplate the matter on the footing of *presumptions* merely—and laying out of the case such ground for acceptance as the works themselves may be found to afford, I wish to be clearly understood, in what I say as to the considerations, which in the present instance, may appear to operate in favour of the experiment, of receiving into the field of legislation the labour of a foreign hand. They are reducible to this simple circumstance vizt. that of the existence of a person, by whom so large a portion of time and study has been bestowed upon the business, coupled with the assumption that, neither in the British Empire nor in the United States, does there exist that other person, by whom, upon any comprehensive plan an *equal* portion of time and study—I might perhaps add *any* portion of time and study—has been employed with any ameliorative views.

One thing I am ready to admit and am fully assured of; and *that* is, that if, on general grounds, and setting aside any such casual opportunity, a resolution were come to, in your Country to set about the drawing up a *Pannomion*, reasons for looking beyond the American States (I mean on the ground of abstract aptitude and setting aside those which have reference to local jealousies and partialities) would not be to be found.

No, Sir: not the smallest doubt have I, but that, if in both Countries, a *Pannomion* were to be drawn up, and in both Countries hands were to be looked out for, in the class of practising lawyers, the hand of an American lawyer would, even for the use of England, present beyond comparison a fairer premise than that of a lawyer of the English school.

What this persuasion has for its ground is, the observation of the improvements—the prodigious improvements—which in matter and even in stile, since its voyage to America, the law of England has received from American hands.

Laying out of the case those necessary changes, which, in the constitutional branch, have been produced by the emancipation and the change in the form of Government—(subjects to which my attention neither has turned, nor is disposed to turn itself) those which on this occasion I have in view are those which through the medium of materials, as I have been hitherto able to collect, I have had the opportunity of observing in the *penal* branch, in the *civil* branch, and in the system of procedure.

Among these, though there may be some, which, being the result of the change in the constitutional branch, could not, consistently with the existing constitutional system, be introduced into the Mother Country, yet there are others—and those the greatest part, which, with as much advantage, and with as little inconvenience, might be effected in England, as they have been in the United States.

Accordingly, but for the adverse interest of professional men, and the lazy and stupid confidence with which the bulk of the people have resigned their best interests into the hands of these their natural and irreconcilable enemies, long ago would these same amendments have been made in this Country.

In America, the work would not fall into the hands of any persons, to whom the practice of amendment was not familiar: who had not been in use not only to see amendments made and made to a great extent, but made with manifest and undeniable good effect: whereas in *this* country (saving exceptions in too small a number to be mentioned) any past Work would look in vain for operators, to whom the very idea of amendment was not an object of unaffected terror, and undisguised enmity.

In this state of things, suppose any person, myself for example, after making up a list of these amendments, were to come forward with the proposal to introduce the same amendments here: what would be the reception it would meet with? "Oh! *You want to republicanize us do you?*" This would be the cry set up by the men of law—echoed by all others (a countless multitude) who have any share in the profit of the existing abuses: and in this cry would be found a full and sufficient answer. Foundation, it is true, it would have none. But, such is still the blindness and indifference of the people at large—so bigotted their admiration, so prostrate their adoration, of their natural and implacable enemies and oppressors.

*(Do you doubt this? Sir, I will put you in a way to make the experiment. I will find you some fit person, who, without possibility of profit to himself, merely being indemnified against the expense, shall write the book and publish it. Sir, if you accept the offer you will be a loser by it. I mean of course in the account of *money:* if you look for indemnification, honour to yourself and country is the only shape, in which you will receive it.)

Such is the bigotry and indifference which in this Country is still prevalent. How long is it destined to continue? This is more than a prudent man will venture to answer. Thus much, however, I will venture to predict, Vizt. that, before this century, not to say this half century, has passed away, this shame to England will likewise have passed away.

I beg your pardon Sir, no sooner is the proposal made than I have to beg your permission to withdraw it. For without those, or any other conditions,

---

*Note Though the fact is true, it is requested that publicity be not given to either of these two passages inclosed in brackets.

the friend to both Countries, who will do this, is already found. A Periodical publication is chosen as a vehicle for it: the subject to go on from number to number in continuance. I have the honor to be, Sir, With all respect,
Your most obedient and very humble Servant

JEREMY BENTHAM [17]

P. S.

In the event of acceptance I would beg the favor of you Sir, to give the
necessary orders for the forming as Speedily as may be, a collection as complete as possible of the Laws of the several States as well as of those of
Congress down to the then present time, and transmitting them to me
here.

Immediately on delivery the expense (purchase money, freight and all
other necessary charges included) will be thankfully paid by me to the person by whom delivery is made.

To these I would beg might be added three Copies of the latest statistical
account extant of the United States—that by Blodget would I suppose be
the book.[18] About 3 years ago I had a momentary sight of it, year of publication I believe 1806 or 1807, but from that time to this, all my endeavours
to obtain the property, or so much as a sight of a Copy have been without
effect.

Also a Copy of the Works of Genl. Alexander Hamilton lately published
at New York 3 Vol. 8 Vo.[19]

Also of such Papers as have been published under the name or in the
character of official Reports—whatsoever promise to be serviceable in any
way to the intended purpose.

Underneath is a List of all the Books of United States Law I have been
able to procure, and for most of them I have been indebted to various accidents—enquiries made at the Booksellers for others, and in particular for
information of the Laws of Congress have proved fruitless.

1 Computation of the several Independent States of America—2d Edition
8 vo by the Revd. W Jackson London 1783.

2. A Review of the Laws of the United States of America—the British
Provinces & West India Islands Anonymous London 8vo: Printed for
Otridge Strand 1790.

3 A Defence of the Constitution of Government of the United States of
America against the attack of M Turgot in his Letter to Dr Price dated
22nd March 1778 by John Adams L.L.D. &c In 3 Vol 8vo: New Edition
London Printed for Stockdale 1794.

4. The Pensylvania State Trials, containing the Impeachment Trial & Acquittal of Francis Hopkinson & Jn. Nicholson Esqr. 8vo. Vol 1 Philadelphia Printed by Francis Busby for Edmund Hogan 1794.

5 A System of the Laws of the State of Connecticut in Six Books by Zepha-

niah Swift 2 Vol: 8vo: Windhams printed by John Byron for the Author Vol 1—1795.—Vol 2 1796.

6. Acts passed at the First Congress of the United States of America begun and held at the City of New York 4 March Anno 1789 Philadelphia Printed by Francis Child Printer of the Laws of the United States 1795.

7 Do. of the Second Congress begun & held at the City of Philadelphia 24 Octr. 1791 ibid 1795.

8. Do. of the Third Congress Do 2 Octr 1793 ibid 1795.

9. Do. of the first Session of the 4th. Congress begun and held at Philadelphia 7th Decr. 1795. Printed by Thomas Dobson 1797.

10 Do. of the second Session of the 4th Congress begun and held at Philadelphia 5 Decr. 1796 ibid Printed by T Dobson 1797.

List of the Works sent with this Letter.

Panopticon 3 Vol:
Essay on Political Tactics
Defence of Usury.
Views of the Hard Labour
Sketches relative to the Poor 4 Nos.
Draught of a Plan for the Judicial Establishment in France
Address to the National Convention of France, proposing the emancipation of their Colonies.
Escheat vice Taxation.
Protest against Law Taxes
Traités de Législation 3 Vol:
Panopticon versus New South Wales & Plea for the Constitution
Summary view of a Plan for a Court & Lords Delegates
Scotch Reform
Théorie des Peines et des Récompenses

Works not sent, being out of print and not procurable

An introduction to the Principles of Morals and Legislation, printed in the year 1780, and now first published by J Bentham Esqr. of Lincoln's Inn, London Printed for T. Payne and Son at the Mews Gate 1789.
A Fragment on Government.

RC (DLC); FC (GBLUc: Bentham Mss). RC sent as enclosure in Henry Brougham to William Pinkney, 1 Nov. 1811 (DLC), and forwarded in Pinkney to JM, ca. 9 Mar. 1812 (DLC). RC in the hand of a copyist and signed by Bentham; docketed by JM. RC misdated 30 Oct. 1812 in the *Index to the James Madison Papers*. FC printed in Jeremy Bentham, *Papers Relative to Codification and Public Instruction* (London, 1817), pp. 1–65 (JM's copy of this work is in the Madison Collection, Special Collections Department, University of Virginia Library). Filed with the FC are notes entitled "Marginals of Codification Papers to US.," dated 14–30 Aug. 1811. Variations between the RC and the FC have not been noted.

1. JM did not reply to Bentham's letter until 8 May 1816, pleading as his apology the "occupations incident to preparations for an anticipated war, which was in fact the result of the anxious crisis" (GBL).

2. In his covering letter to Pinkney enclosing the letter, Brougham conveyed a warning to JM that Bentham's "style is somewhat peculiar—and that, both from excessive subdivisions and from a practice of coining new terms (in some measure arising out of his original turn of thinking & his ancient love of conciseness & precision) his writings are apt to wear an aspect not very favorable in the eyes of a cursory reader."

3. Pierre-Etienne-Louis Dumont (1759–1829), a Genevan-born writer and political associate of Mirabeau, was the first major editor and publisher of Bentham's writings. He resided in England from 1792 to 1814.

4. Bentham referred to the *Code civil de français*, otherwise known as the *Code Napoléon*, promulgated in 1804.

5. Bentham referred to *Application de la théorie de la législation pênale . . . rédigé en projet pour les états de sa majesté le roi de Bavière* (Paris, 1807), a work compiled by the French jurist Scipion-Jérôme-François Bexon.

6. Bentham was one of seventeen foreigners, including JM, who were offered French citizenship by the National Assembly on 26 Aug. 1792 (see *PJM*, 14:381).

7. On 8 Apr. 1803 the *corps législatif* commended Bentham's *Traités de legislation civil et pénale* and ordered that it be deposited in its library (Paris *Gazette Nationale ou Le Moniteur Universel*, 9 Apr. 1803).

8. Bentham's *Preliminary Sketches Relative to the Poor* (1797) and *Pauper Management Improved* (1798) were translated by Adrien Cyprien Duquesnoy as *Esquisse d'un ouvrage en faveur des pauvres* (Paris, 1802).

9. "Of all laws I think that that is the most iniquitous and least like a law, which Lucius Flaccus, the interrex, passed in regard to Sulla—that his acts, whatever they were, should be ratified," Cicero, *De lege agraria*, 3.2.5 (*Cicero in Twenty-Eight Volumes*, Loeb Classical Library [1967 reprint], 6:489).

10. Jean-Charles-Léonard Simonde de Sismondi, *Histoire des républiques italiennes du moyen âge* (16 vols.; Paris, 1809–18).

11. John Adams, *Defence of the Constitutions of Government of the United States of America* (3 vols.; London, 1787).

12. *Draught of a New Plan for the Organization of the Judicial Establishment in France* (London, 1790).

13. *Scotch Reform* (London, 1806).

14. Bentham referred to James Mill (see Mill to Bentham, 25 July and 26 Oct. 1809, Stephen Conway, ed., *The Correspondence of Jeremy Bentham* [9 vols.; Oxford, 1968–83], 8:38, 58).

15. *Essay on Political Tactics, Containing Six of the Principal Rules to Be Observed by a Political Assembly in the Process of Forming a Decision* (London, 1791).

16. Bentham referred to the Louisiana Purchase.

17. Jeremy Bentham (1748–1832), a graduate of Oxford University, had read law at Lincoln's Inn. He did not practice his profession, but by virtue of his application of the principles of utilitarianism, he became both a celebrated jurisconsult and a leading exponent of the ideas of philosophical radicalism.

18. Samuel Blodget, *Economica: A Statistical Manual for the United States of America* (Washington, 1806; Shaw and Shoemaker 10004).

19. *The Works of Alexander Hamilton* (3 vols.; New York, 1810; Shaw and Shoemaker 20274).

§ From John Murray & Sons and Others. *31 October 1811, New York.* The subscribers recommend John Gilmour, who is a respectable and intelligent gentleman and a fit person for a consulship.

RC (DNA: RG 59, LAR, 1809–17, filed under "Gilmour"). 2 pp. Signed by Murray & Sons and twelve others, including Henry Remsen. Docketed by Monroe as a "recommdn of a Consul for Glasgow." Probably enclosed in Gilmour to Monroe, 2 Dec. 1811 (ibid.), where Gilmour requested that the president be informed that he wished to be appointed consul in Glasgow.

Memorandum from Albert Gallatin

[ca. 1 November 1811]

Notes on President's message

————

sheet page

1.   1.   Do the words "considerations drawn from the posture of our foreign affairs" afford a satisfactory reason for the earlier meeting of Congress?

4.   The additional proofs of the repeal of French decrees are mentioned only incidentally & not as a distinct subject; and the mention of the Naples cases (subqt. to 2 Nover apparently under those decrees & at all events very offensive) is omitted.

2. 3 & 4. The war paragraphs. Two questions—1. is it more eligible to resort to war than to rely on the effect of non-importation?— 2. if more eligible, is it proper and consistent with policy to recommend it? To the 1st question I would be disposed to answer in the negative less from a conviction of the prompt efficacy of non-importation in bringing G. B. to terms than from the uncertainty in every respect of the effect of a war. The resources of the Country both in men & money can be drawn but with great difficulty, and will be found much less than a view of its population & wealth would lead us at first to believe. Exclusively of accumn. of debt tending at the conclusion of the war to weaken us and retarding our natural progression, the measures necessary to carry on the war must be unpopular and by producing a change of men may lead to a disgraceful peace, to absolute subserviency hereafter to G. B., and even to substantial alterations in our institutions: whilst we can calculate almost with certainty all the evils and inconveniencies of the non-importation. If however the spirit of the Nation, or an opinion

535

that hostilities not repelled by corresponding measures would be still more pernicious than any possible effect of a war, shall lead to an answer in the affirmative to the first question, the propriety and policy of the recommendation must still be examined. Notwithstanding the general power to recommend vested in the President, I cannot at least in this instance be perfectly reconciled with the attempt to give a tone on the question of war different from what might otherwise govern the decision of the body with whom our constitution has exclusively vested the power of making war. (If it be said that the hostilities of G. B. are already war, the Executive would have a right to repel it even without the previous sanction of Congress.) But it is above all the policy which appears questionable. If war is certainly to ensue, it is better, as soon as we are sufficiently ready, to make it at once, instead of announcing before hand that determination and thereby enabling the enemy to strike at once, to sweep our commerce, to send a fleet & reinforcements on our coast and vicinity. The only argument in favr. of the measure is that the fear of a war may induce G. B. to recede. This is doubtful: but if the experiment is attempted, the recommendation must be so framed as not to convey any threat too offensive to their pride to be digested, and yet to carry a conviction that war must be the final tho' not immediate effect of their not receding. (I say not immediate, because if they considered it as such & concluded not to recede they would strike at once). It may be impossible to frame a recommendation precisely to that effect, but that proposed in the message may be improved. Thus the expressions "the period is arrived," "direct & undisguised hostility" "authorising reprisals" and allusion to a lapse of the present session &a. may be softened or omitted.[1] (Note that it seems that the first sentence of that paragraph which alludes to an extension of defensive preparations might be omitted as a special recommendation follows the ensuing paragraph).

sheet page

2.   4.   last paragraph. A recommendation to encrease revenue & raise money would seem immediately connected with this. Or shall it be reserved for financial paragraph.

3.   1.   *Navy.* Having alluded to our limited resources, it may be added that any misapplication of these will be fatal. Looking at the aggregate of resources actually in the possession of & expended by Congress during the revoly. war, paper money, foreign loans, and requisitions & advances actually paid by individual States,

it has appeared to me incomprehensible that the very moderate army in actual service had not been well fed, clothed & even paid. I can account for it only on a supposition that those resources were partly mis-applied; how much was mis-applied on a navy? how much on other objects would not be an useless enquiry. But the general fact is certain, and the same remark is applicable to almost every other country. G. Britain alone has succeeded in establishing a system of debt & taxation as yet equal to the most profligate expenditure & mis-application of resources. Bonaparte is, at least in his military expenditure, a model of a judicious application of the resources which he can command; & to this system he has been forced by his inability of borrowing. The support even of our present Navy, say 2 millions a year, must either entrench on our other force which would be most fatal, or compel us to borrow 2 millions more a year. The difference between borrowing six millions a year and borrowing eight, is that the six may be borrowed at 6 p% and that if obliged to push the loan to eight, the whole of it must be borrowed at a higher interest, perhaps 8 p%. The effects on the public credit, on the war itself &a., are evident. Unless therefore great utility can be proven, the employment of that force will be a substantial evil. I believe myself that so far from there being any utility it will in its very employment diminish our means of annoying the enemy, & that every sailor engaged in public service would be more usefully employed on privateers. In a country where the resources & spirit of enterprize are great, and the command of Govt. over those resources extremely moderate, it is necessary as far as practicable to induce individuals to apply those resources of their own accord against the enemy. On land that is impossible; but on the Ocean it is our natural & a very formidable weapon. Let us apply all our resources to the defence of our seaports & of Louisiana, and to the attack of the adjacent British provinces: and let individuals attack the British commerce in every sea.[2] I would omit altogether any recommendation on that subject, or allusion as contained in another paragraph to its utility in guarding the rights of our coast.

sheet page

3.   1.   *Spanish colonies.* The only objection which strikes me agt. mentioning this subject is that it will hurt the pride, & may be said to be an improper interference in the concerns of Spain. If it be thought proper to allude to the subject, I think that it would be

better to omit the anticipation of unfriendly views originating in misguided councils or ambition and which appears to allude to Spain & England.

" 3. protection of navigation & manufactures. The present time, when all our plans are controuled by the belligerent decrees & by the measures either of restriction or aggression which we must oppose to them, is not very proper to digest & adopt any permanent & regular system for the protection of our navigation. The subject is in public estimation absorbed in the much greater wrongs inflicted by the Belligerent nations. On the other hand the effect of the recommendation in favr. of manufactures is lessened by its being blended with that for navigation to which from the tenor of the paragraph it appears but secondary.

Blank paragraph—

Indians Will it not be good policy particularly as to G. Britain to present this subject in as favorable view as consistent with truth. It may otherwise give improper encouragement to that Nation.

Finances. Our returns are not all in. But an estimate will be furnished. It will be favorable for the present year, but shew a bad prospect for the next & will render it necessary to recommend an increase of duties and an authority to borrow.

It is proper &a. to observe that France has, subsequent to the revocation of her edicts so far as they violated the neutral commerce of the United States, authorized illegal depredations by her privateers and public vessels in the Baltic and on the high seas. I abstain however at this time from recommending any specific measures with respect to that Nation, under the expectation that the result of the Negotiations still pending between our Minister at Paris and that Government will be ascertained before your adjournment, so as to enable us to decide with certainty on the course &a.[3]

*Or, The communications which accompanied the Message of the   [4] have apprized you that France &a.

#Here may be added—Nor has any reparation been made or promised for the detention & confiscation of our Merchants property under the Rambouillet decrees.

Ms (DLC: Rives Collection, Madison Papers). In Gallatin's hand. Undated. Dated 5 Nov. 1811 in the *Index to the James Madison Papers.* Date assigned here on the assumption that Gallatin's remarks referred to an earlier draft (not found) of JM's message to Congress on 5 Nov. 1811 (see n. 1). Docketed by JM "as to proposed Message to Congs."

1. Gallatin's objections to JM's choice of words here suggest that the draft he received was more strongly worded than the final version of the message JM delivered to Congress on 5 Nov. 1811. If this was the case, one of the factors influencing JM's drafting of the message could have been his reaction to a 29 Oct. 1811 *National Intelligencer* report of a meeting the

British cabinet held on 6 Sept. 1811. The account was taken from the London *Courier*, here described as being "usually considered as the ministerial print," and announced that the cabinet had decided on "a measure of retaliation" against JM's policy of nonintercourse. The decision was justified on the grounds that there was no evidence that France had repealed the Berlin and Milan decrees, and the contents of Robert Smith's *Address* was cited in support of the contention that JM and his administration themselves "did not believe that the French decrees are repealed." Under such circumstances, the *Courier* declared, it would be "an imbecility and absurdity" for Great Britain to remove its orders in council. The report also contained the news that, in order to encourage JM to remove American restrictions against British trade and shipping, a new order in council had been signed the previous day "prohibiting American vessels from entering British ports, except such as are laden with flour and wheat, and providing that they carry back cargoes consisting of the produce of this country and its colonies."

Other American newspapers printed similar reports as well as accounts of how the British cabinet had retracted its decision on 8 Sept. after its announcement had led to a decline of stock prices in London. The *National Intelligencer* therefore concluded that "the cabinet of Great-Britain is as oscillating and indecisive in determining on its policy in relation to us, as it has shewn itself assuming and absurd in its pretensions whenever its interests have come into collision with those of neutrals." In the final analysis, no such order in council was issued at this time, nor did the British cabinet send fresh instructions to Augustus John Foster in Washington (see Wellesley to Foster, 22 Oct. 1811, Mayo, *Instructions to British Ministers*, pp. 332–33).

2. Gallatin's argument suggests that JM's draft, in addition to containing suggestions on naval policy, may have also called on Congress either to legislate for letters of marque and reprisal or to permit merchantmen to arm in self-defense. Such recommendations, however, did not appear in the final version of the message JM sent to Congress on 5 Nov. 1811. The *Index to the James Madison Papers* lists under the date of 5 Nov. 1811 a draft paragraph in JM's hand recommending "the expediency of authorizing merchant vessels to arm for self-defence," taking into view "the unprecedented dangers, incident to neutral navigation on the high seas, that captures continue to be made of American vessels engaged in commerce guaranteed by the acknowledged law of nations; and that in many cases, the evil might be obviated by defensive equipments to be made by the parties interested" (DLC: Rives Collection, Madison Papers; 1 p.). However, as this draft was written on the verso of a cover addressed to JM at Washington (probably by Harry Toulmin) and franked with a postmark dated 5 Nov. at Washington, Mississippi Territory, it is perhaps unlikely that JM composed this paragraph recommending the arming of merchantmen for self-defense on or about 5 Nov. 1811. This paragraph, more probably, was a draft for a message contemplated, but not sent, by JM at some earlier time, either during the second session of the Eleventh Congress between 27 Nov. 1809 and 1 May 1810 or in the first days of the third session of the Eleventh Congress in December 1810.

3. This paragraph and the notes to it are written on a smaller sheet of paper.

4. Left blank by Gallatin.

§ From Robert Williams. *2 November 1811, Washington, Mississippi Territory.* Offers to fill a judicial vacancy in the Orleans Territory occasioned by the death of Judge Mathews.[1] States that he is making this application because some of his "most respectable neighbours & acquaintances" are about to relocate in the Opelousas and Attakapas, and they wish that he "should make one of their number, & fill this appointment"; the fact that the price of cotton is low and likely to get worse, while the reverse is the case with the price of sugar, "is the principal reason for this removal." Points out that his past public services have been expensive and without emolument, and that his four years' administration of the territory cost him about $3,600 more than his annual salary. If JM thinks it proper to make this appointment, he could both serve his country and recover partially some of his earlier sacrifices. Declares that JM knows him too well to require him to say more and requests an acknowledgment of his letter.

RC (DLC). 3 pp. Marked "Confidential." Docketed by JM. Printed in Carter, *Territorial Papers, Orleans*, 9:952–53.

1. The report of the death of George Mathews, Jr., was erroneous, as he resigned his territorial judgeship on 11 July 1812. The son of Gen. George Mathews of Georgia, he had been appointed to the bench in the Orleans Territory in January 1806 (ibid., 9:573–74, 1021 n. 43).

§ From the Berkshire Agricultural Society. *4 November 1811, Pittsfield, Massachusetts.* "The executive Committe[e] of the Berkshire Agricultural Society tender their profound respects & Veneration to the President of the United States—and request his acceptance of the inclosed. They also request he will have the goodness to transmit the inclosure directed to the late President."

RC (DLC). 1 p. Docketed by JM. Enclosure not found.

Index

NOTE: Persons are identified on pages cited below in boldface type. Identifications in earlier volumes of this series are noted within parentheses. Page numbers followed only by n. (e.g., 272 n.) refer to the provenance portion of the annotation.